American Indian Policy in Crisis

AMERICAN INDIAN POLICY IN CRISIS:

Christian Reformers and the Indian, 1865-1900

❀❀❀❀❀❀❀

by Francis Paul Prucha

University of Oklahoma Press : Norman

By Francis Paul Prucha

Broadax and Bayonet: The Role of the United States Army in the Development of the Northwest, 1815–1860 (Madison, 1953)

American Indian Policy in the Formative Years: The Indian Trade and Intercourse Acts, 1790–1834 (Cambridge, 1962)

The Sword of the Republic: The United States Army on the Frontier, 1783–1846 (New York, 1969)

American Indian Policy in Crisis: Christian Reformers and the Indian, 1865–1900 (Norman, 1976)

Maps by Rafael D. Palacios on pages 39 and 359 used with permission of Macmillan Publishing Co., Inc. from *The Long Death*, by Ralph K. Andrist. Copyright © 1964 by Ralph K. Andrist.

Library of Congress Cataloging in Publication Data

Prucha, Francis Paul.
    American Indian policy in crisis.

    Bibliography: p. 405
    1. Indians of North America—Government relations—1869–1934.
2. Indians of North America, Civilization of. I. Title.
E93.P964   323.1′19′7073   75–4957

Preface

This book tells the story of the development of the policy of the United States government toward the American Indians in the last third of the nineteenth century, the most critical period in the whole history of Indian-white relations in the United States. I have focused my attention on a group of humanitarians and their friends in government who set about to "reform" Indian affairs. These men and women, acting in large part upon Christian impulses, decided that the Indians were no longer to be treated as tribal entities, segregated from the mainstream of American life and entitled to special treatment as one-time nations. The Indians instead were to be individualized and Americanized, becoming in the end patriotic American citizens indistinguishable from their white neighbors. By marshaling enough public sentiment to force their major proposals through Congress, the reformers revolutionized American Indian policy. At the end of the century, the legislation on which they placed their reliance had been enacted. All that remained, they believed, was the efficient administration of the policy they had managed to write into the law of the land.

I am concerned only incidentally with the dramatic military encounters between the troops of the United States army and the red warriors of the plains and mountains that filled much of the period, for they have frequently been described in great detail by others. The Indian wars, moreover, destructive as they were, were not the most important element of the story. The use of military force was but one part of an all-encompassing policy of acculturating and assimilating the Indians into white American society.

In recounting the history of the reform movement, I have tried not to blame or to praise the reformers, but only to understand them and to see how they fitted into the American society in which they lived. I have reported in considerable detail, often in their own words, what they proposed for the Indians. The writings and speeches of the Christian men and women were full of value-laden words like "savage" and "heathen" and "civilization," terminology that we would use with more circumspection today. But I have not softened any of their remarks and have attempted to re-create their arguments with all the biases and prejudices open to view. I have limited my inquiry, however, to the purposes of the reformers and have not sought to delve into their subconscious motives.

It is not a pretty story, yet it is one that we must face if we wish to understand the situation of the Indians and their place in American society in our own day.

I do not pretend that this book is "Indian history." The native Americans enter into the narrative, to be sure, but they are not the subject of my story. I am writing about the white humanitarians, about the sincere, religious-minded men and women who believed intensely that only one solution was possible for the problem they saw facing the United States in its relations with the Indians—complete Americanization. It is possible to write about them as a single entity, for by and large they were closely united both in outlook and in goals, and they were supported by government officials of like mind. They had a single program which they meant to apply to all the Indians.

The reaction of the Indians to the reformers' program was an equally important element in the history of Indian-white relations in the United States, but it has not been my purpose to describe that fully here. In fact, I am not sure that it is possible, except in a very general way, to describe Indian reaction as though it were uniform throughout the great diversity of groups to whom it was applied. Each Indian tribe—in many cases each individual Indian—received the program in a particular way, and the story of each calls for separate telling. Many of the stories, of course, have already been well told in the specialized studies of such historians as Arrell M. Gibson, Angie Debo, Donald J. Berthrong, George E. Hyde, Roy W. Meyer, and William T. Hagan.

My thanks are due to the National Endowment for the Humanities for a fellowship grant that allowed me a free year for research and writing on this project and to the director and staff of the Charles Warren Center for Studies in American History, Harvard University, for providing remarkably pleasant and effective facilities in which to do the work. The staffs of the Harvard University Library, the Library of Congress, the National Archives, the State Historical Society of Wisconsin, the Marquette University Library, the Milwaukee Public Library, and other depositories have been invariably helpful. I must thank Ray Allen Billington, too, who first encouraged me to undertake a study of this particular segment of the history of American Indian policy.

Part of Chapter 5 has been published in different form in an essay entitled "Indian Policy Reform and American Protestantism, 1880–1900," and some of the ideas expressed here were included in an introduction to an edition of selected writings of the reformers, 1880–1900.

Francis Paul Prucha, S.J.

Marquette University
January, 1973

Contents

Illustrations

Maps

American Indian Policy in Crisis

CHAPTER 1

BEGINNINGS
OF REFORM

During the first half century after the formation of the Government the flow of population on our continent was confined to a movement from the Atlantic coast westwardly, and the process of displacement of the aboriginal race was comparatively simple; the Indian receded as the white man advanced. Latterly, however, new tides of population have set in from the shores of the Pacific, and the two mighty currents are now commingling their waters amid the gold-bearing ranges of the interior. The emigrant from Minnesota meets in the fields of Montana the miner from Oregon and California. With the termination of our great war, now near its close, a migration will spring up of which the world has as yet known no parallel; and in a few short years every tract capable of settlement and cultivation will pass into the occupancy of the white man.

What is to become of the Indians as the races of the world thus draw together from the opposite shores of the continent? Caught between the upper and the nether millstones—now so remorselessly approaching each other—what is to be his fate?

—IGNATIUS DONNELLY, in the
House of Representatives,
February 7, 1865

✿✿✿✿✿✿✿

Indian affairs in the United States were at a crisis when the Civil War ended in 1865. Ignatius Donnelly, Congressman from Minnesota, in an eloquent plea for the Indians in February of that year spoke of the problem in terms of vast tides of migration of the whites from east and west, crushing the Indians between them. General William Te-

3

cumseh Sherman saw the destruction of the Indians following upon the "construction of two parallel railroads right through their country" which would "prove destructive to the game on which they subsisted, and consequently fatal to themselves."[1] The signs were there for all to read, and the plight of the Indians and the threat of their imminent destruction did not escape the attention of Christian men and women, whose humanitarian impulses made them cry out for the unfortunate red men.

Even during the great holocaust of the Civil War, attention had not been diverted from the Indians completely. In some respects, indeed, the period furnished fertile soil for the seeds of reform to sprout. The weakened control in the West that came with the withdrawal of regular army troops fostered a restlessness among the western tribesmen, and ineffective and fraudulent operations in the Indian service became the rule. Nor did white pressures upon the Indians cease with the conflict between the North and the South, since westward movement of population continued in spite of the war. The concern for the Negroes that was amplified by the war was to some extent reflected in new concern for the other oppressed and wronged racial minority, the Indians, and President Lincoln's deep sympathy made him a sincere listener to pleas made on behalf of the Indians.[2]

There was no concentrated movement for Indian reform during the war years, but private individuals kept the issue alive. Two of these persons were especially insistent: John Beeson, an Oregonian who already had a long history of agitation on behalf of the Indians to his credit, and the Protestant Episcopal Bishop of Minnesota, Henry Benjamin Whipple.

[1] *Reform of the Indian System: Speech of Hon. Ignatius Donnelly, of Minnesota, Delivered in the House of Representatives, February 7, 1865* (n.p., n.d.); William T. Sherman, *Memoirs of Gen. W. T. Sherman, Written by Himself* (4th ed., 2 vols., New York, 1891), II, 412.
[2] The movement for Indian reform in the Civil War and immediate post-Civil War periods is fully discussed in Robert Winston Mardock, *The Reformers and the American Indian* (Columbia, Missouri, 1971), and more briefly in the same author's "The Anti-Slavery Humanitarians and Indian Policy Reform," *Western Humanities Review*, XII (Spring, 1958), 131–46. A brief study of the Lincoln administration is Harry Kelsey, "William P. Dole and Mr. Lincoln's Indian Policy," *Journal of the West*, X (July, 1971), 484–92. See also Henry E. Fritz, *The Movement for Indian Assimilation, 1860–1890* (Philadelphia, 1963), and Loring Benson Priest, *Uncle Sam's Stepchildren: The Reformation of United States Indian Policy, 1865–1887* (New Brunswick, 1942).

Beeson was an Englishman who came to America in 1830 and settled in Illinois in 1834. Two decades later he was struck by the "Oregon fever" and moved to the western territory in 1853. When the Rogue River war broke out between the Indians and the white settlers, Beeson's deep religious convictions led him to defend the Indians and to charge that the war was the result of white aggression. Such nonconformity with frontier attitudes made Beeson's life in Oregon impossible, and he returned to the East, where he devoted much of his time to promotion of Indian causes. He published in New York in 1857 *A Plea for the Indians*, in which he gave a history of the Oregon war and condemned the white savages for destroying the Indians, and in 1859 he spoke at Fanueil Hall in Boston, where he shared the platform with Edward Everett, Wendell Phillips, and other reformers in an appeal for Indian rights. In the following year, he began publication of *The Calumet*, meant to be a vehicle for promoting reform in Indian affairs. Only one issue of the journal came from the presses, however, for the secession crisis turned attention away from Indian matters.[3]

The Civil War did not curb all of Beeson's activities. Firmly convinced that the war was not caused by slavery but was "an extension of the unneighborly, unChristian, and destructive practice which for generations had been operating against the Aborigines," he insisted that redress of Indian wrongs was "the first step in the order of national reform and self preservation." The reformer was received sympathetically by Lincoln, and in a meeting in 1864 the President told him: "My aged Friend. I have heard your arguments time and again. I have said little but thought much, and you may rest assured that as soon as the pressing matter of this war is settled the Indians shall have my first care and I will not rest untill Justice is done to their and your Sattisfaction."[4]

[3] John Beeson, *A Plea for the Indians* (New York, 1857); Beeson, *Are We Not Men and Brethren?: An Address to the People of the United States* (n.p., 1859). There is an autobiographical sketch by Beeson in *The Calumet*, I (February, 1860), 4–9, and sketches are given in Fritz, *Movement for Indian Assimilation*, pp. 34–38, and in Mardock, *Reformers and the American Indian*, pp. 10–14. There is a brief appraisal of Beeson as an example of the "fanatic fringe" of Indian reform in Priest, *Uncle Sam's Stepchildren*, pp. 59–60.

[4] Beeson to Lincoln, November 18, 1862, Department of the Interior, Indian Division, Letters Received, Miscellaneous, National Archives Record Group 48; Lincoln's statement is quoted in Beeson to E. P. Smith, June 25, 1873, Office of Indian Affairs, Letters Received, Miscellaneous P. 520 (M234, Roll 466, frame 302), National Archives Record Group 75.

Beeson interviewed other national leaders, memorialized Congress, and organized public meetings in the cities in the East. When his funds ran out, he returned to Oregon in 1865, but his interest in Indian reform flared up periodically as he joined his voice to others who took up the cause of the Indians.[5]

Paralleling Beeson's activities was the more influential agitation of Bishop Whipple, whose stature as an Indian friend eventually made him a correspondent and confidant of important national leaders and whose powerful voice condemning wrongs could not be ignored as could the more fanatical utterances of Beeson.[6] Whipple, after serving in a parish in Rome, New York, and for two years among the poor on the south side of Chicago, was elected first Bishop of Minnesota in 1859. In 1860 he took up residence at Faribault, which was to be his home for the rest of his life. Having thus been thrust into contact with both the Chippewas and the Sioux on this still primitive frontier, the new bishop investigated the condition of the Indians and became painfully aware of the injustices in the government's Indian system. He began an active crusade to right the wrongs the Indians suffered, bombarding with letters and memorials government officials all the way up to the President himself. Notable was his letter to President Lincoln of March 6, 1862, asking "only justice for a wronged and neglected race." He pointed to the rapid deterioration that had taken place among the tribes since they had signed away much of their land in treaties with the United States, and he especially excoriated the Indian agents, who were selected to uphold the honor and faith of the government without

[5] Beeson wrote many letters to government officials, in some of which he was seeking government employment as some sort of special commissioner to the Indians. See, for example, Beeson to E. P. Smith, July 29, 1873, May 14, 1874; Beeson to President Hayes, October 15, 1877, May 1, 1878, May 16, June 5, 1879; Beeson to Commissioner of Indian Affairs, October 27, 1878; Beeson to Carl Schurz, June 1, June 3, 1879—all in Office of Indian Affairs, Letters Received, Miscellaneous, National Archives Record Group 75. Beeson suggested using phrenology to pick out suitable agents, "such as have the requisite amount of benevolence, conscientiousness and intellect." *Plea for the Indians*, p. 126. In 1875 Beeson again proposed that Indian agents be "tested by the science of phrenology" so that appointments could be based on "native qualities and approved character." Address to the People of the United States, September 23, 1875, copy inclosed in Beeson to President Hayes, October 15, 1877.

[6] Whipple's career as an Indian reformer can be followed in his autobiography, *Lights and Shadows of a Long Episcopate* (New York, 1899), and in the Henry B. Whipple Papers, Minnesota Historical Society. See also the useful sketch by Grace Lee Nute, "Henry Benjamin Whipple," *Dictionary of American Biography*, XX, 68–69.

6

any attention to their fitness. "The Congressional delegation desires to reward John Doe for party work," the bishop charged, "and John Doe desires the place because there is a tradition on the border that an Indian Agent with fifteen hundred dollars a year can retire upon an ample fortune in four years." He asked for simple honesty, for agency employees who were men "of purity, temperance, industry, and unquestioned integrity" rather than "so many drudges fed at the public crib." He wanted the Indian to be treated as a ward of the government, with aid in building a house and opening a farm and with adequate schools for his children. And he insisted that law be provided for the Indians as it was for the whites. Whipple was not ready to submit a detailed plan for a new Indian system, but he urged instead that a commission of three men be appointed to investigate Indian affairs and propose a new plan to remedy the evils, a commission composed of men "of inflexible integrity, of large heart, of clear head, of strong will, who fear God and love man" and who would be "so high in character that they are above the reach of political demogogues."[7]

Lincoln graciously acknowledged the communication and passed the matter on to the Secretary of the Interior, Caleb Smith, who indicated his agreement with Whipple and in turn sent the bishop's letter to the chairmen of the House and Senate committees on Indian affairs.[8] Whipple worked hard, too, with Minnesota's two senators, Henry M. Rice and Martin S. Wilkinson, and with Congressman Cyrus Aldrich. Rice was sympathetic and promised to do whatever he could, although he confessed he feared "the demagogue, the politician, & those *pecuniarally interested*." But Wilkinson and Aldrich openly expressed their doubt that the Indians would profit much from any attention.[9]

Whipple's premonitions of serious trouble if the Indian system were not reformed were tragically fulfilled by the Sioux outbreak in Minnesota in August, 1862.[10] By treaties signed in 1851 at Traverse des Sioux

[7] Whipple, *Lights and Shadows*, pp. 510–14.

[8] Lincoln to Whipple, March 27, 1862, and Caleb Smith to Whipple, March 31, 1862, in Whipple Papers.

[9] Correspondence between Whipple and these men, April–June, 1862, in Whipple Papers.

[10] An admirable brief narrative of the uprising, which skillfully weighs the evidence

and Mendota, these Indians had been located on narrow reservations along the upper Minnesota River, and white settlers rushed into the twenty-four million acres of rich land vacated by the Sioux. The Indians had many grievances arising out of the treaties. They disliked the new reservations, complained that they had been tricked into providing for traders' claims in the treaties, and often were forced to wait unduly long for the annuity payments that had been promised. Crop failures led to near-starvation conditions in the winter of 1861–1862, and the specially tardy arrival of the annuities in 1862 and the niggardliness of the agent and the traders in distributing supplies aggravated the misery. Nor were the Sioux unaware that the regular army troops had been withdrawn to fight the Confederacy and had been replaced by inexperienced volunteers. Under such conditions, an unplanned killing of white settlers by a handful of Indians on August 17, 1862, turned into a major uprising. The Sioux attacked the agencies, murdered unprotected settlers, mounted an attack on Fort Ridgely a few miles below the Lower Agency, and laid siege to the settlement at New Ulm. In the end, at least 450 whites were dead; some estimates claimed as many as 800.

The State of Minnesota and the federal government quickly mobilized against the Indians.[11] Governor Alexander Ramsey gave a colonel's commission to Henry H. Sibley, who gathered volunteer infantry and cavalry to put down the uprising. A fur trader of long experience among the Sioux, although without previous military experience, Sibley moved effectively against the hostiles. He decisively defeated them at Wood Lake, and friendly Indians were emboldened to bring in white captives taken during the outbreak. Little by little the hostile Sioux laid down their arms, some two thousand Indians in all. A hastily assembled military commission tried the Indians who had

is Kenneth Carley, *The Sioux Uprising of 1862* (St. Paul, 1961); I have relied upon it for my account. An excellent older account is William Watts Folwell, *A History of Minnesota* (4 vols., St. Paul, 1921–1930), II, 109–301. A popular account which emphasizes the stories of settlers caught in the war is C. M. Oehler, *The Great Sioux Uprising* (New York, 1959).

[11] The federal government created the Department of the Northwest, with General John Pope in command, to meet the crisis. The story is told fully in Robert Huhn Jones, *The Civil War in the Northwest: Nebraska, Wisconsin, Iowa, Minnesota, and the Dakotas* (Norman, 1960). Pope's western career is traced in Richard N. Ellis, *General Pope and U.S. Indian Policy* (Albuquerque, 1970).

participated in the war. Working routinely and often without sufficient evidence, the commission tried 392 prisoners, of whom sixteen were given prison terms and 307 were sentenced to death. Sibley and General John Pope, commander of the Department of the Northwest, wanted the immediate execution of the condemned Indians.

Bishop Whipple's zeal for the rights and welfare of the Indians was not cooled by the war. He went immediately to the scene of the disaster, taking care of the wounded and comforting the bereaved, and then took a courageous stand in support of the Indians by publishing in the St. Paul newspapers a plea to his fellow citizens not to wreak vengeance on the Indians, whose uprising had been the result of intolerable evils worked upon them by the Indian system. He went personally to Washington to plead with Lincoln for clemency for the Indians condemned to death by the military commission, arguing that they should be treated as prisoners of war, not as murderers.[12] His plea was not completely in vain, for the President, against cries for vengeance from many Minnesotans, approved death sentences for only thirty-nine, one of whom was reprieved at the last moment.

Working through Senator Rice, Whipple continued to urge the President to bring about a wholesale reform in Indian affairs.[13] Lincoln heard the appeal and in his state of the union address of December 1, 1862, told Congress: "I submit for your especial consideration whether our Indian system shall not be remodeled. Many wise and good men have impressed me with the belief that this can be profitably done."[14] This favorable reaction encouraged Whipple, who kept hammering on the idea that a commission should be appointed to set up the reforms.[15] Lincoln continued to recommend reform and his Commissioner of Indian Affairs, William P. Dole, pushed for a carefully managed reservation system, but Congress, too busy with the war and much concerned about vested interests in the current Indian system, took no

[12] Nute, "Henry Benjamin Whipple," p. 69.

[13] Letters of Rice to Whipple, November, 1862, in Whipple Papers.

[14] Fred L. Israel, ed., *The State of the Union Messages of the Presidents, 1790–1966* (3 vols., New York, 1966), II, 1074.

[15] Whipple wrote to General Henry W. Halleck shortly after Lincoln's message: "This Indian system is a sink of iniquity. The President has recommended reform. You have his ear. Do, for the sake of these poor victims of a nations wrong, ask him to put on it [the commission] something better than politicians." Whipple to Halleck, December 4, 1862, in Whipple Papers.

action.[16] Senator Rice reported ruefully in February, 1863: "I have no hope of anything being done to improve the condition of the Indians by this Administration." And Senator Wilkinson justified postponement of action on the basis that he was "greatly perplexed as to the details of the system to be adopted" and that any new system would take long and careful thought. The new Congressman from Minnesota, Ignatius Donnelly, took up Whipple's cause, but he expected to get nothing but hostility from those whose frauds he uncovered, and he urged the bishop to keep up his fight to arouse public opinion.[17]

Whipple continued to propagate his accusations against the agency system and against the lack of adequate law to govern and protect the Indians.[18] When the Civil War ended, other voices were added to his and Beeson's in support of a new day in Indian affairs. By then new horrors on the frontier had added support to their charges of the whites' inhumanity to the Indians.

Not all the Sioux involved in the Minnesota uprising surrendered. A considerable number, perhaps 4,400 from the two agencies, fled into Dakota, where it was rumored they were joined by Yankton and Yanktoni bands. General Pope feared that the Indians would attack the Minnesota frontier in the summer, and early in 1863 he sent a punitive expedition into Dakota. One column under Sibley moved northwest from Fort Ridgely toward Devils Lake; a second column under General Alfred Sully moved up the Missouri from Fort Randall. Although the columns did not meet as planned, encounters with the Sioux left large numbers of the Indians dead and much of their property destroyed. Yet the expedition had failed to end the fighting power of the bands, and in 1864 General Sully led another expedition up the Missouri, which successfully dispersed the Sioux.[19]

While Pope was seeking to control the Indians in his Department of

[16] See Lincoln's messages of December 8, 1863, and December 6, 1864, Israel, *State of the Union Messages*, II, 1092–93, 1104.

[17] Rice to Whipple, February 3, 1863; Wilkinson to Whipple, March 1, 1863; Donnelly to Whipple, June 12, 1864, in Whipple Papers.

[18] Whipple, "The Indian System," *North American Review*, XCIX (October, 1864), 452–54.

[19] Robert M. Utley, *Frontiersmen in Blue: The United States Army and the Indian, 1848–1865* (New York, 1967), pp. 261–80.

the Northwest, war hit the central plains between the Platte and the Arkansas, as Cheyenne, Arapaho, and Sioux bands, taking advantage of the engagement of the United States in the Civil War, attacked the encroaching whites in scattered raids. Depredations over a wide area made it difficult to separate hostile Indians from peaceful ones, and white officials feared a confederacy or conspiracy among the tribes to wipe out the white settlements. It was enough to alarm the Colorado settlements to the point of panic. Governor John Evans of Colorado Territory and Colonel John M. Chivington, Methodist minister turned soldier and politician, who commanded the Colorado Military District, reacted strongly; they urged military action to crush the offending Indians and restore security to the territory.

One group of Cheyennes under Black Kettle and White Antelope, joined by a small number of Arapahos, sought peace with the whites. The Indian leaders met with Governor Evans and Colonel Chivington at Camp Weld near Denver on September 28, 1864. The whites sought only to determine the attitude of the Indians and made no formal peace arrangements, but their remarks were interpreted by the chiefs to mean peace, and the Indians turned in their arms at Fort Lyon and moved northward to a camp along Sand Creek. Here, on the morning of November 29, they were attacked without warning by Colonel Chivington with troops of the First Colorado Cavalry and one-hundred-day enlistees of the Third Colorado Cavalry. Black Kettle raised an American flag and a white flag before his tent to indicate the peaceful nature of the camp, and White Antelope stood with his arms folded in a peaceful gesture as the whites advanced. To no avail. The soldiers slaughtered the defenseless Indians in the most brutal manner, killing men, women, and children indiscriminately and mutilating in revolting fashion the bodies of those who fell. Black Kettle and others escaped, but about one hundred and fifty Indians, including White Antelope, were killed in this Sand Creek Massacre.[20]

[20] The literature on Sand Creek is extensive, for the complexity of the event and its origins has puzzled and intrigued historians and popular writers. Useful accounts are Stan Hoig, *The Sand Creek Massacre* (Norman, 1961); Raymond G. Carey, "The Puzzle of Sand Creek," *Colorado Magazine*, XLI (Fall, 1964), 279–98; Janet Lecompte, "Sand Creek," *ibid.*, 315–35; Lonnie J. White, "From Bloodless to Bloody: The Third Colorado Cavalry and the Sand Creek Massacre," *Journal of the West*, VI (October, 1967), 535–81. For a discussion of the historical controversies about Sand Creek, see Michael A. Sievers, "Sands of Sand Creek Historiography," *Colorado Magazine*, XLIX (Spring,

The inhabitants of Denver considered it a stunning victory and hailed the troops as heroes, but when the details of the massacre reached the East, disgust and indignation soon reverberated across the land. There was no dearth of information, for three formal investigations of the event collected extensive testimony and spread it before the public in official reports. On January 10, 1865, the House of Representatives directed the Joint Committee on the Conduct of the War to investigate the attack. In March the committee heard testimony in Washington, gathered affidavits, correspondence, and official reports, and added testimony from Chivington in Denver. The report, signed by Senator Benjamin F. Wade, was a devastating condemnation. Its description of the massacre was lurid and its criticism harsh. The soldiers, it said, "indulged in acts of barbarity of the most revolting character; such, it is to be hoped, as never before disgraced the acts of men claiming to be civilized." It spoke of the "fiendish malignity and cruelty of the officers who had so sedulously and carefully plotted the massacre," and accused Chivington of deliberately planning and executing "a foul and dastardly massacre which would have disgraced the veriest savage among those who were the victims of his cruelty."[21]

At the same time, another Congressional inquiry was in progress, as the Joint Special Committee headed by Senator James Doolittle undertook an extensive study of the condition of the western Indians. One part of the committee, assigned to study Kansas, the Indian Territory, and the territories of Colorado, New Mexico, and Utah, made a special investigation of Sand Creek. It too took testimony in Washington in March and then traveled west to Fort Riley, Fort Lyon, and Denver, where interviews were held with participants and other interested parties.[22] Finally, a military fact-finding commission, presided over by

1972), 116–42. There is a good account of the massacre, its antecedents, and its aftermath in Donald J. Berthrong, *The Southern Cheyennes* (Norman, 1963), pp. 174–244. The event is placed in its military context in Utley, *Frontiersmen in Blue*, pp. 280–97. Background information is supplied in William E. Unrau, "A Prelude to War," *Colorado Magazine*, XLI (Fall, 1964), 299–313, and Harry Kelsey, "Background to Sand Creek," *ibid.*, XLV (Fall, 1968), 279–300.

21 "Massacre of Cheyenne Indians," *Report of the Joint Committee on the Conduct of the War*, in *Senate Report* No. 142, 38 Congress, 2 session, serial 1214, pp. iii–v. Appended to the report itself are more than one hundred pages of testimony.

22 "The Chivington Massacre," in "Condition of the Indian Tribes: Report of the Joint Special Committee," *Senate Report* No. 156, 39 Congress, 2 session, serial 1279, pp. 26–98.

Samuel F. Tappan, was assembled in Denver to investigate the conduct of Colonel Chivington.[23] The voluminous hearings furnished tremendous ammunition for those who were aghast at the government's handling of Indian affairs and wanted immediate reform. No matter that the testimony on Sand Creek was often contradictory, that evidence was admitted without any critical norms, and that the investigators made no claim to objectivity.[24] No matter that the attack was undertaken by local troops and was not a result of official United States policy or plans. The Sand Creek Massacre became a cause célèbre, a never-to-be-forgotten symbol of what was wrong with United States treatment of the Indians, which reformers would never let fade from view.[25]

Sand Creek intensified Indian hostilities on the plains, if it did not indeed set off the new Indian warfare. Black Kettle and others who escaped got aid from the Northern Cheyennes and Arapahos and from the Comanches and Kiowas, and the Indians fought off the troops sent out to quiet them. While the army planned an extensive campaign, however, humanitarian outcries over Sand Creek and the desire of the Indians themselves for peace led to negotiations. A United States commission met with chiefs of the Cheyennes and Arapahos, Comanches, Kiowas, and Kiowa-Apaches on the Little Arkansas. On October 14, 1865, the Cheyennes and Arapahos present signed a treaty, in which they agreed to give up their lands in Colorado and accept a reservation which lay partly in Kansas and partly in the Indian Territory. Although permitted to range over their old lands, they agreed not to disturb the roads, military posts, and towns of the whites. The government agreed to pay annuities for forty years. Three days later a similar agreement was concluded with the Kiowa-Apaches, and on the following day, one with the Comanches and Kiowas, who were to get a reser-

[23] "Proceedings of a Military Commission Convened by Special Orders No. 23, Headquarters District of Colorado, Denver, Colorado Territory, Dated February 1, 1865, in the Case of Colonel J. M. Chivington, First Colorado Cavalry," *Senate Executive Document* No. 26, 39 Congress, 2 session, serial 1277, pp. 2–228.

[24] See the remarks on the quality of the investigations in Carey, "Puzzle of Sand Creek," pp. 297–98.

[25] The Sand Creek Massacre gets emphatic treatment, for example, in Helen Hunt Jackson, *A Century of Dishonor* (New York, 1881), pp. 343–58, and in Dee Brown, *Bury My Heart at Wounded Knee* (New York, 1970), pp. 67–102. For a novelized treatment, see Michael Straight, *A Very Small Remnant* (New York, 1963).

vation in the Indian Territory and in the panhandle of Texas. The treaties, although bringing a temporary peace, did not solve the problem since the reservations to be established never materialized; Texas' control of her lands nullified the agreement with the Comanches and Kiowas, and Kansas refused to allow a reservation within her boundaries.[26]

The war on the plains and especially the Sand Creek Massacre made it clear that the situation in the West needed investigation at least, if not a thorough overhaul. To this end, Senator James R. Doolittle of Wisconsin, a member of the Senate Committee on Indian Affairs, introduced on January 9, 1865, a joint resolution which directed the appointment of a committee to inquire into the condition of the Indian tribes and their treatment by the civil and military authorities. Doolittle argued that since unscrupulous army officers and dishonest agents were blamed for the Indian disturbances, the government should investigate the charges and report to Congress suggestions for improving the administration of Indian affairs.[27]

The Joint Special Committee, authorized on March 3, 1865, was composed of three senators and four members of the House, with Doolittle serving as chairman.[28] These men went about their task with great seriousness and tremendous energy. After dividing up the Indian country, the committee in the spring split into three groups, each one heading west to investigate affairs in a different section of the Indian frontier. To supplement its on-the-spot observations, the committee sent detailed questionnaires to military commanders, agents, and other persons acquainted with the West, asking about forces working toward the deterioration of the Indians, the best forms of land tenure, the effects of schools and missions, the use of annuities, and whether the

[26] William H. Leckie, *The Military Conquest of the Southern Plains* (Norman, 1963), pp. 24–27. The treaties are in Charles J. Kappler, ed., *Indian Affairs: Laws and Treaties* (2 vols., Washington, 1904), II, 887–95.

[27] *Senate Journal*, 38 Congress, 2 session, serial 1208, pp. 56, 63, 84, 321; *Congressional Globe*, 38 Congress, 2 session, pp. 326–27.

[28] *United States Statutes at Large*, XIII, 572–73. The members appointed in addition to Doolittle were Lafayette S. Foster of Connecticut and James W. Nesmith of Oregon from the Senate and Asahel W. Hubbard of Iowa, William Higby of California, Lewis W. Ross of Illinois, and William Windom of Minnesota from the House.

Indian Bureau should be under the War or Interior Department. The answers filled nearly seventy pages in the committee's report and formed a basis for the committee's recommendations and conclusions.[29]

The report itself, submitted on January 26, 1867, made five points. It noted that, except for the tribes in the Indian Territory, the Indians were everywhere rapidly decreasing in number because of disease, intemperance, war, and the pressure of white emigration. The wars, which were a major concern, it traced in a large majority of cases to "the aggressions of lawless white men," and it cited as an especially horrible example the Sand Creek Massacre. A potent cause of decay, it said, was the loss of Indian hunting grounds and destruction of the game on which many tribes depended for subsistence, and it noted the powerful effect of the railroads on the diminution of the buffalo. The committee decided in favor of leaving the Indian Bureau in the Department of the Interior, but in its final point, arguing that the evils came not so much from the government's Indian policy as from abuses in the system, it recommended a system of five inspection districts, each to be served by a three-man inspection committee to be composed of an assistant commissioner of Indian affairs, an officer of the regular army detailed annually by the Secretary of War, and a third person chosen by the President from the recommendations of church groups or missionary boards.[30]

Senator Doolittle introduced a bill incorporating the inspection provisions in March, 1866, which passed the Senate but never came to a vote in the House.[31] This was clearly patchwork rather than radical revolution in Indian policy. The committee and its report, however, marked a beginning of a new approach to Indian affairs emphasizing peace and justice, that was strikingly in contrast with the demands of

[29] The questionnaire and responses were appended to the committee's report in *Senate Report* No. 156, 39 Congress, 2 session, serial 1279, pp. 424–92. There is a summary and analysis of the responses to the questionnaire in Donald Chaput, "Generals, Indian Agents, Politicians: The Doolittle Survey of 1865," *Western Historical Quarterly*, III (July, 1972), 269–82.

[30] "Condition of the Indian Tribes: Report of the Joint Special Committee, Appointed under Joint Resolution of March 3, 1865, with an Appendix," *Senate Report* No. 156, 39 Congress, 2 session, serial 1279, pp. 3–10.

[31] *Senate Journal*, 39 Congress, 1 session, serial 1236, pp. 235, 243, 246. See Doolittle's support of the measure and debate on it in *Congressional Globe*, 39 Congress, 1 session, pp. 1449–50, 1485–92.

some military men for the rapid subjugation of the tribes and military control of the reservations.

Even while Doolittle's report was being formulated, renewed warfare in the West drove home once again the need for some better policy. The discovery of gold in the mountains of Montana necessitated means of transportation and communication to tie this remote region to the East. Movement up the Missouri to Fort Benton, although the most economical route, was roundabout and for much of the year problematic. What was desired was a shorter, more direct, overland passage; one was soon established through the Powder River country of present-day Wyoming—the Bozeman Trail. Branching off from the Oregon Trail just north of Fort Laramie, the trail ran north, skirting east of the Big Horn Mountains, then west to Bozeman, Virginia City, and other mining centers. The road ran through the favorite hunting grounds of the Sioux, and the Indians resisted this latest encroachment with incessant attacks upon the wagon trains. Heeding the cry of the miners for protection, the army in 1865 and 1866 built and maintained a string of small forts along the road—Fort Reno, where the trail crossed the Powder River, Fort Phil Kearny, sixty-five miles to the north, and Fort C. F. Smith in southern Montana. The forts lived in a state of siege, and wood-cutting and haying parties were regularly attacked by the Sioux. On December 21, 1866, a detachment of eighty troops from Fort Reno under Captain William J. Fetterman, lured into an ambush by the Indians, were killed to the last man. The Fetterman disaster electrified the nation, and renewed Indian attacks on the three forts intensified eastern concern.[32]

Prevention of large-scale war was essential, and whatever might work toward that purpose was worth trying. In February, 1867, the President appointed a commission of military officers and civilians to

[32] A full work on the Bozeman Trail is Grace Raymond Hebard and E. A. Brininstool, *The Bozeman Trail: Historical Accounts of the Blazing of the Overland Routes into the Northwest, and the Fights with Red Cloud's Warriors* (2 vols., Cleveland, 1922). There is a useful analysis of the military situation in Robert A. Murray, *Military Posts in the Powder River Country of Wyoming, 1865–1894* (Lincoln, 1968), pp. 3–12, 73–101. Red Cloud's part in the Indians' fight against the road is discussed in James C. Olson, *Red Cloud and the Sioux Problem* (Lincoln, 1965), pp. 27–57.

investigate the Fetterman affair and to determine which tribes were friendly and which hostile.[33] But at the same time, in an attempt to satisfy the demands for military action coming from the panicked frontiersmen, General Winfield Scott Hancock, commanding the Department of the Missouri, moved into the central plains.

The unsettled conditions on the frontiers made it easy to predict a new outbreak. Cheyenne Dog Soldiers who had not signed the treaties of 1865 stayed on their hunting grounds in Kansas, and although they promised to remain peaceful, rumors of trouble were rampant. The news of the Fetterman ambush and of raiding parties into Texas increased the tension. Such reports stirred Hancock into action. Without checking to measure the truth of the report of Indian dangers, he was convinced that there would be a major outbreak in the spring of 1867. To meet the threat, he assembled an impressive expedition at Fort Harker by April 1 and soon thereafter moved to Fort Zarah and then to Fort Larned on the Arkansas, determined to overawe the Indians. Hancock conferred at Fort Larned with Cheyenne leaders, but he struck a belligerent stance and despite the advice of the Indian agent marched westward to a Cheyenne village. The Indians, fearing a repetition of Sand Creek, fled on his approach. Hancock interpreted the move as hostility and burned the deserted village; the Indians retaliated by attacks on railroad construction and on isolated stage stations. Although Hancock himself returned to Fort Leavenworth in May, he left Lieutenant George A. Custer with the Seventh Cavalry in the field. The peace of the spring had now turned into war, with hostile Indians terrorizing the regions on both sides of the Platte. Instead of overawing the horsemen of the plains, Hancock had irritated and frightened them into open hostility. By the end of the summer, the frontier in Kansas was in a state of siege.[34]

---

[33] Report of the Commissioner of Indian Affairs, 1867, in serial 1326, pp. 2–3. Reports of the members of the commission are in *Senate Executive Document* No. 13, 40 Congress, 1 session, serial 1308.

[34] Leckie, *Military Conquest of the Southern Plains*, pp. 30–62. Correspondence, reports, and other documents on the hostilities of 1867 are printed in "Difficulties with Indian Tribes," *House Executive Document* No. 240, 41 Congress, 2 session, serial 1425. See also the condemnation of the warfare in the report of John B. Sanborn, May 18, 1867, in *Senate Executive Document* No. 13, 40 Congress, 1 session, serial 1308, pp. 111–13.

The investigating commission reported in July, 1867, that most of the Indians in the West wanted peace, and it recommended an end to aggressive campaigns against the Indians. And Commissioner of Indian Affairs Nathaniel G. Taylor submitted a series of suggestions looking toward a peaceful resolution of the crisis on the plains.[35] Congress was now ready to try a serious peace offensive. On July 20, 1867, it authorized a Peace Commission to carry the olive branch to the restless Indians. The commission was directed to determine the reasons for the Indian hostility and at its discretion to make treaty arrangements with the Indians (under the direction of the President and subject to the action of the Senate) which would remove "all just causes of complaint" on the Indians' part and at the same time establish security along the railroads under construction and other lines of communication, and "such as will most likely insure civilization for the Indians and peace and safety for the whites." For Indians not then occupying reservations under treaty agreements, the commissioners were to select reservations which would become the permanent homes for the Indians and from which all whites were to be excluded except for officers and employees of the United States. But there was also an iron hand in this velvet glove, for if the commissioners failed to get the Indians to settle on reservations and failed to secure peace, the Secretary of War was authorized to call for volunteers for "the suppression of Indian hostilities."[36]

The Peace Commission was an impressive aggregation of military commanders and civilian peace advocates. Chairing the group was Indian Commissioner Taylor, a former Methodist minister of evangelical spirit and deep humanitarian concern for the Indians. He spoke for those who wanted liberal treatment of the Indians and was a staunch defender of civilian control of Indian affairs. Seconding him was a Bostonian who had moved to Colorado, Samuel F. Tappan—noted supporter of Indian rights, who had a tinge of fanaticism in his makeup and who had chaired the military commission investigating Colonel Chivington and Sand Creek. Aligned with them was Senator John B. Henderson of Missouri, chairman of the Senate Committee on Indian

[35] *Ibid.*, pp. 5–6. Taylor's suggestions are paraphrased in Report of the Commissioner of Indian Affairs, 1867, in serial 1326, pp. 5–7.

[36] *United States Statutes at Large*, XV, 17. See the discussion in *Congressional Globe*, 40 Congress, 1 session, pp. 756–57.

Affairs and sponsor of the legislation that created the commission. A fourth was John B. Sanborn, a native of Minnesota, who had risen to the rank of major general in the army, but who in 1867 was out of the service and practicing law in Washington. He had served on the commission which investigated the Fetterman massacre. These four men had been named explicitly in the law that established the commission.[37] In addition to these the President appointed three army officers, well qualified men who had had considerable experience in the West and, although firm believers in military control of the Indians, not averse to reasonable attempts at peace maneuvers. General William T. Sherman was in command of the Division of the Missouri and had over-all responsibility for peace on the frontier. With him was Major General Alfred H. Terry, commander of the Department of Dakota, a scholarly young man of forty, who had an excellent military record. The third general was William S. Harney, now retired in St. Louis, who had served on the Indian frontier and had many personal friends among the Indians. An extra member was Major General Christopher C. Augur, commander of the Department of the Platte, who at first substituted for Sherman but then became a regular member of the commission. A reasonable mixture of military firmness and humanitarian leniency, the commission boded well for a successful move toward peace.

The group convened in St. Louis in August and made its plans for conferences with the Indians. They directed attention first to the northern tribes and in September held a conference at North Platte, Nebraska, with delegations of Sioux and Cheyennes. It was here, in the words of the report, "that the hitherto untried policy in connection with Indians, of endeavoring to conquer by kindness, was inaugurated."[38] But this first conference settled nothing, for Red Cloud and the Indians from the Powder River region did not attend. After an-

[37] Congressman William Windom of Minnesota had been named as a member of the commission, but he begged off because of other duties and suggested Tappan in his place. *Congressional Globe*, 40 Congress, 1 session, p. 756.

[38] "Report of Indian Peace Commissioners," *House Executive Document* No. 97, 40 Congress, 2 session, serial 1337, p. 4. The report is also printed in *House Executive Document* No. 1, 40 Congress, 3 session, serial 1366, pp. 486–510. There is a good discussion of the Peace Commission and its work in Henry George Waltmann, "The Interior Department, War Department, and Indian Policy, 1865–1887" (unpublished Ph.D. dissertation, University of Nebraska, 1962), pp. 134–55.

nouncing a new council meeting in November at Fort Laramie, the commissioners returned to St. Louis and made preparations for dealing with the Indians in the south. In October they met at Medicine Lodge Creek in southern Kansas to present a ready-made treaty to the Cheyennes, Arapahos, Kiowas, Comanches, and Kiowa-Apaches, by which the tribes were to locate on designated reservations. Many of the Indians were hesitant to come in to the council grounds, but in the end they collected their presents and signed the treaties, which assigned them to two reservations in the western section of the Indian Territory, where the United States would furnish them rations and other goods needed to turn them into happy farmers. The treaties were pronounced very satisfactory, and indeed they not only seemed to secure peace for the future (an assumption which was soon to be proved false), but they advanced notably the policy of concentrating the Indians of the southern plains in a large colony south of the Arkansas River. There was less success in the north. Red Cloud did not appear at Fort Laramie for the council in November and declared that he would not consider peace until the Bozeman Trail forts were removed. The commission decided on a new meeting for the spring and adjourned.[39]

The report of the Peace Commission, submitted on January 7, 1868, was in tune with the humanitarian reformers' views, and the rhetoric of the report marked it as the work of Commissioner Taylor. The commissioners reviewed the causes of Indian hostilities and returned a powerful indictment against the whites:

> Among civilized men war usually springs from a sense of injustice. The best possible way then to avoid war is to do no act of injustice. When we learn that the same rule holds good with Indians, the chief difficulty is removed. But, it is said our wars with them have been almost constant. Have we been uniformly unjust? We answer, unhesitatingly, yes! We are aware that the masses of our people have felt kindly toward them, and the legislation of Congress has always been conceived in the best intentions, but it has been erroneous in

[39] "Report of the Indian Peace Commissioners," pp. 1–5. The Medicine Lodge Creek treaties are in Kappler, *Indian Affairs: Laws and Treaties*, II, 977–89. A detailed story of the negotiations of the treaties from the reports of newspapermen who covered the event is Douglas C. Jones, *The Treaty of Medicine Lodge: The Story of the Great Treaty Council as Told by Eyewitnesses* (Norman, 1966).

fact or perverted in execution. Nobody pays any attention to Indian matters. This is a deplorable fact. Members of Congress understand the negro question, and talk learnedly of finance, and other problems of political economy, but when the progress of settlement reaches the Indian's home, the only question considered is, "how best to get his lands." When they are obtained the Indian is lost sight of. While our missionary societies and benevolent associations have annually collected thousands of dollars from the charitable, to be sent to Asia and Africa for purposes of civilization, scarcely a dollar is expended or a thought bestowed on the civilization of Indians at our very doors. Is it because the Indians are not worth the effort at civilization? Or is it because our people, who have grown rich in the occupation of their former lands—too often taken by force or procured in fraud—will not contribute? It would be harsh to insinuate that covetous eyes have possibly been set on their remaining possessions, and extermination harbored as a means of accomplishing it. As we know that our legislators and nine-tenths of our people are actuated by no such spirit, would it not be well to so regulate our future conduct in this matter as to exclude the possibility of so unfavorable an inference?[40]

The commissioners did not, however, mean to put an end to white advance and did not deny "that civilization must not be arrested in its progress by a handful of savages." They desired the speedy settlement of the territories and the development of their agricultural and mineral wealth by "an industrious, thrifty, and enlightened population." But they voiced a strong doubt about "the purity and genuineness of that civilization which reaches its ends by falsehood and violence, and dispenses blessings that spring from violated rights."[41]

The answer was to bring the Indians into the folds of white civilization, and to this end the English language was to be the great and indispensable tool. "Through sameness of language is produced sameness of sentiment and thought," the report asserted; "customs and habits are moulded and assimilated in the same way, and thus in process of time the differences producing trouble would have been

[40] "Report of the Indian Peace Commissioners," p. 16.
[41] Ibid., p. 7.

21

gradually obliterated." The Indians should be provided reservations where they could be protected, agriculture and manufactures should be introduced as rapidly as possible, schools should be established where their "barbarous dialects" could "be blotted out and the English language substituted." Missionary groups and benevolent societies should turn their attention to the Indians.

The object of greatest solicitude should be to break down the prejudices of tribe among the Indians; to blot out the boundary lines which divide them into distinct nations, and fuse them into one homogeneous mass. Uniformity of language will do this—nothing else will. As this work advances each head of a family should be encouraged to select and improve a homestead. Let the women be taught to weave, to sew and to knit. Let polygamy be punished. Encourage the building of dwellings, and the gathering there of those comforts which endear the home.[42]

As practical suggestions, the commissioners recommended that money annuities be abolished forever and that domestic animals and agricultural and mechanical implements be substituted, that the intercourse laws be thoroughly revised, and that all agents and superintendents be relieved of office and only the competent and faithful reappointed. They declared that since peace not war with the Indians was the object, Indian affairs should be under civilian not military control, and they recommended the formation of an independent Indian department.[43] The generals as well as the civilians signed the full report, including the statement that Indian affairs belonged under civilian control. But General Sherman later asserted that the report did not accurately reflect the officers' views. "We did not favor the conclusion arrived at," Sherman explained, "but being out-voted, we had to sign the report."[44]

Settlement with the northern tribes came at Fort Laramie in 1868. The way had been prepared by the government's willingness to withdraw its posts from the Powder River country. As the Union Pacific moved westward, it would soon be possible to supply a new route to

[42] *Ibid.*, pp. 17–18.
[43] *Ibid.*, pp. 18–22.
[44] Sherman to Senator E. G. Ross, January 7, 1869, quoted in Waltmann, "The Interior Department, War Department, and Indian Policy," p. 149.

Montana west of the Big Horn Mountains, and General Grant instructed Sherman on March 2, "I think it will be well to prepare at once for the abandonment of the posts Phil Kearney, Reno, and Fetterman and to make all the capital with the Indians that can be made out of the change."[45] Little by little the tribes came in. A treaty was signed with the Brulé Sioux on April 29, with the Crows on May 7, and with the Northern Cheyennes and Northern Arapahos on May 10. But the other bands of Sioux only slowly appeared at the fort to affix their signatures to the treaty. The offending posts were dismantled and burned during the summer, and Red Cloud finally signed the treaty in November. Meanwhile the commissioners had gone about their business of negotiating with other western tribes at Fort Sumner, New Mexico, and at Fort Bridger, Utah. The objectives were all the same—to bind the Indians to keep the peace, to provide suitable reservations with fixed boundaries, and to furnish the means for the education and the civilization of the tribes.[46]

The peace party could claim success. Minor collisions between Indians and frontiersmen occurred, but there were for a time no serious disturbances. Then in August, 1868, a party of Cheyennes with a few Arapahos and Sioux shattered the agreements made at Medicine Lodge Creek by an outbreak on the Salina and Solomon rivers in Kansas. The army, now under Major General Philip Sheridan, who had replaced Hancock in command of the Department of the Missouri, was poorly prepared for the roving war parties which killed and burned and raped on the frontiers of Kansas and Colorado. Additional troops were found by enrolling hardy frontiersmen to act as scouts against the Indians, but the scouts, commanded by Brevet Colonel George A. Forsyth, while pursuing hostiles up the Arikaree Fork of the Republican River were attacked by the Indians. The troops were besieged on an island in the river (called Beecher's Island after Lieutenant F. H. Beecher, who was killed there), and were rescued only after nine days of gallantry and misery. It was a spectacular battle, but it hardly stopped the

[45] Grant to Sherman, March 2, 1868, quoted in Olson, *Red Cloud and the Sioux Problem*, p. 71.
[46] Kappler, *Indian Affairs: Laws and Treaties*, II, 998–1024.

Indian marauders, who continued their raids over much of the southern plains.[47]

In the Indian country, meanwhile, General Sherman had already increased military control. He had been designated by Congress as the disburser of the funds provided for carrying out the treaties, and although the Secretary of the Interior asserted that the relations between the department and the Indians were to remain unchanged, Sherman had in fact acted otherwise. In August he created two military districts, one for the Sioux under General William S. Harney and one for the Cheyennes, Arapahos, Kiowas, and Comanches under General W. B. Hazen. The army officers were to act as "agents" for the Indians not on reservations.[48]

When the Peace Commission met again in Chicago in October, there was no longer agreement. Senator Henderson was detained in Washington over the business of President Johnson's impeachment, and only Taylor and Tappan were left to defend a conciliatory position. The rest had been convinced by the summer's warfare that military force was needed to coerce the hostile Indians, and the resolutions they passed reversed much of the previous report. The commissioners now urged provisions at once to feed and clothe and protect the tribes "who now have located or may hereafter locate permanently on their respective agricultural reservations" and that treaties with these tribes be considered to be in force whether ratified or not. The depredations committed by the Indians, the resolutions declared, justified the government in abrogating the clauses of the Medicine Lodge treaties which gave the Indians the right to hunt outside their reservations, and military force should be used to compel Indians to move to the reservations. The tribes, insofar as existing treaties permitted, should no longer be considered "domestic dependent nations," and the Indians should be individually subject to the laws of the United States. Finally, in a sharp reversal of its previous stand, the commission recommended the transfer of the Bureau of Indian Affairs to the War Department.[49] Commissioner Taylor, as chairman, signed the resolutions, but it was clear from his annual report that he vigorously disagreed with them.

[47] Leckie, *Military Conquest of the Southern Plains*, pp. 63–87.
[48] Olson, *Red Cloud and the Sioux Problem*, p. 78.
[49] Resolutions dated October 9, 1868, *House Executive Document* No. 1, 40 Congress, 3 session, serial 1366, pp. 831–32.

Sherman and Sheridan determined upon a winter campaign to drive the tribes to their reservations and to harry and kill those who refused to settle down, with none too great care to separate those who were actually hostile from those who hoped to remain at peace. Custer attacked the sleeping village of Black Kettle's Cheyennes on the Washita River on November 27, killing more than one hundred, including Black Kettle, and taking women and children prisoners. And Sheridan ordered a sweep against other Cheyenne villages down river toward Fort Cobb, where Kiowas and Comanches had turned themselves in and promised peace. Hostile Cheyennes and Arapahos were pursued south until most of them were defeated and returned to the reservation. But the reservations for many of these southern plains Indians were merely places to recoup their strength between raids.[50]

The report of the Peace Commission and the continuing fire of Indian warfare in the West gave new impetus to reformers interested in the Indians—the latter because it re-emphasized the urgent necessity to do something radical about ending conditions that led to war, the former because it gave hope that the government would listen to men who promoted peace and justice. One cry came from Lydia Maria Child, the noted abolitionist, who exclaimed after she had read the original report of the Peace Commission, "Thank God! . . . we have, at last, an Official Document, which manifests something like a right spirit toward the poor Indians!" She quickly penned an emotional essay, *An Appeal for the Indians*, which first appeared in *The National Anti-Slavery Standard* on April 11, 1868, and then was circulated in pamphlet form. She objected to certain proposals of the commission, however, such as the recommendation that Indian children be instructed in English, in which she saw "our haughty Anglo-Saxon ideas of force." A strong believer in the doctrine of evolutionary progress, Mrs. Child wanted the Indians to be viewed "simply as younger members of the same great human family, who need to be protected, instructed and encouraged, till they are capable of appreciating and

[50] Leckie, *Military Conquest of the Southern Plains*, pp. 88–132. A sympathetic history of Sheridan and his aggressive action against the Indians is Carl Coke Rister, *Border Command: General Phil Sheridan in the West* (Norman, 1944).

sharing all our advantages."[51] Another abolitionist who took up the Indian cause was Wendell Phillips, who like Mrs. Child had been moved by the report of the Peace Commission. His great idea was racial equality, and he applied the principle rigorously to the Indians as well as to the blacks. He urged that the Indians be given the rights and responsibilities of citizenship, from which he believed civilization would follow.

Although Mrs. Child and Phillips frequently spoke out critically on Indian affairs and were joined in their appeals and criticism by other antislavery men, the direct effect of abolitionist leaders in post-Civil War Indian reform was slight. Partly because they had already expended a large part of their reservoir of reforming energies, partly because they did not center their whole attention on Indian reform but kept active in a variety of movements, and partly because they did not create effective or long-enduring organizations through which to channel their work, they did not shape the course of Indian policy. But this is not to deny their importance in helping to stir up public interest, in attracting other reformers to the cause, and in contributing substantial weight to the whole movement.[52]

A related agitation for reform came from Peter Cooper, a New York inventor, manufacturer, and philanthropist, whose Cooper Institute was a center not only for the education of working men, with its classes in such subjects as chemistry and engineering, but also a forum for humanitarian causes. At Cooper's invitation, a group of clergymen and philanthropists met on May 18, 1868, and resolved to form an association "for the protection and elevation of the Indians, and to cooperate with the United States government in its efforts to prevent

[51] Lydia Maria Child, *An Appeal for the Indians* (New York, n.d.), pp. 3, 8, 10.

[52] Mardock in *The Reformers and the American Indian* and in "The Anti-Slavery Humanitarians and Indian Policy Reform" argues the importance of antislavery reformers in Indian reform after the Civil War. He opens his book with the statement: "Most of the men and women who took up the cause of Indian rights during the post-Civil War years had previously been involved with the anti-slavery movement. Their work for the liberation of the Negro slaves had helped to prepare them for action in the movement to improve the condition of the Indians." But the evidence in his own book tends to disprove this statement. It is certainly not true that the *leaders* in the post-Civil War Indian reform movement had been *leaders* in the antislavery movement. The abolitionists cited by Mardock (Lydia Maria Child, Wendell Phillips, Henry Ward Beecher) had no sustained effect on the Indian reform movement after the war. It is instructive to note that some biographies of Mrs. Child and Phillips, for example, say nothing at all about their concern for Indians.

desolation and wars on the frontiers of our country."[53] The result was the United States Indian Commission, a private organization of humanitarians with a deceptively official-sounding name. Cooper was the guiding spirit, but he enlisted important support. John Beeson found the commission a good platform, and Henry Ward Beecher spoke at Cooper Institute on Indian Bureau corruption. The commission drew into its work men like William E. Dodge, a wealthy New York merchant, and Vincent Colyer, leader of the YMCA and secretary of the United States Christian Commission during the Civil War, who became influential members of the later Board of Indian Commissioners. Indicative of the United States Indian Commission's aims and spirit was its memorial to Congress of July 14, 1868:

> It has long been the conviction of the humane amongst us, that our aboriginal inhabitants have been the victims of great wrongs, cruelties, and outrage; but it is only recently that the particular nature, the atrocious character, and the frightful results of these crimes have been brought distinctly before us. The recent reports of the Indian peace commissioners, and of the joint special committee of the two houses of Congress, have, in some degree, disclosed the nature and sources of them; and the disclosure is at once so painful and humiliating, as to call for the most prompt and vigorous measures of redress and remedy, for the reason that it concerns alike the honor and the interests of the nation.
>
> We stand charged before the civilized world, by the testimony of our own witnesses, with having been "uniformly unjust to the Indians;" and it is stated by General Sherman and his associate commissioners, that this injustice has been the cause of all the wars which they have waged against us.[54]

It saw the causes of the Indian wars in unjust treaties, failures of the government to live up to treaty obligations, outrages and murders of Indians by white citizens and white soldiers, encroachments on the Indians' lands, the failure of appropriated funds to reach the Indians,

[53] United States Indian Commission memorial, June 6, 1868, quoted in Mardock, *The Reformers and the American Indian*, p. 33.

[54] "Indian Tribes: Memorial on Behalf of the Indians, by the United States Indian Commission," *House Miscellaneous Document* No. 165, 40 Congress, 2 session, serial 1350, p. 1.

and the impossibility for Indians to get justice in the courts. It condemned the presence of troops in the Indian country, since the Indian race thereby was becoming "not only morally degraded, but also physically undermined, by the most loathsome disease which infects our civilization." And it pointed to the need of "honest and faithful agents, with sufficient power to control the rapacity of frontier practice." "It is the object of the association which we represent," the memorial concluded, "to array on the side of justice and humanity the influence and support of an enlightened public opinion, in order to secure for the Indians that treatment which, if in their position, we should demand for ourselves."[55]

The United States Indian Commission kept up agitation on specific Indian cases. It petitioned Congress to reject an Osage treaty in February, 1869, because the treaty would prevent the Indians from getting full value for their lands, and it sent out its secretary, Vincent Colyer, to answer General Hazen's request for a visitor to investigate the condition of the Kiowas and Comanches. In 1870 the commission drew up a detailed plan for the treatment of the Indians, which emphasized the segregation of the Indians on reservations away from white influences and the appointment of high-minded men to serve as agency personnel.[56] It extended its hospitality, too, to Red Cloud and other Sioux chiefs who toured the East in 1870 and offered them the platform afforded by Cooper Union.[57] But the association soon passed from the scene. It had recommended that to secure the Indians justice the government should enlist the services of reliable men, free of political bias and pecuniary interest. When this was in substance accomplished by the formation of the Board of Indian Commissioners in 1869, much of the purpose of Cooper's group was undertaken by the new official board.

Still another voice raised for reform in Indian affairs came from the organized peace movement in the United States. A small radical group under the leadership of Alfred H. Love had refused to accept the Civil War and in 1866 founded the Universal Peace Society (later called Universal Peace Union), which besides antimilitarism worked for the

[55] *Ibid.*, pp. 1–2.
[56] *A Specific Plan for the Treatment of the Indian Question* (New York, 1870).
[57] A description of the Indians' tour of the East is given in Mardock, *The Reformers and the American Indian*, pp. 74–78.

reconciliation of the North and South, women's rights, and abolition of capital punishment. To these goals, appropriately, Love and his organization added humanitarian treatment of the Indian.[58] In August, 1867, John Beeson informed the Commissioner of Indian Affairs that Love was thinking of making Indian rights a primary topic for his society and urged Taylor that it would be sound policy to accept and use its moral influence to further the reform of Indian policy. At peace meetings in Washington and Philadelphia in 1868 Indian matters held an important place in the discussion, and in November the Universal Peace Union sent a memorial to the Senate urging citizenship for the Indians and the removal of military men and corrupt agents from contact with the Indians. At times of crisis in the movement for a peaceful approach to Indian problems, Love and the Peace Union were ready to lend moral support.[59]

Such stirrings of concern for the Indians could not go unheeded. Influential groups were sufficiently aroused to demand of the government a fundamental change in its administration of Indian affairs.

[58] On Love's concern for Indian affairs, see Robert W. Mardock, "Alfred Love, Indian Peace Policy, and the Universal Peace Union," *Kansas Quarterly*, III (Fall, 1971), 64–71.

[59] Mardock, *The Reformers and the American Indian*, pp. 39–40. That a relatively small part of the Peace Union's activities were devoted to Indian matters is shown in *A Brief Synopsis of Work Proposed, Aided and Accomplished by the Universal Peace Union During the Last 31 Years, (from 1866 to 1897,) Under the Direction of Its President, Alfred H. Love, of Philadelphia* (Philadelphia, 1897).

CHAPTER 2

THE PEACE POLICY

The duty of the nation toward the original occupants of the soil, who have become the wards of the nation by the fortunes of conquest and territorial acquisition, seems to me plainly marked out. The Executive is endeavoring in good faith, and in what is deemed the most proper and efficient manner, to fulfill the nation's duty toward a helpless and benighted race. He has sought to combine influences which may effect their physical and moral elevation and improvement. The missionary authorities have an entire race placed under their control, to treat with in accordance with the teachings of our higher Christian civilization. Their work is immense, and while results may not be encouraging within a very short time, they must lose faith in the power of our aggressive civilization if they refuse to accept the truth or forego their efforts in this direction until complete success is attained.

—Secretary of the Interior
COLUMBUS DELANO, 1872

✳✳✳✳✳✳

The answer to the demands for reform was President Grant's "peace policy," which was almost as many-faceted as the Indian problem it hoped to solve. Basically it was a state of mind, a determination that since the old ways of dealing with the Indians had not worked, new ways which emphasized kindness and justice must be tried. Because states of mind do not begin and end abruptly with the passage of a law, the establishment of a commission, or a military disaster, but more subtly change and grow until they dominate an era, the peace policy cannot be precisely dated nor can it be rigidly defined.[1] An official description of the policy in its early days appeared in a statement in 1873 by Grant's Secretary of the Interior, Columbus Delano, which listed the aims and purposes of the administration's policy. In the first place, Delano noted, the policy aimed to place the Indians on reservations where they could be kept from contact with frontier settlements and could be taught the arts of agriculture and other pursuits of civilization through the aid of Christian organizations co-operating with the federal government, and where "humanity and kindness may take the place of barbarity and cruelty." Second, it sought to combine with such humane treatment "all needed severity, to punish them for their outrages according to their merits, thereby teaching them that it is better to follow the advice of the Government, live upon reservations and become civilized, than to continue their native habits and practices." Third, it meant a determination to see that the supplies furnished the Indians were of high quality and reasonably priced so that funds appropriated for the Indians might not be squandered. Fourth, through the aid of religious organizations, it wanted to procure "competent, upright, faithful, moral, and religious" agents, to distribute the goods and to aid in uplifting the Indians' culture. Finally, "through the instrumentality of the Christian organizations, acting in harmony with the Government," it intended to provide churches and schools which would lead the Indians to understand and appreciate "the comforts and benefits of a Christian civilization and thus be prepared ultimately

---

[1] A number of scholars have studied the peace policy or particular aspects of it and each has his own definition of what the policy included. The following are the most important works. Fritz, *Movement for Indian Assimilation*; Robert H. Keller, Jr., "The Protestant Churches and Grant's Peace Policy: A Study in Church-State Relations, 1869–1882" (unpublished Ph.D. dissertation, University of Chicago, 1967); Priest, *Uncle Sam's Stepchildren*; Peter J. Rahill, *The Catholic Indian Missions and Grant's Peace Policy, 1870–1884* (Washington, 1953); Elsie Mitchell Rushmore, *The Indian Policy During Grant's Administrations* (Jamaica, New York, 1914); Robert Lee Whitner, "The Methodist Episcopal Church and Grant's Peace Policy: A Study of the Methodist Agencies, 1870–1882" (unpublished Ph.D. dissertation, University of Minnesota, 1959). See also Martha L. Edwards, "A Problem of Church and State in the 1870's," *Mississippi Valley Historical Review*, XI (June, 1924), 37–53; Henry E. Fritz, "The Making of Grant's 'Peace Policy,'" *Chronicles of Oklahoma*, XXXVII (Winter, 1959–1960), 411–32; Robert M. Utley, "The Celebrated Peace Policy of General Grant," *North Dakota History*, XX (July, 1953), 121–42.

to assume the duties and privileges of citizenship."[2] Forty years later, a formal description of the peace policy spoke broadly of "such legislation and administration in Indian affairs as by peaceful methods should put an end to Indian discontent, make impossible Indian wars, and fit the great body of Indians to be received into the ranks of American citizens."[3]

Underlying this new departure in Indian policy was the conscious intent of the government to turn to religious groups and religiously minded men for the formulation and administration of Indian policy. The "peace policy" might just as properly have been labeled the "religious policy."

There had, of course, been a long history of co-operation between the federal government and missionary groups in Indian matters. Money appropriated for the promotion of civilization among the Indians was used to stimulate missionary groups to work among the Indians, and many Commissioners of Indian Affairs relied heavily on church aid. "In every system which has been adopted for promoting the cause of education among the Indians," Commissioner William Medill said in 1847, "the Department has found its most efficient and faithful auxiliaries and laborers in the societies of the several Christian denominations, which have sent out missionaries, established schools, and maintained local teachers among the different tribes. Deriving their impulse from principles of philanthropy and religion, and devoting a large amount of their own means to the education, moral elevation and improvement of the tribes, the Department has not hesitated to make them the instruments, to a considerable extent, of applying the funds appropriated by the government for like purposes."[4] But early examples of church-state co-operation in Indian affairs had been limited chiefly to educational and religious activities. In the decades

[2] Report of the Secretary of the Interior, 1873, in serial 1601, pp. iii–iv.

[3] Merrill E. Gates, "Peace Policy," in Frederick Webb Hodge, ed., *Handbook of American Indians North of Mexico* (2 vols., Washington, 1907–1910), II, 218–19. Gates was chairman of the Board of Indian Commissioners, 1890–1899, and later its secretary.

[4] Report of the Commissioner of Indian Affairs, 1847, in serial 503, p. 749; *ibid.*, 1844, in serial 449, p. 436. See also Francis Paul Prucha, "American Indian Policy in the 1840's: Visions of Reform," in John G. Clark, ed., *The Frontier Challenge: Responses to the Trans-Mississippi West* (Lawrence, Kansas, 1971), pp. 81–110; R. Pierce Beaver, *Church, State, and the American Indians: Two and a Half Centuries of Partnership in Missions Between Protestant Churches and Government* (St. Louis, 1966).

following the Civil War church groups and religious-minded men were welcomed into fuller partnership; to a large extent they came to dominate the official government policy and administration of Indian matters, at first by direct participation, then by stirring up and channeling public opinion.

In turning to religious groups, the federal government abdicated much of its responsibility in Indian administration. Specific governmental functions were handed over to church groups, a development that indicated not only the failure of the governmental processes in regard to the "Indian question" but also the pervasive moral and religious influences on the national outlook. Two structural components of Grant's peace policy illustrate the new departure, the Board of Indian Commissioners and the apportionment of Indian agencies among church groups. Each of these resulted from a multiplicity of influences, ideas, and pressures, so that it is impossible to pinpoint their precise origin, but the major events are clear.

The Board of Indian Commissioners was established by Congress on April 10, 1869. The President was authorized to organize a board of not more than ten persons "to be selected by him from men eminent for their intelligence and philanthropy, to serve without pecuniary compensation." The stated purpose of the board was to exercise "joint control with the Secretary of the Interior" over the disbursement of funds appropriated for the Indians.[5] The idea of such a board of independent and high-minded men, not subject to the political pressures that plagued the Indian Office, had long been in the air. Bishop Whipple in 1862 advocated a "Council of appointment made up of men who shall hold their office *ex officio*, who receive no compensation, and who would deem it a high privilege to work in the elevation of an heathen race." Such a group, he thought, could choose Indian agents of high character and guide them with wise oversight.[6] A treaty with the Chippewas in 1863 authorized the President to appoint a board of visitors, to be chosen from such Christian denominations as he might designate. This group of two or three persons was to attend annuity

[5] *United States Statutes at Large*, XVI, 40.
[6] Henry Benjamin Whipple, "What Shall We Do with the Indian," 1862, in *Lights and Shadows*, p. 518.

payments and to report annually on the qualifications and behavior of all persons living on the reservation.[7] The Joint Special Committee under Senator Doolittle in 1867 recommended inspection boards that were to have considerable powers for overseeing the execution of treaties and examining the conduct and competence of Indian agents. In 1868, the New York reform group, the United States Indian Commission, memorialized Congress on behalf of the Indians and urged, among other reforms, enlisting the services of "capable and reliable men, independent of political or party bias, who shall not be remunerated from the public treasury, and who shall have no pecuniary interest to swerve them from the objects of their appointment."[8]

An important pattern for the Board of Indian Commissioners was the United States Christian Commission, which had provided religious literature and church services for the Union soldiers during the Civil War. The commission, organized by the Young Men's Christian Association and supported by the government, offered a good example of close co-operation between religious groups and the federal officers. Indeed, when Secretary of the Interior Jacob D. Cox wrote to men asking them to serve on the Board of Indian Commissioners, he told them that the group was "to act as auxiliary to this Department in the supervision of the work of gathering the Indians upon reservations, etc.," and he remarked, "The design of those who suggested the Commission, was that something like a Christian Commission should be established having the civilization of the Indians in view, & laboring to stimulate public interest in this work, whilst also cooperating with the Department in the specific purpose mentioned."[9]

The final instigation of the measure came from the Philadelphia

[7] Treaty with the Red Lake and Pembina Bands of Chippewa, October 2, 1863, in Charles J. Kappler, *Indian Affairs: Laws and Treaties*, II, 854. Instructions from Indian Commissioner William P. Dole to the board (Bishop Whipple, Roman Catholic Bishop Thomas L. Grace of St. Paul, and the Reverend Thomas S. Williamson of Davenport, Iowa), August 4, 1863, are in the Report of the Commissioner of Indian Affairs, 1863, in serial 1182, pp. 458–59.

[8] "Condition of the Indian Tribes: Report of the Joint Special Committee," *Senate Report* No. 156, 39 Congress, 2 session, serial 1279, pp. 8–10; "Indian Tribes: Memorial on Behalf of the Indians by the United States Indian Commission," *House Miscellaneous Document* No. 165, 40 Congress, 2 session, serial 1350.

[9] Copy of Cox to William Welsh, April 15, 1869, in Henry B. Whipple Papers, Minnesota Historical Society. A similar letter is cited in Charles Lewis Slattery, *Felix Reville Brunot, 1820–1898* (New York, 1901), p. 143. Several members of the Board of Indian

philanthropist William Welsh. Encouraged by Grant's inaugural statement on the Indians that he would favor "any course toward them
which tends to their civilization and ultimate citizenship," Welsh and
a committee of influential friends had a "long and most satisfactory"
interview with the President and the Secretary of the Interior on
March 22, 1869, to propose a commission to supervise the disbursement of funds provided by the recent treaty with the Sioux. Welsh
spoke frankly to Cox. "I told the Secretary," he reported to Bishop
Whipple, "that altho' the community had perfect confidence in him
that unless there was a commission to free him from the thraldom of
party politics, intelligent philanthropists would not rally to his support, for *his* department had always been the prey of the most thievish
party politicians and what had always been, might be again." Welsh
felt he was presumptuous in thus telling the Secretary what he should
do, but Grant and Cox agreed that there should be such a board, not
for the Sioux alone, but for the Indians as a whole.[10]

The legislation establishing the Board of Indian Commissioners did
not have entirely clear sledding, for the spoilsmen whom Welsh and
his group aimed to block were not without influence, and interdenominational rivalry already was a factor to be reckoned with. Some
Quakers feared that the board would be the tool of Episcopalians,
evangelicals, and "their self-constituted com[er] [Welsh]."[11] Others,
conversely, were afraid that the Quakers themselves might become too
subservient to the administration and appear too eager for political
power. When Grant assured Quaker leaders that they would not lose
their agencies and could appoint Quakers to the board, however, their
opposition was dispelled.

The relationship of the board to the churches was not defined in the

Commissioners had served on the Christian Commission. George H. Stuart was chair-
man of the commission; John V. Farwell and Clinton B. Fisk were members; and William
E. Dodge, Nathan Bishop, and Vincent Colyer were associated with its work. See
United States Christian Commission, "Address of the Christian Commission," January
13, 1862, and *Facts, Principles, and Progress* (Philadelphia, 1864); Lemuel Moss,
Annals of the United States Christian Commission (Philadelphia, 1868).

10 Welsh to Whipple, March 26, 1869, in Whipple Papers; William Welsh, *Taopi and
His Friends, or the Indians' Wrongs and Rights* (Philadelphia, 1869), pp. 76–79; William Welsh, *Indian Office: Wrongs Doing and Reforms Needed* (Philadelphia, 1874),
pp. 1–2; George H. Stuart, *The Life of George H. Stuart, Written by Himself* (Philadelphia, 1890), pp. 239–40.

11 Keller, "Protestant Churches and Grant's Peace Policy," p. 80.

law, but it was very intimate, and the first board was composed of prominent laymen from a variety of Protestant denominations—Episcopalian, Presbyterian, Baptist, Methodist, Congregational, and Quaker. The members were not official representatives of their specific churches, but they all represented American Christianity with its dominant Protestant character. All were wealthy men, able to devote their time to the Indian cause without pay. "It was in every way a representative body of men," wrote the biographer of one of the members, "being carefully chosen from different Christian communions and from different political parties."[12] William Welsh, fittingly, was elected first chairman of the board.

On May 27, 1869, the new board met with Grant and Cox in the White House, where the President assured them of his desire to reform abuses in Indian affairs and delineated the main lines of his Indian policy—abandonment of the treaty system, protection of the Indians on reservations where they could be taught the arts of civilization, strict redemption of the government's pledges to the Indians, and secure Indian titles to "such lands as they could be induced to cultivate." The President and the Secretary wanted the board to have "the fullest authority over the whole subject that could be given by them consistently with their own responsibility by law" and promised full support, as did the Secretary of War and General William T. Sherman, whom the members visited on the same day.[13]

[12] Slattery, *Brunot*, p. 143. The first members of the board were Felix R. Brunot, an Episcopalian and partner in a Pittsburgh steel mill; Robert Campbell, a St. Louis merchant and banker, probably a Presbyterian; William E. Dodge, a prominent Presbyterian layman of New York with mining and railroad interests; George H. Stuart, a Philadelphia dry goods merchant, a Presbyterian; John V. Farwell, Methodist, a Chicago merchant; Edward S. Tobey, a Congregationalist from Boston; Henry S. Lane, Methodist, former governor and United States Senator of Indiana; William Welsh, Episcopalian merchant from Philadelphia; Vincent Colyer, a New York leader in the Young Men's Christian Association; Nathan Bishop, a Baptist educator from Boston. The Quaker John Lang replaced Welsh when he resigned a month after the board was established. Fritz, *Movement for Indian Assimilation*, p. 75, says "all the members of the Board . . . were nominated by the various religious denominations." But this does not seem to have been strictly the case. Stuart recalled that Grant had told him, "I want you to name some leading men from different sections of the country, who will be willing to serve the cause of the Indians without compensation," and Stuart named prominent men from various cities, most of whom were then appointed. *Life of George H. Stuart*, pp. 240–41. See also Keller, "Protestant Churches and Grant's Peace Policy," pp. 134–35.
[13] Minutes of May 27, 1869, Records of the Board of Indian Commissioners, Minutes of Board Meetings, vol. I, pp. 6–7, National Archives Record Group 75.

The official duties of the group were set forth in special instructions from the Commissioner of Indian Affairs, Ely S. Parker, and in regulations promulgated by President Grant. Parker, accepting the board's desire to work with the President and other officers for the "humanization, civilization, and Christianization of the Indians," urged the members to visit and inspect as many of the tribes, "especially the wild and roving ones," as they could and to come back with suggestions as to what should be done, and he asked them to inspect the accounts of the agents and report on the efficiency of those officers. Moreover, he spelled out in great detail specific questions which he wanted the board to answer, from the viability of the treaty system, to methods of paying annuities, to the line where civil rule should cease and military rule begin in dealing with conflicts between the Indians and white citizens. More specific guidelines for their activity came in President Grant's executive order. The members were to be furnished full opportunity to inspect the records of the Indian Office, to inspect superintendencies and agencies, to be present at annuity payments and councils with the Indians, and to supervise superintendents and agents in the performance of their duties. They were authorized to be present at the purchase of goods for the Indians and to inspect such purchases. They were to forward complaints, advise as to changing modes of purchasing goods or the conduct of Indian affairs, and recommend plans for civilizing the Indians. All the officers of the Indian service were enjoined to give the board members full access to records, to pay respectful heed to their advice, and to co-operate with them "in the most earnest manner, to the extent of their proper powers, in the general work of civilizing the Indians, protecting them in their legal rights, and stimulating them to become industrious citizens in permanent homes, instead of following a roving and savage life."[14]

These powers and responsibilities were not strong enough to satisfy William Welsh, who wanted the Board of Indian Commissioners to have the full joint control with the Department of the Interior that he felt was demanded by the legislation of Congress and not to be a "mere council of advice." He resigned on June 29, only a month after the organization of the board, and on November 17, Felix Brunot, a Pitts-

[14] Parker to board members, May 26, 1869, in *Report of the Board of Indian Commissioners*, 1869, pp. 3–4; Grant order, June 3, 1869, *ibid.*, pp. 4–5.

burgh industrialist, was elected chairman in his stead.[15] For five years, the members of the board, with the determination not to give up the opportunity the new organization offered, worked selflessly and often against great odds to bring a higher level of competency and of integrity to Indian affairs.

They did this in several ways, not the least of which was arousing public opinion in support of the Indians and the need for fair treatment. The strongest statement of the necessity for a new beginning was the first annual report of the board, submitted by Brunot on November 23, 1869. It was a vehement indictment of past government policy toward the Indians. While noting the desire of the United States to deal generously with the Indians, the report declared that the actual treatment the Indians had received had been "unjust and iniquitous beyond the power of words to express" and that the history of the government's relations with the tribes had been "a shameful record of broken treaties and unfulfilled promises." The report excoriated the frontiersmen who wronged the Indians and placed the primary blame for Indian wars on them. "Paradoxical as it may seem," the report continued, "the white man has been the chief obstacle in the way of Indian civilization," and the Indians, who despite the hindrances thrown in their way had made progress toward civilization, were applauded. All the Indians needed to induce them to work and to advance, the board asserted, was a proper incentive.[16]

Such invective furnished wonderful material for righteous confessions of the white man's guilt, and Helen Hunt Jackson later quoted large sections of the report in *A Century of Dishonor*. Although such utterances gave substance to the charge that the Board of Indian Commissioners were sentimentalists out of touch with the realities of the frontier, the statements of the board were a strong indication that new influences were to be brought to bear upon the policies governing the relationships between the government and the Indians. The report was an apt initial statement of what the peace policy was to mean during the ensuing quarter of a century.

15 Welsh, *Indian Office: Wrongs Doing and Reforms Needed*, pp. 1–2; Minutes of November 17, Records of the Board of Indian Commissioners, Minutes of Board Meetings, vol. I, p. 13.
16 *Report of the Board of Indian Commissioners*, 1869, pp. 7–9.

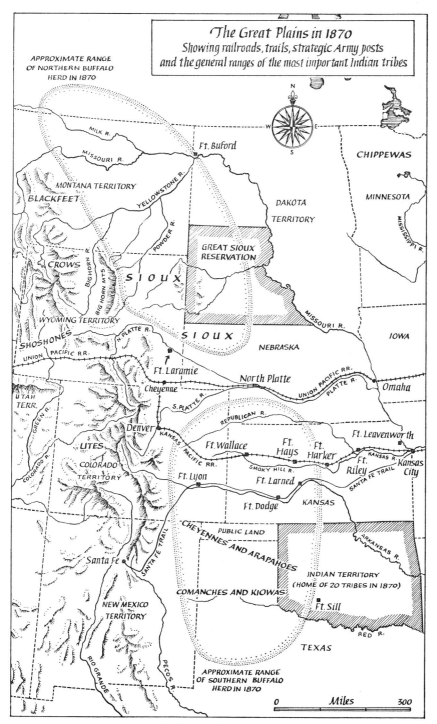

APPROXIMATE RANGE
OF NORTHERN BUFFALO
HERD IN 1870

MILK R.

MISSOURI R.

Ft. Buford

CHIPPEWAS

MONTANA TERRITORY

BLACKFEET

YELLOWSTONE R.

DAKOTA
TERRITORY

MINNESOTA

MISSISSIPPI R.

POWDER R.

CROWS

BIGHORN R.

BIG HORN MTS.

SIOUX

GREAT SIOUX
RESERVATION

WYOMING TERRITORY

N. PLATTE R.

SHOSHONES

SIOUX

MISSOURI R.

UNION PACIFIC RR.

NEBRASKA

IOWA

UTAH
TERR.

GREEN R.

Ft. Laramie

Cheyenne

North Platte

Omaha

UNION PACIFIC RR.

PLATTE R.

S. PLATTE R.

REPUBLICAN R.

Denver

KANSAS PACIFIC RR.

Ft. Leavenworth

UTES

Ft. Wallace

Ft.
Hays

Ft.
Harker

KANSAS R.

Ft.
Riley

Kansas
City

COLORADO
TERRITORY

COLORADO R.

SMOKY HILL R.

Ft. Lyon

Ft. Larned

SANTA FE TRAIL

Ft. Dodge

KANSAS

PUBLIC LAND

CHEYENNES AND ARAPAHOES

ARKANSAS R.

Santa Fe

SANTA FE TRAIL

INDIAN TERRITORY
(HOME OF 20 TRIBES IN 1870)

COMANCHES AND KIOWAS

Ft. Sill

NEW MEXICO
TERRITORY

RIO GRANDE

PECOS R.

RED R.

TEXAS

APPROXIMATE RANGE
OF SOUTHERN BUFFALO
HERD IN 1870

0   Miles   300

The Great Plains in 1870

Having delivered its blast of condemnation, the board devoted the remainder of the report to its preliminary proposals. Recognizing that it could not reach satisfactory conclusions by mere "theorizing" but would have to base them on "personal observation and knowledge, as well as testimony," it did not propose in its first report to be final or exhaustive. Yet the recommendations put forth already exhibited much of the pattern of reform that was to dominate the rest of the century. The board urged the concentration of the Indians on small reservations with ultimate division of the land in severalty, discouragement of tribal relations, citizenship for the Five Civilized Tribes in the Indian Territory, abolition of the treaty system, abandonment of money annuities which "encourage idleness and vice," establishment of schools with teachers employed by the government to teach English to every tribe, and nomination of the teachers by religious bodies and the encouragement of Christian missions. "The religion of our blessed Saviour," it declared, "is believed to be the most effective agent for the civilization of any people." In addition, the board proposed "the honest and prompt performance of all the treaty obligations to the reservation Indians," judicial tribunals in the Indian Territory for the prompt punishment of crime, and selection of superintendents and agents on the basis of moral as well as business qualifications and without political considerations. The legal status of the uncivilized Indians, it declared, should be that "of wards of the government; the duty of the latter being to protect them, to educate them in industry, the arts of civilization, and the principles of Christianity; elevate them to the rights of citizenship, and to sustain and clothe them until they can support themselves."[17]

The board members went about their duties with tremendous goodwill. In order to acquaint themselves with the conditions in the West, they arranged annual tours of inspection, dividing the country into northern, southern, and western divisions, with a subcommittee of the board assigned to each. Information gathered on the tours furnished a basis for the conclusions and recommendations of the board. Brunot, especially, was tireless in his exertions. For five years he devoted nearly all his time to his duties as chairman of the Board of Indian Commissioners, and each summer he spent three or four months among the Indian tribes. Vincent Colyer, the secretary of the board, in the first

[17] *Ibid.*, pp. 9–11.

year alone submitted reports on the condition of the Indians he visited in Kansas, the Indian Territory, Texas, New Mexico, Arizona, and Colorado, as well as a long report on the Indians in Alaska, and in 1871 he submitted another long report on the Apaches of New Mexico and Arizona.[18] Other members of the board performed comparable service. If they carried with them their own background and prejudices and saw Indian matters completely from their own perspective, they nevertheless furnished a continuing element of articulate concern for the Indians that could be ridiculed and often pushed aside but never completely ignored.

Of more practical and immediate significance was the board's supervisory work in the procuring of supplies for the Indians. Perhaps no element in the Indian service had been more open to criticism than the purchase and distribution of annuity and other goods. Fraud was rampant, poor goods were contracted for at high prices, and the merchants and their friends got rich by cheating the government and the Indians. The Board of Indian Commissioners was established in large measure precisely to see that the moneys appropriated for the Indians gave full benefit to the Indians, and in July, 1870, Congress directed that the board inspect all goods purchased for the Indians.[19] A special purchasing committee devoted year after year of unheralded service to correct abuses. The experienced businessmen who made up the committee on purchases recommended changes in the method of purchases in order to secure strict impartiality in the acceptance of bids and rigid inspection of the goods delivered to see that they conformed to the samples supplied. The committee was optimistic that its work could achieve great good. It was convinced, it reported in 1871, "that all 'Indian rings' can be broken up, and that the wards of the nation, who have been so long the victims of greedy and designing men, ought and must be treated in a manner worthy of the highest moral obligations of a Christian government." But there were so many avenues of fraud that it was difficult to watch them all at once, and the costs of transportation as well as of the supplies themselves had to be controlled. Despite the

[18] *Ibid.*, pp. 30–55, 81–164; *ibid.*, 1871, pp. 32–86. The latter report was printed separately as *Peace with the Apaches of New Mexico and Arizona: Report of Vincent Colyer, Member of the Board of Indian Commissioners, 1871* (Washington, 1872).
[19] *United States Statutes at Large*, XVI, 360.

loopholes, however, the committee's reports indicate substantial savings over previous years and a rise in the quality of the goods.[20]

A similar attempt to check corruption was the work of the executive committee of the board in examining the accounts and vouchers presented to the Indian Office for payment, an additional duty given to the Board of Indian Commissioners by Congress in 1871.[21] The task was thought to be very onerous and had not been solicited, but it was considered essential by the board if it was to share responsibility with the Department of the Interior in the disbursement of appropriated funds. The members examined vouchers and bills representing disbursements of millions of dollars each year, approving most but rejecting or postponing payment on large amounts that were improper or unreasonable.[22] Although the Secretary of the Interior could overrule the board and frequently did, the vigilance of the philanthropists saved the government large sums.

Another function of the board was its liaison between the government and the missionary societies that were involved in Indian matters. Each winter in Washington, the board met with the secretaries and other representatives of the mission groups for a discussion of their work among the Indians and of Indian affairs in general. The reports from the various denominations supplied the board members and the Commissioner of Indian Affairs (who usually attended the meetings) with necessary information and with the views and suggestions of men working in the field. These conferences were a valuable forum for discussion of Indian reform. Since the meetings were composed of like-minded people and thus were seldom if ever shaken by strong dissenting opinions, they served to confirm and strengthen the

[20] Report of the Board of Indian Commissioners, 1870, pp. 21–23; ibid., 1871, p. 161. See the reports of the purchasing committee in the annual reports of the board. The report for 1875, pp. 19–24, is a long recital of specific cases which revealed "the tricks, subterfuges, evasions, and combinations" that the committee experienced and its attempts to defeat them. George H. Stuart, who served as chairman of the purchasing committee, tells of its work in Life of George H. Stuart, pp. 242–45.

[21] United States Statutes at Large, XVI, 568.

[22] In 1871, for example, the executive committee examined 1,136 vouchers, representing a cash disbursement of $5,240,729.60, of which it rejected or suspended $153,166.20. In 1873 it examined 1,656 vouchers, representing disbursements of $6,032,877.65, of which 39 vouchers representing $426,909.96 were turned down as fraudulent or questionable. Report of the Board of Indian Commissioners, 1871, pp. 11–12; ibid., 1873, p. 9.

reform sentiment of the age. They brought the churches into closer association with men who helped to formulate Indian policy and furnished a substantial platform from which to preach the reforms devised.

The board members began their work in a halcyon atmosphere. "They have shrunk from no self-sacrifice, toil, or danger in endeavoring to make the policy you have adopted toward the Indians an entire success," Secretary of the Interior Cox informed President Grant at the end of 1870. "The healthful effect of their influence and advice is cheerfully acknowledged by the Department and the Indian Bureau, and has inspired a just confidence in the honesty of the transactions which have been concluded under their supervision." His successor spoke of the board's "wholesome influence in establishing the new policy, and its active aid and co-operation in carrying out the measures of the Government."[23] But all was not as serene as these superficial reports indicated. The board, in fact, soon found its attempts to do good blocked by powerful forces and its advice and recommendations ignored or contradicted. Goodwill and integrity on the part of the board's members met greed from the "Indian ring" and corruption among public officials. The board nearly succumbed altogether; it underwent a crisis in 1874 from which it only slowly recovered.

The heart of the problem was the question of the authority of the Board of Indian Commissioners. Could there be in fact "joint authority" in Indian affairs, or in any part of them, between the Department of the Interior and the quasi-private group of unpaid, religious-minded businessmen? Felix Brunot, conscientious about his responsibilities as chairman of the board, tried hard to find out precisely what power the board had in supervising expenditures, the most critical of its functions. He gathered together the documents relating to the formation of the board and inquired of the Attorney General for a ruling. The ruling upheld the authority of the board, but in practice the members found that their recommendations could be arbitrarily set aside. More serious was the fact that many disbursements were not cleared through the

[23] Report of the Secretary of the Interior, 1870, in serial 1449, p. ix; *ibid.*, 1871, in serial 1505, p. 3.

43

Board of Indian Commissioners at all and that contracts were awarded without competitive bids.[24]

By 1871 the Board of Indian Commissioners and the Department of the Interior were already clearly at odds, as the department grew increasingly jealous of its prerogatives. An attack upon Commissioner Parker was one element in the conflict. Leading the attack was William Welsh, who lost none of his interest in Indian affairs by his resignation from the board and who intended to carry on reform as an unofficial member. By uncovering evidence of Parker's questionable dealings in procuring Indian supplies, he forced a Congressional investigation of the Bureau of Indian Affairs. Although the committee found "irregularities, neglect, and incompetency, and, in some instances, a departure from the express provisions of law for the regulation of Indian expenditures, and in the management of affairs in the Indian Department," it absolved Parker himself of all fraud or corruption. Despite the favorable outcome of the investigation, however, the commissioner resigned in July, 1871. He charged the whole affair to the enmity of those "who waxed rich and fat from the plundering of the poor Indians," and declared it was "no longer a pleasure to discharge patriotic duties."[25]

Opponents of the Indian ring were jubilant. *The Nation* declared that a revolution had taken place by "the complete overthrow of a most gigantic system of wrong, robbery, hypocrisy, greed, and cruelty, and in the triumph of right, of official integrity, of administrative economy, and of the principles of a Christian civilization." The formation of the Board of Indian Commissioners, it asserted, had been a staggering blow against the Indian ring, but that reform had been set back when Commissioner Parker had fallen under the ring's control. The journal exulted in the news report that Brunot would become the

[24] *Report of the Board of Indian Commissioners,* 1873, pp. 6–9. Congress in 1872 provided that the approval of the board was not a prerequisite for payment of vouchers. *United States Statutes at Large,* XVII, 186.

[25] Welsh, *Indian Office: Wrongs Doing and Reforms Needed;* William Welsh, *Summing Up Evidence Before a Committee of the House of Representatives, Charged with the Investigation of Misconduct in the Indian Office* (Washington, 1871); "Affairs of the Indian Department," *House Report* No. 39, 41 Congress, 3 session, serial 1464, p. ii; "Writings of General Parker," *Publications of the Buffalo Historical Society,* VIII (1905), 526–27. Arthur C. Parker, *The Life of General Ely S. Parker* (Buffalo, 1919), pp. 150–61, has nothing but praise for Parker's career as Commissioner of Indian Affairs.

new commissioner, for it believed that "the snake had been scotched, but we are afraid not yet killed."[26]

Brunot was offered the commissioner's post by Secretary of the Interior Delano on October 17, 1871, in a flattering letter that spoke of the need of "a man of good business habits, of sound judgment, of integrity, above suspicion, of quick perception, and one who is prompt to act when his judgment had arrived at settled conclusions," a person true to the best interests of both the Indians and the government, and "a sincere friend of the President and his Indian policy." Brunot refused to accept the challenge. He must already have had suspicions that conditions were hostile to the reform he envisaged, although he wrote a note of refusal that carried a strong word of confidence in Delano's determination to deal with the Indians on principles of justice and mercy and to put an end to peculation and other mismanagement in the Indian Office.[27] The position went to Francis A. Walker, an eminent scholar and a man of sterling qualities, whose appointment gave hope to Brunot and the board. But Walker was unable to end the influence of forces hostile to the board and its vision of reform. The forced resignation of Parker was countered by the forcing from office of Vincent Colyer, the secretary of the Board of Indian Commissioners, whose investigations and reports on Indian affairs in the Southwest won him the enmity of Delano.[28]

By 1874, matters had come to an impasse between the board and the Secretary of the Interior. Brunot, sensing that some immediate reform was necessary, urged the separation of the Indian Office from the Department of the Interior and the establishment of an independent Indian Department. When the recommendation was ignored, Brunot and the rest of the original members of the board resigned. "It was obvious, towards the close of 1873," Brunot's biographer wrote, "that the original members of the Board of Indian Commissioners could not serve much longer. They freely gave of their busy lives for the sake of the Indian, but when they found repeatedly during the last

[26] *Nation*, XIII (August 17, 1871), 100–101.
[27] Delano to Brunot, October 17, 1871, Records of the Board of Indian Commissioners, Minutes of Board Meetings, vol. I, p. 61; Brunot to Delano, October 19, 1871, *ibid.*, p. 62.
[28] Keller, "Protestant Churches and Grant's Peace Policy," p. 152.

year that their recommendations were ignored, that bills, laboriously examined by them and rejected by them, were paid, that gross breaking of the law in giving contracts was winked at, and that many important matters were not submitted to them at all, then they decided that their task was as useless as it was irritating."[29] The failure to set up an Indian Department was but the straw on the camel's back. The board was convinced that the Interior Department from the secretary down was corrupt. The passing of the original members of the board marked the end of an era in the board's existence; the new members appointed in 1874 were of a different breed, who were less inclined to set themselves up in opposition to the official government departments.[30]

Unable by direct action to assume responsibility for Indian finances or for Indian policy in general, the Board of Indian Commissioners broke its head in an attempt to do what was impossible. But the seeds it planted would germinate and blossom later. The new board, weak though it was, perpetuated the idea that the moral and religious sentiments of the people should be represented in the formulation and administration of Indian policy. Brunot and his colleagues were the first example of highly motivated men in a corporate, united attempt to change the course of government action from outside the administrative structure. The idea would not die; it lived on in the formulation of Indian reform sentiment in the 1880's and 1890's.

The second structural component of Grant's peace policy was the apportionment of the Indian agencies among church groups, with the understanding that the missionary boards would nominate the agents and the other employees at the agencies. By such an arrangement, it was hoped that the evils resulting from dishonest and incompetent agents would be obviated. This extreme measure, an admission by the government that it was unable to carry out its obligations by ordinary procedures, was a striking example of the conviction in public as well

[29] Slattery, *Brunot*, p. 217. See also D. Stuart Dodge, *Memorials of William E. Dodge* (New York, 1887), pp. 177–78.
[30] Congressional debates on the board and its continued existence and internal dissension within the board itself are discussed in Priest, *Uncle Sam's Stepchildren*, pp. 47–52. Priest, however, takes too limited a view of the board's work and its successes.

as private circles that only by emphasis on moral and religious means would the Indians be led along the marked-out path to civilization.

The roots of the policy were diverse. It was perhaps an obvious conclusion that if evils were caused because bad men were appointed agents, then the evils could be corrected by appointing good men. If religious men had been such positive influences for good among the Indians as teachers and missionaries, why could they not increase their good effects by broadening the scope of their activities? Even before the Civil War, Bishop Whipple, writing to President Buchanan "as a Christian bishop may write to the Chief Magistrate of a Christian Nation," urged the securing of "practical Christian teachers . . . to teach the Indians the peaceful pursuits of agriculture and the arts of civilization." And in the *North American Review* in 1864, in a devastating attack upon the "Indian system," Whipple urged that the Indian agents be placed beyond the reach of political removal and that "men of the highest character, receiving good salaries, and holding their office during good behavior" be appointed.[31] Army officers, too, noted that missionaries had succeeded with the Indians where military and civilian officers had failed, and there were examples of the good work done by occasional agents who were ministers of Christian denominations.[32]

The post-war allotment of agencies to religious bodies began with the Quakers. This was entirely fitting, for the Society of Friends had long been interested in the humane treatment of the Indians, and the public mind (relying on the story of William Penn and his fair dealings with the red men) came to equate Quakers and peaceful management of Indian affairs. The unhappy condition of the Indians after the Civil War brought considerable response from the Quakers. Delegations of Friends visited key members of Congress, and memorials were sent to urge a more humanitarian policy and to suggest that in the appointment of agents care should be taken to select men of unquestioned integrity.[33]

In January, 1869, delegates from seven Yearly Meetings of Friends

[31] Whipple to Buchanan, April 9, 1860, in Whipple, *Lights and Shadows*, pp. 50–53; Whipple, "The Indian System," *North American Review*, XCIX (October, 1864), 463.
[32] Keller, "Protestant Churches and Grant's Peace Policy," pp. 57–58.
[33] The concern of the Quakers in Indian matters is well treated in Rayner W. Kelsey, *Friends and the Indians, 1655–1917* (Philadelphia, 1917). See especially Chapter VIII, "Grant's Peace Policy," pp. 162–99.

met in Baltimore to discuss the problem of the Indians. They memorialized Congress with a strong statement of the need to turn from the wars devastating the West to a policy of peace and kindness, and they supported the proposal that had been introduced in the House for a separate department of Indian affairs.[34] Fearing that Indian affairs might be turned over to military control by the new President, a delegation from the meeting met with Grant on January 25 and spoke to him of plans for an Indian policy based on peace and Christianity, urging the selection of religious employees as far as practicable. To this group Grant is said to have replied: "Gentlemen, your advice is good. I accept it. Now give me the names of some Friends for Indian agents and I will appoint them. If you can make Quakers out of the Indians it will take the fight out of them. Let us have peace."[35] A similar committee of Philadelphia Friends also visited the President-elect. The committees were impressed by Grant's cordial attitude and his apparently earnest desire to begin a more peaceful and humane policy toward the Indians.[36]

Grant moved quickly to implement the Quakers' proposal. On February 15, 1869, Ely S. Parker, then Grant's aide-de-camp, wrote to Benjamin Hallowell, secretary of the Quaker conference, asking for a list of Quakers whom the Society would endorse as suitable persons for Indian agents. He added that Grant also wished to assure him "that any attempt which may or can be made by your Society, for the improvement, education, and Christianization of the Indians, under such Agencies, will receive . . . all the encouragement and protection which the laws of the United States will warrant him in giving."[37] The Quakers, after some hesitation about accepting posts on the distant and exposed frontiers, responded favorably, and by the middle of June both the Orthodox and the Hicksite Friends had appointed superintendents

[34] "Memorial of Yearly Meetings of the Society of Friends, Relative to the Treatment of the Indians," January 21, 1869, *House Miscellaneous Document* No. 29, 40 Congress, 3 session, serial 1385.

[35] T. C. Battey in introduction to Lawrie Tatum, *Our Red Brothers and the Peace Policy of President Ulysses S. Grant* (Philadelphia, 1899), pp. 17–18.

[36] *Report of the Joint Delegation Appointed by the Committees on the Indian Concern of the Yearly Meetings of Baltimore, Philadelphia and New York* (Baltimore, 1869); Kelsey, *Friends and the Indians*, pp. 166–67.

[37] The letter is printed in Kelsey, *Friends and the Indians*, p. 168, and appears in many of the Quaker reports since it was considered the basic authorization for their participation.

and agents and had organized special committees to deal with Indian matters. The Hicksite Friends were given the Northern Superintendency, comprising six agencies in Nebraska; the Orthodox Friends received the Central Superintendency, comprising the Indians in Kansas and the Kiowas, Comanches, and a number of other tribes in the Indian Territory. The agents were selected without forewarning, it would seem. Lawrie Tatum, the agent selected for the Kiowas and Comanches, declared: "I was living on a farm in Iowa, and knew nothing about being nominated for an Indian agent until I saw my name in a newspaper with others who had been appointed Indian agents, and confirmed by the Senate." But he went dutifully to his post.[38]

For the other agencies Grant appointed army officers, a move that was not surprising in the light of the reduction of the army that came in 1868. The new system of Indian agent appointments was explained by Secretary of the Interior Jacob D. Cox in his report at the end of 1869:

> These sweeping changes were made because it was believed that the public opinion of the country demanded a radical re-organization of this branch of the service. The selection of the officers of the army was made partly for economical reasons, as they were on pay though not on duty, and the salaries of many civil officers could thus be saved, and partly because it was believed they furnished a corps of public servants whose integrity and faithfulness could be relied upon, and in whom the public were prepared to have confidence.
> The Friends were appointed not because they were believed to have any monopoly of honesty or of good will toward the Indians, but because their selection would of itself be understood by the country to indicate the policy adopted, namely, the sincere cultivation of peaceful relations with the tribes and the choice of agents who did not, for personal profit, seek the service, but were sought for it because they were at least deemed fit for its duties.[39]

This solution to the problems of political patronage in the Indian service was soon upset by Congress, for by the army appropriation bill

---

[38] Tatum, *Our Red Brothers*, p. 24.
[39] Report of the Secretary of the Interior, 1869, in serial 1414, p. x; see also Report of the Commissioner of Indian Affairs, 1869, in serial 1414, p. 447.

of July 15, 1870, army officers were forbidden to accept civil appointments.[40] Although such action can be explained by the desire of spoilsmen to regain a foothold in the Indian service by means of political appointments, there had been strong opposition to the army officers on the part of reform elements as well. The massacre of Piegan Indians by troops under Colonel E. M. Baker on January 23, 1870, an action approved by General Sheridan, caused a great humanitarian outcry. Such was the effect of army attempts to civilize the Indians, the critics declared. In the House of Representatives, during debate on the Indian appropriations bill, Daniel Voorhees of Indiana pointed to the "curious spectacle" of the President of the United States "upon the one hand welcoming his Indian agents in their peaceful garments and broadbrims coming to tell him what they have done as missionaries of a gospel of peace and of a beneficent Government, and upon the other hand welcoming this man, General Sheridan, stained with the blood of innocent women and children!"[41]

Vincent Colyer, secretary of the Board of Indian Commissioners, was convinced that missionaries and soldiers as agents formed an inconsistent combination. He feared, however, that if the army officers were removed, the evils of political appointments would return. He therefore began a campaign to enlist other denominations besides the Quakers in the Indian service. In the spring of 1870, he suggested to the Secretary of the Interior that the Quaker plan be extended to include other churches, and he won the approval of Cox, who forwarded the proposal to Grant. Colyer then proceeded to enlist help from the various missionary boards. Having received word of Grant's approval, he began to write officially to the denominations and slowly gained their support. When the prohibition against army officers appeared, the way was open for turning all the remaining agencies over to religious groups. Colyer's goal was clearly a humanitarian one. He contended against army control because that would mean only policing of the Indians, not reclaiming or civilizing them, and by extended church control the efforts of the politicians to regain their sway would be thwarted.[42]

[40] *United States Statutes at Large*, XVI, 319.

[41] *Congressional Globe*, 41 Congress, 2 session, p. 1581. See the discussion of the Piegan incident in Mardock, *The Reformers and the American Indian*, pp. 67–73.

[42] Colyer's view and his successful efforts to enlist other denominations in the work

President Grant's motives are more difficult to isolate. Some observers credited his experience as a young army officer in the Pacific Northwest for his concern to right the wrongs the Indians had suffered. His own religious views and religious experience were hardly strong enough to have been a dominant element in his policy-making, yet it seems reasonable that his desire to end the warfare that had so long marked Indian-white relations could lead him to accept the Quakers and other sincerely religious men as instruments to that end. Grant, at any rate, justified his initial action in his first annual message to Congress. "The Society of Friends is well known as having succeeded in living in peace with the Indians in the early settlement of Pennsylvania, while their white neighbors of other sects in other sections were constantly embroiled," he said. "They are also known for their opposition to all strife, violence, and war, and are generally noted for their strict integrity and fair dealings. These considerations induced me to give the management of a few reservations of Indians to them and to throw the burden of the selection of agents upon the society itself. The result has proven most satisfactory." When the army agents were removed, it was a logical step to expand the system, to offer the agencies to other religious groups, who could be expected "to Christianize and civilize the Indian, and to train him in the arts of peace." Grant expressed the hope that the policy would "in a few years bring all the Indians upon reservations, where they will live in houses, and have schoolhouses and churches, and will be pursuing peaceful and self-sustaining avocations, and where they may be visited by the law-abiding white man with the same impunity that he now visits the civilized white settlements."[43]

To accomplish such goals, Grant knew that the Indian service could not be given back to the spoilsmen. General Sherman declared that when the sponsors of the act to deny the use of army officers as civilian

of nominating agents are seen in his correspondence with officials of the various churches, printed in *Report of the Board of Indian Commissioners*, 1870, pp. 93–100. See also Keller, "Protestant Churches and Grant's Peace Policy," p. 83.

[43] Israel, *State of the Union Messages*, II, 1199, 1216–17. Henry G. Waltmann, "Circumstantial Reformer: President Grant and the Indian Problem," *Arizona and the West*, XIII (Winter, 1971), 323–42, attempts an evaluation of Grant's personal contribution to the reform of Indian policy. He concludes that "Grant was a well-intentioned, but short-sighted and inconsistent would-be Indian reformer whose identification with the Peace Policy was, in some respects, more symbolic than substantial."

agents visited Grant to announce their design, the President replied: "Gentlemen, you have defeated my plan of Indian management; but you shall not succeed in *your* purposes, for I will divide these appointments up among the religious churches, with which you dare not contend." In testimony before a Congressional committee in 1878, Sherman made the same contention and added, "This may be good politics, but surely is bad statesmanship."[44]

Grant's subordinates praised his humanity and his wisdom. Cox emphasized the importance of the church agents who would support rather than obstruct the mission schools. Indian Commissioner Parker remarked: "The plan is obviously a wise and humane one. Under a political management for a long series of years, and the expenditure of large sums of money annually, the Indians made but little progress toward that healthy Christian civilization in which are embraced the elements of material wealth and intellectual and moral development. . . . Not, therefore, as a denier resort to save a dying race, but from the highest moral conviction of Christian humanity, the President wisely determined to invoke the coöperation of the entire religious element of the country, to help, by their labors and counsels, to bring about and produce the greatest amount of good from the expenditure of the munificent annual appropriations of money by Congress, for the civilization and Christianization of the Indian race."[45] These high-sounding sentiments were not mere rhetoric. Cox and Parker, if not Grant as well, were convinced that a peace policy must work. The assignment of the agencies to the churches appeared to be a wonderful solution, in tune with the idealistic, humanitarian sentiments of the day.

Vincent Colyer, so much involved in the formulation and promotion of the scheme, was soon at work in the allotting of the agencies to the various denominations. The only enunciated principle appeared at the end of 1870 in Grant's annual message to Congress, in which he declared his determination "to give all the agencies to such religious

---

[44] *Memoirs of Gen. W. T. Sherman, Written by Himself* (4th ed. rev., 2 vols., New York, 1891), II, 437; "Testimony Taken by the Joint Committee Appointed to Take into Consideration the Expediency of Transferring the Indian Bureau to the War Department," *Senate Miscellaneous Document* No. 53, 45 Congress, 3 session, serial 1835, p. 227.

[45] Report of the Secretary of the Interior, 1870, in serial 1449, p. ix; Report of the Commissioner of Indian Affairs, in serial 1449, p. 474.

denominations as had heretofore established missionaries among the Indians, and perhaps to some other denominations who would undertake the work on the same terms, i. e., as a missionary work."[46] But this was much too vague to be satisfactory, and Colyer was forced to make an initial division on the basis of his own scanty information about the agencies and the missionary work being performed at them. In a letter to the Secretary of the Interior on August 11, 1870, he declared, "I have made a rapid sketch of localities where the various Christian denominations of our country may most naturally follow up their work, in most instances already commenced, on behalf of the Indians." He noted where the various mission groups were at work and which seemed to have the best claim if there were more than one, and he suggested tribes of Indians which might be aggregated to existing mission work.[47]

Colyer's original plans, which he admitted were "simply suggestions," were modified when the agencies were actually assigned, and changes in apportioning the agencies occurred throughout the existence of the policy. In 1872, out of seventy-three agencies assigned, the Methodists had fourteen agencies (54,473 Indians), Orthodox Friends ten (17,724), Presbyterians nine (38,069), Episcopalians eight (26,929), Catholics seven (17,856), Hicksite Friends six (6,598), Baptists five (40,800), Reformed Dutch five (8,118), Congregationalists three (14,476), Christians two (8,287), Unitarians two (3,800), American Board of Commissioners for Foreign Missions one (1,496), and Lutherans one (273).[48]

The distribution caused immediate dissatisfaction, as one religious group after another complained that it had been slighted or overlooked. The vagueness of criteria for appointment was partly to blame. Different principles were proposed, as they fitted the purposes of the churches concerned. One argument was that the agency belonged to

[46] Israel, *State of the Union Messages*, II, 1216.
[47] Colyer to Cox, August 11, 1870, in *Report of the Board of Indian Commissioners*, 1870, p. 98.
[48] Report of the Commissioner of Indian Affairs, 1872, in serial 1560, pp. 461–62. The *Report of the Board of Indian Commissioners*, 1872, pp. 29–46, gives a slightly different listing. For a tabular listing of apportionments for 1870, 1872, and 1875, with a complete list of agencies assigned to each group and a statement of previous missionary efforts at each agency, see Keller, "Protestant Churches and Grant's Peace Policy," Appendix I, pp. 334–36.

the group that had the first mission there, whether or not it had been a success. Catholics insisted that agencies, according to Grant's statement, should be assigned to churches that had missionaries at them in 1870 and if more than one group was represented, to the one that had been there first. At other times Catholics argued that the Indians themselves should be able to choose which denomination they wanted. A Baptist member of the Board of Indian Commissioners proposed distribution according to denominational size, since the Baptists felt cheated in getting fewer than the Episcopalians and Presbyterians, who had fewer adherents. The Board of Indian Commissioners argued that no church had a *right* to any agency and that quality of work done by the churches or simple resolution of competing claims might call for a change. The welfare of the Indians, it insisted, was paramount to the benefit to be received by any church. Sometimes the rival groups were simply left to work out exchanges and other agreements among themselves.[49]

What the government wanted from the churches was a total transformation of the agencies from political sinecures to missionary outposts. The religious societies were expected not only to nominate strong men as agents but to supply to a large extent the subordinate agency personnel. Teachers especially were looked for, men and women with a religious dedication to the work that would make up for the low pay and often frightening conditions. The churches, too, it was assumed, would pursue more energetically and more effectively the strictly missionary activities already begun now that conflicts between government agents and religious missionaries would no longer be an obstacle.[50] Agency physicians, interpreters, and mechanics, if they were of solid moral worth, could all contribute to the one goal of civilizing and Christianizing the Indians. At first the utopia seemed to be within grasp. The reports of the Secretaries of the Interior and the Commissioners of Indian Affairs and the Board of Indian Commissioners, and those of Grant himself, rang loud with praises of the new policy.

[49] *Ibid.*, pp. 85–86.

[50] Commissioner of Indian Affairs Francis A. Walker, in fact, asserted that "the importance of securing harmony of feeling and concert of action between the agents of the Government and the missionaries at the several agencies, in the matter of the moral and religious advancement of the Indians, was the single reason formally given for placing the nominations to Indian agencies in the hands of the denominational societies." Report of the Commissioner of Indian Affairs, 1872, in serial 1560, p. 461.

It did not take long for serious cracks to appear in the new edifice. Fundamentally, the missionary societies were not prepared to handle the tremendous responsibility suddenly cast upon them. It was not as simple as many sanguine persons had thought to supply competent Christian men to run the agencies. Such men were not available in large numbers, even with the greatest of religious motivation, and the missionary boards were none too astute in selecting agents. Amidst the words of praise for the new system in the official reports are clear statements that men of inadequate character and competence had been appointed. As early as 1871, the Board of Indian Commissioners, although noting a "manifest improvement" in the agencies where the policy was in effect, reported that in several cases the missionary boards had been deceived in the character of the persons appointed and the appointees had to be summarily dismissed. "In one or two instances," it added, "the society making a nomination has not yet acted on the implied obligation to take a missionary interest in behalf of the Indians thus committed to their care." Two years later, when one might assume that initial rough spots in establishing the new policy would have been smoothed away, the situation appeared little better. The Board of Indian Commissioners noted that "a vastly better class of men" had been given to the Indian service and that "at the present time a large majority of the agents are, it is believed, honest men." But the fundamental criticism remained: some of the agents were men who had no real sympathy with the missionary effort. Of the eight hundred agency employees who might be under the control of the religious bodies, many did not display Christian character, and some of them were from the worst classes of the country. Until such difficulties were overcome, the work of Christianization would yield little fruit.[51]

Nor were the auxiliary services of education and missionary work effectively pursued, for most of the missionary boards found providing for the Indian service a distasteful responsibility. Among many of the churches, the Indians had to compete with foreign infidels, who captured the imagination of the communicants and most of the missionary funds. In truth, the internal effectiveness of the whole policy was open to serious doubt, although the response to the demands of the agencies

---

[51] Report of the Secretary of the Interior, 1872, in serial 1560, p. 9; *Report of the Board of Indian Commissioners*, 1871, p. 11; *ibid.*, 1873, pp. 24–25.

was met differently by the different churches. The Quakers and the Episcopalians, who helped to originate the peace policy, met the challenge most effectively. The Roman Catholics, although they felt they were persecuted, also performed well. The Methodists, who had been most favored in the distribution of the agencies, did the least.[52]

As serious as the lack of sustained interest on the part of the churches was the interdenominational rivalry. It was unfortunately the case that maintaining a position against a conflicting group was often more powerful motivation than concern for the welfare of the Indians. Examples of these fights abound, and they are all disedifying if not scandalous. If many can be explained by pettiness and denominational bias, the conflict between the Protestant mission groups and the Roman Catholics was nothing less than flagrant bigotry. Anti-Catholicism was a continuing phenomenon in American history, and the close ties between the churches and government in Indian matters were finally cut by the sharp knife of intolerance. The peace policy of Grant came at a time when Protestant missionary interest in the Indians was waning and Catholic activity in Indian missions and Indian schools had begun a remarkable upsurge. This changing relationship in the strength of the rival mission groups in itself explains much of the friction, for the Protestants, whose long dominance had not been seriously challenged before, now faced a threat from growing "Romanism."[53]

In its origins, the peace policy, both in the Board of Indian Commissioners and in the plan for allotting the agencies to the churches, was a Protestant affair. When the allotments were made, the Catholics were shocked to receive only seven agencies, when on the basis of their previous missionary work they expected to get thirty-eight. Their leaders protested, but once the assignments had been made, to respond to Catholic complaints would have meant taking agencies away from

[52] Keller, "Protestant Churches and Grant's Peace Policy," p. 100. Keller gives a denomination-by-denomination evaluation of the Protestant performance, pp. 100–33. The work of the Methodists is treated exhaustively in Whitner, "The Methodist Episcopal Church and Grant's Peace Policy." Whitner concludes: ". . . the record of the Missionary Society of the Methodist Episcopal church as a participant in the peace policy was largely a failure. It did little to improve the service or the condition of the Indian. It did much to perpetuate sectarianism and intolerance and bigotry in America." Whitner, p. 281.
[53] There are extended discussions of denominational conflict in Keller's and Whitner's dissertations. See also the account in Priest, *Uncle Sam's Stepchildren*, pp. 31–36.

groups to which they had been given. In order to protect their interests against what appeared to them as a unified bloc of Protestants, therefore, the Catholics in 1874 organized a central agency, the Bureau of Catholic Indian Missions, to direct the work of the missions in the field and to lobby in Washington for mission needs. The conflicts were numerous on the reservations, where Catholic and Protestant agents and missionaries carried on quite un-Christian feuds.[54]

Much was made of the question of religious liberty. Did assignment of an agency to a particular religious group exclude other denominations from the reservation? The Catholics particularly, cut off by apportionment from a number of reservations where they had traditionally done missionary work, insisted on the right to preach and to teach the Indians on reservations officially assigned to Protestants. The controversy grew to considerable proportions, and no solution seemed in sight until a Protestant group in turn was excluded from carrying on its ministrations to Indians at a Catholic agency. Then the whole matter took on a new light and ultimately a regulation from Secretary of the Interior Carl Schurz in 1881 declared that Indian reservations would be open to all religious denominations, except where "the presence of rival organizations would manifestly be perilous to peace and order" or where treaty stipulations would be violated.[55]

But religious liberty was not very broadly conceived in nineteenth-century America. The Mormons, for example, who had done a good deal of missionary work among the Indians, did not participate in the peace policy. What was more serious was the complete disregard for the religious views and the religious rights of the Indians themselves.

[54] Strong Catholic attacks on Grant's policy appeared in *Address of the Catholic Clergy of the Province of Oregon, to the Catholics of the United States, on President Grant's Indian Policy, in Its Bearings upon Catholic Interests at Large* (Portland, Oregon, 1874), and *Catholic Grievances in Relation to the Administration of Indian Affairs: Being a Report Presented to the Catholic Young Men's National Union, at Its Annual Convention, Held in Boston, Massachusetts, May 10th and 11th, 1882* (Richmond, Virginia, 1882). A thorough study of the Bureau of Catholic Indian Missions and of the work of the Catholics under the peace policy in the Sioux agencies is Rahill, *Catholic Indian Missions and Grant's Peace Policy.* Rahill is too laudatory of Catholic efforts, but Fritz's condemnation of them in *Movement for Indian Assimilation* is too severe. A criticism of both Rahill and Fritz on the matter is in Keller, "Protestant Churches and Grant's Peace Policy," pp. 119–20 note.

[55] Rahill, *Catholic Indian Missions and Grant's Peace Policy*, pp. 273–307; Beaver, *Church, State, and the American Indian*, pp. 157–61; Keller, "Protestant Churches and Grant's Peace Policy," pp. 280–90. Schurz's statement is quoted by Rahill, p. 306.

Quakers, Methodists, Episcopalians, and all the other Protestants fighting for the religious liberty of their own groups on the reservations, made no move to grant so much as a hearing to the Indian religions. The record of the Catholics was no better. They criticized Protestant bigotry and called for freedom of conscience, but that freedom did not extend to native religions, which were universally condemned. The missionaries were not interested in the Indian's right to maintain and defend his own religion. By religious freedom they meant liberty of action on the reservations for their own missionary activities. "The Indians have a right, under the Constitution, as much as any other person in the Republic," one Catholic statement asserted, "to the full enjoyment of liberty of conscience; accordingly they have the right to choose whatever Christian belief they wish, without interference from the Government."[56]

The assignment of agencies to the churches did not solve the "Indian problem." Good intentions of Christian men were not enough to correct evils of a complex nature or overcome a long history of mismanagement. Failure to study or appreciate the Indian side of the question, to adopt or build upon the societal forms that persisted in the Indian communities, weakened all the missionary efforts. And although most of the church groups professed a sincere regard for the well-being and advancement of the Indians, all this was thought of completely in terms of transforming the Indians into acceptable Christian citizens. Catholics and Protestants alike saw nothing worth preserving in the Indian groups they sought to convert and civilize.

Internal weaknesses and dissensions in the various missionary groups, together with the interdenominational bickering and open conflict alone would have doomed the policy. But external forces, too, were at work. In times of the highest moral rectitude in governmental circles, the policy of church-run agencies would have had difficulties; in fact, it was attempted in a decade noted in American history as a low point in public morals. "Grantism" became a term for fraud and corruption in high federal office, and the Indian service was one of the more lucrative areas in which politicians and spoilsmen could grow rich. It is under-

[56] *Address of the Catholic Clergy of the Province of Oregon*, p. 12.

standable that rapacious individuals would not stand idly by when the source of rich spoils was cut off by the missionary policy. Almost from the very start of the program, pressures of political patronage were at work, undermining the system. Secretary of the Interior Cox, who was a man of high integrity and one of the architects of the peace policy, resigned in October, 1870. Under his successor, Columbus Delano, the Interior Department provided one scandal after another, and Delano was forced to resign in 1875. During his term of office, he made it clear to the churches that he had the final say in the appointment of agents, and he frequently presented agents to the missionary boards for their rubber-stamp approval. He pointedly informed the Board of Indian Commissioners at his first meeting with the board and the missionary societies in January, 1871, that he had the ultimate judgment on the agents, and he lectured the humanitarians on the political facts of life. He reserved the right, he told them, "to chop off the political heads of your friends whenever occasion may require it, and you must not complain of this. We treat congressmen in the same way; that is, we accept their recommendations for nominations, and then, when their candidates are in office, we reserve to ourselves the right to judge whether they shall remain in their places." Being "a good Christian brother" was not enough, he said, to make a man a satisfactory agent.[57]

The White House, too, manipulated agency appointments for political friends, and even the Board of Indian Commissioners itself on occasion interfered for special appointments. More subtle but even more significant were the pressures exerted by Congress, many of whose members and their constituents did not understand or could not abide a church-dominated Indian service. If the agents themselves might be church appointed, at least room among the subordinate officials on the reservations could be made for a host of friends in need of a job. Missionary boards did not know just how to counteract senatorial pressure for or against confirmation of particular individuals and often gave in rather than fight the issue. Frequently senators insisted that agents be appointed from men who lived in the state concerned, thus severely limiting the churches' freedom of choice. But the politicians

[57] *Report of the Board of Indian Commissioners*, 1870, p. 112.

were not the only group with unclean hands. Church leaders, too, were not above some conniving to satisfy friends of the church.[58]

Public denunciation of the peace policy was rare in the East, where the press was favorable to the humane attempt to deal with the Indians. If Grant was attacked, little or nothing was said about the Indian policy. Western opinion, though not unanimous, was hostile. In areas where Indians were close at hand and often warlike, "peace" policies did not win much support. Extermination of the Indians was openly advocated; but a Montana paper declared sarcastically that the government would never allow any more punitive expeditions against the Indians because "some poor red-skinned pet of the Government, with its Quaker policy would get hurt, and tender-hearted philanthropists in the east would be thrown into convulsions of grief."[59] How much the rabid utterances of the western press affected the course of the policy is difficult to determine. Extreme ranting most likely only confirmed the eastern humanitarians in their resolve. Voter influence on representatives in Congress was not uniform, for western delegations did not vote as a bloc in opposition to the Grant policies.[60]

When Hayes succeeded Grant in 1877, the policy of church appointed agents was clearly on a downhill course. Humanitarians feared that the peace policy of Grant might suffer with the change of administrations, and agitation arose for a continuation and expansion of the peace efforts. On the surface, there was little to fear, for no attack was made on the basic principles of fair and humane treatment of the Indians as the means to peaceful relations. The Board of Indian Commissioners in 1877, in fact, reported consultations with the President, Secretary of the Interior, and Commissioner of Indian Affairs and noted that all these executive officers expressed "their hearty approval of the peace policy and their earnest desire to continue the effort for Indian civilization which has been steadily pursued since 1869."[61]

But Carl Schurz, the reform-minded Liberal Republican, whom

[58] Keller, "Protestant Churches and Grant's Peace Policy," pp. 161–68.

[59] *Montanian* (Virginia City), August 24, 1871, quoted *ibid.*, p. 170. For other western views see the discussion in Keller, pp. 168–71, and Fritz, *Movement for Indian Assimilation*, pp. 109–19.

[60] Keller, "Protestant Churches and Grant's Peace Policy," pp. 176–77, discusses early Congressional debate on the peace policy.

[61] *Report of the Board of Indian Commissioners*, 1877, p. 3.

Hayes appointed Secretary of the Interior, in outlining his Indian policy developed quite a different tone from that of the previous administration. He offered a list of practical goals—concentration on smaller reservations where agriculture could be promoted, private ownership of property, extension of United States law over the reservations, and the like—rather than an appeal to philanthropy to Christianize the Indians. The new Commissioner of Indian Affairs, Ezra A. Hayt, although recently a member of the Board of Indian Commissioners, wrote in the same tone. One of the points in his list of goals was "opportunity for the free access to the Indians of Christian teachers and missionaries, in order to reclaim them from a debasing paganism, and to win them to a purer and more ennobling faith," but the bulk of his proposals followed the practical line of his superior.[62] Schurz was famed for his attempts to reform the Interior Department and to eliminate the fraud which had become associated with it, but his solution did not depend upon church aid. "The Indian service has been reorganized in several of its branches," he wrote in 1878. "It was found necessary to remove a number of agents on account of improper practices or lack of business efficiency, and great care has been taken in filling their places with new men."[63] The religious character of the men did not seem any longer to be of prime importance.

Schurz no doubt had been influenced by the report of the board of inquiry he had appointed soon after taking office to investigate irregularities in the Indian service. The board criticized the appointment of agents "because of a sentiment" rather than on the basis of business qualifications and said that to entrust the church-appointed agents with such great power and responsibility was to "undertake through pigmies the solution of a problem that has engaged the best efforts of statesmen and philanthropists ever since the days of the republic." Although admitting that it was possible for business acumen and religious convictions to coexist, the board asserted that religious convictions alone were not enough to stem the corruption in the Indian service nor to prevent the avarice of contractors and frontiersmen. "Downright honesty," it said, "is a great desideratum, yet when un-

[62] Report of the Secretary of the Interior, 1877, in serial 1800, pp. x–xii; Report of the Commissioner of Indian Affairs, in serial 1800, pp. 397–98.
[63] Report of the Secretary of the Interior, 1878, in serial 1850, p. iv.

accompanied by capacity oftenest suffers when brought into contact with the sharp contests characteristic of western life."[64]

The churches became less and less involved in the appointment of the agents, and the denominations which had been in the forefront in instigating the policy became disillusioned and withdrew. The Friends, finding co-operation with Commissioner Hayt impossible and suffering from a general weariness, resigned from the duty of supplying agents.[65] The Episcopalians, too, lost interest, and their nominations were ignored. In 1882, when the secretary of the Methodist board, J. M. Reid, wrote to Secretary of the Interior Henry M. Teller to inquire why the nominations for the Michigan and Yakima agencies had not been honored, the Secretary replied that he would no longer consult religious bodies in the appointment of Indian agents. He asserted that since the religious groups had taken over "some of the grossest frauds have been perpetrated on the Indians and the government known in the history of Indian Affairs," and he felt that no benefits had accrued from the system. "I do not believe," he said, "that the government has discharged its duty when it shall have made its appropriations and then turned the matter over to the churches of the land to deal with as their different interests may dictate."[66] So the Methodists, like all the rest, were, as the chairman of the Board of Indian Commissioners remarked, "mustered out of the service," and one of the structures of Grant's peace policy collapsed.

Unless one equates the peace policy simply with the church appointment of agents, however, it is not true to say that "by 1879 the Peace Policy was in ruins."[67] Secretary Teller took a practical line with Reid. "You mention the peace policy of the government as if it was connected

[64] *Report of Board of Inquiry Convened by Authority of Letter of the Secretary of the Interior of June 7, 1877, to Investigate Certain Charges against S. A. Galpin, Chief Clerk of the Indian Bureau, and Concerning Irregularities in Said Bureau* (Washington, 1878), p. 63.

[65] Tatum, *Our Red Brothers*, pp. 285–86; Kelsey, *Friends and the Indians*, pp. 184–85, 196. There is an account of the Friends' difficulties under Hayes in *Extracts from the Minutes of a Convention of Delegates from the Seven Yearly Meetings of Friends Having Charge of the Indians in the Northern Superintendency* (Philadelphia, 1878).

[66] J. M. Reid to H. M. Teller, July 31, 1882, and Teller to Reid, August 5, 1882, printed in *Report of the Board of Indian Commissioners*, 1882, pp. 52–54. The discussion at the meeting of the Board of Indian Commissioners and the church groups at which these letters were read indicated that the policy had come to an end with all the groups.

[67] Keller, "Protestant Churches and Grant's Peace Policy," p. 317.

with and dependent on the system of selecting agents," he told him bluntly. "I do not think there is any connection between the two. I do not know what you mean by the peace policy of the government, and therefore I am unable to say whether I agree with you on that point or not. If, however, you mean that peace is better than war, and that civilization and labor are better for the Indian than his past and present condition, I agree with you."[68] Grant's attempt to solve the Indian problem, rather than being an utter failure, left an important heritage, which was built upon by later Indian reformers.

A concomitant movement for fundamental change in American Indian policy that came to a culmination early in Grant's administration was an attack on the treaty system. From President Grant down, the Indian reformers called for the abandonment of the system which had been an essential element in the relationships between the United States government and the Indian tribes from the inception of the nation. Those who had some historical sense realized that at first the treaties had been a good deal more than "a mere form to amuse and quiet savages, a half-compassionate, half-contemptuous humoring of unruly children," as Indian Commissioner Walker observed in 1873. The Indians at one time had had enough power to make a favorable cession of lands a diplomatic triumph for the United States. "The United States were clearly the stronger party in every such case," Walker noted; "but the Indians were, in the great body of instances, still so formidable, that to wrest their lands from them by pure, brutal violence would have required an exertion of strength which the government was ill prepared to make."[69]

Not many years passed, however, before the relationship had so changed that perceptive men saw the incongruity of treating the Indian tribes as equals. Andrew Jackson, for one, argued in 1817 that it was absurd to continue old forms when times had changed, and he said in 1820 that it was high time to do away with the "farce of treating with Indian tribes." Jackson believed that the Indians should be legislated

---

[68] Teller to Reid, August 5, 1882, *Report of the Board of Indian Commissioners*, 1882, p. 53.
[69] Francis A. Walker, *The Indian Question* (Boston, 1874), pp. 8–9.

for just as other subjects were, and Secretary of War John C. Calhoun concurred. But Calhoun was unable to get Congress to amend the system, and treaties continued to be the formal means of dealing with the Indians.[70] The decisions of Chief Justice John Marshall in the early 1830's strengthened the position of the Indian tribes. Marshall in *Cherokees vs. Georgia* described the Indians as "dependent domestic nations"; in *Worcester vs. Georgia* he argued that Congress had always treated the Indians as nations, and that the trade and intercourse act of 1802, still in force, manifestly considered the Indian nations "as distinct political communities, having territorial boundaries, within which their authority is exclusive, and having a right to all lands within those boundaries."[71]

But as demands for reform in Indian affairs grew in number and vehemence during and immediately after the Civil War, the treaty system came under increasing scrutiny. The attack on the system was part of the movement to end the tribal organization of the Indians and make the individual Indians wards of the state and then ultimately individualized and absorbed as citizens. The disparities between the United States and the tribes were noted along many lines. A statement on Indian reform drawn up by Bishop Whipple and sent to the President in 1862 by the General Conference of the Episcopal Church, declared that it was "impolitic for our Government to treat a heathen community living within our borders as an independent nation, instead of regarding them as our wards." Whipple's statement two years later in the *North American Review* was even stronger. "Our first dealing with these savages is one of those blunders which is worse than a crime," he wrote. "We recognize a wandering tribe as an independent and sovereign nation. We send ambassadors to make a treaty as with our equals, knowing that every provision of that treaty will be our own, that those with whom we make it cannot compel us to observe it, that they are to live within our territory, yet not subject to our laws, that they have no government of their own, and are to receive none from us; in a word, we treat as an independent nation a people whom we will not permit to exercise one single element of that sovereign power

[70] Francis Paul Prucha, *American Indian Policy in the Formative Years: The Indian Trade and Intercourse Acts, 1790–1834* (Cambridge, Massachusetts, 1962), pp. 234–35.
[71] 5 Peters 1 (1831); 6 Peters 515 (1832).

which is necessary to a nation's existence." To Whipple the treaties seemed usually to be "conceived and executed in fraud." Ostensibly the United States government and the Indians were the parties to the treaties, but in actuality the *"real* parties" were the Indian agents, the traders, and the politicians, the real design to pay worthless debts due to traders and to create places where political favorites could be rewarded.[72]

The disdain for the Indians that animated good men in their desire to end the treaty system was set forth in startling fashion by the Reverend Edward D. Neill, a Minnesota minister and historian, who wrote to the Commissioner of Indian Affairs in 1868 about failures in Indian policy. He asserted that the United States had lowered its own dignity in dealing with the tribes as separate nationalities and in thus "encouraging their heathen customs." "Why should we, a civilized people," he asked, "condescend to attend councils with a company of savages who have passed hours in decorating themselves with more care than Parisian fops? If it was once understood that no Indian could be admitted to the presence of a government official, except in a civilized dress and with a clean face and a clean shirt, and that they must transact business according to the usages of business men, quickly would the streaking of their bodies with vermillion, chrome green, or lamp black be discarded, and they would learn to dress in modern coats, perhaps at first like the robe of Joseph, of many colors, but in time they would become neat and less gaudy."[73]

More fundamental was the problem of land cession, which was the major purpose of most of the treaties. Reformers came to blame the treaty system itself for the conflicts and wars which arose between the Indians and the whites over land. In stinging words, Felix Brunot, as chairman of the Board of Indian Commissioners, indicted the whole system:

> The United States first creates the fiction that a few thousand savages stand in the position of equality in capacity, power, and

[72] Whipple, *Lights and Shadows,* p. 139; Whipple, "The Indian System," pp. 450–51.

[73] Edward D. Neill, *Effort and Failure to Civilize the Aborigines: Letter to Hon. N. G. Taylor, Commissioner of Indian Affairs* (Washington, 1868), p. 11. Taylor, finding in the letter "a number of facts, frequently needed for reference not only in the Indian Office, but by all interested in the preservation and elevation of the aborigines," had the letter printed at government expense.

right of negotiation with a civilised nation. They next proceed to impress upon the savages, with all the form of treaty and the solemnity of parchment, signatures and seals, the preposterous idea that they are the owners in fee of the fabulous tracts of country over which their nomadic habits have led them or their ancestors to roam. The title being thus settled, they purchase and promise payment for a portion of the territory, and further bind themselves in the most solemn manner to protect and defend the Indians in the possession of some immense remainder defined by boundary in the treaty, thus becoming, as it were, *particeps criminis* with the savages in resisting the "encroachments" of civilisation and the progressive movement of the age. Having entered into this last-named impracticable obligation, the fact of its non-performance becomes the occasion of disgraceful and expensive war to subdue their victims to the point of submission to another treaty. And so the tragedy of war and the farce of treaty have been enacted again and again, each time with increasing shame to the nation.[74]

Brunot's colleagues on the Board of Indian Commissioners echoed his sentiments. The board in its first report recommended unequivocally: "The treaty system should be abolished." And it went a step farther in proposing that when a "just method" could be devised, existing treaties should be abrogated. Individual members of the board, in their inspection reports, repeated the same principle.[75]

The highest government officials agreed with the reformers. Commissioner of Indian Affairs Ely S. Parker, who was himself an Indian and who had a long career of upholding the rights of the Seneca tribe to which he belonged, declared flatly in 1869 that the treaty system should no longer be continued. "A treaty involves the idea of a compact between two or more sovereign powers," he explained, "each possessing sufficient authority and force to compel a compliance with the obligations incurred. The Indian tribes of the United States are not sovereign nations, capable of making treaties, as none of them have an organized government of such inherent strength as would secure a faithful obedience of its people in the observance of compacts of this

[74] Slattery, *Brunot*, p. 156.
[75] *Report of the Board of Indian Commissioners*, 1869, p. 10; see also John V. Farwell to Brunot, November 4, 1869, *ibid.*, pp. 28–29.

character." Parker considered the Indians to be wards of the government, whose title to the land they claimed was a "mere possessory one." He condemned the treaty procedures for falsely impressing upon the tribes a notion of national independence. "It is time," he said, "that this idea should be dispelled, and the government cease the cruel farce of thus dealing with its helpless and ignorant wards."[76] President Grant remarked when he first met the Board of Indian Commissioners that the treaty system had been a mistake and ought to be abandoned.[77]

Before the post-Civil War reformers could organize effectively enough to bring an end to treaty-making, however, the system was destroyed by Congress for reasons that had little to do with humanitarian reform. The end came as the result of a drawn-out conflict of authority between the House of Representatives and the Senate. The fundamental problem was that treaty-making was a function of the President and the Senate, and if dealings with the Indians were confined to treaties, the House of Representatives was left out completely except to be called upon to appropriate funds for arrangements it had had no hand in making.

One crucial point at issue was the disposition of Indian lands by treaty arrangements. The Indian Office, by negotiating treaties with the Indians which needed only Senate ratification, could manipulate the land cessions made by the Indians in the interests of railroads or land companies. The lands freed of Indian title would not revert to the public domain and thus not become subject to the land laws which frontier settlers had so long fought to gain in their own interests. By means of the treaty process, a quarter of the lands of Kansas passed

[76] Report of the Commissioner of Indian Affairs, 1869, in serial 1414, p. 448. In a later autobiographical statement, Parker repeated his condemnation of the treaty system and said: "I, perhaps, ought to be the last person to find fault with such a condition of things. I suppose that I ought to be very proud, I ought to swell out as a turkey-cock, that, with a few hundred ignorant Indians at my back, I can consider myself the head of a strong, independent sovereignty, and treat with the great United States as if I were Russia, or Germany, or China, or Japan. But I have no such feeling. On the contrary I am humiliated. For I know too well the great wrecks of violated Indian treaties that are strewn in the historical pathway of the United States." "General Parker's Autobiography," *Proceedings of the Buffalo Historical Society*, VIII (1905), 532–33.

[77] Minutes of May 27, 1869, Records of the Board of Indian Commissioners, Minutes of Meetings, vol. I, pp. 6–7.

from Indian ownership to individuals, land-speculating companies, and railroads without ever becoming part of the public domain or coming under Congressional control. Such disposal denied settlers the benefits of the Homestead Act of 1862 and gave no voice to the popularly elected House of Representatives, where land reform sentiment was strongest.[78] The most celebrated case was a treaty signed with the Osages in 1868, by which eight million acres of land was to be sold to railroad interests at about twenty cents an acre. News of the treaty precipitated strong opposition in the House, which led to the defeat of the treaty. The treaty was a striking example of what could happen to the entire public land system, and Congressional opponents of the treaty-making power made full use of it in their attacks upon the defenders of the system.[79]

Another problem arose in 1869 in connection with the treaties negotiated in 1867 by the Peace Commission. The Senate inserted into the Indian appropriation bill for the fiscal year 1870 certain funds necessary for implementing the treaties, but the House refused to approve them. The Fortieth Congress ended on March 4, 1869, without providing any funds for the Indian Office for the year beginning July 1. When the Forty-first Congress met, the impasse continued until a compromise was finally reached whereby Congress voted a lump sum of two million dollars over and above the usual funds "to enable the President to maintain the peace among and with the various tribes, bands, and parties of Indians, and to promote civilization among said Indians, bring them, where practicable, upon reservations, relieve their necessities, and encourage their efforts at self-support." The House, refusing to give up its principle of demanding equal voice with the Senate on Indian matters, added the clause: "That nothing in this

[78] Paul Wallace Gates, *Fifty Million Acres: Conflicts over Kansas Land Policy, 1854–1890* (Ithaca, 1954), pp. 6–8.

[79] The debate in the House over the Osage treaty appears in *Congressional Globe*, 40 Congress, 2 session, pp. 3256–66. Gates discusses the matter fully in *Fifty Million Acres*, pp. 194–211. Gates, however, does not notice the other groups of opposition to the treaty-making power and attributes the end to treaty-making too exclusively to the Osage land question. He writes, furthermore, from the standpoint of the settlers, as though their interests were always to be considered paramount. The Indian Office (aside from the temptations to fraud) might very well have negotiated for the sale of Indian lands, with the sale money to be used for the benefit of the Indians, rather than turning all the lands to the public domain to be homesteaded without cost by white settlers.

act contained, or in any of the provisions thereof, shall be so construed as to ratify or approve any treaty made with any tribes, bands, or parties of Indians since the twentieth day of July, eighteen hundred and sixty-seven." This was a meaningless section legally, since the treaties had already been ratified by constitutional procedures, but it assuaged the pique of the House over its inferior position. A similar statement was included in the Indian appropriation bill for 1871, with the added provision that nothing should "affirm or disaffirm any of the powers of the Executive and Senate over the subject." Inadvertently, this disclaimer was omitted from the final engrossed bill, but it was formally passed with the appropriation act for the next fiscal year.[80]

The House realized that it was making little headway, since it was ultimately forced to approve the appropriations needed to carry out treaties ratified by the Senate, and the provisos tacked on to the bills had little if any legal effect. The only solution to granting the House the voice it wanted in Indian affairs was the abolition of the treaty system altogether. Although some members of the House argued that such a move would be unconstitutional, their position was weakened by a decision of the Supreme Court that acts of Congress might supersede or abrogate treaties. Since the Senate was willing to drop the treaty system provided treaties already ratified were held inviolate, the way was cleared for the necessary legislative action.[81] That action came finally in an obscure clause in the Indian appropriation act of March 3, 1871. Added to a sentence providing funds for the Yankton Indians was the statement: "*Provided*, That hereafter no Indian nation or tribe within the territory of the United States shall be acknowledged or recognized as an independent nation, tribe, or power with whom the United States may contract by treaty: *Provided, further*, That nothing herein contained shall be construed to invalidate or impair the obligation of any treaty heretofore lawfully made and ratified with any such Indian nation or tribe."[82]

[80] *United States Statutes at Large*, XVI, 40, 570. Debate on the matter is in *Congressional Globe*, 40 Congress, 3 session, pp. 1698–1708, 1813, 1891; 41 Congress, 1 session, pp. 170–73, 417–18, 557–73; 41 Congress, 2 session, pp. 1575–81, 4971–73, 5606–5608.

[81] See Laurence F. Schmeckebier, *The Office of Indian Affairs; Its History, Activities, and Organization* (Baltimore, 1927), pp. 58–66; Priest, *Uncle Sam's Stepchildren*, pp. 95–99.

[82] *United States Statutes at Large*, XVI, 566.

AMERICAN INDIAN POLICY IN CRISIS

The ending of the treaty system created a paradox. The question of what constitutional basis the federal government had for dealing with the Indians (aside from trade) had been answered largely by pointing to the treaty-making power. Now Congress struck down or admitted to be false this chief constitutional basis.[83] But as a matter of fact, the old processes could not be completely abandoned, and "agreements" rather than "treaties" continued to be negotiated with the Indian tribes. Whether or not a group of Indians was recognized as "an independent nation, tribe, or power," dealings between it and the United States called for some sort of formal agreement by which Indian consent was obtained. This was true, especially, in land cessions. Such agreements differed from the treaties only in that they were ratified not by the Senate alone but by both houses of Congress. Even legislative terminology showed that the old ways and attitudes had not been erased by the law of 1871. The act of May 1, 1876, for example, provided payment for a commission "to treat with the Sioux Indians for the relinquishment of the Black Hills country in Dakota Territory."[84] Congress did not simply legislate for the Indians as for other inhabitants of the United States as Andrew Jackson and others following him had wanted.

The abolition of treaty-making, only to be substituted for by agreement-making, did not satisfy reformers, who objected to the perpetuation of tribal existence that such agreements acknowledged. Equally objectionable was the continuation of treaty arrangements that had been concluded prior to 1871, for these still rested upon a basis of sovereignty within the tribe. The humanitarians concerned with the rights of the Indians for the most part were forced to insist that treaty rights of the past be respected at all costs, but to consider the Indians simultaneously both sovereign peoples and wards of the government, as Indian Commissioner E. P. Smith pointed out in 1873, involved "increasing difficulties and absurdities." "So far, and as rapidly as possible," Smith declared, "all recognition of Indians in any other relation

[83] W. G. Rice, "The Position of the American Indian in the Law of the United States," *Journal of Comparative Legislation and International Law*, 3d series, XVI (1934), 78–95.
[84] *United States Statutes at Large*, XIX, 45. There is a discussion of the end of treaty-making and the substitution of agreements in Felix S. Cohen, *Handbook of Federal Indian Law* (Washington, 1942), pp. 66–67.

than strictly as subjects of the Government should cease," but he admitted that to accomplish this would require "radical legislation."[85] By 1876 the problems arising in the Indian Territory, where the Five Civilized Tribes had maintained a national existence stronger than that among many other tribes, led the Secretary of the Interior to assert that the sooner the idea of treating with the various tribes in the Indian Territory as though they possessed a sort of independent power and nationality were done away with, the earlier would some practical solution for their government be reached. And his Commissioner of Indian Affairs was even more pointed in his remarks: "There is a very general and growing opinion," J. Q. Smith noted, "that observance of the strict letter of treaties with Indians is in many cases at variance both with their own best interests and with sound public policy."[86]

Old ways did not change as easily as the legal forms. Even outside the Indian Territory, Indian tribal leaders in some cases continued to exercise more authority on the reservations than the federally appointed Indian agent, who was supposed to be directing the destinies of the government's wards. And criticism of tribal authority and objections to consulting with the chiefs about government policy grew rather than diminished after the abolition of the treaty system.[87]

[85] Report of the Commissioner of Indian Affairs, 1873, in serial 1601, p. 371.

[86] Report of the Secretary of the Interior, 1876, in serial 1749, p. viii; Report of the Commissioner of Indian Affairs, 1876, in serial 1749, p. 389. A detailed and strong criticism of the treaty system appeared in Elwell S. Otis, *The Indian Question* (New York, 1878), pp. 117–97.

[87] George E. Hyde, *A Sioux Chronicle* (Norman, 1956), gives numerous examples of the conflict and tension between the agents and the Sioux tribal leaders. See also Priest, *Uncle Sam's Stepchildren*, pp. 102–104.

CHAPTER 3

THE MILITARY CHALLENGE
TO THE PEACE POLICY

In the treatment by the National Government of the Indian, the military and civil officers of Government have generally been diametrically opposed, the former believing the Indians to be as children, needing counsel, advice, and example, coupled with a force which commands respect and obedience from a sense of fear, the latter trusting mostly to moral suasion and religious instruction. The absolute proof produced by you that the Indian has a strong religious bias but is absolutely devoid of a moral sense as connected with religion, more than ever convinces me that the military authorities of the United States are better qualified to guide the steps of the Indian towards that conclusion which we all desire, self-support and peaceful relations with his neighbors, than the civilian agents, most of whom are members of some one of our Christian churches.

—GENERAL WILLIAM T. SHERMAN,
in his introduction to Dodge's
Our Wild Indians, 1882

❊❊❊❊❊❊❊

The Indian reform efforts of the post-Civil War decades were largely civilian efforts. The humanitarians who vociferously expressed their concern for the Indians, the missionaries who co-operated in Grant's peace policy, the Board of Indian Commissioners, whose members labored diligently without pay in the hope of eliminating abuses in the Indian service, and the Commissioners of Indian Affairs and Secretaries of the Interior were nearly unanimous in their conviction that the handling of Indian matters had to be a civilian, not a military matter.

The emphasis was on peace, not war; on civilization, not subjugation; on preservation, not extermination.

But for nearly two decades this dominant and ultimately successful position was criticized, condemned, and ridiculed by persons in and out of the army who demanded that Indian affairs be turned over to military control. The basic arguments of the critics made considerable sense and had an inherent logic that kept them alive in Congress and in the press. The reformers had all they could do on several occasions to beat back the attacks which threatened all their dreams for Indian betterment. The fundamental fact was that peace did not universally obtain. The Sioux uprising and the resultant military activities against the hostile Indians, the wars on the central and southern plains, the open hostilities in Montana and Wyoming, with the ultimate disaster on the Little Bighorn, all furnished striking evidence that kind intentions and peaceful gestures did not end hostility and that military force to some extent was indispensable. The necessary reliance on military force led to a duality of control in Indian matters which many persons considered illogical if not disastrous. The cry was for a return of the Bureau of Indian Affairs to the War Department, in order to put the whole concern for Indian affairs into military hands and to provide a unity of action that would, it was argued, eliminate confusion, cut costs, and in the end benefit the Indians themselves as well as the nation.[1]

The precise nature of the proposals varied. There was a good deal of talk about returning to the situation that existed before 1849, when the Bureau of Indian Affairs had been transferred to the newly created Department of the Interior. But the early period had hardly been a period of *military* control, for the Indian Office had been a civilian enterprise under the direction of a civilian Commissioner of Indian Affairs, with civilian superintendents (often *ex officio* the governors of

[1] Priest, *Uncle Sam's Stepchildren*, pp. 15–27, treats of the transfer issue, with special emphasis on congressional action and public opinion. A brief survey article is Donald J. D'Elia, "The Argument over Civilian or Military Indian Control, 1865–1880," *Historian*, XXIV (February, 1962), 207–25. A discussion of the issue in the early post-war years, with special emphasis on Kansas, is Marvin H. Garfield, "The Indian Question in Congress and in Kansas," *Kansas Historical Quarterly*, II (February, 1933), 29–44. See also Waltmann, "The Interior Department, War Department, and Indian Policy."

the territories) and civilian agents and other agency personnel. Only on relatively rare occasions had army officers filled the posts of Indian agents, and conflict between the two services, although under the single jurisdiction of the Secretary of War, had frequently occurred.[2] Persons in the 1860's and 1870's who knew the history of the Indian service did not advocate a simple transfer of the Bureau from one department to another with little change in outlook, activities, or character of personnel. What the advocates of change proposed was to put the Indians into the hands of army men on active military duty. Thus General Sherman argued that since the army was already on hand to keep the peace, it could easily assume the civil duties of the Indian service as well.

> Each military post has its quartermaster and commissary, who can, without additional cost, make the issues directly to the Indians, and account for them; and the commanding officer can exercise all the supervision now required of the civil agent, in a better manner, because he has soldiers to support his authority, and can easily anticipate and prevent the minor causes which have so often resulted in Indian wars. In like manner, our country is divided into military departments and divisions, commanded by experienced general officers named by the President, who can fulfill all the functions now committed to Indian superintendents; and these, too, have near them inspectors who can promptly investigate and prevent the incipient steps that are so apt to result in conflict and war.[3]

The transfer proposal was not a new idea. The Indian wars of the 1850's had led responsible men to question whether military control of the whole Indian service might not be wise, and both Secretary of War John B. Floyd and Secretary of the Interior Jacob Thompson in 1860

---

[2] Francis Paul Prucha, *Broadax and Bayonet: The Role of the United States Army in the Development of the Northwest, 1815–1860* (Madison, Wisconsin, 1953), pp. 93–95.

[3] Sherman to W. A. J. Sparks, January 19, 1876, in *House Report* No. 354, 44 Congress, 1 session, serial 1709, p. 9. It should be noted that in the face of criticism against military control, Sherman later suggested that the War Department could employ civilian agents for the peaceful tribes and use military ones only for warlike tribes. Sherman to Alvin Saunders, November 27, 1878, in *Senate Miscellaneous Document* No. 53, 45 Congress, 3 session, serial 1835, p. 220. Sherman's role in dealing with the Indians is fully discussed in Robert G. Athearn, *William Tecumseh Sherman and the Settlement of the West* (Norman, 1956).

responded affirmatively to a Senate resolution asking about the expediency of moving the Bureau of Indian Affairs back to the War Department. As Thompson observed, the War Department had superior facilities for controlling and managing "the wild, roving, and turbulent tribes of the interior, who constitute the great majority of the Indians." A transfer bill was introduced in May, 1860, but it quickly died. Lincoln's cabinet discussed the subject on several occasions, but the cabinet members were divided and no action was recommended.[4]

At the end of the Civil War, Ulysses S. Grant, as commanding general, casually recommended in 1866 "the propriety of transferring the Indian bureau from the Interior to the War Department, and the abolition of Indian agencies, with the exception of a limited number of inspectors." The proposition to him seemed "both obvious and satisfactory," for it would result in greater economy and reduce the conflicts between the Indians and the whites, and he did not feel the need to argue at any great length for his recommendation.[5] When he became President, he followed his convictions by his appointment of army officers to most of the Indian agencies. This seemed so reasonable to him that he did little theorizing about the matter. As humanitarian activity increased, however, the arguments for military control had to be expounded more explicitly. The military men and their supporters asserted that the proposals of the Indian reformers could not be carried out by mere moral suasion. General Sherman, reviewing the work of the Peace Commission in assigning the Indians to reservations, wrote: "To labor with their own hands, or even to remain in one place, militates with all the hereditary pride of the Indian, and *force* must be used to accomplish the result." The War Department, he argued, was the only branch of the government that could act with the promptness and vigor necessary to carry out the plans and purposes of the com-

---

[4] Floyd to Jefferson Davis, March 26, 1860, and Thompson to Davis, March 13, 1860, in *Senate Report* No. 223, 36 Congress, 1 session, serial 1040; *Senate Journal*, 36 Congress, 1 session, serial 1022, p. 441; *Diary of Gideon Welles* (3 vols., Boston, 1911), III, pp. 30, 74, 98–100, cited in Priest, *Uncle Sam's Stepchildren*, p. 16.

[5] Report of Grant, November 21, 1866, in *House Executive Document* No. 1, 39 Congress, 2 session, serial 1285, p. 18. In 1868, Grant renewed his recommendation. "It is unnecessary that the arguments in favor of the transfer should be restated," he wrote; "the necessity for the transfer becomes stronger and more evident every day." Grant to J. M. Schofield, November 24, 1868, in *House Executive Document* No. 1, 40 Congress, 3 session, serial 1376, pp. ix–x.

mission. Nor could he abide a divided command. He wrote his brother John in the summer of 1868 that he would have to spend the rest of his days on the Indian frontier "unless the Indians are wholly taken charge of by the War or Interior Dept."[6]

The arguments of the military men were moderately but forcefully summarized by Secretary of War J. M. Schofield in 1868:

> It is manifest that any branch of the public service cannot be efficiently and economically managed by *two* departments of the government. If the Interior Department can alone manage Indian affairs, and thus save the large expense of the army in the Indian country, very well. But if the army must be kept there for the protection of railroads and frontier settlements, why not require the army officers to act as Indian agents, and thus save all the expense of the civilians so employed. Besides, an army officer has his military reputation and commission at stake, and is subject to trial by court-martial for any misconduct in office. Thus is afforded the strongest possible security the government can have for an honest administration of Indian affairs by officers of the army; while the civilian agent, being only a temporary officer of the government, and practically exempt from trial and punishment for misconduct, gives the government the *least* possible security for honest administration.[7]

As the peace policy progressed and the Indian agencies were handed over to the representatives of the religious denominations, the opponents of civilian control found a rich field for criticism. Each failure of the peace policy, each act of Indian hostility, could be used to show that the humanitarians from the East, who had little contact with the wild Indians of the West, were unfit to formulate and carry out a practical Indian policy. Instances of failure by peaceful methods were taken to be automatic proof that Indian affairs belonged in the hands of the military. Ely S. Parker, whose efforts at humanitarian reform as Commissioner of Indian Affairs did not blot out his deeply ingrained military attitudes, summed it up cynically after his retirement from public office. After praising the army as a body of men "who when

[6] Report of Sherman, November 1, 1868, *ibid.*, pp. 5–6; Sherman to John Sherman, July 30, 1868, William T. Sherman Papers, Library of Congress.
[7] Report of Schofield, November 20, 1868, in *House Executive Document* No. 1, 40 Congress, 3 session, serial 1367, pp. xvii–xviii.

they make a promise will keep it and when they make a threat will execute it," he declared: "The civilian managers on the contrary, who though they may disgorge themselves of promises, and though they may talk and bluster in Falstaffian style, having no power whatever at their backs are only laughed at for their pains and derided as men of no weight, and when the civilians have eventually succeeded in making as ridiculous a muss as they well can the poor military are called in either to fight or patch up a quasi peace."[8]

Strong support of the army came from the West, where frontier governors, legislators, and newspaper editors called for aggressive military action against the Indians. The *Daily Conservative* of Leavenworth, Kansas, reflected an attitude common in the areas close to the Indian-white conflicts:

> With the routes of travel closed; with our borders beleaguered by thousands of these merciless devils whose natures are compounded of every essential diabolism of hell . . . we present to the civilized world a picture of weakness and vacillation, deliberately sacrificing men and women, one of whose lives is worth more than the existence of all the Indians in America.[9]

The peace policy of the Interior Department received small acclaim in Kansas, whose state legislators memorialized Congress to transfer the Indians to military control and whose representatives in Congress supported the army proposals.[10]

Nor did transfer lack support in the East. After the Fetterman disaster *The Nation* recommended transfer as the "primal remedy for our evils." Lamenting the *divisum imperium* that marked Indian management, it supported Sherman's stand of sole military control. What

---

[8] "General Parker's Autobiography," *Publications of the Buffalo Historical Society*, VIII (1905), 536.

[9] August 11, 1867, quoted in Garfield, "The Indian Question," p. 44.

[10] *Ibid.*, pp. 29–37. Memorials to Congress from the Kansas legislature in 1869 and 1874 urging transfer are printed in *Senate Miscellaneous Document* No. 29, 40 Congress, 3 session, serial 1361, and *Senate Miscellaneous Document* No. 75, 43 Congress, 1 session, serial 1584. Similar memorials from the California legislature in 1876 and 1878 are in *House Miscellaneous Document* No. 92, 44 Congress, 1 session, serial 1701, and *House Miscellaneous Document* No. 19, 45 Congress, 2 session, serial 1815. General western views on the peace policy are discussed in Fritz, *Movement for Indian Assimilation*, pp. 109–19, but he does not explicitly deal with the transfer issue.

could the troops do if they had sole responsibility, the editor asked. "The answer is," he declared, "The troops could *corral* the Indians; they could keep them away from the emigrant routes; could establish a healthful state of non-intercourse; could remove the temptations to plunder by forcing the Indians away from certain prescribed regions. In this way they would effectually police the 'short route' to Montana and the Pacific."[11]

The Protestant churches were strongly committed to the Interior Department and its civilian peace program and universally opposed transfer, but the Catholic position was mixed. Catholic missionaries, squeezed out of some reservations by the allotment of agencies under Grant's peace policy, hoped that army control might give them a free hand to operate where they chose. Felix Brunot asserted that all denominations opposed transfer "except the Roman Catholics," and Indian Commissioner E. A. Hayt, in a personal letter to the Secretary of the Baptist Home Missionary Society in 1878, remarked, "If the transfer to the Army takes place, which seems extremely probable, the Catholics boast that they will then be allowed to go to every agency in the United States, and I think their boast is not an empty one."[12] *The Council Fire*, the Indian reform journal of Alfred B. Meacham, warned its readers that Catholics favored transfer because they had not received the agencies they thought they were entitled to, and that if the Indian service was returned to the War Department, Protestant missions would be abandoned to Roman Catholics.[13] The Bureau of Catholic Indian Missions, which aligned itself with the Indian Bureau in opposing transfer, clearly did not speak for all Catholics interested in the Indians. James A. McMaster, the lay Catholic editor of the *Freeman's Journal* in New York and a vigorous opponent of the Catholic bureau, condemned the "Quaker Plan," which he considered a complete failure, and called for a return of the Indian service to the War Department. Bishop James O'Connor of Nebraska and the Benedictine

[11] *The Nation*, IV (January 17, 1867), 52. But note that the journal modified its position by 1879; see *ibid.*, XXVIII (January 2, 1879), 7–8. Priest notes the inconstancy of public opinion on the transfer issue in *Uncle Sam's Stepchildren*, p. 23.

[12] Slattery, *Brunot*, pp. 229–30; Hayt to S. S. Cutting, June 3, 1878, Records of the Office of the Commissioner of Indian Affairs, vol. 1878, p. 113, National Archives Record Group 75.

[13] *The Council Fire*, I (July, 1878), 98.

Abbot Martin Marty of Dakota both supported the transfer measure introduced in 1878.[14]

The arguments of the advocates of transfer seem moderate and mild-mannered in comparison with the outbursts of their opponents. The peace policy of the humanitarian reformers was launched in fear of military control of Indian affairs and developed in an atmosphere of constant threat that the stately ship of Indian reform would be scuttled by reassertion of army dominance. Such insecurity kept the reformers alert to the least wind blowing in the direction of military control.

At first everything seemed promising. The Joint Special Committee on the Condition of the Indian Tribes in its report of 1867, after weighing carefully the arguments for and against the transfer of the Indian Bureau, concluded unanimously that the Bureau should remain in the Department of the Interior.[15] The Peace Commission, likewise, after a careful analysis of conditions in the West, decided against transfer in its initial report of January 7, 1868. "If we intend to have war with them [the Indians] the bureau should go to the Secretary of War," it declared. "If we intend to have peace it should be in the civil department." The plan for civilizing the Indians that the commission outlined saw the chief tasks of the Indian Office to be educating and instructing the Indians in peaceful acts. "The military arm of the government," it flatly asserted, "is not the most admirably adapted to the discharge of duties of this character." Not one army man in a thousand, the commissioners thought, would like to teach Indian children to read and write or the Indian men to farm.[16] But renewal of war in the West in the summer of that year led to the reversal of the commission's stand at a meeting at Chicago in October.

To counteract the change of mind of such a distinguished group, which would threaten the hopeful goals of the reformers, Commissioner of Indian Affairs Taylor, who as president of the Peace Commission had refused to vote for transfer when the commission as a

[14] Rahill, *Catholic Indian Missions*, pp. 120–21, 160, 204–205.
[15] "Condition of the Indian Tribes: Report of the Joint Special Committee," *Senate Report* No. 156, 39 Congress, 2 session, serial 1279, pp. 6–7.
[16] "Report of the Indian Peace Commissioners," January 7, 1868, *House Executive Document* No. 97, 40 Congress, 2 session, serial 1337, pp. 20–21.

whole reversed its position, issued a powerful report. His eleven-point indictment of military control of Indian matters, issued as part of his annual report on November 23, 1868, exhausted the arguments of the civilian reformers. Taylor's comprehensive and forceful statement was a manifesto to which later militants could add little. Like many other reformers, however, Taylor was abler in pointing out the evils he considered inherent in military control than in offering convincing proof that civilian control could furnish the answer to the Indian problem. In a strange mixture of reformers' rhetoric, evangelical preaching against evil, and innuendoes about the motives of the military men, he set forth his arguments. That the intemperance of his language and the absurdity of some of his charges might weaken his position seems not to have crossed his mind. Here is a summary of his report:[17]

1. The direction of Indian affairs is too large and important a burden to be added to the existing duties of the Secretary of War. The War Department is already varied and complex. To add to it the intricate and difficult duties involved in Indian affairs would be unreasonable and wrong.

2. The transfer would necessitate the maintenance of a large standing army in the field. And peace is not the time for a large standing army. "Surely Congress is not prepared to transfer the Indian Bureau to the War Department merely to create the necessity to keep up the army, and with it the taxes."

3. "Our true policy towards the Indian tribes is peace, and the proposed transfer is tantamount . . . to perpetual war." The very presence of troops would arouse hostility in the Indians. "It should not be forgotten . . . that almost all the Indian wars which have depleted the treasury and desolated our frontiers ever since the bureau was given to the Interior Department, had their origin in the precipitate and ill-considered action of the military stationed in the Indian country."

4. Previous military management of Indian affairs was a failure and must "in the very nature of things, always prove a failure." Soldiers are trained for war; civilians are taught the arts of peaceful civilization. "Has not military management essentially failed in civilizing the Indians? When and where did it turn their minds from war and the chase and fix them upon agriculture or pastoral life? When and where

[17] Report of the Commissioner of Indian Affairs, 1868, in serial 1366, pp. 467–75.

80

did it reduce the cost of Indian affairs? It has only succeeded in illuminating our Indian history with bloody pictures, in surcharging the hearts of our tribes with hatred and revenge, and spending the money of the people by the fifty million dollars, oft repeated." If the army seeks peace through extermination, even that is an absurdity because of the costs involved, "unless we could get the Indians under the protection of the flag in large masses, surround and butcher them as at Sand Creek."

5. It is "inhuman and unchristian . . . to destroy a whole race by such demoralization and disease as military government is sure to entail upon our tribes." Military posts in the Indian country are subversive of domestic morals, and the "most loathsome, lingering, and fatal diseases" are spread broadcast. "If you wish to exterminate the race, pursue them with ball and blade; if you please, massacre them wholesale, as we sometimes have done; or, to make it cheap, call them to a peaceful feast, and feed them on beef salted with wolf bane; but for humanity's sake, save them from the lingering syphilitic poisons, so sure to be contracted about military posts."

6. The conduct of Indian affairs is incompatible with the nature and objects of the War Department. The goal is to civilize the Indians and this is a civilian not a military job, for which the soldiers are not trained. "Will you send professional soldiers, sword in one hand, musket in the other, and tactics on the brain, to teach the wards of the nation agriculture, the mechanic arts, theology, and peace? You would civilize the Indian! Will you send him the sword? You would inspire him with the peaceful principles of Christianity! Is the bayonet their symbol? You would invite him to the sanctuary! Will you herald his approach with the clangor of arms and the thunder of artillery?"

7. Transfer to the War Department will be offensive to the Indians, who cannot forget past injuries heaped upon them by the army.

8. The reversal of the Peace Commission's decision on transfer is subject to "severe criticism." "I think I can readily understand, however, why my colleagues of the army might desire the transfer. It is but natural they should desire it. It is the history of power to seek more power, and the dispensation of patronage is power. Besides, it is but natural that gentlemen educated to arms, and of the army, should desire to see the aggrandizement of the army."

81

9. Military management is "utterly irreconcilable with the relation of guardian and ward." The primary duty toward the Indians is to teach, enlighten, and civilize them. "If teaching means the instruction given to the Aztecs by Cortez and Pizarro; if enlightening signifies the conflagration of Indian villages; if civilization means peace, and peace means massacre *a la* Sand creek, then by all means let us have the transfer. To every unprejudiced mind the mere mention of the military in connection with the relation of guardian and ward discloses the absurdity of the association."

10. The transfer will entail increased expenditures. War is more costly than peace and transfer will lead to war. "If economy is desirable in our present financial situation, the proposed transfer will, in my judgment, be disastrous."

11. A large military establishment in peacetime endangers the supremacy of the civil authority and the liberties of the people. History is full of striking illustrations of this truth.

A similar fear of what might happen if the army gained control of the Indian Office loomed large in the motivation of the reformers—men like Bishop Whipple, William Welsh, Vincent Colyer, and their Quaker and other religious supporters—who hastened to Washington to promote their peace plans when Grant was elected to the Presidency. When they won over the new President and Grant and his administration supported a radically religious and humanitarian peace policy, the crisis passed. Relative peace returned to the West, and the peace policy seemed to be fulfilling its goals. The War Department and the Interior Department, moreover, were able in the early 1870's to agree on a program of co-operation that worked for a time. Indian Commissioner Parker in 1869 reported what he called "a perfect understanding" between the officers of the two departments, by which Indians who refused to locate on the reservations provided for them were to be subject to the military authorities, while the civil authorities would carry on the work of advancing in civilization the Indians on the reservations.[18]

Francis A. Walker, Parker's successor, likewise saw no inconsistency in making use of the soldiers when Indians needed chastisement while at the same time pursuing the peace policy on the reservations, and his

---

[18] Report of the Commissioner of Indian Affairs, 1869, in serial 1414, pp. 447–48.

82

attitude eased friction between the two services.[19] Walker's appointment was hailed by the reformers, for he was a man of integrity and high intellectual attainments. A noted political economist, he was installed as Commissioner of Indian Affairs for a year to keep him in government employ when the Bureau of the Census, which needed his expert services, lacked necessary funds to retain him. Walker had little patience with recalcitrant Indians and little sympathy for their situation. Touched by popular criticism that the government was inconsistently feeding Indians who threatened hostility and feasting their delegations in Washington while neglecting those who were established in friendship, Walker fell back upon the argument of expediency. "It is not a whit more unreasonable," he argued, "that the Government should do much for hostile Indians and little for friendly Indians than it is that a private citizen should, to save his life, surrender all the contents of his purse to a highwayman; while on another occasion, to a distressed and deserving applicant for charity, he would measure his contribution by his means and disposition at the time." If this was temporizing with evil, it did not worry Walker, for he considered temporizing that would speed along the destruction of an evil that was already doomed by inescapable forces an act of "the highest statesmanship." Nor did he think it harmful to the honor of the nation to deal thus with the Indians. "There is no question of national dignity, be it remembered, involved in the treatment of savages by a civilized power," he asserted. "With wild men, as with wild beasts, the question whether in a given situation one shall fight, coax, or run, is a question merely of what is easiest and safest."

Walker thus had no qualms about occasional use of the military arm to restrain or chastise refractory Indians, and he insisted that such action was no abandonment of the peace policy nor any disparagement of it. The reservation policy from the beginning, he said, demanded "that the Indians should be made as comfortable on, and as uncomfortable off, their reservations as it was in the power of the Government to make them" and he saw the use of military force not as war but as

---

[19] Walker outlined his views on Indian policy at great length in Report of the Commissioner of Indian Affairs, 1872, in serial 1560, pp. 391–401. See also Walker, *The Indian Question*, which reprints part of his 1872 report and two articles dealing with the Indian question in general and with Indian citizenship. The quotations in the paragraphs that follow are taken from the official report.

discipline. He seemed to regret that the government had been somewhat tardy in applying force to Indians who left the reservations without authority, but he attributed the tardiness to "a legitimate deference
to the conviction of the great body of citizens" that the Indians in the
past had been unjustly and cruelly treated and that the nation now
should treat them with great forbearance. Walker optimistically believed that three years would see the "alternative of war" eliminated
from the Indian question. The advance of the railroads and the
strengthening of agricultural settlements would result in the submission of the Indians. This was, after all, their only hope, for the westward
course of the white population could be neither denied nor delayed,
and the Indians could only yield or perish. "There is something that
savors of providential mercy," he said, "in the rapidity with which their
fate advances upon them, leaving them scarcely the chance to resist
before they shall be surrounded and disarmed." Thus defeated, the
Indians should be subjected to "a rigid reformatory discipline" to save
them from themselves.

The success that Walker saw in the government's judicious use of
military force was marred by serious eruptions on the southern plains.
The Kiowas and Comanches, for whom raiding had become a way of
life, would not stay confined to their reservation. Led by aggressive
leaders, these Indians left the reservation time and again to raid across
the Red River into Texas. Lawrie Tatum, the Iowa Quaker farmer who
had been sent to the Kiowas as agent in 1869 under the peace policy,
tried desperately to make a non-violent policy work. He seemed for a
while to make some headway, but he resorted to withholding rations to
force the chiefs to return white captives taken on their raids, and when
such coercion proved insufficient to restrain the Indians, he ultimately
called for military assistance. Having thus violated the basic tenets of
the peaceful Quakers, he got into trouble with his superiors, and at the
end of March, 1873, he resigned. Periodic promises of peace on the
part of the Indians, interspersed with murderous raids off the reservation kept the Red River frontier in a state of turmoil. The Cheyennes,
too, joined in the depredations, and in June, 1874, an attack by Kiowas,
Comanches, and Cheyennes on a trading establishment at Adobe Walls
in the Texas Panhandle signaled the beginning of a full-scale war.
Strong columns of troops were sent into the western part of the Indian

HENRY B. WHIPPLE (1822–1901), Episcopal bishop of Minnesota, was a strong critic of government Indian policy and an ardent promoter of reform. (Prince photograph, Library of Congress)

ELY S. PARKER (1828–1895), a Seneca Indian who served as General Grant's military secretary, was appointed Commissioner of Indian Affairs in 1869. Attacked by reformers, he resigned in 1871. (Brady photograph, Library of Congress)

FELIX R. BRUNOT (1820–1898), a Pittsburgh industrialist, devoted five years of his life to Indian affairs as chairman of the Board of Indian Commissioner, 1869–1874. He wanted justice for the Indians but was willing to cut down Indian land holdings as a means of incorporating them into white society. This portrait served as the frontispiece for the biography of Brunot by Charles Lewis Slattery. (State Historical Society of Wisconsin)

JACOB D. COX (1828–1900), an able Ohio Republican, served briefly as Grant's first Secretary of the Interior. He played an important role in initiating the peace policy. (Brady photograph, Library of Congress)

INDIAN PEACE COMMISSION, 1887. To end warfare on the plains, Congress authorized a special commission to deal with the Indians. This photograph shows the commissioners at Fort Laramie—from left to right, Generals Terry, Harney, and Sherman, a Sioux woman, Indian Commissioner Taylor, S. F. Tappan, and General Augur. (National Archives)

TREATY OF MEDICINE LODGE CREEK, 1867. The meeting of the Peace Commission with the southern plains Indians was depicted in a drawing by Hermann Stieffel, a private of the Fifth Infantry. (Smithsonian Institution)

WILLIAM T. SHERMAN (1820–1891), who commanded in the West immediately after the Civil War and then served as general commanding the army, 1869–1883, was an outspoken advocate of military control of Indian affairs. (Library of Congress)

ALFRED B. MEACHAM (1826–1882), at one time superintendent of Indian affairs for Oregon, was a member of the ill-fated peace commission to the Modocs in 1873. Partially scalped by the Indians, Meacham recovered and spent the remainder of his life promoting reform in Indian policy. This portrait is from the frontispiece of his book, *Wigwam and War-path.* (Marquette University Library)

EDWARD R. S. CANBY (1817–1873) was the only general of the regular army killed in the Indian wars. His murder by the Modoc Indian, Captain Jack, at a peace mission in 1873 was a serious blow to the peace policy of the humanitarian reformers. (Library of Congress)

CAPTAIN JACK (1837?–1873), Indian leader in the Modoc War, was hanged for the murder of the peace commissioners. (Heller photograph, National Archives)

RED CLOUD DELEGATION. Sioux delegations went to Washington to negotiate concerning the reduction of the great Sioux reservation and on other tribal business. This group of Oglala Sioux leaders in 1880 includes, left to right, Red Dog, Little Wound, Red Cloud, American Horse, and Red Shirt. The interpreter John Bridgman stands in the background. (National Archives)

Territory and into the Staked Plains of northwestern Texas to corral and subdue the Indians and force them to the reservations. But not until June, 1875, were the last of the hostiles rounded up, the Red River War brought to a close, and the Indian prisoners of war sent to Fort Marion, Florida. With the defeat of the three tribes peace finally came to the southern plains.[20]

The peace policy was severely tried also by the Modoc War, a flaring up of hostilities along the Oregon-California border in 1872–1873 that grew out of Indian resistance to white pressures on their homelands.[21] The Modocs lived around Tule Lake, which stretched across the border, and they included in their lands along the southern edge of the lake a forbidding region of lava beds which furnished a remarkable stronghold against attacking forces. The Modocs were little affected by the mining frontier, for no gold was found in their vicinity, but the grasslands, especially north of Tule Lake, attracted ranchers, who soon clamored to have the Indians out of the way. In 1864, in response to these white pressures, the United States government negotiated a treaty with the Indians by which they were moved to a reservation twenty-five miles to the north.[22] They had to share the reservation with the Klamath tribes, and the Modocs, on alien ground and outnumbered by the Klamaths, were restless and unhappy. One of the Modoc leaders, called Captain Jack by the whites, soon led his

[20] Leckie, *The Military Conquest of the Southern Plains*, pp. 133–235, gives a full, well-documented account. There are many details on the conflict in W. S. Nye, *Carbine and Lance: The Story of Old Fort Sill* (Norman, 1937). The Quaker agent's own story is in Tatum, *Our Red Brothers*.

[21] The best history of the war is Keith A. Murray, *The Modocs and Their War* (Norman, 1959). A more popular account is Doris Palmer Payne, *Captain Jack, Modoc Renegade* (Portland, Oregon, 1938). Jeff C. Riddle, *The Indian History of the Modoc War and the Causes That Led To It* (n.p., 1914), is an account written, with the help of D. L. Moses, by the son of Frank and Tobey Riddle, interpreters in the negotiations between the whites and the Modocs. Erwin N. Thompson, *Modoc War: Its Military History & Topography* (Sacramento, 1971), is a detailed analysis of the military action prepared originally for the National Park Service. Official documents dealing with the war and the trial of the murderers from both War Department and Interior Department files are printed in "Modoc War," *House Executive Document* No. 122, 43 Congress, 1 session, serial 1607. See also "Report of A. B. Meacham, Special Commissioner to the Modocs, Upon the Late Modoc War," *House Executive Document* No. 1, 43 Congress, 1 session, serial 1601, pp. 442–50.

[22] Kappler, *Indian Affairs: Laws and Treaties*, II, 865–68.

followers back to their old homes along Lost River, which ran into Tule Lake from the north. But in the Indians' absence, white ranchers had moved in, and the return of Captain Jack and his band caused consternation and panic. Early negotiations with Captain Jack, endeavoring to get him to return to the reservation, came to nothing.

When Grant became President in 1869, he appointed as Superintendent of Indian Affairs for Oregon a faithful Republican named Alfred B. Meacham, who was an ardent temperance man and a person moved by deep reforming instincts. Born in Indiana in 1826, Meacham had moved to Iowa with his family in 1841, and when gold fever struck he had migrated to California with his brother. In 1863, he moved once more, this time to Oregon, where he had some success as a proprietor of a hotel and of a toll road. As Indian superintendent, he was a staunch supporter of Grant's peace policy and undertook to carry out its reform principles. He had some success in correcting abuses at the Klamath reservation and then talked Captain Jack into returning to the reservation. But pressures from the Klamath Indians and the Indian agent drove Captain Jack again to Lost River in April, 1870. Use of army troops in the attempt to force the Modocs back to the reserve led in 1872 to armed conflict, and the Modoc War was under way. The Indians holed up in the lava beds, from which the army without enthusiasm and without success sought to dislodge them, although General Edward R. S. Canby, commanding the Department of the Columbia, himself assumed direction of the campaign.

To overcome this expensive and embarrassing impasse, a peace commission was appointed on January 29, 1873, headed by Meacham, who had been relieved of his Indian superintendency early in the previous year. General Sherman acquiesced in the request of the Interior Department that offensive action against the Indians be stopped and directed Canby to order no attacks, since the President seemed "disposed to allow the peace men to try their hands on Captain Jack."[23] Negotiations, however, made little headway. The Modocs themselves were divided, and the army tightened the pressure on the area held by the Indians. Captain Jack, forced by more desperate members of his band, at length agreed to the treacherous murder of General Canby and the peace commissioners when they came unarmed to the next

[23] Sherman to Canby, January 31, 1873, "Modoc War," in serial 1607, p. 65.

council. On Good Friday, April 11, 1873, the deed was done. At a signal from Captain Jack, the Indians rose up armed, and Jack himself, drawing a pistol he had concealed under his coat, shot General Canby at point-blank range. Canby gathered sufficient strength to run a short distance, but he soon fell, was shot again, stabbed by Captain Jack, and stripped of his clothing. The Reverend Eleasar Thomas, a member of the peace commission, was quickly killed by an Indian named Boston Charley. Meacham, starting to flee when the trouble broke out, was grazed by bullets and fell unconscious. He was partially scalped when a cry that soldiers were coming drove his assailant off, and he was found still alive when the rescuers arrived. The other member of the commission escaped unharmed.

The disaster shocked the nation. Much of the sympathy that had supported the Modocs, who had been far outnumbered by the soldiers in the conflict, was destroyed, and cries for vengeance against the murderers resounded. The army intensified its drive until at last, giving up before hopeless odds, the Indians surrendered. Some of the criminals were granted amnesty for aiding in the capture of Captain Jack, but six of the Modocs were tried on July 1–9 before a military commission at Fort Klamath for the murder of Canby and Thomas.[24] The Indians had no defense counsel (although Meacham at one point was tempted to volunteer) and, since they understood little English, were probably unaware of all that was going on. The six were sentenced to be hanged, and on October 3, Captain Jack and three of his companions were executed at Fort Klamath; two lesser participants had their sentences commuted by President Grant to life imprisonment at Alcatraz.

The Modoc murders touched off a nationwide attack on Grant's peace policy. Western opposition was intense. At Jacksonville, Oregon, the citizens hanged Secretary Delano in effigy, and across the nation criticism of the peace policy exploded.[25] Even supporters of the policy were stunned by the murder of the commissioners and agreed that stiff punishment was in order. Meacham himself wrote to the Secretary of the Interior five days after the attack that "complete subjugation by the

<hr>

[24] "Proceedings of a Military Commission Convened at Fort Klamath, Oregon, for the Trial of Modoc Prisoners," *ibid.*, pp. 131–83.

[25] There is a discussion of the Modoc War and its relation to the Indian reform movement in Mardock, *The Reformers and American Indian*, pp. 115–28.

military is the only method by which to deal with these Indians."[26] But it did not take long for the peace advocates to renew their insistent urging that the peace policy itself be continued, and they spoke strongly against recurring white attacks upon the Indians, which they charged deserved as strict an accounting as that meted out to the Modocs. Some urged clemency for the convicted murderers and argued that the military trial had been biased and illegal. Meacham came to blame the affair to a large degree on the military.[27]

After the execution of the sentences of the military tribunal, the remainder of the tribe, 153 in number, were exiled from their homeland. They were taken by the army to Fort McPherson, Nebraska, and there turned over to agents of the Interior Department, who moved them to the Indian Territory and placed them in charge of the Quapaw agency. "The Indian is greatly attached to his tribal organization," Secretary Delano asserted, "and it is believed that this example of extinguishing their so-called national existence and merging their members into other tribes, while in reality a humane punishment, will be esteemed by them as the severest penalty that could have been inflicted, and tend by its example to deter hostile Indians in future from serious and flagrant insurrection."[28] The Modocs lived quietly and productively as farmers in Indian Territory until, in 1909, those who were left were allowed to return to the Klamath reservation in Oregon.

One reason why the Modoc War did not scuttle the peace policy was the one-man crusade for Indian reform carried on by Meacham. Having survived the ordeal of his scalping and making a rapid although incomplete recovery, Meacham, instead of turning bitter against the Indians who had sought to murder him, devoted the rest of his life to propagandizing for Indian reform.[29]

[26] Meacham to Delano, April 16, 1873, "Modoc War," in serial 1607, p. 287.

[27] Address to President Grant by the Universal Peace Union, July 12, 1873; Memorial to Grant from John Beeson, July 18, 1873; and statements on the activity of the American Indian Aid Association, *ibid.*, pp. 309–22. See also "The Tragedy of the Lava-Beds," printed in T. A. Bland, *Life of Alfred B. Meacham* (Washington, 1883), p. 48.

[28] Report of the Secretary of the Interior, 1873, in serial 1601, pp. ix–x.

[29] Biographical details are found in Meacham's own writings: *Wigwam and Warpath; or the Royal Chief in Chains* (Boston, 1875), *Wi-ne-ma (The Woman-Chief) and Her People* (Hartford, 1876), and "The Tragedy of the Lava-Beds," in Bland, *Alfred B.*

He sought first a career as a public lecturer on Indian matters and traveled as far as Boston, where he gave his lecture "The Tragedy of the Lava Beds" at the Park Street Church on May 24, 1874. His early successes on the platform led him to organize a lecture company that combined addresses with Indian exhibitions. Although undoubtedly hoping to make money by capitalizing on his experiences and the growing interest in Indian affairs, he had a deep and genuine concern for reform.

The lecture company, unfortunately, was not a success, and the strain drove Meacham close to physical and nervous collapse. At that crucial point, he made the acquaintance of Dr. Thomas A. Bland, who with his wife Cora (also trained as a physician) mended Meacham's health and gave him encouragement and considerable assistance in his Indian reform efforts. The Blands promoted Meacham's lectures (now without the formality of a company and the presence of Indians) and periodically gave him the medical attention he needed.[30] As a complement to the lectures, Meacham also prepared written accounts of his experiences with the Indians. The first of these, a 700-page book called *Wigwam and War-path; or the Royal Chief in Chains* appeared in Boston in 1875. A shorter book, prepared with the hope of better sales at the lectures, *Wi-ne-ma (The Woman-Chief) and Her People*, was published in 1876.

After returning to the East from a lecture tour in the summer of 1877, Meacham, encouraged and aided by the Blands, resolved to begin publication of a journal, to call attention to the wrongs of the Indians and to promote reform in Indian policy, a journal that was envisaged as another *Liberator*. The first issue of the magazine, called *The Council Fire*, appeared in Philadelphia in January, 1878, but after the March issue, Meacham moved to Washington, where he continued to live with the Blands, who had taken up residence there. The themes of Meacham's lectures were repeated in the new journal: recognition of the Indian's manhood, the necessity of the Indians' accepting civilization as the only alternative to extermination, the importance of dis-

---

Meacham. The fullest account of Meacham's life and works is Edward Sterl Phinney, "Alfred B. Meacham, Promoter of Indian Reform" (unpublished Ph.D. dissertation, University of Oregon, 1963).

[30] Bland, *Alfred B. Meacham*, pp. 7–9.

tributing land in severalty, and specific reforms in the agency system.[31]

The influence of *The Council Fire* under Meacham's editorship is difficult to judge. Paid subscriptions were never more than a thousand, although almost an equal number of copies were distributed free to senators and congressmen, other government officials, Indian agents, and missionaries. It is difficult to determine, too, how much of the journal was the work of the Blands. To broaden the base of the magazine, its title was changed in January, 1882, to *The Council Fire and Arbitrator* and it took up the cause of peace and arbitration as well as Indian reform. This move was clearly the work of Bland, who was a member of the National Arbitration League. And as Meacham undertook commissions from the Department of the Interior—as a disbursing officer in the Indian Territory in the summers of 1878 and 1879 and then for a year and a half as a member of the Ute Commission in 1880–1881—*The Council Fire* was handled completely by his associates.[32] When Meacham died in February, 1882, the journal was continued by Dr. Bland, and it became the vehicle for his particular brand of Indian reform and for the Indian Defence Association which he founded in Washington in 1885.

Whenever hostilities arose and the military advocates renewed their attacks on Indian policy, the peace party trotted out once more its stable of arguments. Renewed agitation for transfer in the mid-1870's led the Board of Indian Commissioners to seek information from the reservations in support of its own position. On August 1, 1875, the board sent a circular letter to each agent, asking whether military forces were stationed at or near the agency, what the troops were used for, and how the Indians reacted to the military presence. The agent was to report his own judgment on the influence of the troops "in respect to morality, good order, and progress in civilization" and to furnish other information "bearing upon the wisdom of increasing or diminishing the use of the Army in the management of Indian affairs."

[31] Phinney, "Alfred B. Meacham," pp. 247–52, gives a good account of the founding of *The Council Fire* and of its program during Meacham's time as editor.

[32] Phinney, "Alfred B. Meacham," pp. 258, 260; Bland, *Alfred B. Meacham*, pp. 10–12.

In a related question, the agents were asked about the use of Indian police and whether they might replace military forces. The replies substantiated the antimilitary leanings of the board. Nearly all the agents who had had experience with troops near the reservation reported that the Indians viewed the troops with dislike and apprehension and that the effect of the common soldiers upon the moral condition of the Indians was universally bad.[33]

The board could thus report its views with confidence. The work, it insisted, was now to educate and civilize the Indians, not to subdue them, and this was eminently civilian not military work. Charging that the men who enlisted in the army during times of peace were "among the most vicious of our population," the board asserted that when a military post and an agency were close together bad results were certain to follow. Moreover, the army acted arbitrarily and with the use of force, which in itself led to more Indian hostilities. So the members righteously concluded: "We cannot see any benefit whatever that is likely, or even possible, to result from relegating the care of the Indians to the Army. The Army is admirable in its place, but its function is not that of civil government in a republic like ours."[34] The Commissioner of Indian Affairs backed up the position of the board. In a long discussion of the whole transfer issue, Edward P. Smith argued that the Peace Commission had voted against transfer in 1868 and that conditions in 1875 called for it even less. He noted that at five-sixths of the agencies no soldiers were needed and at half the remainder troops were required only to assist the agent in the arrest of turbulent men. "So far, then, as eleven-twelfths of the Indian agencies are concerned," he concluded, "the question of putting them under the control of the War Department has no more pertinency than that of putting the almshouse and city schools under the metropolitan police." Rather, the very process of civilization was hindered by the presence of the soldiers. "The first lesson to be given the Indian is that of self-support by labor with his own hands," he said, "—the last lesson which a man in uniform teaches." And he added the usual little piece on "the inevitable demoralization of intemperance and lewdness" which the soldiers brought to Indian reservations. Smith, however, was more than willing

[33] *Report of the Board of Indian Commissioners,* 1875, pp. 64–103.
[34] *Ibid.,* pp. 14–15.

91

that the onerous task of supplying the Indian agencies be taken over by the army.[35]

A few reformers faltered. William Welsh, who had taken such an active part in initiating the peace policy, finally despaired of ridding the Indian service of graft and came out for army control, but he was almost alone and his defection brought other men back into the fray. Felix Brunot, then no longer on the Board of Indian Commissioners, published an open letter, dated May 22, 1876, to his former colleague on the board, William E. Dodge, which was a new testimonial to the antimilitary policy. He pointed once more to the good effects of the peace policy and counted up the acres plowed, the cattle raised, and the Indian children in school. And he ridiculed the idea that military control would mean economy, one of the chief arguments of the army men. Most of the agencies were not even near a military post, and he asked whether it was intended to move the Indians to the forts, or the forts to the reservations. "If it is merely proposed to detach army offi- cers from the posts to perform the duties of agents," he added, "I reply that any one acquainted with the nature of those duties must be aware that the agent can have time for nothing else, and if there are enough superfluous officers of a proper rank who can be spared from the posts to perform them, the army needs to be reduced." Bishop Whipple wrote to thank Brunot for his stand: "I think your manly letter at the time Mr. Welsh was disposed to turn our Indians over to the army prevented it."[36]

The last great challenge to civilian control of the Indians came in the conflicts with the Sioux. The Treaty of Fort Laramie in 1868 had left unceded lands in the Powder River country as hunting lands of the Sioux but it had also set aside the Great Sioux Reserve west of the Missouri River in Dakota, and the chiefs had agreed to settle at the agencies and accept reservation life. Many of the Indians in fact went to the agencies, lured by the government's rations, but some, like Sitting Bull, remained on the unceded lands and refused to settle down. The non-reservation Indians were considered "hostile," for they

[35] Report of the Commissioner of Indian Affairs, 1875, in serial 1680, pp. 520–23.
[36] Slattery, *Brunot*, pp. 233, 236–37. The full letter is given on pp. 229–36.

occasionally raided the Montana settlements and fought the advancing railroad surveyors who entered their lands. The Sioux were irritated, too, by the invasion of the Black Hills by a military expedition under George A. Custer in 1874, which confirmed the rumors that gold was there and stimulated the miners to invade the forbidden hills.

As long as the Indians were able to subsist by hunting in the Powder River valley, it was impossible to control them fully. Only on the reservations would they be completely dependent upon the United States, and in December, 1875, runners were sent to the Sioux to announce that all who were not at the agencies by January 31, 1876, would be hunted down by the army and brought in by military force. The midwinter deadline made compliance impossible, but the Indians did not intend to obey in any event. On February 1, 1876, the Secretary of the Interior declared that all the Indians not on the reservations were to be considered hostile and asked the Secretary of War to take appropriate action. General Sheridan, now in command of the Division of the Missouri, wanted a winter campaign, but delays prevented a full-scale attack until April and May, when three columns moved in toward the Sioux and their Cheyenne allies. One column headed eastward from Fort Ellis in Montana, a second moved northward along the old Bozeman Trail from Fort Fetterman, and a third, including the Seventh Cavalry under Custer, traveled west from Fort Abraham Lincoln on the Missouri. Seriously underestimating the size of the opposing Indian force, Custer launched a premature attack upon the Indian camp on the Little Bighorn on June 25, and he and his entire force were annihilated.[37]

The battle of the Little Bighorn shocked the nation, and heavy army reinforcements were sent into Montana to hunt down the bands of Sioux and Cheyenne who scattered after the fight. Such pressure was more than the Indians could withstand, and little by little during the fall and winter the bands surrendered at the agencies. Even the most recalcitrant at length came in. Crazy Horse with a band of more than a thousand surrendered at Camp Robinson, Nebraska, on May 6, 1877.

[37] Perhaps more has been written about Custer's battle than about any other Indian-related event in United States history. A reasonable, detailed account is Edgar I. Stewart, *Custer's Luck* (Norman, 1955). For an excellent brief survey that illuminates the strategy and the tactics, see Robert M. Utley, *Custer Battlefield National Monument, Montana* (Washington, 1969), a publication of the National Park Service.

Sitting Bull with his adherents fled into Canada determined never to submit to reservation life, but finally he, too, came back and gave up in July, 1881. The Sioux war had accomplished what the peace policy had been unable to; it had forced the Indians to abandon their hunting grounds and accept government control on the reservations.

The reformers kept up the fight against all threats of transfer. The Board of Indian Commissioners made a great stir about the question of economy in its report of 1877, providing comparative figures to show that costs had been greater under the War Department than under the Interior Department. But it did not want such practical issues to crowd out the main issue. "In all our dealings with the Indians, in all our legislation for them," it declared, "their civilization and ultimate citizenship should be the one purpose steadily pursued. That is the only aim worthy of us as a great Christian nation. And the attainment of this end will hardly be possible by military means." In the following year, it repeated once again all the old arguments, emphasizing now, how-ever, that the Indians themselves were opposed to transfer to military control.[38] The Five Civilized Tribes publicly denounced the proposed transfer. The delegates of these nations in the capital met on February 12, 1878, to oppose a new transfer bill, addressing a long memorial to Congress in which they praised the peace policy inaugurated under Grant and echoed the reformers' pleas for keeping the Indians out of the hands of the military. "Do you desire to save from further destruc-tion your Indian population?" they asked Congress. "Is it your purpose to civilize and christianize them, so as to prepare them eventually for citizenship? Then in the name of civilization, christianity, and human-ity, we earnestly ask you to make no change in the present general man-agement unless it be to create an independent Indian department."[39]

In this campaign the opponents of transfer had the support of *The Council Fire*. Meacham was particularly aggressive. He wrote in May, 1878:

[38] *Report of the Board of Indian Commissioners*, 1877, pp. 5–6; *ibid.*, 1878, pp. 9–16.
[39] *The Indians Opposed to the Transfer Bill: United Action of the Delegations of the Cherokee, Creek, Seminole, Chickasaw, and Choctaw Nations in Opposition to the Measure: They Protest against It, and Give Their Reasons for So Doing* (Washington, 1878), p. 10.

94

What means the clamor for a transfer of the Indian to the War Department?

It means to make business for the War Department. No well-informed man will assert that it is for *the good of the Indian*. Everybody knows better. Those who clamor for change give as a reason that by so doing we will get rid of the Indian rings. This is all bosh. The Indian rings are no worse than the army rings. . . . If West Point is the only institution which graduates honest men then our Christian civilization is a lie. It is an insult to our peace-loving people to intimate that military men are superior to civilians in business integrity.[40]

For the defeat of transfer—"that unwise and barbarous measure"—the journal took much of the credit.[41] Former Commissioner of Indian Affairs George W. Manypenny also entered the lists, although a bit late to affect the outcome of the contest, with a detailed recital of military inhumanity to the Indians, in a book called *Our Indian Wards*.[42]

The opposing sides were careful to seek their supporting evidence from their friends. The Board of Indian Commissioners, gathering data in 1875 about the effect of military forces on the Indians and the wisdom of increasing or lessening military influences, sent its questionnaires to the civilian agents who were part of the Interior Department structure and who would have been eliminated under the army's proposals. No wonder that the respondents were almost unanimous in asserting that what was needed was civilian effort to educate and civilize the Indians. The House Committee on Military Affairs in 1876,

[40] *The Council Fire*, I (May, 1878), 66.

[41] Article by A. B. Meacham, December, 1878, reprinted *ibid.*, VI (October, 1883), 139–40; address of M. C. Bland, *ibid.*, VI (March, 1883), 38–39. See also *ibid.*, I (May, 1878), 72; II (January, 1879), 5–6; (March, 1879), 36.

[42] George W. Manypenny, *Our Indian Wards* (Cincinnati, 1880), pp. 373–94. In his introduction Manypenny said: "It is submitted that the facts given ought to silence, now and hereafter, the clamor in which military officers have indulged against the civil administration of Indian affairs, and forever dispose of the question of the restoration of the Indian bureau to the war department—a theme on which these officers (with but few exceptions) have indulged, with an assurance amounting to audacity." P. xxv. Theodore Roosevelt characterized *Our Indian Wards*, with Jackson's *A Century of Dishonor*, as "worse than valueless" and described Manypenny's book as "a mere spiteful diatribe against various army officers." *The Winning of the West* (6 vols., New York, 1889–1896), I, 262. See also Henry E. Fritz, "George W. Manypenny and *Our Indian Wards*," *Kansas Quarterly*, III (Fall, 1971), 100–104.

on the other hand, seeking advice on the expediency of transferring the Indian service to military control, sent its questionnaires to sixty high-ranking army officers, all but two of whom recommended the transfer as a measure of "expediency, wisdom, and economy." Not until 1878 was there an attempt by an investigating group to get both sides of the story, and then the report was a four-to-four split.[43]

While the ideological battle over transfer was raging in the official reports and in the public press, the issue was fought out in the halls of Congress. But as is so often the case, the congressional battle lines could not be drawn sharply on a basis of theory or principle. Conflicts between the House and Senate over jurisdiction in Indian matters, between eastern and western legislators, and between Democrats and Republicans all entered into the final outcome.[44]

Debate first arose at the end of January, 1867, when a bill for transfer passed the House of Representatives by a narrow margin. Although western senators urged the need of force to manage Indian affairs, the Senate defeated the bill.[45] The report of the Peace Commission against transfer, signed as it was by Generals Sherman, Augur, and Terry, dampened the agitation for the measure, but when the commission reversed its decision, the way was cleared for a new attempt, and on December 8, 1868, a new transfer bill, introduced by Congressman James Garfield, passed the House by a substantial margin. The Senate again refused to conform, despite attempts made in February, 1869, to add an amendment providing for transfer to the Indian appropriation bill.[46] Then the inauguration of Grant's peace policy made a strong movement toward military control out of the question for the time being. Military actions like that of Major Baker against the Piegans in

[43] *Report of the Board of Indian Commissioners*, 1875, p. 64; *House Report* No. 354, 44 Congress, 1 session, serial 1709, pp. 4–5; *Senate Report* No. 693, 45 Congress, 3 session, serial 1837.

[44] These matters are treated well in Priest, *Uncle Sam's Stepchildren*, pp. 17–23. Congressional action in regard to transfer is also discussed in some detail in D'Elia, "Civilian or Military Indian Control," pp. 210–23, and in Garfield, "The Indian Question," pp. 31–37.

[45] House debate is in *Congressional Globe*, 39 Congress, 2 session, pp. 891–98; Senate debate, *ibid.*, pp. 1712–20.

[46] House debate is in *Congressional Globe*, 40 Congress, 3 session, pp. 17–21, 880–83; Senate debate, *ibid.*, pp. 39–43, 1376–78.

Montana in January, 1870, were made the most of by critics of the army's handling of Indian affairs, and no doubt it had an important effect upon the outcome of the issue. The increased incidence of Indian hostilities in the 1870's, however, kept the issue alive, and political considerations in the election year of 1876 again made the transfer measure an important one, even before the Custer massacre added new fuel. On April 21, 1876, the House passed a new measure, but it failed again to get by the Senate, which continued to side with the civilian reformers.[47]

The next campaign came in 1878, when the House added a transfer amendment to the army appropriation bill on May 28. This move the Senate met by successfully urging the appointment of a joint committee to investigate the subject. But after exhaustive testimony, which repeated endlessly all the old arguments on both sides, the committee members could not overcome their partisan differences, and separate reports were submitted by the Democratic members (urging transfer) and the Republican members (opposing transfer). With the split decision of the committee, the measure failed again. By this time, the issue had lost much of its urgency, and later congressional action was indecisive if not half-hearted.[48]

Much of the credit belongs to Secretary of the Interior Carl Schurz, whose reform of the Indian Bureau was an important element in the fight against the military. Schurz had appointed a special board of inquiry in 1877 to investigate charges of wrongdoing in the Indian service. The commission—composed of one member from the Interior Department, one from the War Department, and a third from the Department of Justice—submitted a startling report, which accused the Indian Bureau of inefficiency and dishonesty and charged that the management of Indian affairs had been a reproach to the whole

[47] House debate is in *Congressional Record*, IV, 2657–74, 2682–86; Senate debate, *ibid.*, 3962–65. The report of the House Committee on Military Affairs, March 9, 1876, in favor of transfer with supporting testimony from army officers is in *House Report* No. 354, 44 Congress, 1 session, serial 1709; the report of the House Committee on Indian Affairs, March 14, 1876, is in *House Report* No. 240, 44 Congress, 1 session, serial 1708.

[48] House debate is in *Congressional Record*, VII, 3876–77; Senate debate, *ibid.*, 4192–4200, 4234–39, 4685–86. The testimony taken by the joint committee is printed in *Senate Miscellaneous Document* No. 53, 45 Congress, 3 session, serial 1835. See also majority and minority reports of the House Committee on Indian Affairs, February 25, 1878, in *House Report* No. 241, 45 Congress, 2 session, serial 1822. For later congressional action, see Priest, *Uncle Sam's Stepchildren*, pp. 20–21.

nation.[49] The Secretary moved bravely ahead to clean out these Augean stables, starting with the dismissal of the Commissioner of Indian Affairs, John Q. Smith. His success in correcting a corrupt administration of Indian affairs weakened one of the main lines of attack by military men against Interior Department control, and he publicly stood up to the generals who criticized civilian administrators. On the other side, in 1876, just at a crucial point when military advocates seemed to be winning, the impeachment of Secretary of War William W. Belknap for malfeasance in office and his subsequent resignation gave the opponents of War Department control of Indian affairs a new argument. Did the nation, they asked, want Indian affairs turned over to such a corrupt office? One congressman spoke of the spectacle of the "House marching to the Senate for the impeachment of the head of that Department, a Department all bad and worse with every revelation, and at the same time giving it new privileges and powers and fresh responsibilities."[50]

At all events, the humanitarians had won. The Board of Indian Commissioners rejoiced in 1879 that the "general sentiment of the country sustained our views and Congress refused to endorse a measure so fraught with evil and so subversive of the good results of the last ten years of humane policy adopted by the government."[51] Schurz, in his final report as Secretary of the Interior in 1880, renewed once more the arguments for civilian as against military handling of the Indian service, but he noted how little military significance there was then in Indian affairs and his tone indicated that he knew the fight was over.[52] Since the question of the need for military force was no longer of great importance, the issue died. The reformers directed their attention then, among other things, toward improving the condition of the Indians through civil service reform of the Indian service. With the goal of eliminating political patronage from the appointments to the agencies,

[49] *Report of Board of Inquiry Convened by Authority of Letter of the Secretary of the Interior of June 7, 1877, to Investigate Certain Charges against S. A. Galpin, Chief Clerk of the Indian Bureau, and Concerning Irregularities in Said Bureau* (Washington, 1878).

[50] Priest, *Uncle Sam's Stepchildren,* p. 22; *Congressional Record,* IV, 2658. See also the discussion of Schurz's role in Claude Moore Fuess, *Carl Schurz, Reformer* (New York, 1932), pp. 255–57.

[51] *Report of the Board of Indian Commissioners,* 1879, p. 8.

[52] Report of the Secretary of the Interior, 1880, in serial 1959, pp. 16–19.

they scarcely batted an eye when in 1892 army officers were again appointed as Indian agents.

The bitter tirades of the civilian advocates against the army should not be allowed to obscure the sincere concern that some military men showed for the Indians and their welfare. It is true that generals like Sherman and Sheridan advocated immediate and harsh punishment of hostile Indians and military control without civilian interference. It is also true that the army officers in the West agreed that Indians who committed depredations should be punished and that they often ridiculed the ineffectiveness of civilian peace proposals. But the officers of the United States army who served on the Indian frontiers cannot simply be lumped with rabid frontiersmen as exterminationists. A number of them, in fact, have been called "the humanitarian soldiers."[53]

Outstanding, perhaps, was General George Crook, a man who served in the West for a third of a century and who had a well-deserved reputation as an aggressive Indian fighter. But he also developed a philosophy of Indian relations based on honesty, justice, and concern for Indian civilization. He supported the Ponca Indians in their flight from the Indian Territory, spoke out in support of the Cheyenne Chief Dull Knife and of the Bannock Indians in their conflicts with the United States, and during his second tour in Arizona, 1882–1886, worked out a positive program for the economic welfare of the Apaches that sought to convert them into capitalistic farmers.[54] In his later years, his views toward Indian policy were almost indistinguishable from those of the civilian reformers, with whom he came to have close contacts. His words in 1884 on teaching the Indians the value of money

[53] This theme has been developed in two articles by Richard N. Ellis, "The Humanitarian Soldiers," *Journal of Arizona History*, X (Summer, 1969), 53–66; and "The Humanitarian Generals," *Western Historical Quarterly*, III (April, 1972), 169–78.

[54] James T. King, "George Crook: Indian Fighter and Humanitarian," *Arizona and the West*, IX (Winter, 1967), 333–48. King asserts that Crook "conceived and put into practice one of the most enlightened Indian policies in the history of the American frontier" and that his career provides "insight into the element of humanitarianism which lies neglected among the more martial characteristics of the military frontier." *Ibid.*, pp. 333–34. See also James T. King, " 'A Better Way': General George Crook and the Ponca Indians," *Nebraska History*, L (Fall, 1969), 239–56. Crook's own story has been edited by Martin F. Schmitt, *General George Crook: His Autobiography* (Norman, 1946).

fitted well into the sentiments of the Gilded Age and could have come from any of the leading humanitarian reformers:

> No sermon that was ever preached on the "Dignity of Labor" could print upon the savage mind the impression received when he sees that *Work* means *Money* and that the exact measure of his industry is to be found in his pocket book. The next important idea inculcated is that money will grow exactly as a tree does; that is, if he invest his little accumulations in Calves and Colts, they will keep on growing and multiplying by night as well as by day. You see this process is rapidly transforming the Apache from an Ishmaelite into a property owner, and [any] property at all makes its possessor conservative. The Indian sees that peace has its advantages.[55]

Crook believed firmly in the Indians' competence to survive and advance if given a chance. "I wish to say most emphatically," he wrote, "that the American Indian is the intellectual peer of most, if not all, the various nationalities we have assimilated to our laws, customs, and language. He is fully able to protect himself, if the ballot be given and the courts of law not closed against him." When the general died in 1890, he was eulogized as "a tower of strength to all who labored for Indian civilization."[56]

Another western commander of moderate views was General John Pope. When first appointed to command the Department of the Northwest, he spoke openly of exterminating the hostile Sioux responsible for the Minnesota outbreak of 1862, but he later changed his tune. His long subsequent career in the West—he commanded the Department of the Missouri from 1870 to 1883—taught him much about the Indians and about the shortcomings of existing Indian policy. Although he directed campaigns against the warring Indians, he voiced concern for the Indians' future, relieved their suffering at the end of the wars, and sought to protect them from rapacious whites. His goal, like that of the reformers, was the eventual assimilation of the Indians into

[55] Crook to Herbert Welsh, July 16, 1884, quoted in King, "George Crook: Indian Fighter and Humanitarian," p. 345.

[56] Crook to Herbert Welsh, January 3, 1885, printed in *Letter from General Crook on Giving the Ballot to Indians* (Philadelphia, 1885), a leaflet distributed by the Indian Rights Association; "Resolution Adopted by the Executive Committee of the Association upon the Announcement of the Death of Major-Gen. George Crook, U.S.A.," April 2, 1890, in *Report of the Indian Rights Association*, 1890, pp. 52–53.

white society.[57] General Oliver Otis Howard, too, was more than an Indian fighter. Known as the "Christian general" and renowned for his work as head of the Freedmen's Bureau, Howard approached the Indians with deep religious sentiments. His piety irritated some of his associates, but he sincerely hoped for peaceful means of dealing with the Indians. Like so many others, he concluded that there would be no lasting end to Indian troubles until the Indians got land in severalty and protection of the law and were assimilated into American culture. He pushed for Indian education and for an end to the reservation system.[58] Other officers, like Benjamin Grierson, who co-operated closely with the Quaker agent among the Kiowas and Comanches, Ranald Mackenzie, who fed the defeated and starving Indians, and Richard Henry Pratt, whose assignment to care for the prisoners of the Red River War started him on a lifelong career in Indian education and assimilation, add further testimony.

While the transfer issue had been debated, an alternative to the either-or proposition of Interior Department or War Department management of Indian affairs had also been considered. A recommended solution to the disturbing conflict was that the Indian Bureau be elevated into an independent department on a par with Interior and War, although this, clearly, was less satisfactory to the military side than to the civilian reformers. Commissioner Taylor, after his long condemnation of the threatened transfer in 1868, admitted that management of Indian affairs had not proved much more satisfactory under the Interior Department than it had under the War Department prior to 1849. "There is too much cargo for the capacity of the vessel," he wrote, "and too much vessel and freight for the power of the machinery. We have crammed into a bureau, which under the supervisory and appellate power is a mere clerkship, all the large, complex, difficult and delicate affairs that ought to employ every function of a first-class

[57] Ellis, "Humanitarian Generals," pp. 174–76. For a full account of Pope's western career, see Richard N. Ellis, *General Pope and U.S. Indian Policy* (Albuquerque, 1970); pp. 230–42 summarize Pope's views on Indian policy and his proposals.
[58] John A. Carpenter, *Sword and Olive Branch: Oliver Otis Howard* (Pittsburgh, 1964), pp. 267–68; Ellis, "Humanitarian Generals," pp. 169–70. Howard's own story is given in *My Life and Experiences Among Our Hostile Indians* (Hartford, 1907).

department." The remedy was simple: launch a new Department of Indian Affairs. It was an intelligent and reasonable suggestion, and the Peace Commission in January, 1868, had in fact indicated it as its own ultimate preference.[59]

The idea frequently recurred, but it made little headway. An independent department as the solution to fraud and graft in the Indian service was pushed by Felix Brunot and the original Board of Indian Commissioners in 1874, and the failure of the administration to give the proposal a hearing was used as an excuse by the board for resigning en masse. The report of the joint committee in 1879 noted the proposal and asserted its agreement because it thought that the Indian Office was of such importance that its chief should communicate directly with the President. The committee, however, did not urge immediate legislation on the subject. Carl Schurz alluded to the idea in his final report; he was favorable to it but he was not sure that it was wise to enlarge the size of the cabinet.[60] The proposal never got the aggressive support needed to make it a reality.

The transfer issue was the greatest challenge that the peace program of the Christian Indian reformers had to meet. The persistent advocacy of military management of Indian affairs was an explicit denial that civilian methods, on which the peace policy depended, were successful. The contest kept the air filled with charges and countercharges, forced the reformers to defend their policy both in theory and by practical accomplishments, and kept the public agitated over the Indian question. Scraping by with the narrowest of victories in Congress, the reformers stuck to their position until the succession of crises passed and they were able to begin anew with an aggressive humanitarian program for turning the Indians into standardized Americans.

[59] Report of the Commissioner of Indian Affairs, 1868, in serial 1366, pp. 473–75; "Report of Indian Peace Commissioners," January 7, 1868, *House Executive Document* No. 97, 40 Congress, 2 session, serial 1337, p. 21. See also S. F. Tappan to William T. Sherman, February 8, 1868, in Sherman Papers.

[60] *Senate Report* No. 693, 45 Congress, 3 session, serial 1837, p. xix; Report of the Secretary of the Interior, 1880, in serial 1959, p. 19.

CHAPTER 4

DEVELOPMENT OF RESERVATION POLICY

It has long been the policy of the government to require of the tribes most nearly in contact with white settlements that they should fix their abode upon definite reservations and abandon the wandering life to which they had been accustomed. To encourage them in civilization, large expenditures have been made in furnishing them with the means of agriculture and with clothing adapted to their new mode of life.

A new policy is not so much needed as an enlarged and more enlightened application of the general principles of the old one. We are now in contact with all the aboriginal tribes within our borders, and can no longer assume that we may, even for a time, leave a large part of them out of the operation of our system.

I understand this policy to look to two objects: First, the location of the Indians upon fixed reservations, so that the pioneers and settlers may be freed from the terrors of wandering hostile tribes; and second, an earnest effort at their civilization, so that they may themselves be elevated in the scale of humanity, and our obligation to them as fellowmen be discharged.

—Secretary of the Interior
Jacob D. Cox, 1869

❀❀❀❀❀❀❀

The post-Civil War Indian reformers inherited a reservation policy that had developed gradually during the previous decades. The great Indian country west of a definite boundary line marked off quite precisely in treaty after treaty had been a prominent feature of Indian-white relations. The line had been steadily moved to the west, from the watershed of the Appalachians, designated as the boundary of colonial settlement in 1763, to the "permanent Indian frontier," planned along the western border of Missouri and Arkansas in the 1830's. But no sooner had the Indian problem been "settled" by the movement of eastern Indians into the Indian country in the West, which was to remain theirs forever, than new conditions arose that upset the stability of the relationships once again. In the decade of the 1840's, there was a strong movement to consolidate the Indians in the north and in the south so as to open a wide swath of free country across the central plains which could serve as a corridor of travel and communication with the newly opened lands on the Pacific coast.[1]

As early as 1841, officials spoke of a northern Indian territory to serve as a counterpoise to the southwestern Indian territory, which had received the great bulk of the Indians removed in the 1830's. By the end of the decade this principle of division was far advanced. In 1848 the Commissioner of Indian Affairs reported: "It may be said that we have commenced the establishment of two colonies for the Indian tribes that we have been compelled to remove; one north, on the head waters of the Mississippi, and the other south, on the western borders of Missouri and Arkansas, the southern limit of which is the Red river." When the movements he contemplated had taken place, he said, the nation would have "an ample outlet of about six geographical degrees" into which the American population could expand or pass through to the Pacific.[2]

These officials argued that the concentration of the Indians would benefit the Indians in their march toward civilization as well as provide open territory for American expansion. To its advocates, the whole idea of removal was to keep the Indians away from the whites for their own good. Thus Secretary of War W. L. Marcy in 1847 spoke of the "wise policy of separating the Indians residing in States and organized Territories from contiguity to, and intermingling with, the white

---

[1] The breakdown of the Indian country west of the Mississippi up to the passage of the Kansas-Nebraska Act is studied in James C. Malin, *Indian Policy and Westward Expansion* (Bulletin of the University of Kansas, Humanistic Studies, vol. II, no. 3, Lawrence, 1921).

[2] Report of the Commissioner of Indian Affairs, 1841, in serial 401, p. 231; *ibid.*, 1848, in serial 537, pp. 388–90.

population, and of settling them in a quiet home, removed as far as practicable from the reach of influences so pernicious to their well being." Increasingly, extensive territory in itself came to be considered a positive disadvantage to the Indians, for it encouraged them to hold fast to the futile attempt to subsist by the chase, instead of "concentrating and applying themselves with any regular or systematic effort to agriculture and other industrial pursuits."[3]

These theories were acted upon in the 1850's. Treaties with the tribes in Nebraska and Kansas opened up large sections in the eastern parts of those territories. But instead of clearing the Indians out altogether—a constant frontier principle—the treaties negotiated by Indian Commissioner George W. Manypenny provided small diminished reserves for the Indians where they were, in the hope that they could be induced to cultivate them according to white practice.[4] The problems of the Indians in the newly acquired territories in the Southwest, also, were to be solved by a reservation system—concentrating the Indians in designated areas, which would be protected for them in a manner similar to reservations in older regions.[5]

Lincoln's Commissioner of Indian Affairs, William P. Dole, came to see in the reservation system, in fact, "the fixed policy of the government" and the only method by which the defects in the present policy could be amended. In the course of his four-year term, he developed considerable theory about a reservation system and what should be expected from it. Simply assuming as necessary and inevitable the negotiating of treaties of cession with the Indians because the country was being so rapidly filled with whites, Dole couched his pronouncements in terms of justice and aid to the Indians. "The change from savage to civilized life is very great, and is, at best, beset with difficulties and perplexities," he declared in 1861. "As the ultimate object of all our operations among the Indians should be to better their condi-

[3] Report of the Secretary of War, 1847, *Senate Executive Document* No. 1, 30 Congress, 1 session, serial 503, p. 69; Report of the Commissioner of Indian Affairs, 1849, in serial 570, pp. 945–46.

[4] The land problems in Kansas resulting from these treaties are discussed at length in Gates, *Fifty Million Acres*. See also Annie Heloise Abel, "Indian Reservations in Kansas and the Extinguishment of Their Titles," *Transactions of the Kansas State Historical Society*, VIII (1903–1904), 72–109.

[5] See Alban W. Hoopes, *Indian Affairs and Their Administration, with Special Reference to the Far West, 1849–1860* (Philadelphia, 1932).

tion, it will be my duty, as well as of all other employés of the government, to endeavor to secure for them reservations of such dimensions, and possessing such natural facilities in climate, soil, and all other desirable qualities, as will, so far as possible, remove the obstacles in the way of their advancement, and present to them the greatest inducements to abandon savage and adopt civilized modes of life." Dole saw no possibility of red men and white occupying the same territory without the rapid contamination and ultimate extinction of the Indians. Only by segregation could the Indians be reclaimed, then "instructed and gradually conducted along the difficult paths by which all nations who have attained civilization have travelled." But he looked forward to the day when the reservations could be subdivided and allotted to the Indians in severalty, creating from the sale of the surplus land a fund for aiding the Indians to begin their new mode of life.[6]

Dole criticized the creation of many small reservations, which only served to increase the evils that came from contact between the whites and the Indians. He wanted to concentrate all the Indians onto a few large reservations—he believed that the number should not exceed five and might be reduced to three—where only soldiers and civilian officials of the government would reach them while they acquired the arts of civilized life. Whether considered as "a measure of justice and humanity to the Indians, in its economical aspects, or as a measure designed to reclaim a barbarous and heathen race," he commended his plan to all who worked for Indian civilization.[7]

The next administration went along with Dole's proposal, considering it "no doubt the best, if not the only, policy that can be pursued" to preserve the Indians from extinction. The Commissioner of Indian Affairs in 1867 urged the consolidating of the Indians on large reservations where they could be educated intellectually and morally, taught to be self-supporting, and ultimately clothed with the rights of citizenship. For the northern Indians, he recommended the territory north of Nebraska and west of the Missouri River as far as the Rocky Mountains and for the southern tribes an extension of the Indian Territory to include the staked plains of Texas and as much of New Mexico

[6] Report of the Commissioner of Indian Affairs, 1861, in serial 1117, pp. 635, 646–47; *ibid.*, 1863, in serial 1182, pp. 129–30; *ibid.*, 1864, in serial 1220, p. 149.

[7] *Ibid.*, 1863, in serial 1182, pp. 129–30; *ibid.*, 1864, in serial 1220, p. 172.

as might be necessary. Reservations on the Pacific coast would care for the Indians west of the Rockies.[8]

The Indian Office's solution to special or local problems was in terms of this master plan. The Indians of Colorado, it thought, were not likely to improve their condition until they were all concentrated upon reservations. For the Idaho superintendency, likewise, it was the purpose of the Indian Office to move the tribes to reservations, where they could be aided by schools, a supply of provisions and agricultural implements, and instruction in industrial arts and where they would give the white settlers fewer occasions to complain of Indian outrages.[9]

While the theorists were enunciating their plans in Washington, the Peace Commission was in the West trying to make them a reality. In the treaties negotiated at Medicine Lodge Creek in October, 1867, the southern plains Indians were assigned to two reservations, where the United States would furnish them rations and other goods needed to turn them into happy farmers. The commission was unanimous in its opinion that it was necessary to collect the Indians east of the Rockies into reservations north of Nebraska and south of Kansas as rapidly as possible.[10] In the north the treaty-making went more slowly, and the implementation of the treaties was still another matter, for Congress was slow to appropriate the necessary funds, and the Indians were not easily kept within the boundaries marked out for their reservations.

The difficulties did not deter the reformers. The reservation policy became firmly fixed, and when General Grant inaugurated his famous peace policy, the concentration of the Indians on reservations was the presumed underpinning of the new procedures. Commissioner Parker's question to the new Board of Indian Commissioners asking, "should the Indians be placed upon reservations?" was met with an immediate and unanimous opinion that they should be. The first report of the board declared:

> The policy of collecting the Indian tribes upon small reservations

[8] Report of the Secretary of the Interior, 1866, in serial 1284, pp. 7–8; Report of the Commissioner of Indian Affairs, 1867, in serial 1326, p. 5. The commissioner's report summarized a special report prepared by Indian Commissioner N. G. Taylor in response to a Senate resolution of July 8, 1867.

[9] Report of the Commissioner of Indian Affairs, 1867, in serial 1326, pp. 13–15.

[10] A strong statement of this opinion is the report of General W. T. Sherman, November 1, 1868, *House Executive Document* No. 1, 40 Congress, 3 session, serial 1367, p. 2.

contiguous to each other, and within the limits of a large reservation, eventually to become a State of the Union, and of which the small reservations will probably be the counties, seems to be the best that can be devised. Many tribes may thus be collected in the present Indian territory. The larger the number that can be thus concentrated the better for the success of the plan; care being taken to separate hereditary enemies from each other. When upon the reservation they should be taught as soon as possible the advantage of individual ownership of property; and should be given land in severalty as soon as it is desired by any of them, and the tribal relation should be discouraged.[11]

These views accorded well with those of responsible men in Grant's administration. Secretary of the Interior Cox saw that larger concentrations would obviate many of the evils that arose when small reservations were surrounded by the unscrupulous frontier whites, and he hoped that the moving of less advanced tribes into contact with more civilized ones would have a beneficial result. He was sanguine about the prospects of concentration of the tribes in the Indian Territory and the organization of a territorial government over them. In the north, and west of the Rockies, he wanted the same sort of development, although he realized that there it would take more time.[12]

The idea of consolidating the tribes in the Indian Territory became almost an obsession with Columbus Delano, who began to play a numbers game, trying to fit all the Indians into one large reservation. He counted 172,000 Indians outside of the Indian Territory, occupying 96,155,785 acres, a per capita acreage of 558. In the Indian Territory itself he found only one person to every 630 acres. "Could the entire Indian population of the country, excluding Alaska and those scattered among the States . . . be located in the Indian Territory," he decided, "there would be 180 acres of land, *per capita*, for the entire number, showing that there is ample area of land to afford them all comfortable homes." At the same time he candidly admitted that the acres given up by the assembling tribes could be thrown open to white settlement and cultivation. He wanted the Indians to realize that if they did not co-

[11] *Report of the Board of Indian Commissioners*, 1869, pp. 3, 9; Minutes of May 26, 1869, Minutes of the Board of Indian Commissioners, vol. I, p. 4, National Archives Record Group 75.
[12] Report of the Secretary of the Interior, 1869, in serial 1414, pp. viii–ix.

operate in this scheme to preserve them in the consolidated reservation, they would inevitably be inundated or crushed by the rapidly growing tide of white emigration. Because it furthered his purpose, Delano rejoiced in the rapid disappearance of the game upon which the widely scattered tribes had historically depended. While abundant game existed, the Indians showed little disposition to abandon the chase. "When the game shall have disappeared," Delano noted, "we shall be well forward in the work in hand."[13]

The efforts of the Indian Office, as Delano remarked in 1873, were "unremitting," and he reported satisfactory progress in exchanging reservations lying within the range of advancing settlements and railroad construction for other locations. During the year, negotiations had been concluded with the Crows by which their reservation was to be reduced by four million acres, and with the Utes for release of between four and five million acres. All of which was "the legitimate result of the working of the existing policy."[14]

In this work of reducing the Indians' reservations, Felix Brunot of the Board of Indian Commissioners played a large part—the humanitarian reformer working toward an end that pleased the westerners who were avaricious for the Indian lands. The agreement with the Crows by which they were to cede their reservation on the Yellowstone River in southern Montana and accept one in the Judith Basin instead delighted the people of Montana, whose governor wrote to Brunot to thank him in the name of the people of the territory for negotiating the treaty, which would have opened to settlement one of the finest and most extensive valleys in the West. The governor attributed the success of the negotiations to "the ability and patience by which the negotiations were conducted, aided by the friendly feeling that has been brought about by the humane policy of the President towards the Indian tribes." Brunot justified his position by arguing that the Crows in the new reservation would be away from the railroad and in a place better suited to their needs.[15] To the disappointment of the whites,

13 *Ibid.*, 1871, in serial 1505, pp. 6–7; *ibid.*, 1872, in serial 1560, pp. 5–7.

14 *Ibid.*, 1873, in serial 1601, pp. vii–viii.

15 Slattery, *Brunot*, pp. 207–13. The agreement is in Kappler, *Indian Affairs: Laws and Treaties*, IV (*Senate Document* No. 53, 70 Congress, 1 session, serial 8849), 1142–47. The lands in question are shown in Charles C. Royce, ed., *Indian Land Cessions in the United States* (Eighteenth Annual Report of the Bureau of American Ethnology, Part 2, Washington, 1899), Cession No. 635, Plate 39, and Cession No. 557, Plate 40.

Congress failed to ratify the agreement, and the Crows stayed for the time being on their lands along the Yellowstone, but the case shows the sincere desire of humanitarians like Brunot to reduce the Indians' land holdings and how the "friendly feeling" which was a conscious part of the peace policy worked toward the ultimate dispossession of the Indians.

An even more personal involvement of Brunot in the reduction of the reservations came in his dealings with the Utes. Ouray, the chief of the Utes, was steadfast at first in his refusal to agree to any sale of lands. In 1872, at an unsuccessful council with the Utes, Brunot had met Ouray. The chief told him of his young son captured fifteen years before by a party of Cheyennes and Arapahos and not heard from since. Brunot took down the details of the story in his notebook, and he and the secretary of the Board of Indian Commissioners, Thomas Cree, undertook to recover the long-lost son. The boy was found in Texas and united with his father in the office of the Board of Indian Commissioners in Washington. The young Indian, unfortunately, died on his way home. "But the gratitude which he [Ouray] felt toward Mr. Brunot and Mr. Cree," Brunot's biographer wrote, "did what a special commission could not do, and when Mr. Brunot told him he thought it right for him to sell a portion of his reservation, Ouray threw all his strong influence in favour of the sale, though a year before he intended opposition to the bitter end." Brunot did "what neither commissioners nor armies could accomplish"; after six days of patient negotiation on his part the Utes ceded five million acres, the southern half of their reservation in southwestern Colorado.[16]

Even the Sioux in Dakota and Montana did not escape Secretary Delano's solicitous attention. He noted the unproductive soil and the severity of the winters in those northern regions, conditions that hindered all attempts to improve the condition of the Indians by agriculture or grazing. Rejecting the older idea of a northern as well as a southern reserve, he wanted to move these northern Indians en masse to the Indian Territory, where "both climate and soil are so favorable

[16] Slattery, *Brunot*, pp. 191–92, 214–15. The agreement of September 13, 1873, ratified on April 29, 1874, is in Kappler, *Indian Affairs: Laws and Treaties*, I, 151–52. The area ceded is shown in Royce, *Indian Land Cessions*, Cession No. 566, Plate 9. The story of Ouray's lost son is told in Ann W. Hafen, "Efforts to Recover the Stolen Son of Chief Ouray," *Colorado Magazine*, XVI (January, 1939), 53–62.

for the production of everything necessary to sustain and make them comfortable." The Sioux along the Missouri River, too, were in a country insufficient to supply their wants and they continued to rely on government aid, a situation that in itself prevented their advance toward complete self-support. They, like the others, were to be removed to the Indian Territory at the earliest possible moment. Delano lamented the obstinacy of the Sioux, who refused to move, but he thought that time would ultimately overcome their objections.[17]

Delano's schemes ran into snags which he himself was forced to recognize. Many of the Indians, once confined to the reservations designed for them, refused to stay within the set limits. Especially noteworthy were the forays off the reservations of Sioux, Arapahos, Cheyennes, Kiowas, and Comanches in 1873. The tribes at Fort Sill were notorious for raiding parties into Texas, which then returned to the safety of the reservation to "secure their spoils, and be fed and recuperated for fresh outrages." Delano's only solution was a display of military force sufficient to keep the Indians at home. "It will be found to be a measure of mercy to all," he said, "if such Indians can be punished as they deserve."[18]

Delano's plans did not die when he was forced out of office in 1875. His successor, Zachariah Chandler, continued to urge them, although he was willing to use a reservation in Minnesota and another in the southern part of Washington Territory in addition to the Indian Territory as the new permanent homes for the scattered Indians. He also seemed less enthusiastic about what all this would do for the Indians and more concerned about saving money and trouble for the government. In his report of 1876 he neatly summed up the arguments:

> Briefly, the arguments are all in favor of the consolidation; expensive agencies would be abolished, the Indians themselves can be more easily watched over and controlled, evil-designing men be the better kept away from them, and illicit trade and barter in arms, ammunition, and whiskey prevented; goods could be supplied at a great saving; the military service relieved; the Indians better taught, and friendly rivalry established among them, those most civilized

[17] Report of the Secretary of the Interior, 1874, in serial 1639, p. xii.
[18] Report of the Commissioner of Indian Affairs, 1873, in serial 1601, pp. 373–76; Report of the Secretary of the Interior, 1873, in serial 1601, p. vi.

hastening the progress of those below them, and most of the land now occupied as reserves, reverting to the General Government, would be open to entry and sale.[19]

It might be suspected that men like Delano, whose record was none too clean, were more interested in the freeing of the Indians' lands for white exploitation than in Indian welfare, but they no doubt honestly believed that the Indians had to be moved from their present situation if they were to survive and advance. It was the almost universal opinion of the age and a doctrine that went back clearly as far as Thomas Jefferson. Views like Delano's on Indian consolidation were accepted as part of the humanitarians' package of Indian reform. "Since the inauguration of the present Indian policy," the Board of Indian Commissioners declared in 1876, "this board has not ceased to recommend the consolidation of agencies where it can be effected without infringing existing treaties. The time has now arrived when the Government must, if it would see an impulse given to the work of Indian civilization, take decided ground and prompt action upon this important subject." It was convinced that "the public sentiment in and out of Congress will see the great advantage of this important advance movement in Indian civilization." Tribes occupying small reservations and making little progress, if moved to large reservations, would profit by the example and encouragement of their more advanced brethren and would learn by daily observation "that thrift, enterprise, and energy do always produce their legitimate fruits of civilization and self-dependence." Moreover, a system of law could be more easily introduced, early allotment of land could be provided, and tribal relations could be broken up. Such action, the board concluded, would "go far toward the successful solution of the Indian problem, which has so long perplexed our nation, puzzled our statesmen, and disturbed our philanthropists."[20]

[19] Report of the Secretary of the Interior, 1876, in serial 1749, p. vi. Secretary Chandler was merely repeating the arguments and proposals put forth by Commissioner of Indian Affairs John Q. Smith, in his report of October 30, 1876, in serial 1749, pp. 385–87. Two years later, Commissioner E. A. Hayt drew up a bill to further consolidate the tribes. Report of the Commissioner of Indian Affairs, 1878, in serial 1850, p. 440.

[20] *Report of the Board of Indian Commissioners*, 1876, pp. 4–6. The board repeated its recommendations in subsequent years. In 1878, a resolution submitted to the Senate asserted that there were 300,000 Indians on 300,000,000 acres of public land in the United States, or about 1000 acres for each Indian, while whites were restricted to a 160-acre homestead for a family. The creation of four Indian reservations or territories

These theorists reckoned too little with the Indians whom they were so willing to move around like pieces on a chessboard. The Indians were deeply attached to their homelands, and the topographical and climatic conditions were psychologically if not physically of tremendous importance to their well-being. Sioux, long acclimated to the barren northern plains, foresaw only misery and disaster if they had to move to the actually better lands to the south in the Indian Territory. In the 1870's, while the government officials and the humanitarians were concocting fine schemes to remove the Indians to a few large reservations in order to save money and at the same time speed forward the civilization of the tribes, three disastrous removals propelled the issue into the public consciousness.

The most famous removal was that of the Ponca Indians from their reservation along the Missouri River to the Indian Territory. It was, in fact, the spark that ignited a new flame of concern for the rights of the Indians. The cause was just, the propaganda arising from it was spectacular, and the interest of eastern philanthropists in the Indians burned with new intensity.[21]

The Poncas, a small peaceful Siouan tribe, in 1865 had been guaranteed a reservation of 96,000 acres along the Missouri north of the Niobrara River. Three years later, however, the United States in the treaty with the Sioux at Fort Laramie—without consulting the Poncas—ceded the entire Ponca reservation to the Sioux, who had been traditional enemies of the tribe.[22] Although the transfer to the Sioux was admitted by the United States to have been a mistake, the government's resolution of the problem was not a restoration of the lands,

was proposed, two west of the Rockies and two east, with the provision that Indians who cut loose from the tribe could take out homesteads where they were. *Senate Miscellaneous Document* No. 16, 45 Congress, 2 session, serial 1785.

[21] The story of Ponca removal is traced in Earl W. Hayter, "The Ponca Removal," *North Dakota Historical Quarterly*, VI (July, 1932), 262–75; and Stanley Clark, "Ponca Publicity," *Mississippi Valley Historical Review*, XXIX (March, 1943), 495–516. An account by one of the men who fought for the Poncas' rights, with reprints of important documents, is Zylyff [Thomas Henry Tibbles], *The Ponca Chiefs: An Attempt to Appeal from the Tomahawk to the Courts* (Boston, 1880; reprinted with an introduction by Kay Graber, Lincoln, 1972). An excellent account of the Ponca affair and the reaction of the reformers is in Mardock, *The Reformers and the American Indian*, pp. 168–91.

[22] Kappler, *Indian Affairs: Laws and Treaties*, II, 875–76, 998.

which might have irritated the Sioux, but removal of the Poncas to the Indian Territory. Over their objections, the Indians in 1877 were escorted south by federal troops and settled on the Quapaw reserve.

The hardships of the journey and the change in climate brought great misery and many deaths to the Poncas, and even when they found a new and more favorable location within the Indian Territory, they remained restless and unhappy and longed to return to their old home in the north. "I am sorry to be compelled to say," Commissioner of Indian Affairs Hayt lamented, "the Poncas were wronged, and restitution should be made as far as it is in the power of the government to do so." Secretary of the Interior Schurz echoed these sentiments, but Congress paid no heed to the reports, and the Indians' condition remained precarious.[23]

One of the chiefs, Standing Bear, could endure the situation no longer. With the body of his dead son, who had succumbed to malaria, and followed by a small portion of the tribe, he started out in January, 1879, to return to the north. Reaching Nebraska early in the spring, the group settled down for the time being with the Omaha Indians, their long-time friends. The plight of Standing Bear and his followers had by this time become a public issue, and a group of citizens of Omaha took up their case. When federal troops arrived to arrest the runaways and return them to the Indian Territory, prominent lawyers of the city drew up a writ of habeas corpus to prevent the chief's return, and on April 30 the matter was brought before Judge Elmer S. Dundy of the United States District Court. In the celebrated case of *Standing Bear vs. Crook*, Judge Dundy ruled: "That an Indian is a 'person' within the meaning of the laws of the United States, and has, therefore the right to sue out a writ of habeas corpus in a federal court." Since he could find no authority for forcing the Poncas back to the Indian Territory, Dundy ordered their release.[24]

The Ponca removal had important repercussions on Indian reform, for a man much involved in the origins of the Standing Bear case in Omaha soon mounted a campaign in the East to stir up public support for the Poncas. This man was Thomas Henry Tibbles, one of the

[23] Report of the Secretary of the Interior, 1877, in serial 1800, pp. vii–viii; Report of the Commissioner of Indian Affairs, 1877, in serial 1800, pp. 417–19. The quotation from Hayt is in Report of the Commission of Indian Affairs, 1878, in serial 1850, p. 467.
[24] 25 *Federal Cases*, 695–701. The quotation is at 700–701.

strangest characters in the history of Indian reform.[25] He had been a member of John Brown's band in Kansas, a guide and scout on the plains, an itinerant preacher, a Pullman car conductor, and a newspaper reporter. When the Ponca affair occurred, he was an assistant editor of the Omaha *Herald*. According to his own testimony, he was the prime mover in the Standing Bear case, and after the chief's release he resorted to the lecture platform to keep the Ponca issue alive. Accompanied by Standing Bear and Suzette LaFlesche, an Omaha Indian girl who was known as Bright Eyes, he appeared in Chicago and in several eastern cities to relate the wrongs of the Poncas, condemn the government for its actions, and appeal for support of the Indians' cause.

His greatest success was in Boston, where a group of prominent men (including John D. Long, Governor of Massachusetts, and Frederick O. Prince, Mayor of Boston) organized the Boston Indian Citizenship Committee to fight for the rights of the Poncas and other Indians. The principal thrust of the group's program was to demand respect for the Indians' rights, including the return to their original reservation, and bitter denunciation of the federal government for its part in the Ponca removal. Tibbles fitted well into the program and spoke to enthusiastic audiences in Boston. Bright Eyes and Standing Bear, appearing on stage in Indian dress, added a strong personal touch to the proceedings.

The bête noire of Tibbles and the Boston reformers was Secretary of the Interior Schurz, who had assumed his duties just as the actual movement of the Poncas to the Indian Territory got under way. In public speeches and in published letters, the Boston Committee and its supporters on one side and Secretary Schurz on the other engaged in an acrimonious debate, in which neither side adhered strictly to the facts of the case. The atrocity stories of Tibbles and Bright Eyes were countered by Schurz's descriptions of the favorable condition of the

[25] W. J. Ghent, "Thomas Henry Tibbles," *Dictionary of American Biography*, XVIII, 522–23; Publisher's Preface in Thomas Henry Tibbles, *Buckskin and Blanket Days: Memoirs of a Friend of the Indians* (Garden City, New York, 1957), pp. 7–10. Autobiographical material appears in *Buckskin and Blanket Days*, and in Zylyff, *The Ponca Chiefs*. Tibbles also wrote a crudely constructed fictionalized account of the Indian ring: *Hidden Power: A Secret History of the Indian Ring, Its Operations, Intrigues and Machinations, Revealing the Manner in Which It Controls Three Important Departments of the United States Government, A Defense of the U.S. Army, and a Solution to the Indian Problem* (New York, 1881).

Poncas in the Indian Territory. At a public meeting in Boston on December 3, 1880, presided over by Governor Long, Tibbles delivered an enthusiastically received diatribe against Schurz and his handling of the Ponca case, and other speeches were made by Long, Prince, Bright Eyes, and Wendell Phillips. Schurz replied to the talks in an open letter to Governor Long, dated December 9, 1880, in which he urged that justice be accorded the government officials as well as the Indians and stated his position that to move the Poncas back to Dakota, as the Boston group demanded, would cause new misery to the Indians and open the door to white invasions of the Indian Territory. This brought a long and denunciatory reply from the Boston group, which renewed the charges against the Secretary.[26]

Schurz was engaged also in a public exchange of opinions with Helen Hunt Jackson, who had heard Tibbles and Bright Eyes in Boston in November, 1879, and had become a zealous convert to the cause of Indian reform. Schurz quashed an attempt to carry the Standing Bear case to the Supreme Court, and he urged Mrs. Jackson and her friends, who were collecting funds for more legal action on Indian rights, to use the money for Indian education rather than pour it into the pockets of attorneys in futile cases.[27]

Still another of Schurz's opponents was Senator Henry L. Dawes of Massachusetts, with whom he tangled over the accidental killing of Standing Bear's brother, Big Snake, at the Ponca agency on October 31, 1879.[28] Big Snake had been considered a troublemaker by the Ponca agent, who fearing for his own safety, had ordered in troops to arrest the chief. Big Snake insisted that he had done nothing to warrant arrest and refused to depart with the soldiers, forcibly resisting their attempts

[26] T. H. Tibbles, *Western Men Defended: Speech of Mr. T. H. Tibbles in Tremont Temple, Boston, Mass., December, 1880* (Boston, 1880); Schurz to Long, December 9, 1880, in Frederic Bancroft, ed., *Speeches, Correspondence and Political Papers of Carl Schurz* (6 vols., New York, 1913), IV, 50–78; Schurz to Edward Atkinson, November 28, 1879, *ibid.*, III, 481–89; *Secretary Schurz: Reply of the Boston Committee, Governor John D. Long, Chairman: Misrepresentations Corrected and Important Facts Presented* (Boston, 1881).

[27] The exchange of letters is printed in Jackson, *A Century of Dishonor*, pp. 359–66. Another expression of Schurz's views appears in his brief statement, "The Removal of the Poncas," *The Independent*, XXXII (January 1, 1880), 1.

[28] Reports on the killing of Big Snake are printed in *Senate Executive Document* No. 14, 46 Congress, 3 session, serial 1941. See also the testimony in *Senate Report* No. 670, 46 Congress, 2 session, serial 1898, pp. 245–51. A useful article is J. Stanley Clark, "The Killing of Big Snake," *Chronicles of Oklahoma*, XLIX (Autumn, 1971), 302–14.

to handcuff him. In the melee that followed, one of the soldiers shot him dead. Dawes, on January 31, 1881, in a Senate inquiry into the killing of Big Snake, insinuated that the government had plotted the shooting of the Ponca chief and then made an allusion to Schurz's German background:

> It has been a relief to me, however, in examining our treatment of these weak and defenseless people, to find that these methods are not American in their origin, but bear too striking a resemblance to the modes of an imperial government carried on by espionage and arbitrary power. They are methods which I believe to be unique, and which I trust will never be naturalized.[29]

In reply Schurz addressed an open letter to Dawes and gave every senator a copy on his desk as his only means of replying to Dawes's privileged congressional remarks. It was a devastating refutation of the senator's charges. The agitation in the Big Snake affair was, said Schurz, a new illustration of the fact that it was "difficult to exaggerate the malignant unscrupulousness of the speculator in philanthropy hunting for a sensation."[30]

The verbal combat between the reformers and the Secretary of the Interior did not prevent the working out of a solution to the Ponca problem, although nearly every move of the administration was subject to critical attack. A special Senate committee, of which both Senator Dawes and Senator Samuel J. Kirkwood were members, investigated the Ponca removal in 1880, taking massive testimony on the wrongs done and the miseries endured. The committee reported that it could "find no language sufficiently strong in which to condemn the whole proceedings and trace to it all the troubles which have come upon the Poncas, and the hardships and sufferings which have followed

[29] *Congressional Record*, XI, 1958.

[30] Carl Schurz, *An Open Letter in Answer to a Speech of Hon. H. L. Dawes, United States Senate, on the Case of Big Snake* (Washington, 1881). The letter, dated February 7, 1881, is printed also in Bancroft, *Speeches of Schurz*, IV, 91–113. The quotation is from p. 102. An account of the controversy, based in large part on the Dawes Papers in the Library of Congress, is in Priest, *Uncle Sam's Stepchildren*, pp. 78–79. Schurz's biographer, Claude Moore Fuess, in *Carl Schurz, Reformer* (New York, 1932), pp. 252–77, believes that Schurz was completely vindicated in his conflicts with the humanitarian reformers. It is interesting to note that Dr. T. A. Bland was a vigorous critic of Tibbles; see *The Council Fire*, II (August, 1879), 120; III (August, 1880), 122–23.

them since they were taken by the United States from their old reservation and placed in their present location in the Indian Territory." The majority report advocated returning the tribe to its old home on the Missouri. With this Kirkwood disagreed, and in a minority report he supported Schurz in his proposal to indemnify the Poncas but keep them where they were.[31] Finally on December 18, 1880, President Hayes appointed a special commission to confer with the Poncas, both those in the Indian Territory and those in Nebraska, and to recommend action. The commission, headed by General George Crook and made up of General Nelson A. Miles, William Stickney of the Board of Indian Commissioners, and William Allen of Boston, recommended that the Poncas in the Indian Territory remain there and that provision be made as well for those who wanted to stay in the north with Standing Bear. The decision of the commission was in accord with a declaration of wishes presented to the President by a delegation of Poncas from the Indian Territory on December 27, 1880, in which they evinced their desire to remain on the lands they then occupied and to relinquish all interest in their former reservation on the Missouri.[32]

Hayes recommended that immediate action be taken in line with the recommendations of the Crook commission and the Ponca request.[33] At last action was forthcoming; on March 3 Congress appropriated $165,000 to enable the Secretary of the Interior "to indemnify the Ponca tribe of Indians for losses sustained by them in consequence of their removal to the Indian Territory, to secure to them lands in severalty on either the old or new reservation, in accordance with their wishes, and to settle all matters of difference with these Indians." All that remained was to gain the approval of the Sioux for the Poncas of Standing Bear's party to remain in the north, and this was accomplished by a special agreement drawn up with a Sioux delegation in Washington in August, 1881.[34]

[31] *Senate Report* No. 670, 46 Congress, 2 session, serial 1898. The quotation is on pp. viii–ix.

[32] The commission's report and a copy of its proceedings are in *Senate Executive Document* No. 30, 46 Congress, 3 session, serial 1941. Included is a minority report submitted by Allen, who was unwilling to believe that the Indians had genuinely decided to stay in the Indian Territory.

[33] Letter of February 1, 1881, in *Senate Executive Document* No. 30, 46 Congress, 3 session, serial 1941, pp. 1–4.

[34] *United States Statutes at Large*, XXI, 422. Specifications were made for how the

Although it kept the country much alive to Indian problems, the controversy over the Poncas between Schurz and the reformers was unfortunate, for it obscured the fundamental agreement of both sides in their desire to promote justice to the Indians. In large part, no doubt, the attacks on Schurz by the evangelical reformers reflected the fundamental differences of the two parties. Schurz was a severely practical, unsentimental man. His program was one of "policy" not of religious motivation. A man more different in background and outlook from the general run of Indian reformers can hardly be imagined, yet Schurz's Indian policy—attack upon corruption and inefficiency in the Indian Office, support of civilian as opposed to military control of Indian affairs, allotment of land in severalty and selling "surplus" lands, and an aggressive educational program for Indians—were all in line with what the friends of the Indian came to espouse so ardently later in the decade of the 1880's.

Senator Dawes, for his part, learned the danger of opposing the administration. After Schurz left office, Dawes wrote concerning the new Secretary of the Interior, Kirkwood, who had defended Schurz's position on the Poncas: "Of course we widely differ from him but an open conflict with this new administration, as with the last, on the Indian policy, must be avoided if possible, or we shall be very much disabled. . . . Let us, Boston and all, try to pull with Washington, but to be sure and pull the hardest!"[35] The reform groups learned, too, to base their arguments on sound information and not to be carried away, as they had been in the first flush of their reform enthusiasm, by such exaggerated tales as those told by Tibbles and Bright Eyes.[36]

sum was to be broken down to accomplish these purposes. The agreement with the Sioux is printed in *House Executive Document* No. 1, 47 Congress, 1 session, serial 2018, pp. 39–40.

[35] Dawes to Allen, August 11, 1881, Dawes Papers, quoted in Priest, *Uncle Sam's Stepchildren*, p. 79.

[36] Tibbles, whose first wife died in 1879, married Bright Eyes in 1881. Alonzo Bell, who served as Assistant Secretary of the Interior under both Schurz and Kirkwood, wrote to the former on August 5, 1881:

I was greatly rejoiced on my return from a sea-trip to find that the Ponca war was at last ended, that Bright Eyes had capitulated to Tibbles, and that Tibbles had surrendered to Bright Eyes. I very much fear, however, that this last act of the pale-face is in the line of other wrongs perpetrated upon this most unfortunate band of Indians, and that the confiding Indian maiden will some day feel that the fate of Big Snake was preferable to the unhappy one which she has chosen.

Will Dawes hold the Department responsible for this? Will Governor Long add it

The flight of a band of Northern Cheyennes from the Indian Territory in 1878 was another celebrated case that indicated the weaknesses of the consolidation policy.[37] In the summer of 1877, following an agreement made the previous September, a party of these Indians (937 in number) was escorted to the reservation of the Cheyennes and Arapahos near Fort Reno. The Indians suffered greatly in their new home, and the subsistence supplied them by the government was inadequate. On September 9, 1878, about three hundred of them led by chiefs Dull Knife and Little Wolf fled from the reservation and headed north to join their friends the Sioux. When troops of the United States army were sent to stop the Indians and return them to the Indian Territory, the flight became a running fight, and the Cheyennes killed some forty settlers in their passage through Kansas.

When the Indians reached the Platte, they separated into two groups. One of them under Dull Knife moved westward toward Fort Robinson; the party was captured on October 23 and imprisoned at the fort. The post commandant received orders on January 5, 1879, to transport the Indians back to the Indian Territory, but the Indians steadfastly refused to go, and the officer attempted to freeze and starve them into submission by cutting off fuel, food, and finally even water. Able to endure the torture no longer and frightened by the seizure of one of their leaders, Wild Hog, the Indians broke out of their quarters on the night of January 9. Weakened by the ordeal of their imprisonment, they were easy prey for the soldiers who pursued them, and fifty or sixty men, women, and children were killed in flight. Some were captured and returned to the south, while Dull Knife and others escaped to the Sioux. The other group, led by Little Wolf, had continued north, hoping to reach Montana. They were induced to surrender on

---

to his long list of indictments? Let us hope that both may take a rose-colored view of the union between the dusky daughter of the forest and the gay professional philanthropist who buried all the wrongs of her race in a greater one upon herself. I fear poor Bright Eyes has made a mistake, but I am willing to forgive her if the act has effectually disposed of Tibbles. Even so great a sacrifice may be rare economy if it gives the Nation a rest from the vexatious borings of the Tibbles school of philanthropy. Bancroft, *Speeches of Schurz*, IV, 147–48.

[37] A full account of the event is given in George Bird Grinnell, *The Fighting Cheyennes* (New York, 1915), chapters 19–20. Mari Sandoz, *Cheyenne Autumn* (New York, 1953), tells the story of the Indians in dramatic style. See also Verne Dusenberry, "The Northern Cheyenne," *Montana Magazine of History*, V (Winter, 1955), 23–40.

March 25, 1879, and were taken to Fort Keogh, where they were allowed to remain.

Commissioner Hayt looked upon the flight from the reservation as an "outbreak" and blamed the affair upon the unwarranted dissatisfaction of the Indians, asserting that Dull Knife's band contained "the vilest and most dangerous element of their tribe." With elaborate statistics he attempted to prove that the Indians had not been maltreated or underfed in the Indian Territory.[38] But other evidence was soon available. A select committee of the Senate appointed to investigate the case of the Northern Cheyennes returned a critical report in June, 1880, based on abundant testimony taken at Fort Reno and on interviews with Indians imprisoned in Kansas. Its findings sharply contradicted the report of Hayt and described the government's lack of compliance with treaty agreements and the disastrous conditions that resulted from the shortage of supplies. "It is impossible to say," the committee reported, "that these were or were not the causes that led three hundred Indians in a body to escape from the Territory and to return to Dakota. They were doubtless provoking causes to that hegira, but the Indians were also strongly impelled by a longing desire to return to their native country, and by a feeling of disgust towards their new location."[39] The committee noted, too, that the band had not left the reservation as a marauding party but simply with the intention of escaping to their former homes, and that they began to fight only when attacked by the army. The handling of Dull Knife's band at Fort Robinson received severe condemnation:

The process of starving and freezing women and children, *in order to compel men into obedience*, is not justifiable in the eyes of civilized men. The outbreak was a most daring and desperate choice of

[38] Report of the Commissioner of Indian Affairs, 1878, in serial 1850, pp. 455–57. Hayt's views were supported by Schurz, *ibid.*, pp. vii–ix. Further details are provided in the Report of the Commissioner of Indian Affairs, 1879, in serial 1910, pp. 80–82. A useful narrative of events is in a letter of T. J. Morgan, April 23, 1890, *Senate Executive Document* No. 121, 51 Congress, 1 session, serial 2686, pp. 2–9.

[39] *Senate Report* No. 708, 46 Congress, 2 session, serial 1899, p. xvi. The committee was composed of Senators S. J. Kirkwood, J. T. Morgan, H. L. Dawes, J. E. Bailey, and P. B. Plumb. The report, submitted June 8, 1880, included 327 pages of testimony. The failure of the attempt to force the Cheyennes into white agricultural patterns is studied in Ramon Powers, "Why the Northern Cheyenne Left Indian Territory in 1878: A Cultural Analysis," *Kansas Quarterly*, III (Fall, 1971), 72–81.

alternatives, which the Indians expressed in the following language: "We have got to die, but we will not die here like dogs; we will die on the prairie; we will die fighting."[40]

The committee's conclusion was decisive: There was no hope of civilizing the Indians and making them self-supporting in a location where they were discontented. Unless they were living in a place they could look upon as home, there was little probability that they would ever gain the independence of feeling that would lead them to work for their own living. "If they are compelled to accept a prison as a home," the report said, "they will naturally prefer to compel the keepers to feed and clothe them. They will remain pensioners upon our humanity, having lost all pride of character and all care of anything except to live." Moreover, the concentration of Indians in large numbers in one place was out of line with the changing relations between the government and the Indians. "They are already surrounded and separated into limited districts by the intervening white settlements," the senators noted, "and the time is near at hand when they must become members of the same communities with the white people."[41]

Ironically, at the very time that Dull Knife and Little Wolf were fleeing northward, another band of Northern Cheyennes, led by Little Chief, was moving south into the Indian Territory from western Nebraska. This group, too, was severely dissatisfied with its new surroundings and in the summer of 1879 sent a delegation to Washington to beg permission to join their tribesmen at Fort Keogh. Although Commissioner Hayt reported that the delegation was induced to return cheerfully to the Indian Territory, the case was by no means closed. In 1881, after continued petition, Little Chief's band was transferred to the Sioux reservation at Pine Ridge, and in 1883, under congressional authorization, the Northern Cheyennes still in the Indian Territory were allowed to follow.[42]

The Sioux reservation in Dakota, however, did not completely satisfy the Cheyennes, and little by little they drifted west into Montana to

[40] *Senate Report* No. 708, 46 Congress, 2 session, serial 1899, p. xviii.
[41] *Ibid.*, p. xxi.
[42] The story of Little Chief and of the transfer of the Cheyennes to Dakota can be traced in Report of the Commissioner of Indian Affairs, 1880, in serial 1959, p. 109; *ibid.*, 1881, in serial 2018, pp. 41–42; *ibid.*, 1882, in serial 2100, p. 50; *ibid.*, 1883, in serial 2191, p. 39.

join their brethren, for whom a reservation on the Tongue River had been established by executive order on November 26, 1884.[43] No attempts were made to restrain this voluntary migration of the Indians. Captain J. M. Bell, acting agent at Pine Ridge, urged in 1886 that the departing Cheyennes be brought back by force or imprisoned when they arrived at Fort Keogh. "Until measures of this kind are adopted," he reasoned, "they will continue roaming from place to place, and will accomplish nothing in the way of civilization." But Commissioner of Indian Affairs Hiram Price demurred, and Secretary of the Interior L. Q. C. Lamar declared: "These straying Indians, a restless element at their old agencies, appear to be satisfied in their new location, and it is not deemed advisable to force them to return to the Sioux Reservation."[44] It was a clear admission of the failure of the concentration policy.

Chief Joseph's band of Nez Percés furnished still another example of the impossibility of forcing northern Indians into the Indian Territory against their will.[45] When the Nez Percé reservation was reduced in 1863, cutting off the Wallowa Valley in Oregon and other areas once the home of the tribe, some of the Indians, chiefly those who had resisted the attempts to convert them to Christianity, refused to accept the treaty. Chief Joseph was among these "non-treaty" Indians, and he and his band continued to live in their beloved Wallowa Valley. The increasing white encroachments laid the groundwork for troubles, and the United States was eager to persuade these tribesmen to join their relatives on the Lapwai reservation in Idaho. It seemed to be a hopeless endeavor. Two special commissions sent to investigate the matter

[43] The order is printed in *House Document* No. 153, 55 Congress, 3 session, serial 3807, p. 145.

[44] Letters of J. M. Bell, J. D. C. Atkins, and L. Q. C. Lamar, in *Senate Executive Document* No. 212, 49 Congress, 1 session, serial 2341. The movement of the Cheyennes on their own accord from Pine Ridge to Tongue River upset the supply of subsistence, and the Indian Office repeatedly asked Congress for aid in relieving the misery of these Indians. See *Senate Executive Document* No. 208, 48 Congress, 1 session, serial 2168; *House Executive Document* No. 17, 49 Congress, 1 session, serial 2387; *Senate Executive Document* No. 212, 49 Congress, 1 session, serial 2341; and *Senate Executive Document* No. 121, 51 Congress, 1 session, serial 2686.

[45] The Nez Percés and the war of 1877 have received much attention from historians. Histories of the tribe which include accounts of the conflict and its aftermath are Francis Haines, *The Nez Percés: Tribesmen of the Columbia Plateau* (Norman, 1955);

in 1873 reached contrary conclusions about the appropriateness of forcing the band to move, and in 1876 a new group composed of David H. Jerome, General O. O. Howard, Major H. C. Wood, and two members of the Board of Indian Commissioners, William Stickney and A. C. Barstow, made a new attempt to reach a solution. The commission placed most of the blame upon the religious prophets, the "dreamers," who taught that the Indians had the right to any and all land, and it recommended that all the dreamers be sent back to their proper agencies or, if they refused to go, transported by force to the Indian Territory. It urged, however, that, as long as it remained peaceful, Joseph's band be allowed to remain in the Wallowa Valley, with troops sent in to ensure order. If the band did not quietly settle down there, it should be forced to move to the Lapwai reservation. On General Howard was placed the primary responsibility for the peace, and in a series of meetings with Chief Joseph he finally won the Indian's consent to go to the reservation.[46]

Before the movement could be accomplished, hostilities broke out. In June, 1877, young men of the band, avenging the murder of an Indian by whites, killed a party of settlers. General Howard's troops were ordered in and the war began. The Indians' choice was flight. By skillful maneuvers, Joseph and the military leaders of the band moved east through the Lolo Pass into the Bitterroot Valley of Montana, down into Yellowstone Park, and then headed north seeking to reach asylum in Canada. Pursued by Howard's soldiers and with occasional military encounters, the fleeing Indians executed one of the great military movements in history. They had almost reached their objective when they were cut off by troops from Fort Keogh under General Nelson A. Miles. With many warriors dead and the rest exhausted and the women

Alvin M. Josephy, Jr., *The Nez Perce Indians and the Opening of the Northwest* (New Haven, 1965). Histories specifically of the war are Merrill D. Beal, *"I Will Fight No More Forever": Chief Joseph and the Nez Perce War* (Seattle, 1963); Mark H. Brown, *The Flight of the Nez Perce* (New York, 1967). General Howard's popular account appears in O. O. Howard, *Nez Perce Joseph: An Account of His Ancestors, His Lands, His Confederates, His Enemies, His Murders, His War, His Pursuit and Capture* (Boston, 1881), while an Indian's retelling of the events is *Yellow Wolf: His Own Story*, edited by Lucullus Virgil McWhorter (Caldwell, Idaho, 1940). See also Mark H. Brown, "The Joseph Myth," *Montana, the Magazine of Western History*, XXII (Winter, 1972), 2–17.

[46] Report of the Commissioner of Indian Affairs, 1877, in serial 1800, pp. 405–409; "Report of Civil and Military Commission to Nez Percé Indians, Washington Territory and the Northwest," December 1, 1876, *ibid.*, pp. 607–13.

and children cold and starving, Chief Joseph surrendered at Bear Paw Mountains on October 5.

General Miles promised that the defeated Indians, who had won his respect and sympathy, might return to Idaho in the spring to settle down peacefully on the reservation. But General Sherman overruled the humane decision of Miles. Declaring that the Indians were prisoners of war and that they "should never again be allowed to return to Oregon or to Lapwai," Sherman directed that the Nez Percés be imprisoned at Fort Leavenworth until they could be turned over to the Indian Office for disposition.[47] Transported down the Yellowstone and the Missouri to Fort Leavenworth, the miserable Indians were encamped in unhealthy lowlands along the Missouri, where, ill provided for and pining for the clear mountain streams of their homeland, they succumbed to sickness and many died.

Commissioner Hayt had noted in his report for 1877 that "humanity prompts us to send them back and place them on the Nez Percé reservation." But he saw an "insuperable difficulty in the way." The murder of the whites by members of Chief Joseph's band at the beginning of the outbreak meant that the Indians would find neither peace nor safety in their old haunts. Indictments had in fact been issued in Idaho for certain of the Nez Percés, and the memory of the murders would continue to be an obstacle to the return of the band. "But for these foul crimes," Hayt asserted, "these Indians would be sent back to the reservation in Idaho. Now, however, they will have to be sent to the Indian Territory; and this will be no hardship to them, as the difference in the temperature between that latitude and their old home is inconsiderable."[48] The Nez Percés at Fort Leavenworth were turned over by the army to agents of the Indian Office, and on July 21, 1878, they headed south to be settled on a section of the Quapaw reservation. It was hoped that here under the guidance of the Quaker agent, H. W. Jones, the desolate Indians would soon come to be self-supporting, just as the Modocs had done in the same location.[49]

[47] Report of Sherman, November 7, 1877, *House Executive Document* No. 1, 45 Congress, 2 session, serial 1794, p. 15.

[48] Report of the Commissioner of Indian Affairs, 1877, in serial 1800, p. 409.

[49] Two thoroughly documented studies of the Nez Perces in the Indian Territory are J. Stanley Clark, "The Nez Percés in Exile," *Pacific Northwest Quarterly,* XXXVI (July, 1945), 213–32; Berlin B. Chapman, "Nez Percés in Indian Territory: An Archival Study," *Oregon Historical Quarterly,* L (June, 1949), 98–121.

The Indians did not recover, and more of the band sickened and died. Two members of the Board of Indian Commissioners who visited them in August, 1878, found Joseph absolutely averse to remaining in the Indian Territory. "Seldom have we been in councils where the Indians more eloquently or earnestly advocated their side of the question," they reported. "Joseph's arraignment of the Army for alleged bad faith to him after the surrender of himself and people to General Miles was almost unanswerable."[50] The commissioners ordered medical supplies for the Indians and made arrangements for a better tract of land on the Quapaw reserve for the Nez Percés, but these actions hardly struck at the heart of the matter.

When Hayt visited Joseph in the following October, he was informed in unmistakable terms of the chief's dissatisfaction. The Indian insisted that he had been promised by Miles and Howard that he would be allowed to return to Idaho and that he had surrendered under that condition, and he complained about the quality of the region selected for his people in the Indian Territory. Hayt, like all who came in contact with the Nez Percé leader, was impressed with his intelligence, character, and integrity, and he tried to convince the chief that his people were prevented from returning to Idaho for their own protection and welfare. He attempted a limited accommodation, moreover, by taking Joseph on an exploring trip to the west to seek out a better spot in the Indian Territory for his band. A place on Salt Creek in the Cherokee Outlet near the Poncas seemed to please the chief, and Hayt believed that he would agree to settle there.[51] Hayt had been accompanied by E. M. Kingsley, a member of the Board of Indian Commissioners, who was favorably impressed with Joseph's argument about Miles's promise and about the bad conditions in the Indian Territory. "This statement is believed to be true in the main," Kingsley noted, "and, if so, Joseph stands before the American people a victim of duplicity; his confidence wantonly betrayed; his substance pillaged; and involuntary exile from home and kindred; his 'cause' lost; his people rapidly wasting by pestilence; an object not of haughty con-

[50] "Report of Visit of Commissioners Fisk and Stickney to Colorado and Indian Territory," August 22, 1878, *Report of the Board of Indian Commissioners*, 1878, pp. 47–48.
[51] Report of the Commissioner of Indian Affairs, 1878, in serial 1850, pp. 464–65.

tempt or vulgar ridicule, but of generous, humane treatment and consideration."[52]

Chief Joseph refused to give up his demand to be allowed to return to the Northwest, and he became a symbolic hero of those who lamented the wrongs done to the Indians and crusaded for their rights. In January, 1879, Joseph went to Washington to plead his case, and he impressed the assembled congressmen and government officials who heard him speak. His message, recorded later in an interview, was printed in the *North American Review* for April, 1879, and the words of the chief touched every reformer's heart.

I have shaken hands with a great many friends, but there are some things I want to know which no one seems able to explain. I can not understand how the Government sends a man out to fight us, as it did General Miles, and then breaks his word. Such a Government has something wrong about it. I can not understand why so many chiefs are allowed to talk so many different ways, and promise so many different things. . . .

When I think of our condition my heart is heavy. I see men of my race treated as outlaws and driven from country to country, or shot down like animals.

I know that my race must change. We can not hold our own with the white men as we are. We only ask an even chance to live as other men live. We ask to be recognized as men. We ask that the same law shall work alike on all men. If the Indian breaks the law, punish him by the law. If the white man breaks the law, punish him also.

Let me be a free man—free to travel, free to stop, free to work, free to trade where I choose, free to choose my own teachers, free to follow the religion of my fathers, free to think and talk and act for myself—and I will obey every law, or submit to the penalty.[53]

The wheels of justice moved very slowly and none too surely. Still reluctant to send the Indians back among hostile frontiersmen, the

[52] "Report of Commissioner Kingsley," December, 1878, *Report of the Board of Indian Commissioners*, 1878, p. 51.

[53] "An Indian's View of Indian Affairs," *North American Review*, CXXVIII (April, 1879), 431–33. An introduction to the piece was written by the missionary bishop, William H. Hare. See the rejoinder in Oliver Otis Howard, "The True Story of the Wallowa Campaign," *North American Review*, CXXIX (July, 1879), 53–64.

government in June settled the Nez Percés on the new tract picked out in the Cherokee Outlet. Joseph was not reconciled. He told the reformer Alfred B. Meacham in July: "You come to see me as you would a man upon his deathbed. The Great Spirit Chief above has left me and my people to our fate. The white men forget us, and death comes almost every day for some of my people. He will come for all of us. A few months more and we will be in the ground. We are a doomed people."[54] Such dire predictions were not fulfilled and the tribe's condition got better as the Indians engaged in agriculture and stock raising, but the basic dissatisfaction remained.

Finally in 1883, arrangements were made for the return of thirty-three women and children to Idaho. Philanthropists, encouraged no doubt by this break in the government's position, carried on a campaign to return the rest of the Nez Percés to the Northwest, and numerous memorials were sent to Congress for that purpose.[55] Congress now acted. A law of July 4, 1884, authorized the Secretary of the Interior to remove the Nez Percés from the Indian Territory if he judged proper. In May, 1885, 118 of the band settled at the Lapwai reservation in Idaho, where they were warmly received by friends and relatives. The remaining 150, because of continuing threats from Idaho citizens against some of the Indians, were sent on to the Colville reservation in Washington, where adjustment was slow.[56] Chief Joseph's eternal hope that he might eventually return to the Wallowa Valley was never fulfilled.

These cases uncovered evils in forced removals that no one could hide and that policy-makers could not ignore, whatever theoretical advantages there might have been in moving small tribes into large reservations and consolidating the agencies. Men who had held firmly to a removal policy were forced by the course of events to change their ground. Carl Schurz noted in 1880 that when he had taken charge of

[54] *The Council Fire*, II (October, 1879), 145.

[55] The memorials can be traced through the indexes to the House and Senate *Journals*, 48 Congress, 1 session. Some of the memorials came from citizens of Kansas, who may have been moved as much by a desire to free the Cherokee Outlet as by philanthropic motives.

[56] *United States Statutes at Large*, XXIII, 90, 378; Report of the Commissioner of Indian Affairs, 1885, in serial 2379, p. 57.

the Department of the Interior three and a half years earlier, the prevailing opinion seemed to be that it was best for the Indians to be gathered together where they could be kept out of contact with the whites and where their peaceful conduct might be ensured by a few strong military posts. He had accepted that view himself, but as he learned more from experience he realized that it was a "mistaken policy." In his new wisdom, he argued that it was more in accordance with justice as well as wise experience to respect the home attachments of the Indians, introducing them to agricultural and pastoral pursuits in the lands they occupied, provided the lands were capable of sustaining the tribe. Moreover, he began to see that large reservations would become impracticable as the pressure of white settlement increased. "The policy of changing, shifting, and consolidating reservations . . . ," he declared, "was therefore abandoned."[57]

In 1881, Schurz's successor, Samuel J. Kirkwood, tried to return to a policy of consolidation. He counted 102 reservations west of the Mississippi, occupied by about 224,000 Indians. Attached to these reservations were sixty-eight agencies and nearby, for the protection of the whites and the Indians, were thirty-seven military posts. The expenses of this multiplication of agencies and posts disturbed him, and he believed that, if all the Indians could be gathered together into four or five reservations, the savings would be great and the benefit to the Indians proportionate. He urged Congress to appoint a commission to make recommendations about consolidation.[58] But he could not reverse the new trend of thought. The humanitarian reformers resolved in 1884 that "careful observation has conclusively proved that the removal of Indians from reservations which they have long occupied, to other reservations far distant from the former and possessing different soil and climate, is attended by great suffering and loss of life." The reformers were moving rapidly away from support of any kind of reservation system, whether scattered or consolidated, and urged now that the Indians be given the right to take homesteads on the lands they traditionally had occupied.[59] Consolidation of the Indians in the Indian Territory met strong and vociferous objections also from the

[57] Report of the Secretary of the Interior, 1880, in serial 1959, pp. 3–4.
[58] Ibid., 1881, in serial 2017, pp. v–vi.
[59] Lake Mohonk Conference Proceedings, 1884, pp. 15–16.

white population in Missouri, Kansas, Texas, and Arkansas, who objected to the concentration of more Indians in their vicinity. Although in fact they had nothing to fear, the fuss they raised convinced the Secretary of the Interior by 1885 that the scheme was impracticable. "The policy of change and unsettlement," Lamar said, "should give way to that of fixed homes with security of title and possession, and hereafter the civilizing influences and forces already at work among the Indians should be pushed forward upon the lands which they now occupy."[60]

Yet the idea of Indian removals and concentration within the Indian Territory could not be completely scotched. Commissioner of Indian Affairs J. D. C. Atkins in the late 1880's, in the hope of easing white pressure upon vacant lands within the Indian Territory, advocated anew filling up the area by moving in various Indian groups. He met violent opposition from the reformers. "We ought by this time to have learned something from the experience in regard to such removals," one wrote. "Nearly all of our wars have originated in irritations growing out of them; our pauperizing policy of feeding and clothing Indians grew out of them, as this was an inducement offered, and it would be difficult to find a tribe whose removal has not proved to be a long step backward in their progress. The Commissioner should make a study of the past before he urges to its adoption this policy which has been fruitful of evil, and evil alone, hitherto."[61]

But if consolidation of reservations was given up as a realizable ideal, the reduction of the existing reservations continued to be strongly pushed. Secretary Kirkwood, although preferring consolidation, at least wanted to cut the size of those reservations which were "entirely out of proportion to the number of Indians thereon." Henry M. Teller, late Senator from Colorado, who followed Kirkwood as Secretary of the Interior, strongly advocated such reduction. He admitted the necessity of the reservations but did not think their size should be disproportionate to the needs of the Indians. "Very many of these reservations," he noted, "contain large areas of valuable land that cannot

---

[60] Report of the Secretary of the Interior, 1885, in serial 2378, pp. 27–28. Lamar repeats largely the Report of the Commissioner of Indian Affairs, 1885, in serial 2379, pp. 8–12.

[61] Report of the Commissioner of Indian Affairs, 1886, in serial 2467, pp. 88–90; Charles C. Painter, *The Proposed Removal of Indians to Oklahoma* (Philadelphia, 1888), p. 6.

be cultivated by the Indians, even though they were as energetic and laborious as the best class of white agriculturists. All such reservations ought to be reduced in size and the surplus not needed ought to be bought by the government and opened to the operation of the homestead law, and it would then soon be settled by industrious whites, who, as neighbors, would become valuable auxiliaries in the work of civilizing the Indians residing on the remainder of the reservation." The reduced lands should be vested in the tribe in fee simple. His plan he urged for the Crow Reservation in Montana Territory. Of the 4,713,000 acres in the reserve, Teller estimated that at least 3,000,000 acres might be disposed of, still leaving the Indians about 600 acres apiece, sufficient for them to become self-sufficient in agriculture or stock raising. The proceeds from the sale of the surplus lands should be used, he said, to buy herds for the Crows and, if properly used, could make the Indians self-supporting in a few years.[62]

The reformers continued to see great advantages in such a program. The pressure of the whites on Indian lands would be lessened if not entirely removed, the land left in Indian hands could be given a sure title, the proceeds from the sale of the excess lands could replace direct appropriations for Indian subsistence and welfare, and the Indians would be driven closer to an agriculturalist pattern.

[62] Report of the Secretary of the Interior, 1881, in serial 2017, pp. v–vi; *ibid.*, 1882, in serial 2099, p. viii; *ibid.*, 1884, in serial 2286, pp. xiii–xiv. The Crow reservation, however, was not reduced until 1891.

CHAPTER 5

THE NEW CHRISTIAN REFORMERS

. . . Our constituency is a happy combination of elements, combining representatives of the various religious bodies who are active in Christian and educational work among the Indian tribes.

From the Indian Rights Association, with their thorough business aims and methods for the solution of the Indian problem; from the Women's National Association, who respond to the cry of the most needy of our tribes, and whose devotion to the Indian women and Indian homes ought to receive the God-speed and hearty support of all who would uplift the Indian race; from the Indian Committee of Boston, whose magnificent services for the Indian for the last ten years entitle them to the gratitude of all people; from the Board of Indian Commissioners, and from the ranks of the noble and philanthropic men and women all over this land, hither come the best and truest friends of the Indian, men and women who love justice, and whose persevering wisdom stands and knocks at the portals of power until "whatsoever things are just" are to be conferred upon their clients, the American Indian.

—CLINTON B. FISK, at the
Lake Mohonk Conference, 1887

❁❁❁❁❁❁

The last two decades of the nineteenth century witnessed a new and concerted movement of Indian reform. The victory of arms over the southern plains Indians in the Red River War of 1874–1875, the corralling of the Sioux that followed the defeat of Custer at the Little Bighorn in 1876, and the surrender of Chief Joseph and the Nez Percés in 1877 marked a virtual end to the Indian wars that had occupied the

132

army and so disturbed the humanitarians in the first decade following the Civil War. The physical conquest of the western half of the continent that had begun before the Civil War, and continued to advance even during that conflict, by 1880 had clearly demonstrated that the plains and the mountains, as well as the Pacific slope were to be peopled and exploited by the rapidly multiplying Americans. Railroads tied the nation together with ever tightening bands of steel. There seemed to be no place in this destiny for enclaves of still primitive peoples, clinging desperately to their traditional ways and holding reservations of territory (although already greatly reduced) that were barriers to white advance and considered stumbling blocks to the Indians' own progress. Subdued by military force, dependent in large measure upon the federal government for subsistence to replace their old means now destroyed, yet refusing to disappear into the mainstream of American society, the Indians became the object of a new reform movement that engaged the energies and the emotions of many people. The "Indian problem" at last, it was agreed, was within sight of solution.

The era was marked by the advent of new organizations devoted to Indian affairs, which seemed to spring up spontaneously and to attract enough membership and public response to keep them viable.[1] One of these was the Boston Indian Citizenship Committee, which grew out of the furor created by the Ponca affair of the late 1870's and the eastern agitation in its regard by the Omaha newspaperman T. H. Tibbles and the Indian girl Bright Eyes. At a public meeting of the merchants of Boston held in the Exchange on November 25, 1879, a committee of five prominent men was appointed to investigate the wrongs of the Ponca Indians and the general management of Indian affairs. The committee, in a report addressed "To the People of the United States," found in favor of the Poncas and against the government. In considering Indian affairs in general, it noted two evils, "absence of protection

[1] These reform movements have been treated by historians of post-Civil War Indian policy in connection with their general accounts. See Priest, *Uncle Sam's Stepchildren*, especially Chapter 7; Fritz, *Movement for Indian Assimilation*; and Mardock, *Reformers and the American Indian*, especially Chapters 10–12. Some of the material in this chapter has appeared in Francis Paul Prucha, "Indian Policy Reform and American Protestantism, 1880–1900," in Ray Allen Billington, ed., *People of the Plains and Mountains: Essays in the History of the West Dedicated to Everett Dick* (Westport, Connecticut, 1973), pp. 120–45.

133

of law, and insecurity of titles to lands," and it took as its platform the fulfillment of treaties, recognition of the Indian as a person and as a fellow-citizen, granting of Indian reservations to the tribes in fee simple (but inalienable for twenty-five years), and individual allotments of lands to Indians who wanted them.[2] Although spending much of its energy at first in its controversy with Secretary of the Interior Carl Schurz over the Ponca tragedy, the Boston Indian Citizenship Committee continued to keep interest alive in Indian welfare. Some of its members played a continuing role among the Indian reformers, emphasizing the need to secure for the Indians their political and civil rights.

At the same time that the Boston group began its work, a similar organization was getting under way in Philadelphia, led and supported by Mary L. Bonney, principal of the Chestnut Street Female Seminary, who like the Boston businessmen had been aroused by injustices to the Indians and who hoped to stir up the people of the United States to demand reform in Indian affairs. With the aid of Amelia S. Quinton, who served as general secretary of the organization, Miss Bonney sought to unite the Christian women of the nation. The work began in the spring of 1879 in an informal fashion, but it quickly got organizational structure, first as the Central Indian Committee of the Women's Home Mission Society of the First Baptist Church of Philadelphia, then as an independent group. In June, 1881, it took the name The Indian Treaty-Keeping and Protective Association and in October, 1883, The Women's National Indian Association.[3]

---

[2] *The Indian Question: Report of the Committee Appointed by Hon. John D. Long, Governor of Massachusetts* (Boston, 1880). The report included a large number of short extracts from government reports in support of its contentions.

[3] See *Sketch and Plans of the Indian Treaty-Keeping and Protective Association, with Suggestions to Workers* (Philadelphia, 1881). The history of the origin of the association and its early years is given in Amelia S. Quinton, "Care of the Indian," in Annie Nathan Meyer, ed., *Woman's Work in America* (New York, 1891), pp. 373–91; Mary E. Dewey, *Historical Sketch of the Formation and Achievements of the Women's National Indian Association in the United States* (Philadelphia, 1900); *Annual Meeting and Report of the Women's National Indian Association* (Philadelphia, 1883), pp. 6–7; *Fourth Annual Report of the Women's National Indian Association* (Philadelphia, 1884), pp. 7–8. The constitution appears in *Fourth Annual Report* (1884), pp. 57–59. The word "Women's" was included to distinguish the group from the Indian Rights Association, but in 1901 the organization's title reverted to simply The National Indian Association. Mary Bonney was replaced as president by Mrs. Mary Lowe Dickinson in November, 1884, and in November, 1887, Mrs. Quinton became president.

The work of the association was manifold.[4] Its most cherished projects at the beginning were petitions sent to the President and to Congress, the first of which, with 13,000 signatures condemning the invasion of the Indian Territory by white settlers, was sent to Washington in February, 1880. Two years later a mammoth petition, claiming to represent no fewer than 100,000 persons and wrapped in white bunting tied with red, white, and blue ribbons, was delivered to President Arthur by a committee of the association.[5] It was presented in the Senate on February 21, 1882, by Senator Dawes of Massachusetts, who warmly supported the petitioners and their pleas. The petition itself and a memorial letter accompanying it, both of which were read to the Senate by Dawes, gave a dramatic picture of the thrust of the sentimental reform movement which the women's organization signally represented. The petition asked four things: the maintenance of all treaties "with scrupulous fidelity" until they were abrogated or modified with the free consent of the Indians involved; provision of common schools on the reservations "sufficient for the education of every child of every tribe" and of industrial schools as well; allotment of land in severalty (160 acres in fee simple, inalienable for twenty years) to all Indians who desired it; and giving to the Indians full rights under the law, making them amenable to the laws of the United States, granting full religious liberty, and encouraging the Indians in industry and trade. The memorial pointed to the swelling popular support stirred up by the women's crusade:

> Among the petitioners are many hundreds of churches which have adopted the petition by a unanimous rising vote, this often having been taken at a regular Sabbath service; various popular meetings have also here presented their plea similarly expressed; while the roll contains names of members of legislative bodies, of governors, judges, and lawyers; names of bishops and of many hundreds of the clergy—among the latter the entire ministry of three denominations in the city of Philadelphia, numbering nearly three hundred; names of the professors and students of theological seminaries like

[4] Useful discussion of the works of the association appears in *Fourth Annual Report* (1884), pp. 14–15, and in a pamphlet, *Our Work—What? How? Why?* (Philadelphia, 1893).

[5] The petitions and memorial letters of the first three years are printed in footnotes in Quinton, "Care of the Indian."

those at Hartford, Cambridge, Rochester, and Upland; colleges and universities like Yale, Harvard, Brown, Cornell, Rochester, Washington and Lee; names of editors of leading periodicals; the boards of hundreds of missionary and other benevolent societies, not a few of these being national ones, with names of art, literary, and social clubs. Besides all these the roll contains the signatures of hundreds of business and manufacturing firms who control capital to the amount of many millions of dollars, and who employ many thousands of operatives—all showing that not only has there been a rapid growth of sentiment among the religious and intellectual leaders of the community demanding legislation which shall end oppression of Indians and secure to them full opportunity for industrial, mental, and religious development, but that the commercial interests of our land also are fast coming to demand a just and speedy settlement of the Indian question.[6]

Senators Preston B. Plumb of Kansas and Henry M. Teller of Colorado made telling arguments against the petition and memorial. "I have noticed . . . ," Plumb remarked, "that interest of a certain kind in the Indian is in the exact ratio of distance from him, and perhaps I might add in increased ratio to their knowledge of him or his actual need." And he complained that there were "barrels of tears, oceans of sympathy for the Indians, and a fragmentary and passing word only for the men who suffered at their hands." Teller insisted, as he had frequently before, that the Indians were eager for neither land in severalty nor the white man's education. Dawes's plea, he said, was "full of pathos and full of enthusiasm, but utterly lacking in common sense."[7] But such criticism did little to stay the flood of reform sentiment.

A second work of the Women's National Indian Association was the circulation of literature. The women distributed copies of their annual reports and thousands of copies of leaflets printed by the association on Indian reform topics, as well as the pamphlets printed by the Indian Rights Association. It made efforts also to gain wide circulation for

[6] The petition, memorial, and remarks of Dawes are in *Congressional Record*, XIII, 1326–27. Extracts are given in *The Council Fire*, V (March, 1882), 88–92.
[7] *Congressional Record*, XIII, 1327–29.

books which agreed with its positions on the Indian question—George W. Manypenny's *Our Indian Wards*, Helen Hunt Jackson's *A Century of Dishonor* and *Ramona*, and the unsuccessful Indian novel by William J. Harsha, *Ploughed Under*. Third, it furnished information on the Indian question to the press. The local branches secured the publication in both religious and secular papers of articles on Indian education, on national duty to the Indians, and on missionary work, together with extracts of pamphlets and books. The association in Portland, Maine, for example, by 1884 had published sixty-seven articles, the one in Hartford, Connecticut, more than 130. Finally, the women presented their cause at public meetings which they organized, often with the co-operation of church groups, bringing in if possible important speakers such as Senators Dawes or Teller, the Commissioner of Indian Affairs, members of the Board of Indian Commissioners, or dedicated Indian reformers like Herbert Welsh. Mrs. Quinton herself, in 1884, traveled more than 10,000 miles in promoting the work of the association and addressed more than one hundred meetings in the East and Middle West.[8]

The success of the petitions as well as of other work of the association depended on the active support of branches organized throughout the country. By 1886 there were eighty-three such branches furthering the program of the national organization, and contributions rose rapidly, a sure sign of rising national interest. Some of the branches became important in their own right; those of Connecticut and Massachusetts were especially active.[9] In order to have a medium of communication between the national headquarters and the branches, the association in 1888 began publication of a monthly paper called *The Indian's Friend*. The paper recorded current legislation concerning Indians, made appeals for help in the association's work, and chronicled the efforts being made by other reform groups.[10] One of the women's special projects was providing aid to young Indian couples in

[8] *Fourth Annual Report* (1884), pp. 14–15, 27–30.

[9] Quinton, "Care of the Indian," pp. 385–86. Funds rose from $3,880 in 1885 to $16,500 in 1890. On the Connecticut branch, see Ellen Terry Johnson, *Historical Sketch of the Connecticut Indian Association from 1881 to 1888* (Hartford, 1888).

[10] See notice inside the front cover of *Our Work—What? How? Why?*. *The Indian's Friend* ceased publication in 1951.

building houses, and the association established a special Indian Home Building Department.[11]

In 1883 the Women's National Indian Association moved from concentration on propagandizing Indian reform to more direct missionary activity because, as Mrs. Quinton said, "Providence has answered our prayers by bringing the gentlemen's INDIAN RIGHTS ASSOCIATION into existence to pursue as their chief work, and with great advantages, this very object, thus leaving our own society free to devote, not by any means all, but a portion of our work to uplifting Indian homes; to aiding the vastly needed work within Indian hearts, minds, and souls, while not intermitting the effort to secure to the race civil rights." The women's group formally resolved to co-operate with the new organization, and the Indian Rights Association in turn looked to the women for assistance and support.[12]

The Indian Rights Association soon became the most important of the reform organizations, perhaps because it was the most businesslike. It was founded in December, 1882, in Philadelphia, a direct outgrowth of a visit of two young Philadelphians, Henry S. Pancoast and Herbert Welsh, to the great Sioux reservation in Dakota during the previous summer.[13] "This visit," Welsh later recorded, "resulted in a revolution

[11] Alice C. Fletcher was given special credit for promoting this work. Quinton, "Care of the Indian," p. 376.

[12] Annual Meeting and Report (1883), pp. 10, 16–17; Report of the Indian Rights Association, 1884, p. 13. The Women's National Indian Association also co-operated with other groups. It appointed a committee of one in 1884 to work with the Woman's Christian Temperance Union, and in 1892, noting that the "present transitional period of Indian civilization often calls for assistance in way of temperance legislation, or its enforcement," the association directed appeals on this subject to the national or state W. C. T. U. Fourth Annual Report (1884), pp. 49–50; Our Work—What? How? Why?, p. 32. On this co-operation with other groups see Priest, Uncle Sam's Stepchildren, pp. 82–83. Mrs. Quinton regularly reported on the work of her organization at the meetings of the reformers; see, for example, Lake Mohonk Conference Proceedings, 1889, pp. 103–107, and Report of the Board of Indian Commissioners, 1891, p. 131.

[13] Accounts of the trip to Dakota and the subsequent founding of the Indian Rights Association are in Henry S. Pancoast, Impressions of the Sioux Tribes in 1882, with Some First Principles in the Indian Question (Philadelphia, 1883); Herbert Welsh, Four Weeks Among Some of the Sioux Tribes of Dakota and Nebraska, Together with a Brief Consideration of the Indian Problem (Germantown, Pennsylvania, 1882); Report of the Indian Rights Association, 1883, p. 5; Herbert Welsh, The Indian Question Past and Present (Philadelphia, 1890), pp. 14–16; Herbert Welsh, "The Meaning of the Dakota Outbreak," Scribner's Magazine, IX (April, 1891), 439.

of many preconceived opinions and in fixing in our minds clearly and firmly two important truths:—1st. That the Indians were capable of civilization, and 2d. That it was largely due to the injustice or inefficiency of the government's dealings with him that the Indian had attained to civilization so imperfectly." Welsh and his companion were struck by the solid accomplishments of the missionaries whose work they inspected, which pointed to a humane solution to the Indian problem, but they were disturbed that so few of the general public were aware of what they themselves had witnessed. "The Indian must have just and faithful friends," Welsh decided, "who will plead his cause with the people, who will represent him in the East and at Washington, until his rights are accorded, and his days of tutelage are over."[14]

Back in Philadelphia, these young humanitarians determined to establish an organization to promote their views. In December, at a meeting in Welsh's home, the Indian Rights Association was founded, and it quickly became a dominant force in Indian affairs. Welsh, son of John Welsh, former Minister to Great Britain, and nephew of the ardent Indian reformer, William Welsh, became the secretary and for all practical purposes the guiding genius of the organization. The goals and purposes were clearly set forth:

> The Association seeks to secure the civilization of the two hundred and ninety thousand Indians of the United States (inclusive of the thirty thousand natives of Alaska), and to prepare the way for their absorption into the common life of our own people. The Indian as a savage member of a tribal organization cannot survive, ought not to survive, the aggressions of civilization, but his individual redemption from heathenism and ignorance, his transformation from the condition of a savage nomad to that of an industrious American citizen, is abundantly possible. This change can be fully accomplished only by means of legislation.[15]

While not denying or denigrating the good accomplished in the past by missionaries, teachers, and government agents, the association argued that complete success was impossible without vital legislation. "No man in these United States to-day," it asserted, "can be rightly

---

[14] Welsh, *The Indian Question Past and Present*, pp. 14–15.
[15] *Report of the Indian Rights Association*, 1884, p. 5.

termed civilized, nor can his position be considered a safe one, who is removed from both the protection and the punishment of law, who is denied a protected title to land and the right of holding it as an individual, or who is deprived of the blessings of a practical education." Since this condition did not obtain for the Indians, the Indian Rights Association was necessary, and it claimed the moral and financial support of the general public. In incisive statements, it set forth its aims for the Indians.

I. *Law*, and to awaken that spirit of even-handed justice in the nation which will alone make law, when secured, fully operative.
II. *Education*. Signifying by this broad term the developing for their highest use physical, intellectual and moral powers.
III. *A protected individual title to land*. This is the entering-wedge by which tribal organization is to be rent asunder.[16]

The methods by which this was to be accomplished were just as clearly enunciated.[17] Branch associations were organized in principal cities throughout the nation, which kept in close contact with the central headquarters, receiving information on questions of concern to the association. Representatives were sent out to the Indian reservations in order to get complete information, independent and accurate knowledge on which to base recommendations. Here lay much of the reason for the association's success, for it soon became evident to reasonable men that the Indian Rights Association, although often aggressively promoting its own point of view, had abundant facts behind it. When it investigated an alleged evil or some unjust treatment of the Indians, it could not easily be dismissed as a group of unthinking sentimentalists who did not know what they were talking about. Some-

[16] *Ibid.*, p. 6. The Constitution of the Indian Rights Association included the following statements of purpose:
"II. The object of this Association shall be to secure to the Indians of the United States the political and civil rights already guaranteed to them by treaty and statutes of the United States, and such as their civilization and circumstances may justify."
"IV. For the purpose of carrying out its object, the Association shall endeavor in every proper way to influence public opinion and the legislation of Congress, and assist the executive officers of the Government in the enforcement of the laws passed for the protection and education of the Indians."
[17] *Report of the Indian Rights Association*, 1884, pp. 7–8. A useful account of the association is Herbert Welsh, *A Brief Statement of the Objects, Achievements and Needs of the Indian Rights Association* (Philadelphia, 1887).

times a mere statement from the association was enough. Thus, in 1885, when relief for starving Indians in Montana was delayed in Congress, a letter from the Indian Rights Association published in the *New York Tribune* was sufficient to speed action. And the association, by its investigation and condemnation of President Arthur's opening of the Crow Creek Reservation to settlement, caused President Cleveland to revoke the order and uphold the tribe's title to the land.[18]

To place its information and its program before the public the Indian Rights Association embarked on an extensive publication program. It circulated in pamphlet form the reports of its own members' trips of investigation, and it reprinted and spread abroad newspaper articles, speeches, and other materials to further its program. In 1884 it issued eleven titles, with a total printing of 29,250; in 1885, twenty-one titles with 33,650 copies; in 1886, twenty-eight items with 50,000 copies; in 1887, twenty-six titles with 50,000 copies; and year after year the distribution continued.[19] These were channels of information to the newspapers of the country as well as to thousands of individuals in many states and territories. The association declared in 1890 that these publications had been "an essential factor in that marked change in public sentiment for the better, which has been noticeable during recent years."[20] Moreover, Welsh and his associates lectured frequently to interested groups, spelling out their ideas and eliciting support. In the first years of the organization, Welsh alone averaged more than

---

[18] These examples are given in Priest, *Uncle Sam's Stepchildren*, p. 84. See also the Indian Rights Association pamphlet, *Crow Creek Reservation, Dakota: Action of the Indian Rights Association, and Opinions of the Press, West and East, Regarding Its Recent Occupation by White Settlers, Together with the Proclamation of the President Commanding the Removal of the Settlers and Restoring the Lands to the Indians* (Philadelphia, 1885).

[19] See *Report of the Indian Rights Association*, 1884–1887, for titles and number of copies printed of each. Examples of the reports on field investigations are Samuel C. Armstrong, *Report of a Trip Made in Behalf of the Indian Rights Association, to Some Indian Reservations of the Southwest* (Philadelphia, 1884); Herbert Welsh, *Report of a Visit to the Navajo, Pueblo, and Hualapais Indians of New Mexico and Arizona* (Philadelphia, 1885); Charles C. Painter, *A Visit to the Mission Indians of Southern California, and Other Western Tribes* (Philadelphia, 1886); Herbert Welsh, *Civilization Among the Sioux Indians: Report of a Visit to Some of the Sioux Reservations of South Dakota and Nebraska* (Philadelphia, 1893); Charles F. Meserve, *A Tour of Observation Among Indians and Indian Schools in Arizona, New Mexico, Oklahoma, and Kansas* (Philadelphia, 1894).

[20] *Report of the Indian Rights Association*, 1890, p. 55.

141

forty talks a year, usually before church groups or local Indian reform associations.

Year after year the Indian Rights Association informed the public about Indian affairs, through publications and speeches that lost no effectiveness because they often were matter-of-fact rather than spectacular. This educational effort was high on the list of Herbert Welsh's priorities, for he never tired of referring to the remark reportedly made by Secretary of War Stanton to Bishop Whipple, when the latter urged the government to take action on behalf of the Indians: Congress never redresses a wrong until the people demand it. Secure the ear of the people, and then come to Washington with your story. "The Indian Rights Association," its executive committee reported in 1885, "follows with literal exactness this wise and pungent bit of advice."[21]

Even more important was the direct and effective lobbying in Washington done by the Indian Rights Association's full-time representative in the capital, Charles C. Painter, and after Painter's death in 1895, Francis E. Leupp. Painter followed the progress of legislation on Indian matters, brought information to the attention of the members of the Indian committees of the House and Senate and other legislators, and pressed for measures deemed beneficial to the Indians and opposed those considered injurious. In his work, he kept in close touch with Welsh in Philadelphia and as much as possible with branches of the association. To gain firsthand information to aid him in his work, Painter made frequent visits to the Indian country.[22]

The grandiose schemes for a massive uniting of the people across the land were not matched by the actual numbers who actively joined the Indian Rights Association. By 1892 only 1,300 members could be counted in all parts of the country, but the influence of Welsh and his friends cannot be measured in membership statistics. Welsh's own evaluation is accurate: "It is fair to claim that out of all proportion to its members or its expenditures has been its influence upon public sentiment and upon legislation and executive management. It has won general public respect and confidence by the general accuracy of its statements of fact, and by its impartial attitude, its freedom from partisan bias in judging men and measures within the range of Indian

[21] *Ibid.*, 1885, p. 6.

[22] The work of Painter and Leupp can be followed in their contributions to the annual reports of the association.

work."[23] The Indian Rights Association co-operated effectively with other Indian reform groups, and the program Welsh enunciated at the start of his career had been largely enacted by 1900.

The work of the various reform groups came to a focus in a conference held each autumn at a resort hotel on Lake Mohonk, near New Paltz, New York. Here in a beautiful sylvan setting, the self-denominated "Friends of the Indian" met to discuss Indian reform, to hear speakers on matters of concern, and to formulate resolutions which could be broadcast to the public and used to lobby for specific goals in Congress and with government officials. The instigator of the Lake Mohonk conferences and a continuing presence behind them was a Quaker schoolteacher, Albert K. Smiley, who with his brother Alfred had purchased the Lake Mohonk property in 1869 and had developed it into a summer resort which quickly gained popularity with a substantial, religious-minded clientele. Smiley, who had been appointed a member of the Board of Indian Commissioners in 1879, found the meetings of the board in Washington with the representatives of the missionary societies too short to allow time for adequate consideration of Indian matters. Smiley had also taken part in the summer of 1883 in an impromptu meeting of men concerned with Indian reform at the Santee Agency in Nebraska. He and General Eliphalet Whittlesey, who had been sent west by the Board of Indian Commissioners to investigate the attempt to break up the Great Sioux Reserve, had met with Herbert Welsh and a number of missionary leaders to discuss the matter. "That council opened my eyes," Smiley later reported, "and I determined to repeat at Mohonk on a larger scale the conference which had proved so helpful. I invited them all to meet at Mohonk the ensuing autumn, and promised to have a large gathering to discuss leisurely the whole Indian question." The first group assembled at Lake Mohonk in October, 1883. It was a small gathering to begin with, but as the idea took hold, the yearly conferences grew in size until they averaged in the late 1880's and early 1890's more than 150 persons. The format of the meetings was set, yet relaxed. The mornings were devoted to formal sessions in the spacious parlors of the hotel. A president

---

[23] *Report of the Indian Rights Association*, 1892, p. 4.

of the conference was designated (regularly a member of the Board of Indian Commissioners), a resolutions and platform committee chosen, the group welcomed by Smiley, and opening remarks made by the president as the conference got under way. Prepared papers on Indian reform matters by a variety of experts often served as the focus for discussion. The afternoons were free for informal conversations, often on walks through the well-kept grounds of the resort, while the evenings were devoted again to formal sessions.[24]

The Lake Mohonk Conference of the Friends of the Indian had no official status other than as a loose extention of the Board of Indian Commissioners. It was not charged by law as the original Board of Indian Commissioners had been to perform set duties or to co-operate with the Indian Office, nor did it have any supervisory functions. In fact, the Board of Indian Commissioners itself had lost some of its responsibilities.[25] The work at Lake Mohonk, instead, was the deliberate focusing of public opinion behind specific measures of Indian policy and aggressive propagandizing of these measures in the press and in the halls of government. The aim, as Smiley expressed it, was "to unite the best minds interested in Indian affairs, so that all should act together and be in harmony, and so that the prominent persons connected with Indian affairs should act as one body and create a public sentiment in favor of the Indians."[26] Through its widely circulated

[24] For Smiley's accounts of the founding of the conferences, see *Lake Mohonk Conference Proceedings*, 1885, p. 1, and *ibid.*, 1894, p. 38. A brief history of the conferences is Larry E. Burgess, " 'We'll Discuss It at Mohonk,' " *Quaker History: The Bulletin of Friends Historical Association*, XL (Spring, 1971), 14–28. The story of the Lake Mohonk resort with numerous pictures of the buildings and grounds is told in Frederick E. Partington, *The Story of Mohonk* (Fulton, New York, 1911; 2d ed. with additions by Daniel Smiley, Jr., and Albert K. Smiley, Jr., 1932). See also "Mohonk and Its Conferences," *New England Magazine*, XVI (June, 1897), 456–62, and Merrill E. Gates' article in Frederick Webb Hodge, ed., *Handbook of American Indians North of Mexico* (2 vols., Washington, 1907–1910), I, 928–29. There is material on the organization of the conferences and on their participants in the Smiley Family Papers, Quaker Collection, Haverford College Library.

[25] An act of May 17, 1882, provided: "And hereafter the commission shall only have power to visit and inspect agencies and other branches of the Indian service, and inspect goods purchased for said service, and the Commissioner of Indian Affairs shall consult with the commission in the purchase of supplies." *United States Statutes at Large*, XXII, 70. The later work of the board has been studied by Henry E. Fritz in a paper, "The Board of Indian Commissioners and Ethnocentric Reform, 1878–1893," read at the National Archives Conference on the History of Indian-White Relations in the United States, June 16, 1972.

[26] *Lake Mohonk Conference Proceedings*, 1885, p. 1.

annual reports, through coverage of its activities and recommendations in the press, especially the religious press, and through close co-operation with Indian reform groups such as the Indian Rights Association and the Women's National Indian Association, the Lake Mohonk Conference did indeed become what its promoters had intended—a dominant force in the formulation of Indian policy in the last decade and a half of the nineteenth century, when the formulations for solving the "Indian problem" were finally set. "The Lake Mohonk Conference is and has been a power," Lyman Abbott said in 1889; "but why? It does not represent a solid constituency; it casts no vote; it exercises no political influence, in the ordinary sense of that term; nor does it exercise any ecclesiastical or church influence." The answer was clear to Abbott and his associates at Lake Mohonk. The conference, he said, represented "the conscience of the American people on the Indian question." And he drew the lesson from history that "when the conscience of the American people is aroused, it is the most potent factor in American politics, defeating and bringing to shame the cunningly devised schemes of politicians that disregard or condemn it."[27]

One reason for the unanimity with which the Lake Mohonk conferences presented their recommendations to the public was the closely knit composition of the group. On the surface, indeed, it appeared that the net had been thrown wide to bring in the members in attendance. In the years from 1883 to 1900, nearly eight hundred different persons took part in the conferences. But the large number is deceiving, for about two-thirds of these came only once or twice and did not play an important continuing role in the formulation of Indian policy, although they confirmed and supported what the leaders proposed. There was a small core of dedicated men who gave the drive and the direction to the movement—such persons, among others, as Merrill E. Gates, President of Rutgers College and then of Amherst, who served on the Board of Indian Commissioners from 1884 to 1922, as its president from 1890 to 1899, and then as secretary until 1911; Lyman Abbott, liberal theologian and editor of the *Christian Union* (later the *Outlook*) and strong

---

[27] *Ibid.*, 1889, p. 13. When the United States at the end of the century acquired overseas possessions, the Lake Mohonk Conference expanded its interests and became "Friends of the Indians and Other Dependent Peoples." Smiley also developed an interest in arbitration and instituted a second series of annual conferences on that subject at Lake Mohonk.

advocate of immediate and forceful assimilation of the Indians; Senator Henry L. Dawes, who as chairman of the Senate Committee on Indian Affairs became the best known spokesman in Congress for the Indian reformers; Herbert Welsh, powerful and zealous secretary of the Indian Rights Association, and Philip C. Garrett, influential member of the executive committee of the association; General Eliphalet Whittlesey, member of the Board of Indian Commissioners from 1882 to 1909 and its secretary for many years; Samuel A. Armstrong, prominent in Indian as well as Negro educational reform as head of Hampton Institute; Thomas J. Morgan, Commissioner of Indian Affairs under Benjamin Harrison, who looked to the Lake Mohonk Conference for direction and who helped to carry out its leading proposals; Amelia S. Quinton of the Women's National Indian Association; and Joshua Davis, H. O. Houghton, and Frank Wood of the Boston Indian Citizenship Committee. These persons attended regularly and appeared to direct the conferences, with Smiley and his wife and brother serving as the gracious hosts rather than as managers of the conferences. Others in regular attendance were editors of Christian papers, army officers, representatives of the Interior Department, members of nearby chapters of the Indian Rights Association or other Indian reform groups, assorted Protestant ministers from the area, some public school administrators, and representatives of missionary societies involved in Indian work. The membership was almost entirely from New England and the Middle Atlantic States. Occasionally an Indian agent or missionary from the West came to report on his work, and frequently Indian students from Carlisle Indian Industrial School were on hand, but proximity to Lake Mohonk seems to have been for many a deciding factor.[28]

Critics of these reformers pictured them as Easterners, far removed from the Indians they championed and ignorant of Indian ways and Indian problems. Yet such charges were hardly valid when applied to

[28] The annual reports include lists of the members in attendance. Special attention was given to the editors of religious periodicals in the opening address of Clinton B. Fisk at the conference of 1889: "In fact, our editorial group is something to be proud of. In this Conference sit Dr. Abbott of the *Christian Union*, Dr. Ward of the *Independent*, Mr. Barrows of the *Christian Register*, Dr. Buckley of the *Christian Advocate*, Dr. Ferris of the *Christian Intelligencer*, Dr. Wayland of the *National Baptist*, Dr. Dunning of the *Congregationalist*, Dr. Gilbert of the *Advance*, and a large representation of the secular press." *Lake Mohonk Conference Proceedings*, 1889, p. 6.

the most prominent of the humanitarians, for these men and women took special pains to gain firsthand knowledge of Indian affairs. The members of the Board of Indian Commissioners, year after year, made extended tours of investigation in the West as part of their regular duties, and the reports of their visits were published for a wide audience. And when Congress in 1882 severely cut back the board's responsibilities, it retained the periodic investigations of conditions on the reservations. Herbert Welsh was indefatigable in his search for information. "During the past nine years," he wrote in 1891, "while conducting the work of the Indian Rights Association, I have three times visited the Sioux of Dakota, travelling on horseback or by wagon through all parts of the reservation, camping out at night, or receiving the hospitality of army officers, civil agents, missionaries—both white and native—and of Indians. I have also paid three visits to the Navajos and Pueblos of New Mexico and Arizona, and one to the Apaches of the latter territory. During this period I have been brought into constant contact with men and women whose experience made them valuable contributors to an understanding of the Indian question— officers of the army, officials of the Interior Department, members of Congress, missionaries on the reservations, Indian agents, and teachers in Indian schools."[29] The Indian Rights Association lobbyist in Washington was frequently on the road investigating Indian matters, and the leaders of the missionary boards, of course, kept in close contact with their missionaries in the field. Alice C. Fletcher, a regular participant in the Lake Mohonk meetings, was an ethnologist of note, who spent much of her life among the Omahas, Winnebagos, and other Indians.

The harmony that marked the Lake Mohonk conferences was based on a common philanthropic and humanitarian outlook expressed in Christian terms, for the reform organizations represented there had a strong religious orientation. The Women's National Indian Association, which had been established under Baptist auspices, assumed a nondenominational posture, but it consciously drew on church support.

[29] Herbert Welsh, "The Meaning of the Dakota Outbreak," *Scribner's Magazine*, IX (April, 1891), 439.

Its executive board in 1884 comprised members from eight Protestant denominations—Baptist, Presbyterian, Episcopal, Congregational, Methodist, Quaker, Reformed, and Unitarian—and in the previous year had included Lutherans also. The support of Christian congregations throughout the land was essential for the success of its Indian reform crusade, as the petition of 1882 demonstrated, and the churches often formed the nuclei for local branches. In 1883, moreover, the organization specifically added missionary and school work to its efforts and took on many of the characteristics of a home missionary society. The new work was a direct endeavor to supply Christian training for the Indians in areas where no other group was providing it and then, whenever possible, to resign the work to the care of some regular missionary group.[30] The leaders quoted with approbation in their publications the remarks of the Reverend Joseph Cook in 1885: "The first motto of all Indian reformers should be Indian evangelization. . . . Let us not depend on politicians to reform the Indian. We cannot safely depend even on the Government Schools to solve the Indian problem. The longest root of hope for the Indians is to be found in the self-sacrifice of the Christian Church."[31]

This missionary work was in the tradition that had long marked Christian endeavors among the Indians and was defined in the general secretary's report, adopted in 1883:

> The kind of work to be done. This will be teaching children to speak [,] read and write English, also to work and become self-supporting; teaching young parents and others how to make comfortable and attractive homes out of scanty materials; teaching the women how to cook the foods of civilization, and how to care for their children, and, most surely, teaching all within reach in the simplest way, redeeming Christian truths.[32]

By 1892 the association had established twenty-five mission stations,

---

[30] The missionary work is reported in the annual reports and in special pamphlets published by the association. See, for example, *Missionary Work of the Women's National Indian Association, and Letters of Missionaries* (Philadelphia, 1885); *Christian Civilization and Missionary Work of the Women's National Indian Association* (Philadelphia, 1887); *Sketches of Delightful Work* (Philadelphia, 1893).

[31] Title page of *Missionary Work* (1885).

[32] *Annual Meeting and Report* (1883), p. 12.

which had been transferred to Methodist, Episcopal, Baptist, Presbyterian, or Moravian care.[33]

The Indian Rights Association, too, acknowledged the Christian motivation of its work. Herbert Welsh asserted that the Indian needed to be "taught to labor, to live in civilized ways, and to serve God." "The best Christian sentiment of the country," he said, "is needed to redeem the Indian, to stimulate and guide the constantly changing functionaries of the government who are charged with the task of his civilization."[34]

It was at the Lake Mohonk conferences that the atmosphere of deep religiosity in which the reformers worked was most notable. The meetings were begun with an invocation, and the discussions were redolent of religious spirit and religious terminology. Part of this was due, no doubt, to the influence of the Quaker host; part, also, to the heavy clerical participation in the gatherings. Of the names listed in the membership rosters, 1883–1900, more than a fourth were ministers, their wives, and representatives of religious groups, and a great many more were prominent lay leaders in their churches. The editors of the leading religious journals and papers, too, were regularly on hand. All had strong religious motivation for their work in Indian affairs. President Gates's remarks at the opening of the 1899 conference were not unrepresentative of the mood. He noted the beauty of the natural surroundings and then continued:

> But though we cannot forget the beauty of the Indian summer we come together in no spirit of mere enjoyment—no mood of thoughtless gayety. We believe in the government of a God whose will is at once beauty in the material world, and moral order in the world of will and action. We believe in the moral government of the universe; and we rejoice in the beauty of the physical earth as part of God's ordained order. We assemble as those who have faith in Him; and believing in the reign of his holy will we delight in the beauty with which he surrounds us. But we come with earnest purpose, too. We recognize that we are not here for pleasure alone. We believe that we have a duty to the less-favored races; and in considering together the problems connected with these peoples we are touching

33 *Our Work—What? How? Why?*, p. 4.
34 Welsh, *The Indian Question Past and Present*, pp. 15, 18.

almost every question of social reform and governmental administration.[35]

The conviction that it was Christian work in which they were engaged was repeatedly expressed and universally assumed. "[I]t may be taken for granted," Lyman Abbott observed at Lake Mohonk in 1885, "that we are Christian men and women; that we believe in justice, good-will, and charity, and the brotherhood of the human race." And President Gates declared in 1891: "This is essentially a philanthropic and Christian reform. Whatever may be our views, our slight differences of view or differences that may seem to us profound, we all gather here believing that the Lord of the world is the Lord Jesus Christ; believing that, ever since God himself became incarnate, for a man to see God truly, he must learn to see something of God in his fellow-man, and to work for his fellow-men. We come in the spirit of service."[36]

The word "Christian" dropped unselfconsciously from the lips of the reformers as they set about to do God's will, to guide the Indian "from the night of barbarism into the fair dawn of Christian civilization," as Herbert Welsh expressed it in 1886. The only hope for a solution to the Indian problem, Gates declared at the end of nearly two decades of organized humanitarian effort, was to bring the Indians "under the sway of Christian thought and Christian life, and into touch with the people of this Christian nation under the laws and institutions which govern the life of our States and Territories." As he welcomed the members of the Lake Mohonk Conference of 1900, he recalled the Christian foundation of their work for Indian reform. "Nothing less than decades of years of persistent effort," he said, "years of effort prompted by that love of one's fellow-men which has its perennial root in the love of Christ for us, can do the work which here we contemplate and discuss." He welcomed especially the devoted missionaries who worked so diligently for the Indians, but he gave a clue to the pervasive Christianity of the age when he turned to welcome, too, representatives of the Indian Bureau, whom he described as "Christian men of high purpose, whose aim in the issuing of regulations and the administration

[35] *Lake Mohonk Conference Proceedings*, 1899, p. 9.
[36] *Ibid.*, 1885, p. 50; *ibid.*, 1891, p. 11.

of Indian affairs is identical with the aims of the Christian workers in the field, and the Christian friends of the Indian who gather here."[37]

Sentiments such as these gave the tone to their public meetings, but the unity of the reformers was of a more fundamental nature than these pious expressions of Christian goodwill. Although there were debates and differences of opinion among the prominent men and women working for reform in Indian affairs in the 1880's and 1890's, there was strong underlying agreement in outlook and in goals. If we seek the foundation of this agreement, we find it principally in American evangelical Protestantism, which defined what the term "Christian" meant to the friends of the Indian.

The entire history of the United States throughout the nineteenth century, of course, was marked by a strong evangelical movement.[38] So dominant was this force that one historian of American religion has asserted that the story of American Evangelicalism is "the story of America itself in the years 1800 to 1900, for it was Evangelical religion which made Americans the most religious people in the world, molded them into a unified, pietistic-perfectionist nation, and spurred them on to those heights of social reform, missionary endeavor, and imperialistic expansionism which constitute the moving forces of our history in

---

[37] *Ibid.*, 1886, p. 13; *ibid.*, 1900, pp. 13, 21. It had not been uncommon to find religiously oriented men in the office of Commissioner of Indian Affairs. Nathaniel G. Taylor (1867–1869), Edward P. Smith (1873–1875), and Thomas J. Morgan (1889–1893), for example, were Protestant ministers. Of Hiram Price (1881–1885), *The Council Fire*, IV (May, 1881), 67, reported: "Mr. Price is a very prominent member of the Methodist Church, and no layman has been a truer friend, or done more for Methodism in Iowa, than the newly nominated Indian Commissioner. He is a man of large wealth, and his money, influence and personal efforts and labors, has been given as the needs of the church have required. . . . Coming to this work with a life-long record as a thorough Christian temperance man, we shall expect to see a rigid enforcement of the treaty stipulations with various Indian tribes, wherein the United States has covenanted to furnish agents and teachers of good moral character to manage the local affairs of the agencies and to teach the Indian our civilization."

[38] For my understanding of evangelical Protestantism, I have learned much from Robert T. Handy, "The Protestant Quest for a Christian America," *Church History*, XXII (March, 1953), pp. 8–20; Robert T. Handy, *A Christian America: Protestant Hopes and Historical Realities* (New York, 1971); Martin E. Marty, *Righteous Empire: The Protestant Experience in America* (New York, 1970); William G. McLoughlin, ed., *The American Evangelicals, 1800–1900: An Anthology* (New York, 1968); and Sidney E. Mead, *The Lively Experiment: The Shaping of Christianity in America* (New York, 1963).

that century."[39] The evangelicals, in fact, set out to create a "righteous empire" in America. They set out with considerable success "to attract the allegiance of all the people, to develop a spiritual kingdom, and to shape the nation's ethos, mores, manners, and often its laws."[40]

This religious circumstance had important consequences for the nation's dealings with the Indians. The thrust to incorporate all into the "empire" had not by-passed the Indians—witness the continuing efforts, beginning early in the century, to educate, civilize, and Christianize the Indians and thus bring them into the national fold.[41]

What marked the last decades of the century, however, was an intensification of the desire for unity, a new energization of the "quest for a Christian America," and an increasing emphasis on a secularized as opposed to a theological formulation of goals and activities. And it was exactly at this time—for better or for worse—that the "Indian problem" demanded solution. The coincidence of an ultimate crisis in Indian affairs, brought about by the overwhelming pressure of aggressively expanding white civilization upon the Indians and their reservation homes, and the intensified religious drive for a unified American society led to the new program of Indian policy reform. It had consequences for the Indians and for the United States as significant as the dramatic military encounters with the plains tribes that electrified the nation after the Civil War.

The distinguishing mark of American evangelicalism was its insistence on individual salvation. The concern was for the conversion and reformation of individuals as the means of correcting evils or wrongs in society. The Indian reformers eventually realized the fundamental conflict between this principle and the communal life and customs of the Indians. Rather than approach the Indian problem in Indian terms, the reformers insisted adamantly on the individualization of the Indians and their acculturation of individuals freed from bondage to the tribe. "The philosophy of the present [Indian] policy,"

[39] McLoughlin, *American Evangelicals*, p. 1. He concludes: "The history of American Evangelicanism is then more than the history of a religious movement. To understand it is to understand the whole temper of American life in the nineteenth century." *Ibid.*, p. 26.

[40] Marty, *Righteous Empire*, Foreword.

[41] For examples of these efforts, see Robert F. Berkhofer, Jr., *Salvation and the Savage: An Analysis of Protestant Missions and American Indian Response, 1787–1862* (Lexington, Kentucky, 1965).

Senator Dawes said in January, 1884, "is to treat him as an individual, and not as an insoluble substance that the civilization of this country has been unable, hitherto, to digest, but to take him as an individual, a human being, and treat him as you find him." Thomas J. Morgan, as Commissioner of Indian Affairs, urged that the tribal relation be broken up, socialism destroyed, and "the family and the autonomy of the individual substituted." Merrill Gates saw in individualism "the key-note of our socio-political ideas of this century" and thought he could find sympathetic vibrations of it even among the Indians.[42] He epitomized the sentiments of the reformers as he summed up their work in 1900:

We have learned that education and example, and, pre-eminently, the force of Christian life and Christian faith in the heart, can do in one generation most of that which evolution takes centuries to do.

But if civilization, education and Christianity are to do their work, they must get at the individual. They must lay hold of men and women and children, one by one. The deadening sway of tribal custom must be interfered with. The sad uniformity of savage tribal life must be broken up! Individuality must be cultivated. Personality must be developed. And personality is strengthened only by the direction of one's own life through voluntary obedience to recognized moral law. At last, as a nation, we are coming to recognize the great truth that if we would do justice to the Indians, we must get at them, one by one, with American ideals, American schools, American laws, the privileges and the pressures of American rights and duties.[43]

The fight for individualization was carried on on many fronts by the evangelical reformers. They intended to break up tribal ownership of land and to substitute allotment of Indian lands in severalty. They wanted to break up tribal jurisdiction and to treat the Indians as individual citizens before the law. Their individualism, moreover, was tied closely to the Puritan work ethic. Hard work and thrift were virtues that seemed to be at the very basis of individual salvation. No

[42] *Report of the Board of Indian Commissioners*, 1883, p. 69; Report of the Commissioner of Indian Affairs, 1889, in serial 2725, p. 4; Merrill E. Gates, "Land and Law as Agents in Educating Indians," *Report of the Board of Indian Commissioners*, 1885, p. 26.
[43] *Lake Mohonk Conference Proceedings*, 1900, p. 14.

transformation for the Indians could be conceived in the reformers' minds that did not include self-support. Annuities to the tribes and rations to subsist the Indians were imposing blocks that prevented realization of the ideal. Until these were abolished and the Indians made to labor to support themselves and their families, there would be no solution to the Indian problem. Allotment of land in severalty to the Indians was insisted upon because the reformers believed that without the personal labor needed to maintain the private homestead the virtue of hard work could never be inculcated.

It was common for the reformers to see in labor a fulfillment of an essential command of God, as Gates did in 1885 when he criticized past efforts to aid the Indians. "Above all else we have utterly neglected to teach them the value of honest labor," he said. "Nay, by rations dealt out whether needed or not, we have interfered to suspend the efficient teaching by which God leads men to love and honor labor. We have taken from them the compelling inspiration that grows out of His law, 'if a man will not work, neither shall he eat!' "[44] The precepts of work and thrift re-echoed again and again in Gates's addresses to the Lake Mohonk gatherings. In 1896 he explained once more the common goal and spoke of wakening in the Indian broader desires and ampler wants:

> To bring him out of savagery into citizenship we must make the Indian more intelligently selfish before we can make him unselfishly intelligent. We need to *awaken in him wants.* In his dull savagery he must be touched by the wings of the divine angel of discontent. Then he begins to look forward, to reach out. The desire for property of his own may become an intense educating force. The wish for a home of his own awakens him to new efforts. Discontent with the teepee and the starving rations of the Indian camp in winter is needed to get the Indian out of the blanket and into trousers,—and trousers with a pocket in them, and with a *pocket that aches to be filled with dollars!*[45]

Without personal property, Gates argued, there would be no strong

[44] *Report of the Board of Indian Commissioners,* 1885, p. 18.
[45] *Lake Mohonk Conference Proceedings,* 1896, p. 11.

development of personality, and he noted that the Savior's teaching was full of illustrations of the right use of property.

Individual development and the stimulation of honest labor, in the evangelical Protestant worldview, were possible only in the perspective of the family. Glorification of hearth and home was an essential element in their program for Christian living, for the Christian purity and virtues that they extolled could take root and be nurtured to full maturity only within the Christian family.[46] What the reformers saw of Indian life, therefore, seriously offended their sensibilities. Not understanding a culture and a family life that differed so markedly from their own experience, the humanitarians saw only heathen practices which they felt it their duty to stamp out as quickly and as thoroughly as possible. Polygamy was a special abomination, and the whole tribal arrangement was thought to create and perpetuate un-Christian modes of life. Gates's lengthy attack upon tribalism in 1885 was premised fundamentally on the belief that it destroyed the family. "The family is God's unit of society," he declared. "On the integrity of the family depends that of the State. There is no civilization deserving of the name where the family is not the unit in civil government." But the tribal system, he believed, paralyzed both "the desire for property and the family life that ennobles that desire." As allegiance to the tribe and its chiefs grew less, its place would be taken "by the sanctities of family life and an allegiance to the laws which grow naturally out of the family."[47]

The goals envisaged for the Indians were deemed possible because of the belief in the unity of mankind held by the humanitarians. If the Indians were basically no different from other human beings—except for the conditioning coming from their environment—then there could be no real obstacle to their assimilation. "Let us forget once and forever the word 'Indian' and all that it has signified in the past," Charles

[46] McLoughlin, speaking of the middle third of the century, notes: "It is difficult to find a collection of Evangelical sermons in this period which does not devote at least one sermon to 'The Christian Home' and another to 'Motherhood.' It was the Evangelicals who made home and hearth the central features of American sentimentalism." *American Evangelicals*, p. 17.
[47] *Report of the Board of Indian Commissioners*, 1885, pp. 27–29.

C. Painter told the Lake Mohonk Conference in 1889, "and remember only that we are dealing with so many children of a common Father." The doctrine of the brotherhood of man was a cardinal principle of the reformers, who wanted to erase all lines of distinction that marked the Indians off from the rest of the nation. And in the process traditional Indian customs were to be simply pushed aside as unimportant. In speaking of the proposal for severalty legislation, Philip C. Garrett said in 1886: ". . . if an act of emancipation will buy them life, manhood, civilization, and Christianity, at the sacrifice of a few chieftain's feathers, a few worthless bits of parchment, the cohesion of the tribal relation, and the traditions of their race; then, in the name of all that is really worth having, let us shed the few tears necessary to embalm these relics of the past, and have done with them; and, with fraternal cordiality, let us welcome to the bosom of the nation this brother whom we have wronged long enough." Commissioner of Indian Affairs Morgan, in speaking of Indian children, stressed first of all "their kinship with us." "They, too, are human and endowed with all the faculties of human nature," he observed; "made in the image of God, bearing the likeness of their Creator, and having the same possibilities of growth and development that are possessed by any other class of children."[48]

The reformers accepted the traditional view that mankind had passed through distinct stages of society as it advanced from savagery to civilization. They realized that their own ancestors had once existed at the level at which they now found the Indians and that it had taken thousands of years for the slow evolutionary process to work. Their goal was to speed up the process by educational and other civilizing programs—to accomplish in one generation what nature alone had taken eons to effect. In so doing, they paid little heed to the scientific elaboration of the theory of stages of society as it was refined and amplified by Lewis Henry Morgan, whose writings on the Iroquois won him the title "Father of American Anthropology." In his last great work, *Ancient Society: or, Researches in the Lines of Human Progress from Savagery through Barbarism into Civilization*, published in 1877, Morgan established a series of ethnic periods, each marked by distinct char-

[48] Charles C. Painter, "The Indian and His Property," *Lake Mohonk Conference Proceedings*, 1889, p. 88; Philip C. Garrett, "Indian Citizenship," *ibid.*, 1886, p. 11; Thomas J. Morgan, *A Plea for the Papoose: An Address at Albany, N.Y., by Gen. T. J. Morgan* (n.p., n.d.), pp. 2–3.

acteristics, through which human society progressed. Morgan had deep concern for the welfare of the Indians. He had hoped in 1861, in fact, to be appointed Commissioner of Indian Affairs by Lincoln, only to be disappointed when the office went to William P. Dole in payment for political favors, and he had continued to exhibit an interest in Indian policy.[49]

Morgan's views, if fully understood by the Christian reformers, could have given them little encouragement, for the scientist saw no possibility of greatly speeding up the evolutionary process. He urged, instead, adapting Indian policy to the circumstances at hand and developing the Indians of the plains into a pastoral people. In a letter in *The Nation* in 1878, he explained his position:

> We have overlooked the fact that the principal Indian tribes have passed by natural development out of the condition of savages into that of barbarians. In relative progress they are now precisely where our own barbarous ancestors were when, by the domestication of animals, they passed from a similar into a higher condition of barbarism, though still two ethnical periods below civilization. Their great progress commenced, as we have reason to suppose, when they gained, through flocks and herds of domestic animals a permanent meat and milk subsistence. We wonder that our Indians cannot civilize; but how could they, any more than our own remote barbarous ancestors, jump ethnical periods? They have the skulls and brains of barbarians, and must grow towards civilization as all mankind have done who attained to it by a progressive experience.[50]

Lewis Henry Morgan died in 1881, just as the revitalization of Indian reform began to take effect. The humanitarians quietly ignored him as they set about to revolutionize the status of the Indians in America without regard for "ethnical periods." Nor were they affected by other scientific studies of the last half of the nineteenth century which claimed Indian inferiority, a position that would have weakened or

---

[49] Morgan's career is ably recounted in Carl Resek, *Lewis Henry Morgan: American Scholar* (Chicago, 1960).

[50] Lewis Henry Morgan, "The Indian Question," *The Nation*, XXVII (November 28, 1878), 332. For other statements of Morgan on Indian policy, see his "The Hue and Cry Against the Indians," *ibid.*, XXIII (July, 1876), 40–41, and "Factory System for Indian Reservations," *ibid.*, 58–59.

negated the programs aimed at rapid Americanization and assimilation of the Indians.[51]

What especially marked the last decades of the nineteenth century in the development of evangelical Protestantism and gave it its peculiar flavor was the subtle transformation that brought about an almost complete identification of Protestantism and Americanism. It was the culmination of a movement extending through the century. In the first half of the century the co-ordination of the two elements had already been very close; Americanism and Protestantism protected each other. "So close was the bond, so deep the union," says Martin Marty, "that a basic attack on American institutions would have meant an attack on Protestant Christianity itself. Positively, defense of America meant a defense of the evangelical empire."[52] This "ideological amalgamation of Protestant denominationalism and Americanism," as Sidney Mead calls it, was not simply an acceptance of evangelical religion by the officials of the state. It came increasingly to be a complacent defense of the social and economic status quo by the churches. "Protestants, in effect," Mead notes, "looked at the new world they had created, were proud of its creator, and like Jehovah before them, pronounced it very good." Ironically, despite warnings of the necessity of separation of church and state, the churches gave a religious endorsement to the American way of life. Thus, under a system of official separation, Protestants eventually became "as completely identified with nationalism and their country's political and economic system as had ever been known in Christendom."[53] The perceptive English observer Lord

[51] See the discussion in John S. Haller, Jr., *Outcasts from Evolution: Scientific Attitudes of Racial Inferiority, 1859–1900* (Urbana, Illinois, 1971), pp. 35, 100, 111–12, 140–41. A superficial treatment of Presidential views on race is George Sinkler, *The Racial Attitudes of American Presidents from Abraham Lincoln to Theodore Roosevelt* (Garden City, New York, 1971). Sinkler concludes: "As a matter of fact, when it came to the question of the biological acceptibility of racial minorities, 'Lo, the poor Indian' led all the rest. As the aboriginal inhabitants lost their hunting grounds to white despoilers, many of the Presidents expressed a surprising willingness to see red men assimilated into American life, without the usual reservations against intermarriage and social equality which were applied to blacks and less often to Orientals." *Ibid.*, p. 379.

[52] Marty, *Righteous Empire*, p. 89.

[53] Mead, *Lively Experiment*, pp. 142, 156–57.

Bryce noted in 1885: "Christianity is in fact understood to be, though not the legally established religion, yet the national religion."[54]

As the nineteenth century drew to a close, two tendencies or forces intensified the union between Protestantism and Americanism. One was the weakening of traditional theological interest, so that the principles of Americanism became in large part the religious creed. The other was the growing threat to the dominance of the "righteous empire" by new forces in the United States, principally the influx of millions of European immigrants, many of whom did not fit the Anglo-Saxon Protestant pattern of America, and the growing industrialization and urbanization of the nation, which upset the foundations of the traditional rural Protestant outlook. Afraid that the unity of America was being weakened, the churches sought to strengthen union and conformity.

The Indians were engulfed in this flood of Americanism. Their Americanization, indeed, became the all-embracing goal of the reformers in the last two decades of the century. "The logic of events," Commissioner Morgan declared in his first annual report, "demands the absorption of the Indians into our national life, not as Indians, but as American citizens."[55] Nor were the Indians to be allowed to stand in the way of American progress. The reformers were convinced of the divine approbation of the spread of American culture, and the development of the West as an indication of that progress was part of the Protestant mission. There was no intention among the friends of the Indian to protect tribal rights that would obstruct the fruitful exploitation of the nation's domain. Thus Carl Schurz saw that there was no way to stop the powerful advance of an enterprising people, and he hoped to persuade the Indians to accept individual allotments of land that could be protected. "This done," he said, "the Indians will occupy no more ground than so many white people; the large reservations will gradually be opened to general settlement and enterprise, and the Indians, with their possessions, will cease to stand in the way of the 'development of the country.' " He hoped to maintain peace and to

---

[54] Quoted in McLoughlin, *American Evangelicals*, p. 26. See also John Edwin Smylie, "National Ethos and the Church," *Theology Today*, XX (October, 1963), 313–21.
[55] Report of the Commissioner of Indian Affairs, 1889, in serial 2725, p. 3.

protect the Indians "by harmonizing the habits, occupations, and interests of the Indians" with those of the nation.[56]

Whereas Schurz lamented the inability of the government to protect the Indians against the march of progress, the more radical reformers advocated absorbing the Indians as a matter of principle. "Three hundred thousand people have no right to hold a continent and keep at bay a race able to people it and provide the happy homes of civilization," Lyman Abbott told his colleagues at Lake Mohonk. "We do owe the Indians sacred rights and obligations, but one of those duties is not the right to let them hold forever the land they did not occupy, and which they were not making fruitful for themselves or others." The Indian reservations should be abolished, letting the full blast of civilization rush in upon the Indians. "Christianity is not merely a thing of churches and school-houses," Abbott insisted. "The post-office is a Christianizing institution; the railroad, with all its corruptions, is a Christianizing power, and will do more to teach the people punctuality than schoolmaster or preacher can."[57]

Although the staunch Protestant reformers, in their drive to promote Americanism, fought successfully to prevent the use of government funds for missionary schools because they objected to the support this gave to Roman Catholics, they did not want the Indian schools to be devoid of religious influences. Great emphasis was placed on Christian endeavor outside the formal school system. When President Edward H. Magill of Swarthmore College addressed the Lake Mohonk gathering in 1887, he noted that the Dawes Act opened the way to the civilization of the Indians, but he added, "for the realization of all our highest hopes for the Indian, for his education and training, for his introduction as an equal among a civilized people, and for his preparation for the high and responsible duties of American citizenship, we must look largely, if not chiefly, to the religious organizations of our country." Commissioner Morgan, while fighting government appropriations for missionary schools, admitted the need for "the influence of the home, the Sabbath-school, the church, and religious institutions of learning" and for "consecrated missionary work."[58]

[56] Carl Schurz, "Present Aspects of the Indian Problem," *North American Review*, CXXXIII (July, 1881), pp. 17, 23.

[57] *Lake Mohonk Conference Proceedings*, 1885, pp. 51–52.

[58] *Ibid.*, 1887, p. 60; Report of the Commissioner of Indian Affairs, 1889, in serial 2725, p. 97.

The Christian reformers insisted in 1895: "The government alone cannot solve the Indian problem. Our American civilization is founded upon Christianity. A pagan people cannot be fitted for citizenship without learning the principles and acquiring something of the spirit of a Christian people." As the government made progress in providing secular education, so the duty of the churches was increased "to furnish that contribution which nothing but unofficial, voluntary, and Christian service can furnish toward the emancipation and elevation of the Indian."[59] How this was to be done was eloquently explained by Merrill Gates:

> Only as men and women who are full of the light of education and of the life of Christ go in and out among these savage brothers and sisters of ours, only as the living thought and the feeling heart touch their hearts one by one, can the Indians be lifted from savagery and made into useful citizens. . . . As we get at them one by one, as we break up these iniquitous masses of savagery, as we draw them out from their old associations and immerse them in the strong currents of Christian life and Christian citizenship, as we send the sanctifying stream of Christian life and Christian work among them, they feel the pulsing life-tide of Christ's life.[60]

The reformers represented by the Lake Mohonk conferences were stimulated by the memory of a person whose commitment to the Indian cause was without question, Helen Hunt Jackson. Born Helen Maria Fiske in Amherst, Massachusetts, in 1830, she married an army engineer, Edward B. Hunt, in 1852 and when he died accidentally in 1863, she returned to New England and began a literary career. She

[59] *Lake Mohonk Conference Proceedings*, 1895, pp. 106–107. In her introduction to Kate C. McBeth, *The Nez Perces Since Lewis and Clark* (New York, 1908), Alice C. Fletcher stressed the importance of Christianity in preparing the Indians for allotment and citizenship.

[60] *Lake Mohonk Conference Proceedings*, 1893, p. 12. This personal and persuasive approach, which marked Protestant missionary effort, was in contrast with the more sacramental approach of the Roman Catholics. For an excellent comparison of the two groups of missionaries on a single reservation, see Howard L. Harrod, *Mission Among the Blackfeet* (Norman, 1971). A very sentimental view of the goal of Christian work among the Indians is presented in Henry L. Dawes, *Past and Present Indian Policy* (New York, 1892), p. 5. This pamphlet prints an address given to the annual meeting of the American Missionary Association in 1892.

wrote articles for *The Independent* and other journals, published travel pieces, and in 1870 brought out a book of poetry, *Verses.* While passing the winter of 1873–1874 in Colorado Springs, Colorado, she met a Quaker businessman, William Sharpless Jackson, whom she married in 1875. From then on Colorado Springs was her home, but she continued her writing, producing a series of novels and shorter stories.[61]

By chance, Mrs. Jackson was in Boston in the winter of 1879–1880, when the great furor over the Poncas was at its height. In November, 1879, she heard Chief Standing Bear and Bright Eyes lecture on the wrongs of the Poncas, and although never noticeably interested in Indians before, she was suddenly fired by a tremendous indignation and threw herself headlong into the controversy that raged over the Ponca affair. She attacked Secretary of the Interior Carl Schurz in a letter in the *New York Tribune,* December 15, 1879, and when his reply did not satisfy her, carried on direct correspondence with him, some of which was printed in the *Tribune* and in the *Boston Daily Advertiser.*[62]

To confirm her position that the government was to blame for the Indians' troubles, she undertook extensive research in the Astor Library in New York City, and as she came across evidence of broken treaties or unjust treatment, she wrote up and published her findings. In a whirlwind of activity, she became a veritable one-person reform movement, circulating petitions and tracts, rebuking editors, army officers, clergymen, college presidents, and Congressmen, and filling the columns of the *Independent,* the *New York Tribune,* and the *New York Times* with stinging letters.[63] The material she had gathered from the beginning of the year she finally incorporated into her famous volume, *A Century of Dishonor,* which she finished writing by the end of May. The book was published in January, 1881, with a preface by Bishop Whipple and an introduction by President Julius H. Seelye of Amherst.

A Century of Dishonor is a strange book, a disorganized, cluttered

---

[61] There is a sketch of Helen Hunt Jackson by Louise Pound in *Dictionary of American Biography,* IX, 541–43. A full, scholarly biography is Ruth Odell, *Helen Hunt Jackson (H.H.)* (New York, 1939). A sympathetic appraisal by a close friend is Thomas Wentworth Higginson, *Contemporaries* (Boston, 1899), pp. 142–67.

[62] The correspondence is printed in Jackson, *A Century of Dishonor,* pp. 359–66.

[63] Odell, *Helen Hunt Jackson,* pp. 163–64. Odell in her bibliography provides a chronological listing of Mrs. Jackson's articles.

compilation of fragments, which sets forth the story of the government's dealings with seven tribes. It is a polemic work, not balanced history, and everywhere there is evidence of the haste with which the book was put together. Thrown into the appendix was a further miscellany of data—letters, extracts of reports, abridgements of treaties, and the like. Mrs. Jackson's intention was to awaken the conscience of America to the flagrant wrongs that had been perpetrated upon the Indians. "The history of the United States Government's repeated violations of faith with the Indians . . . ," she wrote in the introductory pages of the book, "convicts us, as a nation, not only of having outraged the principles of justice, which are the basis of international law; and of having laid ourselves open to the accusation of both cruelty and perfidy; but of having made ourselves liable to all punishments which follow upon such sins—to arbitrary punishment at the hands of any civilized nation who might see fit to call us to account, and to that more certain natural punishment which, sooner or later, as surely comes from evil-doing as harvests come from sown seed." When the people were aroused, they would demand that Congress right the wrongs. And she took care to see that the congressmen got her message direct, for at her own expense she sent a copy of the book to every member of Congress. "What an opportunity for the Congress of 1880," she exclaimed, "to cover itself with a lustre of glory, as the first to cut short our nation's record of cruelties and perjuries! the first to attempt to redeem the name of the United States from the stain of a century of dishonor!"[64]

The book was a sentimental overdramatization of a complex problem, and what effect it had on the statesmen who had to wrestle with the practical solutions to the Indian question it is impossible to tell. But as Allan Nevins has pointed out in appraising Helen Hunt Jackson's work, dramatization, if it does not show *how* a problem can be solved, at least drives home the fact that a solution is needed. "The function of the propagandist is to deal with public sentiment and to make it more malleable to the labors of the realistic statesman," Nevins wrote. "That function, in dealing with the Indian question, the intense and noble-hearted if somewhat too emotional Mrs. Jackson admirably discharged."[65]

[64] Jackson, *A Century of Dishonor*, pp. 29, 31.
[65] Allan Nevins, "Helen Hunt Jackson, Sentimentalist vs. Realist," *American Scholar*,

Mrs. Jackson's writings on the Indians brought her public fame, and in 1883 she was appointed to serve with Abbot Kinney on a special commission to investigate the condition of the Mission Indians in California. The report, written largely by Mrs. Jackson, and submitted on July 13, 1883, was a strong but matter-of-fact statement of the crucial situation among these neglected Indians and a series of proposals to correct the patent injustices.[66]

Helen Hunt Jackson was not yet finished. She turned her hand finally to a fictionalized treatment of the California Indian story, *Ramona*, which appeared in 1884. The novel, despite the fact that it was severely criticized for its literary weaknesses, enjoyed more popular success than *A Century of Dishonor*, although it never quite fulfilled its author's hope that it would be another *Uncle Tom's Cabin* in the drive for racial justice. But the strain of her crusade had been too much. Mrs. Jackson died in Colorado Springs in August, 1885, keeping up her concern for the Indians to the very last. A few days before her death she wrote to President Cleveland:

> From my deathbed I send you a message of heartfelt thanks for what you have already done for the Indians. I ask you to read my "Century of Dishonor." I am dying happier for the belief I have that it is your hand that is destined to strike the first steady blow toward lifting this burden of infamy from our country and righting the wrongs of the Indian race.[67]

X (Summer, 1941), 270, 285. Theodore Roosevelt, *The Winning of the West* (New York, 1889), I, 257–64, has a biting criticism of *A Century of Dishonor*: "The purpose of the book is excellent, but the spirit in which it is written cannot be called even technically honest. As a polemic, it is possible that it did not do harm (though the effect of even a polemic is marred by hysterical indifference to facts). As a history it would be beneath criticism, were it not that the high character of the author and her excellent literary work in other directions have given it a fictitious value and made it much quoted by the large class of amiable but maudlin fanatics concerning whom it may be said that the excellence of their intentions but indifferently atones for the invariable folly and ill effect of their actions. It is not too much to say that the book is thoroughly untrustworthy from cover to cover, and that not a single statement it contains should be accepted without independent proof; for even those that are not absolutely false are often as bad on account of so much of the truth having been suppressed."

[66] The report is reprinted in *Senate Executive Document* No. 49, 48 Congress, 1 session, serial 2162, pp. 7–37, and in subsequent Senate reports. In abbreviated form it was circulated as a pamphlet, *Report of Mrs. Helen Hunt Jackson and Abbot Kinney on the Mission Indians in 1883* (Boston, 1887).

[67] Letter dated August 8, 1885, quoted in Odell, *Helen Hunt Jackson*, p. 219.

With her recitation of wrongs, Helen Hunt Jackson looked to the past rather than to the future, and her death, just as the great thrust in Indian reform was starting, meant that, except for the Mission Indians, she did not become a part of the positive movement for reform. But the title of her book, if not its substance, stuck in men's minds, and her name became irrevocably associated with nineteenth-century Indian reform.[68]

The humanitarian Indian reformers enjoyed a near unanimity. To be sure, they were faced by western sentiment expressed by men like Senators Plumb and Teller, who claimed that easterners were unacquainted with the Indians and offered impractical solutions to problems they did not really understand, but there was little counterreform activity on the part of eastern philanthropists. The notable exception was Dr. Thomas A. Bland, who began his reform career as the associate of Alfred B. Meacham in the 1870's. Meacham and Bland in the early pages of their publication, *The Council Fire*, did not depart materially from the programs that were so enthusiastically promoted by the new reform organizations. Even when Bland succeeded to full control of the journal on Meacham's death early in 1882, he did not appear to be in opposition to the main currents of Indian reform. *The Council Fire* reported favorably on the 1882 petition of the Women's National Indian Association and strongly sympathized with Dawes's support of the petition against the western senators. The editor welcomed the formation of the Indian Rights Association and other reform organizations and offered them the columns of *The Council Fire* for communicating with each other and with the general public. The allotment of land in severalty to the Indians, a key proposal of the reformers, was also agreed to in principle, and the journal supported the Coke Bill, which safeguarded the rights of the Indians by providing for approval of two-thirds of the adult male Indians before a reservation could be divided up.[69]

[68] Tributes of the reformers to Helen Hunt Jackson appear in *Lake Mohonk Conference Proceedings*, 1885, pp. 68–71.

[69] *The Council Fire*, VI (September, 1883), 121–22; (October, 1883), 137–38; V (March, 1882), 88–92; VI (June, 1883), 84; VII (January, 1884), 7.

But soon Bland parted company with the rest of the reformers. In November, 1885, he organized the National Indian Defence Association and gathered supporters in the East, who took a conservative stance on the elimination of Indian ways, and among the chiefs and squaw men on the reservations, who held fast to the old ways which tended to benefit them. The National Indian Defence Association hoped to slow down if not stop the movement for land in severalty and for citizenship. It argued that the immediate dissolution of the tribal relations would be an impediment to the civilization of the Indians, that individual allotments would motivate the Indians to part with their holdings, and that while education might help the next generation, it could not solve the problems of the present one.[70] Bland and his friends actively promoted their views in Washington and in the press and appeared to have some influence in high places.

The Indian Rights Association fought strongly against that influence, insisting upon the view of Indian policy espoused by the Lake Mohonk reformers. When President Cleveland, in a meeting with Charles C. Painter, asked whether the Indian Rights Association might not reach an understanding with the Indian Defence Association, Painter answered bluntly: "No Sir! Our views of the policy to be pursued are diametrically opposite. . . . we are entirely opposed to the ideas of that Association. It seems to me as if they are defending the Indian's right to be an Indian, and would perpetuate the conditions which must force him to remain Indian."[71] In a long letter printed in the *Boston Herald* on December 27, 1886, and then circulated in pamphlet form, Herbert Welsh made the same sort of analysis of the "irreconcilable difference of opinion" that separated Dr. Bland and his association from Senator Dawes and "other prominent defenders of Indian rights":

> Dr. Bland's efforts have been directed toward keeping the Indian as he is, his tribal relations untouched, his reservations intact; and in opposing the sale of his unused lands, upon no matter how equitable conditions, for white settlement. . . . Senator Dawes and the Indian

[70] *Preamble, Platform, and Constitution of the National Indian Defence Association* (Washington, 1885).

[71] Charles C. Painter to Herbert Welsh, January 22, 1887, in Indian Rights Association Correspondence, Welsh Collection, Historical Society of Pennsylvania. See also Painter to Welsh, January 8, 1886, and February 9, 1887, *ibid.*

Rights Association, on the other hand, believe that such a theory is prejudicial to the best interests of the Indians, and even were it not so that it is wholly impracticable, that the settlement of the Indian question, in view of the uncontrollable pressure of white civilization upon the reservations, can only be reached through a careful, wise and equitable adjustment of the rights and needs of the white man and of the Indian; that under fair conditions the Indian should be persuaded to sell unused and unneeded land, upon which the white should be permitted to enter for *bona fide* settlement. It is upon this theory that such measures as the general land in severalty bill, and the Sioux bill, have been based; and upon this theory, I trust, will rest the Indian legislation of the future.[72]

Bland's attempts to defeat the severalty bill and his threat to challenge it in the courts were met by accusations that he was in the pay of the chiefs who opposed the reforms.[73]

Bland's views, if not his methods, look better in the perspective of time than many of those of the united humanitarian reformers, who in the 1880's regarded the criticisms of the National Indian Defence Association as little more than the nipping of a dog at their heels. "Vituperation from that source," Senator Dawes declared in 1887, "is considered by all acquainted with it as a certificate of fidelity to public trust."[74]

It is clear that the important Indian reformers of the late nineteenth century were not, as they have sometimes been depicted, a small, peripheral group of men and women, who by clever machinations and unjustified propaganda foisted a program of reform upon Congress and

[72] Herbert Welsh, *The Indian Problem: Secretary Welsh of the Indian Rights Association Reviews and Criticises Dr. Bland's Recent Statements—Dr. Sunderland a Self-Confessed Novice* (Philadelphia, 1886), p. 6.
[73] See one-page flyer of the Indian Rights Association, "Friendship That Asks for Pay: Pretended Friends of the Indians and Their Methods," reprinting an article from the *New York Tribune*, March 13, 1887; Frank Wood to Dawes, December 23, 1886, and T. H. Tibbles to Dawes, March 16, 1887, in Dawes Papers, Library of Congress. A reasonable statement of Bland's opposition to the Dawes Severalty Act is "The New Indian Policy: Land in Severalty," *The American*, XIV (May 21, 1887), 73–74.
[74] Dawes to John J. Janney, April 29, 1887, Dawes Papers, Letter Book, p. 139.

the Indian service.[75] Neither the men nor their impact can be understood in this narrow perspective. Rather, they represented or reflected a powerful and predominant segment of Protestant church membership, and thereby of late nineteenth-century American society. When they spoke, they spoke for a large majority of the nation, expressing views that were widely held, consciously or unconsciously. They were the chief channel through which this Americanism came to bear upon the Indians.[76]

It was the fate of the Indians that the solution of the "Indian problem," which had troubled the conscience of many Americans throughout the nineteenth century, should have been formulated at the end of the century when such a group was in command. The friends of the Indian set about with good intentions to stamp out Indianness altogether and to substitute for it a uniform Americanness; to destroy all remnants of corporate existence or tribalism and to replace them with an absolute rugged individualism that was foreign to the traditions and to the hearts of the Indian peoples.

[75] This is the view expressed in George E. Hyde, *A Sioux Chronicle* (Norman, 1956). See his chapter, "The Brethren," pp. 145–63.
[76] The religious men and women who met each year at Lake Mohonk to plot the course of Indian policy represented conservative lines of evangelicalism. They emphasized private elements in their tradition—the emphasis upon the conversion and salvation of the individual. The growing social movements in American Protestantism that appeared in response to the problems of industrialization and urbanization were little represented. Of the leaders in humanitarian Indian reform in the 1880's and 1890's, only Lyman Abbott was a notable figure in the movement we label the "Social Gospel." For a discussion of "Private" Protestantism and "Public" Protestantism, see Marty, *Righteous Empire*, p. 179.

CHAPTER 6

RESERVATION PROJECTS OF THE REFORMERS

For many years the whites of Dakota have sought to cut a great highway for civilization through the heart of the Sioux reserve, so that easy communication might be established between eastern and western Dakota, and Indian lands, practically unused, might be opened to white settlement. It was to the highest interests of both whites and Indians that this should be done—if done wisely and fairly. . . . [The reformers] saw clearly that sooner or later the opening of the reserve must be devoted to making the changes contribute to the Indians' advancement. The reservation could not be permitted permanently to block progress, and the Indian could not be allowed to rest in an isolation which kept him from contact with civilization, and nurtured savagery.

—HERBERT WELSH in 1891

⚙⚙⚙⚙⚙⚙⚙

The reformers seized upon any issue that promised to advance their vision of justice and well-being for the Indians, setting themselves in opposition to men they considered ready and willing to sacrifice Indian rights for selfish private gain. Thus they fought earnestly for reservation policies that they believed would protect the Indians' title to limited land holdings on which the tribesmen could then be hastened along the white man's road. In the 1880's two causes attracted their special attention: the reduction of the Great Sioux Reserve in Dakota and the establishment of legally guaranteed reservations for the Mission Indians of California. For much of the decade, these matters were joined with the general allotment bill as the principal legislative program of the Indian rights organizations.

169

The Great Sioux Reserve was the most blatant case of agitation to reduce large reservations as a humanitarian measure and to force the Indians into an economic and social pattern acceptable to the whites. Driven by the fear that if the Indians did not agree to give up some of their holdings for fair compensation they were likely to lose them all without recompense, the reformers led the movement to cut down the reservation held by the Teton Sioux in Dakota.[1]

The Great Sioux Reserve, stretching from the Missouri River to the western boundary of Dakota, had been set off for the Indians in the treaty of 1868. In that year, the government, after two years of incessant fighting to keep open the Bozeman Trail from the Platte through the Powder River valley to the gold fields of Montana, capitulated to the Indians, withdrew from the string of little military posts along the road, and guaranteed the Powder River country as hunting grounds for the tribes. But the treaty also set up new boundaries for the Sioux reservation and won agreement from the chiefs to settle down there, little inclined as they were toward the civilization program that reservation life was intended to promote. Provisions were made, during a limited period, for schools, teachers, blacksmiths, farmers, physicians, and sundry supplies. Individuals who wished to commence farming were permitted to select 320 acres from the common holdings and withdraw them for private use. Then as an assurance that no further limitations on their land claims would be forced upon them, Article 12 of the treaty specified that no future cession of any part of the reservation held in common would be valid until signed by at least three-fourths of the adult male Indians occupying or interested in it.[2]

It was not long before the discovery of gold in the Black Hills in the southwestern portion of the Sioux reserve upset the 1868 arrangements. Whites swarmed into the area, eager for gold, and the government found it difficult to live up to its pledges to guarantee the reservation for the Sioux. There soon began the familiar tactics of attempting to persuade the Indians to cede the coveted section. A commission headed by Senator William B. Allison of Iowa was appointed on June 18, 1875, to treat with the Sioux for the relinquishing of the Black Hills,

[1] An excellent brief account, which emphasizes the effect on the Sioux, is Robert M. Utley, *The Last Days of the Sioux Nation* (New Haven, 1963), pp. 40–59. A somewhat more detailed account is Olson, *Red Cloud and the Sioux Problem*, pp. 286–319.

[2] Kappler, *Indian Affairs: Laws and Treaties*, II, 998–1003.

but its meetings with the Indians accomplished nothing, and it ended its report with the recommendation that Congress should simply fix a fair price for the Black Hills and present the matter to the Indians "as a finality."[3]

After the defeat of Custer, while the army was still engaged against the hostiles, Congress decided on such an ultimatum. On August 15, 1876, it directed that the Indians were to receive no further subsistence unless they relinquished all claims to land outside the 1868 reserve and all of that reservation lying west of the 103^d meridian (an area including the Black Hills).[4] The President appointed a commission to carry this word to the Sioux. The commission—headed by George W. Manypenny, former Commissioner of Indian Affairs, and including among others Newton Edmunds, one-time governor of Dakota Territory, and Bishop Henry B. Whipple, the old reformer—met with the Indians at the Red Cloud Agency in early September. Here Manypenny laid down the government's terms, and other commissioners lectured the Indians about the paths to civilization. Although it seems clear from the speeches of the Indians at the signing that they did not fully understand the import of the agreement, the chiefs marked their X's, and the scene was repeated at each of the agencies. "We finished our labors in the Indian country," the commissioners said, "with our hearts full of gratitude to God, who had guarded and protected us, and had directed our labors to a successful issue." They had won the cession of the Black Hills, but only by ignoring Article 12 of the treaty of 1868. They had settled for the signatures of the chiefs and headmen of each tribe, but this seemed not to trouble the good men on the commission. They concluded their report with a fine-sounding plea for good faith and justice.[5]

The commission's report was enthusiastically received by the Board

[3] "Report of the Commission Appointed to Treat with the Sioux Indians for the Relinquishment of the Black Hills," Report of the Commissioner of Indian Affairs, 1875, in serial 1680, pp. 686–702. The quotation is from page 701.

[4] United States Statutes at Large, XIX, 192.

[5] The commission's report, dated December 18, 1876, is in Senate Executive Document No. 9, 44 Congress, 2 session, serial 1718. The document also includes the journal of proceedings. The agreement, ratified by Congress on February 28, 1877, is in United States Statutes at Large, XIX, 254–64. Note that the report includes a long argument against transfer of the Indian service to the War Department. This was quite in keeping with Manypenny's agitation against the army's conduct of Indian affairs.

of Indian Commissioners. The report, the Board said, "so truthfully reflects the firm convictions of the members of this board, that we would, if possible, emphasize those views by adopting them as our own," and it included a copy of the commission's report in its report for the year. This blindness of the commission and of the board to the basic disregard of the treaty stipulations calling for consent of the Indians is hard to understand, yet so strong was their belief in the necessity of the change of the Indians into counterparts of white farmers, that they vividly saw past wrongs but did not notice the ones they themselves were perpetrating. In good faith the Board of Indian Commissioners concluded its praise of the commission's work:

> We would, if possible, have the public conscience aroused to a full comprehension of the utter want of good faith, the oft-repeated violations of the most sacred promises and agreements, which have characterized the intercourse of this nation with its helpless wards.
>
> Let us hope, for the sake of our common humanity, for the honor of the nineteenth century, the credit of Christianity, and our boasted civilization, that a better day is about to dawn upon this unfortunate race, and that justice, tardy though it be, is to be recognized in our future dealings with them.[6]

The whites' land hunger was not sated by the large bite into the Sioux homelands made by the agreement of 1876. By the early 1880's, new pressures had built up along the borders of the reservation that were all but irresistible. The Chicago and Northwestern Railroad had reached Pierre, and the Chicago, Milwaukee, and St. Paul had built as far as Chamberlain, one hundred miles south on the Missouri. Here they were stopped in their drive to reach the Black Hills beyond, and it seemed to Dakota promoters as though civilization had come to a halt, blocked by the Great Sioux Reserve to the west. On August 7, 1882, at the instigation of Richard F. Pettigrew, Dakota delegate in Congress, a rider to the sundry civil appropriations bill provided for negotiations with the Sioux in order to modify existing treaties.[7] To

---

[6] *Report of the Board of Indian Commissioners*, 1876, p. 4.
[7] *United States Statutes at Large*, XXII, 328.

carry out this mandate Secretary of the Interior Henry M. Teller named a commission headed by Newton Edmunds, by now an experienced Indian negotiator, and comprising Peter Shannon, one-time chief justice of the Dakota territorial supreme court, and James H. Teller, of Cleveland, Ohio, his own brother. Samuel D. Hinman, a missionary who had often participated in councils with the Sioux, served as interpreter.[8]

The Edmunds commission presented to the Indians an agreement which it had already prepared. The document called for the cession of reservation lands between the White and Cheyenne rivers and for the lands north of the Cheyenne and west of the 102^d meridian—altogether some eleven million acres, including a wide corridor from the Missouri River to the Black Hills. What was left was to be divided into five separate reservations, one for each of the already established agencies— Standing Rock, Cheyenne River, Lower Brulé, Rosebud, and Pine Ridge. In return, each head of a family was to be allowed to choose a 320-acre tract, plus 80 acres for each minor child. Those who made a selection of land were to receive a cow and a team of oxen. And the government agreed to provide 25,000 cows and 1,000 bulls (all carrying the brand of the Indian Department and not to be sold or slaughtered without permission) as a foundation herd to be divided among the reservations according to population.[9] By cajolery and threats the commission gathered the signatures of a number of chiefs and headmen, and disregarding the requirement that cessions of land required approval of three-fourths of the adult males, submitted the agreement as an accomplished fact. Secretary Teller sent it to the President to be forwarded to Congress for ratification with the remark that he considered it "favorable alike to the Indians and the Government."[10]

Outcries of protest immediately arose from the Indians, who claimed with good cause that they had been victimized, and from the newly organized Indian Rights Asssociation and other humanitarian friends of the Indians, who pointed to the failure to attain the necessary consent of the Sioux.[11] Senator Dawes was able to block the measure, and

[8] Documents on the formation of the commission as well as its report are in *Senate Executive Document* No. 70, 48 Congress, 1 session, serial 2165.
[9] The agreements are printed *ibid.*, pp. 34–41.
[10] Teller to the President, February 1, 1883, *ibid.*, p. 31.
[11] See letters of Senator Dawes to Teller, *ibid.*, part 2.

the commission was sent back for more signatures. The second round, entrusted to Hinman, was little more successful than the first, and Congress would not approve the agreement.

The reformers now entered the picture in full force; here was a cause in which they could fight for Indian rights and justice and at the same time promote the advance of civilization. The Indian Rights Association, successsful in its drive to defeat the Edmunds agreement, determined to push the matter to the fullest. In May, 1883, Herbert Welsh visited the Sioux at the Dakota agencies and produced a lengthy report which roundly condemned the terms of the Edmunds agreement and the methods of the commission.[12]

Welsh was not alone in his investigation. The Board of Indian Commissioners sent two of its members, Albert K. Smiley and E. Whittlesey, to visit the Sioux agencies during the same summer to study "the condition of the several Sioux tribes and their attitude towards the proposed reduction of their reservation."[13] And they were joined in Dakota by representatives of missionary boards who kept close tab on the Sioux situation because of their mission establishments among those Indians. On June 1, Welsh, the two members of the Board of Indian Commissioners, and a group of missionaries met at the Santee Agency in Nebraska to discuss the 1882 agreement. A committee of missionaries was appointed, with Bishop William H. Hare as chairman, to draw up a statement expressing the views of the meeting, and the statement which the committee brought back to the conference on June 2 was fully discussed and then adopted.

> A proposition having been submitted to the Sioux Indians for the cession of a portion of their lands, the undersigned missionaries among these Indians feel called upon to make the following statement, for the enlightenment of the Indians who look to them for counsel, and for the information of their white friends, neighbors, and fellow citizens.
>
> The undersigned advocate the division, in any just way, of the Great Sioux Reservation into a number of separate reserves for the

[12] Herbert Welsh, *Report of a Visit to the Great Sioux Reserve, Dakota, Made During the Months of May and June, 1883, in Behalf of the Indian Rights Association* (Philadelphia, 1883).

[13] *Report of the Board of Indian Commissioners*, 1883, p. 3. The report of Smiley and Whittlesey is printed *ibid.*, pp. 33–38.

several tribes, and the cession, on equitable terms, of a portion of the present reservation to the United States for settlement by the whites. The reservation in its present shape and size is, in their opinion, a serious hindrance to the prosperity and welfare of the whites, and a great impediment to the civilization of the Indians. But, while holding this opinion, they think that the method of division provided for in the proposed agreement is not just, and that the consideration offered is not equitable.[14]

The statement scored the Edmunds agreement for not including *"comprehensive* provision" for taking of land in severalty and the development of farming, by which means the Indians could get sure possession of their land, and pointed out that in fact the agreement would dispossess many worthy Indians of their farms and homes. The terms of the cession the missionaries thought inequitable because the cows and teams of oxen provided families were already due under the treaty of 1868, the 26,000 cattle offered in payment were worth far less than the land to be ceded, there were no provisions for the creation of a specific education and civilization fund, and no guarantees were included to prevent settlers from wresting away from the missionaries the lands and improvements they held on the reservation. "The undersigned deeply regret," the statement concluded, "that they may seem to their fellow citizens to play the part of 'obstructives.' In fact, they desire most earnestly that opening up of the country which the popular voice calls for. They believe that the effects in the proposed agreement put this consummation in peril. They would cordially use their influence among the Indians in favor of an equitable proposition, and they believe that such a proposition could be promptly carried to a successful issue."[15]

Welsh eagerly accepted this position, and his report reinforced the missionaries' statement. He was especially outspoken on the pressure that had been used to force the reluctant Indians to sign. The young Indian Rights Association for whom he spoke, in fact, forged ahead energetically to accomplish the end in view. In this they were strongly seconded by the Lake Mohonk Conference, which met in October,

[14] *Ibid.*, p. 34.
[15] *Ibid.*, pp. 34–35.

1883. The first topic on the agenda, as was fitting in the light of the part the Santee Agency meeting had played in Smiley's determination to call the conference, was the Sioux agreement, and the conference re-iterated in formal resolutions what Welsh and the others had con-cluded from their visits. The Board of Indian Commissioners at its January meeting with the representatives of the missionary boards adopted another resolution of the same tenor.[16]

These reform groups soon got official support for their position from Senator Dawes. When the Senate refused to approve the Edmunds commission agreement, largely at Dawes's insistence, it appointed a select committee with Dawes as its chairman to investigate the Sioux reservation situation. Dawes's committee visited all the Sioux agencies, interviewed Indians and agency personnel, and interrogated as well the Edmunds commission. Its condemnation of the commission was, if anything, stronger than that of Welsh and the missionaries, with whose general line of argument it substantially agreed.[17] The report declared:

> The conclusions of the committee are that at the present time the Sioux Nation is practically unanimous in its opposition to this pro-posed agreement. Indeed the committee did not find, among all these Indians at the different agencies, and called into council by their agents, more than one or two Indians whose opposition to this agreement is not now outspoken and decided.... Of the few Indians who signed the agreement most of them claimed that they did not understand it at the time. Quite a number of them assert that they were directly misled. Some of them claimed that they were forced to sign the agreement under threats that they would be removed to the Indian Territory; others stated that they were informed that the agreement already had a sufficient number of names, and unless they joined in assenting to it they would be "left out in the cold."[18]

Many Indians, the committee found, thought that the agreement merely divided up the Great Sioux Reserve into separate reservations

[16] *Report of the Indian Rights Association*, 1883, pp. 13–14; *Lake Mohonk Con-ference Proceedings*, 1883, pp. 4–8; *Report of the Board of Indian Commissioners*, 1883, pp. 68–69.

[17] The Dawes committee report, dated March 7, 1884, is in *Senate Report* No. 283, 48 Congress, 1 session, serial 2174.

[18] *Ibid.*, p. v.

and did not realize that half the reserve was to be ceded to the United States for homesteading. Nor did they appreciate that the 26,000 cattle were intended as payment for the land cession but rather considered them in the light of a gratuity. Dawes spoke harshly of the commission's disregard of treaty obligations in failing to get the honest approval of the necessary Indian majority, argued that payment only in livestock was inappropriate for the Indians in their present circumstances, and in the end firmly recommended that Congress should not approve the agreement in its present form.

But Dawes was no more in favor of the status quo of the Sioux in Dakota than were Welsh and his friends. He much favored cutting up the large reservation and opening part of it to white settlement if it could be done without violating treaty stipulations, and he hoped to convert what he considered the useless and unnecessary lands into a permanent fund, whose annual income could be devoted to "the civilization, education, and advancement in agriculture and other self-supporting pursuits" for the Sioux.[19]

Dawes submitted with the report of his select committee a bill which incorporated the changes he advocated.[20] The main point of the bill was the establishment of the permanent fund Dawes had in mind. It was to total one million dollars and be held in the Treasury to the credit of the Indians at 5 per cent interest, one half of the income to be used for the promotion of "industrial and other suitable education" and the other half in whatever way the Secretary of the Interior would judge best for the advancement of the Indians "in civilization and self-support." All the land acquired by the bill was to be disposed of under existing homestead acts, except that for land so taken the settler was to pay fifty cents an acre, in four equal annual payments. The money thus received was to reimburse the government for the one million dollar permanent fund, for the purchase of stock for the Indians to encourage them in herding (up to 26,000 head), and to pay the expenses of the government in administering the act. Thus, as Dawes noted, the whole process would ultimately cost nothing to the government, which would in fact be free thereafter of annual appropriations for the welfare of the Sioux.

[19] *Ibid.*, p. ix.
[20] Senate bill 1755, 48 Congress, 1 session.

The bands were to receive a patent in fee for the reduced separate reservations, although the lands were to be held in trust by the United States for twenty-five years. Beyond this, however, the President was authorized to issue allotments in severalty to the Indians who seemed to him to be ready for them (according to provisions similar to those incorporated into the Dawes Act of February 8, 1887), and patents for such individual allotments were to override those granted to the tribe for lands held in common. The Indians residing on the lands to be ceded were allowed to take their allotments there, and the lands of the missionary societies were guaranteed to them. The education benefits of the treaty of 1868 were to be continued for twenty years. Finally, the act provided explicitly that the law would be null and void without the consent of three-fourths of the Indian men.

The Dawes committee was confident that the assent of the Indians could be obtained to this measure, that the bill would obtain all the benefits to the whites sought in the earlier agreement of the Edmunds commission, while at the same time be of "the greatest benefit to the Indians."

The passage of this bill, known as "Senator Dawes's Sioux Bill," became one of the primary objectives of the reform groups. The Indian Rights Association, warmly supporting the bill, declared that it was open to "none of the objections raised to the terms of the original Sioux Agreement, but embodies the wishes of the friends of the Indians; it does justice to both parties and is desirable for both whites and Indians."[21] In order to promote the measure, Welsh prepared an abstract of the bill together with arguments in favor of its passage, which he widely circulated as a means of stirring up public sentiment that would influence Congress. He pointed first to the benefits to the whites, for the cession would furnish a "magnificent highway" between "the civilization of Eastern and Western Dakota," and thus provide a "grand step forward in the march of prosperity" for the people of Dakota Territory. But second, in an argument "of equal weight," he noted that the bill would provide "ample justice for the Sioux Indians" and "swell the number of that class among them which is looking and striving toward civilization."[22] The Board of Indian Commissioners urged the

21 *Report of the Indian Rights Association,* 1884, pp. 14–15.
22 *Lake Mohonk Conference Proceedings,* 1884, pp. 17–19.

prompt passage of the bill; and the Lake Mohonk Conference heartily approved of the bill, proferred its thanks to Senator Dawes, and commended the bill to all friends of the Indians.[23]

Like other pieces of legislation promoted by the Indian reformers, Dawes's Sioux bill had little trouble in the Senate; it was passed in the Forty-eighth Congress on April 16, 1884, and when reintroduced in the Forty-ninth Congress on December 8, 1885, it passed again on February 1, 1886.[24] But it bogged down in the House, and the reformers exerted all their efforts to gain its passage.[25] The year 1886 saw a peak of activity, as the Sioux bill was joined with the land-in-severalty bill and a bill to provide relief for the Mission Indians in California as the essential package of legislation demanded by the humanitarians. They were especially distressed by the failure of the House to take up the measures after they had passed the Senate; days were set on the House calendar for consideration of the Indian bills at the end of May, 1886, only to be pushed aside at the last minute by other matters.[26] Although the general allotment bill was passed in early 1887, the other two measures were again put off, and the reformers continued to direct attention to them.[27]

The reformers were sincere in their belief that allotments in severalty

[23] *Report of the Board of Indian Commissioners*, 1884, p. 11; *Lake Mohonk Conference Proceedings*, 1884, p. 16. Secretary Teller urged the passage of the measure in Report of the Secretary of the Interior, 1884, in serial 2286, p. xiii.

[24] *Senate Journal*, 48 Congress, 1 session, serial 2161, p. 541; *Senate Journal*, 49 Congress, 1 session, serial 2332, pp. 49, 232–33.

[25] *Report of the Indian Rights Association*, 1885, pp. 13–14; *Report of the Board of Indian Commissioners*, 1886, p. 4; *Lake Mohonk Conference Proceedings*, 1886, p. 47. The importance of the measure in the minds of its promoters can be seen in a letter of Senator Dawes to Herbert Welsh, April 6, 1886: "I think you will be very much shorn of your influence if you should accept the office of commissioner from Mr. Cleveland. You can do a great deal in Dakota helping along the bill if you hold no official position. I think you will be indispensable, but I do not want to see your locks shorn. There are a great many things you can wisely do if you are not responsible to the government. By taking office you may be committed to methods you would not adopt were you perfectly free. I say this in the full belief, however, that the government is with us in the wish to have the bill accepted. I have no fear of President Cleveland vetoing the bill." Indian Rights Association Papers, Box 1, Historical Society of Pennsylvania.

[26] For two strong statements on this situation, see Welsh's statement in *The Helplessness of Indians before the Law; with an Outline of Proposed Legislation* (Philadelphia, 1886), and Charles C. Painter's statement in *Oleomargarine versus the Indian* (Philadelphia, 1886), both pamphlets published by the Indian Rights Association. The association also issued on February 23, 1886, an untitled leaflet promoting the Sioux bill.

[27] See *Report of the Indian Rights Association*, 1886, p. 10; *ibid.*, 1887, p. 7.

for agricultural purposes were essential for the welfare and civilization of the Indians and that reduction of reservation size would move them necessarily toward the desired goal. But as men attuned to their age, they were also eager for the advance of white society and its well-being. In the burgeoning expansion of post-Civil War America, these men could not envisage rights of the Indians that could obstruct the onward march of American development and prosperity. To their minds this progress was not only a good thing but was in fact inevitable; their purpose was to see that in the process the Indians were treated justly and compensated equitably for the land they would have to give up. Commissioners Smiley and Whittlesey, returning from the Sioux reservation in 1883, reported, for example: "Everywhere in Dakota we saw evidences of rapid growth. New farms opened, new towns built, and new settlers moving in. It is very clear that the Dakota Indians cannot long hold the vast reservation which they now claim."[28] Welsh called the railroads poised to build across the reservation "the forerunners of a civilization, which, sooner or later, will make its way through the reservation." He considered it of the greatest importance that "the irruption of civilization into Indian lands should be lawful, just, and restrained by wise conditions." There was a tone of urgency in what he wrote. "*We cannot stop the legitimate advance of emigration and civilization if we would,*" he said, "*and, we add most emphatically, we would not if we could*; but, on the other hand, we strenuously oppose unlawful violent or ill-advised acquisition of Indian lands whether by the Government or individuals." It is easy to understand how a man of this frame of mind pushed so desperately for the Sioux bill, which he hoped would bring order, before the unchecked pressures of the whites could wreak havoc on the Indian lands. "The waves of an importunate civilization that cannot long be either staid or stopped, at the bidding of any man," Welsh concluded, "are breaking incessantly upon the border of the Great Reservation. It is the deep conviction of the Indian Rights Association that sound policy now demands the opening of a lawful channel for the advance of this mighty tide. Hesitation at the present critical time invites a possible catastrophe."[29]

The House at last bowed to the pressure. On April 30, 1888, Dawes's

[28] *Report of the Board of Indian Commissioners*, 1883, p. 38.
[29] Indian Rights Association leaflet, February 23, 1886.

measure became law in substantially its original form.[30] Under its provisions Secretary of the Interior William F. Vilas appointed a commission to submit the act to the various bands of Sioux in order to get their
consent. This time there was to be no misleading the Indians into signing a document they did not understand. The agents were to draw up
lists of Indian men, and when these men were assembled at each
agency, the act was to be read and interpreted to them and "its provisions fully, fairly, and plainly explained so as to be understood by
them." Enough copies of the act together with a colored map showing
the existing reservation and proposed changes were to be provided so
that each Indian eligible to vote could have a copy. To supplement this
official document, the Indian Rights Association issued an extract of
the law in the Dakota language and distributed it freely to the Indians.
Each Indian was to sign either the act or a document signifying rejection—and, to allow no mistakes, the act was to be printed in black
and the rejection document in red. Stenographers were to take down
all the proceedings. There was, however, to be no negotiation; the
commissioners were to inform the Indians that Congress had drawn
up the agreement with care and that the President after wise scrutiny
had approved it and that it embodied "the desire and purpose of the
Government of the United States for the advancement and civilization" of the Sioux. The commissioners, moreover, were to impress upon
the Indians the fact that new conditions made the old reservation no
longer viable and that if they did not accept the "generous and beneficent" arrangements now proposed by Congress, their future would be
"problematical and uncertain."[31]

To head the commission, Vilas appointed Captain Richard Henry
Pratt, head of the Carlisle Indian School and the most radical and uncompromising of the reformers in his advocacy of civilization and assimilation of the Indians. With him, to serve as interpreter, was the
Reverend William J. Cleveland, a missionary of long experience among
the Sioux. The third member of the commission was Judge John V.
Wright of Tennessee.

The Pratt commission made little headway against the intransigence

---

[30] *United States Statutes at Large*, XXV, 94–104.
[31] Instructions of Vilas to commissioners, July 9, 1888, in *Senate Executive Document*
No. 17, 50 Congress, 2 session, serial 2610, pp. 30–33.

of the Indians, who united in opposition to the new agreement. Having been severely burned before, the Sioux were now careful to stay far away from the fire. Only a few could be induced to give their approval; many refused even to accept the copies of the act and the map, and large numbers would sign no document, not even the one indicating rejection of the proposal. Distrust about the intentions of the commission was everywhere evident, and deep fear pervaded the Indian councils. After a month of palaver at Standing Rock Agency, only twenty-two signatures were secured in favor of the act out of the agent's count of nearly eleven hundred eligible voters. At Crow Creek and Lower Brulé agencies there was some success, but the state of mind at Cheyenne River, Rosebud, and Pine Ridge indicated the uselessness of proceeding there to get assent to the reduction of the reserve.[32]

At this impasse Captain Pratt hastened to Madison, Wisconsin, to confer with Vilas, and the decision was made to convene a special council of chiefs and headmen with a view toward ascertaining if there was any hope of achieving success and to determine what changes in the proposal might bring assent. The conference in September at Lower Brulé strengthened the conviction that no substantial number of signatures could be obtained. Whereupon arrangements were made for the tribal leaders to travel to Washington for a conference with the government officials, in the hope that the Indians' objections might be overcome through further explanations and negotiations. Although there was an underlying resistance to surrendering any of the reservation, the question of price and terms of payment seemed open to negotiation. Vilas, after talking to the President and the chairmen of the Indian committees of the Senate and the House, drew up a set of amendments which he presented to the delegation. Principally he proposed to double the permanent fund to two million dollars and to charge the homesteaders one dollar per acre for the first three years, seventy-five cents for the next two years, and fifty cents thereafter.

[32] A summary account of the work of the commission is given in Report of the Secretary of the Interior, 1888, in serial 2636, pp. lvi–lxvi. The commission's full report, November 24, 1888, is in *Senate Executive Document* No. 17, 50 Congress, 2 session, serial 2610.

Although a minority of the delegation reacted favorably to the government's suggestions, the majority wanted to raise the price still more—to $1.25 an acre, clear of all expenses, placed to their credit in the Treasury with interest at five per cent. And they objected to the complicated scheme for reducing the price of the lands sold, since they feared that delays would lead to sale at the minimum price. Vilas considered this ultimatum excessive and beyond what he was willing to submit to Congress, and he sent the delegation home. The price they demanded, he wrote, would require for the small area to be ceded almost as much as was paid France for all of the Louisiana Purchase, and then only to extinguish the right of occupancy, since the fee was already theoretically in the United States. Nor did he think that large sums would benefit the Indians, for the interest would yield so much money for distribution "as to remove the incentive for their personal effort at subsistence and improvement."[33] Both Vilas and Pratt charged that the Indian delegation had been pressured by whites in Washington, no doubt Dr. Bland and his associates. "During their stay in Washington," the Pratt report noted, "these Indians were constantly beleaguered by persons, male and female, who claimed to be par excellence the friends of the Indians, that they are the especial guardians of these unhappy people, and their protectors against the oppressions and wrongs sought to be imposed upon them by the Government. Every possible argument was used to induce the Indians to reject the offers of the Government."[34] It is unlikely, however, that such advice was a deciding factor in the Indians' rejection of the government's proposals.

The Pratt commission report, submitted on November 24, 1888, was full of the reformers' views. It excoriated the nonprogressive chiefs who controlled the bands in order to keep things as they were and thus prevent the elevation of the masses. "In brief," it said, "the defeat of this act was a victory for indolence, barbarism, and degradation as against the influence of the farm, the work-shop, the schools, and the Gospel. We failed to get behind these chiefs and bring the provisions of the act to the consideration of the people in general." Nor did Pratt like the provisions in the act itself which he was asking the Indians to

[33] Report of the Secretary of the Interior, 1888, in serial 2636, p. lxv.
[34] *Senate Executive Document* No. 17, 50 Congress, 2 session, serial 2610, p. 13.

approve, for they offered "a fresh installment of means whereby the Indians may continue their life of living without work, with no additional requirements laid upon them to better their condition by their own exertions." He charged that the payment for the cession would extinguish the ambition to improve by their own exertion and do them injury instead of good. Pratt's strong attitude about what was good for the Indians can hardly have won him friends among the tribesmen with whom his commission was sent to deal, and his righteousness undoubtedly hindered the work. Pratt could not refrain from ending his report with a typical aphoristic pronouncement on the Indian:

> Any policy which brings him into the honest activity of civilization, and especially into the atmosphere of our agricultural, commercial, industrial examples, assures to him mutual, moral, and physical development into independent manhood. Any policy which prolongs the massing, inactive, herding systems continues to lead to destruction and death. It is folly to hope for substantial cure, except there be radical change in the treatment.[35]

The supporters of the program were not yet ready to give up, for the urgency of the need had increased with the passage of the Omnibus Bill in February, 1889, providing for the admission to statehood of North and South Dakota in November. The Indian appropriation bill, passed March 2, 1889, authorized a new commission to negotiate for the reduction and division of the Sioux reservation, and a separate act approved the same day set forth a new and decidedly more generous agreement which the commission proposed to the Indians for their consent.[36] The permanent fund was increased to three million dollars, and homesteaders were to pay $1.25 an acre for the first three years, seventy-five cents for the next two, and fifty cents thereafter, and the expenses of the program were no longer to be deducted from the income. Allotments in severalty were not to be undertaken on any of the reservations until favored by a majority of adult males, and the size of the allotment was raised from 160 to 320 acres. Unrelated to the main issue, but helpful in getting assent to the agreement, was a provision to pay for ponies seized by the army during the war of 1876.

[35] *Ibid.*, pp. 23, 29–30.
[36] *United States Statutes at Large*, XXV, 888–99, 1002.

For the new Sioux commission, President Harrison appointed as chairman Charles Foster, former governor of Ohio, William Warner of Missouri, national commander of the Grand Army of the Republic, and Major General George Crook. Since the first two had had no experience with Indians, the leadership of the group fell naturally to Crook, who used his long experience and his knowledge of Indian temperament and ways to succeed where previous commissions had failed.[37] The Sioux, united again under tribal leaders, had agreed to resist all pressures, and even Crook was tempted to look upon the whole work as hopeless. But little by little the Indians' will to resist was broken down. The commission put on feasts for the Indians, permitted tribal dances that had long been proscribed, and in general put the Sioux at ease. There seemed to be no hurry to force the agreement upon the Indians and none of the overt threats that had marked previous encounters. Yet the members of the commission were persistent in carrying out the government's designs, for they, like the reformers generally, were convinced that if the Sioux could not be induced to accept the relatively generous terms of the new proposal, they might in the end be forced to accept less. Crook spoke bluntly to the Indians:

> Last year when you refused to accept that bill, Congress came very near opening this reservation anyhow. It is certain that you will never get any better terms than are offered in this bill, and the chances are that you will not get so good. And it strikes me that instead of your complaining of the past, you had better provide for the future.[38]

Ultimately the commission took to working behind the scenes. It discovered that nothing could be done in general councils, where the groups sustained the previous tribal decisions. It was necessary, therefore, to endeavor to convince individuals of the benefits that would accrue from the bill, and slowly the united front was broken. "For a time the task seemed almost hopeless," the commission reported, "but persistence prevailed and interest was awakened. As soon as the ques-

[37] The report of the Sioux commission, dated December 24, 1889, with proceedings and other related material is in *Senate Executive Document* No. 51, 51 Congress, 1 session, serial 2682.

[38] *Ibid.*, p. 172, quoted in Utley, *Last Days of the Sioux Nation*, p. 50. Utley gives an excellent account of the work of the commission in winning Sioux approval, pp. 50–54.

tion became debatable, the situation changed and success was secured."³⁹ Finally, out of 5,678 eligible to vote, 4,463 signified their approval.⁴⁰

The paradox of the reformers' position had become apparent. The Indian Rights Association had declared in 1885, in its advocacy of the Sioux bill, that "it provides for the *inevitable advance of white civilization*, and, at the same time, secures to the Indian an adequate and wise compensation for lands, to the relinquishment of which *his consent must be obtained*."⁴¹ If the inevitability of the white advance was conceded, as it was, any free consent on the part of the Indians could be only a mockery, as it turned out to be.

Crook and his associates on the commission voiced their concern about the conditions they discovered on the reservation. "The average Sioux Indian believes himself 'the ward of the Government,' " they wrote. "He recognizes no dignity in labor, or credit in 'earning his bread by the sweat of his brow.' Ten years ago it would have been easier to have taken these Indians fresh from the war-path, full of the energy of their wild life, and set them to work on farms than in their present enervated condition." The solution they saw was that of the philanthropists; it lay "in industrial and other education, in the cultivation of the soil and the raising of stock, to the end that he may become self-respecting and self-supporting." The Indian "must take his land in severalty, settle upon it, and work."⁴² In these views they were firmly supported by Secretary of the Interior John Noble. He praised the commission for its good work and declared that the Indians would be much benefited by what they had accomplished—". . . for the breaking up of this great nation of Indians into smaller parts and segregating from the national domain separate reservations for each of said parts marks a long step toward the disintegration of their tribal life and will help them forward to their lands in severalty; settling down to civilized

³⁹ *Senate Executive Document* No. 51, 51 Congress, 1 session, serial 2682, p. 21.
⁴⁰ A table showing the number of eligible voters and the number signed at each agency is given *ibid.*, p. 35. Crook wrote at Pine Ridge on July 9: "Lovely day. Tuned different Indians up. Got a good many signatures by different young Indians who were made to see that they must think for themselves, and in this way it is breaking down the opposition of the old, unreconstructed chiefs." Martin F. Schmitt, ed., *General George Crook: His Autobiography* (Norman, 1946), p. 286.
⁴¹ *Report of the Indian Rights Association*, 1885, p. 14. Emphasis added.
⁴² *Senate Executive Document* No. 51, 51 Congress, 1 session, serial 2682, p. 22.

habits and pursuits and earning their support by their individual daily labor."[43]

These fine commitments to ultimate goals, unfortunately, did not solve immediate problems on the Sioux reservation, and the Sioux commission made a number of recommendations for improving conditions that were supported by the executive branch. But Congress could not be forced, and its slash in appropriations for Indian subsistence brought a cut in rations that led the Indians to conclude that they had been tricked once again. Then on February 9, 1890, President Harrison announced the Indians' acceptance of the land agreement and opened the ceded territory to white settlement, before any of the Indians on those lands had been enabled to take out allotments. The President, to be sure, sent to Congress a draft of a bill incorporating the recommendations of the Sioux commission and asking the necessary appropriations to carry out the agreement with the Sioux, but although the Senate passed it on April 26, the House refused.[44] The Indian reform organizations took little notice. Having won the legislative enactment they wanted in the Sioux bills of 1888 and 1889, they considered their battle won and busied themselves with other matters.

While the Indian Rights Association and the other humanitarian reformers were carrying on their fight for Dawes's Sioux Bill, they did not neglect another group of Indians crying for special attention, the Mission Indians of California, "a singularly helpless race in a singularly anomalous position."[45] These Indians, gathered into the missions established by the Franciscans in the eighteenth and early nineteenth centuries, were peaceful and submissive and made considerable advance under the missionaries. After the secularization of the missions by Mexico, however, they lost much of the property that had been divided up among them and fell into a miserable condition. The coming of the Americans after the Mexican War brought a new attack upon their land holdings and thereby upon their very existence. These Indians did not have treaty relations with the United States government

[43] Report of the Secretary of the Interior, 1889, in serial 2724, p. xi.
[44] Utley, *Last Days of the Sioux Nation*, pp. 54–59.
[45] The phrase is quoted from Helen Hunt Jackson and Abbot Kinney, *Report on the Condition and Needs of the Mission Indians of California* (Washington, 1883), pp. 6–7.

to give them special protection. Indeed, when negotiations were entered into with them in 1851, the treaties signed were never confirmed by the Senate, a special committee of which decided that the United States in acquiring possession of the territory from Mexico succeeded to all rights in the soil and that, as the Indians had no rights in the land, the United States was under no obligation to treat with them for the extinguishment of title.[46]

As reform sentiment grew after the Civil War, the dispossession of the Mission Indians became a concern of the humanitarians and of the Indian Office. The Board of Indian Commissioners in 1871 asserted that the Indians were "slaves in all but name" to the rich rancheros and demanded the serious attention of the government, and it recommended that the Indians be given clear title to their lands. In 1873 the Indian Office sent out a special agent, John G. Ames, to investigate the condition of the Mission Indians. His report recommended that lands be clearly set aside for the Indians, that as far as possible individual allotments for families should be made, that schools should be provided, and that a permanent agent be appointed for them. Edward P. Smith, Commissioner of Indian Affairs, supported his recommendations, and Smith continued to urge action upon Congress with a recitation of cases in which the rights of the Indians had been disregarded, but no action was forthcoming. In 1880 the Commissioner of Indian Affairs could report only that "the condition of the Mission Indians of California becomes, yearly, more deplorable."[47]

Then came the new burst of reforming energy and the stirring up of public sentiment to demand a righting of all Indian wrongs. The Mission Indians were not forgotten. In January, 1883, Helen Hunt Jackson was appointed to investigate the condition of the Mission Indians and to make recommendations for correcting injustices. With the aid of Abbot Kinney, a Californian of sympathetic views, she submitted a report on July 13, 1883. Declaring that, with such long neglect and

[46] Report of the Commissioner of Indian Affairs, 1869, in serial 1414, pp. 457–58; Charles C. Painter, A Visit to the Mission Indians of Southern California, and Other Western Tribes (Philadelphia, 1886), p. 14. A discussion of the unratified treaties is in Harry Kelsey, "The California Indian Treaty Myth," Southern California Quarterly, LV (Fall, 1973), 225–38.

[47] Report of the Board of Indian Commissioners, 1871, pp. 9–10; Report of the Commissioner of Indian Affairs, 1873, in serial 1601, pp. 397–409; ibid., 1875, in serial 1680, pp. 511–14; ibid., 1880, in serial 1959, pp. 99–101.

multiplication of wrongs, it was no longer possible to render the Indians a full measure of justice and that what was possible was only some measure of atonement, Mrs. Jackson and Kinney made ten recommendations, which focused on confirmation of land titles to the Indians, appointments of lawyers to safeguard the Indians' rights, more schools, and agricultural and other assistance.[48] The recommendations were incorporated into a bill by the Indian Office and submitted to Congress, where it passed the Senate but was not acted upon by the House.[49] The failure of the House to act became a continuing phenomenon.

Mrs. Jackson used material from her California investigations in her popular novel *Ramona*, which romanticized the Mission Indians and dramatized their plight, but the failure of Congress to act disheartened her, and she wrote to Senator Dawes in August, 1884, "I am sick at heart, and discouraged, I see nothing more I can do, or write."[50] She was considerably cheered, however, by the fact that the Indian Rights Association took up the cause. The association's Washington agent, Charles C. Painter, visited her shortly before her death and accepted for the Indian Rights Association a "most solemn obligation" to carry on where she left off, a trust the reform group earnestly accepted. Most of this responsibility came to rest upon Painter. His first visit to the Mission Indians in 1885 left him with a conviction of their deplorable condition, but also that they had title to the land that could be vindicated in the courts.[51] In 1886 Painter traveled to California again, this time not only as the agent of the Indian Rights Association, but delegated as well by a special committee on the Mission Indians appointed by the Lake Mohonk Conference in October, 1886. His task was to

[48] Jackson and Kinney, *Report on the Condition and Needs of the Mission Indians of California*, pp. 7–13. The report is summarized in Report of the Commissioner of Indian Affairs, 1883, in serial 2191, pp. 36–37. It furnished the basis for the program of the reformers in regard to the Mission Indians.
[49] The bill and Indian Commissioner Price's support of it are in *Senate Executive Document* No. 49, 48 Congress, 1 session, serial 2162, pp. 2–7. See also *Senate Journal*, 48 Congress, 1 session, serial 2161, pp. 204, 745, 904; Report of the Commissioner of Indian Affairs, 1884, in serial 2287, p. 29.
[50] Jackson to Dawes, August 27, 1884, Dawes Papers, Box 26, Library of Congress.
[51] Painter, *A Visit to the Mission Indians* (1886), pp. 12, 14–18; Indian Rights Association, *The Case of the Mission Indians in Southern California, and the Action of the Indian Rights Association in Supporting the Defense of Their Legal Rights* (Philadelphia, 1886), p. 4.

investigate legal means of supporting the Indians' rights and to find legal counsel in California to undertake the work, an indication of the sort of practical approach that became characteristic of the Indian Rights Association's action. "We are approaching the end of the period," Painter wrote, "when mere agitation can accomplish anything of great value." Even legislation in the Indians' favor was not enough; someone had to pay attention to particular cases of wrong and hardship as they arose and devote the time, labor, and money required in the defense of Indian rights. It was this work in which Painter and the Indian Rights Association intended to be engaged.[52] In fact, the Indian Rights Association paid the expenses of the special attorney appointed by the government to defend the Mission Indians when government funds were not forthcoming. In 1887 Painter went once again to California as agent of the Indian Rights Association and of the Lake Mohonk committee, to survey in detail the circumstances of the Indians and search out intelligent solutions.[53]

The reformers' pressure brought some action on the part of the Indian Office, which did what it could to remove intruders from lands on which the Indians lived. And on January 31, 1888, the Supreme Court of California, in the case of *Byrne vs. Alas et al.*, decided in favor of Indian rights to the land. Painter received the decision with great joy. "In this case," he said, "we turn down the last page of the history of our shame, and are about to enter upon a brighter and more creditable chapter, in which is to be recorded our atonement for these wrongs." The Commissioner of Indian Affairs declared the decision "the most valuable thing which has been definitely secured for these Indians since public attention has been turned to their sufferings and wrongs."[54]

The judicial support of Indian titles in California did not put an end to pleas for Congressional action, for although the Senate had passed bills for their relief in the Forty-eighth, Forty-ninth, and Fiftieth Con-

---

[52] Charles C. Painter, *A Visit to the Mission Indians of California* (Philadelphia, 1887), pp. 4, 18. The Lake Mohonk committee was a strong one, including among others Philip Garrett of Philadelphia, Austin Abbott of New York, and J. W. Davis of Boston.

[53] Charles C. Painter, *The Condition of Affairs in Indian Territory and California* (Philadelphia, 1888), pp. 49–102.

[54] *Ibid.*, p. 92; Report of the Commissioner of Indian Affairs, 1888, in serial 2637, p. lxiv. Both Painter and the Commissioner of Indian Affairs reprinted the decision in full, so important did they deem it.

gresses, the House still refused to act.[55] The reformers kept up their pressure, for as delay continued, the situation of the Indians deteriorated.[56] Finally the House gave in. On January 12, 1891, an "Act for the relief of the Mission Indians in the State of California" became law, providing that the Secretary of the Interior should appoint three disinterested persons as commissioners to arrange a just and satisfactory settlement. The commissioners were to select reservations for the Indians to be held in trust by the government for twenty-five years. White settlers were to be removed and compensated for their improvements. Allotments were to be provided for individuals judged by the Secretary of the Interior to be "so advanced in civilization as to be capable of owning and managing land in severalty." The act allowed each head of family not more than 640 acres of grazing land plus 20 acres of arable land, and smaller amounts were designated for single persons. The allotments were to be granted in fee simple after a twenty-five year trust period. Individual patents were to override those granted to a tribe or band as a whole.[57]

The Lake Mohonk Conference in October formally thanked Congress for righting the wrongs against which the conference had so long protested. "We may soon expect to see these Indians holding firm titles to their own individual lands," the report said.[58] Appropriately, two of the commissioners under the act were Albert K. Smiley, the host of the Lake Mohonk conferences, and Charles C. Painter, the indefatigable agent of the Indian Rights Association.[59]

The law fitted perfectly into the patterns of land tenure that the humanitarian reformers had decided upon for the Indians, emphasizing individual holdings in fee simple but with restrictions against

[55] For Congressional action on the bill submitted to the Forty-ninth Congress, see *Senate Executive Document* No. 15, 49 Congress, 1 session, serial 2333, pp. 2–4, and *House Report* No. 2556, 49 Congress, 1 session, serial 2442; for reports on the Senate bill of the Fiftieth Congress, see *Senate Report* No. 74, 50 Congress, 1 session, serial 2519, and *House Report* No. 3282, 50 Congress, 1 session, serial 2607.

[56] *Report of the Board of Indian Commissioners*, 1888, pp. 8, 126; Report of the Secretary of the Interior, 1890, in serial 2840, pp. xxxii–xxxiii.

[57] *United States Statutes at Large*, XXVI, 712–14. Except for the size of individual allotments, the provisions were practically the same as in the bill drawn up in 1884 by the Indian Office.

[58] *Lake Mohonk Conference Proceedings*, 1891, pp. 13, 112.

[59] For recommendations of the Mission Indian Commission and some of its problems, see *House Executive Document* No. 96, 52 Congress, 1 session, serial 2954.

alienation for a term of years. The Mission Indians were no more successful in attaining the great benefits envisaged than were the majority of American Indians, who soon lost much of the land the reformers had hoped to guarantee to them forever. But with the passage of the law, the reformers rejoiced that they had accomplished their goal, and concern for the Mission Indians ceased to be a major element in Indian reform.

CHAPTER 7

RESERVATIONS AS INSTRUMENTS OF CIVILIZATION

When an Indian tribe had given up fighting, surrendered to the whites, and taken up a reservation life, its position was that of a group of men in the stone age of development, suddenly brought into contact with modern methods, and required to renounce all they had ever been taught and all they had inherited; to alter their practices of life, their beliefs, and their ways of thought; and to conform to manners and ways representing the highest point reached by our civilization. It is beyond the power of our imagination to grasp the actual meaning to any people of such a condition of things.

—GEORGE BIRD GRINNELL

in 1899

❀❀❀❀❀❀❀

The reservations of the post-Civil War decades segregated the Indians from the whites in order to prevent violent conflict between the races, but the reformers initially gave them enthusiastic support as hothouses in which the seedlings of civilization could get a protected start. Because the reservations were to serve this purpose, humanitarians had always had an interest in agency affairs. Thus it was that in the pre-Civil War period, missionary groups, with government encouragement and material support, had busied themselves with churches and schools on the reservations. The assignment of agencies to Quakers and then to other religious societies in the Grant administration was a "peace" measure, but it was intended by the government and accepted by the churches as a means to bring about radical transformation in the Indian societies by direct instruction and by the more important stimulus of good example, both in economic endeavor and in Christian faith.

As the nineteenth century waned and the Indians were all forced to accept reservations and then squeezed ever more tightly together as their land holdings were reduced, the reservations and the agencies that governed them became of greater and greater critical concern. Since the great majority of the Indians with whom the reformers were concerned lived on the reservations, these land areas were the places in which the Indian policies were applied. The allotment of lands in severalty was to take place within the reservations; most of the schools established for Indians were to be on the reservations; plans for securing law for the Indians were largely schemes for extending United States law over the reservations. But the reservations were in a sense looked upon also as a means to transform the Indians into American citizens, for the segregation and isolation which they provided would allow the civilization process to proceed unhindered by outside forces. The reservations were to be a controlled society in which, the sooner the better, tribal ways were to fall before the ways of the dominant white society.

The inhabitants of a reservation, however, were not a homogeneous group in their reaction to the purposes the government and the reformers had in mind. Most reservations, in fact, were split into two factions, designated by the reformers as "progressives" and "non-progressives" or "conservatives." Herbert Welsh in 1891 described the divisions among the Sioux in typical terms:

There are two great and sharply defined parties among the Sioux Indians to-day, either of which is the creation and representative of an idea. These ideas are antagonistic and irreconcilable.

First. There is the old pagan and non-progressive party. Inspired by sentiments of hostility to the Government and to white civilization, it believes in what is Indian, and hates what belongs to the white man. It delights in the past, and its dream is that the past shall come back again—the illimitable prairie, with vast herds of the vanished buffalo, the deer, the antelope, all the excitement of the chase, and the still fiercer thrill of bloody struggles with rival savage men. Consider what has been the education of the men who form this party—eating Government rations paid them in lieu of ceded lands, idleness, visits to distant relatives and friends, constant feasts and dances, with oft-repeated recitals from the older men of their own deeds of valor and the achievements of their ancestors. . . .

Second. A new, progressive, and what may properly be termed Christian party, whose life was begotten, nourished, and trained by missionary enterprise and devotion. . . . In these Christian Indians is to be found abundant food for a study of the germs and first awakenings of civilized life rich in variety and suggestion. They present all possible differences of age, condition, and of moral and mental attainments. . . . And yet in all this diversity to be found in the progressive party among the Sioux is clearly shown one controlling principle—an awakened moral purpose, newborn, or well-developed, the stirring of an enlightened conscience, and of a long-dormant intellect.[1]

It was the reformers' mission to encourage the progressives and to stamp out the nonprogressives, to support men and measures that promoted the former and restricted or crushed the latter.

The key figure in the process was the Indian agent. The regulations for the Indian service promulgated by the Bureau of Indian Affairs said bluntly: "The chief duty of an agent is to induce his Indians to labor in civilized pursuits. To attain this end every possible influence should be brought to bear, and in proportion as it is attained, other things being equal, an agent's administration is successful or unsuccessful."[2]

[1] Herbert Welsh, "The Meaning of the Dakota Outbreak," *Scribner's Magazine*, IX (April, 1891), 43–45.

[2] *Regulations of the Indian Department* (Washington, 1884), paragraph 486, p. 84. The same paragraph was repeated when the *Regulations* were reissued in 1894, paragraph 563, p. 102. The section in the *Regulations* in which this paragraph appears is headed "Civilization" and contains directives on employment of Indians, on suppressing the liquor traffic, and on other civilizing duties.
There is a considerable literature on the Indian agents and their work. For general studies, see, for example, Flora Warren Seymour, *Indian Agents of the Old Frontier* (New York, 1941), and Ruth A. Gallaher, "The Indian Agent in the United States Since 1850," *Iowa Journal of History and Politics*, XIV (April, 1916), 173–238. One strong agent's account of his experiences is James McLaughlin, *My Friend the Indian* (Boston, 1910). An evaluation of the agents, which challenges the traditional view that civilian agents were corrupt, inefficient individuals, is William E. Unrau, "The Civilian as Indian Agent: Villain or Victim?," *Western Historical Quarterly*, III (October, 1972), 405–20.
The work of the agents was supplemented by special inspectors, appointed under an

If the agent was a man of strength and integrity, who could control the conservative chiefs and who would aggressively foster the civilization programs, he won the commendation of the humanitarians and their support against attack. One such darling of the reformers was Dr. Valentine C. McGillicuddy, agent of the Oglalla Sioux at Pine Ridge, a man of uncompromising spirit, who ruled his agency like a little despot and who proved to be more than a match for Chief Red Cloud, who rallied around himself considerable dissident elements. Using all the means at his disposal—cutting off rations, employing the agency police, or threatening to call in the soldiers—McGillicuddy was able to survive a repeated clash of wills with the nonprogressive leaders. He enthusiastically adopted the reformers' program for ending the power of the chiefs who represented the old tribalism—although he had little hesitation in building up and using the influence of chiefs who followed the progressive path.[3]

An instance of the reformers' support of the agent was the case of Dr. Thomas A. Bland, in whom Red Cloud found a friend and patron. Emphasizing the need to let the Indians themselves decide what they wanted to do and how fast they wanted to be acculturated, and preaching the wisdom of building upon the good points in the Indian culture, Bland filled his paper, *The Council Fire*, with attacks upon McGillicuddy and his friends.[4] When he personally attempted to investigate affairs at Pine Ridge in the summer of 1884, he was ejected from the reservation by McGillicuddy, and he made use of the event to heighten his crusade against the agent. Bland was openly challenged by the

act of February 14, 1873 (*United States Statutes at Large*, XVII, 463). These inspectors were responsible to the Commissioner of Indian Affairs until March 25, 1880; thereafter they reported directly to the Secretary of the Interior. They were responsible for annual inspections of the agencies and had power to suspend agents and superintendents. For information on their duties and powers, see Schmeckebier, *The Office of Indian Affairs*, p. 408.

[3] The work of McGillicuddy and other agents of the Sioux is discussed briefly in Utley, *Last Days of the Sioux Nation*, pp. 27–30. For a longer account of McGillicuddy's struggles with Red Cloud, see Olson, *Red Cloud and the Sioux Problem*, pp. 264–85. The agent's own account is recorded in Julia B. McGillicuddy, *McGillicuddy, Agent: A Biography of Dr. Valentine T. McGillicuddy* (Stanford University, California, 1941), a book written by the agent's second wife. Hyde, *A Sioux Chronicle*, bitterly condemns the program of the government and the reformers as it affected the Sioux.

[4] *The Council Fire*, volumes VI and VII, *passim*. For an example see VII (September, 1884), 121–22.

mainline reformers. When the *Springfield Republican* on August 5, 1884, printed an editorial entitled "Red Cloud's Sioux and Their Agent," which was based on Bland's material, Senator Dawes replied at once with an open letter, published in the *Republican* on August 7 and later circulated in pamphlet form by the Indian Rights Association. In it Dawes described Bland as "a very strange man," who was "as wild in his attempts to state facts as he is in his ideas of what is the proper policy toward the race he thinks he serves." McGillicuddy expressed his thanks to Dawes, and Dawes was congratulated by other reformers for his stand.[5]

The official personnel of the agency and others permitted by law to live on the reservation were deemed to be instruments for carrying out the program of civilization. Of these the most problematical were the licensed traders, who supplied the goods which the Indians were unable to procure for themselves and who profited by the money that flowed to the Indians from various treaty arrangements. Fulfilling a necessary function on the reservation, they were nonetheless often elements of discord. It was the traders, conniving with venal agents, who supplied the foundation for the stories of Indian "rings" scandalously exploiting the Indians' condition. There were frequent calls for tightening the regulations under which the traders operated, so that they might better conform to the educative purposes of the reservations.

One of the most insistent demands for reform was made by Indian Commissioner Hayt in 1877. Remarking that the agency traders in their daily intercourse with the Indians had "unlimited opportunities to influence them for good or evil," he found that much of the influence had been for evil, since the true interests of the Indians were not always in accord with the selfish interests of the traders. Cheating the Indians by overcharging for their goods and supplying them with guns and ammunition and with liquor were clearly deleterious. In addition, the traders' desire for profitable buffalo robes was stimulating the Indians

[5] Henry L. Dawes, *The Case of McGillicuddy* (Philadelphia, 1884); McGillicuddy to Dawes, August 17, 1884, Dawes Papers, Box 26, Library of Congress. The story of Bland's visit to the reservation is told in Olson, *Red Cloud and the Sioux Problem*, pp. 294–99.

to continue their buffalo hunts, which Hayt considered "a relic of barbarism and an obstruction to the progress of Indian civilization." Hayt issued instructions for control of the traders' activities in order to develop a system of fair trading that would make the traders "most potent instruments in the civilizing process."[6]

The tightened regulations seemed to have some effect, and in 1886 the Commissioner of Indian Affairs pronounced the status of the trade to be "creditable and gratifying," but the profit motive of the white or half-blood traders was too strong to eliminate altogether a certain amount of extortion on the part of the unscrupulous. The Indian Office began to think, then, about making the Indians self-reliant and self-sustaining to the point where they could handle their own trading needs.[7] When Thomas J. Morgan assumed office as Commissioner of Indian Affairs in 1889—as one would expect from a man of his reforming zeal—new measures were taken to insure that the traders fitted into the scheme of civilization. "No branch of the Indians' preparation for citizenship," Morgan noted in his first report, "has perhaps received less attention than that which pertains to commerce." To make up for the oversight, Morgan issued instructions to his special agents to pay particular attention to the traders:

> You will carefully ascertain and report as to the general reputation of each trader for honesty, fair dealing with the Indians, and good influence among them. You will also report specifically as to the quality and sufficiency of the stock of goods kept by the trader; whether he deals in articles whose sale is injurious to the Indians; whether the prices charged are reasonable; whether the schedule of prices is displayed so that the Indians can be well informed thereof; whether the trader sells intoxicating liquor under any guise, or arms or fixed ammunition, or trades with the Indians for goods furnished them by the Government . . . ; whether his store is kept open on Sunday; whether it is used as a resort for loafers; whether gambling, demoralizing dances, or any other practices or amusements hurtful to the Indians are allowed upon the premises, and, in general, whether the trader and his employés are sober, respectable people

[6] Report of the Commissioner of Indian Affairs, 1877, in serial 1800, pp. 404–405.
[7] *Ibid.*, 1886, in serial 2467, pp. 115–16.

whose conduct and example among the Indians will tend to elevate the Indians morally and socially instead of the reverse.[8]

But Morgan soon realized that times were changing. The system of the licensed trader he came to consider "a relic of the old system of considering an Indian as a ward, a reservation as a corral, and a tradership as a golden opportunity for plunder and profit." He sought to encourage competition of trade on the reservations and to stimulate the Indians themselves to engage in the trade as one of the "civilized pursuits" which they were to adopt as a means of livelihood.[9]

What might be expected from an enterprising trader was described by the Indian Rights Association in its report for 1895, under the heading, "Civilization Across a Store-Counter":

One thing which any visitor to the Southern Ute Reservation must note is the suggestion there found of the possibilities of a post-trader's store as an instrument of civilization. The only storekeeper for several years past who has had faith enough in the stability of things on the reservation to take any enterprising step is the present one, George H. Kraus. The building which his predecessors had used he discarded as too small and inconvenient; and, allowing it to remain as an ell, he put up a new and very creditable main building, which he stocked, not with the mere necessaries of subsistence known to the Indians, but with a liberal supply of white men's goods. Soaps of the better sort, hair and toothbrushes, tables, cups and saucers, bedsteads and mattresses, attractive shawls for the women, and cheap but neat-looking blue flannel suits for the men, were among the features of his display. He took as much pains with their arrangement on his shelves and in his show-cases as if they had been intended to capture the best custom of a white village. The effect promptly showed itself. Curiosity was developed among his Indian customers, especially among the women, who are by no means unintelligent as a rule. To stimulate this instinct, and also to satisfy it in a measure, he fell upon the habit of leaving the doors of his living

[8] *Ibid.*, 1889, in serial 2725, p. 30. This list of unacceptable practices parallels the reports of earlier investigations. See, for example, the report of E. N. Stebbins, a member of the Board of Indian Commissioners, in *Report of the Board of Indian Commissioners, 1878*, p. 82.
[9] Report of the Commissioner of Indian Affairs, 1890, in serial 2841, pp. lix–lx.

quarters open, so that all could look in and see what use he made of the various conveniences of toilet and table. It was not long before one of the more inquisitive of his visitors was moved to buy some of the same things for her own tepee. This excited emulation in another, and so on. Then he began to turn the tide of fashion to still more profitable account by refusing to sell a mattress to an Indian who had not a bedstead to put it on, or a plate, cup, and saucer where there was no table. Of course, in nearly every case the bedstead and the table had to come out of his own stock, but the Indian who bought them was lifted off the ground by the purchase, so that the profit to the store-keeper's till was at the same time a modest investment in civilization. More than one Indian brave, who has declined to exchange blanket and leggings for the musty-fusty dirt-colored, uninviting garments which the Government doles out to him on issue-day, has come into the trader's store, bought a blue flannel suit, retired to the back room to put it on, and walked proudly out to exhibit himself to his fellows.[10]

As towns developed near the reservation, however, the absolute dependence of the Indians upon the licensed reservation trader diminished and with it the importance of the traders in the scheme of reservation life.[11]

If the traders were somewhat dubious agents of civilization on the reservations, there were no doubts about the importance of the agency physicians as instruments of change. The drive of the reformers and the government officials to replace the Indians' cultural patterns with their own civilization was often slowed by the "medicine men," who worked effectively to preserve the old ways. If the belief in "sorcery and evil spirits" could be overcome, Commissioner Price remarked in 1884, "a long stride would be made in the work of civilization." No one had greater opportunities in this direction, he felt, than the agency

---

[10] *Report of the Indian Rights Association*, 1895, pp. 48–49.
[11] Clark Wissler in *Indian Cavalcade; or Life on the Old-Time Indian Reservations* (New York, 1938), pp. 97–116, gives a sympathetic picture of the traders. For a detailed account of traders in the Southwest, see Frank McNitt, *The Indian Traders* (Norman, 1962).

physician. Commissioner Atkins, two years later, instructed the doctors not only to educate the Indians in the proper care of the sick but to use every effort to overcome the influence of the native "medicine men," and he reported some success. He recommended, furthermore, the establishment of agency hospitals as an effective means of weakening the hold of ancient superstitions and traditions upon the Indians.[12]

The physicians faced a difficult task, for they worked in a situation that lacked adequate sanitary facilities. They were expected to care for the sick, to improve the hygienic conditions on the reservation, and to instruct the pupils in the schools on elementary principles of health; but as members of a complicated bureaucracy they were also plagued with monthly reports to be filled out on diseases treated and sanitary conditions observed and were expected to promote harmony on the reservation by prompt and cheerful obedience to the agent. The physician was told by Commissioner Morgan, however, that he would be compensated for his poor accommodations and low salary among the Indians by the realization of "the noble part he may perform in helping to lift this people out of their superstitious regard for the grotesque rites of the 'medicine men.' "[13] The good repute in which the doctors were held on the reservations and the influence they had with the Indians came from their concern for their charges and their success in healing their physical ills. Few, apparently, made it their business to mount a frontal attack upon the traditional Indian culture.[14]

Pre-eminent supporters of the agent were the Indian police, quasi-military forces under his command that came into being as a substitute for army control of the reservations.[15] Some sort of police force was necessary in the best ordered societies, it was argued, and to think that the Indian reservations, whose traditional tribal governments were weakened by the white reformers' attacks, could get along without

[12] Report of the Commissioner of Indian Affairs, 1884, in serial 2287, p. 28; *ibid.*, 1886, in serial 2467, pp. 116–17.

[13] *Ibid.*, 1889, in serial 2725, pp. 12–13.

[14] Some account of the doctors' work is given in Wissler, *Indian Cavalcade*, pp. 140–58.

[15] An excellent thorough treatment of Indian police and Indian judges is William T. Hagan, *Indian Police and Judges: Experiments in Acculturation and Control* (New Haven, 1966).

law enforcers was absurd. It was all very well to condemn military management of Indian affairs, but if army troops were not on hand, the agent had to find some other way to back up his decisions.

The idea of a constabulary force of Indian policemen arose spontaneously on several reservations. Indians enrolled by the army as scouts had performed well, and it was not a difficult step to conceive of Indians as a temporary or even a permanent civilian corps. When Benjamin F. Lushbaugh became agent of the Pawnees in 1862, he was immediately annoyed by the frequent thefts, chiefly of horses, by the young men of the tribe. "For the purpose of facilitating the recovery of property thus taken," he wrote to the Indian Office, "I have revived a former police system, by the appointment of a number of the most reliable braves, who are designated soldiers, and am having them drilled in the manual and provided them with suitable uniforms. This excites in them a spirit of martial pride and emulation which is productive of good results. They are very efficient in preserving order in the villages and reporting any depredations that may be committed."[16] In 1872–1873 a group of Navajo policemen, placed under a war chief, served well in preventing depredations and in expediting the return of stolen stock. Similar expedients for preserving order were used with success among the Klamaths, the Chippewas in Wisconsin, and the Sioux and Blackfeet.[17]

The example *par excellence* was the Apache police force established by John P. Clum, the extraordinary young agent at the San Carlos Reservation. Clum had been nominated by the Dutch Reformed Church, who had been allotted the agency under Grant's peace policy, and who, having no missionaries of their own willing to accept the hazards of the post, had turned to Rutgers College to find recruits. Clum had attended there briefly before going west with the United States Weather Service, and former classmates recommended him for the position. He arrived at San Carlos on August 8, 1874, a cocky twenty-two year old, "with instructions to assume *entire* control of the San Carlos agency." This meant forcing out the military and setting up

[16] Lushbaugh to Charles E. Mix, September 15, 1862, in Report of the Commissioner of Indian Affairs, 1862, in serial 1157, p. 266.

[17] Oakah L. Jones, Jr., "The Origins of the Navajo Indian Police, 1872–1873," *Arizona and the West*, VIII (Autumn, 1966), 225–38; Hagan, *Indian Police and Judges*, pp. 25–27, 39–40.

his own enforcement agency. Two days after his arrival, Clum held a big talk with the Apaches and explained his plans. "I then told them that I intended to appoint some Indians as police-men," he later wrote; "that we would establish a supreme court for the trial of offenders; that I would preside as chief justice, and four or five Apache chiefs would serve as assistant justices; that Indians would be called as witnesses at the trials. Under this system, all Apache offenders would be arrested by Apache police, brought before an Apache court, with Apaches as witnesses, and, if convicted, sentenced by Apache judges, and finally delivered into the custody of Apache guards." The self-government plan worked, and Clum controlled the volatile Apaches without the aid of the army. The Indian Office and the Dutch Reformed Church supported him, and his Apache police were accepted as an integral part of the agency.[18]

The Board of Indian Commissioners raised the question of Indian police formally in its report for 1874. In a section entitled "Enforcement of Order," it noted that the power of the chiefs was limited and that outside intervention was resented. The result was that although the wild tribes had treaty obligations to maintain order, to educate their children, to apprehend and deliver offenders for punishment, and to labor for their own support, no machinery existed for the enforcement of these stipulations and they had remained nugatory. The solution would be a "police or constabulary force" made up of the Indians themselves. Noting the successful attempts along this line at the various reservations, the board concluded that there was abundant evidence to prove that a small disciplined and well-instructed police force of Indians would be a safe and effective means of preserving

[18] Woodworth Clum, *Apache Agent: The Story of John P. Clum* (Boston, 1936), pp. 119–21, 132, 134–35. Clum's annual reports appear in the annual reports of the Commissioner of Indian Affairs, 1874–1877. Clum in late life wrote about his Apache police in "The San Carlos Apache Police," *New Mexico Historical Review*, IV (July, 1929), 203–19; V (January, 1930), 67–92. Never hesitant to praise his own work, Clum declared: ". . . the distinguished services rendered by the San Carlos Apache Police Force during 1874, 1875, 1876, and 1877, furnished the model and inspiration for the national system provided for by the Act of Congress approved May 27, 1878, authorizing the organization of the *United States Indian Police Force.*" *Ibid.*, p. 219. For a detailed, heavily documented account of Clum's career as agent, with emphasis on his struggle with the military, see Ralph Henrick Ogle, *Federal Control of the Western Apaches, 1848–1886* (Albuquerque, 1940; reprinted with an introduction by Oakah L. Jones, Jr., 1970), pp. 144–78. See also the account of Clum and his police in Hagan, *Indian Police and Judges*, pp. 27–39.

order and of assisting the tribe in enforcing its treaty obligations. And such a force in many cases, the board asserted, would obviate the necessity of a military post near the agency.[19]

In the following year the board moved ahead vigorously with its scheme. On August 1, 1875, it sent a circular letter to all the Indian agents as part of its campaign against military control of the reservations. After requesting information about the existence of military forces in their vicinity and the effect of the troops on the Indians, the letter posed a specific question about Indian police: "Would the organization of an armed Indian police, under proper restrictions and discipline, for the enforcement of order, arrest of criminals, and the prevention of incursions of evil-disposed persons upon your reservation, prove safe or advisable; and to what extent would such an organization supersede the necessity of a military force?" A number of the agents saw no need for a police force since their charges were peaceful and well ordered, and some believed that Indian distaste for taking punitive action against other Indians would make such a police force useless, but the great majority replied favorably, some even enthusiastically. Agents who had already employed Indians as police of one sort or another pointed to the success of their efforts.[20]

It took some time for the work of the board to bear fruit. Commissioner Hayt picked up the recommendation in 1877, and urged the creation of a general system of Indian police. He noted the successes where such police had already been tried and the practice of using police in Canada. The police system, he said, would relieve the army from police duty on Indian reservations, would save lives and property, and would "materially aid in placing the entire Indian population of the country on the road to civilization."[21] But Congress, where supporters of military control of the reservations were numerous and influential, held back. Finally, on May 27, 1878, the Indian police got Congressional authorization. A section of the Indian appropriation act provided $30,000 to pay for 430 privates at five dollars a month and fifty officers at eight dollars a month, "to be employed in maintaining order and prohibiting illegal traffic in liquor on the several Indian

[19] *Report of the Board of Indian Commissioners*, 1874, p. 9.
[20] *Ibid.*, 1875, pp. 64–103.
[21] Report of the Commissioner of Indian Affairs, 1877, in serial 1800, pp. 398–99.

reservations." By the end of the year, the commissioner reported success at the thirty agencies where police forces had been organized, and in 1879 Congress doubled the number of police authorized. By 1880 there were police at forty agencies and a decade later at fifty-nine.[22]

The police were immediately useful to the agents, an extension of whose authority they were. The tasks they performed were in many cases hardly police duties at all. An Indian policeman was the "reservation handyman." The police served as couriers and messengers, slaughtered cattle for the beef ration, kept accounts of births and deaths in the tribe, and took censuses for the agent; and they added to the labor force of the agency by building roads, clearing out irrigation ditches, and other chores. In all this they contributed substantially to the smooth operation of the agency. Routine labor, however, did not obscure the enforcement of order, which had been foremost on the minds of the advocates of the police system. The Indian police were armed and often mounted, at the beck and call of the agent when disorder threatened or force was needed to see that rules and regulations on the reservation were properly observed. The police arrested or turned back intruders on the Indian lands and tore out the squatters' stakes, arrested horse thieves, escorted surveying parties, and served as scouts. They acted as guards at annuity payments, preserved order at ration issues, protected agency buildings and other property, and returned truant children to school. They searched for and returned lost or stolen goods, prevented depredations in timber, and brought whisky sellers to trial. They arrested Indians for disorderly conduct, drunkenness, wife-beating, and theft, and reported the comings and goings of strangers on the reservation.[23]

The reformers soon became aware, if they had not been from the very first, that these duties and responsibilities of the Indian police were means to an end of greater worth than the day-to-day good order on the reservations. The police were to become important chiefly for their moral influence. The police force on a reservation impressed the

---

[22] *United States Statutes at Large*, XX, 86, 315; Report of the Commissioner of Indian Affairs, 1878, in serial 1850, pp. 471–72; *ibid.*, 1880, in serial 1959, pp. 88–89; *ibid.*, 1890, in serial 2841, p. xciv.

[23] *Ibid.*, 1880, in serial 1959, pp. 88–89; Report of the Secretary of the Interior, 1880, in serial 1959, pp. 10–11; Report of the Commissioner of Indian Affairs, 1881, in serial 2018, p. 13. See also Hagan, *Indian Police and Judges*, Chapter 4, "Agents of the Civilization Process," pp. 69–81.

Indians with the supremacy of law; it discouraged the traditional practice of personal revenge; it imbued a sense of duty and personal responsibility, subjected the policemen themselves to strict discipline and self-control, and inspired them with a pride of good conduct; it taught respect for the personal and property rights of others; by strengthening the authority of the government agent against that of the chiefs, it prepared the Indians for the dissolution of their tribal relations and pushed them forward toward incorporation into American society. The police force, Commissioner Hiram Price said in 1881, was "a perpetual educator."[24]

The Indian police taught by good example as well as by the enforcement of precepts. They were expected to have only one wife, and to dress in the accepted white man's costumes, with short hair and unpainted faces. All this was difficult enough, but the Indian policemen as well had to be the agent's men when the crackdown came on deeply ingrained traditions and religious practices and to support the agents against the medicine men of the tribe, in a word to uphold the progressives against the conservatives.

All in all, the Indian police worked remarkably well in fulfilling the reformers' designs. Four years after the program began, the Commissioner of Indian Affairs reported: "Tried as an experiment, it has proved a decided success. It has accomplished all that was claimed for it, and at many agencies has become an absolute necessity." Compared with white police forces throughout the country, he declared two years later, the Indian police could not be surpassed for "fidelity, faithfulness, and impartial performance of duty." And this was all the more remarkable considering that the police were asked to enforce against members of their own race laws which were made by white officials and many of which went strongly against established practices and customs, often of a religious nature.[25]

The success of the police rested to a large extent on the fact that the police forces often paralleled or replaced similar institutions within the tribes themselves. The soldier societies that had regulated much of

24 See the reports of the Commissioner of Indian Affairs cited in note 23.
25 Report of the Commissioner of Indian Affairs, 1882, in serial 2100, pp. 35–36; *ibid.*, 1884, in serial 2287, p. 12. See also the favorable report, *ibid.*, 1888, in serial 2637, pp. xxvii–xxix. The Report of the Commissioner of Indian Affairs, 1890, in serial 2841, pp. xci–xciv, appends extracts of agents' reports praising the Indian police.

tribal life performed functions not unlike those assigned to the Indian police, and, wittingly or unwittingly, agents drew their policemen from the membership of such societies.[26] The fidelity of the police to the agent was remarkable, even when there was considerable risk to themselves. The police played the key role in the killing of Sitting Bull as he resisted arrest at the Standing Rock Reservation in December, 1890, and six of the Indian police lost their lives in the melee. Herbert Welsh, in publishing an account of the death of the chief written by the agent, James McLaughlin, remarked: "The unostentatious courage and fidelity of the Indian police, who did not hesitate to sacrifice their lives in the service of a Government not of their own race, is worthy of remembrance."[27] In another case, in which seven of the police at the Cheyenne River Agency were brought to trial for murder after killing in self-defense a man they had been sent to arrest, the Indian Rights Association successfully undertook their legal defense. The account of the case published by the association included this encomium: "No men have rendered more faithful service to the Government of the United States in our western country than the members of the native Indian police force. . . . These men have proved themselves susceptible of thorough discipline, they have shown a remarkable sense of responsibility, and in no case known to us have they betrayed their trust. Where commanded by a strong superior, in whom they have confidence, they have often shown distinguished courage—even heroism."[28]

There were of course some nay sayers. The strongest argument made against the Indian police was that they gave too much power to the agent. The Chairman of the House Committee on Indian Affairs argued strongly in 1880 against the continuation of the police on that basis. "This provision turns him [the Indian] over, bound hand and foot, to the agents," he said. "These men had authority before almost without restriction, except as they are restricted by the want of physical force. Now we give them eight hundred men armed and equipped,

---

26 Wissler, *Indian Cavalcade*, pp. 128–29; Hagan, *Indian Police and Judges*, p. 161.

27 Untitled Indian Rights Association leaflet, January 19, 1891, p. 1. The role of the Indian police in the death of Sitting Bull has been told many times; an excellent account is Utley, *Last Days of the Sioux Nation*, pp. 146–66.

28 *The Attorney-General and Seven Indian Policemen of Cheyenne River Agency— A Case Where to Serve Faithfully Came Near Meaning the Gallows* (Philadelphia, 1895), p. 1. See also *Report of the Indian Rights Association*, 1895, pp. 38–40.

and thus the fullest authority is allowed with fearful power to execute not known laws, but the will of the agent."[29] There was no doubt that an obedient police force in the hands of an authoritarian or unscrupulous agent would be a dangerous thing. The vocal opponents of McGillicuddy at Pine Ridge accused him of running the reservation as a tyrant with his police. But such isolated examples hardly outweighed the overwhelmingly favorable impression made by the Indian police on white observers.[30]

The Indian policemen were shortly joined by another experiment in self-government on the reservations, the so-called courts of Indian offenses. Judicial organization on many reservations was rudimentary or nonexistent. The agent was usually the judge as well as legislator and executive, and a logical complement to the police force was a system of courts staffed by Indian judges. The establishment of the courts, however, originated less from a desire to fill out a skeletal system of self-government under the agent's control than explicitly to end a series of Indian practices that were considered by the whites to be inimical to civilization.

The instigator of the courts was Secretary of the Interior Henry M. Teller, who in December, 1882, called attention to "a great hindrance to the civilization of the Indians, viz, the continuance of the old heathenish dances, such as the sun-dance, scalp-dance, etc." Such practices, he insisted, led to a war spirit and demoralized the young. Furthermore, he objected to the practice of polygamy among the Indians, a practice that could not be afforded when the Indians supported themselves by the chase, but which now seemed to flourish when the government furnished rations. A third hindrance to the advancement of the Indians he found in the influence of the medicine men, who kept children from attending school and promoted the heathenish customs. Nor could he abide the practice among the Indians of giving away or destroying the property of a man who dies. "It

---

[29] *Congressional Record*, X, 2487. Several other members of the House spoke strongly in favor of the police, and the objection was not sustained. See the debate, *ibid.*, 2487–89.

[30] Hyde, in *A Sioux Chronicle*, generally supports the critics' position, but Hagan's *Indian Police and Judges* gives a more sober and more favorable evaluation of the police.

will be extremely difficult to accomplish much towards the civilization of the Indians," Teller concluded, "while these adverse influences are allowed to exist."[31]

Following the Secretary's orders, Commissioner of Indian Affairs Hiram Price issued a directive to the agents on April 10, 1883. The judges were to be "intelligent, honest, and upright and of undoubted integrity," and could not practice polygamy. The courts were to meet twice a month and rule upon all questions presented to it for consideration by the agent. Specific jurisdiction was granted over the dances objected to by Teller, polygamous marriages, interference of the medicine men with the civilization program, thefts and destruction of property, intoxication and the liquor traffic, and misdemeanors. The civil jurisdiction of the courts was the same as that of justices of the peace in the state or territory where the courts were located.[32] "There is no good reason," Price asserted, "why an Indian should be permitted to indulge in practices which are alike repugnant to common decency and morality; and the preservation of good order on the reservations demands that some active measures should be taken to discourage and, if possible, put a stop to the demoralizing influence of heathenish rites."[33]

The courts were to be composed of the first three officers in rank of the police force, if the agent approved, otherwise of three other persons selected by the agent, and in all cases, like the police, the courts were an extension of the agent's authority. Punishments were usually in the form of a fine, although imprisonment also could be ordered. All the decrees of the court were subject to the approval or disapproval of the agent and appeal could be made to the Commissioner of Indian Affairs. There was no intention that the courts should handle major crimes. Courts of Indian offenses were not established for the Five Civilized Tribes, the Indians of New York, the Osages, Pueblos, and Eastern Cherokees, since these tribes had recognized tribal governments. On other reservations, they were set up as Commissioners of

[31] Teller to the Commissioner of Indian Affairs, December 2, 1882, in Report of the Secretary of the Interior, 1883, in serial 2190, pp. xi–xii.

[32] Rules for the Courts of Indian Offenses, April 10, 1883, cited in Hagan, *Indian Police and Judges*, pp. 109–10. A revision of these rules is in Report of the Commissioner of Indian Affairs, 1892, in serial 3088, pp. 28–31.

[33] Report of the Commissioner of Indian Affairs, 1883, in serial 2191, p. 11.

Indian Affairs saw need; at the height of the system, about 1900, approximately two-thirds of the agencies had courts.[34]

The legal basis on which the courts of Indian offenses rested was extremely vague. Congress in 1888 authorized pay for the judges, but that was as close as the courts came to legislative formalization, despite continual requests from the Indian Office.[35] The courts were later compared with those maintained by common consent in mining camps or logging districts far removed from official tribunals, "where nobody knows just what the law is on any subject, but where everyone recognizes the necessity of some fixed center of authority as a refuge from anarchy."[36]

Everyone spoke favorably of the work of the courts. Teller was enthusiastic from the beginning, and Price after a year's experience with the system noted that the decisions of the judges had been quietly accepted and peaceably enforced and that at some agencies the courts had been instrumental in abolishing "many of the most barbarous and pernicious customs that have existed among the Indians from time immemorial." Within a few years he looked for the complete end to "polygamy and the heathenish customs of the sun dance, scalp dance, and war dance." Reports from agents substantiated his opinion. In 1886 Commissioner Atkins declared that the courts had been a great help to the Indians in preparing them for self-government and citizenship. And Thomas J. Morgan, though speaking of them as "a tentative and somewhat crude attempt" to break up superstitious practices and to provide a rudimentary knowledge of legal processes, considered them a great benefit to the Indians and of substantial help to the agents.[37]

The specific offenses listed in the rules for the courts were geared to the promotion of civilization, and in 1892 the revised rules added as another provision "that if an Indian refuses or neglects to adopt the

[34] Hagan, *Indian Police and Judges*, p. 109.

[35] *United States Statutes at Large*, XXV, 233. Schmeckebier, *Office of Indian Affairs*, p. 259, sees the authority for the courts resting on general authority over Indian affairs granted by the laws of July 9, 1832 (organizing the Indian Department) and of June 30, 1834 (trade and intercourse law).

[36] Francis E. Leupp, *The Indian and His Problem* (New York, 1910), p. 241.

[37] Report of the Secretary of the Interior, 1884, in serial 2286, pp. ix–x; Report of the Commissioner of Indian Affairs, 1884, in serial 2287, pp. 6–8; *ibid.*, 1886, in serial 2467, p. 103; *ibid.*, 1889, in serial 2725, pp. 26–27.

habits of industry, or to engage in civilized pursuits or employments, but habitually spends his time in idleness and loafing, he shall be deemed a vagrant and guilty of a misdemeanor."[38]

No tribal custom on the reservations was overlooked by the zealous reformers. One that particularly distressed them was the practice among the Sioux of killing the annuity beef cattle in ways reminiscent of the bygone buffalo hunts. The cattle were driven out of the corrals, pursued over the prairies, and killed in flight by the excited warriors. A member of the Indian Rights Association, who visited the Sioux reservations in the summer of 1886, was appalled by what he saw and even more by the apparent acceptance of the practice by whites as a sporting event. His disgust is evident in his description:

> As we drive homeward, threading our way between the bloody groups around the flayed and dismembered beasts, many Indians are already beginning their feast. They are seated on the ground, eating the raw blood-hot liver. . . . The next day, at the great Government boarding school, the principal told us that his boys and girls had behaved so well through the term that he meant to take them out in a body to see the next beef issue as a reward for their good conduct. It is a brutal and brutalizing spectacle.[39]

The Sioux commission of 1888, headed by Pratt, was equally dismayed. "A beef-killing day on an Indian reservation is a spectacle which is a disgrace to our civilization," the report said. "It can not but serve to perpetuate in a savage breast all the cruel and wicked propensities of his nature. It is attended with scenes enacted in the presence of the old and the young, men, women, and little children, which are too disgusting for recital." The recommended solution of this commission was to substitute bacon and pork for the beef—which it considered a more economical as well as a more civilized disbursement.[40]

The beef issue was seized upon by Thomas J. Morgan with his usual

[38] *Ibid.*, 1892, in serial 3088, p. 30.
[39] J. B. Harrison, *The Latest Studies on Indian Reservations* (Philadelphia, 1887), pp. 128–29.
[40] *Senate Document* No. 17, 50 Congress, 2 session, serial 2610, p. 19.

forcefulness when he became Commissioner of Indian Affairs. In the memorandum he wrote indicating the accomplishments of his term of office, the subject had a prominent place. It had been customary, he noted, "to turn the cattle loose on the prairie and allow the Indians, mounted on their ponies, to chase, torture, cripple and kill them by degrees, when the squaws and children cut them up on the bare ground, the blood and offal being consumed." It became Morgan's goal to end this "savage sport," and to substitute properly equipped slaughterhouses where the slaughter of the cattle and the handling of the beef could be done as painlessly and as cleanly as possible.[41] To this end, he issued on July 21, 1890, a set of "Instructions to Agents in Regard to Manner of Issuing Beef," which gave detailed directions on the killing and the distribution of the beef. The slaughtering was to be done by competent men, with proper implements, and in a private place where cleanliness could be provided. Women and children were specifically forbidden to be present. Consumption of the blood and the intestines—a "savage and filthy custom"—was strictly prohibited, since it served "to nourish brutal instincts" as well as being a source of disease. Morgan directed that men cut up the beeves and that the meat be distributed to the Indian men, not to the women, except in special exigencies. "In short," he declared, "I intend that this branch of the work, which at many agencies has been so conducted as to be a scandal on the service and a stimulus to the brutal instincts of the Indians, shall become an object lesson to them of the difference in this respect between the civilized man and the savage."[42] When he left office, he considered the reform almost entirely successful.

The Indian Office and its humanitarian supporters waged an incessant war, which they never quite won, against intruders and other discordant elements on the reservations. The treaties and executive orders by which the reservations were established uniformly pro-

[41] Memorandum of Morgan, Records of the Office of the Commissioner of Indian Affairs, Letters Sent, 1890–1892, p. 486, National Archives Record Group 75. There is a description of a "mimic buffalo hunt" in Report of the Secretary of the Interior, 1890, in serial 2840, pp. xlvi–xlvii.

[42] "Instructions to Agents in Regard to Manner of Issuing Beef," July 21, 1890, in Report of the Commissioner of Indian Affairs, 1890, in serial 2841, p. clxvi.

hibited the entrance of whites who were not official agency personnel or licensed for some special purpose to come within the boundaries. Casual intruders were expelled by the agents and their police forces, and in serious cases, of which the infiltrations into the Indian Territory were most notorious, a call could be made upon the troops of the United States army. Two groups, however, caused special trouble.

The first of these were white men who had married Indian women and lived as members of the tribe. Known at the time as "squawmen," they sometimes exploited the Indians by using without charge large portions of the reservations for grazing or agricultural purposes, but often they merely lived off the tribe with little work. Everywhere they were a discordant element, backed the chiefs in their resistance to change, and earned the enmity of the reformers. A member of the Board of Indian Commissioners, E. N. Stebbins, who toured the Dakota agencies in 1878 was strong in his denunciation of the class:

> The Missouri River is infested from Yankton to Fort Benton with a low class of white men, a large portion of whom are of French origin. At some agencies I find the squaw-men with their children number as many as five hundred and fifty persons. I cannot believe it is the intention of the government to increase this class of lazy half-bloods. These persons form an element which is with difficulty controlled, for they are in some cases outlaws from the East, and a crafty, unscrupulous set of men. They in many cases sow dissension among the Indians, inducing them to complain of their treatment for some trivial cause, while they themselves make a pretense of friendship to the agent. Without doubt they are often the sole cause of outbreaks, often poisoning the minds of the Indians by misrepresenting the best intentions of the agent, and in this way, as in many others, exerting a damaging influence on all concerned. These persons are justly dreaded by the agent, who on this account allows them many favors.[43]

Dr. McGillicuddy spoke strongly against the squawmen in his testimony before the Dawes committee in 1883, charging that the Indians were unduly influenced by these men, who were opposed to advancement of the Indians toward self-support. McGillicuddy continued to

---

[43] *Report of the Board of Indian Commissioners,* 1878, pp. 81–82.

place on them much of the blame for opposition to government policies. "The squawmen and half breeds and chiefs," he wrote to Dawes in 1889, "may be expected on general principles to oppose the opening of the reservation, land in severalty, and anything else that tends to interfere with their present non-progressive condition or break up their herding privileges. . . . Poor old Red Cloud is simply a tool in all these men's hands."[44]

In the western parts of the Indian Territory, where grazing possibilities were inviting to enterprising whites, squawmen made use of their marital connections with the tribes to benefit where otherwise they would have been excluded. They were disturbers of the peace, who profited shamelessly from their special situation and made life miserable for anyone who opposed their schemes, and they were intimately involved in the factionalism and politics that were part of reservation life.[45] Secretary of the Interior Lamar in 1885 condemned them as bad and vicious men, who "foment discord among the Indians themselves, disturb their peaceful inclinations towards the settlers in the country surrounding the reservation, and incite opposition on the part of the Indians to the measures adopted and regulations prescribed by the Department for their advancement and civilization." He recommended legislation that would end their privileges within the tribes by making Indian women who married whites give up their tribal status and become citizens of the United States. But no attention was paid to his proposal, and when the anthropologist Clark Wissler made the rounds of the reservations at the beginning of the twentieth century, the squawmen remained much in evidence.[46]

A second serious challenge to the isolation which the reservations

[44] *Senate Report* No. 283, 48 Congress, 1 session, serial 2174, p. 175, quoted in Olson, *Red Cloud and the Sioux Problem*, p. 293; McGillicuddy to Dawes, April 10, 1889, Dawes Papers, Box 28. Harry H. Anderson, "Fur Traders as Fathers: The Origins of the Mixed-Blooded Community Among the Rosebud Sioux," *South Dakota History*, III (Summer, 1973), 233–70, emphasizes the importance of the mixed-bloods and their influence on tribal decisions.

[45] William T. Hagan, "Squaw Men on the Kiowa, Comanche, and Apache Reservation: Advance Agents of Civilization or Disturbers of the Peace?" in John G. Clark, ed., *The Frontier Challenge: Responses to the Trans-Mississippi West* (Lawrence, Kansas, 1971), pp. 171–202.

[46] Report of the Secretary of the Interior, 1885, in serial 2378, pp. 28–29; Wissler, *Indian Cavalcade*, pp. 159–75.

were supposed to provide came from the intrusion of white cattlemen and their herds upon the Indian lands. The reservation of the Cheyennes and Arapahos in the Indian Territory was an especially attractive target, for the sparse population left vast acres of grassland lying vacant. In 1883 enterprising men entered into agreements with certain Indians within this reservation at minimal fees and began to exploit the lands. Of 4,297,771 acres in the reservation, only 465,651 were left in Indian hands. Similar leases were made on other reservations.[47] Such actions were opposed by the reformers. The members of the Lake Mohonk Conference in 1883 considered the leasing of Indian lands for grazing as "inexpedient"; they wanted the Indians themselves to become herders on these lands and suggested that Congress appropriate money to buy herds to get the Indians started. And *The Council Fire*, not yet in sharp conflict with the other reformers, fought vigorously against leasing of the reservations to whites for any purpose. "The rule is," the editors declared, "that when white men get any sort of possession of Indian lands they never surrender them."[48]

The government, unfortunately, was caught without a policy. The Indian Department declined to approve the leases because it doubted its legal authority to do so, but it permitted the Indians to make them under the pretense that they were merely licenses granted by the Indians to the whites to enter the reservations. The average annual rental price, however, ran to about two cents an acre, which the government officials considered altogether too low. Lamar charged in 1885 that the assistance given by the Indian agents in the making of the leases was "directed more for the interest of the cattlemen than that of the Indians placed under their care and supervision." The Senate during the Forty-eighth Congress directed two inquiries into the matter of the leasing, and when the Attorney General was asked for a ruling, he decided in July, 1885, that "no general power appears to be conferred

[47] An account of the leases is given in Report of the Secretary of the Interior, 1885, in serial 2378, pp. 14–19. There is a table showing leases made, number of acres, length of lease, and rental price, *ibid.*, pp. 15–16. Full accounts of the Cheyenne-Arapaho leases are in Edward Everett Dale, "Ranching on the Cheyenne-Arapaho Reservation 1880–1885," *Chronicles of Oklahoma*, VI (March, 1928), 35–59; and Donald J. Berthrong, "Cattlemen on the Cheyenne-Arapaho Reservation, 1883–1885," *Arizona and the West*, XIII (Spring, 1971), 5–32.

[48] *Lake Mohonk Conference Proceedings*, 1883, p. 9; *The Council Fire*, VII (December, 1884), 167–68.

by statute upon either the President or Secretary or any other officer of the Government to make, authorize, or approve leases of lands held by Indian tribes," and that "Indian tribes cannot lease their reservations without the authority of some law of the United States."[49]

The leases of the Cheyennes and Arapahos, meanwhile, had caused great dissension among the Indians themselves. Powerful traditionalist groups within the reservation fought against the presence of the cattlemen and their herds, and the factionalism threatened to result in open conflict. President Cleveland, thereupon, issued a proclamation on July 23, 1885, declaring the leases null and void and calling for the removal of the whites and their cattle from the Indian lands. By the end of the year, the cattlemen and their herds were gone.[50]

On the Kiowa, Comanche, and Apache reservation, lying southeast of the Cheyennes and Arapahos along the Texas border, the encroachment of cattlemen was less successfully resisted. Texas cattlemen moved across the Red River with large herds, and leases signed with influential chiefs gave a color of legality to their operations. The Indian Office, unsure of its ground, let the leases stand. The cattlemen here formed a powerful lobby supporting the Indians in opposition to the allotment of their lands in severalty and the opening of the surplus to white settlement, but their presence was in many ways harmful to the Indians. The money they poured into the pockets of the Indians corrupted the leaders, contributed to tribal factionalism, and did little to stimulate personal economic effort on the part of the tribesmen. The isolation, moreover, that the reservations were intended to provide, was destroyed.[51] At the reservations in the Pacific Northwest, too,

[49] Report of the Secretary of the Interior, 1885, in serial 2378, p. 17; the Attorney General is quoted *ibid.*, p. 18. The Senate inquiries led to the publication of *Senate Executive Document* No. 54, 48 Congress, 1 session, serial 2165, and *Senate Executive Document* No. 17, 48 Congress, 2 session, serial 2261, both of which contain extensive documentation pertaining to the leases.

[50] See the discussion in Berthrong, "Cattlemen on the Cheyenne-Arapaho Reservation," pp. 29–32. He concludes that the two and one-half years of occupation by the white cattlemen revealed that "the power of the traditional social and political organization of the Cheyennes and Arapahoes was not yet completely eroded away. When the crisis reached its peak, the soldier societies and the chiefs whom they supported were able to enforce their will against the Indian agent, the mixed-bloods, and those of their fellow tribesmen who had succumbed to white institutions. . . . This, however, was the last time that the Cheyenne and Arapaho warriors and chiefs were able to protect their reservation land."

[51] William T. Hagan, "Kiowas, Comanches, and Cattlemen, 1867–1906: A Case

cattlemen moved in unbidden to make use of the grasslands, and the efforts to remove them were continuous but largely ineffective.[52] The problem of the white cattlemen on the reservations was never satisfactorily faced because of the ambivalence of the government and of the reformers toward the matter. Vast areas of the reservations were lying empty and unused—a condition abhorrent to men imbued with the exploitative sentiment of the day. If the lands were not profitably used by the Indians, should they not be used by others who would pay for the use and provide funds for the benefit of the Indians? And could not the Indians learn by observing the profit-making enterprise of the whites in their midst? Would not such benefits outweigh the evils of white infiltration? No final answers were forthcoming. The solution instead was to eliminate the questions by doing away with the unused acres of the reservations, cutting down the holdings of the Indians as they were moved toward accepting land in severalty, and making the surplus lands directly accessible to the whites.

A strong argument for segregating the Indians had always been that a special curse of drunkenness afflicted Indians who were in contact with frontier whites. A vile breed of whisky traders seemed to appear as if by magic wherever there were Indians with goods or money that could be exchanged for intoxicating liquor. Such vendors had been the bane of every frontier from the Atlantic coast to the Pacific, and increasingly stringent laws to prevent their nefarious business had never been quite effective.[53] In the decades after the Civil War, the condem-

Study of the Failure of the U.S. Reservation Policy," *Pacific Historical Review*, XL (August, 1971), 333–55. See also Martha Buntin, "Beginning of the Leasing of the Surplus Grazing Lands on the Kiowa and Comanche Reservation," *Chronicles of Oklahoma*, X (September, 1932), 369–82. An excellent discussion of the problem of grazing leases on the Cherokee Outlet is in William W. Savage, Jr., *The Cherokee Strip Live Stock Association: Federal Regulation and the Cattleman's Last Frontier* (Columbia, Missouri, 1973).

[52] J. Orin Oliphant, "Encroachments of Cattlemen on Indian Reservations in the Pacific Northwest, 1870–1890," *Agricultural History*, XXIV (January, 1950), 42–58.

[53] See Prucha, *American Indian Policy in the Formative Years*, pp. 102–38; William E. Johnson, *The Federal Government and the Liquor Traffic* (Westerville, Ohio, 1917), pp. 183–238; Otto F. Frederikson, *The Liquor Question Among the Indian Tribes in Kansas, 1804–1881* (Lawrence, Kansas, 1932). A thorough analysis of Indian liquor laws is in Cohen, *Handbook of Federal Indian Law*, pp. 352–57.

nation of the liquor traffic on or near the reservations was a strident echo of earlier charges, and the attempts to plug all the loopholes by legislation were intensified.

The secretary of the Board of Indian Commissioners declared that liquor was the greatest obstacle to Indian civilization, that, notwithstanding the rigor of the laws, Indians had little difficulty in procuring liquor when they wanted it, and that whole tribes were being slowly but surely destroyed by the vice of drunkenness. Commissioner of Indian Affairs Hiram Price expressed a common view in his assertion in 1882 that "whiskey is the one great curse of the Indian country, the prolific source of disorder, tumult, crime, and disease, and if the sale could be utterly prohibited, peace and quiet would almost uniformly exist among the Indians from the Mississippi to the Pacific."[54]

The problem seemed almost insuperable. In order to obviate the difficulty of the divided jurisdiction between the federal and state governments, a law of 1862 had made it a crime to sell or give liquor to any Indian who was under the care of a superintendent or an agent without specifying that the act had to be done on a reservation. Permission was given to Indian superintendents and agents and to military post commanders to search for and seize liquors; any person in the service of the United States was permitted to destroy any such liquor found in the Indian country, and in 1864 that permission was changed to an obligation.[55] But the strongly worded laws were emasculated by the provision of maximum penalties but not minimum ones, for the judges in the West seldom applied penalties stiff enough to deter the whisky merchants. Nor did the laws block all the channels through which intoxicants flowed into the reservations. One of these was the army, for the laws exempted the War Department from their provisions, and liquor intended for the soldiers too often found its way into Indian hands. Another was the reservation traders, some of whom stocked a variety of items with an alcohol base that served well to intoxicate the Indians—concoctions described by a member of the Board of Indian Commissioners in 1878 as "bottled patent medicine contain-

[54] Report of the Board of Indian Commissioners, 1873, p. 31; Report of the Commissioner of Indian Affairs, 1882, in serial 2100, p. 11.

[55] Act of February 13, 1862, United States Statutes at Large, XII, 339; Act of March 15, 1864, ibid., XIII, 29.

ing principally alcohol, and used for drink, consisting of bay-rum, ginger, cologne, &c., prepared expressly for the Indians."[56]

Commissioner Price fumed against these problems during his four years in office, with a crescendo of complaint. He recommended a law prohibiting the manufacture or sale of liquor in any territory of the United States or, if that was impossible, within twenty miles of any Indian reservation. He was vehement against allowing the introduction of whisky by the army. "Fire should not be permitted near a powder-magazine," he said, "nor whiskey near an Indian reservation. Army whiskey is no better than other whiskey; it does not appear that its effects are any more desirable." He opposed, too, the exclusion of malt liquors from the prohibiting legislation. While he asked for and got an appropriation to aid in ferreting out and prosecuting persons who furnished the Indians with liquor, he considered this insufficient and called for the establishment of stiff minimum fines and imprisonment, since "some of the courts are extremely tender-hearted when sentence is to be pronounced on a wretch who furnishes liquor to Indians." The Indians themselves, he claimed, wanted the government to act. "What must an Indian think of a Government claiming to be governed by the principles of Christianity," he asked, "and urging them to abandon their heathenish practices and adopt the white man's ways, which at the same time allows the meanest and vilest creatures in the persons of white men to demoralize and debauch their young men by furnishing them with that which brutalizes and destroys them?"[57]

Price's agitation was in vain, but the evangelical reformers, whose organizations to aid the Indians came into full bloom during his administration of Indian affairs, carried on the crusade. These men and women, of course, had a strong temperance bent. Mrs. Amelia Quinton had had an active career as an organizer for the Woman's Christian Temperance Union (founded in 1874) and as a temperance lecturer before she started work in Indian reform.[58] Lyman Abbott, although

[56] *Report of the Board of Indian Commissioners*, 1878, p. 82.

[57] Report of the Commissioner of Indian Affairs, 1881, in serial 2018, pp. 24–25; *ibid.*, 1882, in serial 2100, p. 12; *ibid.*, 1883, in serial 2191, pp. 2–4; *ibid.*, 1884, in serial 2287, p. 5.

[58] The temperance activities of Mrs. Quinton are discussed in the biographical sketch of her by Irene Joanne Westing in *Notable American Women, 1607–1950: A Biographical Dictionary* (3 vols., Cambridge, Massachusetts, 1971), III, 108–10.

eschewing the extremes of prohibitionism, held firmly to temperance principles. He and his brothers had written a temperance novel in 1855, and as editor of the Tract Society's *Illustrated Christian Weekly* and then of the *Christian Union* he promoted the temperance cause.[59] The strongest anti-liquor figure among the important Indian reformers, however, was Clinton B. Fisk, an ardent Methodist who had distinguished himself as a Civil War general, an agent of the Freedmen's Bureau, and founder of Fisk University for Negroes. President Grant had appointed him to the Board of Indian Commissioners in 1874, and from 1881 until his death in 1890 he served as president of the board. As a total abstainer, he developed an interest in the Prohibition Party, and in 1888 he was the party's nominee for President.[60] Such leaders, backed by the ranks of Baptists, Methodists, and other evangelicals who staffed the reform organizations, easily made the liquor problem on the reservations one of their concerns. The Indian Office, too, continued to contribute its share of strong temperance men. Notable were Commissioner Morgan, an ordained Baptist minister, and his Superintendent of Indian Schools, Daniel Dorchester, a Methodist minister, who had written a number of temperance tracts and who served as president of the National League for the Suppression of the Liquor Traffic.[61]

Morgan first of all hit at the problem through means at his disposal and in accord with his views of educating the Indians to a high state of morality. He dismissed agency personnel who were themselves guilty of intemperance and refused to appoint anyone who would not pledge to abstain from drinking. "I do not wish to demand too much of an Indian agent," he said, "but it does seem as if sobriety might be reasonably required of those who represent, or are supposed to represent, to the Indians the civilization which we are trying to induce them to accept in lieu of their present condition." He also used the Indian school system to "inculcate principles of temperance" and instituted

[59] Ira V. Brown, *Lyman Abbott, Christian Evolutionist: A Study in Religious Liberalism* (Cambridge, Massachusetts, 1953), pp. 17, 62, 81.

[60] Frederic L. Paxson, "Clinton Bowen Fisk," *Dictionary of American Biography*, VI, 413–14.

[61] See Daniel Dorchester, *Latest Drink Sophistries versus Total Abstinence* (Boston, 1883), and *Non-Partisan Temperance Effort Defined, Advocated, and Vindicated* (Boston, 1885). Dorchester also wrote a long history of the liquor problem, *The Liquor Problem in All Ages* (New York, 1884; revised edition, 1888).

instruction in the evil effects of alcohol and narcotics.[62] But Morgan did not cease the campaign for stronger legislation, and he rejoiced that Congress in 1892 heeded his repetition of Price's demand that malt liquors as well as spirituous liquors be excluded from the Indian Territory and other Indian lands.[63]

The very civilization programs that the reformers promoted, however, weakened their temperance crusade. For the question soon arose whether the Indians who adopted the white man's ways could still be subject to special prohibitory legislation. One difficulty came from Indians who enlisted in the United States army. They bought liquor with their army pay and not only indulged to excess themselves but also supplied the Indians on nearby reservations, and it was questioned whether persons who sold liquor to these Indian soldiers could be indicted. The Indian Office in 1893 in answer declared its position that "the United States is not relieved from the responsibility assumed by it for the protection of Indians against influences calculated to degrade them morally and prevent them from advancing in the knowledge and customs of civilization by the mere fact of their having been enlisted in the armies of the Government."[64] The courts upheld this decision.

A more serious challenge to prohibition on the reservations came with the allotment of lands in severalty to the Indians under the Dawes Act of 1887. Indians who had received allotments and thereby had become citizens of the United States were judged by some courts no longer to fall under the laws forbidding the sale of liquor to Indians. Such a judicial interpretation seemed to counteract any advantages coming from allotments with the danger of opening the reservations to whisky sellers.[65] The solution would have to be new legislation that would explicitly provide for the allotted Indians.

[62] Report of the Commissioner of Indian Affairs, 1890, in serial 2841, pp. liv, lvii.

[63] Act of July 23, 1892, *United States Statutes at Large*, XXVII, 260–61; Report of the Commissioner of Indian Affairs, 1891, in serial 2934, pp. 74–76. Secretary of the Interior Noble said: "The law is now believed to be sufficient to give all possible protection to the Indians of the Indian Territory, or elsewhere, from the evil results of intemperance, and when enforced by the courts, as I confidently expect and hope they will be." Report of the Secretary of the Interior, 1892, in serial 2087, p. lxx.

[64] Report of the Commissioner of Indian Affairs, 1893, in serial 3210, pp. 57–58.

[65] The problem is discussed in the Report of the Commissioner of Indian Affairs, 1894, in serial 3306, pp. 60–64. The difficulties in enforcing the laws are illustrated in George Bird Grinnell, *The Enforcement of Liquor Laws a Necessary Protection to the Indians* (Philadelphia, 1893), a pamphlet published by the Indian Rights Association.

Such a bill was introduced in the House by Congressman George Meiklejohn of Nebraska on April 13, 1894, but although it passed the House on March 2, 1895, in the last hours of the Fifty-third Congress, there was no time for its consideration by the Senate.[66] At the urging of the Indian Office a similar measure was introduced by Meiklejohn on December 6, 1895, in the Fifty-fourth Congress. The bill attempted to strengthen the existing legislation in three ways. It made it unlawful to sell or give to the Indians "any essence, extract, bitters, preparation, compound, composition, or any article whatsoever under any name, label, or brand, which produces intoxication"—thus hitting at the patent medicines and at the practice of providing pickles, fruits, and other articles of diet with an alcoholic base for the Indian trade. Secondly, it changed the penalty for offenses from a maximum to a minimum imprisonment of not less than sixty days and a fine of not less than one hundred dollars for the first offense and not less than two hundred dollars for each subsequent offense. Finally, it defined the term "Indian" to include those who had received allotments as long as the allotment was held in trust by the government, any Indian under the charge of a superintendent or agent, as well as mixed-bloods over whom the government exercised guardianship.[67] The bill had the support of all the reforming elements. The Commissioner of Indian Affairs pushed it strongly, as did the Indian Rights Association and the Lake Mohonk Conference. Passed by the House on January 18 and by the Senate on January 25, the bill became law on January 30, 1897, and it was immediately hailed as a great step forward. It was, said the Commissioner, "of unusual importance to the service," and he sent copies of the law to every Indian agent, school superintendent, and special agent. The Indian Rights Association called it a piece of legislation "in which every friend of the red race will rejoice." Good results seemed to follow the law even though the problem of Indian drunkenness was by no means solved.[68]

[66] *House Journal*, 53 Congress, 2 session, serial 3196, pp. 333, 489; *House Journal*, 53 Congress, 3 session, serial 3291, pp. 110, 192. See also *House Report* No. 1781, 53 Congress, 3 session, serial 3346.

[67] *Senate Report* No. 1209, 54 Congress, 1 session, serial 3461. The legislative history of the bill (H.R. 280), is traced in *House Journal*, 54 Congress, 1 session, serial 3367a, pp. 20, 388, and *House Journal*, 54 Congress, 2 session, serial 3476a, pp. 92, 113, 144.

[68] Report of the Commissioner of Indian Affairs, 1896, in serial 3489, p. 55; *Report of the Indian Rights Association*, 1895, pp. 12–13; *Lake Mohonk Conference Proceed-*

The reformers were more successful in enacting programs for "elevating" the Indians than they were in providing for the basic human needs of the Indians in the process. The plains tribes, who got most of the attention, had been self-sufficient in their hunting culture. With the buffalo gone, these Indians were supposed to become self-sustaining agriculturalists almost immediately. For a short period the government was willing to provide subsistence—either through annuity arrangements or as gratuities—and it publicly proclaimed that it was cheaper to feed the Indians than to fight them. The rations in many cases, however, had to continue indefinitely, for the conversion to agriculture came slowly if at all, and large numbers of the former energetic and aggressive warriors became enervated and dispirited recipients of the dole. In such an unlooked-for circumstance, it was perhaps understandable that the rations supplied were insufficient and often poor in quality. Starvation and near-starvation conditions were prevalent, and the reformers and the Indian Office again and again had to make special appeals to stir Congress into making the necessary appropriations to prevent disaster. Cattle supplied for the purpose of starting a grazing economy among the Indians frequently disappeared to assuage hunger before they could begin to thrive. Other goods—clothing and farming implements, for example—were of bad quality and not plentiful enough to answer the Indians' needs.[69]

Such circumstances made the reservations appear to be mammoth poorhouses rather than nurseries of civilization, and they seriously undercut the positive efforts made to convert the Indians into American citizens. The reformers had looked with optimism to the reservations as halfway houses in which the native Americans could make a more or less speedy transition from their traditional ways to full acculturation. The change was to be made from the nomadic life of a buffalo hunter to the sedentary life of a small farmer, from communal patterns to fiercely individualistic ones, from native religious ceremonials to Christian practices, from Indian languages and oral tradi-

ings, 1896, p. 16; Report of the Commissioner of Indian Affairs, 1897, in serial 3641, pp. 56–57; *Report of the Indian Rights Association*, 1897, p. 32. See also *Lake Mohonk Conference Proceedings*, 1897, p. 115. The law is in *United States Statutes at Large*, XXIX, 506–507.

[69] I have been helped by a paper by William T. Hagan, "The Reservation Policy: Too Little and Too Late," read at the National Archives Conference on the History of Indian-White Relations in the United States, Washington, D.C., June 16, 1972.

tions to spoken and written English. For most of the reservation Indians, the changes were a shattering experience, demoralizing rather than uplifting the people. The self-reliance and self-support which underlay the hopes of the reformers for the Indians were little in evidence.[70]

The realization that the Indians were not changing as the reformers had so confidently believed they would led to an outright condemnation of the reservations as an unmitigated evil to be destroyed. The strongest voice raised against the reservations was that of Lyman Abbott, the vigorous proponent of so many reforms. Abbott admitted that his knowledge of the Indians was limited—that he had never visited an Indian reservation and had never known more than ten Indians—but his convictions about what was best for the Indians were absolute. The solution to the Indian problem, he believed, lay "in the annihilation of the reservation system root and branch."[71] To make sure that his views had wide impact, Abbott published them in his paper, *The Christian Union.*[72] But more than that, he hoped to have them adopted by the Lake Mohonk Conference. To that end, he called a preliminary meeting at his editorial offices in New York on July 7, 1885, to prepare for the coming meeting at Lake Mohonk in October. At hand were Albert K. Smiley and Eliphalet Whittlesey of the Board of Indian Commissioners, Samuel C. Armstrong of Hampton Institute and Richard H. Pratt of Carlisle Indian School, James E. Rhoads and Herbert Welsh of the Indian Rights Association, and the ethnologist Alice C. Fletcher. Senator Dawes was unable to attend. It soon became clear that Abbott's views were too radical to suit the rest of the reformers, for he argued that treaties made with the Indians should be unilaterally abrogated by the United States if they stood in the way of the abolition of the reservation system. Herbert Welsh took it upon

[70] For an excellent account of how the goals of the reformers fell short of accomplishment on the Kiowa and Comanche reservation, see William T. Hagan, "Indian Policy After the Civil War: The Reservation Experience," *American Indian Policy: Indiana Historical Society Lectures 1970–1971* (Indianapolis, 1971), pp. 20–36.

[71] Lyman Abbott, *Reminiscences* (Boston, 1915), pp. 425–26. The story of Abbott's work in Indian reform is well told in Brown, *Lyman Abbott*, pp. 89–98.

[72] For a condemnation of the reservation system, see Abbott's editorials in *The Christian Union*, XXXII (July 16, 1885), 3; (July 23, 1885), 3; (July 30, 1885), 4–5; (August 6, 1885), 3–4. A strong attack upon treaties and insistence that they should be "simply set aside" if the Indians would not consent to change them appears *ibid.*, XXXII (August 13, 1885), 4.

himself to head off "the crude and radical views" of Abbott, speaking against them to his colleagues and writing to Dawes to enlist his support.[73]

At Lake Mohonk Dawes spoke eloquently against Abbott's position, insisting that the treaties with the Indians were inviolate and could not in justice be overthrown. He referred to the petition submitted to Congress in 1883 by the Women's National Indian Association, which urged first of all that treaty obligations be observed, and he noted that members in both Houses had pledged themselves to maintain the treaty obligations of the United States. "I beg of you," he said, "not to ask of these men in Congress, who stand before the country, committed, that they shall openly violate the solemn treaties they have made."[74]

Abbott was not easily put down and spoke his mind forcefully at the conference. "If we have made a bad contract," he said, "it is better broken than kept. . . . It is not right to do a wrong thing, and if you have agreed to do a wrong thing, that agreement does not make it right." And he continued:

> I declare my conviction then that the reservation system is hope-lessly wrong; that it cannot be amended or modified; that it can only be uprooted, root, trunk, branch, and leaf, and a new system put in its place. We evangelical ministers believe in immediate repentance. I hold to immediate repentance as a national duty. Cease to do evil, cease instantly, abruptly, immediately. I hold that the reservation barriers should be cast down and the land given to the Indians in severalty; that every Indian should be protected in his right to his home, and in his right to free intercourse and free trade, whether the rest of the tribe wish him so protected or not; that these are his individual, personal rights, which no tribe has the right to take from him, and no nation the right to sanction the robbery of.[75]

Most of his listeners were not quite ready for immediate repentance,

[73] On Abbott's planning for the Lake Mohonk Conference and reaction thereto, see copy of "Proceedings of Informal Indian Meeting Held by Request of Dr. Lyman Abbott," sent to Dawes by Herbert Welsh, in Dawes Papers, Box 27. Welsh's concern over Abbott's views and his attempts to get support for opposition to Abbott at Lake Mohonk are shown in Welsh to Dawes, July 25, August 19, and August 31, 1885, *ibid.* The letter of July 25 is quoted in Priest, *Uncle Sam's Stepchildren*, pp. 245–46.
[74] *Lake Mohonk Conference Proceedings*, 1885, p. 41.
[75] *Ibid.*, pp. 50–53.

for they were strongly committed to maintaining the formal treaty rights of the Indians. Although Abbott served on the resolutions committee at the conference, he was unable to swing the gathering completely to his way of thinking. The platform adopted was a compromise. It agreed to the principle of allotting the lands of the reservations in severalty, and it urged that negotiations be undertaken to modify existing treaties and that "these negotiations should be pressed in every honorable way until the consent of the Indians be obtained." But it rejected the proposal to abrogate the treaties or to force severalty upon the Indians.[76]

There could be little doubt, however, that the powerful drive then under way for general allotment of land in severalty and for extending United States law over the Indians was intended ultimately to destroy the reservation system.

[76] *Ibid.*, p. 49. On October 11, 1885, two days after the Lake Mohonk meeting, Mrs. Henry L. Dawes wrote to her daughter, Anna: "The Abbott phase was *managed.* Dr. Abbott made a *very good* and effective speech on his side, but the current was set strongly the other way. Some of the *wisest* of the men said that your Father smashed him!!" Dawes Papers, quoted in Brown, *Lyman Abbott,* p. 269.

CHAPTER 8

ALLOTMENT OF LANDS IN SEVERALTY

There can be but little doubt that this [Dawes Act] is one of the most vital and important steps ever taken by Congress in its dealings with the Indians. It may be said to make an era; to be the beginning of a new order of things. In its very nature it is a new departure on the part of Congress. Legislation on this subject in the past has consisted largely of provisions for the needs of some particular tribes, in appropriation bills, or in some necessary regulations as to the intercourse between whites and Indians. But here is a law of practically general application, which is neither a matter of temporary expediency nor of immediate necessity, but which means that Congress has at last inaugurated a definite and comprehensive policy in regard to the Indians. That policy is the broad and obvious one which has been urged for years by sensible and practical friends of the Indians and by this Association. The policy which tempers the danger of ultimately radical changes with the wise safeguards of conservative restrictions; which would help the Indians to become independent farmers and stock men by making them individual land holders; which looks to the gradual breaking up of the reservations on which the Indians are shut from all wholesome contact with our civilization; which loosens the fatal tribal bonds by bringing the Indians under our laws, and making the way broad for their entrance into citizenship.

—The Indian Rights Association in 1887

❁❁❁❁❁❁❁

No panacea for the Indian problem was more persistently proposed

227

than the allotment of land to the Indians in severalty. It was an article of faith with the reformers that civilization was impossible without the incentive to work that came only from individual ownership of a piece of property.

The faith had deep roots in the American tradition; by no means was severalty a latter-day solution thought up to meet the crisis in Indian affairs in the 1880's. Historians have found the idea in early colonial days, when the General Court of Massachusetts in 1633 ordered that Indians who came to the English plantations and lived in a civil and orderly manner should have "allotments amongst the English, according to the custom of the English in like cases."[1] But advocacy of individual ownership of property as a means of transforming the Indians into acceptable members of white society first became strong in the early days of the republic. Henry Knox, the humanitarian-minded first Secretary of War, admitted in 1789 that the civilization of the Indians would be "an operation of complicated difficulty," but he did not doubt its possibility. A first step, he thought, would be an attempt to instill in the Indians a "love for exclusive property," and to this end he recommended gifts of sheep and other stock to the chiefs and their wives.[2] Thomas Jefferson, hoping to fasten upon the Indians the pattern of the yeoman farmer which he revered, urged holding land in severalty. "Let me entreat you . . . on the land now given you," he told a delegation of chiefs in 1808, "to begin to give every man a farm; let him enclose it, cultivate it, build a warm house on it, and when he dies, let it belong to his wife and children after him." Jefferson tried to convince the Indians that the only way to prevent the loss of lands was to have individual ownership of farms, which the tribe could not take away or sell.[3]

Although the government was generally unwilling to grant the allotments of land in fee simple that Jefferson's proposals envisaged, the idea of individual holdings made considerable headway in treaties with the Indians, which provided reservations of land for chiefs and

---

[1] J. P. Kinney, *A Continent Lost—A Civilization Won: Indian Land Tenure in America* (Baltimore, 1937), p. 82. Kinney's book is a comprehensive cumulation of information about Indian land tenure and United States policy in regard to it.

[2] Knox to George Washington, July 7, 1789, *American State Papers: Indian Affairs* (2 vols., Washington, 1832–1834), I, 53–54.

[3] Address of Jefferson to Indian chiefs, December 21, 1808, *Writings of Thomas Jefferson*, ed. Andrew A. Lipscomb (20 vols., Washington, 1903–1904), XVI, 452–53.

other persons when land cessions were negotiated.[4] The holdings were not usually in fee, since provisions were attached which prevented free alienation of the land; the allotments were to revert to the United States if voluntarily abandoned and could be disposed of only in restricted ways or with specific permission of the President.

The removal years of the 1830's saw an increasing emphasis on severalty. Lewis Cass, announcing in his first report as Secretary of War in 1831 that "a crisis in our Indian affairs has evidently arrived, which calls for the establishment of a system of policy adapted to the existing state of things, and calculated to fix upon a permanent basis the future destiny of the Indians," proposed among other things that the Indians be encouraged to adopt severalty of property. His Commissioner of Indian Affairs, Elbert Herring, presented a more fully formulated theory of private property as a *sine qua non* of advancement in civilization for the Indians:

> The unrestrained authority of their chiefs, and the irresponsible exercise of power are of the simplest elements of despotic rule; while the absence of the *meum* and *tuum* in the general community of possessions, which is the grand conservative principle of the social state, is a perpetual operating cause of the *vis inertiae* of savage life. The stimulus of physical exertion and intellectual exercise, contained in this powerful principle, of which the Indian is almost entirely void, may not unjustly be considered the parent of all improvements, not merely in the arts, but in the profitable direction of labor among civilized nations. Among them it is the source of plenty; with the Indians, the absence of it is the cause of want, and consequently of decrease of numbers.[5]

These ideas were widely accepted by men concerned with Indian affairs. "Unless some system is marked out by which there shall be a separate allotment of land to each individual whom the scheme shall entitle to it," one official wrote in 1838, "you will look in vain for any general casting off of savagism. Common property and civilization

[4] For an able discussion of the Senate's hesitancy to grant lands to Indians in fee simple, see Robert W. McCluggage, "The Senate and Indian Land Titles, 1800–1825," *Western Historical Quarterly*, I (October, 1970), 415–25.

[5] Report of the Secretary of War, 1831, *House Executive Document* No. 2, 22 Congress, 1 session, serial 216, pp. 27, 34; Report of the Commissioner of Indian Affairs, 1832, in serial 233, p. 163.

cannot co-exist." Individuality of property, in his view, was the very foundation of the social system and the stimulus that produced energy and enterprise, contributed to the good morals of men, and provided "all the delights that the word home expresses." He was convinced that the Indians would have to adopt the practice, and he felt that they would do so rapidly. Extensive fields, rich pastures, and valuable stock belong to the man "who is conscious that what he ploughs is his own, and will descend to those he loves." Among those who do not know by what tenure they hold the land, "laziness and unthrift will be so general as not to be disgraceful."[6]

The implementation of these ideas came slowly but steadily. A notable example was the provision made for New York Indians in Wisconsin. Congress in 1839 authorized the allotment of lands in fee simple to Brotherton Indians in the area east of Lake Winnebago ceded by the Menominees and the granting of full citizenship to the Indians. A law of 1843 made similar provisions for the Stockbridge Indians in the same region.[7] The great bulk of allotment provisions, however, came through treaties rather than congressional legislation. Between March 4, 1853, and his annual report of November 22, 1856, Indian Commissioner George W. Manypenny reported the negotiation of fifty-two treaties, a considerable number of which had as their primary purpose the permanent settlement of individuals on separate tracts of land or homesteads and the gradual abolition of the tribal character.[8]

Manypenny's successors continued his principles. James W. Denver in 1857 objected to the policy of granting large areas to Indian tribes to hold in common since this tended "directly to prevent the Indians from acquiring settled habits and an idea of personal property and rights, which lie at the very foundation of all civilization." And Charles M. Mix, the following year, indicated that one important element in his Indian policy was locating tribes on reservations with only sufficient land for their actual use, dividing this land among them in severalty, and requiring the Indians to live on and cultivate the tracts allotted to them. In 1859 Secretary of the Interior Jacob Thompson spoke en-

---

[6] *Ibid.*, 1838, in serial 338, pp. 454–55.
[7] *United States Statutes at Large*, V, 349–51, 645–47.
[8] Report of the Commissioner of Indian Affairs, 1856, in serial 875, p. 571. Kinney has a discussion of Manypenny's treaties in *A Continent Lost*, pp. 114–24. A critical account of these allotments is in Gates, *Fifty Million Acres*.

thusiastically about the success already achieved. "Wherever separate farms have been assigned within the limits of a tribal reservation to individual Indians, and the owners have entered into possession," he reported, "a new life is apparent, comparative plenty is found on every hand, contentment reigns at every fireside, and peace and order have succeeded to turbulence and strife." He spoke of allotment in severalty as "the fixed policy of the government" and the "leading idea in all the treaties recently negotiated with the Indians."[9] There was no letup during subsequent administrations. Commissioner William P. Dole, so eager to confine the tribes on tidy reservations, pushed allotment in severalty to the Indians as "the best method yet devised for their reclamation and advancement in civilization." The only error in practice, he thought, was making allotments to all members of a band or tribe regardless of the dispositions and abilities of each individual. He wanted allotment to be a special mark of favor and approbation from the government to be given to Indians of good conduct, industry, and a disposition to abandon the ancient customs of the tribe.[10]

By the end of the treaty-making period approximately seventy treaties had included specific provisions for allotment of lands to individuals meeting certain requirements, and a large number of other treaties had provided for granting tracts of land in severalty to chiefs, mixed-bloods, and other special classes of persons. The great majority of the treaties concluded in 1853 and afterward contained provisions for the division of lands in severalty as a primary feature.[11]

The upsurge of humanitarian concern for Indian reform in the two decades following the Civil War gave a new impetus to the severalty principle, which was almost universally accepted and aggressively promoted, until Congress finally passed a general allotment law. This is

[9] Report of the Commissioner of Indian Affairs, 1857, in serial 919, p. 292; *ibid.*, 1858, in serial 974, p. 355; Report of the Secretary of the Interior, 1859, in serial 1023, p. 99. Thompson repeated the same ideas the next year.
[10] Report of the Commissioner of Indian Affairs, 1862, in serial 1157, p. 169; *ibid.*, 1863, in serial 1182, p. 130.
[11] Kinney, *A Continent Lost*, p. 156. See the "Statement showing number of patents for land issued to individuals of the several Indian tribes up to September 1, 1885," which also indicates the treaties and laws under which the patents were issued, in Report of the Commissioner of Indian Affairs, 1885, in serial 2379, pp. 546–47. There is a valuable discussion of allotments in Paul W. Gates, "Indian Allotments Preceding the Dawes Act," in John G. Clark, ed., *The Frontier Challenge: Responses to the Trans-Mississippi West* (Lawrence, Kansas, 1971), pp. 141–70.

not surprising in the light of the long history of provision for allotments; what is surprising is the almost blind enthusiasm with which the policy was advocated despite considerable evidence from the previous half-century of experience that allotment had not been an unmixed blessing. But allotment of land in severalty was part of the drive to individualize the Indian that became the obsession of the late nineteenth-century Christian reformers and did not stand by itself. The breakup of tribalism, which was a major goal of this Indian policy, had been moved forward by the abolition of the treaty system and would be carried on by a government educational system and by the extension of American law over the Indian communities. For many years, however, the dissolution of the communal lands by allotment in severalty, together with the citizenship attached to private land owning, was a central issue.

The various advocates of the peace policy spoke almost in unison. The General Assembly of the Society of Friends that met in Baltimore in January, 1869, memorialized Congress: "It is our belief that the sooner the tribal relation is broken up, and the Indian population permanently attached to the land, and brought under the same laws, privileges, and responsibilities with the rest of the community, the better it will be for the whole country." Ely S. Parker, Grant's first Commissioner of Indian Affairs, spoke of the requests of the Indians for allotments in severalty as an "indication of progress," and he declared that under this plan the Indians would advance more rapidly in civilization than if they continued to hold lands in common. Commissioner Edward P. Smith asserted that a "fundamental difference between barbarians and a civilized people is the difference between a herd and an individual," and that the starting point of individualism for the Indian lay in personal possession of his portion of the reservation.[12]

Little by little the movement gained momentum. The Board of Indian Commissioners in its first report recommended giving land in severalty as soon as it was desired by any of the Indians, and it continued from that time on to push the measure. Secretaries of the In-

[12] Memorial on treatment of the Indians, January 21, 1869, *House Miscellaneous Document* No. 29, 40 Congress, 3 session, serial 1385; Report of the Commissioner of Indian Affairs, 1870, in serial 1449, p. 473; *ibid.*, 1873, in serial 1601, p. 372.

terior Delano and Chandler favored the changes. Indian Commissioner John Q. Smith in 1876 called for a "general law" which would not only permit but require each Indian family to accept the allotment of a tract of land as private property in lieu of any interest in communal tribal possessions. He appreciated the opposition that would arise to such a measure from Indians themselves, and he attributed such attitudes to ambitious men who would lose authority under the new dispensation. "But it is essential," Smith declared, "that these men and their claims should be pushed aside and that each individual should feel that his home is his own; that he owes no allegiance to any great man or to any faction; that he has a direct personal interest in the soil on which he lives, and that that interest will be faithfully protected for him and for his children by the Government." The commissioner, in common with most advocates of severalty, wanted the allotments to be inalienable for a number of years—he specified "at least twenty, perhaps fifty years"—to protect the Indians from sharpers and speculators who would surely be on hand to relieve the unwary Indians of their possessions.[13]

What the advocates of change wanted ultimately was general legislation that would permit or require the allotment of lands in severalty for all the Indians on reservations, but they did not hesitate to support halfway measures that pointed in the proper direction. One such measure was provision for Indians to take out homesteads under the Homestead Law of 1862. Extension of the homestead principle to Indians was recommended by Delano in 1874, with a further recommendation that the homesteads patented by Indians should be inalienable except by permission of the President.[14] In the next year, Congress

[13] Report of the Secretary of the Interior, 1873, in serial 1601, pp. v–vi; *ibid.*, 1876, in serial 1749, pp. vi–vii; Report of the Commissioner of Indian Affairs, 1876, in serial 1749, p. 387.

[14] In support of his proposal Delano cited the usual litany of benefits: "An extension to the Indians of the benefits of the homestead-laws, under the safeguards mentioned, and such others as the wisdom of Congress may suggest, will greatly facilitate the work of their civilization. It will rapidly break up tribal organizations and Indian communities; it will bring Indians into subjection to our laws, civil and criminal; it will induce them to abandon roving habits; and teach them the benefits of industry and individual ownership, and thus prove highly advantageous in promoting their prosperity." Report of the Secretary of the Interior, 1874, in serial 1639, pp. v, vii.

233

provided that all the benefits of the Homestead Law should apply to the Indians, without their losing any share in tribal funds. To protect the Indians, the lands were declared inalienable for five years after the issuance of the final patent. This was some protection, but it was not enough to satisfy all the reformers.[15]

The Indian homestead legislation had little effect. It was enacted in a hurry as part of a deficiency appropriation bill on the last day of a session and as a result was never debated. The Senate included provisions for the Indians to cut their tribal ties and to become citizens of the United States. When the House refused to concur, the conference committee eliminated the citizenship clause and provided for the continuation of annuity payments and other tribal benefits to Indians taking advantage of the law.[16] Then Congress in 1884 declared that Indians could take full advantage of the homestead laws without paying fees or commissions, and it appropriated the small sum of one thousand dollars to aid them in making selections of land. Indian homesteads were to be held in trust for the Indians by the United States for a period of twenty-five years, at the end of which time they would be conveyed to the Indian or his heirs in fee simple.[17] Government officials, unfortunately, seemed to be unaware of the homesteading opportunities, and few Indians availed themselves of the chance for private land ownership that they furnished.[18]

A pilot case on severalty occurred as a result of an outbreak among the Utes in Colorado in 1879. These Indians, by a treaty of 1868, had been guaranteed a reservation in the western quarter of Colorado. Two agencies were to be maintained, one on the White River for two bands in the north and the other on the Los Pinos River for three bands in the south, and provisions were made for education, for individual home-

[15] *United States Statutes at Large*, XVIII, 420; Report of the Commissioner of Indian Affairs, 1875, in serial 1680, p. 517.
[16] *Senate Journal*, 43 Congress, 2 session, serial 1628, pp. 418, 423, 432; *Congressional Record*, III, 2182, 2205.
[17] *United States Statutes at Large*, XXIII, 96; Report of the Secretary of the Interior, 1884, in serial 2286, pp. xii–xiii; Report of the Commissioner of Indian Affairs, 1884, in serial 2287, p. 8. Commissioner Price had strongly recommended the measure from the beginning of his term of office.
[18] See Priest, *Uncle Sam's Stepchildren*, pp. 180–82.

steads, and for stock, seeds, and implements to start the Utes on the road toward civilization.[19] The expanding mining frontier in Colorado, however, soon encroached upon the reserved lands, and a United States commission, headed by Felix Brunot of the Board of Indian Commissioners, succeeded in gaining from the Indians in 1873 a large cession of land in the southern part of the reservation. The Utes remained at peace and under Chief Ouray exhibited loyalty and friendship to the United States. But white pressures upon the Utes' lands did not let up, and after the admission of Colorado as a state in 1876 they became incessant, as the state's inhabitants, its government, and the press shouted in ever louder chorus, "The Utes must go!" The tension between the two races was aggravated by failures on the part of the government to provide promptly the goods and services it had promised in the treaties.[20]

A violent outbreak might have been avoided but for a change in agents at the White River Agency in 1878. In that year, Agent H. E. Danforth, a nominee of the Unitarians under the peace policy, was replaced by Nathan C. Meeker. Meeker, born near Cleveland, Ohio, in 1817, had had an intriguing career. Something of a visionary, he became converted to the agrarian socialism of Fourier and lived for several years in a phalanx in Ohio. His economic enterprises were seldom successful, and he was constantly on the move, but he was interested in writing and, when his work came to the attention of Horace Greeley, Meeker was hired by the *New York Tribune*. He served as agricultural editor of the *Tribune* and became a national authority on agriculture. But he had not lost his utopian dreams; on a trip to the West in 1869, he determined to set up an ideal agricultural community, and with Greeley's enthusiastic support founded "Union Colony" in eastern Colorado. The community, soon named Greeley, prospered, but Meeker himself seemed always to be in debt. When he was offered the Indian agency at White River, therefore, he saw it as a way to a sure income. But he also looked upon it as an opportunity to

[19] Kappler, *Indian Affairs: Laws and Treaties*, II, 990–93.

[20] The Ute problems and the conflict they led to at White River are discussed in Report of the Commissioner of Indian Affairs, 1879, in serial 1910, pp. 82–97. Two studies which treat the episode in detail are Robert Emmitt, *The Last War Trail: The Utes and the Settlement of Colorado* (Norman, 1954), and Marshall Sprague, *Massacre: The Tragedy of White River* (Boston, 1957).

try his agricultural principles as a solution to the Indian problem—to build a Union Colony among the Utes.[21]

Meeker moved the agency down river to a spot more suitable for his agricultural plans and began to plow, fence, and irrigate the meadows which had been the favored grazing grounds for the Indians' ponies. He met adamant opposition from some members of the tribe, who had no interest in farming and who objected to Meeker's plowing up their lands. When the agent realized their growing antagonism, he called for military support, and troops under Major Thomas T. Thornburgh were dispatched from Fort Fred Steele to strengthen the agent's position. Thornburgh's troops were attacked as they entered the reservation and the major and eleven of his soldiers were killed. At the same time, the agency was assaulted; Meeker and eight others were killed, and Meeker's wife and daughters were taken captive. It was a tragic ending for a good man, whose obstinacy and lack of understanding of the Indians brought his death.[22] Even Clinton B. Fisk, chairman of the Board of Indian Commissioners, who might have been expected to sympathize with the aggressive civilizing program that Meeker attempted, declared the agent "destitute of that particular tact and knowledge of the Indian character which is required of an agent; a man of too many years to begin with, unhappily constituted in his mental organization for any such place." Fisk viewed Meeker's whole administration as a failure.[23]

Although the uprising, the work of a small group of Indians, was quickly quieted through the good offices of Ouray and the concentration of additional troops in the area, the effect upon the Coloradans was electrifying. It was just the occasion they looked for to demand a war of extermination against the Utes.

[21] For biographical information on Meeker, see the article by J. F. Willard in *Dictionary of American Biography*, XII, 497–98; Emmitt, *Last War Trail*, pp. 44–53; Sprague, *Massacre*, pp. 3–60.

[22] Contemporary newspaper accounts are gathered together in Thomas F. Dawson and F. J. V. Skiff, *The Ute War: A History of the White River Massacre and the Privations and Hardships of the Captive White Women among the Hostiles on Grand River* (Denver, 1879; facsimile edition, Boulder, 1964). A wealth of documentation is printed in *Senate Executive Document* No. 31, 46 Congress, 2 session, serial 1882; testimony taken at Los Pinos Agency, November, 1879, to January, 1880, is in "White River Ute Commission Investigation," *House Executive Document* No. 83, 46 Congress, 2 session, serial 1925; and testimony taken in Washington, January to March, 1880, is in *House Miscellaneous Document* No. 38, 46 Congress, 2 session, serial 1931.

[23] *Ibid.*, p. 45.

Carl Schurz as Secretary of the Interior moved at once to prevent an expensive and destructive war, which he was sure would come if the situation of the Utes in Colorado could not be radically changed. He sent a special agent to get back the captives, in the first place, and then to obtain the surrender of the guilty Indians. But Schurz was chiefly interested in a plan for long-range settlement of the difficulties, a plan he expressed in succinct terms: "the settlement of the Utes in severalty, so as to promote the civilization of the Indians, and to open the main part of the Ute reservation to development by white citizens, thus removing a source of constant irritation between the latter and the Utes."[24]

An agreement was signed in Washington on March 6, 1880, by representatives of the Ute tribe, which provided for removal of the White River Utes to the Uintah Reservation in Utah and for the bands of Uncompahgre and Southern Utes to settle on lands on the Grand River and the La Plata River. But more important than the designation of these locations was the provision that allotments of land in severalty were to be made to the Indians—160 acres to the head of a family and lesser amounts for other classes of individuals, with a like amount of additional land for grazing purposes. These allotments were to be inalienable for twenty-five years. All the rest of the original reservation was to be ceded to the United States for a variety of annuities and other payments. Consent of three-fourths of the adult males of the tribes was required before the agreement would take effect.[25] The agreement, when it was sent to Congress for ratification, elicited heated debate, and the arguments for and against severalty were well aired. The later debates on a general severalty law, which followed shortly, were in many respects only a repetition of this earlier debate.[26]

Senator Richard Coke of Texas, chairman of the Committee on

[24] Report of the Secretary of the Interior, 1879, in serial 1910, pp. 16–19. The quotation is from "Agreement with Ute Indians of Colorado," *House Report* No. 1401, 46 Congress, 2 session, serial 1937, p. 2.
[25] The agreement is in *Senate Executive Document* No. 114, 46 Congress, 2 session, serial 1885; it is also printed as part of the law in *United States Statutes at Large*, XXI, 200–202.
[26] The extensive debate in the Senate, April 1–12, 1880, is in *Congressional Record*, X, 2027–30, 2058–67, 2152–64, 2189–2202, 2221–28, 2249–68, 2309–20. Debate in the House appears *ibid.*, 4251–63; House speeches on the topic are printed *ibid.*, Appendix, pp. 100–105, 233–37, 274–76.

Indian Affairs, reported the bill in the Senate and set forth clearly the position of the proponents of severalty:

> The policy of the bill is to break up this large reservation, to individualize the Indians upon allotments of land; to break up their tribal relations and pass them under the jurisdiction of the Constitution and laws of the United States and the laws of the States and Territories in which the lands are situated, to aid them with stock and with agricultural implements, and by building houses upon their allotments of land, to become self-supporting, to be cultivators of the soil; in a word, to place them on the highway to American citizenship, and to aid them in arriving at that conclusion as rapidly as can be done.
>
> The bill is in many respects a departure from the ancient and established policy of the Government with reference to the Indian tribes. The advance of settlements in the West has been so rapid that it has been found inexpedient and impolitic, as leading to collisions between the whites and the Indians, to continue the system of locking or attempting to lock up large tracts of land within their exclusive occupancy. The whites cannot be restrained from intrusion upon these large reservations. The Indians will not use them except for hunting purposes and the whites will not permit them to remain unused.
>
> The bill simply recognizes the logic of events, which shows that it is impossible to preserve peace between the Indians and the whites with these immense bodies of land attempted to be locked up as Indian reservations. . . .[27]

Underlying all the arguments in favor of the bill was the sense of inevitability that Coke expressed. Schurz, in his strong support of the bill before the joint committees on Indian affairs, candidly admitted that the system of large reservations would "in the course of time, become utterly untenable," that as available lands became scarcer and more valuable it was "not unnatural that the withholding of large tracts from settlement and development so as to maintain a savage aristocracy in the enjoyment of their chivalrous pastimes, should be looked upon by many as a system incompatible with the progress of

[27] *Ibid.*, 2059.

civilization and injurious to the material interests of the country." He saw the impossibility of the government's being able always to control the action of the western people. So he urged the "new system." Its ultimate and necessary end, he said, was that "the Indians be gradually assimilated to and merged in the body of citizens."[28]

The inevitability of change also struck the members of the Board of Indian Commissioners as they contemplated the situation of the Utes in a Colorado filling up with a busy and enterprising population.

It is as evident to every reflecting mind that civilization and bar-barism cannot long live side by side as it was to President Lincoln that the country could not long remain "half slave and half free." There is the same "irrepressible conflict" between civilization and barbarism as between freedom and slavery. Barbarism must yield to and accept civilization, flee before it, or sooner or later be overborne by it. As friends of the Indians, our efforts are directed to induce them to accept civilization, while as loyal citizens we use what influence we have to induce the government to be just, patient, kind, and even generous to this weak and ignorant race. . . .

We may moralize over the natural rights of the Indian as much as we please, but after all they have their limit. His right to the soil is only possessory. He has no title in fee. If he will cultivate it and use it as civilized men use their possessions, it will and should be well with him; but it is evident that no 12,000,000 acres of the public domain whose hills are full of ores, and whose valley are waiting for diligent hands to "dress and keep them," in obedience to the divine command, can long be kept simply as a park, in which wild beasts are hunted by wilder men. This Anglo-Saxon race will not allow the car of civilization to stop long at any line of latitude or longitude on our broad domain. If the Indian in his wildness plants himself on the track, he must inevitably be crushed by it. But when he sets his face and his heart towards civilization, as many have done and are doing, then it becomes alike the interest and the duty both of the government and the people to afford all needed aid.[29]

One member of the Board of Indian Commissioners, David H.

---

[28] *House Report* No. 1401, 46 Congress, 2 session, serial 1937, pp. 2–3.
[29] *Report of the Board of Indian Commissioners*, 1879, pp. 11–12.

Jerome, on returning from an investigation of the Indians in Colorado even before the Meeker tragedy, declared: "My judgment is that we should make more progress by working in harmony with the inevitable than to battle for abstract rights. *Occupancy I believe to be the only practical way of holding these lands.*"[30]

The attack upon the Ute bill in Congress was led by Senator Henry Moore Teller of Colorado. A New Yorker by birth who had moved to Colorado shortly before the Civil War, he was elected Senator when Colorado became a state in 1876.[31] He could claim to have more first-hand contact with the Indian problem and a sounder understanding of Indian culture than most of those who wanted to reform Indian policy, and his views on severalty were decidedly negative. He denied that severalty was a means of civilizing the Indians, asserted that it would not work until the Indians were already civilized, and declared that individual ownership of parcels of land went against the customs and the religious beliefs of the Indians. He made some telling points, but the effectiveness of his argument was weakened by his obvious special pleading for the citizens of Colorado (he insisted that the Utes be removed entirely from the state), and by his harsh views of the Indians ("We ought not to forget that we are dealing with savages—brutal, bloody savages—and we never should deal with savages as we deal with civilized people"). He turned his attack upon the principles of the Ute bill into a display of his animus toward Schurz. He cried that the bill was intended not to save the Indians but to save the Indian department; ". . . it is to cover up, under the plea of keeping the peace, the stupidity and ignorance that have signalized the conduct of the Indian Office during the past three years; to direct attention from the many blunders and misfortunes of that office."[32] That Teller's cries to a large extent reflected his personal views was indicated by the support given to the Ute bill by Teller's partner in the Senate, Nathaniel Hill, and by Colorado's Congressman, James B. Belford.[33]

[30] *Ibid.*, p. 50. Italics in the original.
[31] For a biography of Teller which pays considerable attention to his long interest in Indian matters, see Elmer Ellis, *Henry Moore Teller: Defender of the West* (Caldwell, Idaho, 1941).
[32] *Congressional Record*, X, 2059–61.
[33] See Hill's comments in the Senate on April 2, 1880, *ibid.*, 2066–67, and Belford's speech of June 1, 1880, *ibid.*, Appendix, pp. 233–36.

No doubt aided by the exigencies of the Colorado situation, as well as by the support of strong advocates of a fundamental change in Indian policy, the bill passed easily in both House and Senate, and when divergent amendments of the two houses were straightened out in committee, it became law on June 15, 1880. The act provided for a commission of five men to present the amended agreement to the Utes for their approval, to draw up a census of the tribe, and to arrange for the survey of the lands and for their allotment in severalty. The commission, with former Commissioner George W. Manypenny as chairman and the Indian reformer A. B. Meacham as one of its members, obtained the consent of the Indians and set about the task of allotting the lands in severalty.[34]

Meanwhile the drive for a general allotment law was stepped up.[35] Early in 1879, Commissioner of Indian Affairs E. A. Hayt drew up a draft of such legislation, which he announced to the meeting of the Board of Indian Commissioners and the missionary societies on January 15. Then on January 24, he sent the bill to Secretary Schurz, together with a long letter in which he advanced arguments similar to those used to support the Ute bill. The history of the past fifty years, he asserted, had proved that the government was impotent to protect the Indians on their reservations, especially when the lands were held in common. Thus the measures seeking the civilization of the Indians and their advance toward self-support had of necessity failed, as the Indians were continually moved from place to place in front of the oncoming white settlers. Commonalty of lands, furthermore, was pernicious to the Indians, for it "repressed that spirit of rivalry and the desire to accumulate property for personal use or comfort which is the source of success and advancement in all white communities." Hayt pointed to the numerous treaties with allotment provisions as support of his analysis, but criticized them for failure to protect the Indian

[34] *United States Statutes at Large*, XXI, 199–205; "Report of Ute Commission," *Senate Executive Document* No. 31, 46 Congress, 3 session, serial 1943.

[35] A detailed account of the general allotment law, the motives behind it, and its effects is D. S. Otis, *The Dawes Act and the Allotment of Indian Lands*, edited by Francis Paul Prucha (Norman, 1973), a monograph published originally in 1934. The reform movement culminating in the Dawes Act is studied in Priest, *Uncle Sam's Stepchildren*.

allotments adequately from imprudent alienation, and his own proposal included a provision against alienation for a period of twenty-five years. The inefficiency of the old system of common title and of the treaties which granted land in severalty with a title in fee had been demonstrated, he thought, and he believed that his plan with delayed title would solve the problem. By such a measure, he was convinced that "the race can be led in a few years to a condition where they may be clothed with citizenship and left to their own resources to maintain themselves as citizens of the republic."[36] Hayt's bill was sent to the House with strong approval by Schurz; it was introduced on January 31, 1879, and won the support of the House Committee on Indian Affairs. On February 6 a similar measure was introduced in the Senate, but neither bill progressed to a vote.[37]

In April, 1879, in the next session of Congress, general severalty bills were introduced in both houses, but to no avail. Renewed attempts were made in 1880. A revised bill in the House again got support of the Committee on Indian Affairs, although a strong minority report was submitted, but the measure did not get as far as discussion on the floor. In the Senate, new bills were introduced in January and again in May.[38]

The Senate bill introduced on May 19, 1880, by Senator Coke became the center of attention for the advocates of the allotment policy, and it was debated vigorously in the Senate over a period of several days in January and February, 1881.[39] The bill provided that in cases where the President decided that reservations were fit for agricultural purposes, he could direct the allotment of lands in severalty—160 acres to the head of a family, 80 acres to single persons over eighteen years of age, 40 acres to orphans under eighteen, and 20 acres to other children. The sale of the excess lands to the government was to be negotiated

[36] *Report of the Board of Indian Commissioners*, 1878, pp. 122, 129–33; Hayt to Schurz, January 24, 1879, *House Report* No. 165, 45 Congress, 3 session, serial 1866, pp. 2–3. Hayt repeated his arguments in Report of the Commissioner of Indian Affairs, 1879, in serial 1910, p. 70.

[37] *House Journal*, 45 Congress, 3 session, serial 1841, pp. 332, 685; *Senate Journal*, 45 Congress, 3 session, serial 1827, p. 227; *House Report* No. 165, 45 Congress, 3 session, serial 1866.

[38] *Senate Journal*, 46 Congress, 1 session, serial 1868, pp. 82, 139; *House Journal*, 46 Congress, 1 session, serial 1874, p. 127; *House Journal*, 46 Congress, 2 session, serial 1901, pp. 725, 1228, 1343; *House Report* No. 1576, 46 Congress, 2 session, serial 1938; *Senate Journal*, 46 Congress, 2 session, serial 1881, pp. 101, 570.

[39] *Congressional Record*, XI, 778–88, 873–82, 933–43, 994–1003, 1060–70.

with the tribes. The allotment of the reservation could be made only with the consent of two-thirds of the males of the tribe over twenty-one years of age; and the allotments were to be inalienable for twenty-five years. Once the allotments had been made, the laws of the state or territory in which the Indians lived would govern the Indians. The bill did not apply to the Five Civilized Tribes, which consistently opposed the measure.[40]

The Coke Bill had tremendous support from many sides, most importantly, perhaps, from Schurz, who again and again urged its passage. He insisted that the agricultural industry of the Indians would be greatly stimulated if the Indians could be sure of the title to their lands. And he spoke of the Coke Bill as "the most essential step in the solution of the Indian problem." His statement of the advantages that would accrue summed up the views of the reformers generally:

> It will inspire the Indians with a feeling of assurance as to the permanency of their ownership of the lands they occupy and cultivate; it will give them a clear and legal standing as landed proprietors in the courts of law; it will secure to them for the first time fixed homes under the protection of the same law under which white men own theirs; it will eventually open to settlement by white men the large tracts of land now belonging to the reservations, but not used by the Indians. It will thus put the relations between the Indians and their white neighbors in the Western country upon a new basis, by gradually doing away with the system of large reservations, which has so frequently provoked those encroachments which in the past have led to so much cruel injustice and so many disastrous collisions. It will also by the sale, with their consent, of reservation lands not used by the Indians, create for the benefit of the Indians a fund, which will gradually relieve the government of those expenditures which have now to be provided for by appropriations. It will be the most effective measure to place Indians and white men upon an equal footing as to the protection and restraints of law common to both.[41]

[40] A summary of the provisions is given by Senator Coke, *ibid.*, 778–79. See also the abstract of the bill in *Lake Mohonk Conference Proceedings*, 1884, pp. 7–13. The opposition of the Five Civilized Tribes can be seen in their memorial, *Congressional Record*, XI, 781.

[41] Report of the Secretary of the Interior, 1880, in serial 1959, pp. 5–6, 12; see also *ibid.*, 1879, in serial 1910, p. 12.

In this he had the strong and active support of the Commissioners of Indian Affairs. Hayt, as we have seen, pushed aggressively for the law, and his successors, E. M. Marble and Hiram Price, were no less enthusiastic. Price, in fact, made a strong point of the desire of the Indians themselves for lands in severalty. "The Indian wants his land allotted to him," he asserted. "He wants a perfect and secure title that will protect him against the rapacity of the white man. He is not only willing but anxious to learn the ways of civilization. He is desirous of being taught to work and to accumulate property. His mind is imbued with these ideas, and some decisive steps should be taken by the law-making branch of the government to encourage him in his laudable and praiseworthy desires and efforts toward civilization, self-support, and a better and more useful life." In his second report, he went so far as to claim that "very many of the Indian tribes are clamorous for the allotment of their lands in severalty." The system of allotments then in force under various treaties, Price thought were "crude and imperfect" and did not give the Indians sufficient protection. A bill such as Coke's was the first step to be taken to solve the "Indian question."[42]

These sentiments were strongly supported by the Board of Indian Commissioners, who from the very first had included allotments in severalty as part of their basic Indian reform program. In 1880 the board urged the measure as one of "simple justice to the Indians," and accused Congress of turning a deaf ear to the cry of the Indians for such legislation. "Every year strengthens the convictions of the members of the Board," the report stated, "that no single measure of legislation would give such general satisfaction to the Indians, or be productive of more happy results. . . ." The board was convinced that no people could reach a high state of civilization "under the communistic system, and without the incentive to labor and enterprise that the right to individual ownership of property inspires." Their views, the members noted, were in accord with those of all the high officials of the government and with "the feeling of the best people of the land."[43]

The Lake Mohonk Conference in 1884 passed a formal resolution

---

[42] Report of the Commissioner of Indian Affairs, 1881, in serial 2018, pp. 17, 19; ibid., 1882, in serial 2100, pp. 34–35. See also ibid., 1883, in serial 2191, pp. 11–12.

[43] Report of the Board of Indian Commissioners, 1880, p. 10; ibid., 1881, pp. 7–8. See the Memorial of the General Assembly of the Presbyterian Church in the United States, ibid., 1880, pp. 98–99.

CHIEF JOSEPH (1840?–1904) was leader of the Nez Perce Indians in their flight from Oregon in 1877 and was later a noble spokesman for the Indian cause. (Barry photograph, National Archives)

STANDING ROCK INDIAN POLICE. The establishment of Indian police forces on the reservations provided a law enforcing arm for the Indian agents. This photograph shows Sergeants Red Tomahawk and Eagle Man about 1890. (Barry photograph, Western History Department, Denver Public Library)

PINE RIDGE AGENCY. The agency buildings at Pine Ridge on the Oglala Sioux Reservation are shown here as they looked in the mid-1880's. Red Cloud's house is in the distance at the left of the flagpole. (National Archives)

CAPTAIN THUNDERBEAR was captain of the Indian police at Pine Ridge when this picture was taken in 1896. (Dinwiddie photograph, National Archives)

CARL SCHURZ (1829–1906), the reform-minded Secretary of the Interior, 1877–1881, had a strong influence on Indian policy. He believed in individualizing the Indians through education and allotment of land in severalty, and his reform of the Indian Bureau eased attacks on federal policy. (Brady photograph, Library of Congress)

HELEN HUNT JACKSON (1830–1885) became involved in Indian reform when she came into conflict with Carl Schurz over the removal of the Ponca Indians. Her tract, *A Century of Dishonor* (1881), was a stinging indictment of federal Indian policy. (Library of Congress)

CARTOON OF CARL SCHURZ. Although *Harper's Weekly* supported Schurz's reform of the Indian Bureau, its famous cartoonist, Thomas Nast, ridiculed the secretary's efforts. This cartoon appeared on January 25, 1879. (State Historical Society of Wisconsin)

HIRAM PRICE (1814–1901) served as Commissioner of Indian Affairs from 1881 to 1885. A devout Methodist layman from Iowa, he supported the proposals of the Christian reformers. (Brady photograph, Library of Congress)

HENRY M. TELLER (1830–1914), Senator from Colorado, 1877–1882 and 1885–1909, and Secretary of the Interior, 1882–1885, was a long-time student of Indian affairs. He was one of the few to speak out strongly against allotment of Indian lands. (Western History Department, Denver Public Library)

JOHN D. C. ATKINS (1825–1908), Commissioner of Indian Affairs, 1885–1888, was a strong advocate of assimilating the Indians into white society, but his spoils system activities won him the enmity of the reformers. (Brady photograph, Library of Congress)

BUFFALO BILL'S WILD WEST. The participation of Indians in wild west shows was condemned by the reformers because it perpetuated the old Indian ways, but there was no effective way to stop the practice. This photograph shows Indians of Buffalo Bill's show relaxing in 1886. (Sarony photograph, Library of Congress)

DISTRIBUTION OF ANNUITY GOODS. As they were forced to give up their old ways and were settled on restricted reservations, the Indians depended on goods supplied by the United States government. This photograph shows the issuing of annuities at the Crow Agency in Montana, November 10, 1887. (National Archives)

HENRY L. DAWES (1816–1903), Congressman and Senator from Massachusetts, was the best known of the reformers who sought to individualize and Americanize the Indians. His name is attached to the legislation that provided for allotment of land in severalty and to the commission for the allotment of lands of the Five Civilized Tribes, which he headed. (Brady photograph, Library of Congress)

HERBERT WELSH (1851–1941), founder and long-time secretary of the Indian Rights Association, was one of the most influential men in Indian policy reform. He was greatly interested in establishing nonpartisan administration of Indian affairs. (Gutekunst photograph, Historical Society of Pennsylvania)

"earnestly and heartily" approving the Coke Bill, which it characterized as "the best practicable measure yet brought before Congress for the preservation of the Indians from aggression, for the disintegration of the tribal organization, and for the ultimate breaking up of the reservation system." The Indian Rights Association, too, looked upon the Coke Bill with favor, since the bill seemed to provide for the possible difficulties that long experience with allotments had suggested. Even Thomas A. Bland, who later was to fight against severalty legislation, supported Senator Coke's bill, which he printed in full for the readers of *The Council Fire*. The editor said that "its provisions seem to be so well guarded as to appear quite fair to the Indians," and he praised the provisions for Indian consent and for eliminating the Five Civilized Tribes from the scope of the law.[44]

To Lyman Abbott, who often pushed Indian reform measures to extremes, the Coke Bill was not quite satisfactory, but only because it did not go far enough. Abbott wanted to make the action compulsory rather than voluntary—not to authorize allotments but to require them, not to negotiate for the purchase of unallotted lands but to appraise the land and take it by eminent domain. He thought that the experiment of trying to civilize and educate the Indians on reservations had failed. "I would, therefore, abandon this experiment," he said, "abolish the reservations, allow only time enough to work out the abolition, scatter the Indians among the white people, make their lands inalienable for a term of years, give them the rights of citizenship, and trust for their protection to the general laws of the land."[45]

There were, to be sure, a few voices who spoke out against allotment and who criticized the humanitarians' arguments. The minority report of the House Committee on Indian Affairs in 1880 attacked the measure as an experiment without practical basis, a "hobby of speculative philanthropists." An Indian could not be changed into a farmer, these Congressmen argued, merely by giving him a quarter-section of land, since his whole tradition and culture predisposed him against the "scheme for his improvement, devised by those who judge him ex-

[44] *Lake Mohonk Conference Proceedings*, 1884, p. 7; *Report of the Indian Rights Association*, 1884, p. 15; *The Council Fire*, VII (January, 1884), 7; (February, 1884), 9–10.
[45] Abbott to Henry L. Dawes, July 20, 1885, Dawes Papers, Box 27, Library of Congress.

clusively from *their* standpoint instead of from *his*." Nor was the measure logical, since it began by assuming that the Indian was a man like other men, then hedged his allotment round with such restrictions as would make sense only for a ward. Most basic of all, the report charged that the main purpose of the bill was not to help the Indians at all, but to get at the valuable Indian lands and open them up to white settlement. "If this were done in the name of Greed, it would be bad enough," the report concluded; "but to do it in the name of Humanity, and under the cloak of an ardent desire to promote the Indian's welfare by making him like ourselves, whether he will or not, is infinitely worse. Of all the attempts to encroach upon the Indian, this attempt to manufacture him into a white man by act of Congress and the grace of the Secretary of the Interior is the baldest, the boldest, and the most unjustifiable."[46]

By far the strongest of the opponents of the severalty bill was Senator Teller, who repeated many of the arguments he had used in the Ute debate but expanded their applicability. He criticized the reformers' desire for a universal and uniform measure. "An Indian is regarded by the people of the country as an Indian, and all Indians are regarded alike," he said. "The Indians differ as much one from another as the civilized and enlightened nations of the earth differ from the uncivilized and unenlightened nations of the earth. Legislation that is proper and just for one class of Indians will fail to perform the great object that its friends have, to civilize them, if applied to another." He flatly denied the claims of the advocates of severalty that the Indians were clamoring for allotments in fee simple. "There is not a wild Indian living who knows what a fee-simple is," he cried. "There are a good many white men who do not know what it is, and there are certainly very few Indians, civilized or uncivilized, who understand it." For the reports of the agents praising the effects of allotment on the reservations and reporting the eagerness of the Indians for the policy, he had only scorn, charging that the agents were forced to support the "pet theory of the Secretary of the Interior" and that they wrote what their superiors wanted to hear. In Teller's view, the friends of severalty had the whole matter turned around, mistaking the end for the means.

[46] *House Report* No. 1576, 46 Congress, 2 session, serial 1938, pp. 7–10.

Once the Indian was civilized and Christianized and knew the value of property and the value of a home, then give him an allotment of his own, he argued. But do not expect the allotment to civilize and Christianize and transform the Indians. Previous opportunities to take land in severalty had not been accepted by the Indians in any great numbers, he noted, and he asserted that it was part of the Indian's religion not to divide the land. The Senator was not afraid to advance his unpopular view. In a remarkably prescient declaration, he took his stand: "If I stand alone in the Senate, I want to put upon the record my prophecy in this matter, that when thirty or forty years shall have passed and these Indians shall have parted with their title, they will curse the hand that was raised professedly in their defense to secure this kind of legislation, and if all the people who are clamoring for it understood Indian character, and Indian laws, and Indian morals, and Indian religion, they would not be here clamoring for this at all."[47]

Senator Coke answered Teller. He noted that the Senator was at war with the President, at war with the Secretary of the Interior, at war with the Commissioner of Indian Affairs, at war with the peace commissioners, at war with the Committee on Indian Affairs of the Senate, and at war with his own colleague, Senator Hill. In reference to Teller's complaint that he had been thwarted in his views on Indian policy by all these men, Coke likened Teller to the juror who was thwarted by eleven contumacious jurors, and he asserted that the rest of the Senate would try to get along as best it could without Teller's concurrence.[48]

On April 17, 1882, Teller became Secretary of the Interior in President Arthur's cabinet. He was now in a position to promote his own theories, as he had charged that Schurz had promoted his. But he did not find the sycophancy among subordinates that he had charged against his predecessor. He did not change his own position, and he declared in his first annual report, "No greater misfortune can befall the Indian race than when their lands are allotted and patents issue therefor, even though the period of alienation should be fixed at twenty-five years." But the Commissioner of Indian Affairs, Hiram

47 *Congressional Record*, XI, 780–83, 934–35.
48 *Ibid.*, 782.

Price, continued to promote severalty as a measure upon which the future welfare and prosperity of the Indians depended.[49]

Hardly a session of Congress passed without the introduction of severalty measures in both houses. The Coke Bill was passed again in the Senate on April 24, 1882, and on March 26, 1884. It was reported favorably by the House Committee on Indian Affairs in January, 1885, but never reached the floor for debate.[50]

When the severalty bill came before the Senate again on December 8, 1885, it was introduced by Senator Henry L. Dawes of Massachusetts, now chairman of the Committee on Indian Affairs. His name stuck to the final act, although he had been relatively late in climbing on the allotment bandwagon, and Senator Coke was soon forgotten.[51] Dawes, less self-assured and doctrinaire than men like Abbott and some of the other proponents of the panacea, knew the seriousness of the Indian problem, but he admitted that he did not know an easy solution. In a revealing letter to Secretary Teller in September, 1882, Dawes had set forth his misgivings. What worried him were the tremendous pressures of the whites upon the remaining Indian reservations. "I see unmistakable signs," he told Teller, "that you will have the whole Indian race, 'five nations' and all on your hands with no place to put them. I have never seen such an advance made upon them as has been made this last year. 'Civilization' has got after their possession with a greed never before equalled but it is idle to expect to stay it and worse than folly to shut our eyes to the consequences." Dawes alluded to all the talk about land in severalty for the Indians as a solution to the problem, but he was not yet ready to accept it, and he told Teller:

> All this is well in theory, but you and I know that it will not meet the present practical difficulty. Two hundred thousand savages who cannot read a word in any language or speak a word of English, who

[49] Report of the Secretary of the Interior, 1882, in serial 2099, pp. vi–vii; Report of the Commissioner of Indian Affairs, 1882, in serial 2100, pp. 34–35. See also the reports of the Commissioner for 1883 and 1884.

[50] *Senate Journal*, 47 Congress, 1 session, serial 1984, p. 622; *Senate Journal*, 48 Congress, 1 session, serial 2161, p. 469; *Congressional Record*, XIII, 3213; XV, 2240–42, 2277–80; *House Report* No. 2247, 48 Congress, 2 session, serial 2328.

[51] *Senate Journal*, 49 Congress, 1 session, serial 2332, p. 49. Dawes himself declared that to Coke "more than to any other Senator is due the credit of this which I believe will be considered hereafter one of the wisest measures with reference to the Indian." *Congressional Record*, XVII, 1559.

were never taught to work and don't know how to earn their living nor care to learn, who can't read or be made to comprehend the laws they are expected to obey as citizens or know what is meant by a court of justice instituted to enforce them—or even the law of *meum et tuum*, the fundamentum of society, cannot be set up in severalty and left to stand alone any more than so many reeds—can no more be turned loose in society and bid to confide in and respect an unknown and invisible power relied on to enforce right and punish wrong than so many wild beasts. Without doubt these Indians are to be somehow absorbed into and become a part of the 50,000,000 of our people. There does not seem to be any other way to deal with them. But how?[52]

Dawes, perhaps because he despaired of any other answer, perhaps because he became convinced that the restrictions on alienation of the land would be a sufficient protection against the difficulties he foresaw, perhaps because he succumbed to the incessant arguments of the advocates of severalty with whom he was closely associated in Indian reform work, was not long in swinging to their way of thinking. He, in fact, became one of the most active supporters of the individualization of the Indian through private property, answering questions in public meetings about the details of the proposal and ultimately pushing the measure through Congress. An indication of his change of mind, or better, the resolution of his doubts, was an address he gave at a public meeting held in January, 1884, in connection with the annual conference of the Board of Indian Commissioners and the missionary boards. After a critical recital of the evils of the past Indian policy of dispossession and war, he pointed to the contrast of the present:

The philosophy of the present policy is to treat him as an individual, and not as an insoluble substance that the civilization of this country has been unable, hitherto, to digest, but to take him as an individual, a human being, and treat him as you find him, according to the necessities of his case. If he be one who hitherto has been permitted to grow as a wild beast grows, without education, and thrown upon his instincts for his support, a savage, take him, though grown up and matured in body and mind, take him by the hand and set him upon

[52] Dawes to Teller, September 19, 1882, draft in Dawes Papers, Box 26.

249

AMERICAN INDIAN POLICY IN CRISIS

his feet, and teach him to stand alone first, then to walk, then to dig, then to plant, then to hoe, then to gather, and then to *keep*. The last and the best agency of civilization is to teach a grown up Indian to *keep*. When he begins to understand that he has something that is his exclusively to enjoy, he begins to understand that it is necessary for him to preserve and keep it, and it is not a great while before he learns that to keep it he must *keep the peace*; and so on, step by step, the individual is separated from the mass, set up upon the soil, made a citizen, and instead of a charge he is a positive good, a contribution to the wealth and strength and power of the nation.[53]

The bill Dawes proposed in 1886 passed the Senate on February 25, in the first session of the Forty-ninth Congress, but the usual delay occurred in the House. The House Committee on Indian Affairs reported the bill favorably on April 20, but then Indian matters stalled again.[54] The Indian reformers, who were eager to get the enactment not only of the severalty bill but of Dawes's Sioux Bill and the Mission Indian measure as well, were beside themselves; victory for their proposals seemed within grasp if only the bills could be brought to a vote. The House put the bills on the calendar for May 27 and 29, but then the Indian matters were shouldered aside by other concerns. The anguish of the reformers was reflected in a leaflet written by Charles C. Painter and published by the Indian Rights Association on June 3. After noting the agreement to consider the Indian bills on the May dates, Painter lamented:

All of them, and especially the general Severalty and Mission Indian Bill, are most vitally related to the solution of the Indian problem, and to the relief of a most deeply wronged people, whose sad condition has been appealing to the country for years. After a long night of watching and waiting, of praying and working, the friends of the Indians had great hope that at last we were to have conditions supplied, obstacles removed, and opportunity given to deal with the question of the civilization of the Indian. The time allotted in these two days was deemed ample for an intelligent disposition of those bills. The Committee had been overwhelmed with

[53] *Report of the Board of Indian Commissioners*, 1883, pp. 69–70.
[54] *House Report* No. 1835, 49 Congress, 1 session, serial 2440.

petitions and prayers of the best people of the country, begging that these measures should be adopted, and we had come down through the weary months of delay to these days of hope, believing that at last we were to see the beginning of the end.[55]

But at the last minute, the Indian matters were again postponed and the House turned its attention to a proposed tax on the manufacture and sale of oleomargarine as a means of protecting dairy farmers from imitation products. "For a full week," Painter asserted in reference to the oleomargarine question, "the whole House has cowered and shuddered as the finger of the granger has pointed to this ghastly phantom, and all Indian business has been forgotten." He hoped by his pamphlet to stir up enough public sentiment to force the House to take up the Indian bills. Only one honest day's work was needed to dispose of them, he said; failure to pass them would be "a blunder and a crime."[56]

Painter was not the only one at work. J. W. Davis, of the Boston Indian Citizenship Committee, wrote Herbert Welsh on June 9 that his group had been "plying every one we could reach to press the Indian business thro'—." Davis expressed his hope that from Welsh's "societies & friends outside of Phil[a] & Boston there will still be earnest pressure," for he feared that the effectiveness of agitation from Philadelphia and Boston had already reached its limit. Mrs. Quinton spent a week in Washington to fight for the bills, and likely Congressmen—including Samuel Jackson Randall, powerful chairman of the appropriations committee, and B. M. Cutcheon—were solicited for special aid. Hope finally died for quick action. As the first session drew to a close, Cutcheon wrote to Welsh, "The strife for consideration is very great— and as the poor Indian has but few active friends he will be crowded aside."[57]

Early in the second session of the Forty-ninth Congress, the severalty bill at last came before the House. It was debated on December 15, 1886, and passed the following day. Dawes later claimed that the passage of the bill by the House was due to Congressman Randall's

[55] Charles C. Painter, *Oleomargarine versus the Indian* (Philadelphia, 1886).

[56] *Ibid.* The debate on the oleomargarine tax, much of it frivolous in nature, can be followed in *Congressional Record*, XVII, 5009–12, 5032–56, 5074–92.

[57] J. W. Davis to Welsh, June 9, 1886, and B. M. Cutcheon to Welsh, June 19, 1886, in Indian Rights Association Papers, Box 1, Historical Society of Pennsylvania.

daughter, who, inspired by the discussions at Lake Mohonk, persuaded her father that the measure should be passed. "Public sentiment for the Indian has been manufactured *here*," Dawes told the gathering at Lake Mohonk. "Power to carry legislation in Congress has had its inspiration *here*. This Conference it was that insisted upon it that the House of Representatives should pass the allotment bill, which had been twice through the Senate."[58]

The House, however, added significant amendments to the Senate bill—providing that the time allowed for selection of allotments be reduced from five years to two years, that Congress should decide in each case what disposition to make of the money from the sale of surplus lands, and that the measure must be accepted by a majority of the tribe before it was applied to it. The Senate refused to approve the changes, and when the House held firm, a conference committee was appointed to iron out the difficulties. Both houses promptly agreed to the compromises, which allowed four years for selection, provided in the law for the disposal of the money from the sale of surplus lands, and dropped altogether the provision requiring tribal consent. President Cleveland signed the bill on February 8, 1887, and the Dawes General Allotment Act became the law of the land.[59]

The act dealt primarily with the ownership of the land.[60] It authorized but did not require the President, in cases where Indian reservations had good agricultural and grazing land, to survey the reservations or selected parts of them and to allot the land to individual Indians. The amounts to be allotted were close to those specified in the Coke Bill and reflected the strong tradition of a quarter-section homestead for the yeoman farmer. One-quarter of a section (160 acres) was to be allotted to each head of family, one-eighth of a section (80 acres) to each single person over eighteen years of age and to each orphan child under eighteen, and one-sixteenth of a section (40 acres) to other

[58] *Lake Mohonk Conference Proceedings*, 1890, p. 84.
[59] The action can be followed in *Senate Journal*, 49 Congress, 2 session, serial 2447, pp. 81, 82, 90, 91, 98, 99, 124, 140, 186, 198, 308, and in comparable sections of the *House Journal*, serial 2459. See also *Congressional Record*, XVII, 1558–59, 1688, 1762–64; XVIII, 225–26, 972–74. For a discussion of the legislative history of the bill, see Priest, *Uncle Sam's Stepchildren*, pp. 185–87. The law is in *United States Statutes at Large*, XXIV, 388–91.
[60] A clear discussion of the provisions of the act is in James B. Thayer, "The Dawes Bill and the Indians," *Atlantic Monthly*, LXI (March, 1888), 315–22.

single persons under eighteen then living or born prior to the time when the President ordered allotment. In cases where lands were suitable only for grazing purposes, the allotments were to be doubled, and if prior treaty provisions specified larger allotments, the treaty was to govern. If anyone entitled to an allotment did not make the selection within four years after the President directed allotment, the Secretary of the Interior was authorized to direct the agent of the tribe or a special agent to make such selection. Indians who did not live on reservations or whose tribe had no reservation could make their selection on any part of the public domain, surveyed or not surveyed, and receive an allotment under the same provisions. Fees for such entries due the General Land Office were to be paid by the United States.

When the allotments were approved by the Secretary of the Interior, he was to issue to each Indian a patent, which declared that the United States would hold the allotted lands for twenty-five years in trust for the Indian and for his sole benefit or that of his heirs. At the expiration of the twenty-five years, the land would be conveyed to the Indian in fee simple. Any conveyance or contract touching the land during the trust period was null and void, and the President at his discretion could extend the trust period.

After the lands had been allotted on any reservation, or sooner if the President thought it was in the best interests of the tribe, the Secretary of the Interior could negotiate with the tribe for the purchase of the remaining or surplus lands, the purchase to be ratified by Congress before becoming effective. If the lands so purchased were suitable for agricultural purposes, they were to be used only for actual homesteaders in 160-acre tracts. The money paid to the Indians for the surplus lands was to be held in the Treasury for the sole use of the tribes to whom the reservations belonged, and the funds were subject to appropriation by Congress for the education and civilization of the Indians concerned.

Secondarily, the Dawes Act provided for Indian citizenship. Every Indian born in the United States to whom an allotment was made or any Indian who had voluntarily taken up residence apart from his tribe and adopted the habits of civilized life was declared by the act to be a citizen of the United States, without impairing the rights he might have to tribal or other property. When the allotments were completed

253

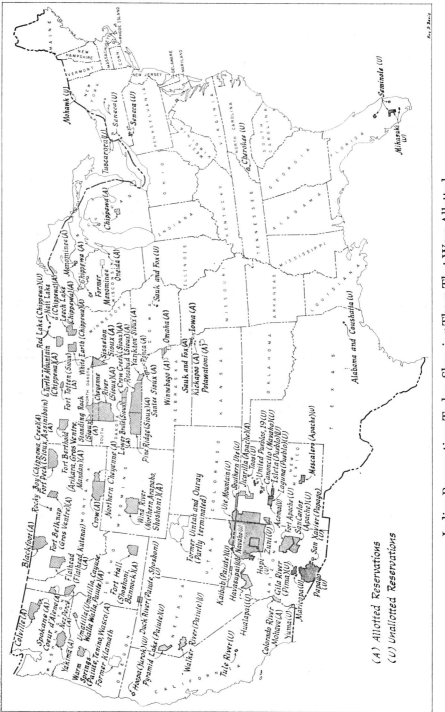

Indian Reservations Today, Showing Those That Were Allotted

Colville (A)
Spokane (A)
Coeur d'Alene (A)
Nez Percé (A)
Yakima (A)
Warm Springs (Paiute, Tenino, Wasco)(A)
Umatilla (Umatilla, Cayuse, Walla Walla, Paiute)(A)
Former Klamath

Blackfoot (A)
Rocky Boy (Chippewa, Cree)(A)
Fort Peck (Sioux, Assiniboin)(A)
Fort Belknap (Gros Ventre)(A)
Flathead (Flathead, Kutenai)(A)
Fort Hall (Shoshoni, Bannock)(A)
Crow (A)
Northern Cheyenne (A)
Wind River (Northern Arapaho, Shoshoni)(A)

Red Lake (Chippewa)(U)
Nett Lake (Chippewa)(U)
Leech Lake (Chippewa)(A)
Turtle Mountain (Chippewa)(A)
White Earth (Chippewa)(A)
Fort Totten (Sioux)(A)
Fort Berthold (Arikara, Gros Ventre, Mandan)(A)
Standing Rock (Sioux)(A)
Cheyenne River (Sioux)(A)
Crow Creek (Sioux)(A)
Lower Brulé (Sioux)(A)
Rosebud (Sioux)(A)
Pine Ridge (Sioux)(A)
Sisseton Sioux (A)
Yankton Sioux (A)
Santee Sioux (A)
Ponca (A)

Chippewa (A)
Menominee (A)
Former Menominee
Oneida (A)
Chippewa (A)

Menominee (A)
Sauk and Fox (U)
Omaha (A)
Winnebago (A)
Sauk and Fox (A)
Kickapoo (A)
Iowa (A)
Potawatomi (A)

Mohawk (U)
Seneca (U)
Seneca (U)
Tuscarora (U)
Oneida

Cherokee (U)

Alabama and Coushatta (U)

Seminole (U)
Mikasuki (U)

Former Uintah and Ouray (Partly Terminated)

Ute Mountain (U)
Southern Ute (U)
Jicarilla (Apache)(A)
Taos (U)
United Pueblos, 19 (U)
Canoncito (Navaho)(U)
Isleta (Pueblo)(U)
Acoma(U)
Laguna (Pueblo)(U)
Zuni(U)
Fort Apache (Apache)(U)
San Carlos (Apache)(U)
Mescalero (Apache)(U)

Huualapai (U)
Kaibab (Paiute)(U)
Havasupai (U)
Hopi (U)
Navaho (U)
San Xavier (Papago)(U)
Papago (U)

Walker River (Paiute)(U)
Tule River (U)
Pyramid Lake (Paiute)(U)
Moapa (Yarok)(U) Duck River (Paiute, Shoshoni)(U)
Colorado River (A)
Mohave (A)
Yuma (U)
Gila River (Pima)(U)
Maricopa (U)

(A) Allotted Reservations
(U) Unallotted Reservations

Rev. D. Davis

for any tribe and patents granted to the allottees, those Indians were made subject to the laws, both civil and criminal, of the state or territory in which they resided.[61]

In short, the Dawes Act enabled the President, if he wished, to give the Indians individual ownership of land and thereby to make them citizens of the United States. It also enabled the United States to acquire the remaining lands on the reservations and open them to white settlement. The Dawes Act did not apply to the Five Civilized Tribes or the Osages, Miamis, Peorias, and Sacs and Foxes in the Indian Territory, to the Seneca Indians in New York, or to the strip of Sioux lands in Nebraska.[62]

That the victory was finally theirs caused great exultation among the reformers who had fought so persistently for the proposal. The tone was set by a pamphlet issued in March by the Indian Rights Association, written by its agent in Washington, Charles C. Painter:

> By signing the Dawes Severalty bill the President has placed the 8th of February among the national anniversaries as a day to be commemorated by the Sons of Liberty. So long as the cosmopolitan population of this country shall remember and celebrate Runnymede and Magna Charta, Independence and Emancipation, will the 8th of February, 1887, also come in for proportionate claim for honorable mention and thrilling memories.

Painter extolled the recognition of the manhood of the Indians and the opening of the doors that had been closed against them. "In securing the passage of this law the Indian Rights Association achieved the greatest success in its history," the executive committee of the association declared, "and its enactment was the most important step forward ever taken by the national Government in its methods of dealing with the Indians." Clinton B. Fisk, chairman of the Board of Indian Commissioners, spoke of a "new epoch in Indian affairs," and called the act

---

[61] The Burke Act of May 8, 1906, provided that citizenship should not be granted and the Indians should not be subject to state and territorial laws until the expiration of the trust period and the issuing of the patents in fee. *United States Statutes at Large,* XXXIV, 182–83.

[62] The act also provided that religious organizations occupying lands subject to the provisions of the act could be confirmed in their possession, up to 160 acres, and it directed that Indians who had availed themselves of the provisions of the act were to be preferred in appointments as Indian police or as other employees of the Indian service.

"the star of the East for the Indian tribes." Secretary of the Interior Lamar called the act "the most important measure of legislation ever enacted in this country affecting our Indian affairs . . . [and] practically a general naturalization law for the American Indians." It was to his mind "the only escape open to these people from the dire alternative of impending extirpation."[63]

Nor did the enthusiasm cool when the first blush of victory passed. Lamar's successor in 1888 asserted that the severalty policy offered "a brighter promise for the adult Indian race" than anything the government had ever done. And as late as 1892 *The Independent* editorialized about the "Red Man's charter of liberty" and compared the Dawes Act once more with Lincoln's Emancipation Proclamation.[64] The opposition to the law, which came largely from the Five Civilized Tribes and the Indian Defence Association of T. A. Bland, was almost completely drowned out by the great chorus of acclaim and was attributed by the victorious reformers to selfish interests of the chiefs and headmen and their white supporters or to misunderstandings about the nature of the legislation.[65]

The Dawes Act was put into operation with a speed that frightened Dawes himself. When President Cleveland signed the bill, he remarked that he intended to apply it at first to only one reservation and then gradually extend its provisions to others. But when the Lake Mohonk Conference met seven months later, Dawes reported that the act had already been applied to half a dozen reservations. Such haste was disturbing to Dawes, who voiced a fear that the land-grabbers would force allotment quickly so that they could get the surplus lands. "There is no danger but this will come most rapidly—," Dawes warned, "too rapidly, I think,—the greed and hunger and thirst of the white man for the Indian's land is almost equal to his 'hunger and thirst for righteousness.' "[66]

[63] Charles C. Painter, *The Dawes Land in Severalty Bill and Indian Emancipation* (Philadelphia, 1887), p. 1; *Report of the Indian Rights Association*, 1887, p. 36; *Lake Mohonk Conference Proceedings*, 1887, p. 2; Fisk to Dawes, December 27, 1886, Dawes Papers, Box 27; Report of the Secretary of the Interior, 1887, in serial 2541, pp. 25–26.
[64] *Ibid.*, 1888, in serial 2636, p. xxxi; *The Independent*, XLIV (April 28, 1892), 586–87.
[65] Painter, *Dawes Land in Severalty Bill*, pp. 1–2. For Bland's opposition, see above, pp. 166–67.
[66] *Lake Mohonk Conference Proceedings*, 1887, p. 67. Another warning came from James E. Rhoads of the Indian Rights Association, who stressed the need to make sure

In general, however, the reformers were eager to see the panacea applied. Why should the remedy to the Indian problem be delayed any longer than was necessary, they asked; and the arguments that had been advanced for the passage of the act were now repeated as justification for its rapid application. The act, Merrill E. Gates told the Lake Mohonk Conference in 1900, was "a mighty pulverizing engine for breaking up the tribal mass."[67] Year by year, in fact, the process of allotment was stepped up, and the surplus lands were rapidly transferred to the whites. The Indians held 155,632,312 acres in 1881; by 1890 they had 104,314,349, and by 1900, only 77,865,373. Of these 77,865,373 acres in 1900, 5,409,530 had been allotted. So successful did the process seem that the reformers looked forward to the day when government supervision over the Indians would disappear entirely and the Indians would all be absorbed into American society.[68]

The reformers were soon disturbed, however, by the provisions of the Dawes Act which authorized allotments of different size for different classes of persons. Almost at once they began to agitate for an equalization of the allotments. Commissioner Thomas J. Morgan in his first annual report in 1889 pointed to the need to protect married women, who were excluded from allotments by the Dawes Act. Indian women could be turned out of their homes by their husbands and then would be without any rights to land. The Board of Indian Commissioners in the same year listened to Alice Fletcher speak in favor of equal allotments to women and to her argument that equalization would benefit as well the young and able-bodied, who under the Dawes Act got only 40 acres while the old and infirm were given 160. The board urged Congress to equalize all the allotments. In January, 1890, Morgan sent a proposed bill to the Secretary of the Interior providing for 160 acres for every Indian, man, woman, and child, and the

that the provisions of the Dawes Act were wisely carried out. See his pamphlet, *Our Next Duty to the Indians* (Philadelphia, 1887).

[67] *Lake Mohonk Conference Proceedings*, 1900, p. 16. Theodore Roosevelt liked that phrase and used it in his first annual message to Congress on December 3, 1901. Israel, *State of the Union Messages*, II, 2047.

[68] The figures on allotment, compiled by the Land Division of the Indian Office, are cited in Otis, *The Dawes Act*, p. 87. Chapter VII of Otis's study gives a detailed analysis of the working out of allotment up to 1900 and evaluates its success and failure.

bill was forwarded to Congress.[69] A leasing bill introduced by Dawes in March, 1890, incorporated Morgan's proposal. As the bill proceeded through Congress, there was considerable debate about the size of the equalized allotments—whether they should be 160 acres or only 80 acres—but little disagreement apparently about the need for equalization. The Senate, originally voting for a uniform 160-acre allotment, in the end gave in to the wishes of the House and agreed to 80 acres, the provision that was finally written into the law.[70]

In another way, too, the reformers were dissatisfied with the Dawes Act, for they soon discovered that the allotment of a homestead to an Indian did not automatically turn him into a practical farmer. The provisions of the act which prohibited the leasing or other such conveyance of the allotments—wisely intended to protect the Indian holdings for an extended period—actually seemed to work a hardship on many Indians. Women and children and Indians who were in some way disabled could not reap the benefits of their allotments because they were unable to farm them. The agent of the Omahas and Winnebagos estimated in 1890 that sixty per cent of the Winnebago land belonged to women, old or infirm men, and minor children, none of whom could cultivate it. Moreover, lands belonging to students who were away at school were lying fallow or were used illegally by whites with no benefit to the Indians. If leasing were allowed for these needy persons, an income from the land could be provided for them. Other Indians, it turned out, did not have the work animals or agricultural implements that were indispensable for effective use of their allotments. If a portion of their land could be rented, the income could be used to provide the tools needed to farm the rest.[71]

There was in addition the question—which many of the reformers

[69] Report of the Commissioner of Indian Affairs, 1889, in serial 2725, p. 17; Report of the Board of Indian Commissioners, 1889, pp. 8–9; Senate Executive Document No. 64, 51 Congress, 1 session, serial 2686, pp. 2–4.

[70] Congressional Record, XXI, 10705; House Report No. 1700, 51 Congress, 1 session, serial 2812; United States Statutes at Large, XXVI, 794–95. The legislative history of the measure is given in Otis, The Dawes Act, pp. 111–14.

[71] Report of Robert H. Ashley, August 26, 1890, in Report of the Commissioner of Indian Affairs, 1890, in serial 2841, p. 137. The best discussion of the leasing of allotments, on which I have relied heavily, is Otis, The Dawes Act, pp. 107–31. See also Everett Arthur Gilcreast, "Richard Henry Pratt and American Indian Policy, 1877–1906: A Study of the Assimilation Movement" (unpublished Ph.D. dissertation, Yale University, 1967), pp. 231–36; Schmeckebier, Office of Indian Affairs, pp. 84, 177–79.

could not shake—of advancing the Indians toward full participation in American society by letting them assume the full responsibility for their own property. To hedge their ownership around with all kinds of restrictions in its use hardly was conducive to Indian growth in maturity. Discussion of a paper on "The Indian and His Property," read at Lake Mohonk in 1889 by Charles C. Painter, indicated considerable support for allowing the Indian to manage his allotment as he saw fit. Supporters of leasing saw still another benefit. It would intersperse white farmers among the Indians, who would furnish object lessons of great value in teaching the Indians how to farm.[72]

It is strange how readily the reformers accepted these arguments, the same groups who had championed allotment in severalty as the way to move the Indians from a state of idleness to a state of hard work on their own property. Only a few voices were raised against the proposals to make leasing legal under set conditions, among them that of Senator Dawes, who in 1890 told the Lake Mohonk Conference:

> I know there are instances of hardship under this inalienable allotment system, and instances of worthy young men who want to leave their allotment and go into some other business or get an education; and in an endeavor to meet those cases we are in danger of overthrowing the fundamental idea of the whole system, that controlling idea that work on one's own homestead is the most potent of all civilizing agencies for the Indian. . . . we forget that the Indian, as a rule, won't work if he can help it, and that the white man has never been known to take his foot off from an Indian's land, when he once got it on.[73]

Dawes saw in leasing the danger of a speedy collapse of the whole allotment system. "Thus the allotment law would be gradually undermined and destroyed," he said, "and the Indian would abandon his own work, his own land, and his own home, which we have talked about as the central pivot of our efforts in attempting to civilize the Indian."[74]

The opposition was too slight to stem the movement, however, and

---

[72] *Lake Mohonk Conference Proceedings*, 1889, pp. 84–89; Report of Ashley, August 26, 1890, serial 2841, p. 137.
[73] *Lake Mohonk Conference Proceedings*, 1890, p. 82.
[74] *Ibid.*, p. 83.

in fact the basic idea was accepted by the reformers provided that safeguards were set up to prevent indiscriminate leasing. By a law of February 28, 1891, Congress made leasing possible. The legislation provided that any Indian who had received an allotment under the Dawes Act or any other act or treaty and who "by reason of age or other disability" was personally unable to occupy and improve his allotment, could lease the land for three years for farming or grazing and for ten years for mining. In addition, the Indians, "by authority of the council speaking for such Indians," could lease for grazing and mining purposes other lands not needed for farming. All the arrangements were subject to the approval of the Secretary of the Interior.[75] The bill had been supported by the reform groups, but little real interest was stirred up, and neither the Lake Mohonk Conference nor the Indian Rights Association noted the legislation in its formal report for the year. Even Dawes relented a little in his opposition, for, as he told the Lake Mohonk gathering in 1891, the Indians got discouraged in their attempts to break the prairie sod, and he thought it wise to let them rent part of the land to white farmers who would prepare it for cultivation. But he insisted that such action would be safe only if the Indian Office was very careful in its administration of the law.[76]

Although the Indian Office did move slowly at first in applying the leasing law, the program soon gained a momentum that swept away the restrictions the advocates had intended. The law provided that approval be given by the Secretary of the Interior to all requests for leasing, but by 1893 the matter of leasing had been placed in the hands of the Indian agents (although their recommendations were subject to department approval), and agents succumbed to pressures put upon them by whites who desired to farm the Indian lands. Moreover, the wording of the law was loosened in 1894 by adding "inability" to age and disability as a reason for leasing allotments and by extending the

[75] *United States Statutes at Large*, XXVI, 795. See Otis, *The Dawes Act*, pp. 111–14, for the legislative history of the bill. In 1893, the Indian Office defined "age" and "disability" in "Rules and Regulations to be Observed in the Execution of Leases of Indian Allotments," in Report of the Commissioner of Indian Affairs, 1893, in serial 3210, pp. 476–77.

[76] *Lake Mohonk Conference Proceedings*, 1891, p. 87. Charles C. Painter later declared that "Senator Dawes and General Whittlesey and I talked this over, and we drew up an amendment, and Mr. Dawes secured its passage, providing for such leases as we thought should be provided for, in cases where there was disability to use the land. That is all that should have been covered by it." *Ibid.*, 1894, p. 86.

period of agricultural and grazing leases to five years and permitting ten-year leases for "business purposes" as well as for mining.[77] The Indian Office reasserted its intention not to allow indiscriminate leasing and directed that if an Indian had physical or mental ability to cultivate an allotment by personal labor or by hired help, leasing should not be permitted. But it was impossible to define "inability" precisely, and the number of leases steadily climbed.[78]

These developments dismayed the reformers. Painter warned the Lake Mohonk Conference in 1894 that the spirit and intent of the allotment law were being set aside and destroyed. And he blamed westerners, who he alleged wanted to sweep away all the restrictions which the severalty law had put on alienation. The Indian Rights Association, too, strongly criticized the course of government policy. "It cannot be said too strongly or urgently that attention should be aroused, and intelligent action at once taken," its executive committee declared in its annual report, "or the severalty law will prove as unavailing as treaties have been to protect the Indian in the possession of his land." The Lake Mohonk Conference recommended in its platform for 1894 that because the recent laws permitting Indians to lease their lands were "widely resulting in dispossessing ignorant Indians of their property rights, without an adequate return, to their great disadvantage and the enriching of designing white men," lease or sale should be approved only by a United States district court on the same principles that protected minor heirs among the whites from alienation of their property.[79]

In 1897 there was a temporary check to the leasing of allotments, as Congress changed the law back to its original form and indeed cut the legal period of leasing for mining and business purposes to five years. There was a drop in the number of leases in 1898, but then the figure shot up again in subsequent years.[80] The effects on the Indians could

[77] *United States Statutes at Large*, XXVIII, 305.

[78] Report of the Commissioner of Indian Affairs, 1894, in serial 3306, p. 33. There were 295 leases in 1894, 330 in 1895, 933 in 1896, and 1,287 in 1897. Otis, *The Dawes Act*, p. 120.

[79] *Lake Mohonk Conference Proceedings*, 1894, pp. 86–87, 149; *Report of the Indian Rights Association*, 1894, pp. 36–38.

[80] *United States Statutes at Large*, XXX, 85. There were 948 leases in 1898, 1,185 in 1899, and 2,590 in 1900. Otis, *The Dawes Act*, p. 121. A law of May 31, 1900, set the maximum period for leases at five years and restricted leasing to farming only. *United States Statutes at Large*, XXXI, 229.

have been predicted. The Indians of the Omaha and Winnebago reservations in Nebraska, who had been the great hope of the promoters of allotment, by the end of the decade were suffering the evil effects of leasing. Out of 140,000 acres allotted on the two reservations by 1898, 112,000 had been leased. And the low character of the whites who thus came to mingle with the Indians contributed further to their demoralization. One student of the Omahas concluded that these Indians, not sufficiently good farmers to make a better or more reliable income than the rent gotten from a white tenant and with no incentive to improve a standard of living that was alien to them, found in leasing a way out. Two-thirds of the men "ceased to make any further economic struggle."[81]

Among the Santee Sioux, to take another example, leasing was widespread even though most of the agents opposed the practice. But on such reservations as the Santee Reservation, leasing was probably a necessary economic arrangement, since it allowed access to the large amounts of land that were the only means of making farming or ranching pay in the unpredictable climate of the region.[82]

There is no doubt that the leasing policy ate deeply into the goals envisaged by the reformers for the allotment policy, for many Indians came to look upon the land as a source of revenue from the labor of a tenant, not as a homestead to be worked personally as an independent small farmer. The leasing, furthermore, was a step toward complete alienation of the allotments by sale, a process that soon began to appear as breaks in the dike of protection that had been erected around the allotments by the reformers.[83]

The allotment of Indian lands, which was intended to fit the Indians into Anglo-Saxon systems of land tenure and inheritance, was complicated by the traditional system of Indian personal names. If the In-

[81] Otis, *The Dawes Act*, p. 130. A variety of views on the effects of leasing can be found in the replies of agents to questions asked by the Board of Indian Commissioners in 1898. *Report of the Board of Indian Commissioners*, 1898, pp. 12–25.
[82] Roy W. Meyer, *History of the Santee Sioux: United States Indian Policy on Trial* (Lincoln, 1967), p. 196.
[83] Otis, *The Dawes Act*, pp. 149–50. By 1916 more than one-third of allotted agricultural lands were leased.

dians were to be fully assimilated into American life, they would have to be renamed. To this end, Commissioner Morgan issued a circular to Indian agents and school superintendents on March 19, 1890. "When the Indians become citizens of the United States, under the allotment act," he said, "the inheritance of property will be governed by the laws of the respective States, and it will cause needless confusion and, doubtless, considerable ultimate loss to the Indians if no attempt is made to have the different members of a family known by the same family name on the records and by general reputation. Among other customs of the white people it is becoming important that Indians adopt that in regard to names." Morgan was not unmindful of Indian interests and directed that whenever possible the Indian name should be retained, and he condemned the translation of Indian names into English, which often resulted in "awkward and uncouth" names. Nor would he tolerate "the habit of adopting sobriquets given to Indians such as 'Tobacco,' 'Mogul,' 'Tom,' 'Pete,' etc., by which they become generally known." He authorized, however, the substitution of English names for Indian ones too difficult to pronounce and the introduction of Christian given names before the surname. Indian names that were "unusually long and difficult" were to be arbitrarily shortened.[84]

Morgan's plan was endorsed by John Wesley Powell, director of the Bureau of Ethnology, who saw the advantages of the renaming for the inheritance of property and for accurate census-taking among the tribes. Powell, in addition, stressed the value of the new system of naming in breaking up the tribal organization, which was "perpetuated and ever kept in mind by the Indian's own system of names." "In selecting aboriginal names," he wrote, "I do not think it will be necessary to limit the choice to such names as Indians already bear. Excellent names may frequently be selected from the Indian's vocabulary of geographic terms, such as the names of rivers, lakes, mountains, etc., and where these are suitable and euphonic, I think they may be substituted for personal names which are less desirable." He optimistically

[84] Morgan's circular is printed with his "Rules for Indian Schools" in the appendix to Report of the Commissioner of Indian Affairs, 1890, in serial 2841, p. clx. An extended discussion of the renaming program is in Daniel F. Littlefield, Jr., and Lonnie E. Underhill, "Renaming the American Indian: 1890–1913," *American Studies*, XII (Fall, 1971), 34–36.

believed that the Indians would readily assume the new names and co-operate with the agents in selecting appropriate ones.[85]

Although Morgan's program was reaffirmed by his successors, progress was slow, and by the end of the century, it was apparent that the attempts to rename the Indians had not fulfilled the hopes of the Americanizers. Allotment moved ahead as best it could under a mixed system of Indian and American names.[86]

[85] J. W. Powell to T. J. Morgan, April 4, 1890, in Report of the Commissioner of Indian Affairs, 1890, in serial 2841, p. clxi; Littlefield and Underhill, "Renaming the American Indian," p. 36.

[86] The work of renaming was carried on after 1900, largely under the stimulus of Hamlin Garland, who enlisted the support of the Indian Office and of the Indian physician, Charles A. Eastman. *Ibid.*, pp. 37–43.

CHAPTER 9

THE PROMOTION
OF INDIAN SCHOOLS

Resolved, That education is essential to civilization. The Indian must have a knowledge of the English language, that he may associate with his white neighbors and transact business as they do. He must have practical industrial training to fit him to compete with others in the struggle for life. He must have a Christian education to enable him to perform the duties of the family, the State, and the Church. Such an education can be best acquired apart from his reservation and amid the influences of Christian and civilized society. . . . But since the great majority of the Indians cannot be educated away from their homes, it is a matter of the highest importance that the Government should provide and liberally sustain good manual labor and day schools on the reservations. These should be established in sufficient number to accommodate all Indian children of school age. The Christian people of the country should exert through the Indian schools a strong moral and religious influence. This the Government cannot do, but without this the true civilization of the Indian is impossible.

—Resolution of the Lake
Mohonk Conference, 1884

❀❀❀❀❀❀❀

There had long been common agreement among those interested in the improvement of the Indians that education in English-speaking schools was absolutely necessary for the Indian youth. Nearly all attempts to assimilate the Indians rested upon the schools; civilization and Christianization, the great goals of the Indian reformers, could be accomplished only through formal educational endeavors. The theory was so firmly held and so strongly advocated for so long a period that the limited scope of the actual educational system and the resultant paucity of results are surprising.[1]

The earliest attention to Indian education was part of Christian missionary effort. The scattered colonial attempts to provide schools for Indians were the work of missionaries who hoped primarily to bring the Gospel message to the heathens, and when Indian schools got their start in the United States, it was again the missionaries who undertook them. Government officials, who had generally preached the importance of civilizing the Indians by transforming them into farmers, welcomed the church efforts and modestly encouraged them, but at the end of the second decade of the nineteenth century, an enumeration of Indian schools showed very little; the Superintendent of Indian Trade counted only four schools in the Indian country and three outside, plus a few "minor and fugitive" schools which he could not precisely locate.[2]

Agitation continued, however, for government aid or stimulus to Indian education, and Congress in 1819 passed an "Act making provision for the civilization of the Indian Tribes adjoining the frontier settlements," which appropriated ten thousand dollars annually to be used at the discretion of the President to employ "capable persons of good moral character, to instruct them in the mode of agriculture suited to their situation; and for teaching their children in reading, writing, and arithmetic." Rather than spend these funds itself, the government decided to spend them through "benevolent societies" who already had Indian schools in operation or were willing to begin them. Secretary of War John C. Calhoun issued a circular on September 3, 1819, in which he invited individuals and groups to apply for a share in the funds by submitting information about their resources, the kind of

[1] There have been few general histories of Indian education. Alice C. Fletcher, *Indian Education and Civilization* (*Senate Executive Document* No. 95, 48 Congress, 2 session, serial 2264, Washington, 1888), was an early attempt to gather together data, but it is not a well-synthesized account. Evelyn C. Adams, *American Indian Education: Government Schools and Economic Progress* (New York, 1946), is a very brief survey. For the post-Civil War decades, see Priest, *Uncle Sam's Stepchildren*, pp. 132–54.

[2] Thomas L. McKenney to John C. Calhoun, August 14, 1819, in Records of the Office of Indian Trade, Letters Sent, vol. E, pp. 298–302, National Archives Record Group 75.

education they proposed to give, and the number of students they would instruct.[3]

Despite attacks from opponents of the scheme, who argued that all previous attempts to civilize Indians had failed, the missionary societies made considerable headway and were stimulated, as Calhoun had hoped, to invest sizable amounts of money of their own. By 1824 there were twenty-one Indian schools in existence, all but three established after 1819. There followed a steady increase in the number of schools, the number of students, and the private funds devoted to Indian education. In addition, treaties with the tribes increasingly made provision for educational funds.[4]

The disruption brought about by mass removal of eastern Indians to lands west of the Mississippi caused setbacks in the educational program, but they were only temporary, and the reforming decade of the 1840's saw a great upsurge in attention to Indian education among the tribes in their new homes.[5] The directors of Indian affairs believed that the inferior position in which the Indians found themselves was remediable. "It is proved, I think, conclusively," T. Hartley Crawford, the Commissioner of Indian Affairs, asserted of the Indian race in 1844, "that it is in no respect inferior to our own race, except in being less fortunately circumstanced. As great an aptitude for learning the letters, the pursuits, and arts of civilized life, is evident; if their progress is slow, so has it been with us and with masses of men in all nations and ages." Buoyed up by such optimism, the men of the 1840's advocated Indian schools with great enthusiasm. "The greatest good we can bestow upon them," Crawford said, "is education in its broadest sense—education in letters, education in labor and the mechanic arts, educa-

[3] *United States Statutes at Large,* III, 516–17; Circular, September 3, 1819, *American State Papers: Indian Affairs* (2 vols., Washington, 1832–1834), II, 201.

[4] Report of House Committee on Indian Affairs, March 23, 1824, *ibid.,* pp. 457–59; Fletcher, *Indian Education and Civilization,* p. 197. In 1825, the Indian schools received $13,620.41 from the government, $11,750.00 from Indian annuities and other treaty provisions, and $176,700.44 from private contributions. *American State Papers: Indian Affairs,* II, 669. There are tables showing the amounts available in 1834 and in 1845 for civilization promotion under treaty arrangements in George D. Harmon, *Sixty Years of Indian Affairs: Political, Economic, and Diplomatic, 1789–1850* (Chapel Hill, 1941), pp. 380–81.

[5] Prucha, "American Indian Policy in the 1840s," in *Frontier Challenge,* pp. 81–110.

tion in morals, and education in Christianity."[6] To accomplish such universal education, manual labor schools, patterned after the one established for the Shawnees in 1839 by the Methodists, were advocated. Here the boys and the girls, taken out of their native homes, would learn to live and to work according to white patterns. Eager cooperation of the Indian Office with missionary groups led to an increase in the number of Indian pupils in school, enough progress to enable the Commissioners and the Secretaries of War, as well as agents and missionaries in the field, to predict ultimate and quick success. Commissioner Orlando Brown, for example, in 1849 described a "great moral and social revolution" taking place among some of the tribes, which he predicted would spread to the rest.[7] These efforts continued into the 1850's, even though the slavery question caused qualms among the New England missionaries about supporting Indian tribes whose members were slaveowners, and the American Board of Commissioners for Foreign Missions had withdrawn from its southern schools by 1860.[8]

Thus when the post-Civil War Indian reformers faced the great mass of new Indians who had come within the immediate scope of American Indian policy and who needed "civilizing," there was a long tradition to fall back upon. The same principles and programs that were promoted so ardently in the 1840's for the Shawnees, the Potawatomis, and the Cherokees were advocated with equal vigor in the 1870's and 1880's for the Sioux, the Cheyennes, and the Comanches. The governmental officials concerned with Indian affairs spoke boldly about the need for education, although they realized the difficulties to be faced. Little could be done during the Civil War, but at its conclusion the Indian Office began once again an active campaign for more and better schools. Commissioner Dennis Cooley in 1866 made an extensive survey of the condition of the schools and endeavored to revive interest in the work of Indian education, which he characterized as "the only means of saving any considerable portion of the race from the life and

[6] Report of the Commissioner of Indian Affairs, 1844, in serial 449, p. 315; *ibid.*, 1842, in serial 413, p. 386.

[7] *Ibid.*, 1849, in serial 570, pp. 956–57.

[8] On the slavery problem, see Robert T. Lewitt, "Indian Missions and Anti-Slavery Sentiment: A Conflict of Evangelical and Humanitarian Ideals," *Mississippi Valley Historical Review*, L (June, 1963), 39–55.

death of heathen." Having recently become aware of the German kindergarten system, he sent books explaining it to several teachers and expressed great hopes that the system might attract to the schools the younger Indian children.[9]

Education, it is clear, was considered to be an essential part of the "peace policy" introduced at the beginning of President Grant's administration. Without education and training in industrial pursuits there could be no hope for any lasting results from the new policy. The church groups who co-operated with the government by assuming responsibility for the Indian agencies were expected to make education one of their primary concerns, and Columbus Delano suggested withholding annuities from Indians who refused or neglected to take advantage of the educational facilities provided. Commissioner Edward P. Smith argued in 1873 that "any plan for civilization which does not provide for training the young, even though at a largely increased expenditure, is short-sighted and expensive." And he thought that with proper facilities half the Indian children then growing up in barbarism could be put into schools. "Four or five years of this appliance of civilization cures one-half of the barbarism of the Indian tribe permanently," he declared. The Board of Indian Commissioners in 1875 noted that in order to civilize the Indians and establish them in a permanent condition of self-support "*education* must be regarded as a fundamental and indispensable factor," and the board proposed a universal common school system supplied by the federal government to all its Indian wards just as the states provided public schools for their children. The government should do this in justice, in return for the rich lands acquired from the Indians. Moreover, it said, "the true policy in dealing with the Indian race, as with every other, for the purpose of elevating them to the social and moral conditions of Christian civilization, consists not so much in feeding or governing the *adults* as in educating the *children*." Secretary of the Interior Zachariah Chandler in 1876 saw no alternative than education to the "gradual extinction of the race."[10]

There was general agreement that the type of education that was needed was industrial or manual training, as well as schooling in read-

[9] Report of the Commissioner of Indian Affairs, 1866, in serial 1284, pp. 20–21.

[10] Report of the Secretary of the Interior, 1871, in serial 1505, pp. 4–5; *ibid.*, 1876, in serial 1749, pp. iii–iv; Report of the Commissioner of Indian Affairs, 1873, in serial 1601, p. 377; *Report of the Board of Indian Commissioners*, 1875, pp. 8–9.

ing, writing, and arithmetic. The manual labor school was as much in vogue among the reformers of the 1870's and 1880's as it had been among those of the 1840's, and the arguments were much the same. The purpose of Indian education, ultimately, was to make the Indians self-supporting—not only as a means to advancing the individual's manhood but, quite practically, to bring an end to the enormous governmental outlays needed to maintain large numbers of Indians who had lost their old means of subsistence and had not taken up any new ones. To this end, training in agriculture or the common trades for the boys and in the domestic tasks of white households for the girls was considered indispensable. Despite the heavier costs of providing such schools—equipping schools with stock, wagons, farming implements, and tools—they were proposed as the only economical policy in the long run.[11]

These manual labor schools had to be boarding schools. Although day schools were provided on the reservations and were an important means of bringing the first lessons of civilization to the young, they were not satisfactory for accomplishing what the reformers had in mind—the complete transformation of the Indian children from their native ways to the ways of white civilization. The day schools, reported the Board of Indian Commissioners in 1871, were "a total or comparative failure in nearly every instance known to the members of the board." The reasons were clear to the reformers. As Commissioner Hayt remarked in 1877, "the exposure of children who attend only day-schools to the demoralization and degradation of an Indian home neutralizes the efforts of the schoolteacher, especially those efforts which are directed to advancement in morality and civilization."[12] How could the Indian child become properly acculturated, the reformers asked, if he were not removed from the irregular life and Indian language of his home? What was needed was a substitute home, and this the boarding school provided. Such a school "takes the youth under constant care, has him always at hand, and surrounds him by an English-speaking community, and above all, gives him instruction in

[11] See, for example, Report of the Commissioner of Indian Affairs, 1882, in serial 2100, pp. 25–34.
[12] Report of the Board of Indian Commissioners, 1871, p. 11; ibid., 1879, p. 14; Report of the Commissioner of Indian Affairs, 1877, in serial 1800, pp. 399–400.

the first lessons of civilization, which can be found only in a well-ordered home."[13]

No one pushed more strenuously for Indian education than Carl Schurz. In his report of 1877, in which he outlined his comprehensive Indian program, he gave extended space to education, and in subsequent years he repeated and refined his ideas. His policy included all the key elements advocated by the humanitarian reformers—compulsory education, boarding schools, and use of the English language—and he emphasized the need for manual and domestic arts training for the boys and the girls, to teach the Indian children how to live as well as how to read and write.[14] Secretary Henry Teller hammered incessantly on the same theme. He wanted to put at least half of the Indian children of school age into manual labor schools, where "more attention should be paid to teaching them to labor than to read." And he urged the annual expenditure of five or six million dollars for fifteen years for such schools and the turning of abandoned military posts into Indian schools. At least half the students, he said, should be girls, who should be taught to spin and weave, to make their own clothing, to take care of the house, and to "become suitable companions of the educated males." Teller, in fact, thought he had found the answer to the Indian problem. "The greatest agency for the civilization of the Indian," he wrote in 1884, "is the manual-labor school. Indeed, I do not think I shall be far out of the way if I say the only agency for that purpose is the manual-labor school. . . . The history of the few manual-labor schools established for the education of Indian children has demonstrated their great value, and that it is only necessary to multiply their number, so as to include all the Indian children of school age, to forever set at rest the question as to 'what shall be done with the Indians.' "[15]

Indian education was given a new impetus and, in a sense, a new direction by the appearance on the scene in the mid-1870's of a re-

[13] Ibid., 1873, in serial 1601, pp. 376–77.
[14] Report of the Secretary of the Interior, 1877, in serial 1800, pp. xi–xii; ibid., 1879, in serial 1910, pp. 10–11; ibid.,1880, in serial 1959, pp. 7–10.
[15] Ibid., 1882, in serial 2099, pp. xi–xvii; ibid., 1884, in serial 2286, p. vii.

markable young army officer named Richard Henry Pratt.[16] Pratt, born in New York in 1840, had only a common school education which ended when he was thirteen. Service in the Civil War as a cavalry officer gave him a taste for military life, and when his post-war business attempts ended in failure, he re-entered the army as a second lieutenant. He was assigned to the Tenth Cavalry, a Negro regiment, and saw considerable action on the southern plains against hostile Indians in 1868–1869 and in the Red River War of 1874–1875. As commander of Indian scouts, he gained firsthand knowledge of the red man's character and capabilities.

When the fighting ended, Pratt was detailed to take a group of seventy-two Indian prisoners to Fort Marion at St. Augustine, Florida. As he cared for the prisoners there, he began a program of education that was to make him a national figure. He got permission to release the Indians from close confinement, replaced their guards with some of the Indians themselves, instituted classes for them, and found useful work for them in the St. Augustine area. Determined to advance the Indians in their progress toward acceptance of white ways by treating them with dignity and providing opportunities for them to mix with whites, he had remarkable success. He interested white benefactors in his cause and persuaded his army superiors to assign him to the work of Indian education, where he could promote and expand the approach to Indian assimilation that he had begun so dramatically at Fort Marion. When the Indians' imprisonment came to an end, Pratt was assigned to Hampton Normal and Agricultural Institute in Virginia,

[16] Pratt's career and the history of his educational work with the Indians can best be followed in his memoirs and related papers printed in *Battlefield and Classroom: Four Decades with the American Indian, 1876–1904,* edited and with an introduction by Robert M. Utley (New Haven, 1964). Valuable also is Pratt's *The Indian Industrial School, Carlisle, Pennsylvania: Its Origin, Purpose, Progress and the Difficulties Surmounted* (Carlisle, 1908). Elaine Goodale Eastman, *Pratt: The Red Man's Moses* (Norman, 1935), is an uncritical biography written by a person who was much involved in Indian reform. A great deal of detail can be found in Carmelita S. Ryan, "The Carlisle Indian Industrial School" (unpublished Ph.D. dissertation, Georgetown University, 1962), and Everett Arthur Gilcreast, "Richard Henry Pratt and American Indian Policy, 1877–1906: A Study of the Assimilation Movement" (unpublished Ph.D. dissertation, Yale University, 1967). See also Robert L. Brunhouse, "The Founding of the Carlisle Indian School," *Pennsylvania History,* VI (April, 1939), 72–85; Louis Morton, "How the Indians Came to Carlisle," *ibid.,* XXXIX (January, 1962), 53–73; Thomas G. Tousey, *Military History of Carlisle and Carlisle Barracks* (Richmond, Virginia, 1939), pp. 273–355; Ruth Shaffner, "Civilizing the American Indian," *The Chautauquan,* XXIII (June, 1896), 259–68.

taking with him twenty-two of his Indian students, who were supported by private benefactors.

Hampton had already become well known for its educational work with freedmen under the direction of General Samuel C. Armstrong, who had commanded colored troops during the Civil War and then served as an agent of the Freedmen's Bureau.[17] Armstrong developed and promoted a plan of combining mental and manual training for the Negroes, and he founded Hampton Institute for that purpose in 1868 with the support of the American Missionary Association and private benefactors. The strong similarity that reformers saw between the needs of the Negroes and those of the Indians in preparing for full participation in American society made it reasonable to provide room for Indians as well as Negroes at Hampton. Pratt and his Indian charges arrived in April, 1878, and soon Pratt was off to the West to recruit more Indians for his educational experiment. He returned with forty-three additional students for the Indian department at Hampton.[18]

Despite this promising beginning, Pratt was dissatisfied at Hampton. His belief in the necessity of manual and industrial training for the Indians matched that of Armstrong, and the two men shared many common views. But Pratt chafed under the conditions at Hampton and feared that popular prejudices against the colored would rub off on his Indians, whom he wished to see associate and mix fully with the whites. He proposed, therefore, to set up an industrial training school solely for Indians, where he could carry out his educational principles unhampered. He importuned his superiors in the Army—for he continued to be on active duty although detailed to Indian educational work—and the officials of the Interior Department for a chance to prove the value of his program. Fortunately for his plans, he found in Secretary Schurz a sympathetic friend, and by a series of bureaucratic maneuvers he got permission to use the abandoned military barracks at Carlisle,

[17] On Hampton Institute, see Francis Greenwood Peabody, *Education for Life: The Story of Hampton Institute* (Garden City, New York, 1919). A eulogy on Armstrong is Herbert Welsh, "Samuel Chapman Armstrong," *Educational Review*, VI (September, 1893), 105–25.
[18] "Report of Lieut. R. H. Pratt, Special Agent to Collect Indian Youths to be Educated at Hampton Institute, Va.," *House Executive Document* No. 1, 45 Congress, 3 session, serial 1850, pp. 669–71.

Pennsylvania, for his experiment.[19] The federal government continued to support Indian students at Hampton until 1912 and for another decade a few Indians still attended, but attention soon became focused on Pratt's new venture.

Pratt went west in the summer of 1879 to recruit students for his school. At the Rosebud Agency, he persuaded Spotted Tail to send his children to Carlisle, and other Sioux there and at Pine Ridge followed the chief's example. Eighty-two children still wearing their tribal costumes, who were in a sense hostages for the good behavior of their parents, made a dramatic entry into Carlisle on October 6, 1879, and the Carlisle Indian Industrial School began its influential history. The Sioux were soon joined by fifty-five students from tribes in the Indian Territory, and on November 1, 1879, the school was officially opened. Enrollment steadily increased as facilities grew and the fame of the school spread until it reached about a thousand students.

Pratt's views on Indian matters were simple. He insisted upon the complete integration of the Indians into white society, and his whole program was geared to that one goal. Anything that tended to isolate or segregate the Indians was to him anathema. Reservations were an unmitigated evil, tribal status a preservation of outmoded ways and attitudes; he condemned what he called "this whole segregating and reservating process."[20] He was only half jesting when he noted that there were about 260,000 Indians in the United States and 2,700 counties and suggested that the Indians be divided up and sprinkled, nine to a county, across the nation.[21] There were no twilight zones in Pratt's mind; his principle shone as a brilliant light, and he wavered not an inch from the path it marked out. He held as tenaciously to his views at the end of his long career as he had at the beginning, despite the setbacks he had received and the friends he had broken with.

Pratt firmly believed that a man was the product of his environment. "There is no 'heart language,'" he insisted. "There is no resistless clog placed upon us by birth. We are not born with language, nor are we

---

[19] Since a special act of Congress was needed to transfer Carlisle Barracks from the War Department to the Department of the Interior, Pratt operated under a temporary arrangement made between the two departments until Congress finally acted in July, 1882.

[20] Eastman, *Pratt*, p. 77.

[21] *Ibid.*, p. 221.

born with ideas of either civilization or savagery. Language, savagery and civilization are forced upon us entirely by our environment after birth." If the Indians were kept in tribal surroundings on the reservations, he said, the nation would "not lack material for Wild West shows which the gaping throngs of great cities may scoff at and the crowned heads of Europe patronize, for centuries to come."[22] He repeatedly pointed to the example of the Negroes, who had learned the white man's language and his customs by associating with him, and to Europeans, who had immigrated in large numbers but were being rapidly integrated. To him the comparison and contrast were compelling. He noted that between 1880 and 1890 more than five million foreigners, representing many nations, had immigrated to the United States, and he wrote:

> They and their children are with us to-day, but where are they? Scattered everywhere in the very midst of the best environment of our America, they have abandoned their language, their Arabia, their Turkey, their Italy, their Russia, their Spain, etc., with all their former habits, and have become Americans. 5,246,616 foreigners made American citizens in ten years. 250,000 Indians, who were Indians ten years ago, are still practically Indians. Why? Simply because we will not allow them the same environment of America and our civilization. Twenty-one foreigners for every Indian! The foreigners made Americans and citizens by being invited, urged, and compelled to that consummation by their surroundings. The Indians remain Indians because they are walled in on reservations and compelled by every force we can apply even to the hedging about with guns, pistols and swords, to remain Indians.[23]

He told the World Convention of Baptists in 1883, "In Indian civilization I am a Baptist, because I believe in immersing the Indians in our civilization and when we get them under holding them there until they are thoroughly soaked."[24]

[22] Richard Henry Pratt, *How to Deal with the Indians: The Potency of Environment* (Carlisle, 1903), p. 3.
[23] *Ibid.*
[24] *Battlefield and Classroom*, p. 335. An excellent statement of Pratt's views is given in his paper, "The Advantages of Mingling Indians with Whites," read at the Nineteenth Annual Conference of Charities and Correction, Denver, 1892.

Pratt was a man of tremendous drive, with an impatience to get things done that could not brook opposition or delay. "If I were asked to characterize in one word Captain Pratt's work for the Indian," one of his contemporaries said, "I should call it *uncompromising*. He does not hesitate—he stops at no half-way measures. His goal is American citizenship; and, while others are working gradually and tentatively *toward* that end, he works directly *for* it—flings himself *at* it with all the force and combativeness of his vigorous nature. There are plenty of smaller minds to creep over obstacles and skirt pit-falls—it is well to have some one of the party who keeps the general direction in his head and sticks sublimely to an impracticable straight line."[25] This single-mindedness carried with it a stubborn streak and an inability to admit mistakes. Those who disagreed with him, he charged with stupidity or jealousy, and he easily imagined plots against him. But he was scrupulously honest and a deeply religious man.

The singlemindedness of his approach was reflected in his manner. He was a great coiner of slogans. "To Civilize the Indian; Get Him into Civilization. To Keep Him Civilized; Let Him Stay"—this mast-head on the Carlisle school paper described his program. One student at Carlisle in later life recalled Pratt entering the school assembly hall in his Prince Albert coat, "tall, of massive frame, square shouldered and military in bearing." Pratt called out questions to the students—"How shall we solve the Indian problem?" And the crowd responded with the prepared slogans that had been drilled into them: "Abolish the reservation system! Abolish the ration system!"[26] The nation was making a great mistake, Pratt said, "in feeding our civilization to the Indians, instead of feeding the Indians to our civilization."[27]

The Carlisle Indian Industrial School was to be but the beginning, a showcase for his educational policies and the prototype of a system of similar schools which would eventually provide assimilatory training for all the Indian youth. Pratt wanted the results to be so convincing that other off-reservation schools would follow until the universal training he envisaged would obtain, and he used his considerable pro-

[25] Elaine Goodale in Indian Rights Association pamphlet, *Captain Pratt and His Work for Indian Education* (Philadelphia, 1886), p. 6.

[26] Gilcreast, "Pratt and American Indian Policy," pp. 53, 92.

[27] Eastman, *Pratt*, p. 264.

motional skills to make sure that the story of Carlisle was widely known. He himself lectured widely, influential men and women were invited to visit the school, and he gave the Carlisle band full exposure at parades and other public gatherings. In this he was much helped by the discovery in the 1890's that the Indians of Carlisle could play great football, holding their own on the gridiron with the best of the Ivy League schools.[28]

The athletic association with Harvard and Cornell and Pennsylvania was a grossly inaccurate indication of the academic level that Carlisle was able to achieve, for its level of instruction was basically that of a grammar school. Indian students came to Carlisle with little or no schooling and some of them had to learn English after they arrived. Not until 1889, a decade after its opening, did Carlisle graduate its first class. Ultimately the course was extended to include the first two years of high school and some teacher training. To the end, Pratt complained about the quality of the students who were sent to his school.

Pratt's success, however, did not depend entirely upon the academic competence and accomplishments of his students. Following Armstrong's lead, he insisted upon education for the hand and the heart as well as the head, and various manual labor or industrial pursuits formed a large part of the training. An essential part of the Carlisle program was the "outing system," a program of placing students during the summer and sometimes throughout the year with rural families in the vicinity of Carlisle, many of whom were Quakers and shared the traditional interest of their church in Indian welfare. The outing system was an exemplification of Pratt's principle of associating the Indian children closely with the whites, so that they could learn by example and observation the benefits of white family and economic life. It was a tightly controlled system, however, in which rigid rules were to be enforced. The formula that the students were required to sign before being sent out gives a good idea of the kind of disciplined experience that Pratt had in mind.

[28] Much information about Carlisle was spread through the school papers published there. The publications—variously called *School News, The Red Man, The Red Man and Indian Helper,* and *The Carlisle Arrow*—provided a vehicle for Pratt's views and were another proof of the capabilities of the students.

Sir:

I want to go into the country.

If you will send me I promise to obey my employer, to keep all the rules of the school.

I will attend Sunday School and Church regularly.

I will not absent myself from my farmhouse without permission of my employer and will not loaf about stores or elsewhere evenings or Sundays.

I will not make a practice of staying for meals when visiting friends.

I will not use tobacco nor spirituous liquors in any form.

I will not play cards nor gamble, and will save as much money as possible.

If out for the winter, I will attend school regularly and will do my best to advance myself in my studies.

I will bathe regularly, write my home letter every month, and do all that I can to please my employer, improve myself and make the best use of the chance given me.

Very respectfully,

————, Pupil[29]

Pratt's prominence made him the focus of attacks by men who opposed the idea of trying to educate the Indians in the East and who objected strenuously to the expenditure of government funds for that purpose. Most outspoken of such critics was Senator Preston B. Plumb of Kansas, who spoke violently against special legislation to supplement Pratt's pay and who continued to harass the captain, publicly calling him a "fraud" and a "swindler," and charging that "his posturing before the country was ridiculous, and only done to make for himself notoriety, and gain credit for doing great things."[30]

[29] Quoted in Tousey, *History of Carlisle*, p. 306. Pratt described the outing system in remarks at Lake Mohonk in *Lake Mohonk Conference Proceedings*, 1891, pp. 60–65. See also George Bird Grinnell, "The Indians and the Outing System," *Outlook*, LXXV (September 12, 1903), 167–73. The outing system did not work so well at the other off-reservation training schools. The public-spirited Quaker farmers and Pratt with his unusual dynamic force were no doubt responsible for the success of the system at Carlisle.

[30] Debate in the Senate over a special grant to Pratt, January 21, 1881, is in *Congressional Record*, XI, 817–21. Other Plumb strictures are quoted in Pratt to Henry L. Dawes, March 18, 1882, cited in Priest, *Uncle Sam's Stepchildren*, p. 144.

That there were good points in Pratt's educational philosophy, however, was recognized by most of the persons who sought to improve the
condition of the Indians. The prominence of Carlisle in the public eye,
moreover, and the unmistakable achievements of many of the students
were convincing proof to many former skeptics that Indians were
indeed educable and could take their places in white society. Although
Pratt's own claims as to the importance and significance of his work
have been discounted, the Carlisle Indian School greatly advanced
public and private interest in Indian education and was an important
factor in the increased appropriations for that purpose by Congress.
Schurz and a succession of Indian Commissioners all spoke highly of
Carlisle and Hampton, and additional off-reservation schools on the
Carlisle model were established by the government, although they
were in the West closer to the reservations and not in the East as Pratt
desired.[31] The Board of Indian Commissioners, too, and the humanitarians at Lake Mohonk rejoiced at Pratt's success, and the captain
was a welcome guest at the early conferences.[32]

Few of the reformers or the officials in the Indian Office, however,
wanted to go down Pratt's single track. After the initial years of enthusiastic support and rich praise, Pratt's doctrine ran into opposition,
and alternative programs were projected which ultimately won the
day. Pratt's position that the Indian problem would be solved only if
every Indian student were enrolled in an off-reservation school, to
move from there to public schools and thence into the mainstream of
white society (with the consequent destruction of reservations and any
other form of segregation), was pushed aside by a more varied and
comprehensive system of Indian education, which emphasized reservation schools instead of those away from the reservations.

The problem that bothered Pratt's critics was the eventual status of
the alumni of the eastern industrial training schools. Were they, in
fact, absorbed into white society as Pratt hoped? Or did they return to
the reservation, and if so did their eastern off-reservation schooling
really fit them for the lives they actually led? A few educated men and

[31] Report of the Secretary of the Interior, 1879, in serial 1910, pp. 10–11; *ibid.*, 1880,
in serial 1959, pp. 8–10; Report of the Commissioner of Indian Affairs, 1881, in serial
2018, pp. 28–29; *ibid.*, 1885, in serial 2379, pp. 13–14.
[32] *Report of the Board of Indian Commissioners*, 1879, p. 14; *Lake Mohonk Conference Proceedings*, 1883, p. 10; *ibid.*, 1884, pp. 13–14.

women returning into the midst of an uneducated mass would soon lose their new ways, it was feared, and then perhaps not adjust well to either culture. The advocates of Hampton and Carlisle published careful reports to show that few graduates reverted to their old ways when they returned to their reservations.[33] But a few striking examples, like the Sioux youth Plenty Horses, who murdered an army officer at Pine Ridge at the time of the Ghost Dance troubles, with the explanation that he had done the deed to wipe out the stain of Carlisle, indicated that problems did exist. The reasonable solution was to raise the general level of education on the reservations so that there would be less disparity between returned students and those they had left behind, and to attain this goal emphasis would have to be placed on reservation schools. Furthermore, it was argued, if most Indians were going to live out their lives on the reservations, schooling there would be more advantageous. Francis E. Leupp, Washington agent of the Indian Rights Association and later Commissioner of Indian Affairs under Theodore Roosevelt, strongly advocated reservation schools and by that token became a foe of Pratt, for he reversed Pratt's view of the transit of civilization. "So the whole subject pivots on the question whether we should carry civilization to the Indian or carry the Indian to civilization," he later wrote, "and the former seems to me infinitely the wiser plan. To plant our schools among the Indians means to bring the older members of the race within the sphere of influence of which every school is a centre."[34] Off-reservation schools like Carlisle could then best serve as a capstone for a system of education beginning with day schools and boarding schools on the reservations, which would feed those youths best qualified for advanced studies to Carlisle and similar academies.

The off-reservation schools suffered because the reservation schools were reluctant to send away all their best students. Although the Indian Office insisted that the transfers be carried out and that the function of the reservation schools was to "work up" the "raw material

[33] Herbert Welsh, *Are the Eastern Industrial Training Schools for Indian Children a Failure?* (Philadelphia, 1886); J. J. Gravatt, *The Record of Hampton's Returned Indian Pupils* (Philadelphia, 1885); *Senate Executive Document* No. 31, 52 Congress, 1 session, serial 2892. The last item is a long report, dated December, 1891, on 639 returned students, with photographs of some of them at home on the reservations.

[34] Francis E. Leupp. *The Indian and His Problem* (New York, 1910), p. 135.

from the camps" which could then be sent to more advanced schools, it decided not to force the attendance of children at off-reservation schools against the wishes of their parents.[35] Pratt opposed the whole program, and he complained bitterly in the pages of the Carlisle school paper: " 'You must not take away my pupils,' 'You must not take my best pupils,' is the never ending whine of a very large number of narrow minded men and women sent to Indian reservations and paid by the government to teach and help it lift the Indian tribes into civilization and citizenship." In 1898, he wrote to the Commissioner of Indian Affairs, "We are not quite full, but I do not get proper students. The home schools hold on to them, and generally allow me to have the rubbish."[36]

As the movement for reservation schools grew, Pratt struck back intemperately at his opponents. He attacked the work of the missionaries for fostering Indian ways. "The missionary goes to the Indian," he said in 1892. "He learns the language. He associates with him—makes him feel that he is friendly and has great desire to help him. He even teaches the Indian English. But the fruits of his labor, by all the examples I have seen, have been to strengthen and encourage him to remain separate and apart from the rest of us."[37] He issued great blasts against the contract schools and against the Catholics who had the bulk of them. Old friends, like General Armstrong, who spoke in support of the contract schools at Lake Mohonk, were bitterly assailed. A similar attack was made against the Indian Rights Association and its secretary, Herbert Welsh, because they openly supported day schools and other schools on the reservations—although they and other humanitarians had long been supporters of Carlisle—and because they came to emphasize civil service reform rather than education as the great panacea for the Indian problem. Pratt was at first enthusiastic about the appointment of Thomas J. Morgan as Indian Commissioner in 1889, but his enthusiasm cooled when he discovered that Morgan's plan called for reservation schools as well as schools like Carlisle and that in fact the number of reservation schools increased during his term of office. After a decade, Pratt was still re-

[35] Report of the Commissioner of Indian Affairs, 1893, in serial 3210, pp. 9–10.
[36] Gilcreast, "Pratt and American Indian Policy," pp. 305–306.
[37] Eastman, *Pratt*, p. 112.

ferring to Morgan's system as a "most-un-American, class, and race perpetuating system of tribal and home schools."[38]

Ethnologists, too, were victims of his tirades, and he accused them of persuading the Indians to remain in their old ways and teaching them to be proud of their race. "Where is the profit to them or to us," he demanded, "in forcing Indian youth to hold on to primitive ideas? . . . Why compel them to carry two loads—to become civilized, and at the same time to remain uncivilized?" The United States Bureau of American Ethnology became a special bête noire. "Ethnology," he said, "revels in war, ghost and other dances, Peyote seances and all other spectacular characteristics and encourages them."[39]

Pratt saved his strongest denunciations for the Bureau of Indian Affairs because of its educational policy and because it dealt with tribes and thought in terms of reservations. He accused the Bureau of seeking only to perpetuate itself and referred to it as a "barnacle to be knocked off some time." His intemperate remarks and cantankerous attitude were too much for Washington officialdom. On June 15, 1904, Pratt was informed by the Commissioner of Indian Affairs that he had been dismissed from his post at Carlisle.[40] One observer commented, "Pratt, the irrepressible, has been suppressed at last. He is an honest lunatic."[41] But he did not quietly fade away. Retired from the army with a rank of brigadier general, he continued to fight singlemindedly until his death in 1924 for the cause and principles he had espoused.

Pratt's goal was never attained, and the system on which he had placed his hope was rejected. His basic assumption that it was possible to eradicate completely the culture of the Indians and assimilate them as European immigrants were assimilated into American society was a questionable one and could not have been accomplished without great human cost. His importance lies not in promoting this impossible dream, but in his part in awakening public opinion to the capabilities of the Indians and in mobilizing forces to promote their education. "General Pratt," Herbert Welsh said, "was, in my opinion, the greatest

---

[38] Gilcreast, "Pratt and American Indian Policy," p. 352. Gilcreast has a long discussion of Pratt's quarrels with the humanitarians, the Catholics, Protestant missionaries, his army superiors, and the Indian Bureau, pp. 252–301.

[39] Eastman, *Pratt*, pp. 194–95.

[40] Gilcreast, "Pratt and American Indian Policy," pp. 380–82.

[41] Quoted from the *Catholic Watchman* in Eastman, *Pratt*, p. 262.

moral force effecting the great change that has taken place in the minds of our citizens touching the Indians."[42]

The fact that Pratt's radical policy for Indian integration was not adopted says a good deal about the movement for Indian reform in the late nineteenth century. Eager as the humanitarians were for the assimilation of the Indians into American life, they were not ready in theory, and certainly not in the real world of American politics and bureaucracy, to wrest the Indian so radically and abruptly from the cultural and economic bearings of the reservations. Although they spoke of rapid acculturation and assimilation, and hoped and worked for it, they intended to move forward from the existing situation. When confronted by the radical extention of their principles in Pratt, they backed away.

The cultural imperialism of the reformers, their utter lack of understanding of or appreciation for Indian culture, was exhibited sharply in the demands that Indian languages be prohibited and that only English be taught or spoken in the Indian schools. There had been early interest in Indian languages, to be sure. Missionaries, interested in bringing the Gospel to all the red men, collected word lists and drew up grammars of the native tongues as a means of learning to communicate with the tribesmen, and the Bible, hymns, and other religious pieces had been laboriously translated. Scientific interest, too, had often rested on a study of Indian language. Most early mission schools

---

[42] Eastman, *Pratt*, p. 8. For a sound evaluation of Pratt, see Robert M. Utley, introduction to *Battlefield and Classroom*, pp. xiii–xviii. Mrs. Ryan, in her dissertation on Carlisle Indian School, concludes that Pratt's ideals were "too high and somewhat questionable. Based in large part on his own experience, Pratt firmly believed that the Indian could make the jump across the centuries through hard work and sheer desire." She criticized Pratt's inability to merge into the educational system of the Bureau. "The school remained a maverick, outside the pale. . . ." (pp. 280–84). Gilcreast, in his dissertation, on the other hand, is strongly on Pratt's side, and criticizes the humanitarian reformers of the nineteenth century and the social science reformers of the twentieth century insofar as they did not agree with Pratt. "As for Pratt," he writes, "it is not too much to say that he comes down to us as a truer reformer than the humanitarians and the social scientists. He had a rare ability to see the heart of the problem and to identify himself with the needs of the individual Indians. He came long before his time, and, unfortunately, was never in a position to alter the course of Indian affairs." (p. 397) Gilcreast concludes about Pratt: "History may yet render the judgment that would have pleased him most—that he was supremely right." (p. 399)

for the Indians, however, were conducted in English (no doubt largely because there were no teachers who spoke the native tongues), and the government schools followed suit. Tribal leaders, like those of the Cherokees and the other civilized tribes, appreciated the value of English in their dealings with the United States, and men who had been educated in English schools—John Ross, John Ridge, and Elias Boudinot among the Cherokees, for example—became the spokesmen of the nation. Learning English had thus been to a large extent a practical matter.

After the Civil War, English for the Indians became a theoretical principle, and its implementation became almost an obsession, not only with Pratt but with all the Indian reformers. If the Indians were to become civilized, the civilization they were to adopt was American civilization, and for that a key means and a key symbol was the English language. The Peace Commission of 1867, in analyzing the problems faced in Indian relations, hit upon the difference in language as an important element in preventing "a proper understanding each of the other's motives and intentions." "In the difference of language to-day," the commission asserted, "lies two-thirds of our trouble." Its proposed solution was the establishment of schools which the Indian children should be required to attend and where "their barbarous dialects should be blotted out and the English language substituted." One of the great goals of the commission was to break down tribal identity of the Indians and thus to "fuse them into one homogeneous mass." To accomplish this, only one means was at hand: uniformity of language.[43]

Carl Schurz stated the principle moderately: "If Indian children are to be civilized they must learn the language of civilization. They will become far more accessible to civilized ideas and ways of thinking when they are enabled to receive those ideas and ways of thinking through the most direct channel of expression." Efforts to draw up Indian grammars and to instruct the Indians in their native languages Schurz dismissed as "certainly very interesting and meritorious philological work" but of little use to the Indians. The policy of teaching English in the government schools was praised by the Board of Indian Commissioners as "eminently wise," for if the Indians were to become

[43] "Report of Indian Peace Commissioners," *House Executive Document* No. 97, 40 Congress, 2 session, serial 1337, pp. 16–18.

useful American citizens, they had to know the common language of the country.[44]

The most radical promoter of English was J. D. C. Atkins, who served as Indian Commissioner from 1885 to 1888. From the very first, he took a strong stand that only English should be taught to the Indians, and he rejoiced that there was not an Indian pupil whose tuition or maintenance in schools was paid for by the United States government who was permitted to study any language but English— "the language of the greatest, most powerful, and enterprising nationalities beneath the sun." The superiority if not supremacy of English was a first principle with Atkins, and he was convinced that the Indians should acquire the language as rapidly as possible. "Every nation is jealous of its own language," he philosophized, "and no nation ought to be more so than ours, which approaches nearer than any other nationality to the perfect protection of its people. True Americans all feel that the Constitution, laws, and institutions of the United States, in their adaptation to the wants and requirements of man, are superior to those of any other country; and they should understand that by the spread of the English language will these laws and institutions be more firmly established and widely disseminated. Nothing so surely and perfectly stamps upon an individual a national characteristic as language." Atkins had no qualms about pushing the Indians' native tongues completely aside. English, he said, "which is good enough for a white man and a black man, ought to be good enough for the red man." To allow the Indian to continue with his native tongue was in fact a detriment to him. "The first step to be taken toward civilization, toward teaching the Indians the mischief and folly of continuing in their barbarous practices, is to teach them the English language."[45]

To make sure that his principles were carried out in practice, Atkins issued a series of regulations to the agents and to the representatives of missionary groups to insist that only English be used as a means of instruction in both the government and the church schools.[46] The direc-

[44] Report of the Secretary of the Interior, 1877, in serial 1800, p. xii; *Report of the Board of Indian Commissioners*, 1881, pp. 10–11.

[45] Report of the Commissioner of Indian Affairs, 1886, in serial 2467, pp. 99–100; *ibid.*, 1887, in serial 2542, pp. 19–21.

[46] These regulations, dated December 14, 1886, February 2, 1887, and July 16, 1887, are printed in the Commissioner's report of 1887, pp. 20–21.

tives raised an immediate storm, largely from missionaries who interpreted them to mean a prohibition on all use of Indian vernacular by missionary teachers. They had been preaching the Gospel in Indian languages and cried that Atkins' order amounted to religious persecution, since the native tongue was the only way to bring Christian teachings to the adult Indian. Nor did all the mission schools restrict their secular teaching of the children to English.[47]

Atkins tried his best to soothe the ruffled feelings of the missionaries and in a final version of the directive made allowances for certain situations in which the Indian vernacular was to be permitted. The full directive, which follows, shows the intensity of Atkins' conviction and his determination to allow few loopholes in his policy.

1. No text-books in the vernacular will be allowed in any school where children are placed under contract, or where the Government contributes to the support of the school; no oral instruction in the vernacular will be allowed at such schools. The entire curriculum must be in the English language.

2. The vernacular may be used in missionary schools, only for oral instruction in morals and religion, where it is deemed to be an auxiliary to the English language in conveying such instruction; and only native Indian teachers will be permitted to otherwise teach in any Indian vernacular; and these native teachers will only be allowed so to teach in schools not supported in whole or in part by the Government, and at remote points, where there are no Government or contract schools where the English language is taught. These native teachers are only allowed to teach in the vernacular with a view of reaching those Indians who can not have the advantages of instruction in English, and such instruction must give way to the English-teaching schools as soon as they are established where the Indians can have access to them.

3. A limited theological class of Indian young men may be trained in the vernacular at any purely missionary school, supported exclusively by missionary societies, the object being to prepare them for the ministry, whose subsequent work shall be confined to preach-

[47] United States Indian Office, *Correspondence on the Subject of Teaching the Vernacular in Indian Schools, 1887–'88* (Washington, 1888), pp. 5–7, 12.

ing, unless they are employed as teachers in remote settlements, where English schools are inaccessible.

4. These rules are not intended to prevent the possession or use by any Indian of the Bible published in the vernacular, but such possession or use shall not interfere with the teaching of the English language to the extent and in the manner hereinbefore directed.[48]

In a special pamphlet issued in April, 1888, Atkins explained at considerable length the aims of his policy and insisted that it was not aimed at strictly religious teaching or preaching.[49] But he did not recede an inch from his basic position. He insisted that "in the schools established for the rising generation of Indians shall be taught the language of the Republic of which they are to become citizens." If the vernacular were allowed in the church-sponsored schools, the Indian students and their parents might be prejudiced against English and against the government schools where it was used exclusively. He stood firm, too, against the charge that his mandatory English struck a cruel blow at the sacred rights of the Indians. "Is it cruelty to the Indian," he asked, "to force him to give up his scalping-knife and tomahawk? Is it cruelty to force him to abandon the vicious and barbarous sun dance, where he lacerates his flesh, and dances and tortures himself even unto death? Is it cruelty to the Indians to force him to have his daughters educated and married under the laws of the land, instead of selling them at a tender age for a stipulated price into concubinage to gratify the brutal lusts of ignorance and barbarism?"[50]

The Commissioner consoled himself in the face of criticism with the argument that he had been governed in his action solely by what he believed to be "the real interests of the Indians," and by the fact that he was supported in his stand by eminent educators and missionaries. Captain Pratt, as might have been expected, came quickly to Atkins' support, declaring that "the first wall to be knocked down is the wall of language," and that there was "more of Indian emancipation in it [Atkins' order] than in the land-in-severalty law." And the agent of the Cheyenne River Agency declared, "to teach the rising generation

[48] *Ibid.*, pp. 11–12.
[49] *Ibid.*, pp. 7–16.
[50] Report of the Commissioner of Indian Affairs, 1887, in serial 2542, pp. 20–22.

of the Sioux in their native tongue is simply to teach the perpetuation of something that can be of no benefit whatever to them."[51]

Considerable progress was made in the system of Indian education in the quarter-century following the Civil War, even though the enthusiastic proclamations of advance made periodically by the Secretaries of the Interior and the Commissioners of Indian Affairs have to be accepted with caution. Commissioner Hayt in 1878 provided statistical tables to show the "steady increase" in the number of Indian children attending school. "The results, after trial during the few years past, of the peace policy, imperfectly carried out as it has been," he asserted, "prove beyond a doubt that the eventual civilization of Indians may be reached through the education of their children; and further, that it can be brought about more speedily by that method than by any other."[52] By 1884, Secretary of the Interior Teller was able to report eighty-one boarding schools, seventy-six day schools, and six industrial or manual labor schools under government control, including new schools at Chilocco, Indian Territory, Lawrence, Kansas, and Genoa, Nebraska. In addition there were fourteen boarding schools and four day schools run by religious denominations under contracts with the government and twenty-three other missionary schools toward which the government provided no support at all.[53]

Secretary Lamar in 1885, noting the progress in the schools, remarked, "The practicability of Indian education is no longer a question." Two years later he transmitted to the President data for a decade of work. At the beginning of the decade, in 1878, there had been 137 Indian schools of all kinds provided by the government, with an average attendance of about 3,500, maintained at a total cost of nearly $196,000. In 1887 there were 231 schools, with over 10,000 students, at a cost of almost $1,200,000. Lamar considered this "a gratifying improvement," that showed how the interest in education was growing among the Indians.[54]

[51] *Teaching the Vernacular in Indian Schools*, pp. 17, 20–21.
[52] Report of the Commissioner of Indian Affairs, 1878, in serial 1850, pp. 457–58; see also *ibid.*, 1879, in serial 1910, pp. 73–74; *ibid.*, 1880, in serial 1959, pp. 85–88.
[53] Report of the Secretary of the Interior, 1884, in serial 2286, pp. iii–v.
[54] *Ibid.*, 1885, in serial 2378, p. 29; *ibid.*, 1887, in serial 2541, p. 29. See also Report

The figures surely indicated a growth, but even a cursory examination of them indicates that the surface had been little more than scratched. A total of ten thousand pupils out of an Indian population estimated at one-third of a million could hardly be considered satisfactory. The fact, of course, did not escape the proponents of Indian education, who kept pounding on the doors of Congress for the additional funds needed to establish a reasonably inclusive system for the Indian children. From Ely S. Parker in 1869, who lamented that Congress had reduced the estimates for educational expenses that he had submitted; to Edward P. Smith in 1873, who argued that a "large expenditure for a few years in the proper direction will be more economical than a smaller expenditure perpetuated"; to Hiram Price in 1881, who noted that the State of Rhode Island spent $600,000 annually for 49,000 students, compared with the government's $215,000 for the same number of Indian children; to Atkins in 1887, who pointed out that the "cost of the schools is immeasurably less than that of the wars they supplant, to say nothing of the sacrifices of lives of both soldiers and Indians"—everyone urged greater appropriations for Indian education.[55]

There was an increasing realization among the proponents of Indian education that compulsion was going to be necessary. Delano thought that it might be well "to establish a system of compulsory education to such an extent, at least, as to withhold annuities from those individuals who refuse or neglect to avail themselves of the educational facilities offered," and Schurz recommended compulsory education "as far as practicable."[56] By 1884, some progress was reported. Compulsory education had been tried at four agencies, at two by the withholding of rations and at the others by withholding annuity payments, and the Commissioner of Indian Affairs noted that as soon as enough school buildings could be provided, all the Sioux could have a similar

of the Commissioner of Indian Affairs, 1887, in serial 2542, pp. 12–15, and the statistics in Report of the Superintendent of Indian Schools, *ibid.*, pp. 757–91. For a table showing annual appropriations for Indian schools from 1877 to 1894, see Report of the Commissioner of Indian Affairs, 1893, in serial 3210, p. 18.

[55] *Ibid.*, 1869, in serial 1414, p. 455; *ibid.*, 1873, in serial 1601, p. 377; *ibid.*, 1881, in serial 2018, pp. 25–30; *ibid.*, 1887, in serial 2542, p. 15.

[56] Report of the Secretary of the Interior, 1871, in serial 1505, pp. 4–5; *ibid.*, 1877, in serial 1800, pp. xi–xii. See also Report of the Commissioner of Indian Affairs, 1877, in serial 1800, pp. 399–400.

system of enforcement applied under the terms of their treaty. But no general regulation was enacted at once, despite repeated recommendations that only compulsory education would save the Indians for civilization.[57] There was a general feeling, no doubt, that the peace approach to civilizing and assimilating the Indians must rest on persuasion, not force. And the failure of the government to provide needed funds to care for the education of the entire population of Indian children made compulsion infeasible. The drive for a universal government Indian school system, however, that came to a climax after the passage of the Dawes Act, carried with it the corollary of compulsory action.

Since the government appropriations, although increasing, were by no means equal to the task, the government continued to rely upon missionary effort for the schools it itself failed to provide. By means of so-called "contract schools," the government gave financial aid to religious groups that set up Indian schools on the reservations. By 1883, these groups were conducting twenty-two boarding schools and sixteen day schools with government aid, in addition to those they conducted entirely on their own. The aggregate monetary contribution to these schools came to $252,016, but this was considered to be only a part of the value contributed by the missionaries. "The influence of men and women whose lives are devoted to the uplifting of the degraded and ignorant cannot be measured by dollars and cents," Commissioner Price asserted. "Moreover, the very fact that he represents a great religious denomination, that a Christian community is his constituency, and that the funds which come into his hands have been consecrated by prayer and self-denial, gives to a man and his work a moral force and momentum which Government patronage does not impart."[58] Price's successors, Atkins and Oberly, continued the system, and the religious groups responded generously, putting more money into Indian school buildings than the government itself. The increase in enrollment between 1887 and 1888, for example, was substantially

[57] Ibid., 1884, in serial 2287, p. 18; Kappler, Indian Affairs, II, 1000. For recommendations on compulsory education, see Report of Superintendent of Indian Schools in Report of the Commissioner of Indian Affairs, 1885, in serial 2379, pp. 113–14; Report of the Secretary of the Interior, 1887, in serial 2541, pp. 29–30.

[58] Report of the Commissioner of Indian Affairs, 1883, in serial 2191, p. 32. For a detailed tabular account of the religious educational work among the Indians in 1883, see ibid., pp. 298–303.

greater in the contract schools than in the government schools because the contract schools had increased their accommodations more than the government schools.[59]

The Christian interest in Indian matters explicitly acknowledged by government officials made such an arrangement seem unexceptionable if not wise and necessary, but both a growing interest in a public school system and increased antagonism of the traditionally Protestant-minded Americans toward the Roman Catholics, who got by far the largest part of the funds granted to contract schools, led to a serious questioning of the whole system. Although the Indian Office declared that its support of the mission schools had been "entirely non-sectarian," and refuted the early charges that Catholics had been favored by pointing out that they had expended larger sums of money than any other denomination in the establishment of schools and therefore had been enabled to accommodate more pupils under contract, the drive against the contract school system helped to force the government to reconsider its role as educator of the red man.[60]

[59] Report of the Commissioner of Indian Affairs, 1887, in serial 2542, pp. 16–17; ibid., 1888, in serial 2637, pp. xii–xv.

[60] Ibid., 1887, in serial 2542, pp. 16–17; ibid., 1888, in serial 2637, p. xv. Oberly noted that the Bureau of Catholic Indian Missions reported an expenditure of $115,000 for Indian school buildings and equipment during the fiscal year ending June 30, 1887, and that the total amount invested by the Catholics in such buildings was about $1,000,000.

CHAPTER 10

EDUCATION FOR PATRIOTIC CITIZENSHIP

Modern studies in ethnology have made us acquainted with the depth to which the distinctions of civilization penetrate. We do not now expect to work the regeneration of a people except by changing the industrial habits, the manners and customs, the food and clothing, the social and family behavior, the view of the world, and the religious conviction systematically and co-ordinately. . . .

On this account the new education for our American Indians as it has been founded in recent years by devoted men and women, undertakes to solve the problem of civilizing them by a radical system of education not merely in books, nor merely in religious ceremonies, but in matters of clothing, personal cleanliness, matters of dietary, and especially in habits of industry.

—WILLIAM TORREY HARRIS,
U.S. Commissioner of
Education, 1889

✿✿✿✿✿✿✿

The early efforts at creating an Indian school system look anemic compared with the earnest drive for Indian education that came after 1887. No sooner had the severalty principle been written into law by the Dawes Act than the reformers began to realize—somewhat belatedly—that neither the homestead nor the citizenship would benefit the Indian if he were not properly prepared to appreciate the responsibilities as well as the benefits of both. The Lake Mohonk Conference of 1888, with a fearful sense of urgency, turned most of its attention to Indian education. The question, as formulated by one member of the conference, was "How can we make the individual red man a member of the white man's civilization?" The answer was obvious: "We have got to train him and fit him for it by the slow process of education."[1] There was a lengthy discussion about how this might best be done, and the conference in the end issued a platform calling for a thorough government system of Indian schools. It noted that the cost of education was only a fraction of the cost of war, declared that "the expense of educating the Indian for self-support [was] less than one-tenth the cost of keeping him in pauperism," and urged the federal government to establish an Indian school system analogous to the public school system. The conference pledged its cordial co-operation in efforts "to remove at once the National dishonor of supporting ignorant and barbaric peoples in the heart of a Christian civilization."[2]

To forward this work the reformers soon had the powerful aid of Thomas Jefferson Morgan, Commissioner of Indian Affairs from 1889 to 1893 and the first significant national figure in the history of American Indian education. Not only was Morgan a professional educator, but he epitomized important intellectual trends of his age. His ardent and aggressive Americanism, his unquestioning belief in the public school system, his professional Protestantism (with its corollary of anti-Catholicism), and his deep humanitarianism brought together strands of American thought that had been slowly but steadily intertwining in the preceding decades. With him the United States government embarked upon a comprehensive system of Indian education that had enduring effects for the Indians and for the nation. Morgan was a symbol of the realization taking shape that education was the indispensable instrument that would make possible the final goal envisaged for the Indians.

This goal was aptly expressed by the title of a book Morgan published two years after he left office, a sort of catechism for public school pupils which expounded the nationalistic fervor that nineteenth-century America reveled in. The book, a distillation of Morgan's philosophy developed during his years as soldier, clergyman, educator, and government administrator, was called *Patriotic Citizenship*.[3] The title expressed Morgan's highest aspiration for the nation he loved. It

[1] Remarks of Seth Low, *Lake Mohonk Conference Proceedings*, 1888, p. 24.
[2] Platform, *ibid.*, pp. 94–95.
[3] New York, 1895.

could serve as well as the motto of his four-year term as Commissioner of Indian Affairs, for he energetically sought to usher the Indians, at last, into the great republican edifice as citizens indistinguishable from other Americans.

Morgan was born in Franklin, Indiana, on August 17, 1839. He graduated from Franklin College in 1861, although he left school during his senior year to enlist in the Union Army. After a short period as a private soldier, he was commissioned a first lieutenant in the Seventieth Indiana Volunteer Infantry, a regiment commanded by Benjamin Harrison. He soon became prominent as a leader of Negro troops, for in November, 1863, he organized the Fourteenth United States Colored Infantry and commanded it as lieutenant colonel and then as colonel. At the battle of Nashville, he commanded two brigades and was brevetted brigadier general on March 13, 1865. His humanitarian concern for the elevation of the Negro was evident from the beginning. In summing up the part the colored troops played at Nashville, he remarked: "It had been shown that marching under the flag of freedom, animated by a love of liberty, even the slave becomes a man and a hero."[4]

When the war ended, Morgan entered Rochester Theological Seminary and in 1869 was ordained a Baptist minister. After two years as corresponding secretary of the New York Union for Ministerial Education and a brief pastorate at Brownville, Nebraska (1871–1872), he began his career as secular educator by accepting the principalship of the Nebraska State Normal School at Peru (1872–1874). From there he moved to the Baptist Union Theological Seminary in Chicago, where he taught homilectics and ecclesiastical history. During his seven years of connection with the Chicago seminary, he spent one semester studying abroad at the University of Leipzig and for two years acted as corresponding secretary. In 1881 he resigned his Chicago post to accept a position as principal at the State Normal School

[4] Thomas J. Morgan, *Reminiscences of Service with Colored Troops in the Army of the Cumberland, 1863–65* (Providence, 1885), cited in Dudley Taylor Cornish, *The Sable Arm: Negro Troops in the Union Army, 1861–1865* (New York, 1956), p. 298. For facts of Morgan's career, see the article by Conrad Henry Moehlman, *Dictionary of American Biography*, XIII, 187–88, and a biographical sketch written by Morgan himself, attached to letter of Morgan to E. W. Halford, January 14, 1889, in Records of the Secretary of the Interior, Appointments Division, "Commissioner of Indian Affairs, 1889," National Archives Record Group 48.

at Potsdam, New York, and after two years there accepted a similar position at the State Normal School at Providence, Rhode Island. That a Baptist clergyman could move so easily between denominational and public institutions is an indication of the dominant place held by Protestants and their general acceptance in the growing public school system of the nation. Morgan's continual insistence upon the need for "Christian education" not only reflected his own personal commitment to religion but was a part of the spirit of the age.

He gained attention in the educational world by his writings and his public addresses. In 1887 he edited a collection of short pieces on educational questions, entitled *Educational Mosaics*, and two years later published *Studies in Pedagogy*, a textbook for normal school students.[5] In addition, he was a regular participant in the annual meetings of the National Education Association and served as a vice-president of that organization in 1887–1888 and 1888–1889. Although he maintained his interest in Baptist educational activities and served as corresponding secretary of the Providence Branch of the Indian Rights Association, it was as a public educator that he prided himself and first sought federal office.

When his old Civil War commander, Benjamin Harrison, was elected to the presidency, Morgan hoped to be appointed United States Commissioner of Education. He wrote to Harrison that the position would be in line with his special training of nearly twenty-five years. And he carefully sent to Harrison's private secretary a full dossier of recommendations and testimonials from men prominent in educational and other public fields.[6] Support of Morgan for the education position was genuine and widespread, although not sufficient to win him the post, which went instead to William Torrey Harris, a more prominent man in educational circles than Morgan. But Morgan's desire for public office was soon satisfied, for Harrison offered him the post of Commissioner of Indian Affairs, which he eagerly accepted. Herbert Welsh, secretary of the Indian Rights Association had worked

---

[5] *Educational Mosaics: A Collection from Many Writers (Chiefly Modern) of Thoughts Bearing on Educational Questions of the Day* (Boston, 1887); *Studies in Pedagogy* (Boston, 1889).

[6] Morgan to Harrison, November 26, 1888, and Morgan to E. W. Halford, January 14, 1889, in Records of the Secretary of the Interior, Appointments Division, "Commissioner of Indian Affairs, 1889," National Archives Record Group 48.

diligently to persuade the new President to retain in office the incumbent Commissioner, John H. Oberly, whose integrity met the high standards of the Indian reformers and whose retention would be a strike against the spoilsmen. But if Oberly could not be kept on under the Republicans, Morgan was considered a more than acceptable substitute. Harrison appointed Morgan on June 10, 1889; the new Commissioner did not report for duty, however, until some days after his job as principal at Providence ended on June 28.[7]

Morgan came to the Indian Office with firm opinions on the value of education as an essential means for the promotion of American citizenship and on the necessity of a public school system. In *Studies in Pedagogy*, he extolled the virtues of the "free schools of America," which would create a universal Americanism. The goal of the teachers, he wrote, should be to bring about a common life among the various peoples who made up the nation. The children of Germans, Italians, and Africans, of Protestants, Catholics, and atheists, of anarchists, socialists, and communists were to enter the classroom representing divergent and often antagonistic groups. They were to leave the schools "speaking the same language, eager in the same pursuits of knowledge, loving the same institutions, loyal to the same flag, proud of the same history, and acknowledging the one God the maker of us all." The instruments for such a transformation were the public schools, which he considered the "safeguards of liberty," the "nurseries of a genuine democracy," the "training schools of character." "They are American," Morgan declared. "Nothing, perhaps, is so distinctly a product of the soil as is the American school system. In these schools all speak a common language; race distinctions give way to national characteristics. . . ."[8] In his new office, Morgan added the American Indian to this vision.

His first annual report as Commissioner of Indian Affairs, submitted on October 1, 1889, presented his general position on Indian affairs—a position clearly in accord with the views advanced by the Board of

[7] Morgan to Harrison, May 22, 1889, and Morgan to John W. Noble, June 13, 1889, *ibid.* For Harris's appointment in place of Morgan, see Kurt F. Leidecker, *Yankee Teacher: The Life of William Torrey Harris* (New York, 1946), pp. 458–60. Welsh's support of Morgan's candidacy is found in *Lake Mohonk Conference Proceedings*, 1889, p. 110; *Report of the Indian Rights Association*, 1889, pp. 10–11.

[8] *Studies in Pedagogy*, pp. 327–28, 348–50.

Indian Commissioners, the Lake Mohonk Conference, and other associated Indian reform groups. He had entered into his office, he said at the beginning of his report, with "a few simple, well-defined, and strongly-cherished convictions." He asserted that the "anomalous position heretofore occupied by the Indians in this country can not much longer be maintained." The reservation system had to cease and the "logic of events" demanded the absorption of the Indians into the national life, not as Indians but as American citizens. The relation of the Indians to the government must come to rest solely upon a recognition of their individuality, and in the end the Indians must conform to American civilization. Morgan was uncompromising in his insistence on this point: "This civilization may not be the best possible, but it is the best the Indians can get. They can not escape it, and must either conform to it or be crushed by it." The tribal relations had to be broken up, he reasserted, socialism destroyed, and the family and the individual substituted. The means to this end were the allotment of land in severalty, establishment of local courts, development of a personal sense of independence, and the universal use of the English language. And, of course, a comprehensive system of education patterned after the American public school system.[9]

The day following the submission of this statement of his philosophy, Morgan appeared at the Lake Mohonk Conference to present in detail a proposal for an Indian educational system. He began with a stance of humility, seeking the counsel of those present. "When President Harrison tendered me the Indian Bureau," Morgan related, "he said, 'I wish you to administer it in such a way as will satisfy the Christian philanthropic sentiment of the country.' That was the only charge that I received from him. I come here, where the Christian philanthropic sentiment of the country focusses itself, to ask you what will satisfy you." He had but one motive, he told the conference: "to embody in administrative work the highest thought which you elaborate in regard to the treatment of the Indians." Then he stated his goal by way of definition:

When we speak of the education of the Indians, we mean that comprehensive system of training and instruction which will convert

9 Report of the Commissioner of Indian Affairs, 1889, in serial 2725, pp. 3–4.

297

them into American citizens, put within their reach the blessings which the rest of us enjoy, and enable them to compete successfully with the white man on his own ground and with his own methods. Education is to be the medium through which the rising generation of Indians are to be brought into fraternal and harmonious relationship with their white fellow-citizens, and with them enjoy the sweets of refined homes, the delight of social intercourse, the emoluments of commerce and trade, the advantages of travel, together with the pleasures that come from literature, science, and philosophy, and the solace and stimulus afforded by a true religion.[10]

Morgan pointed out that the education of the Indians was a responsibility of the national government that could not safely be shirked or delegated to any other party. And he insisted that the government of the United States, "now one of the richest on the face of the earth, with an overflowing treasury," could undertake the work without finding it a burden. To accomplish the work he set forth a series of stipulations.

The system should accommodate all the Indian children. "To resist successfully and overcome the tremendous downward pressure of inherited prejudice, and the stubborn conservatism of centuries," he insisted, "nothing less than universal education should be attempted." And this education must be compulsory; whatever steps were necessary should be taken to place the children under "proper educational influences." Morgan was convinced that with such education the Indians would become "honorable, useful, happy citizens of a great republic." Without it they were "doomed either to destruction or to hopeless degradation."

Indian education, he continued, should be completely systematized. The common schools on the reservations, the agency boarding schools, and the great national industrial schools like Carlisle and Hampton should be properly related to form one whole. There should be a uniform course of study, similar methods of instruction, and standard textbooks, so that the Indian schools would conform to the public school system of the states. The Indian schools should be nonpartisan and nonsectarian, with teachers chosen on a rigid basis of qualification,

[10] *Lake Mohonk Conference Proceedings*, 1889, pp. 16–17. The full address, "The Education of American Indians," is on pp. 16–34. It was also printed separately. The quotations in the paragraphs following are taken from this address.

paid salaries comparable to those of teachers in public schools, with stable tenure of office and subject to a careful inspection system. Although Morgan placed special stress on industrial training that would fit the Indian to earn an honest living, he asked for provision as well for "that general literary culture which the experience of the white race has shown to be the very essence of education." To this end command of the English language was essential, and Morgan proposed that in schools supported wholly or in part by the government only English-speaking teachers be employed and that no language but English be allowed in the schools. The school system, too, should not stop with a common school education but should provide for higher education for the few, those with special capacity or ambition who were destined to be leaders.

"The Indian youth," he said, "should be instructed in their rights, privileges, and duties as American citizens; should be taught to love the American flag; should be imbued with a genuine patriotism, and made to feel that the United States, and not some paltry reservation, is their home." He urged those responsible for educating the Indians to waken in them "a sense of independence, self-reliance, and self-respect." He was worried that Indian youth, after studying at the great industrial schools, would return to the reservations rather than put their former life of the tribe behind them. "Education should seek the disintegration of the tribes, and not their segregation. They should be educated, not as Indians, but as Americans. In short, public schools should do for them what they are so successfully doing for all the other races in this country,—assimilate them."

To accomplish this goal, the education of the Indians would have to be comprehensive, beginning with the Indians while they were still young and susceptible and continue until habits of industry and love of learning had replaced indolence and indifference. Morgan considered one of the chief defects of the existing system of Indian education to be the fact that efforts to educate the Indian youth had not been carried far enough for them to compete successfully with white youth. In order to destroy tribal antagonisms and to develop a feeling of common brotherhood and mutual respect, Morgan wanted to mix the tribes thoroughly in the industrial schools. But ultimately he envisaged the time when the mixing would take place in regular public schools. "Indeed," he said, "it is reasonable to expect that at no distant day, when the Indians shall have all taken up their lands in severalty and have become American citizens, there will cease to be any necessity for Indian schools maintained by the government."

Coeducation was another part of Morgan's plan. It was the surest way, he thought, to lift the Indian women out of their position of "servility and degradation" up to a plane where they would be treated with "the same gallantry and respect which is accorded to their more favored white sisters." For both girls and boys he proposed an extension of the outing system which had been developed at Carlisle. By this means would the Indian children acquire "habits of industry, a practical acquaintance with civilized life, a sense of independence, enthusiasm for home, and the practical ability to earn their own living." In this system he found a promise of their "complete emancipation."

Morgan ended with a nod of approval for the work being done by church societies. He admitted that in addition to the public school system he proposed, the "influence of the home, the Sabbath-school, the church, and religious institutions of learning" would be necessary, and he recognized the urgent need for dedicated missionary work and liberal expenditure of money by individuals and religious groups on the Indians' behalf. The churches should supplement the government's work in Indian education, and he saw no need for conflict or unbecoming rivalry. "If the friends of Indian civilization can be led to unite upon a scheme of which the foregoing is a tentative outline," he concluded, "the so-called 'Indian problem' can be quickly and successfully solved."

A whole day at the Lake Mohonk Conference was devoted to a discussion of Morgan's plan, and he was enthusiastically applauded and supported. Men who often represented quite different views at the conferences rallied behind the Commissioner. Lyman Abbott said he thought the conference was ready to stand behind Morgan and give him cordial and hearty support in his endeavor to provide universal education for the Indians, and his remarks were greeted by warm applause. General Armstrong of Hampton urged strong support. "Let us put ourselves behind the commissioner," he said, "just as the column of black soldiers years ago, whom he led to fight for freedom and right, followed his command." Herbert Welsh spoke vigorously in support;

and the Board of Indian Commissioners, in a special business meeting in which it conferred with Morgan, voted formally to aid the Commissioner in carrying out his plans for the education of the Indians and their progress to full American citizenship.[11]

With such enthusiastic support behind him, Morgan moved ahead boldly with his elaboration of a school system for the Indians. In a "Supplemental Report on Indian Education," submitted to the Secretary of the Interior on December 1, 1889, he explained in specific detail what he proposed for high schools, grammar schools, and primary schools, consciously modeling them on the public school system that he knew. His plans were pervaded by his over-all philosophy of turning Indians as rapidly as possible into patriotic American citizens.[12]

The high schools should develop character. "To this end," he said, "the whole course of training should be fairly saturated with moral ideas, fear of God, and respect for the rights of others; love of truth and fidelity to duty; personal purity, philanthropy, and patriotism. Self-respect and independence are cardinal virtues, and are indispensable for the enjoyment of the privileges of freedom and the discharge of the duties of American citizenship." The high school would promote the liberalizing influences for the Indian that would break "the shackles of his tribal provincialism" and lift him to such a high plane of thought and aspiration that his native ways would become intolerable. The training would be so thorough that the students would not be able to be "dragged down by the heathenish life of the camp." The high school, in short, would be a "gateway out from the desolation of the reservation into assimilation with our national life." Below the high schools, the grammar schools should teach systematic habits and "the marvelous secret of diligence." Indian children should learn in them that labor is not repulsive but honorable and attractive, that waste is wicked. They should become familiar with the forms and usages of civilized life, and a fervent patriotism should be awakened in their minds. The primary schools would be the foundation of all the rest, supplying the lack of

---

[11] *Lake Mohonk Conference Proceedings*, 1889, pp. 107, 110; *Report of the Board of Indian Commissioners*, 1889, p. 4. Memorials in support of Morgan were sent to Congress by the Baptist Conference and by the Women's National Indian Association. *Senate Journal*, 51 Congress, 1 session, serial 2677, pp. 13, 56.

[12] "Supplemental Report on Indian Education," December 1, 1889, in Report of the Commissioner of Indian Affairs, 1889, in serial 2725, pp. 93–114.

home training. Children should be enrolled in them at as early an age as possible, before camp life had made an indelible stamp on them.[13]

Such was Morgan's initial vision of the cultural transformation he hoped to bring about, and as his term of office advanced, he held firm to his conviction that the goal was to turn the American Indian into the Indian American. The support he received encouraged him to move ahead in the direction he had plotted. He noted in 1890 that the United States Commissioner of Education, the National Educational Association, the American Institute of Instruction, the New York State Teachers' Association, and other leading educational bodies had given him hearty endorsement and that the philanthropic groups were all behind him. After a year's practical work in carrying out his ideas, he saw no reason to modify them in any essential aspect. And his optimism was unbounded. If the government would provide the means to establish the schools called for in his supplemental report of the previous year, it would be only a matter of time—"two or three years I think will suffice"—before all Indian youth of school age would be in school.[14]

Systematization was one of Morgan's key principles, and he published in 1890 a detailed set of "Rules for Indian Schools," which formalized the structure of the system, from common day schools through high schools, stipulated a uniform course of study, and prescribed the textbooks to be used.[15] The Indian program covered a period of eight years, which was about equivalent to six years of work in the white public schools, but it added regular industrial training. Secretary of the Interior John W. Noble spoke in praise of Morgan's work, noting the increased efficiency that would result from his methodical arrangement.[16]

Another of Morgan's basic principles was patriotic training for the Indian pupils, for love of America was the keystone in his arch of American citizenship. As part of the students' training, he asserted, it

[13] *Ibid.*, pp. 98–103.

[14] Report of the Commissioner of Indian Affairs, 1890, in serial 2841, pp. vi–viii, xiv–xvii.

[15] "Rules for Indian Schools," *ibid.*, pp. cxlvi–clxv. Similar sets of regulations were issued periodically; see, for example, Office of Indian Affairs, *Rules for Indian Schools, with Course of Study, List of Text-books, and Civil Service Rules* (Washington, 1892).

[16] Report of T. W. Blackburn, *Lake Mohonk Conference Proceedings*, 1890, pp. 22–29; Report of the Secretary of the Interior, 1890, in serial 2840, p. xli.

was important that they understand the significance of national holidays and be encouraged to celebrate them. He sent instructions to the schools for appropriate celebrations of New Year's Day, Washington's Birthday, Decoration Day, the Fourth of July, Thanksgiving, Christmas, and Arbor Day, and he directed that a special holiday (to be called Franchise Day) be celebrated on February 8, the date on which the Dawes Act was signed. "The Indian heroes of the camp-fire need not be disparaged," he said, "but gradually and unobtrusively the heroes of American homes and history may be substituted as models and ideals." The students were to be taught that the highest privilege that could be conferred on them was American citizenship.[17]

As he began his second year in office, Morgan made a three months' tour of the West, leaving Washington on September 5, 1890, for a trip of eight thousand miles. He visited reservations in Idaho, Nevada, California, Arizona, and Oklahoma, and the non-reservation schools in the West and came back well pleased. Student progress was good and advance in manual labor was commendable. Nothing on the trip, he concluded, had shaken his faith in the effectiveness and final triumph of his system of government schools.[18] When he returned he drew up an able paper, which he entitled *The Present Phase of the Indian Question*. In it he reiterated his analysis of what was wrong with America's Indian management and reiterated his proposals. The wide circulation of the pamphlet with its logical arguments considerably strengthened Morgan's position.[19]

Everything he wrote manifested the philosophy of the reform groups he represented. These principles shine through in clearest fashion in a paper he read at Albany under the sentimental title *A Plea for the Papoose*. In a long fantasy in which he spoke for an Indian infant and set forth what the child was dreaming of for himself, Morgan displayed his strong adherence to the theory of the unity of humanity on which so much reform effort rested. The savagery and brutishness of the Indians, he noted, were due "rather to unfortunate circumstances, for which they are not always responsible, than to any inherent

---

[17] Report of the Commissioner of Indian Affairs, 1890, in serial 2841, pp. xviii–xix, clxvii–clxix.

[18] *Ibid.*, pp. cxxxv–cxlv.

[19] *The Present Phase of the Indian Question: Also a Memorial on the Extension of Law to the Indians, by the Boston Indian Citizenship Committee* (Boston, 1891).

303

defect of nature." Granted this basic principle, the need for providing proper environment and training followed logically. "The pretty, innocent papoose has in itself the potency of a painted savage, prowling like a beast of prey," he continued, "or the possibility of a sweet and gentle womanhood or a noble and useful manhood." It was up to the nation to provide the education necessary to make the latter possibility come true.[20]

The great challenge to Morgan's carefully conceived plan for a universal Indian public school system came from the church-run contract schools. The mission schools had developed rapidly in the decade before Morgan took office and had done important work for the Indians, but the fact that the great bulk of the contract school funds were going to Roman Catholics was intolerable to Morgan and the Protestant-orientated Indian reform groups. In 1889, they pointed out, $347,672 out of a total $530,905 was distributed to Catholic schools; the Presbyterians with $41,825 ran a poor second.[21]

Morgan was not the first to be alarmed by such figures. At the Lake Mohonk Conference of 1888 these schools had been a topic of discussion, and underlying anti-Catholic sentiments had come to the surface. But in the end, all had agreed that if missionary schools were suddenly cut off, government efforts could not immediately replace them. The platform, therefore, spoke favorably of the work done by the church schools and of the "essential importance of religious as distinguished from secular education" for the well-being of the Indians. The missionary contract schools, the platform asserted, ought to be continued until the government was able to supply by its own school system all the educational needs of the Indian children.[22]

When Morgan presented his plans to the conference in 1889, there hovered over the discussion the specter of the contract schools and the anti-Catholicism they engendered. The issue came up again and again

[20] A Plea for the Papoose (n.p., n.d.), pp. 2–4.
[21] Figures for the distribution of contract school funds are given in Report of the Commissioner of Indian Affairs, 1890, in serial 2841, p. xvii; they were frequently repeated in argument against the contract school system. An excellent history of church-state co-operation in Indian schools is Beaver, Church, State, and the American Indians.
[22] Lake Mohonk Conference Proceedings, 1888, pp. 11–26, 31–41, 95.

in the discussion of Morgan's paper; it could hardly have been avoided since the universal public school system for the Indians that the Commissioner proposed would ultimately preclude the use of government funds to support church-sponsored schools on the reservations. The topic was treated gingerly, with speakers vying with each other to say kind words about missionary educational work, but there was tension in the air. Morgan himself took an equivocal stand on the matter of continuing the existing contract schools. It was clear, however, that any expansion of the contract school system would not meet his approval and that his love for a public school system was too strong to permit an unbiased view of other schools. Nor would he stand for criticism of the public schools. "If the heterogeneous masses that are coming to us from all parts of the world are to be melted and moulded into a homogeneous mass, if the children that come here with all their inherited prejudices from Germany and France, Italy, and all over the world, are to be blended into a great nationality, it will be because of the work done by the public schools. They seem to be God's machinery of assimilation." And he asked rhetorically: "You say they cannot do this for the Indians?"[23]

In the long discussions of the issue at the Lake Mohonk conferences and at the winter meetings of the missionary boards with the Board of Indian Commissioners, the Catholics were not represented by any spokesmen, official or unofficial. Whether by exclusion or by their own preference, they had no forensic forum in which to hammer out a compromise with their opponents (assuming that such a thing was possible in the Protestant-dominated Indian reform groups). Instead they resorted to political action to protect their interests and to increase if possible government support for the schools they conducted among the Indians. They began a frontal attack upon Morgan and upon Daniel Dorchester, a Methodist minister who had been appointed Superintendent of Indian Education at the same time that Morgan entered the office of Commissioner. The broad attack was aimed at Morgan's character, but the principal charge was that he was an anti-Catholic bigot who was replacing Catholics in the Indian service with Protestants and who intended to ruin the Catholic mission

23 *Ibid.*, 1889, p. 64.

schools. The Catholics' aim was to prevent the confirmation of Morgan and Dorchester by the Senate.

The Catholics were understandably edgy about having two Protestant ministers in such key spots in the Indian service. They had been discriminated against in the apportionment of agencies among various religious groups under Grant's peace policy, and the Board of Indian Commissioners was an exclusively Protestant group.[24] The 1870's and 1880's, moreover, saw a rising tide of anti-Catholicism in the nation. The increased immigration of Catholics from southern and central Europe, the unfortunate emphasis and interpretation given to the declaration of papal infallability, and the impolitic appointment of Monsignor Satolli as Apostolic Delegate gave great concern to the Protestants, whose domination of American culture appeared to be threatened and who consciously and unconsciously fought against the Catholic threat. "Patriotic" organizations, which preached a "pure" Americanism began to thrive and were absorbed largely into a burgeoning American Protective Association at the very time that Morgan served as Commissioner of Indian Affairs. And it was the school question that was the center of much of the bitterness, as Catholics, objecting to the Protestant Christianity that pervaded the "nonsectarian" public schools, established parochial schools and then sought to win support for them from public funds.[25]

Of the two political parties, the Republicans found the greater support from the anti-Catholic factions, and the Catholics were especially alarmed when the Republicans regained the presidency in 1889 and Harrison appointed Morgan and Dochester to the Indian Office. They began at once to fight bitterly to protect their interests in the contract schools for the Indians. To lead and direct the battle, a ready-made organization was on hand, the Bureau of Catholic Indian Missions. Organized in 1874 to co-ordinate the work of the various missions and

[24] The Catholic position is thoroughly discussed in Rahill, *Catholic Indian Missions and Grant's Peace Policy.*

[25] The best account of anti-Catholicism in the late nineteenth century is in Donald L. Kinzer, *An Episode in Anti-Catholicism: The American Protective Association* (Seattle, 1964). See also Humphrey J. Desmond, *The A. P. A. Movement: A Sketch* (Washington, 1912); John Higham, *Strangers in the Land: Patterns of American Nativism, 1860–1925* (New Brunswick, 1955), chapters III and IV; and Robert H. Lord, John E. Sexton, and Edward T. Harrington, *History of the Archdiocese of Boston in the Various States of Its Development, 1604 to 1943* (3 vols., Boston, 1945), III, 100–59.

to furnish a Washington headquarters to lobby for Catholic missions, the Bureau in 1889 was headed by the Reverend Joseph A. Stephan as Director, a Catholic priest of vitriolic temperament, who had served as Catholic agent among the Sioux under Grant's peace policy.[26]

Charges of bigotry against Morgan and Dorchester soon filled the air, as Stephan and the Catholic press, aided by Democratic papers, fought to prevent Senate confirmation of the two men. Despite the continued public assertions by the Indian Office appointees that they had no anti-Catholic bias of any kind, their records were far from clean in Catholic eyes. Dorchester was the more vulnerable, for he had been active in the public school controversy in Boston in 1888 and in that year had published a book called *Romanism* versus *the Public School System*. In it he violently attacked the Catholic school system. "Its crying defect," he declared, "is that its teaching is not only un-American but anti-American, and will remove every one of its pupils, in their ideals, far from a proper mental condition for American citizenship, and enhance the already too difficult task of making them good citizens of a republic."[27]

With such a man in charge of Indian schools, it is no wonder that the Catholics feared for the future of their Indian schools, but for some reason Dorchester was nearly forgotten, and the main attack was leveled against Morgan. Perhaps this was because he was Dorchester's superior and more influential in formulating Indian policy, perhaps because he seemed more vulnerable on grounds other than his religious bias. To be sure, however, Morgan was on record with anti-Catholic statements that matched Dorchester's for sweeping denunciation of the Catholic position on the schools. In a discussion at the National Educational Association meeting in 1888 devoted to the criticism that the public schools failed to cultivate morality and religion, Morgan from the floor lashed out at the Catholics, whom he accused of trying to destroy the public school system and substitute their own. "I have traced this matter to the source," he said. "I have studied it, and it

[26] For the work of the Bureau of Catholic Indian Missions, see Rahill, *Catholic Indian Missions*, and various reports of the Bureau. The character of Stephan is shown also in Harry J. Sievers, "The Catholic Indian School Issue and the Presidential Election of 1892," *Catholic Historical Review*, XXXVIII (July, 1952), 129–55.
[27] Daniel Dorchester, *Romanism* versus *the Public School System* (New York, 1888), p. 185.

simply means that it is a challenge to our civilization, it is a challenge to our Christianity, it is a challenge to our political life, it is a challenge to everything that we Americans cherish today." He denied that the public schools were godless simply because they were not Catholic and urged his listeners not to yield to Catholic criticisms. "If you yield, if you accept the criticism as just," he concluded, "you yield everything that we prize in the civilization of the nineteenth century, represented by Martin Luther, and represented in its outflowering by American ideas; you recognize that all that is a sham and a pretense, that it is to be thrown aside, and that we are all to go back to mediaevalism, with all that condition implies.[28] A man of such mentality was not likely to be enthusiastic about government-supported Catholic Indian schools, no matter how much he protested his impartiality.

Morgan, appointed during a recess of the Senate, had served as Commissioner for more than five months before his name was formally sent to the Senate for confirmation on December 4, 1889. In that time he had formulated his policies and won the support of the influential groups represented by the Board of Indian Commissioners and the Lake Mohonk Conference. But that time also allowed his opponents to organize a campaign against him. The charges of anti-Catholic bias on the part of Morgan were widely circulated in the Catholic press. The *Catholic Columbian* of Columbus, Ohio, was especially active. It printed and distributed ten thousand petition forms to be signed and sent to the Senate protesting against the confirmation of Morgan and Dorchester.[29]

Anti-Catholicism was not the only charge leveled at Morgan, for his enemies dredged out a court-martial from his Civil War career. Although Morgan had been acquitted and subsequently promoted, a fact he pointed to in vindication, the court-martial was not forgotten by his political and religious opponents. The *National Democrat* (Washington) for December 7, 1889, for example, had a long article opposing confirmation on the basis of the court-martial, and Father

[28] National Educational Association, *Journal of Proceedings and Addresses*, 1888, p. 158.
[29] Numerous copies of the petition forms are in the archives of the Bureau of Catholic Indian Missions, Washington, D.C. See also John A. Kuster to Stephan, January 14, 1890, in the same archives. The scrapbooks of newspaper clippings kept by the Bureau give ample evidence of Catholic press opposition to Morgan. See also the account in Sievers, "Catholic Indian School Issue," pp. 141–48, with its extensive citations.

Stephan and his friends never quite let the issue die in their battle with Morgan throughout his term of office. The opponents of Morgan, however, were unable to prevent his confirmation, which came on February 12, 1890, after the charges had been thoroughly aired and answered. Dorchester was confirmed the following day.[30]

Morgan's friends were jubilant at the favorable outcome. "It is gratifying," one of them wrote to Senator Dawes, "to see a chosen victim escape the toils of intolerance." Morgan himself spoke of it as "a great and far reaching victory," and he repeatedly argued that the Senate confirmation meant a complete quashing of all the charges made against him.[31]

The confirmation, however, did not quiet the contract school controversy. The Lake Mohonk Conference in October, 1890, in fact, devoted much of its time to debating the advisability of continuing those schools. Opponents, including the Reverend James M. King, secretary of the National League for the Protection of American Institutions, who read a paper on "The Churches: Their Relation to the General Government in the Education of the Indian Races," argued vehemently that any government appropriation for church schools was unconstitutional. Supporters pointed to the good work being done by the contract schools and insisted that the system of government schools could not at once provide for all Indian children if the mission schools were closed down. In the end the conference unanimously adopted a resolution approving Morgan's proposal for a common school education for all Indian children at government expense, but until that could be done, advising that the work of the contract schools be continued and fostered.[32]

[30] *Journal of the Executive Proceedings of the Senate*, XXVII, 65, 66, 353–54, 449–50, 461–63. The executive proceedings on the confirmations were leaked to the press and appeared in an article in the *Washington Post* for February 12, 1890, reprinted *ibid.*, pp. 461–62.

[31] George W. Norris to Dawes, February 13, 1890, and Morgan to Dawes, February 14, 1890, in Henry L. Dawes Papers, Library of Congress.

[32] *Lake Mohonk Conference Proceedings*, 1890, pp. 51–58; *Report of the Board of Indian Commissioners*, 1890, p. 4. The National League for the Protection of American Institutions was organized in 1889 "to secure constitutional and legislative safeguards for the protection of the common school system and other American institutions, to promote public instruction in harmony with such institutions, and to prevent all sectarian or denominational appropriations of public funds." It proposed a sixteenth amendment to the Constitution to carry out these objectives. Its list of adherents included many

During 1891 the bitter recriminations came to a head as Morgan fought a violent verbal battle with the Bureau of Catholic Indian Missions. When it became clear that neither Morgan nor his philanthropic supporters had changed their ultimate position about the contract schools, a campaign of abuse against Morgan got under way. Morgan's public reaction was circumspect and gentlemanly, but the attack in no way influenced him to weaken his original adherence to the principle of a unitary public school system for the Indians. At the January meeting of the Board of Indian Commissioners with the representatives of the missionary boards, he asserted that he had never "uttered a word either in public or private about suddenly destroying that system [contract schools]." He pointed to the fact that instead the money granted to the contract schools had increased since he took office— $530,000 the year before he entered office, $562,000 during his first year, and $570,000 for the current year. He left no doubt, however, about where he stood in principle. "But I do not believe in the system," he said. "It is utterly untenable." He did not intend to disturb good schools in existence, but he was adamant against extending the system by approving new schools. "I believe the churches would spend their money more wisely," he told the missionaries, "if they spent it in missionary work rather than in the secular education of Indians."[33]

The issue was soon joined between Morgan and the Bureau of Catholic Indian Missions. The Commissioner, in fact, had early identified his foe. In January, 1891, he noted stirrings of opposition to him in Congress, which he attributed partly to partisan purposes and partly to a "little bit of spite" against him by a dismissed clerk. "The gist of the whole matter, however," he wrote to Harrison's private secretary, "is the desire of the Roman Catholic Bureau to get rid of me, because of my attitude on the question of Indian education."[34] Father Stephan, in a letter to Morgan which was entered in the *Congressional Record* for February 14, 1891, accused the Commissioner of "marked religious

---

prominent men, among them active Indian reformers. Kinzer, *Episode in Anti-Catholicism*, pp. 56–57; National League for the Protection of American Institutions, *A Petition Concerning Sectarian Appropriations for Indian Education* (New York, 1892).

[33] *Report of the Board of Indian Commissioners*, 1890, pp. 168–69.

[34] Morgan to E. W. Halford, January 13, 1891, Records of the Office of the Commissioner of Indian Affairs, Letters Sent, vol. 1890–1892, pp. 118–20, National Archives Record Group 75.

bigotry and of treating certain religious denominations with gross unfairness."[35] Morgan replied with a flat denial of bigotry or unfairness, and he pointed to numerous examples of his goodwill toward Catholic incumbents in the Indian service.[36] A continued exchange between Morgan and the Catholic missionary organization did little to soften the asperities on either side, and in the end Morgan refused to deal any longer with the Catholic Bureau and treated instead with the Catholic mission schools individually.[37]

The charges made against the government Indian schools by Catholic critics presented a dilemma. One line of attack was that the nonsectarian schools were "godless." Thus the Jesuit missionary, L. B. Palladino, in a pamphlet entitled *Education for the Indian: Fancy and Reason on the Subject; Contract Schools and Non-Sectarianism in Indian Education,* asserted the absolute necessity of Christianity as a means to civilize the Indians.[38] "The Government," he said, "must either enlist in the cause the services of Christianity, or be doomed to utter failure in its attempt to civilize the Indians." An answer to Palladino appeared in the nondenominational Protestant weekly, *The Independent,* where the editor ridiculed the priest's argument that to make Indian schools nonsectarian was to eliminate Christianity from Indian education. In refutation he cited the case of the government boarding school at Carlisle. "This school," he noted, "is presided over by Captain Pratt, an earnest Christian man, and most of the teachers and other employes connected with the institution are active members in Chris-

[35] *Congressional Record,* XXII, 2709. This was part of a long debate in the House over funds for contract schools as part of the Indian appropriation bill, *ibid.,* pp. 2698–2709.

[36] Morgan to Bureau of Catholic Indian Missions, February 27, 1891, Records of the Office of Indian Affairs, Letters Sent, Education, vol. XXIX, pp. 333–41, National Archives Record Group 75.

[37] Correspondence between Morgan and the Catholic Bureau is printed as an appendix to Report of the Commissioner of Indian Affairs, 1891, in serial 2934, pp. 161–70. The story can be traced in detail in correspondence preserved in the archives of the Bureau of Catholic Indian Missions and in the following collections in the National Archives: Records of the Office of Indian Affairs, Letters Sent (Education) and Letters Received; Records of the Office of Indian Affairs, Summaries of Work Completed and Records Relating to Mission Schools; and Records of the Office of Commissioner of Indian Affairs, Letters Sent.

[38] New York, 1892. Palladino included the information from his pamphlet as well as other attacks on Morgan's Indian school plans in his book, *Indian and White in the Northwest: A History of Catholicity in Montana, 1831–1891* (2d ed. rev., Lancaster, Pennsylvania, 1922), pp. 108–37.

tian churches. There is a preaching service at the school every Sabbath afternoon; there is a Sunday-school exercise for all who desire to attend in the morning; Catholic pupils are expected to attend their own services in the neighboring city of Carlisle; there is a weekly prayer meeting, conducted by the students, and largely participated in by others, there is an active, vigorous Young Men's Christian Association, having close relationship with the Christian associations of the country and doing a valuable work, and in addition to all this there are many influences, directly and indirectly, brought to bear upon the pupils, seeking to develop their Christian characters and to inculcate in their minds the highest ideals of Christian living." Similar work, the editor pointed out, was being done in other "Government non-sectarian schools."[39]

Such an open profession, and it was not untypical of the sentiments of proponents of the government school system, led to the other horn of the dilemma. If indeed the national Indian schools were inculcating Christianity, then they were "sectarian," since whoever taught it would of necessity teach it according to his own denominational views. Father Stephan in December, 1893, charged that "the effort now being made to secularize, to 'non-sectarize' the Indian schools, is a dishonest, hypocritical one, whose sole aim and purpose it is to drive the Catholic Church out of the Indian educational and missionary field, in which it has gained glorious laurels, and to substitute for its influence and teachings the influence and teachings of other religious bodies." Although Stephan's tone was offensive, the point he made was not without merit. "Nonsectarian" was quite a relative term. "If any Christian teaching at all be allowed," he asked, "is not that 'sectarian' as between Christians and Jews, Buddhists and Atheists? Equally, much might be taught that would be 'nonsectarian' as between the views of the leading Protestant denominations, but which would be 'sectarian' as to Catholics."[40]

That the nonsectarian schools advocated by Morgan and his supporters were in fact Protestant schools, if not indeed specifically Baptist or Methodist or Presbyterian, can hardly be questioned, as *The Independent* had made clear. Stephan charged: ". . . the most extreme

[39] *The Independent*, XLIV (May 5, 1892), 624–25.
[40] Stephan's statement and the reaction to it are in *Report of the Board of Indian Commissioners*, 1893, pp. 112–15.

claimants for secularization now would be found incorporating all the elements of their peculiar religious systems in the Indian schools when once they had control, and the sectarian phenomena of 'revivals,' Young Men's Christian associations, Christian Endeavor societies, King's Daughters, and so on, would be introduced in the 'nonsectarian' schools, as they have been hitherto."[41] Morgan's earlier remarks that Catholic schools would threaten American civilization was indicative of his ingrained sentiment. Equally explicit were the remarks of James M. King at the Lake Mohonk Conference of 1892. Referring to an "unscrupulous" attack by Father Stephan on the government schools "because they have the Protestant Bible and Gospel Hymns in them," he went on to make his point: "In this Columbian year it becomes us to remember that our civilization is not Latin, because God did not permit North America to be settled and controlled by that civilization. The Huguenot, the Hollander, and the Puritan created our civilization. Let us not put a premium by national grants on a rejected civilization in the education of a race who were here when Columbus came." Americanism and Protestantism thus coalesced. King concluded that "much Roman Catholic teaching among the Indians does not prepare them for intelligent and loyal citizenship. The solution of the Indian problem consists in educating them for citizenship, as we educate all other races."[42]

Morgan's troubles in promoting his unified system of government schools for the Indians did not all stem from religious controversy. His plan was based on a clear hierarchy of schools, beginning with primary schools on the reservation, proceeding through reservation boarding schools, and culminating in the industrial schools like Carlisle and Hampton far away from the reservations. Unless a steady flow of students could be maintained from the lower to the higher schools, the system of producing American citizens would break down. The number of non-reservation schools, he pointed out to one agent who

[41] *Ibid.*, p. 113.
[42] *Lake Mohonk Conference Proceedings*, 1892, pp. 63–64. King read a paper entitled "Sectarian Contract Schools," in which he discussed the work of the National League for the Protection of American Institutions in fighting against the use of government funds by religious denominations.

complained about students being taken away from his school, had increased from eight to twenty in a comparatively short time and had a capacity of five thousand, and they could not be run economically unless they had full enrollment. Children had to be obtained from the reservation schools and this had to be done "not once, twice or thrice during the year, but many times in order that all these schools may be filled." The reservations schools were to be considered "recruiting stations for the non-reservation schools."[43]

Morgan realized that persuasion alone was not going to succeed in making his theoretically wonderful system work. The depth of his conviction that it must succeed can be seen in his ultimate willingness to resort to force.[44] In November, 1892, he laid bare his own feelings in the matter in a long letter to the Secretary of the Interior.[45] He cited a law of Congress of 1890 which authorized the Commissioner of Indian Affairs "to make and enforce by proper means such rules and regulations as will secure the attendance of Indian children of suitable age and health at schools established and maintained for their benefit," and he noted the great pains that the Indian Office had taken to discharge this serious responsibility. "It has argued with the Indians," he said, "has pleaded with them; has offered every inducement in its power to cause them voluntarily to put their children into school; has, wherever it has seemed wise, resorted to mild punishment by the withholding of rations or supplies, and, where necessary, has directed Agents to use their Indian police as truant officers in compelling attendance." There had been some encouraging results and a sizable increase in the number of pupils in school, and he refused to admit any error in principle. "After 25 years of experience in educational work, with exceptional opportunities for studying the question, I have no hesitation in saying that the present scheme of Government education for Indians has in it the 'promise and potency' of accomplishing for these people all that its most zealous friends have claimed for it."

The theory was fine, but in practice Morgan was confronted with a

---

[43] Morgan to C. W. Crouse, October 24, 1892, Records of the Office of Indian Affairs, Letters Sent, Education, vol. 44, pp. 128–30 (second pagination), National Archives Record Group 75.

[44] See, for example, Morgan to Robert Waugh, October 24, 1892, *ibid.*, pp. 126–27.

[45] Morgan to the Secretary of the Interior, November 30, 1892, copy in Dawes Papers. The data in the paragraphs following are from this letter.

crisis. The advance of the public school system for the Indians was resisted everywhere. Not only did the "enemies of these schools [that is, the Catholics]" thwart the efforts of the government in its "benign purpose," but the Indian parents themselves, not appreciating the immense value of the schools, and the medicine men, who feared the enlightenment of the people, threw themselves against the new movement. The agent at Fort Hall was resisted by violence when he sought to obtain Indians for the school. The transfer of Lumni Indians to the training school at Chemawa, Oregon, was thwarted by the interference of a priest; the Navajo agent was beaten, threatened with death, and forced to promise that he would make no further efforts to put children into the government school at his agency. The Oreiba Indians refused to keep their solemn promise to return their children to school after a summer vacation, and the agent of the Southern Utes was met by taunts and gibes when he tried, with the help of his Indian police force, to secure children for the boarding school established at Fort Lewis.

Morgan might have interpreted such evidence as an indication that perhaps all was not right with his theory, but no such doubts crossed his mind. He remained absolutely convinced that the great work of making acceptable citizens through public education must go on. "I would not needlessly nor lightly interfere with the rights of Indian parents," he wrote. "But I do not believe that Indians like the Bannacks and Shoshones at Fort Hall, the Southern Utes in Colorado, the Apaches, or the Navajoes of Arizona,—people who, for the most part, speak no English, live in squalor and degradation, make little progress from year to year, who are a perpetual source of expense to the Government and a constant menace to thousands of their white neighbors, a hindrance to civilization and a clog on our progress—have any right to forcibly keep their children out of school to grow up like themselves, a race of barbarians and semi-savages. We owe it to those children to prevent, forcibly if need be, so great and appalling a calamity from befalling them." All he asked was a mere show of military force in order to convince the Indians that the government was in earnest in the matter and that the authority of its agents was to be respected. Such a move Morgan believed "to be dictated by every honorable, patriotic, philanthropic, and humanitarian consideration."

Morgan had expressed similar views publicly at the Lake Mohonk

315

Conference in October, 1892, and had won the support of the meeting. The platform adopted at the conference read: ". . . in cases where parents, without good reason, refuse to educate their children, we believe that the government is justified, as a last resort, in using power to compel attendance. We do not think it desirable to rear another generation of savages."[46]

Morgan's duties by then were almost over, for the Harrison administration of which he was such a conspicuous part, did not stand the test of the polls in November, 1892. The verdict was considered by many to be an explicit repudiation of Morgan and his Indian school policy.[47] The Bureau of Catholic Indian Missions fought vigorously against Morgan and did what it could to tie Morgan and his alleged anti-Catholicism to Harrison's coattails. The most notable salvo was a remark in Stephan's 1892 report to the president of the Bureau. The priest referred to "the bigoted Commissioner, and the not much less bigoted President," and the statement soon re-echoed through the religious and the secular press.[48] The Catholic press, considerably more vitriolic than became professedly Christian organs, urged Catholics to throw out the Harrison administration. The campaign was only a continuation of the bitter attacks on Morgan that began at the very start of his government career. The editor of the *Catholic Columbian* had written to Stephan at the time of the fight against Morgan's confirmation: "If Morgan and Dorchester are confirmed the conviction is eternal as truth itself, in the minds of Catholics that the outrage will be resented by the hundreds of thousands of Catholic voters throughout the country. The ballot box will right the wrong."[49]

When Cleveland won in November, the Catholic press was jubilant. The *Catholic Herald* of New York declared: ". . . the Republican Party,

[46] *Lake Mohonk Conference Proceedings*, 1892, pp. 51–54, 121.

[47] The influence of the contract school question on the election of 1892 is treated exhaustively in Sievers, "Catholic Indian School Issue."

[48] *Report of Rev. J. A. Stephan, Director, to Rt. Rev. Bishop M. Marty, President of the Bureau of Catholic Indian Missions, for the year 1891–'92* (Washington, 1892), p. 1.

[49] John A. Kuster to Stephan, January 14, 1890, archives of the Bureau of Catholic Indian Missions. There are numerous clippings from Catholic newspapers exhibiting the virulent attacks upon Morgan in the scrapbooks of the Catholic Bureau. There is no doubt that these attacks were intemperate and in many cases petty.

led by bigots, invaded the sanctuary of the home, usurped parental rights, and robbed the Catholic Indians of their only treasure, their faith; but the people, true to the best traditions of America, hurled it from power. Cleveland's victory was, in truth, the defeat of bigotry."[50] The anti-Catholics, on the other hand, looked at the victory as new evidence of Catholic political power. Both sides tended to over-emphasize the religious aspect of the campaign and the importance of the Indian school question among the general questions of the day.

Morgan offered his resignation on January 10, 1893, to take effect at the end of Harrison's term. On March 1, 1893, he accepted the position as corresponding secretary of the Baptist Home Mission Society and editor of *The Home Mission Monthly*. He thus had an excellent vehicle to continue his agitation for Indian education and other reforms and to renew his interest in Negro education, to which the Baptists were solidly committed. It was also a platform for his anti-Catholicism, which seemed suddenly to burst forth the minute he left public office.[51]

Morgan had succeeded admirably during his four-year term of office in submerging whatever anti-Catholic sentiments he harbored from his earlier days. Even under the violent abuse he received from aggressive supporters of the Catholic contract schools, he seldom replied with anti-Catholic tirades. He objected vigorously to the personal attacks made upon him, but again and again he denied any antipathy or bigotry toward Catholics and any sectarian or partisan influence on him in his official actions. Suddenly, as if the dam holding back his deep sentiments had burst, he gave himself over to a torrent of attacks upon the Catholic Church. The growing American Protective Association, which seized upon the Catholic attacks on the Indian school system and the Catholic influence on the election of 1892, made the Morgan case one of its prime exhibits and eagerly welcomed Morgan to its roster of speakers and writers. Morgan responded with more alacrity

[50] Issue of December 3, 1892, quoted in Sievers, "Catholic Indian School Issue," p. 131.
[51] Morgan to Harrison, January 10, 1893, Records of the Secretary of the Interior, Appointments Division, "Commissioner of Indian Affairs, 1889," National Archives Record Group 48. *The Home Mission Monthly*, XV (April, 1893), carried a picture of Morgan on the cover and a salutation from him. The work of Morgan and the Baptists in Negro education is discussed in James M. McPherson, "White Liberals and Black Power in Negro Education, 1865–1915," *American Historical Review*, LXXV (June, 1970), 1370–74.

317

than was becoming for one who so recently had been proclaiming his lack of bias. He delivered anti-Catholic speeches in cities as far apart as Boston, Minneapolis, and San Francisco, recounting his experiences in Washington with the Catholic Bureau and charging that the Catholics has assumed an attitude on the Indian question that was "un-American, unpatriotic, and a menace to our liberties."[52]

If the election of 1892 was indeed a victory of the Catholics, in which the people of the United States had "beaten bigotry black and blue," it was a hollow victory for the proponents of direct government aid to the mission schools.[53] The removal of Morgan and Dorchester could not stem the tide of support for public schools nor quiet the winds of opposition to the contract schools that had begun before Morgan had taken office and of which he was more the servant than the master. The Protestant denominations at the height of the controversy during Morgan's term had quietly withdrawn from the program, preferring to lose their own meager benefits than to see the Catholics profit, and the anti-Catholic spirit among the reformers continued to be strong. Senator Dawes, speaking to a Protestant missionary group in 1892, pleaded with them not to give up their work among the Indians lest the Catholics move into their places. "Unless you carry out with aggressive energy all the work you have hitherto carried on into every field, by every method and every means," he told them, "you will let go, not only your opportunity, but the prize itself. I appeal to the Protestant churches of the land. Unless you occupy this field others will surely occupy it."[54]

Little by little, Congress wore away the contract school system. In 1896 the funds were reduced to eighty per cent of the previous year, and by 1900 the government support of church-run schools for the Indians was cut off altogether. The Catholics won a favorable decision in regard to money that came from the Indians through treaty rights,

[52] Thomas J. Morgan, *Roman Catholics and Indian Education* (Boston, 1893), p. 2; clippings from *Chicago Herald*, October 14, 1893, and *San Francisco Chronicle*, November, 1895, in Catholic Bureau scrapbooks. See also Morgan's chapter in *Errors of the Roman Catholic Church and Its Insidious Influence in the United States and Other Countries* (St. Louis, 1895), pp. xxxii–xlix.

[53] The phrase is quoted in Sievers, "Catholic Indian School Issue," p. 155.

[54] Henry L. Dawes, *Past and Present Indian Policy* (New York, 1892), pp. 4–5. The official actions of the Presbyterians, Baptists, Episcopalians, Congregationalists, and Methodists in withdrawing from the contract school system are appended to the Report of the Commissioner of Indian Affairs, 1892, in serial 3088, pp. 177–82.

rather than by direct appropriation, but the position represented by Thomas Jefferson Morgan won the day.[55] The Indians were to be educated in government national schools, in order to become exemplary Americans in the Protestant tradition of the nation.

The Indian schools, trying doggedly to convert the Indians from their old customs by a thoroughly American education, had sharp competition in the public eye from another institution, equally American in its enterprising spirit: the Wild West shows. These great entertainment spectacles—so the reformers thought—were a glaring obstacle to the transformation of the Indians, for they perpetuated old ways and hindered an all-out commitment to American civilization.

Indians as showpieces for the satisfaction of the curious or the excitement of the adventure seekers had been known on occasion through most of American history, but in the last decades of the nineteenth century the exploitation of the Indians by promoters of the Wild West and medicine shows reached new heights. The best known of the showmen was "Buffalo Bill" Cody, whose frontier exploits as a scout had brought him a measure of fame, and who turned his dramatic and entrepreneurial talents toward producing theatrical shows on western themes that brought him worldwide renown.[56] Buffalo Bill's Wild West, as he termed his extravaganzas, presented to eager audiences in the United States and in Europe remarkable re-enactments of exciting frontier adventures, from sharpshooting exhibitions and spectacular horsemanship to an Indian attack upon a fleeing stagecoach. An amazingly successful tour of England in 1887–1888 made Cody a celebrity, and until he retired in the early twentieth century he was among the best known of all Americans.

In all the exhibitions the Indians were an essential attraction. In 1885 Cody succeeded in signing up Sitting Bull to join his troupe, and the old enemy of Custer toured the East with great acclaim.[57] For a

[55] Beaver, *Church, State, and the American Indians*, pp. 167–68; Schmeckebier, *The Office of Indian Affairs*, pp. 212–13.

[56] The best account of Buffalo Bill's career is Don Russell, *The Lives and Legends of Buffalo Bill* (Norman, 1960). See also Henry Blackman Sell and Victor Weybright, *Buffalo Bill and the Wild West* (New York, 1955), and Don Russell, *The Wild West: A History of the Wild West Shows* (Fort Worth, 1970).

[57] Sitting Bull's participation is thoroughly explored in Louis Pfaller, " 'Enemies in

quarter of a century and more, Cody enticed Indians to leave their reservations to work for him. It soon became clear to the humanitarians interested in the education of the Indians as American citizens, however, that the Wild West shows were retrogressive, that for both the Indians who performed and the whites who were entertained the image presented of the Indians was the wrong one. The glorification of the savage past was hardly a way to lead the Indians down the paths of decorous white civilization. Nor was the life of the theatrical circuit a suitable introduction of reservation Indians to white manners and customs. By the end of the 1880's, therefore, considerable agitation arose to proscribe the use of Indians in such enterprises. Individual agents noted the deleterious effects on the Indians who took part in the shows; James McLaughlin at Pine Ridge, for example, complained that Sitting Bull was impossible to handle after he returned from his ego-stimulating tours and urged that no further travels as a star in the show be allowed the chief.[58] As requests continued to come in to the Indian Office for permission to engage Indians for exhibition purposes, the federal officials began to voice general disapproval.

John H. Oberly, Commissioner of Indian Affairs in Cleveland's first administration, set the general tone of the opposition in a letter to the Secretary of the Interior in March, 1889:

> The effect of traveling all over the country among, and associated with, the class of people usually accompanying Shows, Circuses and Exhibitions, attended by all the immoral and unchristianizing surroundings incident to such a life, is not only most demoralizing to the present and future welfare of the Indian, but it creates a roaming and unsettled disposition and educates him in a manner entirely foreign and antagonistic to that which has been and now is the policy of the Government, as well as the aim of all good christian people who are doing so much for the welfare and benefit of the Indian.

Oberly argued that the moral, religious, and financial interests of the Indians would all be better served if they stayed on their reservations and made a home for themselves and their families, sent their children

---

'76, Friends in '85'—Sitting Bull and Buffalo Bill," *Prologue: The Journal of the National Archives*, I (Fall, 1969), 17–31.
[58] *Ibid.*, pp. 26–27.

to school, and prepared themselves for the privileges and responsibilities of citizenship.[59]

When the Commissioner hesitated to take action because he did not think he had authority to do so, he was prodded by the reformers. Senator Dawes ridiculed Oberly's reluctance to act. "Don't tell me," he wrote, "that the Government has no power to keep Indians on their reservations. They have for forty years hunted and chased with the whole force of the army, whenever they chose, Indians off their reservations without leave, and brought them back, sometimes in irons." Oberly stuck to his guns and lectured Dawes that the reformers could not have it both ways. He pointed to the case of Standing Bear in 1879, in which the court had acknowledged the right of a peaceful Indian to come and go as he wished with the same freedom accorded to a white man. "The righteousness of this decision and the push which it gave to the advancement of the Indians and the recognition of their rights is unquestioned," he wrote to Dawes. Dawes's own allotment act pointed in the same direction—the removal of the paternal hand of the government and the treatment of the Indians simply as citizens. "The officer [of government]," Oberly noted, "cannot restrain the liberty of the law-abiding person or citizen because in his opinion or the opinion of someone else that person or citizen will make an injudicious use of his liberty."[60] Oberly put his finger on a very tender nerve of the reformers. They fought against government action in regard to Indians that they took to be oppressive or unjust, but they had no qualms about forcing upon the Indians measures which they considered to be for the Indians' own good.

Oberly's successor, Morgan, was more fully in tune with Dawes and other reformers, and he did not share Oberly's concern about the freedom of decision of the Indians. In the same aggressive manner in which he pushed for Indian education, he began an attack upon the Wild West shows. On November 1, 1889, he sent an official circular to the Indian agents, calling for information about the effect of such shows, morally and physically, upon the Indians. The answers he received confirmed his opinion that the shows were diametrically opposed to

[59] John H. Oberly to the Secretary of the Interior, March 20, 1889, copy in Dawes Papers.
[60] Oberly to Dawes, April 15, 1889, *ibid.*

the government's efforts to educate and civilize the Indians.[61] "The influence of these shows is antagonistic to that of the schools," he wrote. "The schools elevate, the shows degrade. The schools teach industry and thrift, the shows encourage idleness and waste. The schools inculcate morality, the shows lead almost inevitably to vice. The schools encourage the Indians to abandon their paint, blankets, feathers, and savage customs, while the retention and exhibition of these is the chief attraction of the shows." The growth of public opinion supporting the possibility of civilizing the Indians, he noted, had led Congress to appropriate nearly two million dollars that year for Indian education. But the impression left by the Wild West shows was that the Indians were incapable of civilization and such an impression worked "directly and powerfully against the Government in its beneficent work."[62]

The agent at Pine Ridge corroborated the Commissioner's views. He reported that Cody and his partner, Nate Salsbury, in the spring of 1889 had hired seventy-two healthy young men for their tour of the Continent. Five of them died abroad and seven others were sent home broken in health and unfit for further service. Similarly, the Kickapoo Medicine Company had seventy-five to one hundred young men in its service, many of whom became stranded in distant states with no means to return to the agency. "The injury already done," the agent asserted, "is irreparable and will prove a curse to these people for many generations to come."[63]

Morgan moved resolutely against the evil he saw. In March, 1890, he sent a circular to the agents advising them of the ruin that awaited Indians who left the reservations for Wild West shows and instructing them to impress upon the Indians the dangers involved. They were to urge the Indians to remain at home and practice more civilized pursuits. Seven months later he reiterated his concern and issued a new peremptory warning. Indians were to be told that if they left the reservations for exhibition purposes, their action would be considered "an open defiance of the authority of the Government" and that prompt

[61] Morgan to Herbert Welsh, June 13, 1891, Records of the Office of Indian Affairs, Letters Sent, Land, vol. 109, pp. 324–25 (second pagination). Welsh had asked to see the answers to the circular, and Morgan sent him the thirty-nine replies he had received as well as a report from the agent at Pine Ridge and a letter from T. A. Bland.

[62] Report of the Commissioner of Indian Affairs, 1890, in serial 2841, pp. lvii–lix.

[63] Report of H. D. Gallagher, August 28, 1890, *ibid.*, pp. 50–51.

measures would be taken to detain them. The agents were instructed to detect and thwart the designs of any persons entering the reservations to engage Indians for shows and to report employees who aided them. If despite such warnings Indians did seek to get away, the agents were to use "every legitimate manner" to prevent them.[64]

Morgan won the support of Secretary of the Interior John W. Noble for his directives, but the pressures were too great and the legal authority too questionable for the practice to be entirely overcome. Although Morgan declared in subsequent years that his views had not changed, in fact there was no way to prohibit the activity, and he resorted instead to attempts to make sure that bonds were provided by the promoters for the proper care and compensation of the Indians who were involved. He rejected the arguments that participation in the shows was advantageous for the Indians and asserted that the employers were interested primarily in their own profits.[65]

His attempts at persuasion, nevertheless, did not cease, and he seized every opportunity to drive home the lesson of the evils of the shows. In early 1893 he received a letter from the United States consul in Sydney, Australia, about two Sioux who had come to Australia with a show and were now in a destitute condition. Morgan sent the letter to the Indian agent at Pine Ridge, as "a good illustration of the usual outcome of Indians who allow themselves to be enticed away by the proprietors of medicine companies, 'Wild West' shows, etc.," and he directed the agent to read the letter to his Indians in order to let them know what happens when they leave the reservation and join such "demoralizing shows."[66]

Cody and Salsbury were generally successful in getting Indians for their performances, no doubt because of their public reputation and their businesslike conduct. In March, 1891, the partners were permitted to enroll one hundred Indians for a new European tour, including a number of Sioux who were prisoners of war at Fort Sheridan

[64] "Instructions to Indian Agents in Regard to Wild West Shows," October 1, 1890, *ibid.*, pp. clxv–clxvi.

[65] Report of the Secretary of the Interior, 1890, in serial 2840, p. xlvii; Report of the Commissioner of Indian Affairs, 1891, in serial 2934, pp. 78–79; *ibid.*, 1892, in serial 3088, pp. 105–106.

[66] Morgan to George LeRoy Brown, February 13, 1893, Records of the Office of Indian Affairs, Letters Sent, Land, vol. 126, p. 188 (second pagination).

as a result of the Ghost Dance disturbances.[67] But the high point of Buffalo Bill's shows came in 1893 with the Columbian Exposition at Chicago. In April of that year, the Indian Office gave permission to Cody and Salsbury to engage one hundred Indians for exhibition at Chicago. The terms of the agreement were intended to protect the Indians from the evils feared by the critics of Indian participation. The promoters agreed to pay the Indians a fair compensation, to feed and clothe them properly, to pay traveling and incidental expenses from the agencies to Chicago and return, to protect them from "all immoral influences and surroundings," to furnish medical care, and "to do everything that may be requisite for their health, comfort, and welfare." Cody and Salsbury were required to furnish a bond of ten thousand dollars for their faithful performance of the agreements they signed with the various Indians.[68] The Wild West show was a tremendous success at Chicago. Unable to gain a spot within the official limits of the Exposition, Cody and Salsbury leased a lot near the entrance to the fair, and to most of the visitors to the Exposition Buffalo Bill's Wild West and Rough Riders of the World seemed an integral part not to be missed.

Unfortunately, the conspicuous and popular participation of the "wild" Indians with Buffalo Bill presented a striking contrast to Commissioner Morgan's attempts to use the Exposition as a means of propaganda for his Indian industrial school system. Morgan had begun to lay plans for an exhibition at Chicago as early as 1891. It was his desire, he said, "to set forth as graphically as practicable the progress made by Indians in the various lines of civilization, especially in industrial pursuits and in education." He wanted displays of products made by the Indians, specimens of the work of school children, and Indians on hand pursuing various occupations. "Great care should be taken," he warned, "to make such a presentation as shall be creditable to a Government which has furnished one of the rare instances in history of a systematic attempt on the part of the conquering power to respect the rights and improve the condition of a conquered people. In spite of the blunders, failures, and disasters which can be cited in what has been stigmatized as a 'century of dishonor,' our Government can claim

[67] Russell, *Lives and Legends of Buffalo Bill*, p. 369.
[68] Report of the Commissioner of Indian Affairs, 1893, in serial 3210, p. 59.

credit and take satisfaction in what it has attempted and is now doing for its Indians, and time and money will be wisely spent in giving the results of its efforts a clear and adequate setting forth at Chicago." He hoped that Congress would make generous provision for representing at the Exposition "the process of evolving United States citizens out of American savages."[69]

The Commissioner's hopes for Congressional generosity were ill-founded. Instead of a lavish, eye-catching display to compete with the grand buildings that created the "White City," the Indian Office was forced to curtail its plans and to cut down expense in every way in order to stay within the meager sums appropriated for its exhibit. What resulted was a two-story frame building, devoid of ornamentation and as inexpensively built as safety permitted. It had a school room, dining room, kitchen, dormitory, sitting rooms, and industrial rooms, and it was plainly furnished to accommodate thirty pupils and half a dozen employees. Morgan's successor, Daniel M. Browning, described the building in September, 1893: ". . . in it since the 15th of May, delegations of Indian boys and girls, accompanied by their instructors, have cooked, eaten, slept, worked, and recited. They bring their own tools, implements, bedding, specimens of school-room work and products of their shops, and, as far as circumstances permit, carry out and exemplify the routine and methods prevailing in their respective schools. Allowing for the peculiar surroundings, the aim has been to give a fair representation on a small scale of an Indian boarding school. Even its lack of some conveniences and of needed space, notably in its school room, might be considered an added realistic touch." The Commissioner reported enthusiastically about the success of the exhibit, pointing to large numbers who observed the model school, and asserting that it showed "concretely and unmistakably" the Indians' readiness and ability for the new conditions of American life upon which they were entering.[70] He was careful, too, to deny any responsibility of the Indian Office for Indians appearing at various anthropological exhibits showing their native ways, other than permission for them to leave their reservations.

[69] *Ibid.*, 1891, in serial 2934, pp. 79–80. See also the remarks of Morgan in *Report of the Board of Indian Commissioners*, 1891, p. 153, and Report of the Commissioner of Indian Affairs, 1892, in serial 3088, pp. 61–62.

[70] *Ibid.*, 1893, in serial 3210, pp. 20–21.

The Commissioner, putting the best light possible on the enterprise, was overly enthusiastic. The secretary of the Board of Indian Commissioners described the exhibit more soberly as "a little, mean-looking building in the midst of those grand and imposing structures." The schoolroom, he thought, was too crowded for many persons to see what was going on and often the exercises had to stop altogether. He lamented that the "grand opportunity to educate hundreds of thousands of the people of the United States upon the subject of civilizing and Christianizing the Indian population" had been lost.[71]

Private enterprise won out over government impecuniousness. Buffalo Bill's romantic and exciting version of the Indians in America was more than a match for the Indian Office's meager display of the new Indians in school on their way to becoming exemplary American citizens.

Governmental Indian schools continued unabated, but so too for a time did the Wild West shows. At the end of the century the two efforts were pulling in their opposite directions on the minds of the Indians as well as of the whites. The Indian Rights Association, always solicitous that Indian reform not be swerved from the single track the humanitarians had in view, noted the paradox in its report for 1899:

> The Government is wholly committed to a definite policy of Indian education. For this it expends large sums and sustains a great teaching force. It is worse than folly for the Government to say to the Indian child, through the school: Think, dress, act like a civilized white man; and then to say, through the show business: Think, dress, act like a savage Indian. The show business teaches the Indian that what the white man really wants of him is amusement furnished by exhibitions of picturesque barbarism; not the acquisition of those sober, unpicturesque but absolutely necessary qualities which alone can make him equal to the battle of life, and able to endure even the humblest forms of competition with the white man. But, second, the shows teach the whites who witness them false ideas about the present condition of the Indians; they represent him only as a savage, and convey no idea of the progress he has made in civilized pursuits. None but those acquainted with actual conditions on Indian reserva-

[71] Remarks of E. Whittlesey, *Lake Mohonk Conference Proceedings*, 1893, p. 134.

tions are fully aware of the pernicious influence exerted by the shows upon Indian life.[72]

But time was on the side of the Indian schools. The Wild West shows lost much of their dynamism when Buffalo Bill passed from the scene, and the dramatic charge of the Indian braves upon the Deadwood coach faded slowly from memory.

[72] *Report of the Indian Rights Association*, 1899, p. 26. A strong condemnation of the effects of the Wild West shows is in the Report of the Commissioner of Indian Affairs, 1899, in serial 3915, pp. 42–43.

CHAPTER 11

LAW AND CITIZENSHIP FOR THE INDIANS

The practical question is this: What are the primary wants of the Indian in order to advance him and fit him for citizenship? and not, how can tribal organizations be improved? He requires that which cannot be dispensed with, even in the case of civilized humanity,— active law with speedy physical punishments, administered with justice and moderation. He needs a stable rule of action to restrain him from committing injuries on the rights and property of others, and should be punished and coerced until he submits to be guided by that rule. The germ of civilization is obedience to law. Implant that in the savage breast, and the beginning of a better state is positively secured.

—ELWELL S. OTIS, in
The Indian Question,
1878

✿✿✿✿✿✿✿

The changing relationship between the Indians and the United States government brought to the foreground a serious problem that had troubled Indian-white affairs for many decades, the question of what kind of law was to govern the Indian communities. It was a problem that the reformers attacked with their usual gusto, and some of them offered a theoretical solution which had all the earmarks of a new panacea.

The historical starting point was clear enough. The Indian tribes were treated as "nations," and although John Marshall characterized them as "domestic" and "dependent" to distinguish them from foreign states, the internal independence of the Indian groups was assumed.

Limitations were placed upon the sovereignty of the tribes, most notably in the American insistence that the Indians did not own the land in fee simple but had only a right of occupancy, and increasing numbers of restrictions relative to trade and intercourse between the Indians and the whites were written into treaties and into the legislation that backed up the treaties. The relations of the Indians among themselves, however, were not considered to be the concern of federal lawmakers or administrators. The series of trade and intercourse laws, culminating in the act of June 30, 1834, were the basic laws that touched upon the legal relationships, and they carefully left to the tribes the responsibility of governing and punishing their own members in matters that did not concern the whites.[1]

The reformers after the Civil War soon discovered weaknesses in this traditional arrangement, and various elements in their program eventually so changed the status of the Indians that the problem of law for the Indians assumed new and threatening dimensions. "A serious detriment to the progress of the partially civilized Indians," the Board of Indian Commissioners declared in 1871, "is found in the fact that they are not brought under the domination of law, so far as regards crimes committed against each other." The board admitted that Indian tribes differed greatly among themselves and that all were not yet suited to white legal norms. "But when they have adopted civilized costume and civilized modes of subsistence," it said, "we owe it to them, and to ourselves, to teach them the majesty of civilized law, and to extend to them its protection against the lawless among themselves."[2]

The sharpest blow at the traditional status of the Indian groups was the legislation of 1871 which declared that thereafter no Indian tribe would be recognized as an independent nation with whom the United States might contract by treaty.[3] Although agreements were still concluded that were no different from previous treaties except in mode of ratification, the formal end of treaty-making and the conscious intention thereby to denigrate the power of the chiefs resulted in a loss of old systems of internal order without the substitution of anything in

[1] For a history of the trade and intercourse laws, see Prucha, *American Indian Policy*.
[2] *Report of the Board of Indian Commissioners*, 1871, pp. 7–8; see also *ibid.*, 1873, p. 6.
[3] *United States Statutes at Large*, XVI, 566.

their place. Francis A. Walker put his finger on the problem as he left the office of Commissioner of Indian Affairs:

> While the Act of 1871 strikes down at a blow the hereditary authority of the chiefs, no legislation has invested Indian agents with magisterial powers, or provided for the assembling of the Indian *demos*. There is at this time no semblance of authority for the punishment of any crime which one Indian may commit against another, nor any mode of procedure, recognized by treaty or statute, for the regulation of matters between the government and the several tribes. So far as the law is concerned, complete anarchy exists in Indian affairs; and nothing but the singular homogeneity of Indian communities, and the almost unaccountable spontaneity and unanimity of public sentiment within them, has thus far prevented the attention of Congress and the country being called most painfully to the unpardonable negligence of the national legislature in failing to provide a substitute for the time-honored policy which was destroyed by the Act of 1871.[4]

Walker's successor, Edward P. Smith, who inherited the problem, was no less concerned, and he recommended the application of United States courts to the Indian territories as a substitute for the former tribal authority.[5] This became the common cry of the reformers both in and out of the government. Even among white men, they asserted, civilization would not long exist without the guarantees of law. How, then, could there be any hope of civilizing the Indians without law? "That the benevolent efforts and purposes of the Government have proved so largely fruitless," the Commissioner of Indian Affairs declared in 1876, "is, in my judgment, due more to its failure to make these people amenable to our laws than to any other cause, or to all other causes combined."[6] From all sides the refrain sounded. Bishop William Hare, the Episcopal missionary among the Sioux, wrote in 1877: "Wish well to the Indians as we may, and do for them what we will, the efforts of civil agents, teachers, and missionaries are like the

[4] Walker, *The Indian Question*, pp. 12–13.
[5] Report of the Commissioner of Indian Affairs, 1873, in serial 1601, pp. 372–73.
[6] *Ibid.*, 1876, in serial 1749, pp. 387–88. See also Report of the Secretary of the Interior, 1876, in serial 1749, p. vii, and Report of the Commissioner of Indian Affairs, 1877, in serial 1800, p. 398.

struggles of drowning men weighted with lead, as long as by the absence of law Indian society is left without a base."[7] Indians, too, were appealed to, and the Commissioner of Indian Affairs in 1878 said that Chief Joseph, the famous Nez Percé leader, believed that the greatest need of the Indians was a system of law by which controversies between Indians and between Indians and whites could be settled without appealing to physical force.[8]

A bill was introduced in Congress early in 1879 which authorized the President to prescribe police regulations for the Indian reservations and provided that the laws of the respective states and territories relating to major crimes should be in force on the reservations.[9] Both Secretary Schurz and Commissioner Hayt strongly supported the measure. The Commissioner declared: "A civilized community could not exist as such without law, and a semi-civilized and barbarous people are in a hopeless state of anarchy without its protection and sanctions. It is true the various tribes have regulations and customs of their own, which, however, are founded on superstition and ignorance of the usages of civilized communities, and generally tend to perpetuate feuds and keep alive animosities. To supply their place it is the bounden duty of the government to provide laws suited to the dependent condition of the Indians."[10] Congress could not be persuaded to enact the bill, but agitation kept the idea strong, and increasing pressure arose for law as a necessary means to bring about the Indian reform and civilization the humanitarians wanted.

By 1882 well worked out arguments began to appear with regularity. They increasingly exhibited a shift in emphasis as the general reform movement which aimed to individualize the Indian gained momentum. Although punishment for crimes committed by Indians on other Indians was not lost sight of, the dominant concern came to be the protection of the individual Indian in his personal and property rights. "That Law is the solution of the Indian problem would seem to be a

---

[7] Quoted in Report of the Commissioner of Indian Affairs, 1883, in serial 2191, p. 7.

[8] *Ibid.*, 1878, in serial 1850, p. 465.

[9] *Senate Journal*, 45 Congress, 3 session, serial 1827, p. 178; *House Journal*, 46 Congress, 1 session, serial 1874, p. 127; a copy of the bill is in Report of the Commissioner of Indian Affairs, 1879, in serial 1910, pp. 105–106.

[10] Report of the Secretary of the Interior, 1879, in serial 1910, pp. 12–13; Report of the Commissioner of Indian Affairs, 1879, in serial 1910, p. 106.

self-evident proposition," declared a writer in the *North American Review* in March, 1882. Everything that was sought for the Indians—inducements to make them labor, educational facilities, and land in severalty—rested, he argued, upon adequate protection of law. To declare that the Indian is "a *person* before the law" was the first and all important thing. "When his possessions are secure," the writer concluded, "his labor will be both profitable and attractive; when he feels himself a man, he will desire his own and his children's education; when he can be protected by law, the granting of land to him in severalty will be something more than a pretentious form."[11]

Similar sentiments were promoted by the Indian Rights Association, which established a standing committee on law under the chairmanship of one of the founders of the association, Henry S. Pancoast. Pancoast, a young lawyer of reforming temperament, returned home from his trip to the Sioux reservations in 1882 with strong convictions about what should be done to solve the Indian problem. "Acknowledge that the Indian is a man," he said, "and as such give him that standing in our courts which is freely given as a right and a necessity to every other man." Because the Indians were neither citizens, nor aliens, nor foreign nations they had no standing in court either individually or collectively and were therefore robbed and cheated with impunity. Their only resort was to demand their rights by force, and if they did so they were crushed by the military power of the United States. "If we want to make them like other people," Pancoast wrote, "we will never do it by studiously treating them differently from everybody else."[12] Two years later Pancoast prepared for the Indian Rights Association a pamphlet called *The Indian Before the Law*, in which he blamed the troubles in Indian relations on the "stubborn outward adherence to a theory, and the disregard or permission of a state of things which is an open contradiction of it." The theory he condemned as no longer relevant was that of Indian tribes as separate and internally independent nations. Under such stimulus the matter continued to be urged upon Congress by both the Indian Office and the Board of Indian Commissioners.[13]

[11] William Justin Harsha, "Law for the Indians," *North American Review*, CXXXIV (March, 1882), 272–92.

[12] Pancoast, *Impressions of the Sioux Tribes*, p. 22.

[13] Henry S. Pancoast, *The Indian Before the Law* (Philadelphia, 1884), pp. 5–6. An

While concern for general Indian rights and recognition of the individual Indian's manhood was thus pushed as an essential part of the program to introduce the Indian into the mainstream of American society as a man like other men, the question of a criminal code for the reservations came again to the forefront in the dramatic case of the Brulé Sioux chief Crow Dog. This Indian was sentenced to death by the territorial court of Dakota for murdering Chief Spotted Tail. In the case of *ex parte Crow Dog*, decided on December 17, 1883, the United States Supreme Court ordered the immediate release of Crow Dog on the ground that the United States had no jurisdiction over crimes committed by one Indian against another. Since Congress had provided no national jurisdiction over Indian crimes, even a murderer could not be punished, and the chief was permitted to return to his tribe.[14]

The decision caused great consternation. Such a state of lawlessness could not be tolerated within the Republic, and the House of Representatives on April 3, 1884, passed an amendment to the Indian appropriation bill to make Indians on the reservations subject to the criminal jurisdiction of the United States. The provision was not supported by the Senate and was struck out by the conference committee because more time was needed to formulate an adequate measure. The Indian Rights Association drew up a bill to establish special courts of criminal jurisdiction on the reservations. But such a temporary expedient did not satisfy all the reformers, many of whom wanted no distinction whatever between the Indians and the whites in legal matters. The Board of Indian Commissioners objected that such a separate code of law for the Indians was not only expensive but would perpetuate the evil that had grown out of the treaty and reservation policies of keeping the Indians apart from the whites. "We believe," the board said, "that the laws which are good enough for all other kindreds and peoples and tribes and nations are good enough for Indians."[15]

appendix to the pamphlet contains a questionnaire sent to Indian agents and others about a system of law for the Indians and their replies. See also Report of the Commissioner of Indian Affairs, 1883, in serial 2191, pp. 7–10; *Report of the Board of Indian Commissioners*, 1884, pp. 6–7.

[14] 109 *U.S. Reports* 556.

[15] *Congressional Record*, XV, 2577, 4112, 5802–5803; *Report of the Board of Indian Commissioners*, 1884, p. 6. See also the discussion in Priest, *Uncle Sam's Stepchildren*, p. 202.

On January 22, 1885, the House passed a measure to extend criminal jurisdiction for serious crimes and civil procedures over the Indians, but the provision was deleted in the Senate. In compromise, the law approved on March 3, 1885, provided only for criminal cases. Jurisdiction was limited to seven major crimes (murder, manslaughter, rape, assault with intent to kill, arson, burglary, and larceny).[16] Even in its final limited form the legislation was revolutionary. For the first time, the United States asserted its jurisdiction over strictly internal crimes of Indians against Indians, a major blow at the integrity of the Indian tribes and a fundamental readjustment in the relations between the Indians and the United States government. When the Supreme Court in *United States v. Kagama* on May 10, 1886, upheld the right of Congress to take this step, the way was open for unlimited interference by the federal government in the affairs of the Indians.[17] "It was laid down in this case, one of the landmarks of our Indian law," explained a leading legal expert of the day, "that the government of the United States has full power, under the Constitution, to govern the Indians as its own subjects, if it sees fit to do so, and to such partial or full extent as it sees fit; that nothing in the tribal relation or in any previous recognition of it by the United States cuts down this legislative power; that this is so not merely in the Territories, but on reservations within the States."[18]

For a while the efforts to bring further legal reforms, measures which would extend civil as well as criminal law over the Indians, were diverted by interest in the land-in-severalty bills that finally resulted in the Dawes Act of 1887. There was no doubt in the reformers' minds that the Dawes Act was a major step in the direction they aimed to go in making the Indians individually indistinguishable from other Americans. The act provided that Indians who had taken allotments would be subject to both the civil and criminal laws of the state or territory where they resided and declared that "no Territory shall pass or enforce any law denying any such Indian within its jurisdiction the equal protection of the law." All Indians to whom an allotment was

[16] *Congressional Record*, XVI, 934–36, 2385–87, 2466; *United States Statutes at Large*, XXIII, 385.

[17] 118 *U.S. Reports* 375.

[18] James Bradley Thayer, "A People Without Law," *Atlantic Monthly*, LXVIII (November, 1891), 677. The case was hailed at the time as of equal importance with John Marshall's Cherokee cases. See, for example, Robert Weil, *The Legal Status of the Indian* (New York, 1888), p. 12.

made under the provisions of the act, moreover, were declared to be citizens of the United States.[19]

Senator Dawes and many others felt that this act answered the needs of the Indians for legal protection and equality. Whenever Indians were judged by the President to be ready for the transition, they would get their homesteads, their citizenship, and their equality before the law and could merge with the general population. As the provisions of the Dawes Act were extended to tribe after tribe, the Indian problem would be solved without resort to hasty or radical measures. When Charles C. Painter suggested at Lake Mohonk in 1887 that the Indian service be reorganized by establishing a special board of commissioners, Senator Dawes objected, for he believed that the allotment act alone would render all such organizations obsolete. "It seems to me," he said, "this is a self-acting machine we have set going, and if we only run it on the track it will work itself all out, and all these difficulties that have troubled my friend will pass away like snow in the spring time, and we will never know when they go; we will only know they are gone."[20] But to reformers interested primarily in the Indian's legal status, the Dawes Act was too slow. Its legal provisions and opportunities for citizenship did not immediately embrace all the Indians, and in the long transition period until the Dawes Act had taken effect everywhere, some further legislation, they felt, was absolutely necessary.

The man most eager for this to happen and most earnest and articulate in its promotion was a learned and highly respected professor in the Harvard Law School, James Bradley Thayer. Torn at first between the ministry and the law, he chose the latter and entered Harvard Law School as a student in 1854. After practicing law with a leading Boston firm, he accepted a post as professor of law at Harvard in 1874, and until his death in 1902 he was an influential member of the faculty, known for his work in constitutional law and the rules of evidence. He was also a deeply religious man and one with an active social conscience, and in the mid-1880's he turned his attention to the Indian question.[21] He strongly supported Senator Dawes in his severalty pro-

[19] *United States Statutes at Large*, XXIV, 390.

[20] *Lake Mohonk Conference Proceedings*, 1887, p. 9.

[21] For Thayer's career see Samuel Williston, "James Bradley Thayer," *Dictionary of American Biography*, XVIII, 405–406; James Parker Hall, "James Bradley Thayer, 1831–1902," in William Draper Lewis, ed., *Great American Lawyers* (8 vols., Philadelphia, 1907–1909), VIII, 345–84.

posal, lecturing to Indian reform groups and writing an intelligent article explaining the Dawes Act to the public.[22]

But the Dawes Act Thayer considered merely "one great step to be followed by others." "We must not leave things alone for one or two generations," he declared, "to be worked out by the Severalty Law unaided."[23] Thayer expressed his views on the need to treat the Indians as individuals under the law from the very first of his interest in Indian matters. Speaking to the Women's Indian Association in Cambridge, Massachusetts, in May, 1886, he declared that it was high time to put an end to "the monstrous situation of having people in our country who are not entitled to the full protection of our national constitution, who are native here and yet not citizens." It mattered little to him whether or not the Indians wanted to abandon their tribal relations. The United States could simply ignore the tribes and deal directly with the individuals. "There is little harm in men associating together," Thayer said, "whether in tribes of Shakers or Oneida communities, or Odd Fellows, or Masons, or Germans, or colored men, or Indians, if they like; but as we do not carry on a separate commerce with the tribe of Shakers we had better stop doing it with the Indians."[24] If a man as learned as Thayer could see no difference between an Indian tribe, with its long history of political nationhood and traditions as a separate people and an Odd Fellows lodge, there was little hope that the Indian view of things would get much attention.

Thayer stressed the foolishness of maintaining a "gigantic, complicated, costly, and, in a great degree, needless body of laws and administration" to handle the Indians. There were fewer Indians in the whole United States than there were people in Boston, Thayer pointed out, and the whole Indian Bureau and its numerous personnel were set up to care for them outside of the American judicial system. This, perhaps, would not have been so bad had it provided a reasonable system of law and administration for the Indians. But instead it resulted in the exercise of arbitrary power over the Indians, which was repugnant to

[22] James B. Thayer, "The Dawes Bill and the Indians," *Atlantic Monthly*, LXI (March, 1888), 315–22.

[23] Thayer, "A People Without Law," pp. 682, 686.

[24] James B. Thayer, *Remarks Made at a Meeting in Cambridge, Mass., Called by the Women's Indian Association of That City, May 3, 1886* (n.p., n.d.).

the American system of government. He expressed himself strongly in 1887:

We have got to a point where we are dealing with these poor people in a manner wholly at variance with the fundamental notions of our English and American liberty. And they are painfully suffering the consequences. We shut them up in their reservations. We send and maintain there at pleasure our own officials, and give them large, dangerous, despotic powers. We keep other people off the reservations. We allow nobody to trade with the Indians except certain persons who get their place by the favors of political officeholders. And all this with results that are often monstrous; there are many frauds and abuses, and all the uncertainty and misery which usually results from mere political control. We give them no courts; for we assume, through our obsolete fiction, that their tribal authorities will furnish these. At the same time our officials displace their chiefs, and break down and undermine and degrade the tribal authorities in all sorts of ways; and the result is great lawlessness and demoralization. There is an amount of irresponsible power over these poor people, in the hands of the President and Secretary of the Interior, the Indian Commissioner, and the other subordinate officials, that, in such a country as ours, is simply amazing and distressing; it ought not to be tolerated for a moment longer.[25]

Much was made of the arbitrary power of the agents by all the reformers who urged the extension of United States law over the Indians. Pancoast had been especially strong in his condemnation. The agents, he thought, were generally a bad lot—"men ignorant, conceited, and narrow-minded in their office, and openly irreligious and immoral in their private lives." The "tyrannical power" of the agents astounded him. "Here in the midst of us is an unauthorized power so despotic as to be utterly irreconcilable with every principle of liberty we profess," he wrote. "The agent is permitted to arrest and imprison Indians without trial. Here in America, in the nineteenth century, does our Government deny these men a right which Englishmen gained for themselves in the thirteenth." That the tyranny of the agent was not infinitely

[25] James B. Thayer, *Remarks Made Before the Worcester Indian Association at Worcester, Mass., February 13, 1887* (n.p., n.d.), pp. 4–5.

337

worse was due, he thought, not to the system but to the good sense and moderation of the agents themselves.[26]

Thayer, Austin Abbott of New York (a brother of Lyman Abbott noted for his legal writings), and Philip C. Garrett of Philadelphia (a lawyer of philanthropic interest in the Indians) were appointed by the Lake Mohonk Conference of 1887 to frame a statute that would accomplish what Thayer and his friends had in mind for the Indians. After consulting persons noted for their practical knowledge of Indian affairs, as well as distinguished lawyers, the committee drew up a bill that was generally known as the Thayer Bill. Senator Dawes, although he himself did not support the measure, was prevailed upon to introduce it in the Senate, which he did on March 29, 1888. It was referred to the Committee on Indian Affairs, and there it languished, while Thayer and many others urged its adoption as the only hope for solving the Indian question.[27]

Thayer's bill provided that all Indians be given the full protection of the law and enabled them to sue and be sued in all courts and to make contracts and enter into trade or business. It provided, furthermore, for the immediate extension over every reservation of the civil and criminal laws of the state or territory in which it was located. To administer these laws, special commissioners' courts were to be established, since until the Indians generally became taxpayers the burden would be too heavy for the local courts to bear. The bill did not apply to the Five Civilized Tribes, the Senecas of New York, or the Eastern Cherokees.[28]

There was strong agitation to have this measure or something like it passed. Thayer spoke in its favor at the Lake Mohonk Conference in 1888, and his co-committeeman, Austin Abbott, published a detailed exposition of the bill in the *Harvard Law Review* in the same year. Abbott emphasized the condition of lawlessness that existed on the

[26] Pancoast, *Impressions of the Sioux Tribes*, p. 25; Pancoast, *The Indian Before the Law*, p. 15.

[27] *Senate Journal*, 50 Congress, 1 session, serial 2503, p. 557. An account of the work that went into the framing of the bill was given by Thayer at Lake Mohonk in 1888. *Lake Mohonk Conference Proceedings*, 1888, pp. 42–48. See also Thayer's remarks in *Report of the Annual Meeting of the American Bar Association*, XIV (1891), 15.

[28] A summary of the provisions of the bill is given in Austin Abbott, "Indians and the Law," *Harvard Law Review*, II (November, 1888), 177–78, and in *Report of the Indian Rights Association*, 1888, pp. 26–27.

reservations and asserted that the necessity of law, for the protection and welfare of both the Indians and the white population, was obvious. The most thoroughgoing anarchist, he said, could find the state of society he aimed to establish already in existence on the reservations. "If justice to the Indians would allow it," he added, "banishment to a reservation might be the most fitting punishment for a convicted anarchist."[29] The Indian Rights Association, with its committee on law under the chairmanship of Pancoast, fought strenuously for the bill and urged Thayer's proposal over other similar measures introduced into Congress. The Boston Indian Citizenship Committee, likewise, continued its efforts. In a memorial of 1891, it urged Congress and the country at large to provide law for the Indians, asserting that "this country has no duty towards the Indians so solemn and so instant as that of bringing these poor people under the protection and the control of the ordinary laws of the land."[30]

Thayer renewed his push for the bill with a long expository article in the *Atlantic Monthly* in 1891, called "A People Without Law."[31] The distinguished New York lawyer, William B. Hornblower, at the meeting of the American Bar Association in 1891, presented a position similar to Thayer's. Hornblower pictured the Indian tribes as "wretched remnants, hanging on the outskirts of civilization," dependent upon the government. The fact of their nationhood had become a fiction. "Let the fiction be abolished," he urged. "Let us enact laws suitable for the present situation, and place the legal status of the Indian upon a rational and practical basis." The American Bar Association passed a resolution, drawn up by Thayer, that the United States should provide as soon as possible for courts and a system of law for the Indian reservations.[32]

Such prestigious backing might have been expected to force the measure through Congress, but there was conflict within the ranks of the reformers themselves over the Thayer Bill. The chief opponent was

[29] Abbott, "Indians and the Law," p. 175.
[30] The memorial is printed as an appendix to Thomas J. Morgan, *The Present Phase of the Indian Question* (Boston, 1891), pp. 22–23.
[31] LXVIII (October, 1891), 540–51; (November, 1891), 676–87.
[32] William B. Hornblower, "The Legal Status of the Indian," *Report of the Annual Meeting of the American Bar Association*, XIV (1891), 277; Resolution, *ibid.*, p. 18. The American Bar Association renewed its stand in 1894. Report of "Special Committee on Indian Legislation," *ibid.*, XVI (1893), 61, 351–63; *ibid.*, XVII (1894), 53, 333–34.

Senator Dawes, who had qualms about the constitutionality of Thayer's proposal and who, more fundamentally, pinned his hopes for Indian salvation on the severalty measure he had sponsored. As the allotment went forward and the Indians became citizens and subject to state and territorial laws, there would be no need for Thayer's radical measure. He opposed its elaborate and expensive solution for a problem that to his mind would soon vanish. One point at issue was the time involved before the Dawes Act reached all the Indians. Thayer argued that the situation was so bad that it could not wait for the slow operation of the allotment system. He would admit that ultimately the Dawes Act would dispose of the Indian problem. "The question is, however," he told the American Bar Association in 1891, "as to the time it will take. Mr. Dawes says, 'Why are you providing for a vanishing state of things?' We say, 'How long is it going to take to vanish?'" Thayer cited information from the Commissioner of Indian Affairs that in the nearly four and one-half years under the Dawes Act somewhere between twelve and thirteen thousand allotments had been taken out. At that rate, he pointed out, it would take sixty years to end the Indian problem. But even half that time was too long "to allow this state of things to continue under which the Indians are a people absolutely without any law."[33]

Thayer sought to break down what he considered Dawes's obstruction to the measure. One move was to write to Bishop Henry B. Whipple for support, which he did on December 31, 1891. "I wish, dear Sir," he wrote, "that your voice might again be heard urging this measure of law upon the reservations and courts through which it can be enforced. In the present state of public opinion, it could not but help powerfully." Thayer charged that Dawes had "a fancy that nothing can be done in time to do any good—they will be enfranchised before law can be provided for them" and that in the meantime he was doing whatever he could to make his prophecy come true by blocking Thayer's bill.[34] Whipple kindly obliged with a long letter addressed to Thayer that was published in the *Christian Union*, charging that the Indians were without law and urging support of Thayer's measure. A strong edi-

[33] *Ibid.*, XIV (1891), 18.
[34] Thayer to Whipple, December 31, 1891, Whipple Papers, Box 21, Minnesota Historical Society. When Whipple printed this letter in his autobiography, he omitted the section critical of Dawes. Whipple, *Lights and Shadows*, pp. 265–66.

BAKING BREAD AT CARLISLE. Vocational training was an important part of the education at Carlisle Indian School. Shown here are the son of High Bear, Rosebud Sioux (at the wheelbarrow), and the son of American Horse, Pine Ridge Sioux. (National Archives)

SIOUX GIRLS AT CARLISLE. American dress replaced Indian apparel for the students at Carlisle Indian School. These carefully posed girls, photographed in the 1880's, were daughters of Sioux Indians at Rosebud and Pine Ridge agencies. (National Archives)

RICHARD HENRY PRATT (1840–1924) was perhaps the most ardent promoter of complete assimilation of the Indians into white American society. The school he founded in 1879 at Carlisle, Pennsylvania, was a means toward that goal. (National Archives)

LAKE MOHONK MOUNTAIN HOUSE. Each year from 1883 to 1916 men and women interested in Indian affairs gathered at this resort hotel near New Paltz, New York, to formulate proposals for the reform of Indian policy. (Photograph supplied by Keith Smiley)

LAKE MOHONK CONFERENCE. This group picture shows the serious men and women who gathered at Lake Mohonk in 1899. (Photograph supplied by Keith Smiley)

LYMAN ABBOTT (1835–1922) was a leader of the reform group at the Lake Mohonk Conferences. A Congregational minister and influential editor of the *Christian Union* (later *Outlook*), he eagerly supported many reform movements. (Purdy photograph, 1901, Library of Congress)

ALBERT K. SMILEY (1828–1912), a Quaker educator and member of the Board of Indian Commissioners, was the founder of the Lake Mohonk Conferences of Friends of the Indian and the host of the conferences at his resort hotel. (Photograph supplied by Keith Smiley)

PINE RIDGE INDIAN BOARDING SCHOOL. A typical reservation boarding
school established by the United States government was this imposing structure
on the Pine Ridge Reservation in South Dakota. (Grabill photograph, 1891,
Library of Congress)

INDIAN SCHOOL AT THE CHICAGO COLUMBIAN EX-
POSITION, 1893. The efforts of the Indian Office to display and
promote Indian educational activities were carried on in this
pitiable building, set among the splendors of the Exposition's
buildings. (Photograph supplied by Dominic B. Gerlach)

THOMAS JEFFERSON MOR-
GAN (1839–1902), a former
Civil War general, Baptist
minister, and public educator, was
Commissioner of Indian Affairs
during Benjamin Harrison's
administration, 1889–1893. He
worked eagerly to Americanize
the Indians, especially through a
government school system. This
portrait appeared on the cover
of the *Baptist Home Mission
Monthly*, which Morgan edited
after he left public office. (State
Historical Society of Wisconsin)

THE GHOST DANCE among the Oglala Sioux was depicted by the
artist Frederick Remington for *Harper's Weekly*, December 6, 1890.
(Library of Congress)

GENERAL NELSON MILES AND STAFF are shown overlooking the hostile Sioux camp near Pine Ridge, January 16, 1891. (Grabill photograph, Library of Congress)

torial, presumably written by Lyman Abbott, reinforced the letter.[35]

This was too much for Dawes, who sent off a letter to the journal objecting to the letter and to the editorial. "Do you mean to impute to the administration of Indian Affairs here," he asked, "the charge that though they have been professedly at work for a dozen years in the effort to lift the Indian out of his savage life into that of a self-support-ing citizen of the United States, and have spent in that effort millions of dollars, that nevertheless it is true that they have so forgotten justice and right as to leave him to-day without law?" He suggested that Whipple was out of touch with Indian matters now and too much in-fluenced by Thayer. For his own view, he referred to his remarks at the 1891 Lake Mohonk Conference, in which he had taken issue with Thayer and his supporters and had argued that the Indians were *not* without law by pointing to the Dawes Act, the act of 1885 providing for the punishment of major crimes, and the courts of Indian offenses organized on many reservations.[36]

Without someone of Dawes's stature to drive the measure through, it made no headway in Congress. Thayer lamented that "the whole Indian question gets little hold on public men, and is crowded aside by tariffs and silver and President-making and office-jobbing and pension-giving," and that too much attention was paid to patching up the present Indian system instead of radically changing the status of the Indian before the law.[37]

Although the questions of law for the Indians and Indian citizenship were intimately related, strong advocates of a system of law like Pancoast and Thayer were careful not to equate the two. Pancoast as-serted that "the idea of declaring all Indians citizens at once, without warning or preparation, is crude and unpractical, devoutly as we may wish it were not so." He pointed to the duties of citizenship for which many Indians were not yet ready and declared that there had to be at

[35] *Christian Union*, XLV (January 30, 1892), 194–95, 234.
[36] Dawes to editors of the *Christian Union*, January 31, 1892, Dawes Papers, Box 29, Library of Congress; *Lake Mohonk Conference Proceedings*, 1891, 43–48. See also Dawes to J. W. Davis, June 5, 1892, Dawes Papers, in which he sets forth his position at length.
[37] "A People Without Law," p. 686.

least "an approximate fitness in the individual Indian for the duties of citizenship" before he could be made a citizen. But that did not preclude measures to make sure that all Indians, citizens or not, were protected by the law. Thayer, too, urged that the ballot and citizenship should not be granted immediately to all, as it had been to the former slaves.[38]

The question of citizenship for the Indians, nevertheless, could not be kept down. To make the Indians into acceptable American citizens was the great goal of the humanitarians and of the Indian Bureau officials. There was little if any controversy about that. But the niceties of the precise legal formulation and how and when legal citizenship should be acquired by the red men were all matters of divided opinion. The immediate granting of citizenship, unlike most of the reforms proposed at the end of the nineteenth century for the Indians, was not universally accepted as a panacea.[39]

The anomalous legal status of the Indians was the major difficulty. As long as the Indians were members of tribes or nations, which treated with the United States as quasi-independent political units but which were also subject to the United States, they could not be considered American citizens. A clear formulation of their dependent status was given by Attorney General Caleb Cushing in 1856:

> The fact . . . that Indians are born in this country does not make them citizens of the United States.
>
> The simple truth is plain, that the Indians are the *subjects* of the United States, and therefore are not, in mere right of home-birth, citizens of the United States. The two conditions are incompatible. The moment it comes to be seen that the Indians are domestic subjects of this Government, that moment it is clear to the perception that they are not the sovereign constituent ingredients of the Government.
>
> This distinction between *citizens* proper, that is, the constituent members of the political sovereignty, and *subjects* of that sovereign-

---

[38] Pancoast, *The Indian Before the Law*, p. 25; Thayer, "A People Without Law," p. 683.

[39] There is a brief survey of the citizenship question in Michael T. Smith, "The History of Indian Citizenship," *Great Plains Journal*, X (Fall, 1970), 25–35.

ty, who are not therefore citizens, is recognized in the best authorities of public law. . . .

But they cannot become citizens by naturalization under existing general acts of Congress. . . .

Those acts apply only to *foreigners*, subjects of another allegiance. The Indians are not foreigners, and they are in our allegiance, without being *citizens* of the United States. Moreover, those acts only apply to "white" men. . . .

Indians, of course, can be made citizens of the United States only by some competent act of the General Government, either a treaty or an act of Congress.[40]

The status of the Indians came into question with the adoption of the Fourteenth Amendment to the Constitution in 1868. That Reconstruction measure provided in Section 1: "All persons born or naturalized in the United States, and subject to the jurisdiction thereof, are citizens of the United States and of the State wherein they reside." Although the amendment was aimed at the recently emancipated Negro slaves, the Indians did not escape attention when the amendment was being debated in Congress. Senator James Doolittle of Wisconsin, assuming that the amendment as worded would make citizens of the Indians as well as of the Negroes, strongly opposed such a move, for he believed that the Indians were not yet prepared for citizenship. He thereupon proposed adding the words, "excluding Indians not taxed," to the section. Other senators, although agreeing with Doolittle's views on Indian citizenship, held that the added phrase was unnecessary, since the Indians with their tribal connections could not be considered "subject to the jurisdiction" of the United States, and Doolittle's amendment was voted down thirty to ten.[41] That such a difference of opinion could obtain among senators, many of whom were well trained in law, indicates the confusion that existed about the precise status of the Indians under the Constitution.

Doolittle's view, in fact, continued to be expressed. In debate in the House on April 6, 1869, on treaty-making, Congressman Benjamin F. Butler of Massachusetts asserted his belief that the Indians became

---

[40] *Opinions of the Attorney General,* VII, 749–50.
[41] *Congressional Globe,* 39 Congress, 1 session, pp. 2890–97.

citizens by virtue of the Fourteenth Amendment, and he went on to argue that the United States could not make treaties with such groups. A year later, the Senate, still in doubt, instructed its Committee on the Judiciary to report on the effect of the Fourteenth Amendment upon the Indian tribes, whether or not the amendment made the Indians citizens, and if so whether the treaties existing between the tribes and the United States were annulled. The report, submitted on December 14, 1870, presented a long historical exposition and then declared that the Indians did not become citizens because they were not subject to the jurisdiction of the United States in the sense meant by the amendment. Moreover, Section 2 of the Fourteenth Amendment, which determined the apportionment of representatives in Congress, excluded "Indians not taxed" from the calculations. The committee's opinion became generally accepted so far as Indians holding tribal relations were concerned, and Congress, subsequent to the adoption of the Fourteenth Amendment, passed special laws granting citizenship to various tribes.[42]

What was still not clear, however, was the citizenship status of Indians who voluntarily severed their connections with their tribes and took up the ways of white society. Did they, by such an act, automatically receive citizenship? The Senate Judiciary Committee seemed to imply that they did, for it limited its restriction to tribes and to "individuals, members of such tribes, while they adhere to and form a part of the tribes to which they belong."[43] This theory was certainly current for more than a decade. In the mid-seventies the anonymous author of a pamphlet entitled *The Political Status of the American Indian* declared that an Indian, unlike an alien of foreign birth, had an "inchoate right of citizenship, which may be perfected by bringing himself wholly within the relation upon which citizenship depends"— that individual members might become citizens "by the mere act of abandoning *in toto* all previous tribal relations, and subjecting themselves fully to the jurisdiction of the United States."[44] And a legal

[42] *Ibid.*, 41 Congress, 1 session, p. 560; *Senate Report* No. 268, 41 Congress, 3 session, serial 1443; G. M. Lambertson, "Indian Citizenship," *American Law Review*, XX (March–April, 1886), 184; Felix S. Cohen, *Handbook of Federal Indian Law* (Washington, 1942), p. 154. See also R. Alton Lee, "Indian Citizenship and the Fourteenth Amendment," *South Dakota History*, IV (Spring, 1974), 198–221.

[43] *Senate Report* No. 268, 41 Congress, 3 session, serial 1443, pp. 10–11.

[44] *The Political Status of the American Indian* (n.p., n.d.), pp. 8–9.

scholar writing in 1881 asserted that, no matter how absolute the power of Congress might be over a tribal Indian living on his reservation, "as soon as an Indian has severed his tribal relation, or come to reside among us without severing his tribal relation, the supreme power of Congress over him ceases,—he then becomes a person within the meaning of the Constitution."[45]

In actual decisions of the Department of the Interior, however, the theory did not hold. The matter came up specifically in connection with making the Homestead Law available to Indians, since that law applied to citizens of the United States. Secretary of the Interior Delano in 1874 saw no problem if an Indian tribe had been dissolved by treaty or by act of Congress (as had happened with certain Ottawa and Chippewa Indians by a treaty of July 31, 1855); the members of such a tribe, he declared, "become *ipso facto* citizens of the United States, and entitled to all the privileges and immunities belonging to other citizens." It was quite different, in his opinion, when an individual Indian withdrew from his tribe and adopted the habits and customs of civilized life. It was, he said, "inconsistent with sound law, as well as with public policy, to permit an individual Indian, by voluntarily withdrawing from his tribe, to become a citizen without some act of the Government recognizing his citizenship." Delano thought the time had arrived for some general law regulating Indian citizenship, but he had to be satisfied with legislation that extended homesteading privileges to Indians without reference to the larger matter of their citizenship.[46]

Not until November 3, 1884, was there a definite answer to questions about the status of an Indian who had withdrawn from his tribe and adopted the ways of white civilization. On that date the Supreme Court handed down its decision in the case of *Elk v. Wilkins*. John Elk, an Indian who had separated from his tribe, was refused permission to register to vote in a local election in Omaha, Nebraska, and when he

[45] George F. Canfield, "The Legal Position of the Indian," *American Law Review*, XV (January, 1881), 33. Priest, *Uncle Sam's Stepchildren*, p. 205, asserts that "by the early eighties most Americans believed either that all Indians were citizens or that they could become so by leaving their tribes." This statement is too strong, for it disregards official decisions that a specific act of Congress was required to make such Indians citizens.

[46] Report of the Secretary of the Interior, 1874, in serial 1639, pp. v–vii, ix. The Chippewa treaty is given in Kappler, *Indian Affairs*, II, 729.

later appeared at the polls he was again refused the right to vote. Elk met the residence and other requirements of the state of Nebraska and of the city of Omaha, but he was turned back because it was alleged that as an Indian he was not a citizen. The majority of the court held against the plaintiff, declaring that an Indian who was born a member of an Indian tribe, although he voluntarily separated himself from the tribe and took up residence among white citizens, was not thereby a citizen of the United States. Some specific act of Congress was necessary to naturalize him. "Indians born within the territorial limits of the United States, members of and owing allegiance to, one of the Indian tribes (an alien though dependent power)," the decision said, "although in a geographical sense born in the United States, are no more 'born in the United States and subject to the jurisdiction thereof,' within the meaning of the first section of the Fourteenth Amendment, than the children . . . born within the United States, of ambassadors or other public ministers of foreign nations."[47]

Granted the necessity, then, of some sort of Congressional action to make Indians citizens, would such an enactment be wise and in the best interests of the Indians and of the United States? It was on this question that disagreement prevailed. Was citizenship a reward to be conferred when an Indian had demonstrated his desire and his competence to live among the whites, or was citizenship to be a means whereby the Indian would advance on the road to civilization? A few men were eager to make all Indians citizens. Senator Richard J. Oglesby of Illinois proposed in 1876 "to make every living one of them, men and women, pappooses and squaws, chiefs, heroes, and medicine-men, citizens of the United States." He knew no one, he said, who was "white enough, or black enough, or red enough not to be an American citizen," and he proposed to offer the Indians "this priceless boon upon easy and reasonable conditions."[48] But most friends of the Indian were not so sure that mass conversion was feasible or desirable. The obstacle they saw was an incompatibility between Indian tribal connections and United States citizenship. Could an Indian maintain his position in a tribe, give allegiance to tribal leaders, continue his right to share in communal property, and enjoy a particular political status

[47] 112 U.S. Reports, 94, 102. Two justices dissented from the majority opinion.
[48] Congressional Record, IV, 1263–64.

in relations with the federal government and special benefits accruing thereto, such as annuity payments and freedom from taxation, and still be a citizen? Could the United States government make "treaties" with a special group of its own citizens? And if an Indian were forced to give all this up when he became a citizen, was he prepared to survive in white society? The position was well stated by Commissioner Hayt in his annual report of 1878:

It has been strongly urged that citizenship should be extended to all the so-called civilized Indians. Such citizenship, if conferred indiscriminately, would, in my judgment, while the Indians are in their present transition state, be of incalculable damage to them. We should move slowly in the process of making Indians citizens, until they are prepared to assume intelligently the duties and obligations of citizens. The experience of the past has shown us that to make them citizens hastily is to make them paupers. Indians of full age are infants in law; and in fact they need a long tutelage before launching them into the world to manage their own affairs. Entire civilization, with education, a knowledge of the English language, and experience in business forms and matters, especially such as relate to the conveyance of lands, should precede citizenship if it is the intention of the government to save the Indians from pauperism and extermination.[49]

The Lake Mohonk Conference in 1883 urged that "the Indians be admitted to United States citizenship so soon, and only so soon, as they are fitted for its responsibilities." In the next year the conference repeated the same doctrine in more detail. It recognized that the Indian must be "forced out into the current of ordinary life; that to make him a citizen is the solution of the Indian problem." Yet the resolutions it passed expressed a strong conviction that "Indians should not be at once made citizens in a mass." The conference urged preparation for citizenship through land in severalty and through broad education.[50]

Beginning in 1874, advocates of Indian citizenship made repeated attempts to get legislation through Congress that would make Indians, or some specific classes of them, citizens. A bill was introduced in the

[49] Report of the Commissioner of Indian Affairs, 1878, in serial 1850, p. 444.
[50] Lake Mohonk Conference Proceedings, 1883, p. 8; ibid., 1884, p. 21.

Senate in April, 1874, and favorably reported by the Committee on Indian Affairs, but it got no further. The Senate in 1875, in considering the bill to allow Indians homesteading privileges, proposed to grant citizenship to Indians who took out homesteads, but only after five years and with the provision that the Indians get testimonials from two neighboring citizens as to their competence, but the amendment was cut out by the conference committee.[51] In the following year, during consideration of the measure to transfer the Indian Bureau to the War Department, the House adopted an amendment to the bill to provide Indian citizenship. The concern about the competence of such Indians was clearly evident in the provisions of the amendment:

> That whenever any Indian belonging to any organized Indian tribe or nation having treaty relations with the United States shall desire to become a citizen of the United States, he may become such citizen by appearing in open court in the United States district court nearest to the reservation of his tribe or nation, and making proof to the satisfaction of the court that he is sufficiently intelligent and prudent to control his own affairs and interests; that he has adopted the habits of civilized life, and has for at least five years been able to support himself and his family; and by taking an oath to support the Constitution of the United States. . . .[52]

A further provision declared that no Indian availing himself of the citizenship procedures should forfeit any interest in tribal property that he might then have or later acquire. But these citizenship measures died in the Senate when the transfer bill to which they were attached was voted down.

The next concerted drive came in 1877, with a bill (S. 107) introduced in October by Senator John J. Ingalls of Kansas, which largely duplicated the House amendment of the previous year. The extended debate on the issue centered on the objection of Senator Allen G. Thurman of Ohio and others that it was inconsistent for the United States to make or to maintain special arrangements through Indian treaties and agreements with particular groups of citizens. Although

---

[51] *Senate Journal*, 43 Congress, 1 session, serial 1579, pp. 485, 540; *Congressional Record*, III, 2182, 2205.
[52] *Ibid.*, IV, 2674.

Ingalls answered that the treaties were no obstacle, for Indian tribes like other groups in the nation could have special corporate interests in property, the bill was ultimately recommitted to the Committee on Indian Affairs and there died.[53] To senatorial questions of principle, moreover, was added strong opposition to the bill from the Five Civilized Tribes in the Indian Territory, who saw serious troubles for themselves if the measure became law. They objected principally to the provisions which would allow the Indian-become-citizen to retain all his tribal rights, including those to property, since such arrangements would violate treaty provisions and cause irritation within the Indian nations.[54]

The efforts to make general provision by law for Indian citizenship having thus far failed, proponents of Indian citizenship came to attach their proposals to land-in-severalty measures. In January, 1881, when the Coke Bill was under consideration, Senator George F. Hoar of Massachusetts proposed to amend the bill by a declaration that all Indians who obtained an allotment under the bill would "become citizens of the United States and entitled as such to the full protection of the Constitution and laws." To this Senator Coke objected, since he thought it inconsistent to make the Indians citizens and at the same time to hedge about their title to the land by restrictions against alienation. Hoar replied that there was no restriction on the *Indian* in Coke's bill; rather the government was granting *land* under conditions of temporary inalienability, and he challenged the senators to show that the United States government could not grant to him a piece of property in Washington with the proviso that he could not sell it for twenty-five years. In the end, however, Hoar's amendment was lost by a vote of twenty-nine to twelve.[55]

[53] *Senate Journal*, 45 Congress, 1 session, serial 1771, pp. 29, 62, 73, 76; *Senate Journal*, 45 Congress, 2 session, serial 1779, pp. 43, 213, 244; *Congressional Record*, VI, 525–27, 549–56; VII, 1130–31.

[54] "Memorial of Delegates and Agents of the Choctaw and Chickasaw Nations of Indians, Remonstrating Against the Passage of Senate Bill No. 107, to Enable Indians to Become Citizens," *Senate Miscellaneous Document* No. 8, 45 Congress, 2 session, serial 1785; "Remonstrance of the Seminole and Creek Delegates Against the Passage of Senate Bill No. 107, to Enable Indians to Become Citizens of the United States," *Senate Miscellaneous Document* No. 18, 45 Congress, 2 session, serial 1785.

[55] *Congressional Record*, XI, 875–82, 908–11, 939.

By the time that Senator Dawes took over the sponsorship of the severalty bill, a significant change had taken place in the agitation of the reformers for Indian citizenship. Whereas in 1883 and 1884 the Lake Mohonk Conference had stressed preparation for citizenship, by the end of 1884 the Board of Indian Commissioners could assert: "The solution of the Indian problem is citizenship, and we believe that the time has come to declare by an act of Congress that every Indian born within the territorial limits of the United States is a citizen of the United States and subject to the jurisdiction thereof." What brought such a shift in opinion cannot be explained completely, but the decision in *Elk v. Wilkins* of November 3, 1884, played an important part.[56]

The movement gained considerable momentum in the next two years. Merrill E. Gates of the Board of Indian Commissioners prepared a paper in 1885 entitled "Land and Law as Agents in Educating Indians." He asked, "For what ought we to hope as the future of the Indian? What should the Indian become?" And he replied, "To this there is one answer—and but one. He should become an intelligent citizen of the United States. There is no other 'manifest destiny' for any man or any body of men on our domain." Gates was no longer willing to wait until the Indians had proved their worth. "[B]y the stupendous precedent of eight millions of freedmen made citizens in a day," he declared, "we have committed ourselves to the theory that the way to fit men for citizenship is to make them citizens."[57] In the following year the Lake Mohonk Conference formally adopted Gates's view:

> It is our conviction that the duties of citizenship are of such a nature that they can only be learned by example and practice, and we believe that quicker and surer progress in industry, education, and morality will be secured by giving citizenship first than by making citizenship depend upon the attainment of any standard of education and conduct; and we therefore urge upon Congress the necessity of ceasing to treat the Indians as incapable of bearing responsibilities, and the advantages of compelling them to undertake

[56] *Report of the Board of Indian Commissioners*, 1884, pp. 7–10.
[57] Gates's paper was endorsed by the Board of Indian Commissioners and attached to its annual report. *Report of the Board of Indian Commissioners*, 1885, pp. 13–35. Quotation is from p. 17.

the same responsibilities that we impose upon all other human beings competent to distinguish right from wrong.[58]

There were more cautious voices, however. Dr. Bland of the Indian Defence Association described citizenship as "just such a policy as those who hang about the borders of Indian reservations, awaiting an opportunity to rob the Indians of their lands, would propose, if they dared." Less radical men than Bland did not want to push the Indians headlong into citizenship without guarding them from a precipitous descent into pauperdom. Secretary of the Interior Lamar, meeting in November, 1885, with a committee from the Lake Mohonk Conference, answered a question about making the Pueblos citizens by declaring: "After swallowing four million black slaves and digesting that pretty well we need not strain at this. We could do that; but in my opinion it would be most sad service to the Indian, and there would not be much of him left if that were done suddenly." But most important was Senator Dawes, the towering figure in Indian reform legislation. He persisted in his opinion that indiscriminate granting of citizenship to all Indians would be bad and held to the position that citizenship should be tied to taking land in severalty.[59] The provisions on citizenship in the Dawes Severalty Act, however, were a compromise:

And every Indian born within the territorial limits of the United States to whom allotments shall have been made under the provisions of this act, or under any law or treaty, and every Indian born within the territorial limits of the United States who has voluntarily taken up, within said limits, his residence separate and apart from any tribe of Indians therein, and has adopted the habits of civilized life, is hereby declared to be a citizen of the United States, and is entitled to all the rights, privileges, and immunities of such citizens, whether said Indian has been or not, by birth or otherwise, a member of any tribe of Indians within the territorial limits of the United States without in any manner impairing or otherwise affecting the right of any such Indian to tribal or other property.[60]

[58] *Lake Mohonk Conference Proceedings*, 1886, p. 46.
[59] *The Council Fire*, IX, 29, quoted in Priest, *Uncle Sam's Stepchildren*, pp. 210–11; *Report of the Board of Indian Commissioners*, 1885, p. 116; Priest, *Uncle Sam's Stepchildren*, pp. 211–12.
[60] *United States Statutes at Large*, XXIV, 390.

As a compromise, it did not fully satisfy either faction. Dawes complained about the House amendment to his bill that had provided citizenship for others than allottees under the severalty provisions of the bill. Advocates of immediate citizenship for all Indians were disappointed because tribal Indians on reservations were still excluded.[61]

The Indians frequently did not welcome federal citizenship, and the effects of citizenship in the end were meager, for the actual situation of the Indians was changed very little. Citizenship did not impair tribal law or affect tribal existence. It was not considered incompatible with federal powers of guardianship, nor was it inconsistent with restriction on the right to alienate property.[62] The great drive to make American citizens out of the Indians that reformers like Indian Commissioner Morgan and the members of the Lake Mohonk Conference undertook in the late 1880's and the 1890's through a system of national Indian schools was not a matter of legal citizenship but of cultural amalgamation of the Indians into the mass of white citizens, a much more comprehensive matter.

[61] The movement toward universal Indian citizenship continued. An act of August 9, 1888, provided that an Indian woman should become an American citizen by marrying a citizen. *United States Statutes at Large*, XXV, 392. An act of May 3, 1901, declared all Indians in the Indian Territory citizens of the United States. *Ibid.*, XXXI, 1447. On November 6, 1919, Congress provided that every Indian war veteran, if he desired, could be granted full citizenship by a court of competent jurisdiction. *Ibid.*, XLI, 350. Finally, on June 2, 1924, all Indians who were not yet citizens, about one-third of the total, were granted citizenship. *Ibid.*, XLIII, 253.

[62] Cohen, *Federal Indian Law*, pp. 155–57.

CHAPTER 12

CIVIL SERVICE REFORM

The just solution of the Indian problem depends upon a wise and comprehensive management of Indian affairs. Such management is as important as legislation regulating Indian citizenship and individual tenure of land. Careful and intelligent training in all civilizing methods and practices is now indispensable, and this can be expected only from an administration of Indian affairs resting upon business principles, and consequently ensuring consistent action and stability of purpose. The happy issue of the Indian question lies, therefore, in the total separation of the Indian Bureau from mere partisan control.

—Report of a Special Committee
of the National Civil-Service
Reform League, 1887

✿✿✿✿✿✿✿

The Indian reformers realized, implicitly if not always explicitly, that their programs and policies for Indian betterment depended upon the quality of the men who administered them. Without honest and competent men in the Indian service, the best laid plans would amount to little. Concomitant, therefore, with other proposals for reform was long-continuing agitation to improve the quality of the agents and of their subordinate personnel, and at times the drive to ensure adequate staffing of the agencies took on the characteristics of a major crusade.[1]

---

[1] In the decades after the Civil War, there was a continual plea on the part of Interior Department officials and the humanitarian reformers for an increase in the pay of Indian agents. The $1,500 per year that agents received was insufficient to attract men of capacity and integrity. See, for example, Report of the Secretary of the Interior, 1867, in serial 1326, p. 9; *ibid.*, 1888, in serial 2636, pp. xxix–xxx; Report of the Com-

One such movement came with Grant's peace policy. The graft that flourished in the Indian Office and on the reservations was a major target of the early post-Civil War reformers, who attacked the political appointments that had corrupted the service. But the dream of turning the agencies into little mission enclaves, with incorruptible Christian agents working for humanitarian reasons and not for financial gain and surrounded by teachers, mechanics, and other workers who were motivated by the same high ideals, did not work. Goodwill was not enough to reform the service permanently. Nor was the alternative of military control acceptable to the reformers, and their opposition prevented transfer of the Indian Bureau to the War Department. After the last great struggle for transfer in 1878, the proposal lost ground, especially since the situation in the West was no longer to any great degree a military one. The advantages that military officers might bring to agency management, however, were not lost sight of.

The cries against evils in the Indian service were in large measure quieted by Secretary of the Interior Carl Schurz's successful drive against corruption in his department. His appointment of a special commission to investigate the Indian service and his relentless removal of corrupt or incompetent workers gave the Indian Bureau an air of respectability that permitted the humanitarian watchdogs to devote their energies to the promotion of land in severalty and other positive programs to solve the Indian question.[2] Yet it was only a temporary calm. By the end of the 1880's a hue and cry was again raised against the politicization of the Indian service and the degradation that followed in its wake. For the better part of a decade a sustained drive to bring civil service reform to the Indian Bureau vied with education and a system of law for the Indians as the major concern of the Indian reformers.

There were several converging developments that gave impetus to the movement for reform in Indian administration. For one thing, the changes in political parties in the executive branch of the government that occurred with four-year regularity between 1884 and 1896

missioner of Indian Affairs, 1873, in serial 1601, pp. 377–78; *Lake Mohonk Conference Proceedings*, 1883, p. 12.

[2] Fuess, *Carl Schurz*, pp. 255–56. See also Report of the Commissioner of Indian Affairs, 1878, in serial 1850, pp. 439–40.

brought the spoils system into new prominence. The Democrats, capturing the presidency for the first time since the Civil War with the election of Grover Cleveland in 1884, had a hunger for the fruits of victory that could not be denied, and the house that had been cleaned out by Schurz began again to show unmistakably the messy accumulations of partisan favors. A special committee of the National Civil-Service Reform League reported that up to November 16, 1886, of sixty-one Indian agents appointed by the previous administration, only eleven remained and that at many agencies not only the agents but nearly all of the employees had been changed. "The conclusion is irresistible," the report concluded, "that the Indian Bureau has been managed in the interest of a party, and not primarily in the interest of the public service, and, consequently, that the administration of Indian affairs has been thrown into an unhappy and confused condition."[3] The chief villains were Commissioner of Indian Affairs J. D. C. Atkins and his Assistant Commissioner, Alexander B. Upshaw, described by the Indian Rights Association as "Tennessee politicians of small range and the most thoroughgoing partisan principles, who . . . regarded the Indian reservations as a green pasture where their political herds might comfortably browse and fatten."[4] The *Nation* exonerated Atkins as "much too simple-minded and good-natured for his place" and settled the blame on Upshaw. But it concluded that the Indian service had suffered as no other department had done from the change of administration in 1884.[5]

A second factor was the state of the Indian reform movement itself. In 1887, just as the worst evils of partisan appointments were beginning to be noticed, the humanitarians won the great victory they had been seeking, for the Dawes Act provided the land-in-severalty program that had been their most hoped for panacea. Individual allotments of land and the citizenship status that followed were considered by many to be the essential ingredients in a solution to the Indian

---

[3] *Extract, Report of the Special Committee of the National Civil-Service Reform League Upon the Present Condition of the Reform Movement* (Philadelphia, 1887), a pamphlet of the Indian Rights Association.

[4] *Report of the Indian Rights Association*, 1888, p. 32. A similar criticism of Atkins and Upshaw appears in Herbert Welsh, "Indian Affairs Under the Present Administration," *The Civil-Service Reformer*, IV (August, 1888), 90–92.

[5] "A Good Field for Reform," *Nation*, XLVI (March 15, 1888), 210–11.

problem. What was needed then was not new legislative programs for the Indians but careful and competent carrying out of the ones already enacted. "It will thus be seen," declared one prominent reformer, "that legislation has largely done its part, and that *administration* of Indian affairs now claims the most serious attention."[6] The key to administration, of course, was the Indian agent and his subordinates. Unless they were appointed on the basis of merit alone, they could hardly be depended upon to carry out the important work of the Dawes Act or the educational program that was coming to the fore.

The third element was the national movement for civil service reform, which provided ready-made principles and rules to govern the Indian reformers in purifying the Indian service. The Pendleton Act of 1883 supplied the necessary structure for reform, and the humanitarian friends of the Indian soon began a campaign to have the whole Indian service classified under the reform legislation.[7]

The driving force behind the growing demand that civil service rules be applied to the Indian service was the Indian Rights Association and most particularly its secretary, Herbert Welsh, who made the reform his principal goal for more than a decade. To Welsh, who hoped to bring good business methods into Indian administration, the matter was a simple one. "Civil-service reform," he said, "is simply the putting into operation of a principle which is universally recognized in all business affairs excepting those of the government. . . . It is the selection of officials and employees on account of fitness, not on account of partisan politics, and their retention, so long as their work is well done."[8] The subject occupied much of the association's attention in 1886 and continued to be one of its primary activities. A long series of pamphlets and flyers began to appear from the press of the association, and its agent in Washington also brought to bear whatever pressure he could. At first it seemed that no headway was possible, but persistence in calling attention to the need and the support of other reforming groups began to tell.

[6] James E. Rhoads, *Our Next Duty to the Indians* (Philadelphia, 1887), p. 5.
[7] A detailed monograph on civil service reform is Adelbert Bower Sageser, *The First Two Decades of the Pendleton Act: A Study of Civil Service Reform* (Lincoln, 1935). The progress of the reform can also be traced in the annual *Report of the United States Civil Service Commission.*
[8] *Lake Mohonk Conference Proceedings*, 1891, pp. 74–75.

As the executive committee reported in 1888: "Messrs. Atkins and Upshaw were pursued in their predatory course by the incessant exposures and criticisms of the Indian Rights Association; these, passing through many channels of influence, finally produced tangible results. The Commissioner resigned his post, to follow less sharply contested ambitions; while the power for evil of the Assistant Commissioner rapidly diminished, if it did not wholly cease, and he also at last resigned."[9] William F. Vilas, who became Secretary of the Interior in January, 1888, was willing to listen to the pleas of the reformers, and in October, 1888, John H. Oberly, a member of the Civil Service Commission who had formerly been Superintendent of Indian Education and a man who met the high standards of public and personal integrity set by the Indian Rights Association, was appointed Commissioner of Indian Affairs.[10] Oberly found a difficult task, that of restoring a disorganized and demoralized service to a state of efficiency, and before the Commissioner had completed a month of service, President Cleveland was defeated at the polls and the Republican Benjamin Harrison elected to the presidency. It seemed that the hard-won victories of the reformers were to be lost and that a new round of spoilsmanship might well begin.

Welsh determined to meet the danger by campaigning to retain Oberly as Commissioner under the new administration. If he could succeed in this, he would strike a blow at the spoils system, set a precedent for future times, and provide an opportunity for an upright Commissioner to retain and to appoint qualified men in the service. Welsh was unable to break such a sturdy barrier, however, and he had to be satisfied with his second choice, Thomas J. Morgan, who saw pretty much eye to eye with the humanitarian reformers and was determined in his own way to improve the quality and efficiency of the Indian service.[11]

Morgan's initial report must have given Welsh and his friends con-

[9] Report of the Indian Rights Association, 1888, p. 32.

[10] Harper's Weekly praised Oberly highly for his experience and his ability and regarded his appointment as "an earnest of the President's wish to put Indian affairs into the most competent hands." XXXII (October 13, 1888), 771.

[11] The Question of Indian Commissioner Oberly's Retention (Philadelphia, 1889), an Indian Rights Association pamphlet, contains statements of Welsh and Charles C. Painter in favor of retaining Oberly. See also Report of the Indian Rights Association, 1889, pp. 10–11.

siderable satisfaction, for the new Commissioner declared, "The chief thing to be considered in the administration of this office is the character of the men and women employed to carry out the designs of the Government." He favored integrity, justice, patience, and good sense, and said that dishonesty, injustice, favoritism, and incompetency had no place in the Indian service.[12]

The disastrous outbreak of the Sioux in 1890, shortly after Morgan had taken office, furnished substantial fuel for the fires of the civil service reformers. The Sioux, indeed, had many grievances, for the goals of the reformers among them had not been attained. The reduction of the Great Sioux Reserve, which men like Dawes believed would move the Indians more rapidly toward acculturation and perhaps quiet once and for all the clamors for opening up tribal lands, was for the Sioux a great disaster. When the rations promised by the Crook Commission failed to come because of Congressional parsimony, frustration and resentment mounted. "Despair came again," Red Cloud said, and the Sioux were ready to grasp at any promise that could restore some of the hope and well-being of the old times.[13]

Then news came of a messiah, who held out a vision of a new paradise. Far to the west in a remote corner of Nevada a Paiute shaman named Wovoka was preaching a wonderful message, compounded of Christian doctrines and Indian mysticism. During an eclipse of the sun in January, 1889, Wovoka, lying delirious with fever, claimed to have been transported to heaven, where he spoke with God and saw departed Indians living in peace and happiness. God gave Wovoka a message to take back to earth: If the Indian people would obey Wovoka's preaching, they might join their ancestors in the heaven Wovoka had seen. The Indians were to remain at peace, living honest, virtuous, and industrious lives, and were to perform a ghost dance that God taught to the messiah. After displays of apparently supernatural control of the elements, the Paiutes followed Wovoka with enthusiasm,

[12] Report of the Commissioner of Indian Affairs, 1889, in serial 2725, p. 4.
[13] The best work on the Sioux troubles is Utley, *Last Days of the Sioux Nation*, and I have relied upon it for my account. Utley has a solid grasp of the pertinent sources, and his judgments are balanced and convincing.

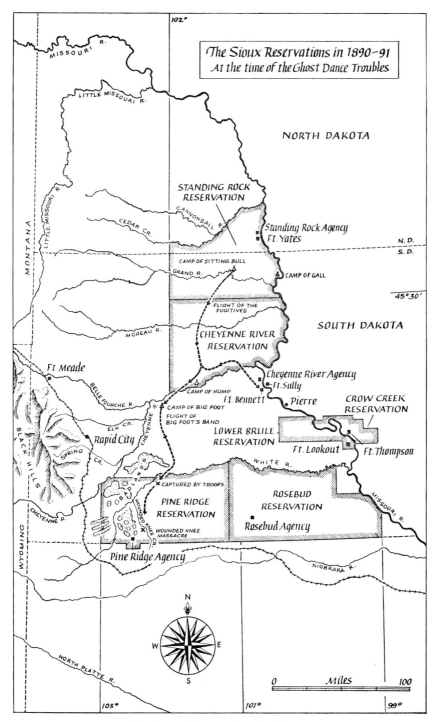

The Sioux Reservations in 1890–91

and news of the wonderworker quickly spread to nearly every reservation in the West.[14]

The Sioux, like many other tribes, sent a delegation to Wovoka to investigate the new religion. The emissaries, returning to the reservations in March, 1890, told wonderful tales of the messiah. Modifying the nonviolent peace message of Wovoka, however, the Sioux made it into one of antagonism toward the whites, who were held responsible for the present misery of the tribes, and they held councils to propagate the new ideas. At first little disturbance was caused, and the Indian agents, though reprimanding the leaders for their councils, did not take the ghost dance religion seriously. Had the troubles of the Sioux not multiplied during the summer of 1890, it is possible that Wovoka's teachings and the ghost dance would have quietly faded away as they did in other tribes. But the specter of hunger still rode over the Dakota reservations, as Congress failed to restore the ration cut and the promising crops of early summer were destroyed by the scorching heat of midsummer. "For the Sioux country in that year was a veritable dust bowl. . . ," wrote one of the schoolteachers on the reservation. "The pitiful little gardens curled up and died in the persistent hot winds. Even young men displayed gaunt limbs and lackluster faces. Old folks lost their hold on life, and heart-broken mothers mourned the last of a series of dead babies."[15] Under such conditions other grievances assumed mountainous proportions. New boundary lines between reservations upset traditional tribal ties, and the taking of a census presaged in the minds of the Indians still another ration cut. The restlessness of the Indians led to movements of troops into uncomfortably close proximity to the reservations.[16]

[14] The most thorough study of the ghost dance religion is James Mooney, *The Ghost-Dance Religion and the Sioux Outbreak of 1890* (Fourteenth Annual Report of the Bureau of Ethnology, 1892–93, Part II, Washington, 1896). A briefer, more popular exposition by the same author is "The Indian Ghost Dance," *Collections of the Nebraska State Historical Society*, XVI (1911), 168–82. For a biography of the messiah, see Paul D. Bailey, *Wovoka, The Indian Messiah* (Los Angeles, 1957). An excellent annotated bibliography of the numerous accounts of the ghost dance among the Sioux and of the outbreak that resulted is in Utley, *Last Days of the Sioux Nation*, pp. 287–301.

[15] Elaine Goodale Eastman, "The Ghost Dance War and Wounded Knee Massacre of 1890–91," *Nebraska History*, XXVI (January-March, 1945), 29.

[16] An excellent, temperate account of the development of the Sioux crisis with a listing of twelve "causes of the trouble" appears in Report of the Commissioner of Indian Affairs, 1891, in serial 2934, pp. 123–35.

The troubles and misery of the summer furnished an occasion for the nonprogressive chiefs once more to assert their leadership in opposition to government policies with a reasonable hope of gaining adherents from the progressive or uncommitted ranks. Sitting Bull at Standing Rock Agency, Hump and Big Foot at Cheyenne River, Red Cloud at Pine Ridge, and a group of conservatives at Rosebud began to take courage that the old ways might yet be saved. The deep distress of the Sioux offered a favorable climate for their efforts, and when the most aggressive of the ghost dance apostles, Kicking Bear, returned in midsummer from a visit to the Arapahos and told of the regeneration of that tribe through Wovoka's religion, he gained important converts. Ghost dances multiplied among the Sioux, the dancers garbed in ghost shirts supposed to be invested with magic qualities that made the wearers invulnerable to bullets. Trances were common, with visions of the earth regenerated and repeopled by the Indians. In alarm, as the craze spread, the Indian agents warned of its dangers and attempted with little success to suppress it with the agency police. Hump and Big Foot enthusiastically espoused the new religion at Cheyenne River Agency, and at Standing Rock Sitting Bull became its apostle.

To meet this growing challenge to government authority, there were new and ineffectual agents, spawned by the spoils system. James McLaughlin at Standing Rock was a man of experience and ability, although he was faced with troubles enough in handling the shrewd Sitting Bull. At Cheyenne River, a Republican without experience, Perain P. Palmer, was cast in the difficult role of dealing with Kicking Bear, Hump, and Big Foot. But the greatest crisis of leadership came at Pine Ridge, where the powerful McGillicuddy had fallen victim to the system. He had been replaced in 1886 by the well meaning but weak Democrat, Hugh Gallagher; in October, 1890, Gallagher in turn was dismissed to make room for the patronage appointment of a South Dakota Republican, Daniel F. Royer, whom the Indians in derision called Young-Man-Afraid-of-Indians. Royer soon lost all control of the situation as the dancers openly defied him and his police. On November 15, the frantic agent telegraphed for troops: "Indians are dancing in the snow and are wild and crazy.... *We need protection and we need it now.*"[17] Two days later the order was given to send troops to Pine

[17] Royer to R. V. Belt, November 15, 1890, quoted in Utley, *Last Days of the Sioux Nation*, p. 111.

Ridge and Rosebud. The coming of the soldiers excited the ghost dancers and united them in armed defiance of the government. The disaffected Pine Ridge and Rosebud Indians massed in the Bad Lands in the northwest corner of the Pine Ridge reservation and threw themselves into a continuous frenzy of dancing, although at other agencies the nearness of the troops seemed to bring a measure of quiet. General Nelson A. Miles, commanding the Division of the Missouri, prepared to restore order on the Sioux reservations, depending on military control rather than on the agents, whom he in principle considered incapable of the task.

To end the troubles, government officials proposed to arrest the ghost dance leaders. High on the government's list was Sitting Bull at Standing Rock. Although Agent McLaughlin opposed immediate arrest, General Miles issued an order to Buffalo Bill Cody, who had employed the Hunkpapa chief in his Wild West show, to arrest Sitting Bull. McLaughlin succeeded in getting Miles's order rescinded, but the problem of the reactionary chief remained. New efforts to arrest the chief by Indian police led to a shooting match between the chief's supporters and the police that left Sitting Bull dead, with seven of his Indians and six of the police.[18] At Cheyenne River Agency, Hump unexpectedly gave up without trouble, but Big Foot, befriending refugees from Sitting Bull's followers, was treated as an outlaw, and with his people he fled south from the reservation.

Meanwhile the hostiles in the Bad Lands, pressed by troops to the north and west and suffering from cold and weariness, moved in toward the Pine Ridge Agency to surrender. When Big Foot approached the Bad Lands, they had already moved out, and Big Foot and his band were intercepted by troops of the Seventh Cavalry under Major S. M. Whitside. Whitside led the band to a spot on Wounded Knee Creek, northeast of the agency, where they were surrounded by more troops from the Seventh Cavalry under Colonel George A. Forsyth, the regimental commander. On the following day, December 29, Forsyth prepared to disarm the Indians. The situation was tense and a small spark would cause an explosion. It soon came, as one of the Indians dis-

18 McLaughlin's own account of his relations with Sitting Bull and the death of the chief is in *My Friend the Indian*, pp. 179–222.

charged a concealed gun and the troops surrounding the camp, inter-preting it as an outbreak, opened fire on the encampment. Both sides fought in fury. Hotchkiss guns mounted on the overlooking hill raked the camp with murderous fire, catching many of the women and chil-dren. Fleeing Indians were shot down by the soldiers without discrimi-nation of age or sex. It was a terrible holocaust. A total of 146 Indians were buried on the battlefield, eighty-four men and boys, forty-four women, and eighteen children, many of whom had been frozen in dis-traught postures by the blizzard that swept down upon the scene after the massacre. Seven more Indians of the fifty-one wounded later died; how many more were carried away by the Indians is not known. The whites lost twenty-five killed and thirty-nine wounded.

The Indians from the Bad Lands who had come in to surrender be-came hostile again when the battle of Wounded Knee occurred. They attacked the agency and small troop detachments, but their efforts were half-hearted and by January 16, 1891, they had been rounded up again and surrendered. When General Miles left Pine Ridge for Chi-cago at the end of January, he took with him twenty-five ghost dance leaders to be imprisoned at Fort Sheridan. It was the end of the Indian wars.

The reaction to Wounded Knee was polarized in the popular press at two extremes.[19] Some papers saw the battle as a victorious triumph of the soldiers over treacherous Indians. Others condemned the action as a brutal revenge for Custer's defeat (the soldiers were of the same regiment), in which women and children had been wantonly butch-ered. Neither position was right, for neither side in the conflict had planned or foreseen the tragedy that occurred. Big Foot and his people sought peace, but they were afraid and suspicious and when the shoot-ing started they reacted violently. The soldiers fought back savagely against what they considered Indian treachery. "It is time that Wounded Knee be viewed for what it was—," a sober historian of the event concludes, "a regrettable, tragic accident of war that neither side intended, and that called forth behavior for which some indi-viduals on both sides, in unemotional retrospect, may be judged cul-

[19] Elmo Scott Watson, "The Last Indian War, 1890–91—A Study of Newspaper Jingoism," *Journalism Quarterly*, XX (September, 1943), 205–19.

pable, but for which neither side as a whole may be properly condemned."[20]

Wounded Knee convinced the advocates of reform more than ever that they were right. Herbert Welsh and his friends declared that the troubles could have been prevented had not the spoils system operated to weaken the administrative control so necessary at Pine Ridge. The executive committee of the Indian Rights Association, issuing a statement in 1891 called "A Crisis in Indian Affairs," discussed a number of causes of the Sioux outbreak—increased opposition of the non-progressive Indians as the progressive party gained strength, extreme suffering among the Sioux because of food shortages, and the religious fanaticism of the messiah craze. But then the committee came to its point: "These causes linked together produced serious conditions, but in our opinion, the danger might have been averted had it not been for the last, most potent and determining cause, viz.:—the spoils system of appointments in the management of the Indian service, which supplied at the two most critical points in the Sioux country—Pine Ridge and Cheyenne River Agencies—a disastrously inadequate management and control." It lashed out at the principle of leaving appointments effectively in the hands of local politicians, for such "home rule" paid no attention to the merits of the appointees. The urgings of the Indian Rights Association through two administrations, it lamented, had been largely in vain, for the spoils system had "continued on its remorseless way." "Perhaps," the committee suggested, "it is one of those evils from which without shedding of blood there is no remission."[21] Francis E. Leupp, the association's Washington agent, forcefully stated the same view: "There is no doubt—now that we can go back and study the Pine Ridge incident in the cold light of history—that all the upheaval, and riot, and bloodshed and suffering might have been spared if the first blunder had not been made in the removal of McGillicuddy—an act of political partisanship utterly hostile to the principles of Civil Service Reform."[22]

[20] Utley, *Last Days of the Sioux Nation*, p. 230.

[21] *A Crisis in Indian Affairs* (Philadelphia, 1891), p. 4. Welsh expressed his views in "The Meaning of the Dakota Outbreak," *Scribner's Magazine*, IX (April, 1891), 439–52.

[22] Francis E. Leupp, *Civil Service Reform Essential to a Successful Indian Administration* (Philadelphia, 1895), p. 7.

The humanitarians drew what comfort they could from the tragedy. Commissioner Morgan, speaking to the missionary boards in January, 1891, noted that the Sioux troubles were confined to a small locality compared with the whole extent of the Indian country and that the number of hostile Indians was less than three thousand compared with the total Indian population of 250,000. He urged his audience not to exaggerate the importance of the Sioux outbreak "in its relation to the great Indian question of the country," and he said with pride: "Do you know that the Government boarding school at Pine Ridge, at the seat of this trouble, has not been interrupted? It goes on to-day."[23] Merrill Gates at Lake Mohonk looked upon the outbreak as a source "of especial encouragement," for it showed that the United States could now deal with small groups of Indians as individuals under law and not undertake a war against a whole Indian nation. "I think that the Dakota disaster shows," he said, "that we shall not need to have taught us again the lesson of the difference between savagery and civilization."[24] The prevention of a general Indian war was proof to the reformers that their policies of education and civilization had been a success. Secretary of the Interior Noble spoke for them in his analysis of the outbreak as he pointed to the good behavior of the majority of the Indians. "They did not go upon the 'warpath' in the usual and aggressive way of Indians generally, and of the Sioux in particular," he noted. "The councils and efforts of much the larger portion of the tribe were for peace, and they rendered good service in persuading their turbulent brethren to submit to the authority of the United States. They were held in check, undoubtedly, by the influences of civilization, which had been brought to bear upon a large number of them by the work of the schools, by the practical training to industry, and by the labors of the faithful missionaries and religious institutions established among them. Christianity, education, and industrial discipline, with an intelligent appreciation by many of the power of the United States restrained them more than arms."[25] The Indian Rights Association offered General Miles "the sincere gratitude of the country" for the way he had managed the campaign, and Dr. Bland, although placing the blame on

---

[23] *Report of the Board of Indian Commissioners*, 1890, p. 166.
[24] *Lake Mohonk Conference Proceedings*, 1891, p. 8.
[25] Report of the Secretary of the Interior, 1891, in serial 2933, pp. lvi–lvii.

Congress and the army, saw "good results of the invasion" in the fact that it would arouse public sympathy for the Sioux and compel the government to redeem its pledges to them.[26]

The peace policy, however, had had to fall back upon military force in the crisis, and General Miles made use of the opportunity to implement his views that the army should run the reservations. In a series of orders in January, 1891, he assigned officers to duties at the Dakota agencies that brought divided authority and came close to negating civilian authority altogether. Commissioner Morgan fought back vigorously for the principle of civilian control. Before an open conflict between the two departments could materialize, however, an army reorganization in July, 1891, removed Miles from authority over the Sioux, and, although a military agent continued to run Pine Ridge, the other agencies returned to civilian management.[27]

The Sioux crisis gave new impetus to the movement for civil service reform. The missionary boards, meeting in January, 1891, passed resolutions in favor of the retention of agents with experience and "the extension of civil-service-reform regulations to the subordinate appointments in the Indian Department." And the Board of Indian Commissioners itself formally petitioned the President to the same end.[28] The pleas were not in vain, for on April 13, 1891, the President extended the civil service rules to cover all physicians, superintendents of schools, assistant superintendents, teachers, and matrons in the Indian service.[29] It was a substantial beginning, and the reformers rejoiced, but the success only whetted their appetites for more. The goal was to bring the rest of the agency employees under the classified service and then, if possible, make sure that the agents, too, were freed from the political rotation that interrupted the smooth continuation of

[26] *Report of the Indian Rights Association*, 1890, p. 31; T. A. Bland, *A Brief History of the Late Military Invasion of the Home of the Sioux* (Washington, 1891).

[27] Utley, *Last Days of the Sioux Nation*, pp. 277–82.

[28] *Report of the Board of Indian Commissioners*, 1890, pp. 4–5, 186.

[29] James D. Richardson, ed., *A Compilation of the Messages and Papers of the Presidents* (10 vols., Washington, 1896–1899), IX, 173; *Eighth Report of the United States Civil Service Commission, July 1, 1890, to June 30, 1891*, p. 72. The number covered was 626, divided as follows: superintendents, 87; assistant superintendents, 7; physicians and clerks, 111; teachers, 311; matrons, 110.

policy. If rules could not formally be extended, the reformers pleaded that the spirit at least of the law be followed.[30] If the Indians were to be fitted for citizenship, the spoils system would have to be abandoned entirely, Welsh declared in 1892. "We may tolerate the spoils system with its false appointments and its wanton removals in our post-offices and custom houses," he said, "but in the Indian service, which concerns the welfare of a people, where the fortunes of human beings—even life and death!—hang in the balance, it is wholly intolerable!"[31]

There was, however, a further expedient that could be employed in removing politics from the Indian service—a return to the assignment of army officers as Indian agents. The use of military men as agents, which President Grant had inaugurated in his attempt to head off partisan appointments, had quickly been stopped by Congress in 1870 by its law that army officers could not keep their commissions if they performed civilian duties, and the attempts in the 1870's to turn the Indian service entirely over to the military had never quite succeeded. Now, more than a decade after the final serious attempt at transfer had been defeated, army officers were again employed. The Indian appropriation bill of July 13, 1892, provided that thereafter when any vacancies occurred, the President was to detail army officers to fill them, although he could appoint civilians if the good of the service would be better promoted thereby. The military men were to act under the orders and direction of the Secretary of the Interior in their duties as agents.[32]

Support for this measure came principally from the Indian Rights Association. Herbert Welsh, returning from a visit to the Sioux reservations in 1892, recommended the appointment of "judiciously selected Army Officers to serve as Agents *at many of the Agencies* whose present incumbents are unsatisfactory," and the reports of the association

[30] *Lake Mohonk Conference Proceedings*, 1891, pp. 112–13; *ibid.*, 1892, pp. 10, 121; *ibid.*, 1893, pp. 141–42; *Report of the Board of Indian Commissioners*, 1891, p. 154; *ibid.*, 1892, p. 9; *ibid.*, 1894, p. 11; *ibid.*, 1895, p. 9; *Report of the Indian Rights Association*, 1894, p. 12.

[31] Herbert Welsh, *How to Bring the Indian to Citizenship, and Citizenship to the Indian* (Philadelphia, 1892), pp. 13–14. Welsh earlier had declared: "It is manifest that the great army of spoilsmen, the political boss, the ward 'rounder up' and 'heeler,' the impecunious, illiterate, hungry relative or hanger-on of representative or senator, is not as a rule suitable material with which to effect the education and civilization of the Indian." *The Civil-Service Reformer*, IV (August, 1888), 91.

[32] *United States Statutes at Large*, XXVII, 120–21.

commended the measure. Francis E. Leupp stressed the continuity that the military appointments would ensure, even to the point that although the officers might change, the uniform remained the same. "In this one respect at least," he noted, "a series of army officers are alike. In dealing with uniformed officers, the Indian does not have forced upon him in quite so pointed a way the fact that he has been passed from hand to hand."[33]

Other humanitarians, remembering no doubt the fearful cry that they had made against military control of Indians, were less sure that the move was a wise one. Commissioner Morgan regarded the policy "with grave apprehension," and although he admitted that the idea of stopping the spoils system was a good one, hoped it might be accomplished in some other way. He re-emphasized the point that the work of an agent was civil not military in nature and that an army officer's training did not fit him for it. The Board of Indian Commissioners, too, protested on the same grounds when the measure was before Congress, but they were willing to withhold judgment until the effects could be evaluated.[34] President Cleveland moved ahead under the new legislation. By the end of 1893, twenty-seven out of fifty-seven agencies were under the charge of army officers.[35]

Another proposal for getting around the political appointment of Indian agents was to eliminate the position altogether. Morgan made such a suggestion in his annual report of 1892, declaring that it was "entirely feasible and very desirable to modify the agency system and prepare the way for its complete abolition by placing the agency affairs, in certain cases, in the hands of school superintendents." He argued that on reservations where allotment had gone forward the work of the agent was greatly reduced, and he noted that the school superintendents were "generally men of high personal character and large business capacity." The Indian appropriations act of March 3, 1893,

[33] Herbert Welsh, *Civilization Among the Sioux Indians; Report of a Visit to Some of the Sioux Reservations of South Dakota and Nebraska* (Philadelphia, 1893), p. 58; *Report of the Indian Rights Association*, 1893, pp. 5–7; Leupp, *Civil Service Reform Essential to a Successful Indian Administration*, pp. 4–5.

[34] Report of the Commissioner of Indian Affairs, 1892, in serial 3088, pp. 10–12; *Report of the Board of Indian Commissioners*, 1893, p. 11. *The Independent* condemned the action of Congress and laid the responsibility on the Democrats seeking to forestall Republican appointments. XLIV (April 21, 1892), 550–51.

[35] Report of the Commissioner of Indian Affairs, 1893, in serial 3210, p. 6.

authorized the Commissioner, with the approval of the Secretary of the Interior, to assign the agent's duties to the superintendent at any agency where he felt the superintendent was qualified for the job. The agent's position at the Eastern Cherokee Agency in North Carolina, in fact, was abolished by the same law and the duties turned over to the school superintendent, but no other such assignments seem to have been made until after 1900.[36]

For employees below the level of agent, the civil service reformers won their case. By direction of President Cleveland, the Department of the Interior on March 30, 1896, amended the classification of the Indian service to include "all physicians, school superintendents, assistant superintendents, supervisors of schools, day school inspectors, school-teachers, assistant teachers, industrial teachers, teachers of industries, disciplinarians, kindergarten teachers, matrons, assistant matrons, farmers, seamstresses, and nurses." All of these, without regard to salary level, were made subject to competitive examination for appointment. Another order of the same date included "all clerks, assistant clerks, issue clerks, property clerks, and other clerical positions and storekeepers at Indian agencies and Indian schools." Furthermore, on May 6, 1896, the scope of the classified service was still further enlarged to include "all officers and employees, of whatever designation, except persons merely employed as laborers or workmen and persons who have been nominated for confirmation by the Senate." These regulations, however, did not apply to Indians themselves, who in increasing numbers were employed at the agencies.[37]

A report on personnel in the field in the Indian service on June 30, 1896, showed how extensively the civil service rules were applied. There were 552 white persons in the classified service and eighty-three in the unclassified service. Of the latter, there were thirty-eight agents, five inspectors, and five commissioners to the Five Civilized Tribes who held positions confirmed by the Senate; seventeen military officers acting as agents, three physicians paid for occasional services, three transportation agents, and twelve employees at compensation below classification levels. In addition there were 1,434 Indians, with Indians

[36] Ibid., 1892, in serial 3088, pp. 9–10; United States Statutes at Large, XXVII, 614; Sageser, Pendleton Act, p. 227.
[37] Report of the Commissioner of Indian Affairs, 1896, in serial 3489, pp. 3–4.

employed at all but two agencies. These figures did not include the Indian schools, which were entirely classified. There were 1,364 whites and 705 Indians employed in the schools. "The recognition of the merit system in the Indian service is a long step forward," the Commissioner of Indian Affairs said in 1896, "and will undoubtedly elevate its standard, improve its morale, and promote its efficiency. The removal of all partisan influence from appointments will give added dignity to the positions and increase the zeal of those engaged in the work."[38]

The Indian Rights Association reported in 1896 that that year had "probably been the most encouraging and satisfactory" that it had ever experienced. Even the fact that the key positions of agents and inspectors were excluded from the classified list could be overlooked, for the Cleveland administration had to a large extent applied the spirit of the reform in making nonpartisan appointments.[39]

The millenium, however, had not yet arrived. The Indian agent, the most important person in the field, was still subject to political machinations. The advent of the McKinley administration brought forebodings to the Indian reformers. The Indian Rights Association feared that a plan was afloat for getting rid of a number of the army officers who served as agents in order to make room for civilian appointees, who were more likely than the officers to serve local or personal interests at the cost of the Indians. And in fact the number of army officers in the service greatly declined.[40] The McKinley administration got low marks in general from the Indian Rights Association, which asserted in 1898 that the advances made in the two previous administrations had been negated and that affairs were worse than ever. After

---

[38] *Ibid.,* pp. 4–5.

[39] *Report of the Indian Rights Association,* 1896, p. 3; *Report of the Board of Indian Commissioners,* 1896, pp. 3–4. The civil service reform efforts of the Indian Rights Association brought the organization into sharp conflict with Richard Henry Pratt, head of the Carlisle Indian Industrial School. Pratt vigorously objected to the application of the civil service rules to Carlisle personnel, and more basically, objected to the emphasis put on civil service reform at the expense of educational efforts by the Indian Rights Association. The story is told in detail in Everett Arthur Gilcreast, "Richard Henry Pratt and American Indian Policy, 1877–1906: A Study of the Assimilation Movement" (unpublished Ph.D. dissertation, Yale University, 1967), pp. 284–99.

[40] *Report of the Indian Rights Association,* 1897, pp. 12–14. There was a steady decline in the number of army officers acting as agents; in 1898 there were only three out of a total of fifty-six agents. Report of the Commissioner of Indian Affairs, 1898, in serial 3757, pp. 1117–18.

noting the positive accomplishments of Harrison and Cleveland, the association concluded: "So far in the present administration the credit sheet remains virtually blank."[41] In 1900 the annual report devoted extensive space to accounts of the appointment of bad agents under the spoils system. The singlemindedness of the Indian Rights Association on this point is evident in its conclusion:

It may seem to the casual reader that an undue amount of space is devoted to the abuse of power on the part of the appointing officer, but when it is considered that the Indian Agent is really the key to the proper solution of the Indian problem, the importance of securing good men for these positions and retaining them so long as they faithfully perform their duties will be apparent. As a matter of fact, a great part of the Association's work during the past eighteen years has been to counteract the disastrous results too often caused by placing unworthy, if not dishonest, men in charge of Indian agencies. Had the Government selected the proper kind of agents and other employees, it is safe to say that the Indian problem would have been solved by this time, and the Indian Rights Association would never have been organized.[42]

The Board of Indian Commissioners, likewise, continued its agitation to include the agents in the classified civil service and for a strict application of the existing laws to correct abuses on the reservations. At the end of the century it repeated its conviction, "never more deeply felt, that *Indian agents should be appointed solely for merit and fitness for the work*, and *should be retained in the service when they prove themselves to be efficient and helpful by their* character and moral influence, as well as by their experience." The evils that still remained in the Indian service it attributed to "the partisan and political influences which still surround the appointment and removal of Indian agents."[43]

Like views about most panaceas, these views were too simple. Bureaucratic personnel, securely protected by civil service rules, were not necessarily enlightened in their administration of Indian affairs, nor

[41] *Report of the Indian Rights Association*, 1898, pp. 4–5; Sageser, *Pendleton Act,* p. 210.
[42] *Report of the Indian Rights Association*, 1900, p. 18.
[43] *Report of the Board of Indian Commissioners*, 1899, p. 22; *ibid.*, 1897, p. 12; *Lake Mohonk Conference Proceedings*, 1897, p. 115.

would perfection in administration alone have been able to solve the Indian problem. Once again the Indian reformers, seizing upon a remedy that was important in the general reform atmosphere of the day, mistakenly thought they had found the answer.

CHAPTER 13

LIQUIDATING THE INDIAN TERRITORY

A vague expectation of a coming change seems to prevail to a considerable extent in all parts of the Territory. . . . One thing is clear: the new order of things must include the abandonment of communism and seclusion. Great progress and improvement cannot be expected without individual ownership of the soil. A permanent home, and a right to all the value that labor may give it, form the great incentive to effort and enterprise. The Indian needs that incentive as much as the white man. The citizens of the Indian Territory need it now to lift them to a higher plane of civilization. . . .

The Indian Territory cannot always remain in seclusion, impeding commerce from ocean to ocean. The rapid growth of the country will ere long demand that it fall into line and join in the march of human progress.

—E. Whittlesey, Secretary
of the Board of Indian
Commissioners, 1882

❊❊❊❊❊❊❊

The dreams of the Indian reformers for the Americanization of all the Indians and the desire of western settlers for Indian lands that lay unused were long frustrated by the Indian Territory. Here were the Five Civilized Tribes—Cherokee, Creek, Choctaw, Chickasaw, and Seminole—who had advanced the farthest along the white man's road and who seemed most apt for final absorption into American society as individualized, land-owning citizens. Here too were rich acres only partially used by the Indians, which were coveted by white farmers as the surrounding states of Arkansas, Texas, and Kansas grew rapidly in population. The drive to destroy the Indian Territory and the independence of the Indians who inhabited it filled much of the period between the Civil War and 1900. It is an instructive story of the ultimate force of the reforming spirit, which, blocked time and again in its efforts to eradicate this last great obstacle to the fulfillment of its promise, by the end of the century, here too had triumphed.[1]

The Indian nations which had been moved to the Trans-Mississippi West in the 1830's had been guaranteed a large measure of independence and self-government. It had been a fundamental argument of those who proposed removal that in the West the Cherokees and other tribes would be free of white interference, no longer subjected to political harassment by state governments, and able to maintain their national identity and customs. When treaties of removal were signed, strong guarantees were included to protect the Indians' lands and their self-determination. The Choctaw treaty of 1830, for example, had these provisions:

> The United States under a grant specially to be made by the President of the U.S. shall cause to be conveyed to the Choctaw Nation a tract of country west of the Mississippi River, in fee simple to them and their descendants, to inure to them while they shall exist as a nation and live on it. . . .
>
> The Government and people of the United States are hereby obliged to secure to the said Choctaw Nation of Red People the jurisdiction and government of all the persons and property that may be within their limits west, so that no Territory or State shall ever have a right to pass laws for the government of the Choctaw Nation of Red People and their descendants; and that no part of the land granted them shall ever be embraced in any Territory or State; but the U.S. shall forever secure said Choctaw Nation from, and against, all laws except such as from time to time may be enacted in their own National Councils, not inconsistent with the Constitution, Treaties, and Laws of the United States; and except such as may,

[1] The most detailed and fully documented history of the changes in the Indian Territory is Roy Gittinger, *The Formation of the State of Oklahoma, 1803–1906* (Berkeley, California, 1917). Other histories of Oklahoma that have useful accounts are Grant Foreman, *A History of Oklahoma* (Norman, 1942); Arrell M. Gibson, *Oklahoma: A History of Five Centuries* (Norman, 1965); and Edward Everett Dale and Morris L. Wardell, *History of Oklahoma* (New York, 1948).

and which have been enacted by Congress, to the extent that Congress under the Constitution are required to exercise a legislation over Indian Affairs.[2]

Subsequent treaties with the other tribes contained similar clauses, and through the years the separate nations developed strong and largely independent governments.[3] Attempts to form a "Western Territory" based on a confederacy of the tribes were successfully beaten down, and the separate nations went their own ways under their own laws and generally prospered.

The Civil War, however, radically disrupted the Five Civilized Tribes. All of the nations, under pressure from the Confederacy and largely abandoned by the Union, signed treaties with the South and joined in the efforts of the war, although the Cherokees, Creeks, and Seminoles had large Union factions. The war ravaged the Indian Territory, and the factionalism of the war continued when the war ended, making reconstruction of the nations very difficult. The United States government intended to deal strongly with the Indians at the end of the war. A special commission, headed by Commissioner of Indian Affairs Dennis N. Cooley, met with tribal spokesmen at Fort Smith, Arkansas, in September, 1865. For its guidelines the commission had a letter of instruction from Secretary of the Interior James Harlan, dated August 16, 1865, and a bill for the organization of the Indian Territory (known as the Harlan Bill), passed by the Senate on March 2, 1865.[4] Cooley offered treaty arrangements to the Indians, in which the following were key stipulations:

1. Each tribe must enter into a treaty for permanent peace and amity with themselves, each nation and tribe, and with the United States....

3. The institution of slavery, which has existed among several of the tribes, must be forthwith abolished, and measures taken for the unconditional emancipation of all persons held in bondage, and for their incorporation in the tribes on an equal footing with the original members, or suitably provided for....

[2] Kappler, *Indian Affairs*, II, 311.
[3] See Creek treaty, *ibid.*, p. 343, and Cherokee treaty, *ibid.*, p. 442.
[4] Harlan's letter is in Annie Heloise Abel, *The American Indian under Reconstruction* (Cleveland, 1925), pp. 219–26.

5. A portion of the lands hitherto owned and occupied by you must be set apart for the friendly tribes in Kansas, and elsewhere, on such terms as may be agreed upon by the parties and approved by the government, or such as may be fixed by the government.

6. It is the policy of the government, unless other arrangement be made, that all the nations and tribes in the Indian territory be formed into one consolidated government after the plan proposed by the Senate of the United States, in a bill for organizing the Indian territory.[5]

That the intention of Secretary Harlan and Commissioner Cooley was to incorporate the Five Civilized Tribes fully into the American political system can be seen from the Harlan Bill. The measure would have erected the existing Indian Territory into a regular territory of the United States, with a governor appointed by the President having an absolute veto over the legislative council and acting *ex officio* as superintendent of Indian affairs. Tribal citizens would elect a council, and the territory thus constituted would send a delegate to Congress.[6]

The Indian nations refused to accede to such an arrangement, and the Fort Smith negotiations accomplished no more than an agreement to renew friendship between the tribes and the United States.[7] In 1866, however, treaties were signed with the Five Civilized Tribes, which while not going as far as the Cooley commission had suggested, specified new relations with the United States. The Indians sold large parts of their land to the United States for use by other Indians, thus dividing the Indian Territory roughly in two; the Five Civilized Tribes retained the eastern half, while the remainder was to be used as homes for western tribes who were to be settled on reservations as part of the government's policy of consolidation. Slavery was prohibited, and the freedmen were granted certain rights within the nations. Finally, the

[5] The stipulations are included in Cooley's report as president of the treaty commission, October 30, 1865, in Report of the Commissioner of Indian Affairs, 1865, in serial 1248, pp. 482–83. Proceedings of the council are printed *ibid.*, pp. 496–537. Accounts of the proceedings at Fort Smith are given in Gittinger, *Formation of the State of Oklahoma*, pp. 71–78, and in Abel, *Indian under Reconstruction*, pp. 173–218.

[6] Senate Bill 459, 38 Congress, 2 session. Abel, *Indian under Reconstruction*, pp. 219–67, has a long discussion of the bill, including a transcript of much of the Senate debate on the matter.

[7] The agreement is in Report of the Commissioner of Indian Affairs, 1865, in serial 1248, pp. 514–15.

treaties, although restoring annuities and other treaty rights cut off during the war and continuing local governmental control by the Indians themselves, pointed toward the organization of a general council of the Five Civilized Tribes and ultimate territorial status.[8]

Agitation began almost immediately to develop the last of these provisions. The pattern was drawn by Ely S. Parker, Commissioner of Indian Affairs, who urged in 1869 that action be taken to organize the general council spoken of in the treaties of 1866. "The accomplishment of this much-desired object," he said, "will give the Indians a feeling of security in the permanent possession of their homes, and tend greatly to advance them in all the respects that constitute the character of an enlightened and civilized people. The next progressive step would be a territorial form of government, followed by their admission into the Union as a State."[9]

After inconclusive meetings of an intertribal council in 1867 and 1869, a new council at Okmulgee in December, 1870, approved a constitution for a unified Indian territory and future Indian state, which it submitted to the federal government. President Grant, in sending this Okmulgee Constitution to Congress, spoke of the action in laudatory terms: "This is the first indication of the aborigines desiring to adopt our form of government, and it is highly desirable that they become self-sustaining, self-relying, Christianized, and civilized. If successful in this their first attempt at territorial government, we may hope for a gradual concentration of other Indians in the new Territory." But the President noted as well that certain elements of the constitution were unacceptable in their exclusion of the United States from the general control it exerted over territories. The constitution, however, failed to be ratified by the Indian nations and never went into effect.[10] The

[8] Kappler, *Indian Affairs: Laws and Treaties*, II, 910–15 (Seminole); 918–31 (Choctaw and Chickasaw); 931–37 (Creek); 942–50 (Cherokee). The Seminoles were completely relocated; the Cherokees did not give up any land but agreed to let friendly Indians settle in tribal reservations on Cherokee lands west of the 96th meridian.

[9] Report of the Commissioner of Indian Affairs, 1869, in serial 1414, pp. 450–51.

[10] Letter of Grant, January 30, 1871, *Senate Executive Document* No. 26, 41 Congress, 3 session, serial 1440, p. 1. This document includes a copy of the Constitution and of the proceedings of the Council. The journal is reprinted in "Journal of the General Council of the Indian Territory," *Chronicles of Oklahoma*, III (April, 1925), 33–44; (June, 1925), 120–36. A good discussion of the Okmulgee Constitution and its failure is in Allen G. Applen, "An Attempted Indian State Government: The Okmulgee Constitution in Indian Territory, 1870–1876," *Kansas Quarterly*, III (Fall, 1971), 89–99.

council continued for some time to meet annually, but no further moves were made toward the unification of the territory that had been the thrust of the constitution; the council, on the contrary, became a strong force opposing federal plans for territorial organization.

The persistent efforts to bring an end to tribal control and to establish a regular territorial government were reflected in the numerous bills introduced into Congress for that purpose.[11] One such measure was that introduced on March 17, 1870, by Senator Benjamin F. Rice of Arkansas, for the organization of the "Territory of Ok-la-homa." The favorable report of the bill by the Committee on Territories proposed the general argument that the Indians, or at least a large proportion of them, were fitted for citizenship and should be admitted to its rights and duties. "It is in consonance with the new policy of the government, born of the war and matured by the fifteenth amendment," the report said, "that no alien race shall exist upon our soil; all shall be citizens irrespective of race, color, or previous condition of servitude. It is a part of the inexorable logic of the times that the Indian must adapt himself to the rights and duties of citizenship. He must wield the franchise and fulfill the obligations imposed thereby, otherwise he will gradually disappear as the waste soil becomes more and more absorbed by the increasing necessities of agriculture."[12] At the heart of the matter was the conviction that there were too few Indians on too much land, that if the Indians could be forced to work 160-acre homesteads of their own, they would find their salvation and the rest of the land could be put into profitable production by whites.[13]

Aside from the purported advantages to the Indians from territorial government, American citizenship, and land in severalty, the advocates of territorial organization made much of what they considered the lawlessness of the Indian Territory. The Indian governments were criticized as ineffective, the courts as inadequate, and the protection of the rights of whites and freedmen as almost completely lacking. What

[11] A list of the principal bills introduced between 1865 and 1879 to organize the Indian Territory or otherwise to extend federal jurisdiction over the area is given in Gittinger, *Formation of the State of Oklahoma*, pp. 221–23.

[12] *Senate Report* No. 131, 41 Congress, 2 session, serial 1409, p. 4.

[13] See statements of this view, for example, in *Senate Report* No. 336, 41 Congress, 3 session, serial 1443; Report of the Secretary of the Interior, 1871, in serial 1505, pp. 7–8.

severely complicated the matter was the growing number of whites within the Five Civilized Tribes. Some of these were intermarried into the tribes or adopted as tribal citizens and caused no special problem. A few others were simply intruders, who infiltrated into the Territory unbidden and unwanted. The great majority, however, were farmers or other laborers who had been invited in by the Indians to work. Although all the Five Civilized Tribes prohibited the leasing of the Indian lands, contracts or permits were given to whites to open up farms in return for a share of the crops. By such means ambitious Indians or mixed-bloods were able to establish large holdings not greatly different from ante-bellum plantations. The discovery of coal near McAlester in 1872 brought an influx of whites to work the mines, and railroad construction in the Indian Territory augmented still more the number of whites within the Indian nations. Since the tribal governments pertained to the Indians alone, the demand arose for an adequate means to protect the personal and property rights of the whites. "The lawless condition of the Territory," Secretary of the Interior Delano noted in 1873, "the growing insecurity of life and property, and the manifest indisposition of the tribes there resident to accept voluntarily any improved form of government whereby existing difficulties might be avoided, would seem to call for some legislation to effect an improvement in the status of the Territory." In the following year the Secretary spoke of the Indian Territory as "a resort for lawless men and criminals, who take refuge thus in order to avoid the restraints incident to an efficient government, or to escape the penalties due for crimes elsewhere committed."[14]

As the years passed and the white population continued to increase, the complaints rose, and the patience of the federal officials was severely strained. Secretary of the Interior Zachariah Chandler declared in 1876 that the necessity of devising some simple and satisfactory form of government for the Indian Territory was growing more and more urgent and soon had to be met. His Commissioner of Indian Affairs, John Q. Smith, was more outspoken. "The anomalous form of government, if government it can be called, at present existing in the Indian Territory must soon be changed . . . ," he wrote. "The idea that that

---

[14] *Ibid.*, 1873, in serial 1601, p. x; *ibid.*, 1874, in serial 1639, p. xiv.

Territory is to consist forever of a collection of little independent or semi-independent nationalities is preposterous."[15]

Congressional pressures did not subside. The Senate in February, 1878, instructed its Committee on Territories to ascertain whether a civil form of government could not be organized over the Indian Territory for the better protection of life and property and whether the lands held in common could not be divided in severalty without confirming the conditional grants of lands made to railroads.[16] The committee took its charge seriously, sending members to the Indian Territory to interview inhabitants and collecting extensive historical documentation. It was the first of a number of extensive investigations of the conditions in the Territory and resulted in a massive volume of evidence.[17] The committee confirmed the previous analysis of the situation. It found twenty thousand white and black citizens of the United States lawfully residing among the Five Civilized Tribes and almost without the protection of any law against violence and crime. The committee recommended the establishment within the Territory of a United States court having criminal and civil jurisdiction, that the Indians should become citizens of the United States, and that they should have representation in Congress similar to that of other territories. It asserted that the lands could be divided in severalty without confirming the railroad grants, but it did not press the matter of individual allotment.[18]

The agitation for changes in the Indian Territory in the 1870's bore no fruit. Bill after bill was introduced in Congress but all failed. Although the arguments were repeated without end and the conditions complained about not only did not disappear but worsened, opponents of territorial organization were able to hold off the threat of radical change.

Among these opponents the Indians themselves were foremost. The

[15] *Ibid.*, 1876, in serial 1749, p. vii; Report of the Commissioner of Indian Affairs, 1876, in serial 1749, p. 390.
[16] Resolution of February 25, 1878, *Senate Miscellaneous Document* No. 77, 45 Congress, 2 session, serial 1786.
[17] *Senate Report* No. 744, 45 Congress, 3 session, serial 1839.
[18] *Ibid.*, pp. i–v.

Five Civilized Tribes had astute and articulate spokesmen, who countered each congressional move toward territorial organization with forceful memorials protesting the action. Many of the memorials were drawn up and presented by the national delegates maintained in Washington to look after tribal interests and to oppose any change in the political status or in the land tenure system. Other protests came from the intertribal council or from principal chiefs of the various nations.[19] An example of the common concern was the Creek protest against the proposed legislation of 1870:

> We need not remind you that the establishment of such a government over us would work our ruin and speedy extinction, by subjecting us to the absolute rule of a people foreign to us in blood, language, customs, traditions, and interest, who would speedily possess themselves of our homes, degrade us in our own estimation, and leave us a prey to the politician and land speculator, thus destroying the unity of our race, and producing national disintegration.[20]

The Indians' first defense was to rely upon the treaties which had guaranteed them self-government without white interference, and their memorials skillfully marshaled the historical evidence in support of their position. They denied, moreover, the condition of lawlessness, which was the foundation for so much of the pro-territorial argument. The Creek and Cherokee delegates in 1873, for example, attacked the report of the House Committee on Territories:

> Throughout this report, and in the arguments used to you against us, it is continually assumed that the Indian country is the theater of violence and lawlessness; that there is no adequate government machinery; that immense herds of Texas cattle are stopped at our border and cannot cross to market; that railroads cannot be built; that emigrants cannot pass; that white men can only be tried in Indian tribunals; that the "necessities of civilization" are in agony,

[19] A convenient listing of these memorials, together with other pertinent documents, appears in Foreman, *History of Oklahoma*, pp. 363–66. For an account of the activity of one of the tribal delegates, see W. David Baird, *Peter Pitchlynn: Chief of the Choctaws* (Norman, 1972), pp. 181–212.

[20] Creek resolution of February 10, 1870, *Senate Miscellaneous Document* No. 76, 41 Congress, 2 session, serial 1408, p. 3.

and that a savage Indian, with war-point and tomahawk, stands guard at the gateway of civilization.

The absurdity of such statements, made to your honorable bodies by outside parties here, is only equalled by its mendacity. It is high time that your confidence should cease to be abused by such mischievous falsehoods.[21]

They made a point by point refutation of the charges.

The thrust of the white policy was well understood by the Indians. The "inexorable logic of the times" brought a sharp rejoinder from the Indian delegates: "Ah! this is the plea of 'manifest destiny' again." The argument signified that "the Indian must be compelled to abandon his present organized government, surrender what he has, and disappear before the white race."[22]

No referendum was taken among the Indians to determine the desires of the Indian population as a whole, and each side claimed that the mass of the people was behind it. When the Board of Indian Commissioners in 1874 made a strong recommendation for territorial organization and claimed that such action "would receive the hearty indorsement of a great majority of the inhabitants of the Territory," the Chickasaws and Creeks immediately responded with memorials strongly contradicting the judgment of the board.[23] The Cherokee advocate of territorial status, Elias Cornelius Boudinot, asserted that the Indians would acclaim such legislation if presented to them fairly and that they had been "humbugged and deceived" by the tribal delegates, but he was not supported by many.[24]

A basic fear of the Indians was that proposed changes would mean the ultimate loss of their lands. Especially disturbing were the conditional land grants made by Congress in July, 1866, to railroad corpora-

[21] Protest of Creek and Cherokee delegates, March 3, 1873, *House Miscellaneous Document* No. 110, 42 Congress, 3 session, serial 1573, p. 2.

[22] Memorial of Cherokee, Creek, and Choctaw delegates, May 23, 1870, *Senate Miscellaneous Document* No. 143, 41 Congress, 2 session, serial 1408, p. 11.

[23] *Report of the Board of Indian Commissioners,* 1874, pp. 12–14, 97–100; Chickasaw memorial, January 15, 1875, *Senate Miscellaneous Document* No. 34, 43 Congress, 2 session, serial 1630; Creek memorial, January 26, 1875, *Senate Miscellaneous Document* No. 71, 43 Congress, 2 session, serial 1630.

[24] Elias Cornelius Boudinot, *Oklahoma: Argument of Col. E. C. Boudinot before the Committee on Territories, January 29, 1878* (Alexandria, Virginia, 1878), p. 32.

tions for building lines through the Indian Territory. Ten or twenty alternate sections of land along the right of way were granted to the companies "whenever the Indian title shall be extinguished by treaty or otherwise" and the lands became part of the public domain.[25] The Indians charged that territorial organization and the end of tribal independence would fulfill the conditions and that the land would then fall to the railroads. Most of the Indian protests adverted to the danger inherent in the railroad grants, and there was impressive support for the Indian position on the matter. Bills proposed for territorial organization at the end of the 1870's added sections specifically repealing the earlier conditional grants.[26]

The Indians, of course, did not lack support. Cattlemen who benefited from leasing of Indian lands fought for the maintenance of the status quo, and many persons agreed with the Indians' analysis of their treaty rights. A strong minority report from the House Committee on Territories was lodged against one of the proposed territory bills on the basis that the bill would contravene treaty agreements and that the movement for territorial organization came from the railroads. "[T]hese soulless corporations," it said, "hover like greedy cormorants over this Territory, and incite Congress to remove all restraint, and allow them to swoop down and swallow over twenty-three million acres of land of this Territory, destroying alike the last hope of the Indian and the honor of the Government."[27] In 1879 the House Committee on Territories reported unfavorably on a bill to organize the Territory and divide the land in severalty, arguing that the measure would conflict with treaty agreements, that there was no need to invalidate the treaties, and that past experience had shown that allotment of land in severalty and granting of citizenship to Indians had had uniformly bad results.[28]

[25] *United States Statutes at Large*, XIV, 238, 291, 294.

[26] See, for example, House Bill 1596, 45 Congress, 3 session.

[27] Report of May 27, 1872, *House Report* No. 89, 42 Congress, 2 session, serial 1543. The absurdity of the 23,000,000-acre figure is clear from the fact that the Dawes Commission found a total of only 19,525,976 acres in the Five Civilized Tribes. Elias C. Boudinot at the time pointed out the exaggeration, charging that the figure was at least 20 million acres off. Boudinot, *Oklahoma*, pp. 27–28.

[28] *House Report* No. 188, 45 Congress, 3 session, serial 1867. The report supplied a long historical argument. It was lauded by the Indian delegates.

The 1880's saw an intensification of white agitation for changes in the Indian Territory, as new elements came to the fore. Western desire for land, played upon by railroad interests, caused a decade of increasing pressure to open parts of the Territory to homesteaders, and federal officials supported by humanitarian reformers found new arguments for dividing the Indians' land in severalty and absorbing the Indians as citizens of the United States.

The business interests were tireless advocates. Aided by Boudinot, they fostered a group of professional promoters called Boomers, who by propaganda and direct action determined to force open the lands in the Territory. Boudinot had wholeheartedly accepted the white vision of the future of the Five Civilized Tribes calling for citizenship and allotment of land.[29] Now he claimed that fourteen million acres of land in the Indian Territory were in fact already in the public domain and subject to homestead entry. Special attention was given to the two million acres of the Oklahoma District, a central area which had been purchased from the Five Civilized Tribes but never assigned as reservations to the immigrating western Indians, but other lands were designated in the Kiowa, Comanche, Cheyenne-Arapaho reservations, and in Greer County, the southwestern section in dispute with Texas. Boudinot made his assertions in an article in the Chicago *Times* for February 17, 1879, and he provided a map of Indian Territory with the "public lands" plainly marked.[30] Such activities, together with a tremendous flood of Boomer literature, led to organized Oklahoma colonies on the borders of the Indian Territory in Kansas and Texas, which claimed the right to homestead in the Territory and which, led by such organizers as C. C. Carpenter, David L. Payne, and William L. Couch, made forays into the Territory and established incipient communities, only to be driven out by federal troops.[31]

The illegal invasions of the Indian Territory stirred new support of

[29] Elias Cornelius Boudinot, "The Indian Territory and Its Inhabitants," *Geographical Magazine*, I (June, 1874), 92–94; Boudinot, *Oklahoma*.

[30] *Senate Executive Document* No. 20, 46 Congress, 1 session, serial 1869, pp. 7–10. A copy of the map is appended to the document.

[31] There is a good survey of Boomer activity in Gittinger, *Formation of the State of Oklahoma*, Chapters VII–X; see also Solon J. Buck, "The Settlement of Oklahoma," *Transactions of the Wisconsin Academy of Sciences, Arts, and Letters*, XV (1907), 325–80; Carl Coke Rister, *Land Hunger: David L. Payne and the Oklahoma Boomers* (Norman, 1942).

the Indians among humanitarians concerned with Indian rights, but the pressure seemed too great to withstand. Secretary of the Interior Carl Schurz told the Indians in 1879 that "the difficulties of protecting the integrity of the Territory might in the course of time increase beyond control," and he urged them to meet the emergency by dividing their lands and obtaining individual titles in fee which could be defended against attack.[32]

The vacant lands of the Oklahoma District were a powerful magnet for land-hungry westerners, and the reformers, too, could not abide continuing non-use of the lands. When Commissioner of Indian Affairs Atkins proposed to move various Indian groups into the District in an attempt to end the agitation for white settlement of the region, Charles C. Painter penned a vigorous reply. "The purpose to fill up Oklahoma [District] with settlers will never sleep, and ought never to sleep, until it is accomplished," he wrote. "Such an anomaly as is there presented can never be sanctioned and made permanent—that of an immense territory, valuable for its vast resources, and needed to meet the demand for homes by our increasing population, kept empty by the use of the army. It must, it will be opened in some way; it will be occupied and used by somebody."[33] But he roundly condemned removal into the area of Indians who had already taken root elsewhere.

Little by little, indeed, the government gave way. Congressional friends of the Boomers regularly introduced bills for opening lands in the Territory for homesteading, and in 1889 initial success was attained. The Indian appropriation bill of March 2, 1889, made provision for homesteading in the Oklahoma District, and President Harrison proclaimed the lands open to settlement at noon on April 22, 1889.[34] Fifty thousand homeseekers lined the area waiting for the signal to advance, and when the blast of the bugle sounded, the first of the dramatic Oklahoma "runs" was under way. For a year the new inhabitants were forced to maintain their own communities, for Congress had failed to provide government for the region. Then on May 2, 1890, with the Oklahoma Organic Act, a formal territorial government was

[32] Report of the Secretary of the Interior, 1879, in serial 1910, p. 15.
[33] Charles C. Painter, *The Proposed Removal of Indians to Oklahoma* (Philadelphia, 1888), p. 3.
[34] *United States Statutes at Large*, XXV, 1005; Proclamation of March 23, 1889, Richardson, *Messages and Papers of the Presidents*, IX, 15–18.

established for the Oklahoma District and for "No Man's Land" (the Oklahoma panhandle), which was joined with it.[35] This was a far cry from the organization of the whole Indian Territory which had been advocated so strenuously, but white settlers had at last broken the barrier and had begun their legal invasion of the once sacrosanct region.

Meanwhile the attack on the independent status of the Five Civilized Tribes went on. J. D. C. Atkins, as Commissioner of Indian Affairs, was especially vehement. He asserted in 1885 that the idea of Indian nationality was fast melting away and that the tribal relations would sooner or later have to be broken up. When the Indians had taken their lands in severalty and become citizens, they would be prepared to dispose of their surplus lands to their own advantage and for the public good. Atkins hammered ceaselessly upon this theme. He insisted that he did not want to do anything contrary to the treaties but only to convince the Five Civilized Tribes to adopt his views. But ultimately he admitted that the feelings of nationality among the Indians should not be the final arbiter. "These Indians," he declared in 1886, "have no right to obstruct civilization and commerce and set up an exclusive claim to self-government, establishing a government within a government, and then expect and claim that the United States shall protect them from all harm, while insisting that it shall not be the ultimate judge as to what is best to be done for them in a political point of view. I repeat, to maintain any such view is to acknowledge a foreign sovereignty, with the right of eminent domain, upon American soil—a thing utterly repugnant to the spirit and genius of our laws, and wholly unwarranted by the Constitution of the United States."[36]

Atkins made much of the recurring argument used by the proponents of forced change in the political arrangements of the Five Civilized Tribes that the nations were controlled by aristocratic leaders who had built up huge land monopolies. He pointed to the large holdings within the nations controlled by certain important men who acquired land that belonged to all in common. "What a baronial estate!" he exclaimed about one such holding. "In theory the lands are held in common under

[35] *United States Statutes at Large*, XXVI, 81–100.
[36] Report of the Commissioner of Indian Affairs, 1885, in serial 2379, p. 13; *ibid.*, 1886, in serial 2467, p. 87.

the tribal relation, and are equally owned by each member of the tribe, but in point of fact they are simply held in the grasping hand of moneyed monopolists and powerful and influential leaders and politicians, who pay no rental to the other members of the tribe. . . ." Such a situation, the Commissioner insisted, needed radical reformation. "Are these the sacred rights secured by treaty, which the United States are pledged to respect and defend?" he asked. "If so, the United States are pledged to uphold and maintain a stupendous land monopoly and aristocracy that finds no parallel in the country except in two or three localities in the far West." He saw the need, he said, for "some potent influence or power to dispel this system and establish a new order of things"—some change that would raise up the downtrodden people to their proper level and bring down the mighty.[37]

The humanitarian reformers who aimed to turn the Indians into land-owning, civilized, Christian citizens of the United States wanted the Five Civilized Tribes to be the model for the rest of the Indian tribes. Not only would the final incorporation of the Cherokees, Creeks, and others into the American system solve the problems that beset the Indian Territory, but it would provide stimulus and encouragement for other Indians to do the same.[38] The reformers, however, were to be disappointed. The insistent opposition of the Five Civilized Tribes to proposed land-in-severalty and citizenship legislation enabled them to be excluded from the Dawes Act in 1887. Thus the very tribes that might have been the first to whom the Dawes Act could be applied and who had been a prime target of such proposals for two decades had slipped out of the net. Secretary of the Interior Lamar at the end of 1887 remarked upon the large surplus lands of the Cherokees and other Indians and their practice of leasing them for grazing purposes. Such a situation, he thought, was not conducive to the future well-being of the Indians, no matter how profitable it might be in the short run. Nor did

[37] *Ibid.*, pp. 82–84.
[38] The Senate Committee on Indian Affairs, in a report presented on June 4, 1886, by Senator Dawes, stressed the high state of civilization among the Five Civilized Tribes and clearly expected them to lead the way to full acceptance of white ways. *Senate Report* No. 1278, 49 Congress, 1 session, serial 2362, pp. i–xxvi. Two volumes of testimony accompany the committee's report, serials 2362 and 2363.

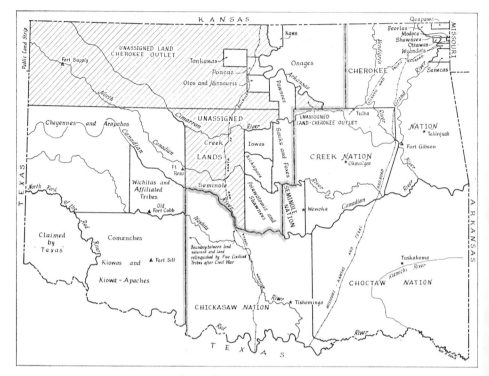

The Indian Territory, 1888

it promote "the general policy of localization of the individuals of the tribes upon separate allotments of land." He noted, too, that the exemption of these tribes made more difficult the enforcement of the severalty law among other groups.[39]

Although the reformers had lost this battle, they had not yet lost the war. New lines of action finally brought about the collapse of the Five Civilized Tribes and the destruction of the Indian Territory: the opening to homesteading of most of the western section of the Territory, the allotment of the lands of the Five Civilized Tribes in severalty, and the accompanying destruction of the self-government of these nations.

The acquisition of lands for homesteading was accomplished by direct negotiation with the Cherokees for sale of the Cherokee Outlet and with other tribes residing west of the Five Civilized Tribes for

[39] Report of the Secretary of the Interior, 1887, in serial 2541, p. 31.

cession of their surplus lands. This work was undertaken by the so-called Cherokee Commission.[40] Senator William M. Springer of Illinois, chairman of the Committee on Territories, had managed to insert in the Indian appropriation bill passed on March 2, 1889, an amendment authorizing the President to appoint three commissioners "to negotiate with the Cherokee Indians and with all other Indians owning or claiming lands lying west of the ninety-sixth degree of longitude in the Indian Territory for the cession to the United States of all their title, claim, or interest of every kind or character in and to such lands." Lands so obtained were to become part of the public domain.[41] In July, 1889, the President appointed the first members of the commission: Lucius Fairchild, former governor of Wisconsin; John F. Hantranft, former governor of Pennsylvania; and Judge Alfred M. Wilson of Arkansas.

The commissioners proceeded first to negotiate with the Cherokees for the Outlet. They offered $1.25 an acre, the price fixed by Congress, but the Cherokees, hoping to gain more from leasing to cattlemen, refused. After long and futile conferring, the negotiations were broken off at the end of December.

Following the death of Hantranft in October, 1889, and the resignation of Fairchild on January 1, 1890, the commission was reconstituted by the appointment of David H. Jerome, former governor of Michigan, and Warren G. Sayre of Indiana, and the new commission (now frequently called the Jerome Commission) began its work in May, 1890. Much opposition came from the Indians, but the persistence of the commissioners resulted finally in eleven agreements ratified by Congress, by which the Indians gave up more than fifteen million acres. The common pattern provided for 160-acre allotments in severalty to each man, woman, and child on the tribal rolls. The remainder of the

[40] The history of the Cherokee Commission is told in a series of articles by Berlin B. Chapman: "The Cherokee Commission, 1889–1893," *Indiana Magazine of History*, XLII (June, 1946), 177–90; "The Cherokee Commission at Kickapoo Village," *Chronicles of Oklahoma*, XVII (March, 1939), 62–74; "The Final Report of the Cherokee Commission," *ibid.*, XIX (December, 1941), 356–67; "How the Cherokees Acquired and Disposed of the Outlet: Part Three—The Fairchild Failure," *ibid.*, XV (September, 1937), 291–321; "How the Cherokees Acquired and Disposed of the Outlet: Part Five—The Cherokees Concede to a Contract," *ibid.*, XVI (June, 1938), 135–62; "Secret 'Instructions and Suggestions' to the Cherokee Commission, 1889–1890," *ibid.*, XXVI (Winter, 1948–1949), 449–58.

[41] *United States Statutes at Large*, XXV, 1005–1006.

land was declared surplus and bought by the government for home-steading. As the areas were opened to white settlers new counties were organized and incorporated into Oklahoma Territory.⁴² The Cherokee Outlet was the largest transfer of land. The Indians' reliance on graz-ing leases there was undercut by a presidential proclamation on Feb-ruary 17, 1890, that such leases were illegal and by an order that all livestock be removed by December, 1890. When the Jerome Commis-sion resumed negotiations in November, 1890, therefore, the Chero-kees were in a more compliant mood and an agreement was reached by which the Indians sold more than six million acres of the Outlet for $8,595,736.12. On September 16, 1893, the Cherokee Outlet was opened to homesteaders, and the greatest of the Oklahoma land runs occurred as a hundred thousand persons rushed in to locate home-steads on the new land.

A second line of attack on the problems of the Indian Territory was the extension of federal judicial jurisdiction over the region. Criminal cases in the Territory involving white citizens of the United States had been handled by the United States District Court at Fort Smith, Arkansas, but the distance and expense involved in bringing cases before the court were so great that only important ones were brought in. There were no courts to handle civil cases. Then in 1889 a United States court was established at Muskogee, with jurisdiction in civil cases affecting citizens of the United States if the amount involved was more than one hundred dollars, and the court was given criminal jurisdiction over cases in which the offense was not punishable by death or imprisonment at hard labor.⁴³ But the more serious cases still had to go to Fort Smith or to the United States District Court at Paris, Texas, which had been designated for criminal cases arising in the Choctaw and Chickasaw nations. In the following year, nine United

⁴² Details on each of the agreements are given in Foreman, *History of Oklahoma*, pp. 244–53. An enlightening discussion of the conflicts that arose between Indians and whites in the Cheyenne-Arapaho reservation after the Indians received allotments and the surplus lands were opened to settlement appears in Donald J. Berthrong, "White Neighbors Come among the Southern Cheyenne and Arapaho," *Kansas Quarterly*, III (Fall, 1971), 105–15. Berthrong speaks of the relations as "tragic" and concludes: "The first full contact of these tribesmen with whites delayed and perhaps even prevented them from attaining the goal of self-support demanded by Congress and the officials of the Bureau of Indian Affairs."
⁴³ *United States Statutes at Large*, XXV, 783–88.

States commissioners for the Indian Territory were authorized and given powers of justices of the peace over United States citizens. The laws of Arkansas were made applicable if not in conflict with federal law.[44] These provisions were a start in furnishing a judicial system for the whites who resided in the Indian nations.

On March 1, 1895, Congress created two new United States courts for the Indian Territory and ended the jurisdiction of the courts in the neighboring states, and the system was gradually expanded. The dissolution of the Indian governments was thus rapidly moved forward. In 1897 Congress provided that after January 1, 1898, all civil and criminal cases should be tried in the United States courts. The Curtis Act of June 28, 1898, abolished tribal laws and tribal courts and brought all persons in the Indian Territory, regardless of race, under United States authority. The act, entitled "an act for the protection of the people of the Indian Territory, and for other purposes," was unilateral action by the United States that signaled the end of the tribal governments; it was practically an organic act for the establishment of the long-sought territorial government.[45]

Paralleling this dissolution of the tribal governments, and in fact a strong force in their destruction, was the work of the Commission to the Five Civilized Tribes (usually known as the Dawes Commission), which accomplished the allotment of land in severalty that had been the goal of the government and of the reformers for nearly three decades.[46] The commission came as the result of the incorporation into the Indian appropriation bill of March 3, 1893, of a proposal first introduced by Senator George G. Vest of Missouri the preceding December. The act authorized the appointment of three commissioners to negotiate with the Five Civilized Tribes for the extinguishment of the national or tribal title to their lands and for consent to measures that

[44] Extensive judicial provisions for the Indian Territory were included in the Oklahoma Organic Act of May 2, 1890; *ibid.*, XXVI, 93–99.

[45] *Ibid.*, XXVIII, 693–98; XXX, 83, 495–519.

[46] Loren N. Brown, "The Establishment of the Dawes Commission for Indian Territory," *Chronicles of Oklahoma*, XVIII (June, 1940), 171–81, and Loren N. Brown, "The Dawes Commission," *ibid.*, IX (March, 1931), 71–105. Official reports and related documents are in the *Annual Report of the Commission to the Five Civilized Tribes*, 1894–1905 (issued under varying titles). See also *Index to the Annual Reports of the Commission to the Five Civilized Tribes for the Years 1894 to 1905, Inclusive* (Washington, 1906), and *Laws, Decisions, and Regulations Affecting the Work of the Commissioner to the Five Civilized Tribes, 1893 to 1906* (Washington, 1906).

would be "requisite and suitable to enable the ultimate creation of a State or States of the Union" out of the Indian Territory. The commissioners were directed to endeavor to procure first the allotment of the Indian lands in severalty and then the cession of any surplus lands to the United States.[47] It is significant that President Cleveland chose Henry L. Dawes, who had retired from the Senate in 1893, to head the commission.[48] Dawes's strong views as to the future of the Indians and the necessity of incorporation into white society through allotment of lands and citizenship made him a fit instrument to carry out the mandate of Congress. There is no doubt of his conviction that the goal was the proper one.

After a preliminary meeting in Washington in December, 1893, the Dawes Commission in January moved to the Indian Territory. It began at once a series of conferences with tribal leaders, to whom it submitted as the basis for discussion a series of proposals dealing with the allotment of lands in severalty, provisions for townsites and mineral lands, and the establishment of a territorial government. The Indians refused to negotiate, and the Dawes Commission could report little but frustration at the end of its first year's work.[49]

The conditions which the Dawes Commission faced were those that had long agitated the reformers. A Senate committee headed by Senator Teller had investigated the Indian Territory in early 1894 and submitted a report in May. This report, as well as the report of the Dawes Commission submitted in November, 1894, emphasized the crisis resulting from the great influx of whites into the Territory and from the monopolization of land by a few individuals. The whites were estimated to number 250,000 or more, and they had for the most part been invited in by the Indians themselves, despite the provisions in the

[47] *United States Statutes at Large*, XXVII, 645–46.

[48] The other two members appointed were Meredith H. Kidd and Archibald S. McKennon. In 1895, the commission was increased to five members, and Thomas B. Cabaniss and Alexander B. Montgomery were appointed new commissioners. Membership continued to change frequently, although Dawes remained as nominal chairman until his death in 1903. He was succeeded as chairman by Tams Bixby, a member of the commission since 1897 and its acting chairman. The Dawes Commission was dissolved in 1905, but its work was continued by a Commissioner to the Five Civilized Tribes, a position held by Bixby until 1907 and then until it was abolished in 1914 by J. George Wright. See Robert L. Williams, "Tams Bixby," *Chronicles of Oklahoma*, XIX (September, 1941), 205–12.

[49] *Annual Report of the Commission to the Five Civilized Tribes*, 1894.

treaties that the lands were to be for the exclusive use of the Indians. The United States, Teller asserted, had made it possible for the Indians to maintain their tribal relations and Indian laws and customs. "And, if now," he continued, "the isolation and exclusiveness sought to be given to them by our solemn treaties is destroyed, and they are overrun by a population of strangers five times in number to their own, it is not the fault of the Government of the United States, but comes from their own acts in admitting whites to citizenship under their laws and by inviting white people to come within their jurisdiction, to become traders, farmers, and to follow professional pursuits." Most of these persons were not subject to the Indian law and lacked adequate protection of life and property.[50]

It had been the theory, the reports noted, that when the government made over title to the lands to the Indian nations that the lands would be held in trust for *all* the Indians. Instead, Teller reported, a few enterprising citizens of the tribe, frequently Indian not by blood but by intermarriage, had become the practical owners of the largest and best part of the lands, even though the title still remained in the tribe. The monopoly was so great that in one tribe a hundred persons were reported to have appropriated fully one-half of the best land. The trust had thus been broken, nor would it ever be properly executed, Teller thought, if left to the Indians. And the question arose as to the duty of the government of the United States with reference to the trust.[51] "These tribal governments," the Dawes Commission asserted, "have wholly perverted their high trust, and it is the plain duty of the United States to enforce the trust it has so created and recover for its original uses the domain and all the gains derived from the perversion of the trust or discharge the trustee." Noted too were the inequities in the condition of the freedmen—despite the clear provisions of the 1866 treaties—and "corruption of the grossest kind, openly and unblushingly practiced" in "every branch of the service of the tribal government."[52]

It was apparent to these official observers that the current system

---

[50] Report of Select Committee on the Five Civilized Tribes, May 7, 1894, *Senate Report* No. 377, 53 Congress, 2 session, serial 3183. The quotation is on p. 7. The same kinds of remarks occur in the *Annual Report of the Commission to the Five Civilized Tribes*, 1894, p. 17.

[51] *Senate Report* No. 377, 53 Congress, 2 session, serial 3183, pp. 11–12.

[52] *Annual Report of the Commission to the Five Civilized Tribes*, 1894, pp. 17, 20.

could not continue. "It is not only non-American," Teller said, "but it is radically wrong, and a change is imperatively demanded in the interest of the Indian and whites alike, and such change cannot be much longer delayed. . . . There can be no modification of the system. It cannot be reformed. It must be abandoned and a better one substituted." There was only one solution: Congress had to act whether or not the Indians liked it. "The United States . . . granted to these tribes the power of self-government not to conflict with the Constitution," the Dawes Commission concluded its report. "They have demonstrated their incapacity to so govern themselves, and no higher duty can rest upon the Government that granted this authority than to revoke it when it has so lamentably failed."[53]

Despite its convictions, the Teller committee made no specific recommendations, preferring, it said, to await the outcome of the Dawes Commission's negotiations. The commission, for its part, continued to treat with the tribal governments. Its report at the end of 1895, however, indicated how hopeless it considered the work to be. It declared that the tribal governments were "wholly corrupt, irresponsible, and unworthy to be longer trusted" and that the promises of self-government made in the treaties were no longer binding under the changed conditions. "It is . . . the imperative duty of Congress," the commissioners declared, "to assume at once the political control of the Indian Territory."[54] The reformers at Lake Mohonk placed themselves firmly on the side of the commission. Their platform for 1895 included this forthright statement:

> The nation possesses a supreme sovereignty over every foot of soil within its boundaries. Its legislative authority over its people it has neither right nor power to alienate. Its attempt to do so by Indian treaties in the past does not relieve it from the responsibility for the condition of government in the reservations and in the Indian Territory; and, despite those treaties, it is under a sacred obligation to exercise its sovereignty by extending over the three hundred thousand whites and fifty thousand so-called Indians in the Indian Terri-

[53] *Senate Report* No. 377, 53 Congress, 2 session, serial 3183, p. 12; *Annual Report of the Commission to the Five Civilized Tribes*, 1894, p. 20.

[54] *Ibid.*, 1895, p. 78.

tory the same restraints and protection of government which other parts of the country enjoy.[55]

Congress heeded the message. A law of June 10, 1896, directed the commission to make out rolls of Indian citizens in preparation for allotment and stated: "It is hereby declared to be the duty of the United States to establish a government in the Indian Territory which will rectify the many inequalities and discriminations now existing in said Territory and afford needful protection to the lives and property of all citizens and residents thereof."[56] Under these new mandates, the Dawes Commission moved rapidly ahead toward the dissolution of the Five Civilized Tribes.

The Indian reformers followed the work of the Dawes Commission with interest and at first with some concern, and Dawes regularly reported to the Lake Mohonk Conference, in person or by letter, on the progress of his work.[57] Critics of the Dawes Commission and its work, however, had broadcast their complaints, charging that the commission aimed to violate the treaty rights of the tribes. Such accusations could not go unnoticed, and the Indian Rights Association, which considered itself the watchdog of Indian rights, decided in 1896 to send a special agent of its own to investigate the conditions in the Indian Territory and the work of the Dawes Commission. The man chosen was Charles F. Meserve, president of Shaw College in Raleigh, North Carolina, and former superintendent of the Haskell Institute.[58]

Brushing aside the complaints he had heard, emanating, he said, "largely, if not wholly, from paid attorneys, from Indian and white coal, cattle, or timber monopolists, from Indian officials or other influential people, all of whom are profiting from the present abnormal condition of affairs, and consequently are interested in the continuance of

[55] *Lake Mohonk Conference Proceedings*, 1895, p. 106.

[56] *United States Statutes at Large*, XXIX, 339–40.

[57] Dawes made substantial remarks on the Indian Territory at the meetings of 1895, 1896, 1897, 1898, 1900, and 1902. See the *Lake Mohonk Conference Proceedings* for those years. His remarks of 1900 were reprinted as "The Indian Territory," *The Independent*, LII (October 25, 1900), 2561–65.

[58] *Report of the Indian Rights Association*, 1896, p. 9.

the *status quo*," Meserve set about to seek the facts for himself.[59] He spent the summer of 1896 in the Indian Territory, and his findings corroborated those of the Dawes Commission and the Teller committee. Meserve saw crime, corruption, and monopoly—and everywhere the overpowering presence of the whites.

> But whom do you see? [he asked] *White* men, *white* men everywhere! The scarcest object is an Indian, and this is the *Indian* Territory, set apart by solemn treaty obligation for the *Indian*. You see here and there large gangs of men cutting, curing, and pressing hay, and loading it into freight cars for shipment to Kansas City and Chicago. You hear the sound of the woodman's axe and the crash of the lord of the forest as he falls to the ground, and anon the whir of the saw and the hum of the planer and other machinery preparing the timber for use in the States, where it finds a market. Now and then you pass a long line of cars heavily laden with coal. Here is a string of coke ovens. Yonder a stone quarry or a vast deposit of asphaltum is giving employment to busy hands. Then you come to square mile after square mile of fenced pasture with innumerable herds. Here in the rich Arkansas bottom is a field of a hundred acres of cotton, and another of a hundred acres of corn. The cotton will yield a bale to the acre and the corn 50 bushels or more, and all this without a pound of fertilizer. The bottom is three miles wide and the soil is black, deep, and rich. This property all belongs to the Indian, but it is white men who are cutting and shipping his hay, white men who are felling, manufacturing, and shipping his timber, white men who are mining and shipping his coal, white men who are hauling his stone and asphaltum, white men who are harvesting the corn and cotton from his rich acres, white men who are pasturing his beautiful waving prairies and shipping the fat herds to the stock yards of Kansas City and Chicago. It is the white man who is omnipresent. The common Indian is well-nigh an alien in the land of his fathers.[60]

In October, 1896, Meserve appeared at Lake Mohonk, where he repeated verbatim large sections of his printed report. He was followed

---

[59] Charles F. Meserve, *The Dawes Commission and the Five Civilized Tribes of Indian Territory* (Philadelphia, 1896), p. 5.
[60] *Ibid.*, p. 12.

on the platform by Dawes, who offered an apologia for the work of his commission, expressed his deep gratitude for the findings of Meserve, and urged the members of the conference to continued support of his efforts. Dawes asked how it was that the Five Civilized Tribes enjoyed an autonomous political status within the territorial limits of the United States, and he answered: "It grows out of the belief of a large portion of the people of the United States that somehow and in some way they have bound themselves to let it be so; the belief that the United States has abdicated authority over this people. If it is really and rightly so, it is to be respected and adhered to so long as public safety will permit *and no longer.*" But for his part, Dawes denied that the United States had ever abdicated authority over any of its territory and in fact did not have the power to do so. The governmental arrangements of the Indians had been made by the United States, he insisted, "and if the government of the United States made it, it can unmake it." He emphasized the fact that the lands of the Indians in the Indian Territory were granted to them to be held in common, lands put in the hands of those nations "as *trustees for each and every one of the citizen Indians.*" Dawes wanted to return to that state of affairs, and he asserted that the commission "has asked for the violation of no treaty obligations. . . . They ask that these treaty stipulations may be enforced." If the Indian governments had failed as trustees and had misappropriated the trust by allowing the monopolization of the land, they should be removed. Dawes understandably placed his primary reliance on the allotment of the lands in severalty and was less concerned about the details of territorial or state governmental arrangements, since he was convinced that once the Indians owned their land individually they would see to it that they got a proper government to protect it.[61]

The touch of sentimentality that had marked Dawes's career as Indian reformer had not disappeared in his old age. In 1897 he told the Lake Mohonk Conference: "Remember that your work is not for the regeneration of a locality, but for a race. And until in every Indian home, wherever situated, the wife shall sit by her hearthstone clothed in the habiliments of true womanhood, and the husband shall stand sentinel at the threshold panoplied in the armor of a self-supporting

[61] *Lake Mohonk Conference Proceedings,* 1896, pp. 44–55.

citizen of the United States,—then and not till then, will your work be done."[62]

Dawes got the support at Lake Mohonk that he was seeking, and in fact his listeners needed little persuading. John Eaton, former United States Commissioner of Education, rejoiced to learn that the work of the Dawes Commission was "a movement in favor of the sacredness of treaties and the sacredness of human character and of those great rights and privileges for which this government exists," and he offered thanks to Dawes, whose aim it was "to keep the treaties solemnly made with these people." The old reformer Bishop Whipple wanted it known that the Indians had forfeited their old treaty rights by taking the side of the Confederacy during the Civil War and that after the war they had been received back into friendship under quite different conditions. "Familiar as I am with Indian wrongs," he concluded, "I have never had my heart more deeply stirred than in listening to Senator Dawes and to Mr. Meserve; and from my heart I can only say, God be praised for raising up such men to do his work."[63]

The desire to see the Indians as individual landowners and the belief that this was necessary for the advance of American civilization were so strong that they seemed to block out other considerations. Thomas J. Morgan, returning to Lake Mohonk in 1895, declared that the condition of things in Indian Territory was so anomalous that it was "irreconcilable with any philosophy of our national life," that the Indian governments had proved inadequate to meet the needs of the time, and that the Indian Territory was obstructing the "march of civilization." The time had come, Morgan said, when "the solution of the problem *must* be reached." It was a hard and perplexing situation, he admitted, but action had to be taken and the Indian Territory moved to territorial and then to state organization. In the final analysis the United States had to act, whether or not the Indians agreed.[64]

Support of the Meserve report by the Indian Rights Association clearly placed that organization on Dawes's side. In an analysis of the question of the Five Civilized Tribes in 1896, the association spokesmen opted for a middle course between "a purely sentimental policy which considers the present situation of the five civilized tribes an

[62] *Ibid.*, 1897, p. 43.
[63] *Ibid.*, 1896, p. 57.
[64] *Ibid.*, 1895, pp. 99–101.

autonomous one" and urges that the Indians be left alone, and a change overriding all rights of the Indians, forced by outside interests not by friends of the Indians—between "land-grabbing and spoliation on the one side; a sentimentalism which takes no account of facts on the other." But ultimately the Indian Rights Association was "quite content to let the tribe go." It noted that all recent Indian legislation had contemplated the extinction of the tribes and that the great majority of Indian reformers were agreed on that policy. The association wanted to do all that could be done wisely "to save and guard the individual Indian."[65]

The tribes finally saw the futility of further resistance and gave in. On April 23, 1897, the Dawes Commission negotiated the Atoka Agreement with the Choctaws and Chickasaws, which determined the fundamental formula of allotment for those nations. An agreement was reached with the Seminoles in 1898, with the Creeks in 1901, and with the Cherokees finally in 1902.[66] Meanwhile the Curtis Act authorized the Dawes Commission to proceed with the allotment of lands as soon as the tribal rolls were completed.

The work of the Dawes Commission was exacting. The lands had to be surveyed, not only for extent but also for quality of land, since the agreements specified that allotments would be based on the value of the land, not simply on acreage.[67] In addition the commission was responsible for determining the eligibility of allottees, a tremendous job since more than 300,000 persons claimed membership in the Five Civilized Tribes. Beginning in 1898 and running until the rolls were closed in 1907, the commission entered 101,506 persons on the rolls.[68]

[65] *Report of the Indian Rights Association*, 1896, p. 12.

[66] The Atoka Agreement was incorporated into the Curtis Act, *United States Statutes at Large*, XXX, 505–13; Seminole agreement, *ibid.*, XXX, 567–69; Creek agreement, *ibid.*, XXXI, 861–73; Cherokee agreement, *ibid.*, XXXII, 716–27. For a detailed listing of agreements with the tribes, see Gittinger, *Formation of the State of Oklahoma*, p. 194n.

[67] See Loren N. Brown, "The Appraisal of the Lands of the Choctaws and Chickasaws by the Dawes Commission," *Chronicles of Oklahoma*, XXII (Summer, 1944), 177–91.

[68] There is a tabulation of the final rolls, showing full-bloods and mixed-bloods, whites, and freedmen enrolled in each tribe in Angie Debo, *And Still the Waters Run* (Princeton, 1940), p. 47. Figures on enrollment differ since some names were removed and the rolls were opened from time to time to admit new members.

The size of the allotments varied from tribe to tribe. Choctaws and Chickasaws received 320 acres each, Cherokees 110 acres, Creeks 160 acres, and Seminoles 120 acres. Freedmen among the Cherokees, Creeks, and Seminoles shared equally with the Indians; those among the Chickasaws and Choctaws received 40-acre allotments. Some part of each allotment was designated a homestead and made inalienable for a period of years. Altogether 19,526,966 acres were surveyed in the Five Civilized Tribes, of which 15,794,400 were allotted to persons on the tribal rolls. The rest comprised land for townsites, schools, and other public purposes, and coal and mineral lands held for tribal benefit. There were no surplus lands within the Five Civilized Tribes to be returned to the public domain and opened to homesteading.[69]

These moves meant that members of the Five Civilized Tribes were to lose their tribal citizenship and become citizens of the United States. Congress in 1890, in fact, had provided that individuals could apply at the federal court at Muskogee for United States citizenship, and the allotment agreements drawn up by the Dawes Commission provided for a switch in citizenship. Finally, in 1901, Congress made every Indian in the Indian Territory a citizen of the United States.[70]

Thus ended the campaign to destroy the exclusiveness of the Indians of the Indian Territory. The tribal governments were allowed to continue until the property was liquidated, and national councils were allowed to meet, but their acts were all subject to approval by the President of the United States. For the Indians it was a sad defeat. The situation of the Chickasaws, described by a historian of the nation, was duplicated in the other tribes.

> ... after 1898 the Chickasaw government was an empty shell. Every substantive function of the tribal government passed from Indian to federal control. The Chickasaw Constitution and laws no longer were operative, and tribal citizens were subject to administrative decrees and to the laws of Congress. Tribal officials, emasculated of

[69] Gibson, *Oklahoma*, pp. 325–26; Gittinger, *Formation of the State of Oklahoma*, p. 230.

[70] *United States Statutes at Large*, XXVI, 99. The Atoka Agreement, for example, provided that "the Choctaws and Chickasaws, when their tribal governments cease, shall become possessed of all the rights and privileges of citizens of the United States." *Ibid.*, XXX, 513. Citizenship for all the Indians in the Territory came fittingly enough as an amendment to the Dawes Act of 1887. *Ibid.*, XXXI, 1447.

their constitutional function, had to stand idly by as federal agents collected tribal revenues, disbursed tribal funds, and moved cases from defunct tribal courts to federal courts. Even the Chickasaw Nation school system passed to federal control. United States agents set curricula and qualifications for teachers, directed the construction of new schools to accommodate the white and Negro children, and appointed teachers.[71]

The Indian nations had succumbed to the pressures of the whites, who could brook no alien enclaves within their completely Americanized society. The Christian reformers believed that they had won a total victory.

[71] Arrell M. Gibson, *The Chickasaws* (Norman, 1971), pp. 276–77. Gibson presents an excellent history of the dissolution of the Chickasaw nation on pp. 247–78. For accounts of the end of the other tribal governments and the reactions of the tribes, see Angie Debo, *The Rise and Fall of the Choctaw Republic* (Norman, 1934); Angie Debo, *The Road to Disappearance* [Creeks] (Norman, 1941); Edwin C. McReynolds, *The Seminoles* (Norman, 1957); and Morris L. Wardell, *A Political History of the Cherokee Nation, 1838–1907* (Norman, 1938). The sad fate of the Indians of the Five Civilized Tribes after the end of tribal autonomy is described in Debo, *And Still the Waters Run*. Her judgment is harsh: "The policy of the United States in liquidating the institutions of the Five Tribes was a gigantic blunder that ended a hopeful experiment in Indian development, destroyed a unique civilization, and degraded thousands of individuals." Pp. viii–ix.

EPILOGUE

The Christian reformers at the end of the century looked at their works and judged them good. They had accomplished what they had set out to do. Congress had enacted their legislative program, which they were convinced would quickly Americanize all the Indians. Tribal organization and communal traditions they had dealt crippling if not fatal blows, and they had established programs and structures to transform the tribesmen into individual citizens of a Christian nation.

The platform of the Lake Mohonk Conference in 1900 reaffirmed the humanitarians' conviction that "it would have been better for the Indians if they had been treated from the beginning as individuals subject to the laws of the land." The problem had been to overcome the errors of the past and to bring the Indians into individual relations with the government of the United States with as little injustice and hardship as possible. "The discontinuance of treaties with the Indian tribes as separate nationalities," the platform noted in a litany of accomplishments, "the allotment of land in severalty, the gradual decrease of rations, the increase of appropriations for providing all Indian children of school age with the essentials of an English education, the consequent discontinuance of the contract school system with the un-American union of Church and State which the system involved, are all parts of one coherent and consistent general policy." All that was needed as the new century began was the continuation of that policy "to its natural consummation." Then the reservations, the agencies, and the Bureau of Indian Affairs itself would wither and disappear.[1]

We know now that the vision of these Christian reformers was

[1] *Lake Mohonk Conference Proceedings*, 1900, pp. 7–8.

clouded, that their goal of rapid and total assimilation for the Indians did not—indeed could not—work. Even in their own day, a few individuals saw that immediate cultural transformation was impossible. Most perceptive, perhaps, was George Bird Grinnell, whose evaluation of the philanthropists and their program in 1899 was quite at variance with the optimistic accounts of the reformers themselves. He wrote:

For many years good people have been endeavoring to devise plans which should at once transform the Indian from a rover and a warrior to a sedentary laborer. Men of various trades and professions, from the soldier to the theologian, have studied the Indian problem, and many different methods have been suggested for rendering the wild man civilized and self-supporting. The author of each has had most perfect confidence that his remedy was the one certain to cure all ills brought to the Indians by contact with the white man. Some of these projects have had fair trial; yet the progress of the race has not been so rapid as to justify the faith that any of these means of civilization—except when engineered with unusual energy and wisdom—would do the work claimed for it, while in some cases the experiments have brought disaster to the Indians.

The sincerity and earnestness of a majority of such philanthropists cannot be doubted, but in all their reasoning about Indians there has been one point of weakness: they had no personal knowledge of the inner life of the people they were trying to help. Their theories appear to have assumed that Indians are precisely like white men, except that their minds are blank and plastic, ready to receive any impression that may be inscribed on them. These friends of the Indian had little acquaintance with Indian character; they did not appreciate the human nature of the people. They did not know that their minds were already occupied by a multitude of notions and beliefs that were firmly fixed there,—rooted and grounded by an inheritance of a thousand years. Still less did they comprehend the Indian's intense conservatism, the tenacity with which he clings to the beliefs which have been handed down to him by uncounted generations.[2]

[2] George Bird Grinnell, "The Indian on the Reservation," *Atlantic Monthly*, LXXIII (February, 1899), 258–59.

The Christian reformers faced the crisis in American Indian policy with honesty and the best of intentions. With singleminded devotion to their cause they brought forth their panaceas—land in severalty, law, education, and efficient administration—and by united effort triumphantly won their way in Congress. With typical reformers' zeal they swept criticism and opposition aside, for they knew that they were supremely right. So much more tragic, then, was their ultimate failure.

BIBLIOGRAPHY

I. RECORDS OF THE NATIONAL ARCHIVES

Although this study relies largely on government sources that have been published, some valuable data were found in the following collections in the National Archives. No attempt was made to search all these collections exhaustively.

Record Group 48. Records of the Office of the Secretary of the Interior.
    Indian Division of the Department of the Interior, Letters Received. Appointments Division.
    Indian Territory Division, Monthly Reports of the Dawes Commission.
Record Group 75. Records of the Bureau of Indian Affairs.
    Office of Indian Affairs, Letters Received.
    Office of Indian Affairs, Letters Sent.
    Office of the Commissioner of Indian Affairs, Letters Sent.
    Records of the Board of Indian Commissioners, Minutes of Board Meetings.
    Summaries of Work Completed and Records Relating to Mission Schools.

II. MANUSCRIPT COLLECTIONS

Bureau of Catholic Indian Missions Archives, Washington, D.C.
Henry L. Dawes Papers. Library of Congress.
Indian Rights Association Papers. Historical Society of Pennsylvania.
William T. Sherman Papers. Library of Congress.
Smiley Family Papers (Lake Mohonk Conference). Quaker Collection, Haverford College.
Welsh Family Papers. Historical Society of Pennsylvania.
Henry B. Whipple Papers. Minnesota Historical Society.

III. ANNUAL REPORTS OF THE COMMISSIONER OF
INDIAN AFFAIRS

The citations below include the names of the commissioners and the location of the annual reports in the serial set of Congressional documents. The reports were also published separately. Footnote references to these documents are abbreviated.

1832–(Elbert Herring), *House Executive Document* No. 2, 22 Congress, 2 session, serial 233.

1838–(T. Hartley Crawford), *Senate Document* No. 1, 25 Congress, 3 session, serial 338.

1841–(T. Hartley Crawford), *Senate Document* No. 1, 27 Congress, 2 session, serial 395.

1842–(T. Hartley Crawford), *Senate Document* No. 1, 27 Congress, 3 session, serial 413.

1844–(T. Hartley Crawford), *Senate Document* No. 1, 28 Congress, 2 session, serial 449.

1847–(William Medill), *Senate Executive Document* No. 1, 30 Congress, 1 session, serial 503.

1848–(William Medill), *House Executive Document* No. 1, 30 Congress, 2 session, serial 537.

1849–(Orlando Brown), *Senate Executive Document* No. 1, 31 Congress, 1 session, serial 550.

1856–(George W. Manypenny), *Senate Executive Document* No. 5, 34 Congress, 3 session, serial 875.

1857–(James W. Denver), *Senate Executive Document* No. 11, 35 Congress, 1 session, serial 919.

1858–(Charles E. Mix), *Senate Executive Document* No. 1, 35 Congress, 2 session, serial 974.

1860–(A. B. Greenwood), *Senate Executive Document* No. 1, 36 Congress, 2 session, serial 1078.

1861–(William P. Dole), *Senate Executive Document* No. 1, 37 Congress, 2 session, serial 1117.

1862–(William P. Dole), *House Executive Document* No. 1, 37 Congress, 3 session, serial 1157.

1863–(William P. Dole), *House Executive Document* No. 1, 38 Congress, 1 session, serial 1182.

1864–(William P. Dole), *House Executive Document* No. 1, 38 Congress, 2 session, serial 1220.

1865–(Dennis N. Cooley), *House Executive Document* No. 1, 39 Congress, 1 session, serial 1248.

1866–(Dennis N. Cooley), *House Executive Document* No. 1, 39 Congress, 2 session, serial 1284.

1867–(Charles E. Mix), *House Executive Document* No. 1, 40 Congress, 2 session, serial 1326.

1868–(Nathaniel G. Taylor), *House Executive Document* No. 1, 40 Congress, 3 session, serial 1366.

1869–(Ely S. Parker), *House Executive Document* No. 1, 41 Congress, 2 session, serial 1414.

1870–(Ely S. Parker), *House Executive Document* No. 1, 41 Congress, 3 session, serial 1449.

1871–(H. R. Clum), *House Executive Document* No. 1, part 5, 42 Congress, 2 session, serial 1505.

1872–(Francis A. Walker), *House Executive Document* No. 1, part 5, 42 Congress, 3 session, serial 1560.

1873–(Edward P. Smith), *House Executive Document* No. 1, part 5, 43 Congress, 1 session, serial 1601.

1874–(Edward P. Smith), *House Executive Document* No. 1, part 5, 43 Congress, 2 session, serial 1639.

1875–(Edward P. Smith), *House Executive Document* No. 1, part 5, 44 Congress, 1 session, serial 1680.

1876–(John Q. Smith), *House Executive Document* No. 1, part 5, 44 Congress, 2 session, serial 1749.

1877–(Ezra A. Hayt), *House Executive Document* No. 1, part 5, 45 Congress, 2 session, serial 1800.

1878–(Ezra A. Hayt), *House Executive Document* No. 1, part 5, 45 Congress, 3 session, serial 1850.

1879–(Ezra A. Hayt), *House Executive Document* No. 1, part 5, 46 Congress, 2 session, serial 1910.

1880–(E. M. Marble), *House Executive Document* No. 1, part 5, 46 Congress, 3 session, serial 1959.

1881–(Hiram Price), *House Executive Document* No. 1, part 5, volume II, 47 Congress, 1 session, serial 2018.

1882–(Hiram Price), *House Executive Document* No. 1, part 5, volume II, 47 Congress, 2 session, serial 2100.

1883–(Hiram Price), *House Executive Document* No. 1, part 5, volume II, 48 Congress, 1 session, serial 2191.

1884–(Hiram Price), *House Executive Document* No. 1, part 5, volume II, 48 Congress, 2 session, serial 2287.

1885–(J. D. C. Atkins), *House Executive Document* No. 1, part 5, volume II, 49 Congress, 1 session, serial 2379.

1886—(J. D. C. Atkins), *House Executive Document* No. 1, part 5, volume I, 49 Congress, 2 session, serial 2467.

1887—(J. D. C. Atkins), *House Executive Document* No. 1, part 5, volume II, 50 Congress, 1 session, serial 2542.

1888—(John H. Oberly), *House Executive Document* No. 1, part 5, volume II, 50 Congress, 2 session, serial 2637.

1889—(Thomas J. Morgan), *House Executive Document* No. 1, part 5, volume II, 51 Congress, 1 session, serial 2725.

1890—(Thomas J. Morgan), *House Executive Document* No. 1, part 5, volume II, 51 Congress, 2 session, serial 2841.

1891—(Thomas J. Morgan), *House Executive Document* No. 1, part 5, volume II, 52 Congress, 1 session, serial 2934.

1892—(Thomas J. Morgan), *House Executive Document* No. 1, part 5, volume II, 52 Congress, 2 session, serial 3088.

1893—(Daniel M. Browning), *House Executive Document* No. 1, part 5, volume II, 53 Congress, 2 session, serial 3210.

1894—(Daniel M. Browning), *House Executive Document* No. 1, part 5, volume II, 53 Congress, 3 session, serial 3306.

1895—(Daniel M. Browning), *House Document* No. 5, volume II, 54 Congress, 1 session, serial 3382.

1896—(Daniel M. Browning), *House Document* No. 5, volume II, 54 Congress, 2 session, serial 3489.

1897—(William A. Jones), *House Document* No. 5, 55 Congress, 2 session, serial 3641.

1898—(William A. Jones), *House Document* No. 5, 55 Congress, 3 session, serial 3757.

1899—(William A. Jones), *House Document* No. 5, 56 Congress, 1 session, serial 3915.

1900—(William A. Jones), *House Document* No. 5, 56 Congress, 2 session, serial 4101.

IV. ANNUAL REPORTS OF THE SECRETARY OF THE INTERIOR

The citations below include the names of the secretaries and the location of the annual reports in the serial set of Congressional documents. The reports were also published separately. Footnote references to these documents are abbreviated.

1859—(Jacob Thompson), *Senate Executive Document* No. 2, 36 Congress, 1 session, serial 1023.

1860—(Jacob Thompson), *Senate Executive Document* No. 1, 36 Congress, 2 session, serial 1078.

1861—(Caleb B. Smith), *Senate Executive Document* No. 1, 37 Congress, 2 session, serial 1117.

1862—(Caleb B. Smith), *House Executive Document* No. 1, 37 Congress, 3 session, serial 1157.

1863—(John P. Usher), *House Executive Document* No. 1, 38 Congress, 1 session, serial 1182.

1864—(John P. Usher), *House Executive Document* No. 1, 38 Congress, 2 session, serial 1220.

1865—(James Harlan), *House Executive Document* No. 1, 39 Congress, 1 session, serial 1248.

1866—(O. H. Browning), *House Executive Document* No. 1, 39 Congress, 2 session, serial 1284.

1867—(O. H. Browning), *House Executive Document* No. 1, 40 Congress, 2 session, serial 1326.

1868—(O. H. Browning), *House Executive Document* No. 1, 40 Congress, 3 session, serial 1366.

1869—(Jacob D. Cox), *House Executive Document* No. 1, 41 Congress, 2 session, serial 1414.

1870—(Jacob D. Cox), *House Executive Document* No. 1, 41 Congress, 3 session, serial 1449.

1871—(Columbus Delano), *House Executive Document* No. 1, part 5, 42 Congress, 2 session, serial 1505.

1872—(Columbus Delano), *House Executive Document* No. 1, part 5, 42 Congress, 3 session, serial 1560.

1873—(Columbus Delano), *House Executive Document* No. 1, part 5, 43 Congress, 1 session, serial 1601.

1874—(Columbus Delano), *House Executive Document* No. 1, part 5, 43 Congress, 2 session, serial 1639.

1875—(Zachariah Chandler), *House Executive Document* No. 1, part 5, 44 Congress, 1 session, serial 1680.

1876—(Zachariah Chandler), *House Executive Document* No. 1, part 5, 44 Congress, 2 session, serial 1749.

1877—(Carl Schurz), *House Executive Document* No. 1, part 5, 45 Congress, 2 session, serial 1800.

1878—(Carl Schurz), *House Executive Document* No. 1, part 5, 45 Congress, 3 session, serial 1850.

1879—(Carl Schurz), *House Executive Document* No. 1, part 5, 46 Congress, 2 session, serial 1910.

1880—(Carl Schurz), *House Executive Document* No. 1, part 5, 46 Congress, 3 session, serial 1959.

1881–(Samuel J. Kirkwood), *House Executive Document* No. 1, part 5, volume I, 47 Congress, 1 session, serial 2017.

1882–(Henry M. Teller), *House Executive Document* No. 1, part 5, volume I, 47 Congress, 2 session, serial 2099.

1883–(Henry M. Teller), *House Executive Document* No. 1, part 5, volume I, 48 Congress, 1 session, serial 2190.

1884–(Henry M. Teller), *House Executive Document* No. 1, part 5, volume I, 48 Congress, 2 session, serial 2286.

1885–(L. Q. C. Lamar), *House Executive Document* No. 1, part 5, volume I, 49 Congress, 1 session, serial 2378.

1886–(L. Q. C. Lamar), *House Executive Document* No. 1, part 5, volume I, 49 Congress, 2 session, serial 2467.

1887–(L. Q. C. Lamar), *House Executive Document* No. 1, part 5, volume I, 50 Congress, 1 session, serial 2541.

1888–(William F. Vilas), *House Executive Document* No. 1, part 5, volume I, 50 Congress, 2 session, serial 2636.

1889–(John W. Noble), *House Executive Document* No. 1, part 5, volume I, 51 Congress, 1 session, serial 2724.

1890–(John W. Noble), *House Executive Document* No. 1, part 5, volume I, 51 Congress, 2 session, serial 2840.

1891–(John W. Noble), *House Executive Document* No. 1, part 5, volume I, 52 Congress, 1 session, serial 2933.

1892–(John W. Noble), *House Executive Document* No. 1, part 5, volume I, 52 Congress, 2 session, serial 3087.

1893–(Hoke Smith), *House Executive Document* No. 1, part 5, volume I, 53 Congress, 2 session, serial 3209.

1894–(Hoke Smith), *House Executive Document* No. 1, part 5, volume I, 53 Congress, 3 session, serial 3305.

1895–(Hoke Smith), *House Document* No. 5, volume I, 54 Congress, 1 session, serial 3381.

1896–(David R. Francis), *House Document* No. 5, volume I, 54 Congress, 2 session, serial 3488.

1897–(Cornelius N. Bliss), *House Document* No. 5, 55 Congress, 2 session, serial 3640.

1898–(Cornelius N. Bliss), *House Document* No. 5, 55 Congress, 3 session, serial 3756.

1899–(Ethan Allen Hitchcock), *House Document* No. 5, 56 Congress, 1 session, serial 3914.

1900–(Ethan Allen Hitchcock), *House Document* No. 5, 56 Congress, 2 session, serial 4100.

V. ANNUAL REPORTS OF THE SECRETARY OF WAR

Footnotes give full citations to the serial set of Congressional documents for the reports used.

VI. CONGRESSIONAL DOCUMENTS (in serial order)

"Massacre of Cheyenne Indians," in *Report of the Joint Committee on the Conduct of the War, Senate Report* No. 142, 38 Congress, 2 session, serial 1214.

Senate Executive Document No. 26, 39 Congress, 2 session, serial 1277. Proceedings of the military commission in the case of Colonel J. M. Chivington.

"Condition of the Indian Tribes: Report of the Joint Special Committee, Appointed under Joint Resolution of March 3, 1865, with an Appendix," *Senate Report* No. 156, 39 Congress, 2 session, serial 1279. Report of the Doolittle Committee.

Senate Executive Document No. 13, 40 Congress, 1 session, serial 1308. Reports on the Fetterman Massacre.

"Report of Indian Peace Commissioners," *House Executive Document* No. 97, 40 Congress, 2 session, serial 1337.

"Indian Tribes: Memorial on Behalf of the Indians, by the United States Indian Commission," *House Miscellaneous Document* No. 165, 40 Congress, 2 session, serial 1350.

Senate Miscellaneous Document No. 24, 40 Congress, 3 session, serial 1361. Petition of Cherokee, Creek, and Choctaw delegates against transfer of the Indian Bureau.

"Resolution of the Legislature of Kansas in Favor of the Transfer of the Control and Management of the Indians from the Interior to the War Department," *Senate Miscellaneous Document* No. 29, 40 Congress, 3 session, serial 1361.

"Memorial of Yearly Meeting of the Society of Friends, Relative to the Treatment of the Indians," *House Miscellaneous Document* No. 29, 40 Congress, 3 session, serial 1385.

Senate Miscellaneous Document No. 76, 41 Congress, 2 session, serial 1408. Creek memorial against organization of a territorial government for the Indian Territory.

Senate Miscellaneous Document No. 83, 41 Congress, 2 session, serial 1408. Cherokee memorial against territorial government.

Senate Miscellaneous Document No. 90, 41 Congress, 2 session, serial 1408. Choctaw memorial against territorial government.

Senate Miscellaneous Document No. 143, 41 Congress, 2 session, serial 1408.

Memorial of Cherokee, Creek, and Choctaw delegates against territorial government.

Senate Report No. 131, 41 Congress, 2 session, serial 1409. Report of Committee on Territories in favor of a "Territory of Ok-la-homa."

"Difficulties with Indian Tribes," *House Executive Document* No. 240, 41 Congress, 2 session, serial 1425. Concerning relations with the Cheyenne, Comanche, Arapaho, Apache, and Kiowa tribes in 1867.

Senate Executive Document No. 26, 41 Congress, 3 session, serial 1440. Proceedings of International Council at Okmulgee, 1870.

Senate Report No. 336, 41 Congress, 3 session, serial 1443. Report of Committee on Territories favoring territorial government for the Indian Territory.

House Miscellaneous Document No. 49, 41 Congress, 3 session, serial 1462. Resolution of Board of Indian Commissioners urging organization of government for the Indian Territory.

"Affairs in the Indian Department," *House Report* No. 39, 41 Congress, 3 session, serial 1464. Report of investigation of Commissioner of Indian Affairs Ely S. Parker.

House Report No. 89, 42 Congress, 2 session, serial 1543. Minority report of Committee on Territories, opposing territorial organization for the Indian Territory.

Senate Executive Document No. 29, 42 Congress, 3 session, serial 1545. Relations with the Modoc Indians.

House Miscellaneous Document No. 110, 42 Congress, 3 session, serial 1573. Protest of Creek and Cherokee delegates against organization of the Indian Territory.

"Resolution of the Legislature of Kansas in Favor of the Transfer of the Bureau of Indian Affairs to the War Department," *Senate Miscellaneous Document* No. 75, 43 Congress, 1 session, serial 1584.

Senate Miscellaneous Document No. 117, 43 Congress, 1 session, serial 1584. Memorial of Indian delegates against appointment of a superintendent of schools in the Indian Territory.

"Modoc War," *House Executive Document* No. 122, 43 Congress, 1 session, serial 1607.

House Miscellaneous Document No. 87, 43 Congress, 1 session, serial 1618. Protest of Indians against territorial government.

House Miscellaneous Document No. 88, 43 Congress, 1 session, serial 1618. Protest of Indian International Council against territorial government.

Senate Miscellaneous Document No. 34, 43 Congress, 2 session, serial 1630.

Memorial of citizens of the Chickasaw Nation against territorial government.

Senate Miscellaneous Document No. 71, 43 Congress, 2 session, serial 1630. Memorial of citizens of the Creek Nation against territorial government.

Senate Miscellaneous Document No. 72, 43 Congress, 2 session, serial 1630. Protest of Osage Indians against territorial government.

Senate Executive Document No. 76, 44 Congress, 1 session, serial 1664. Osage remonstrance against territorial government.

"Transfer of Indian Affairs to War Department," *House Miscellaneous Document* No. 92, 44 Congress, 1 session, serial 1701. Resolution of the legislature of California.

"Transfer of Indian Bureau," *House Report* No. 240, 44 Congress, 1 session, serial 1708. Report of Committee on Indian Affairs.

"Reduction of Army Officers' Pay, Reorganization of the Army, and Transfer of the Indian Bureau," *House Report* No. 354, 44 Congress, 1 session, serial 1709. Report of the Committee on Military Affairs.

Senate Executive Document No. 9, 44 Congress, 2 session, serial 1718. Report and proceedings of the Manypenny commission for reduction of the Sioux Reserve, 1876.

House Report No. 82, 44 Congress, 2 session, serial 1769. Reports on bill for the organization of the Indian Territory.

Senate Executive Document No. 14, 45 Congress, 2 session, serial 1780. Reports on the Nez Percé war.

Senate Miscellaneous Document No. 8, 45 Congress, 2 session, serial 1785. Memorial of Choctaws and Chickasaws against bill to enable Indians to become citizens.

Senate Miscellaneous Document No. 16, 45 Congress, 2 session, serial 1785. Proposal for consolidation of Indian reservations.

Senate Miscellaneous Document No. 18, 45 Congress, 2 session, serial 1785. Protest of Seminole and Creek delegates against bill to enable Indians to become citizens.

Senate Miscellaneous Document No. 82, 45 Congress, 2 session, serial 1786. Memorial of delegates from the Indian Territory against territorial organization.

"Transfer of Indian Bureau," *House Miscellaneous Document* No. 19, 45 Congress, 2 session, serial 1815. Resolutions of the legislature of California.

House Miscellaneous Document No. 32, 46 Congress, 2 session, serial 1815. Indian opposition to authorization of a delegate in Congress from the Indian Territory.

"Transfer of Indians from Civil to Military Management," *House Miscellaneous Document* No. 33, 45 Congress, 2 session, serial 1815. Memorial of Cherokee, Creek, Seminole, Choctaw, and Chickasaw delegates opposing transfer.

"Transfer of the Indian Bureau to the War Department," *House Report* No. 241, 45 Congress, 2 session, serial 1822. Report of the Committee on Indian Affairs.

Senate Miscellaneous Document No. 73, 45 Congress, 3 session, serial 1833. Memorial of Five Civilized Tribes against establishing a United States court in the Indian Territory.

"Testimony Taken by the Joint Committee Appointed to Take into Consideration the Expediency of Transferring the Indian Bureau to the War Department," *Senate Miscellaneous Document* No. 53, 45 Congress, 3 session, serial 1835.

"Report of the Joint Committee Appointed to Consider the Expediency of Transferring the Indian Bureau to the War Department," *Senate Report* No. 693, 45 Congress, 3 session, serial 1837.

Senate Report No. 744, 45 Congress, 3 session, serial 1839. Report of Committee on Territories on organization of the Indian Territory, with massive testimony.

House Report No. 107, 45 Congress, 3 session, serial 1866. Report of Committee on Indian Affairs in favor of bill for relief of the Ponca Indians.

"Lands to Indians in Severalty," *House Report* No. 165, 45 Congress, 3 session, serial 1866. Report of Committee on Indian Affairs.

"Equal Rights to All Religious Denominations among Indians," *House Report* No. 167, 45 Congress, 3 session, serial 1866.

House Report No. 188, 45 Congress, 3 session, serial 1867. Report of Committee on Territories against organization of the Indian Territory.

Senate Executive Document No. 20, 46 Congress, 1 session, serial 1869. Concerning occupation of the Indian Territory by white settlers.

House Miscellaneous Document No. 13, 46 Congress, 1 session, serial 1876. Cherokee, Creek, and Choctaw protest against organization of the Indian Territory.

Senate Executive Document No. 31, 46 Congress, 2 session, serial 1882. Documents concerning the Ute outbreak in Colorado.

Senate Executive Document No. 114, 46 Congress, 2 session, serial 1885. Agreement signed with the Ute Indians.

Senate Miscellaneous Document No. 41, 46 Congress, 2 session, serial 1890. Memorial of Indians against organization of the Indian Territory.

Senate Report No. 670, 46 Congress, 2 session, serial 1898. Report on removal of the Poncas.

Senate Report No. 708, 46 Congress, 2 session, serial 1899. Report on removal of the Northern Cheyennes.

"Report of the Ute Commission," *House Executive Document* No. 1, part 5, 46 Congress, 2 session, serial 1910, pp. 276–87.

"White River Ute Commission Investigation," *House Executive Document* No. 83, 46 Congress, 2 session, serial 1925.

"Testimony in Relation to the Ute Indian Outbreak, Taken by the Committee on Indian Affairs of the House of Representatives," *House Miscellaneous Document* No. 38, 46 Congress, 2 session, serial 1931.

"Transfer of the Bureau of Indian Affairs to the War Department," *House Report* No. 1393, 46 Congress, 2 session, serial 1937.

"Agreement with Ute Indians of Colorado," *House Report* No. 1401, 46 Congress, 2 session, serial 1937.

Senate Executive Document No. 14, 46 Congress, 3 session, serial 1941. On the killing of the Ponca, Big Snake.

Senate Executive Document No. 30, 46 Congress, 3 session, serial 1941. On the removal of the Poncas.

Senate Executive Document No. 31, 46 Congress, 3 session, serial 1943. Report of the Ute Commission.

Senate Miscellaneous Document No. 49, 46 Congress, 3 session, serial 1944. Testimony on the removal of the Northern Cheyennes and of the Poncas.

"Memorial of the Members of the Omaha Tribe of Indians, for a Grant of Land in Severalty," *Senate Miscellaneous Document* No. 31, 47 Congress, 1 session, serial 1993.

"Allotment of Lands in Severalty among Indian Tribes: Memorial of the Creek Nation on the Subject of Lands in Severalty among the Several Indian Tribes," *House Miscellaneous Document* No. 18, 47 Congress, 2 session, serial 2115.

Senate Executive Document No. 49, 48 Congress, 1 session, serial 2162. Concerning relief of the Mission Indians, including report of Helen Hunt Jackson and Abbot Kinney.

Senate Executive Document No. 54, 48 Congress, 1 session, serial 2165. On leasing of lands in the Indian Territory for cattle grazing.

Senate Executive Document No. 70, 48 Congress, 1 session, serial 2165. Document on the Edmunds commission for the reduction of the Sioux Reserve.

Senate Executive Document No. 109, 48 Congress, 1 session, serial 2167. On status of Indians and of lands in the Indian Territory.

Senate Executive Document No. 208, 48 Congress, 1 session, serial 2168. On condition of the Northern Cheyenne Indians.

Senate Report No. 283, 48 Congress, 1 session, serial 2174. Report of Dawes's Select Committee on the Sioux Reserve.

Senate Executive Document No. 17, 48 Congress, 2 session, serial 2261. On leasing of Indian lands in the Indian Territory.

"Allowance of Lands in Severalty to Indians," *House Report* No. 2247, 48 Congress, 2 session, serial 2328. Report of Committee on Indian Affairs.

Senate Executive Document No. 15, 49 Congress, 1 session, serial 2333. On relief for the Mission Indians in California.

Senate Executive Document No. 212, 49 Congress, 1 session, serial 2341. On condition of the Northern Cheyenne Indians.

"Report of the Committee on Indian Affairs, United States Senate, on the Condition of the Indians in the Indian Territory, and Other Reservations, etc.," *Senate Report* No. 1278, 49 Congress, 1 session, serials 2362 and 2363.

"Allotment of Lands in Severalty to Indians," *House Report* No. 1835, 49 Congress, 1 session, serial 2440. Report of Committee on Indian Affairs.

"Mission Indians, State of California," *House Report* No. 2556, 49 Congress, 1 session, serial 2442. Report of Committee on Indian Affairs.

Senate Miscellaneous Document No. 153, 50 Congress, 1 session, serial 2517. Memorial for courts in the Indian Territory.

Senate Report No. 74, 50 Congress, 1 session, serial 2519. On relief for the Mission Indians of California.

"Mission Indians, State of California," *House Report* No. 3282, 50 Congress, 1 session, serial 2607. Report of Committee on Indian Affairs.

Senate Executive Document No. 17, 50 Congress, 2 session, serial 2610. Report of the Pratt commission for the reduction of the Sioux Reserve.

Senate Executive Document No. 51, 51 Congress, 1 session, serial 2682. Report of the Sioux Commission (Crook) for reduction of the Sioux Reserve.

Senate Executive Document No. 78, 51 Congress, 1 session, serial 2686. Concerning the status of the Indians in the Indian Territory.

Senate Executive Document No. 121, 51 Congress, 1 session, serial 2686. On condition of the Northern Cheyennes.

"Allotment of Lands in Severalty to Indians," *House Report* No. 1700, 51 Congress, 1 session, serial 2812. Report of Committee on Indian Affairs urging equalization of allotments.

Senate Executive Document No. 31, 52 Congress, 1 session, serial 2892. Report by Hampton Institute on returned Indian students.

Senate Report No. 281, 52 Congress, 1 session, serial 2912. On extending the jurisdiction of the Supreme Court over the Indian Territory.

"Mission Indians of California," *House Executive Document* No. 96, 52 Congress, 1 session, serial 2954.

Senate Report No. 377, 53 Congress, 2 session, serial 3183. Report of Select Committee on the Five Civilized Tribes (Teller).

"Sale of Intoxicants to Indians," *House Report* No. 1781, 53 Congress, 3 session, serial 3346.

Senate Document No. 182, 54 Congress, 1 session, serial 3353. On conditions in the Indian Territory.

"Sale of Intoxicating Liquors to Indians," *House Report* No. 1209, 54 Congress, 1 session, serial 3461.

VII. OTHER PUBLISHED GOVERNMENT SOURCES

Board of Indian Commissioners. *Annual Reports.* Beginning in 1869 the Board of Indian Commissioners issued an annual report under the title *First Annual Report of the Board of Indian Commissioners*, with appropriate changes for subsequent years. The volumes included a report on the year's activities, reports of committees of the board, proceedings of the annual meetings with the missionary boards, and after 1883 the proceedings of the Lake Mohonk Conference.

———. *Journal of the Second Annual Conference of the Board of Indian Commissioners with the Representatives of the Religious Societies Cooperating with the Government, and Reports of Their Work among the Indians.* Washington: Government Printing Office, 1873. This is the only report of the annual meeting with the missionary societies that was printed separate from the *Annual Report* of the board.

———. *What the Government and the Churches Are Doing for the Indians.* Washington: Government Printing Office, 1874.

Bureau of Indian Affairs. *Correspondence on the Subject of Teaching the Vernacular in Indian Schools, 1887–'88.* Washington: Government Printing Office, 1888.

———. *Regulations of the Indian Department, with an Appendix Containing the Forms Used.* Washington: Government Printing Office, 1884. New revised edition, 1894.

———. *Rules for Indian Schools, with Course of Study, List of Text-books, and Civil Service Rules.* Washington: Government Printing Office, 1892.

Census Office, Department of the Interior. *Extra Census Bulletin: The Five Civilized Tribes in Indian Territory: The Cherokee, Chickasaw, Choc-*

taw, Creek, and Seminole Nations. Washington: United States Census Printing Office, 1894.

Civil Service Commission. *Annual Reports.*

Cohen, Felix S. *Handbook of Federal Indian Law, with Reference Tables and Index.* Washington: Government Printing Office, 1942.

Commission to the Five Civilized Tribes. *Annual Reports.* These were issued under a variety of titles.

———. *Index to the Annual Reports of the Commission to the Five Civilized Tribes for the Years 1894 to 1905, Inclusive.* Washington: Government Printing Office, 1906.

Commissioner to the Five Civilized Tribes. *Laws, Decisions, and Regulations Affecting the Work of the Commissioner to the Five Civilized Tribes, 1893–1906, Together with Maps Showing Classification of Lands in the Chickasaw, Choctaw, Cherokee, Creek, and Seminole Nations, and Recording Districts, Railroads, and Principal Towns of the Indian Territory.* Washington: Government Printing Office, 1906.

Congressional Globe.

Congressional Record.

Hodge, Frederick Webb, ed. *Handbook of American Indians North of Mexico.* 2 vols. Washington: Government Printing Office, 1907–1910.

Israel, Fred L., ed. *The State of the Union Messages of the Presidents, 1790–1966.* 3 vols. New York: Chelsea House, 1966.

Jackson, Helen Hunt, and Abbot Kinney. *Report on the Condition and Needs of the Mission Indians of California, Made by Special Agents Helen Jackson and Abbot Kinney, to the Commissioner of Indian Affairs.* Washington: Government Printing Office, 1883.

Journal of the Executive Proceedings of the Senate.

Journal of the House of Representatives.

Journal of the Senate.

Kappler, Charles J., *Indian Affairs: Laws and Treaties.* 2 vols. Washington: Government Printing Office, 1904.

Report of Board of Inquiry Convened by Authority of Letter of the Secretary of the Interior of June 7, 1877, to Investigate Certain Charges against S. A. Galpin, Chief Clerk of the Indian Bureau, and Concerning Irregularities in Said Bureau. Washington: Government Printing Office, 1878.

Richardson, James D., ed. *A Compilation of the Messages and Papers of the Presidents.* 10 vols. Washington: Government Printing Office, 1896–1899.

Royce, Charles C., ed. *Indian Land Cessions in the United States.* Eighteenth Annual Report of the Bureau of American Ethnology, part 2. Washington: Government Printing Office, 1899.

United States Statutes at Large.

VIII. PUBLICATIONS OF INDIAN REFORM ORGANIZATIONS

Indian Rights Association. Annual Reports. These were published under the title *First Annual Report of the Executive Committee of the Indian Rights Association,* with appropriate changes for successive years.

———. Publications. Each year the Indian Rights Association published pamphlets and booklets for wide distribution. They were original reports by members of the association or reprinted material from a variety of sources. A full listing is given for each year in the *Annual Report.* Those of special value for this study are listed below under "Indian Rights Association" or under the author of the individual publication.

Lake Mohonk Conference. Proceedings. The first two annual reports (1883 and 1884) were called *Address to the Public of the Lake Mohonk Conference Held . . . in Behalf of the Civilization and Legal Protection of the Indians of the United States* and were published by the Indian Rights Association. The later reports were called *Proceedings,* with the following form: *Proceedings of the Seventh Annual Meeting of the Lake Mohonk Conference of Friends of the Indian.* They were published in separate form by the conference itself and were also reprinted each year in the annual reports of the Board of Indian Commissioners.

Women's National Indian Association. Annual Reports. First called The Indian Treaty-Keeping and Protective Association, the organization took the name Women's National Indian Association in 1883. It published annual reports under the following form: *Fourth Annual Report of the Women's National Indian Association.*

———. Publications. The association published a variety of special reports and other pamphlet material. Important items are listed below under "Women's National Indian Association" or under the author's name.

———. *The Indian's Friend.* Beginning in 1888 the association published this monthly magazine, largely for its own membership.

IX. PERIODICALS

In addition to specific articles from contemporary periodicals listed below, the following journals were useful for comment on Indian matters.

The Christian Union
The Council Fire
Harper's Illustrated Weekly
The Independent

The Nation
The Outlook

X. CONTEMPORARY WRITINGS

Abbott, Austin. "Indians and the Law," *Harvard Law Review*, II (November, 1888), 167–79.

Abbott, Lyman. "Our Indian Problem," *North American Review*, CLXVII (December, 1898), 719–28.

———. *Reminiscences*. Boston: Houghton Mifflin Company, 1915.

Address of the Catholic Clergy of the Province of Oregon, to the Catholics of the United States, on President Grant's Indian Policy, in Its Bearings upon Catholic Interests at Large. Portland, Oregon: The Catholic Sentinel Publication Company, 1874.

American Bar Association. "Report of Special Committee on Indian Legislation," *Report of the Sixteenth Annual Meeting of the American Bar Association*. Philadelphia, 1893. Pp. 351–63.

Annual Report of the Indians' Hope Association of Philadelphia, a Branch of the Women's Auxiliary to the Board of Missions, 1875. Philadelphia, 1875.

Armstrong, Samuel C. *Report of a Trip Made in Behalf of the Indian Rights Association, to Some Indian Reservations of the Southwest.* Philadelphia: Indian Rights Association, 1884.

Associated Executive Committee of Friends on Indian Affairs. *Need of Law on the Indian Reservations*. Philadelphia: Sherman and Company, 1878.

Beeson, John. *Are We Not Men and Brethren? An Address to the People of the United States.* New York: National Indian Aid Office, 1859.

———. *A Plea for the Indians*. New York: J. Beeson, 1857.

Blackmar, F. W. "Indian Education," *Annals of the American Academy of Political and Social Science*, II (May, 1892), 813–37.

Bland, Thomas A. *A Brief History of the Late Military Invasion of the Home of the Sioux.* Washington: National Indian Defence Association, 1891.

———. *Life of Alfred B. Meacham: Together with His Lecture, The Tragedy of the Lava Beds.* Washington: T. A. and M. C. Bland, 1883.

———. "The New Indian Policy: Land in Severalty," *The American*, XIV (May 21, 1887), 73–74.

Boudinot, Elias Cornelius. "The Indian Territory and Its Inhabitants," *Geographical Magazine*, I (June, 1874), 92–95.

———. *Oklahoma: Argument of Col. E .C. Boudinot before the Committee on Territories, January 29, 1878.* Alexandria, Virginia: G. H. Ramey and Son, 1878.

———. *Speech of Elias C. Boudinot, a Cherokee Indian, Delivered before the House Committee on Territories, February 7, 1872, in Behalf of a Territorial Government for the Indian Territory, in Reply to Wm. P. Ross, a Cherokee Delegate, in His Argument against Any Congressional Action upon the Subject.* Washington: McGill and Witherow, 1872.

———. *Speech of Elias C. Boudinot, of the Cherokee Nation, Delivered before the House Committee on Territories, March 5, 1872, on the Question of a Territorial Government for the Indian Territory, in Reply to the Second Argument of the Indian Delegations in Opposition to Such Proposed Government.* Washington: McGill and Witherow, 1872.

———. *Speech of Elias C. Boudinot, a Cherokee Indian, on the Indian Question, Delivered at Vinita, Cherokee Nation, the Junction of the Atlantic and Pacific, and the Missouri, Kansas, and Texas Railroads, September 21, 1871.* Washington: McGill and Witherow, 1872.

Burdick, Usher L. *My Friend the Indian, or Three Heretofore Unpublished Chapters of the Book Published under the Title of My Friend the Indian by Major James McLaughlin.* Baltimore: The Proof Press, 1936.

Canfield, George F. "The Legal Position of the Indian," *American Law Review,* XV (January, 1881), 21–37.

Catholic Grievances in Relation to the Administration of Indian Affairs, Being a Report Presented to the Catholic Young Men's National Union, at Its Annual Convention, Held in Boston, Massachusetts, May 10th and 11th, 1882. Richmond, Virginia: Catholic Visitor Print, 1882.

Child, Lydia Maria. *An Appeal for the Indians.* New York: William P. Thomlinson, n.d.

Colyer, Vincent. *Peace with the Apaches of New Mexico and Arizona: Report of Vincent Colyer, Member of the Board of Indian Commissioners, 1871.* Washington: Government Printing Office, 1872.

Crook, George. *Letter from General Crook on Giving the Ballot to the Indians.* Philadelphia: Indian Rights Association, 1885.

Dawes, Henry L. *The Case of McGillicuddy.* Philadelphia: Indian Rights Association, 1884.

———. "The Indian Territory," *The Independent,* LII (October 25, 1900), 2561–65.

———. *Past and Present Indian Policy.* New York [?], 1892.

Dawson, Thomas F., and F. J. V. Skiff. *The Ute War: A History of the White River Massacre and the Privations and Hardships of the Captive White Women among the Hostiles on Grand River.* Denver: Tribune Publishing House, 1879. Facsimile edition, Boulder: Johnson Publishing Company, 1964.

Dewey, Mary E. *Historical Sketch of the Formation and Achievements of*

The Women's National Indian Association in the United States. Philadelphia: Women's National Indian Association, 1900.

Dodge, D. Stuart. *Memorials of William E. Dodge.* New York: Anson D. F. Randolph and Company, 1887.

Dorchester, Daniel. *Romanism* versus *the Public School System.* New York: Phillips and Hunt, 1888.

Ellis, George E. *The Red Man and the White Man in North America from Its Discovery to the Present Time.* Boston: Little, Brown and Company, 1882.

Extracts from the Minutes of a Convention of Delegates from the Seven Yearly Meetings of Friends Having Charge of the Indians in the Northern Superintendency, with Report of Barclay White, Special Agent of the Society of Friends. Philadelphia: Friends' Book Association, 1878.

Fletcher, Alice C. *Indian Education and Civilization.* Senate Executive Document No. 95, 48 Congress, 2 session, serial 2264. Washington: Government Printing Office, 1888.

Foote, Kate. *The Indian Legislation of 1888.* Philadelphia: Women's National Indian Association, n.d.

Gates, Merrill E. "Land and Law as Agents in Educating Indians," *Report of the Board of Indian Commissioners,* 1885, pp. 13–35.

Gravatt, J. J. *The Record of Hampton's Returned Indian Pupils.* Philadelphia: Indian Rights Association, 1885.

Grinnell, George Bird. *The Enforcement of Liquor Laws a Necessary Protection to the Indians.* Philadelphia: Indian Rights Association, 1893.

———. "The Indian on the Reservation," *Atlantic Monthly,* LXXXIII (February, 1899), 255–67.

———. "The Indians and the Outing System," *Outlook,* LXXV (September 12, 1903), 167–73.

Hailmann, William N. *Education of the Indian. Monographs on Education in the United States,* No. 19, edited by Nicholas Murray Butler. St. Louis: Division of Exhibits, Department of Education, Universal Exposition, 1904.

Harrison, J. B. *The Latest Studies on Indian Reservations.* Philadelphia: Indian Rights Association, 1887.

Harsha, William Justin. "Law for the Indians," *North American Review,* CXXXIV (March, 1882), 272–92.

Hornblower, William B. "The Legal Status of the Indian," *Report of the Annual Meeting of the American Bar Association,* XIV (1891), 261–77.

Howard, Oliver Otis. *My Life and Experiences among Our Hostile Indians: A Record of Personal Observations, Adventures, and Campaigns among the Indians of the Great West, with Some Account of Their Life, Habits, Traits, Religion, Ceremonies, Dress, Savage Instincts, and Customs in Peace and War.* Hartford: A. D. Worthington and Company, 1907.

————. *Nez Perce Joseph: An Account of His Ancestors, His Lands, His Confederates, His Enemies, His Murders, His War, His Pursuit and Capture.* Boston: Lee and Shepard, 1881.

————. "The True Story of the Wallowa Campaign," *North American Review,* CXXIX (July, 1879), 53–64.

Howe, M. A. DeWolfe. *Memorial of William Welsh.* Reading, Pennsylvania: Owen, Printer, 1878.

The Indian Question: Report of the Committee Appointed by Hon. John D. Long, Governor of Massachusetts. Boston: Frank Wood, 1880.

Indian Rights Association. *The Attorney-General and Seven Indian Policemen of Cheyenne River Agency—A Case Where to Serve Faithfully Came Near Meaning the Gallows.* Philadelphia: Indian Rights Association, 1895.

————. *Captain Pratt and His Work for Indian Education.* Philadelphia: Indian Rights Association, 1886.

————. *The Case of the Mission Indians in Southern California, and the Action of the Indian Rights Association in Supporting the Defense of Their Legal Rights.* Philadelphia: Indian Rights Association, 1886.

————. *A Crisis in Indian Affairs.* Philadelphia: Indian Rights Association, 1891.

————. *Crow Creek Reservation, Dakota: Action of the Indian Rights Association, and Opinions of the Press, West and East, Regarding Its Recent Occupation by White Settlers, Together with the Proclamation of the President Commanding the Removal of the Settlers and Restoring the Lands to the Indians.* Philadelphia: Indian Rights Association, 1885.

————. *Friendship That Asks for Pay: Pretended Friends of the Indians and Their Methods.* Philadelphia: Indian Rights Association, 1887.

————. *The Helplessness of Indians before the Law; with an Outline of Proposed Legislation.* Philadelphia: Indian Rights Association, 1886.

————. *The Question of Indian Commissioner Oberly's Retention.* Philadelphia: Indian Rights Association, 1889.

The Indians Opposed to the Transfer Bill: United Action of the Delegations of the Cherokee, Creek, Seminole, Chickasaw, and Choctaw Nations in Opposition to the Measure: They Protest against It, and Give Their Reasons for So Doing. Washington: Gibson Brothers, 1878.

Jackson, Helen Hunt. *A Century of Dishonor: A Sketch of the United States Government's Dealings with Some of the Indian Tribes.* New York: Harper and Brothers, 1881.

Jackson, Helen Hunt, and Abbot Kinney. *Report of Mrs. Helen Hunt Jackson and Abbot Kinney on the Mission Indians in 1883.* Boston: Stanley and Usher, 1887.

Johnson, Ellen Terry. *Historical Sketch of the Connecticut Indian Association from 1881 to 1888.* Hartford: Fowler and Miller Company, 1888.

Joseph, Chief. "An Indian's View of Indian Affairs," *North American Review,* CXXVIII (April, 1879), 412–33.

"Journal of the General Council of the Indian Territory," *Chronicles of Oklahoma,* III (April, 1925), 33–44; (June, 1925), 120–36.

Koch, P. "Indian Reservations," *Nation,* XXX (April 15, 1880), 287–88.

Lambertson, G. M. "Indian Citizenship," *American Law Review,* XX (March–April, 1886), 183–93.

Leupp, Francis E. *Civil Service Reform Essential to a Successful Indian Administration.* Philadelphia: Indian Rights Association, 1895.

———. *The Indian and His Problem.* New York: C. Scribner's Sons, 1910.

———. "The Spoils System and the Indian Service," *Public Opinion,* XVIII (May 23, 1895), 570–71.

Linn, J. M. "The Relation of the Church to the Indian Question," *Presbyterian Review,* I (October, 1880), 677–93.

McAdam, Rezin W. "An Indian Commonwealth," *Harper's New Monthly Magazine,* LXXXVII (November, 1893), 884–97.

McLaughlin, James. *My Friend the Indian.* Boston: Houghton Mifflin Company, 1910. See also Burdick, Usher L.

Manypenny, George W. *Our Indian Wards.* Cincinnati: Robert Clarke and Company, 1880.

Marty, Martin. "The Indian Problem and the Catholic Church," *Catholic World,* XLVIII (February, 1889), 577–84.

Meacham, Alfred B. *Wigwam and War-path: or the Royal Chief in Chains.* Boston: John P. Dale and Company, 1875.

———. *Wi-ne-ma (The Woman-Chief) and Her People.* Hartford: American Publishing Company, 1876.

Memoranda of Some of the Proceedings of the Friends of Baltimore Yearly Meeting in Relation to the Western Indians. Philadelphia, 1869.

Memorial of the Society of Friends in Regard to the Indians. n.p., 1868.

Meserve, Charles F. *The Dawes Commission and the Five Civilized Tribes of Indian Territory.* Philadelphia: Indian Rights Association, 1896.

———. *A Tour of Observation Among Indians and Indian Schools in Arizona, New Mexico, Oklahoma, and Kansas.* Philadelphia: Indian Rights Association, 1894.

Miles, Nelson A. "The Indian Problem," *North American Review*, CXXVII (April, 1879), 304–14.

"Mohonk and Its Conferences," *New England Magazine*, XVI (June, 1897), 447–64.

Morgan, Thomas J. *The American Catechism: A Manual of Patriotism*. Boston: American Citizen Company, 1894.

———. *Educational Mosaics: A Collection from Many Writers (Chiefly Modern) of Thoughts Bearing on Educational Questions of the Day*. Boston: Silver, Rogers and Company, 1887.

———. *Indian Education*. United States Bureau of Education, Bulletin No. 1, 1889. Washington: Government Printing Office, 1890.

———. *The Negro in America and the Ideal American Republic*. Philadelphia: American Baptist Publication Society, 1898.

———. *Patriotic Citizenship*. New York: American Book Company, 1895.

———. *A Plea for the Papoose: An Address at Albany, N. Y., by Gen. T. J. Morgan*. n.p., n.d.

———. *The Present Phase of the Indian Question: Also a Memorial on the Extension of Law to the Indians, by the Boston Indian Citizenship Committee*. Boston: Boston Indian Citizenship Committee, 1891.

———. *Reminiscences of Services with Colored Troops in the Army of the Cumberland, 1863–65. Personal Narratives of Events in the War of the Rebellion, Being Papers Read before the Rhode Island Soldiers and Sailors Historical Society*, 3d series, No. 13. Providence: The Society, 1885.

———. "The Roman Catholic Church and the Indians," in *Errors of the Roman Catholic Church, and Its Insidious Influence in the United States and Other Countries*. St. Louis: J. H. Chambers and Company, 1895. Pp. xxxii–xlix.

———. *Roman Catholics and Indian Education*. Boston: American Citizen Company, 1893.

———. *Studies in Pedagogy*. Boston: Silver, Burdett and Company, 1889.

National Civil Service Reform League. *Extract, Report of the Special Committee of the National Civil-Service Reform League Upon the Present Condition of the Reform Movement*. Philadelphia: Indian Rights Association, 1887.

National Indian Defence Association. *Preamble, Platform, and Constitution of the National Indian Defence Association*. Washington: Rufus H. Darby, 1885.

National League for the Protection of American Institutions. *A Petition Concerning Sectarian Appropriations for Indian Education*. New York, 1892.

Neill, Edward D. *Effort and Failure to Civilize the Aborigines: Letter to*

Hon. N. G. Taylor, Commissioner of Indian Affairs. Washington: Government Printing Office, 1868.

Otis, Elwell S. *The Indian Question.* New York: Sheldon and Company, 1878.

Painter, Charles C. *The Condition of Affairs in Indian Territory and California.* Philadelphia: Indian Rights Association, 1888.

———. *The Dawes Land in Severalty Bill and Indian Emancipation.* Philadelphia: Indian Rights Association, 1887.

———. *Oleomargarine versus the Indian.* Philadelphia: Indian Rights Association, 1886.

———. *The Proposed Removal of Indians to Oklahoma.* Philadelphia: Indian Rights Association, 1888.

———. *A Visit to the Mission Indians of California.* Philadelphia: Indian Rights Association, 1887.

———. *A Visit to the Mission Indians of Southern California, and Other Western Tribes.* Philadelphia: Indian Rights Association, 1886.

Palladino, L. B. *Education for the Indian: Fancy and Reason on the Subject: Contract Schools and Non-Sectarianism in Indian Education.* New York: Benziger Brothers, 1892.

———. *Indian and White in the Northwest: A History of Catholicity in Montana, 1831–1891.* Baltimore: John Murphy and Company, 1894. Second edition revised, Lancaster, Pennsylvania: Wickersham Publishing Company, 1922.

Pancoast, Henry S. *Impressions of the Sioux Tribes in 1882, with Some First Principles in the Indian Question.* Philadelphia: Franklin Printing House, 1883.

———. *The Indian Before the Law.* Philadelphia: Indian Rights Association, 1884.

Parker, Ely S. "Writings of General Parker: Extracts from His Letters and an Autobiographical Memoir of Historical Interest," *Publications of the Buffalo Historical Society,* VIII (1905), 520–36.

The Political Status of the American Indian. n.p., n.d.

Pratt, Richard Henry. *Battlefield and Classroom: Four Decades with the American Indian, 1867–1904.* Edited and with an Introduction by Robert M. Utley. New Haven: Yale University Press, 1964.

———. *How to Deal with the Indians: The Potency of Environment.* Carlisle, Pennsylvania: Carlisle Indian School, 1903.

———. *The Indian Industrial School, Carlisle, Pennsylvania: Its Origin, Purposes, Progress and the Difficulties Surmounted.* Carlisle, Pennsylvania: Hamilton Library Association, 1908.

Proceedings on the Occasion of the Presentation of the Petition of the Women's National Indian Association, by Hon. H. L. Dawes, of Massachusetts, in the Senate of the United States, February 21, 1882. Washington, 1882.

Prucha, Francis Paul, ed. *Americanizing the American Indians: Writings by the "Friends of the Indian" 1880-1900.* Cambridge: Harvard University Press, 1973.

Quinton, Amelia S. "Care of the Indian," in Annie Nathan Meyer, ed., *Woman's Work in America.* New York: Henry Holt and Company, 1891. Pp. 373-91.

Report of the Delegates Representing the Yearly Meetings, of Philadelphia, New York, Baltimore, Indiana, Ohio, and Genesee, on the Indian Concern, at Baltimore, Tenth Month, 1871. New York, 1871.

Report of the Joint Delegation Appointed by the Committees on the Indian Concern of the Yearly Meetings of Baltimore, Philadelphia and New York Respectively . . . To Visit the Indians Under the Care of Friends, in the Northern Superintendency, State of Nebraska. Baltimore, 1869.

Rhoads, James E. *Our Next Duty to the Indians.* Philadelphia: Indian Rights Association, 1887.

Ross, William P. *Indian Territory: Remarks in Opposition to the Bill to Organize the Territory of Oklahoma by Wm. P. Ross, Principal Chief of the Cherokee Nation, before the Committee on Territories of the House of Representatives, Monday, February 9th, 1874.* Washington: Gibson Brothers, 1874.

Schurz, Carl. *An Open Letter in Answer to a Speech of Hon. H. L. Dawes, United States Senate, on the Case of Big Snake.* Washington, 1881.

———. "Present Aspects of the Indian Problem," *North American Review,* CXXXIII (July, 1881), 1-24.

———. "The Removal of the Poncas," *The Independent,* XXXII (January 1, 1880), 1.

———. *Speeches, Correspondence and Political Papers of Carl Schurz.* Edited by Frederic Bancroft. 6 vols. New York: G. P. Putnam's Sons, 1913.

Second Annual Report of the Joint Delegation Appointed by the Committees on the Indian Concern of the Yearly Meetings of Ohio and Genesee. Rochester, New York, 1870.

Secretary Schurz: Reply of the Boston Committee, Governor John D. Long, Chairman: Misrepresentations Corrected and Important Facts Presented. Boston: Frank Wood, 1881.

Shaffner, Ruth. "Civilizing the American Indian," *The Chautauquan,* XXIII (June, 1896), 259-68.

Sherman, William T. *Memoirs of Gen. W. T. Sherman, Written by Himself.* 4th ed., 2 vols. New York: C. L. Webster and Company, 1891.

Stephan, J. A. *Report of Rev. J. A. Stephan, Director, to Rt. Rev. Bishop M. Marty, President of the Bureau of Catholic Indian Missions, for the Year 1891-'92.* Washington, 1892.

Stuart, George H. *The Life of George H. Stuart, Written by Himself.* Edited by Robert Ellis Thompson. Philadelphia: J. M. Stoddart and Company, 1890.

Tatum, Lawrie. *Our Red Brothers and the Peace Policy of President Ulysses S. Grant.* Philadelphia: J. C. Winston and Company, 1899.

Thayer, James B. "The Dawes Bill and the Indians," *Atlantic Monthly*, LXI (March, 1888), 315–22.

———. "A People Without Law," *Atlantic Monthly*, LXVIII (October, 1891), 540–51; (November, 1891), 676–87.

———. *Remarks Made at a Meeting in Cambridge, Mass., Called by the Women's Indian Association of That City, May 3, 1886.* n.p., n.d.

———. *Remarks Made Before the Worcester Indian Association at Worcester, Mass., February 13, 1887.* n.p., n.d.

Tibbles, Thomas Henry. *Buckskin and Blanket Days: Memoirs of a Friend of the Indians.* Garden City, New York: Doubleday and Company, 1957. A work written in 1905.

———. *Hidden Power: A Secret History of the Indian Ring, Its Operations, Intrigues and Machinations, Revealing the Manner in Which It Controls Three Important Departments of the United States Government; A Defense of the U.S. Army, and a Solution to the Indian Problem.* New York: G. W. Carleton and Company, 1881.

——— [Zylyff]. *The Ponca Chiefs: An Indian's Attempt to Appeal from the Tomahawk to the Courts.* Boston: Lockwood, Brooks and Company, 1880. Edited with an introduction by Kay Graber, Lincoln: University of Nebraska Press, 1972.

———. *Western Men Defended: Speech of Mr. T. H. Tibbles in Tremont Temple, Boston, Mass., December, 1880.* Boston: Lockwood, Brooks and Company, 1880.

Universal Peace Union. *A Brief Synopsis of Work Proposed, Aided and Accomplished by the Universal Peace Union During the Last 31 Years, (from 1866 to 1897,) Under the Direction of Its President, Alfred H. Love, of Philadelphia.* Philadelphia, 1897.

United States Indian Commission. *A Specific Plan for the Treatment of the Indian Question.* New York, 1870.

Walker, Francis A. *The Indian Question.* Boston: J. R. Osgood and Company, 1874.

Weil, Robert. *The Legal Status of the Indian.* New York, 1888.

Welsh, Herbert. *Are the Eastern Industrial Training Schools for Indian Children a Failure?* Philadelphia: Indian Rights Association, 1886.

———. *A Brief Statement of the Objects, Achievements and Needs of the Indian Rights Association.* Philadelphia: Indian Rights Association, 1887.

———. "Civil Service and the Indian Service," *Good Government,* XIII (October 15, 1893), 41–43.

———. *Civilization Among the Sioux Indians: Report of a Visit to Some of the Sioux Reservations of South Dakota and Nebraska.* Philadelphia: Indian Rights Association, 1893.

———. *A Dangerous Assault Upon the Integrity of the Civil Service Law in the Indian Service.* Philadelphia: Indian Rights Association, 1893.

———. *Four Weeks Among Some of the Sioux Tribes of Dakota and Nebraska, Together with a Brief Consideration of the Indian Problem.* Germantown, Pennsylvania, 1882.

———. *How to Bring the Indian to Citizenship, and Citizenship to the Indian.* Philadelphia: Indian Rights Association, 1892.

———. "Indian Affairs Under the Present Administration," *The Civil-Service Reformer,* IV (August, 1888), 90–92.

———. *The Indian Problem: Secretary Welsh of the Indian Rights Association Reviews and Criticises Dr. Bland's Recent Statements—Dr. Sunderland a Self-Confessed Novice.* Philadelphia: Indian Rights Association, 1886.

———. *The Indian Question Past and Present.* Philadelphia: Indian Rights Association, 1890.

———. "The Meaning of the Dakota Outbreak," *Scribner's Magazine,* IX (April, 1891), 439–52.

———. *Report of a Visit to the Great Sioux Reserve, Dakota, Made During the Months of May and June, 1883, in Behalf of the Indian Rights Association.* Philadelphia: Indian Rights Association, 1883.

———. *Report of a Visit to the Navajo, Pueblo, and Hualapais Indians of New Mexico and Arizona.* Philadelphia: Indian Rights Association, 1885.

———. "Samuel Chapman Armstrong," *Educational Review,* VI (September, 1893), 105–25.

Welsh, William. *Indian Office: Wrongs Doing and Reforms Needed.* Philadelphia, 1874.

———. *Summing Up of Evidence Before a Committee of the House of Representatives, Charged with the Investigation of Misconduct in the Indian Office.* Washington: H. Polkinhorn and Company, 1871.

429

———. *Taopi and His Friends, or the Indians' Wrongs and Rights*. Philadelphia: Claxton, Remson and Hoffelfinger, 1869.

Whipple, Henry B. "The Indian System," *North American Review*, XCIX (October, 1864), 449–64.

———. *Lights and Shadows of a Long Episcopate*. New York: Macmillan Company, 1899.

White, Barclay. *The Friends and the Indians: Report of Barclay White, Late Superintendent of Indian Affairs in the Northern Superintendency, Nebraska, Exhibiting the Progress in Civilization of the Various Tribes of Indians Whilst Under the Care of Friends as Agents*. Oxford, Pennsylvania, 1886.

Women's National Indian Association. *Christian Civilization and Missionary Work of the Women's National Indian Association*. Philadelphia, 1887.

———. *A Few Facts for Workers of the Indian Treaty-Keeping and Protective Association*. Philadelphia, 1881.

———. *Missionary Work of the Women's National Indian Association, and Letters of Missionaries*. Philadelphia, 1885.

———. *Our Work—What? How? Why?* Philadelphia, 1893.

———. *Report on Indian Home Building*. Philadelphia, 1888.

———. *Sketch and Plans of the Indian Treaty-Keeping and Protective Association, with Suggestions to Workers*. Philadelphia, 1881.

———. *Sketches of Delightful Work*. Philadelphia, 1893.

———. *A Thrilling Record*. Philadelphia, 1880.

Wood, Frank. "The Evils of the Reservation System," *Outlook*, LXXV (September 19, 1903), 164–66.

Zylyff. *See* Tibbles, Thomas Henry.

XI. SECONDARY WORKS

Abel, Annie Heloise. *The American Indian under Reconstruction*. Cleveland: Arthur H. Clark Company, 1925.

———. "Indian Reservations in Kansas and the Extinguishment of Their Titles," *Transactions of the Kansas State Historical Society*, VIII (1903–1904), 72–109.

Adams, Evelyn C. *American Indian Education: Government Schools and Economic Progress*. New York: King's Crown Press, 1946.

Anderson, Harry H. "Fur Traders as Fathers: The Origins of the Mixed-Blooded Community Among the Rosebud Sioux," *South Dakota History*, III (Summer, 1973), 233–70.

Andrist, Ralph K. *The Long Death: The Last Days of the Plains Indians*. New York: Macmillan Company, 1964.

Applen, Allen G. "An Attempted Indian State Government: The Okmulgee Constitution in Indian Territory, 1870–1876," *Kansas Quarterly*, III (Fall, 1971), 89–99.

Athearn, Robert G. *William Tecumseh Sherman and the Settlement of the West*. Norman: University of Oklahoma Press, 1956.

Bailey, Paul D. *Wovoka, The Indian Messiah*. Los Angeles: Westernlore Press, 1957.

Baird, W. David. *Peter Pitchlynn: Chief of the Choctaws*. Norman: University of Oklahoma Press, 1972.

Beal, Merrill D. *"I Will Fight No More Forever": Chief Joseph and the Nez Perce War*. Seattle: University of Washington Press, 1963.

Beaver, R. Pierce. *Church, State, and the American Indians: Two and a Half Centuries of Partnership in Missions Between Protestant Churches and Government*. St. Louis: Concordia Publishing House, 1966.

Berthrong, Donald J. "Cattlemen on the Cheyenne-Arapaho Reservation, 1883–1885," *Arizona and the West*, XIII (Spring, 1971), 5–32.

———. *The Southern Cheyennes*. Norman: University of Oklahoma Press, 1963.

———. "White Neighbors Come among the Southern Cheyenne and Arapaho," *Kansas Quarterly*, III (Fall, 1971), 105–15.

Brown, Dee. *Bury My Heart at Wounded Knee*. New York: Holt, Rinehart and Winston, 1970.

Brown, Ira V. *Lyman Abbott, Christian Evolutionist: A Study in Religious Liberalism*. Cambridge: Harvard University Press, 1953.

Brown, Loren N. "The Appraisal of the Lands of the Choctaws and Chickasaws by the Dawes Commission," *Chronicles of Oklahoma*, XXII (Summer, 1944), 177–91.

———. "The Dawes Commission," *Chronicles of Oklahoma*, IX (March, 1931), 71–105.

———. "The Establishment of the Dawes Commission for Indian Territory," *Chronicles of Oklahoma*, XVIII (June, 1940), 171–81.

Brown, Mark H. *The Flight of the Nez Perce*. New York: G. P. Putnam's Sons, 1967.

———. "The Joseph Myth," *Montana, the Magazine of Western History*, XXII (Winter, 1972), 2–17.

Brunhouse, Robert L. "The Founding of the Carlisle Indian School," *Pennsylvania History*, VI (April, 1939), 72–85.

Buck, Solon J. "The Settlement of Oklahoma," *Transactions of the Wisconsin Academy of Sciences, Arts, and Letters*, XV, part II (1907), 325–80.

Buntin, Martha. "Beginning of the Leasing of the Surplus Grazing Lands on the Kiowa and Comanche Reservation," *Chronicles of Oklahoma*, X (September, 1932), 369–82.

Burgess, Larry E. " 'We'll Discuss It at Mohonk,' " *Quaker History: The Bulletin of Friends Historical Association*, XL (Spring, 1971), 14–28.

Carey, Raymond G. "Colonel Chivington, Brigadier General Connor, and Sand Creek," *The 1960 Brand Book* [Denver Westerners], pp. 103–36.

———. "The Puzzle of Sand Creek," *Colorado Magazine*, XLI (Fall, 1964), 279–98.

Carley, Kenneth. *The Sioux Uprising of 1862*. St. Paul: Minnesota Historical Society, 1961.

Carpenter, John A. *Sword and Olive Branch: Oliver Otis Howard*. Pittsburgh: University of Pittsburgh Press, 1964.

Chalmers, Harvey, II. *The Last Stand of the Nez Perce: Destruction of a People*. New York: Twayne Publishers, 1962.

Chapman, Berlin B. "The Cherokee Commission, 1889–1893," *Indiana Magazine of History*, XLII (June, 1946), 177–90.

———. "The Cherokee Commission at Kickapoo Village," *Chronicles of Oklahoma*, XVII (March, 1939), 62–74.

———. "The Final Report of the Cherokee Commission," *Chronicles of Oklahoma*, XIX (December, 1941), 356–67.

———. "How the Cherokees Acquired and Disposed of the Outlet: Part Three—The Fairchild Failure," *Chronicles of Oklahoma*, XV (September, 1937), 291–321.

———. "How the Cherokees Acquired and Disposed of the Outlet: Part Five—The Cherokees Concede to a Contract," *Chronicles of Oklahoma*, XVI (June, 1938), 135–62.

———. "Nez Percés in Indian Territory: An Archival Study," *Oregon Historical Quarterly*, L (June, 1949), 98–121.

———. "Secret 'Instructions and Suggestions' to the Cherokee Commission, 1889–1890," *Chronicles of Oklahoma*, XXVI (Winter, 1948–1949), 449–58.

Chaput, Donald. "Generals, Indian Agents, Politicians: The Doolittle Survey of 1865," *Western Historical Quarterly*, III (July, 1972), 269–82.

Clark, J. Stanley. "The Killing of Big Snake," *Chronicles of Oklahoma*, XLIX (Autumn, 1971), 302–14.

———. "The Nez Percés in Exile," *Pacific Northwest Quarterly*, XXXVI (July, 1945), 213–32.

———. "Ponca Publicity," *Mississippi Valley Historical Review*, XXIX (March, 1943), 495–516.

Clum, John P. "The San Carlos Apache Police," *New Mexico Historical Re-*

view, IV (July, 1929), 203–19; V (January, 1930), 67–92. The same article appeared in *Arizona Historical Review*, III (July, 1930), 12–25; (October, 1930), 21–43.

Clum, Woodworth. *Apache Agent: The Story of John P. Clum*. Boston: Houghton Mifflin Company, 1936.

Cutler, Lee. "Lawrie Tatum and the Kiowa Agency, 1869–1873," *Arizona and the West*, XIII (Autumn, 1971), 221–44.

Dale, Edward Everett. "Ranching on the Cheyenne-Arapaho Reservation, 1880–1885," *Chronicles of Oklahoma*, VI (March, 1928), 35–59.

Dale, Edward Everett, and Morris L. Wardell. *History of Oklahoma*. New York: Prentice-Hall, 1948.

Debo, Angie. *And Still the Waters Run*. Princeton: Princeton University Press, 1940.

———. *A History of the Indians of the United States*. Norman: University of Oklahoma Press, 1970.

———. *The Rise and Fall of the Choctaw Republic*. Norman: University of Oklahoma Press, 1934.

———. *The Road to Disappearance*. Norman: University of Oklahoma Press, 1941.

D'Elia, Donald J. "The Argument over Civilian or Military Indian Control, 1865–1880," *The Historian*, XXIV (February, 1962), 207–25.

Desmond, Humphrey J. *The A. P. A. Movement: A Sketch*. Washington: New Century Press, 1912.

Dusenberry, Verne. "The Northern Cheyenne," *Montana Magazine of History*, V (Winter, 1955), 23–40.

Eastman, Elaine Goodale. "The Ghost Dance War and Wounded Knee Massacre of 1890–91," *Nebraska History*, XXVI (January-March, 1945), 26–42.

———. *Pratt: The Red Man's Moses*. Norman: University of Oklahoma Press, 1935.

Edwards, Martha L. "A Problem of Church and State in the 1870's," *Mississippi Valley Historical Review*, XI (June, 1924), 37–53.

Ellis, Elmer. *Henry Moore Teller: Defender of the West*. Caldwell, Idaho: Caxton Printers, 1941.

Ellis, Richard N. "After Bull Run: The Later Career of Gen. John Pope," *Montana, the Magazine of Western History*, XIX (Autumn, 1969), 46–57.

———. "Copper-skinned Soldiers: The Apache Scouts," *Great Plains Journal*, V (Spring, 1966), 51–67.

———. "General John Pope and the Southern Plains Indians, 1875–1883," *Southwestern Historical Quarterly*, LXXII (October, 1968), 152–69.

433

———. *General Pope and U.S. Indian Policy.* Albuquerque: University of New Mexico Press, 1970.

———. "The Humanitarian Generals," *Western Historical Quarterly*, III (April, 1972), 169–78.

———. "The Humanitarian Soldiers," *Journal of Arizona History*, X (Summer, 1969), 53–66.

Emmitt, Robert. *The Last War Trail: The Utes and the Settlement of Colorado.* Norman: University of Oklahoma Press, 1954.

Ewers, John C. *The Blackfeet: Raiders on the Northwestern Plains.* Norman: University of Oklahoma Press, 1958.

Fee, Chester Anders. *Chief Joseph: The Biography of a Great Indian.* New York: Wilson-Erickson, 1936.

Folwell, William Watts. *A History of Minnesota.* 4 vols. St. Paul: Minnesota Historical Society, 1921–1930.

Foreman, Grant. *A History of Oklahoma.* Norman: University of Oklahoma Press, 1942.

Frederikson, Otto F. *The Liquor Question Among the Indian Tribes in Kansas, 1804–1881.* Bulletin of the University of Kansas, Humanistic Studies, vol. IV, no. 4. Lawrence, 1932.

Fritz, Henry E. "George W. Manypenny and *Our Indian Wards*," *Kansas Quarterly*, III (Fall, 1971), 100–104.

———. "The Making of Grant's 'Peace Policy,'" *Chronicles of Oklahoma*, XXXVII (Winter, 1959–1960), 411–32.

———. *The Movement for Indian Assimilation, 1860–1890.* Philadelphia: University of Pennsylvania Press, 1963.

Fuess, Claude Moore. *Carl Schurz, Reformer.* New York: Dodd, Mead and Company, 1932.

Gallaher, Ruth A. "The Indian Agent in the United States Since 1850," *Iowa Journal of History and Politics*, XIV (April, 1916), 173–238.

Garfield, Marvin H. "The Indian Question in Congress and in Kansas," *Kansas Historical Quarterly*, II (February, 1933), 29–44.

Gates, Paul Wallace. *Fifty Million Acres: Conflicts over Kansas Land Policy, 1854–1890.* Ithaca: Cornell University Press, 1954.

———. "Indian Allotments Preceding the Dawes Act," in John G. Clark, ed., *The Frontier Challenge: Responses to the Trans-Mississippi West.* Lawrence: University Press of Kansas, 1971. Pp. 141–70.

Gibson, Arrell M. *The Chickasaws.* Norman: University of Oklahoma Press, 1971.

———. *The Kickapoos: Lords of the Middle Border.* Norman: University of Oklahoma Press, 1963.

———. *Oklahoma: A History of Five Centuries.* Norman: Harlow Publishing Corporation, 1965.

Gilcreast, Everett Arthur. "Richard Henry Pratt and American Indian Policy, 1877–1906: A Study of the Assimilation Movement." Ph.D. Dissertation, Yale University, 1967.

Gittinger, Roy. *The Formation of the State of Oklahoma, 1803–1906.* Norman: University of Oklahoma Press, 1939. Originally published in 1917 as University of California Publications in History, vol. VI.

Green, Charles Lowell. "The Indian Reservation System of the Dakotas in 1889," *South Dakota Historical Collections,* XIV (1928), 307–416.

Grinnell, George Bird. *The Fighting Cheyennes.* New York: Charles Scribner's Sons, 1915.

Hafen, Ann W. "Efforts to Recover the Stolen Son of Chief Ouray," *Colorado Magazine,* XVI (January, 1939), 53–62.

Hagan, William T. *American Indians.* Chicago: University of Chicago Press, 1961.

———. *Indian Police and Judges: Experiments in Acculturation and Control.* New Haven: Yale University Press, 1966.

———. "Indian Policy After the Civil War: The Reservation Experience," *American Indian Policy: Indiana Historical Society Lectures 1970–1971.* Indianapolis: Indiana Historical Society, 1971. Pp. 20–36.

———. "Kiowas, Comanches, and Cattlemen, 1867–1906: A Case Study of the Failure of U.S. Reservation Policy," *Pacific Historical Review,* XL (August, 1971), 333–55.

———. "Quanah Parker, Indian Judge," in K. Ross Toole *et al.,* eds., *Probing the American West.* Santa Fe: Museum of New Mexico Press, 1962. Pp. 71–78.

———. "Squaw Men on the Kiowa, Comanche, and Apache Reservation: Advance Agents of Civilization or Disturbers of the Peace?" in John G. Clark, ed., *The Frontier Challenge: Responses to the Trans-Mississippi West.* Lawrence: University Press of Kansas, 1971. Pp. 171–202.

Haines, Francis. *The Nez Percés: Tribesmen of the Columbia Plateau.* Norman: University of Oklahoma Press, 1955. A revision of *Red Eagles of the Northwest: The Story of Chief Joseph and His People.* Portland, Oregon: The Scholastic Press, 1939.

Hall, James Parker. "James Bradley Thayer, 1831–1902," in William Draper Lewis, *Great American Lawyers.* Vol. VIII. Philadelphia: John C. Winston Company, 1909. Pp. 345–84.

Haller, John S., Jr. *Outcasts from Evolution: Scientific Attitudes of Racial Inferiority, 1859–1900.* Urbana: University of Illinois Press, 1971.

Handy, Robert T. *A Christian America: Protestant Hopes and Historical Realities.* New York: Oxford University Press, 1971.

———. "The Protestant Quest for a Christian America," *Church History,* XXII (March, 1953), 8–20.

Harmon, George D. *Sixty Years of Indian Affairs: Political, Economic, and Diplomatic, 1789–1850.* Chapel Hill: University of North Carolina Press, 1941.

Harrod, Howard L. *Mission Among the Blackfeet.* Norman: University of Oklahoma Press, 1971.

Havighurst, Walter. *Buffalo Bill's Great Wild West Show.* New York: Random House, 1957.

Hayter, Earl W. "The Ponca Removal," *North Dakota Historical Quarterly,* VI (July, 1932), 262–75.

Hebard, Grace Raymond, and E. A. Brininstool. *The Bozeman Trail: Historical Accounts of the Blazing of the Overland Routes into the Northwest, and the Fights with Red Cloud's Warriors.* 2 vols. Cleveland: Arthur H. Clark Company, 1922.

Higginson, Thomas Wentworth. *Contemporaries.* Boston: Houghton Mifflin and Company, 1899.

Higham, John. *Strangers in the Land: Patterns of American Nativism, 1860–1925.* New Brunswick: Rutgers University Press, 1955.

Hoig, Stan. *The Sand Creek Massacre.* Norman: University of Oklahoma Press, 1961.

Hoopes, Alban W. *Indian Affairs and Their Administration, with Special Reference to the Far West, 1849–1860.* Philadelphia: University of Pennsylvania Press, 1932.

Hopkins, Alphonso A. *The Life of Clinton Bowen Fisk.* New York: Funk and Wagnalls, 1888. Facsimile reprint, New York: Negro Universities Press, 1969.

Howard, Helen Addison, and Dan L. McGrath. *War Chief Joseph.* Caldwell, Idaho: Caxton Printers, 1941.

Hyde, George E. *Red Cloud's Folk: A History of the Oglala Sioux Indians.* Norman: University of Oklahoma Press, 1937.

———. *A Sioux Chronicle.* Norman: University of Oklahoma Press, 1956.

———. *Spotted Tail's Folk: A History of the Brulé Sioux.* Norman: University of Oklahoma Press, 1961.

Johnson, William E. *The Federal Government and the Liquor Traffic.* Westerville, Ohio: American Issue Publishing Company, 1917.

Jones, Douglas C. *The Treaty of Medicine Lodge: The Story of the Great*

Treaty Council as Told by Eyewitnesses. Norman: University of Oklahoma Press, 1966.

Jones, Oakah L., Jr. "The Origins of the Navajo Indian Police, 1872–1873," *Arizona and the West,* VIII (Autumn, 1966), 225–38.

Jones, Robert Huhn. *The Civil War in the Northwest: Nebraska, Wisconsin, Iowa, Minnesota, and the Dakotas.* Norman: University of Oklahoma Press, 1960.

Josephy, Alvin M., Jr. *The Nez Perce Indians and the Opening of the Northwest.* New Haven: Yale University Press, 1965.

Keller, Robert H., Jr. "The Protestant Churches and Grant's Peace Policy: A Study in Church-State Relations, 1869–1882." Ph.D. Dissertation, University of Chicago, 1967.

Kelsey, Harry. "Background to Sand Creek," *Colorado Magazine,* XLV (Fall, 1968), 279–300.

———. "The California Indian Treaty Myth," *Southern California Quarterly,* LV (Fall, 1973), 225–38.

———. "William P. Dole and Mr. Lincoln's Indian Policy," *Journal of the West,* X (July, 1971), 484–92.

Kelsey, Rayner W. *Friends and the Indians, 1655–1917.* Philadelphia: Associated Executive Committee of Friends on Indian Affairs, 1917.

King, James T. " 'A Better Way': General George Crook and the Ponca Indians," *Nebraska History,* L (Fall, 1969), 239–56.

———. "George Crook: Indian Fighter and Humanitarian," *Arizona and the West,* IX (Winter, 1967), 333–48.

Kinney, J. P. *A Continent Lost—A Civilization Won: Indian Land Tenure in America.* Baltimore: Johns Hopkins Press, 1937.

Kinzer, Donald L. *An Episode in Anti-Catholicism: The American Protective Association.* Seattle: University of Washington Press, 1964.

Leckie, William H. *The Military Conquest of the Southern Plains.* Norman: University of Oklahoma Press, 1963.

Lecompte, Janet. "Sand Creek," *Colorado Magazine,* XLI (Fall, 1964), 315–35.

Lee, R. Alton. "Indian Citizenship and the Fourteenth Amendment," *South Dakota History,* IV (Spring, 1974), 198–221.

Leidecker, Kurt F. *Yankee Teacher: The Life of William Torrey Harris.* New York: Philosophical Library, 1946.

Lewitt, Robert T. "Indian Missions and Anti-Slavery Sentiment: A Conflict of Evangelical and Humanitarian Ideals," *Mississippi Valley Historical Review,* L (June, 1963), 39–55.

Lowitt, Richard. *A Merchant Prince of the Nineteenth Century: William E. Dodge.* New York: Columbia University Press, 1954.

McBeth, Kate C. *The Nez Perces Since Lewis and Clark.* New York: Fleming H. Revell Company, 1908.

McCluggage, Robert W. "The Senate and Indian Land Titles, 1800–1825," *Western Historical Quarterly,* I (October, 1970), 415–25.

McGillycuddy, Julia B. *McGillycuddy, Agent: A Biography of Dr. Valentine T. McGillycuddy.* Stanford University, California: Stanford University Press, 1941.

McLoughlin, William G., ed. *The American Evangelicals, 1800–1900: An Anthology.* New York: Harper and Row, 1968.

McNitt, Frank. *The Indian Traders.* Norman: University of Oklahoma Press, 1962.

McReynolds, Edwin C. *The Seminoles.* Norman: University of Oklahoma Press, 1957.

McWhorter, L. V. *Hear Me, My Chiefs! Nez Perce History and Legend.* Edited by Ruth Mordin. Caldwell, Idaho: Caxton Printers, 1952.

Malin, James C. *Indian Policy and Westward Expansion.* Bulletin of the University of Kansas, Humanistic Studies, vol. II, no. 3. Lawrence, 1921.

Mardock, Robert Winston. "Alfred Love, Indian Peace Policy, and the Universal Peace Union," *Kansas Quarterly,* III (Fall, 1971), 64–71.

———. "The Anti-Slavery Humanitarians and Indian Policy Reform," *Western Humanities Review,* XII (Spring, 1958), 131–46.

———. "Irresolvable Enigma? Strange Concepts of the American Indian Since the Civil War," *Montana, the Magazine of Western History,* VII (January, 1957), 36–47.

———. *The Reformers and the American Indian.* Columbia: University of Missouri Press, 1971.

Marty, Martin E. *Righteous Empire: The Protestant Experience in America.* New York: Dial Press, 1970.

Mead, Sidney E. *The Lively Experiment: The Shaping of Christianity in America.* New York: Harper and Row, 1963.

Meyer, Roy W. *History of the Santee Sioux: United States Indian Policy on Trial.* Lincoln: University of Nebraska Press, 1967.

Moody, Marshall. "A History of the Board of Indian Commissioners and Its Relationship to the Administration of Indian Affairs, 1869–1900." M.A. Thesis, American University, 1951.

Mooney, James. *The Ghost-Dance Religion and the Sioux Outbreak of 1890.* Fourteenth Annual Report of the Bureau of Ethnology, 1892–1893, Part II. Washington, 1896.

———. "The Indian Ghost Dance," *Collections of the Nebraska State Historical Society*, XVI (1911), 168–82.

Morton, Louis. "How the Indians Came to Carlisle," *Pennsylvania History*, XXXIX (January, 1962), 53–75.

Murray, Keith A. *The Modocs and Their War*. Norman: University of Oklahoma Press, 1959.

Murray, Robert A. *Military Posts in the Powder River Country of Wyoming, 1865–1894*. Lincoln: University of Nebraska Press, 1968.

Nevins, Allan. "Helen Hunt Jackson, Sentimentalist vs. Realist," *American Scholar*, X (Summer, 1941), 269–85.

Nye, W. S. *Carbine and Lance: The Story of Old Fort Sill*. Norman: University of Oklahoma Press, 1937.

Odell, Ruth. *Helen Hunt Jackson (H.H.)*. New York: D. Appleton-Century Company, 1939.

Oehler, C. M. *The Great Sioux Uprising*. New York: Oxford University Press, 1959.

Ogle, Ralph Henrick. *Federal Control of the Western Apaches, 1848–1886*. Albuquerque: University of New Mexico Press, 1940.

Oliphant, J. Orin. "Encroachments of Cattlemen on Indian Reservations in the Pacific Northwest, 1870–1890," *Agricultural History*, XXIX (January, 1950), 42–58.

Olson, James C. *Red Cloud and the Sioux Problem*. Lincoln: University of Nebraska Press, 1965.

O'Neil, Floyd A. "The Reluctant Suzerainty: The Uintah and Ouray Reservation," *Utah Historical Quarterly*, XXXIX (Spring, 1971), 129–44.

Otis, D. S. *The Dawes Act and the Allotment of Indian Lands*. Edited by Francis Paul Prucha. Norman: University of Oklahoma Press, 1973. Originally printed as "History of the Allotment Policy," in *Readjustment of Indian Affairs* (Hearings before the Committee on Indian Affairs, House of Representatives, Seventy-third Congress, Second Session, on H. R. 7902, Washington, 1934), Part 9, pp. 428–89.

Parker, Arthur C. *The Life of General Ely S. Parker, Last Grand Sachem of the Iroquois and General Grant's Military Secretary*. Buffalo Historical Society Publications, XXIII. Buffalo: Buffalo Historical Society, 1919.

Partington, Frederick E. *The Story of Mohonk*. Fulton, New York: Morrill Press, 1911. Second edition, with additions by Daniel Smiley, Jr., and Albert K. Smiley, Jr., 1932.

Payne, Doris Palmer. *Captain Jack, Modoc Renegade*. Portland, Oregon: Binford and Mort, 1938.

Peabody, Francis Greenwood. *Education for Life: The Story of Hampton*

439

Institute. Garden City, New York: Doubleday, Page and Company, 1919.

Peery, Dan W. "Oklahoma, A Foreordained Commonwealth," *Chronicles of Oklahoma*, XIV (March, 1936), 22–48.

Pfaller, Louis. " 'Enemies in '76, Friends in '85'—Sitting Bull and Buffalo Bill," *Prologue: The Journal of the National Archives*, I (Fall, 1969), 17–31.

Phinney, Edward Sterl. "Alfred B. Meacham, Promoter of Indian Reform." Ph.D. Dissertation, University of Oregon, 1963.

Powers, Ramon. "Why the Northern Cheyenne Left Indian Territory in 1878: A Cultural Analysis," *Kansas Quarterly*, III (Fall, 1971), 72–81.

Priest, Loring Benson. *Uncle Sam's Stepchildren: The Reformation of United States Indian Policy, 1865–1887*. New Brunswick: Rutgers University Press, 1942.

Prucha, Francis Paul. "American Indian Policy in the 1840's: Visions of Reform," in John G. Clark, ed., *The Frontier Challenge: Responses to the Trans-Mississippi West*. Lawrence: University Press of Kansas, 1971. Pp. 81–110.

———. *American Indian Policy in the Formative Years: The Indian Trade and Intercourse Acts, 1790–1834*. Cambridge: Harvard University Press, 1962.

———. "Indian Policy Reform and American Protestantism, 1880–1900," in Ray Allen Billington, ed., *People of the Plains and Mountains: Essays in the History of the West Dedicated to Everett Dick*. Westport, Connecticut: Greenwood Press, 1973. Pp. 120–45.

Rahill, Peter J. *The Catholic Indian Missions and Grant's Peace Policy, 1870–1884*. Washington: Catholic University Press, 1953.

Resek, Carl. *Lewis Henry Morgan: American Scholar*. Chicago: University of Chicago Press, 1960.

Rice, W. G. "The Position of the American Indian in the Law of the United States," *Journal of Comparative Legislation and International Law*, 3d series, XVI (1934), 78–95.

Riddle, Jeff C. *The Indian History of the Modoc War and the Causes That Led To It*. n.p., 1914.

Rister, Carl Coke. *Border Command: General Phil Sheridan in the West*. Norman: University of Oklahoma Press, 1944.

———. *Land Hunger: David L. Payne and the Oklahoma Boomers*. Norman: University of Oklahoma Press, 1942.

Rushmore, Elsie Mitchell. *The Indian Policy During Grant's Administrations*. Jamaica, New York: Marion Press, 1914.

Russell, Don. *The Lives and Legends of Buffalo Bill*. Norman: University of Oklahoma Press, 1960.

———. *The Wild West: A History of the Wild West Shows*. Fort Worth: Amon Carter Museum of Western Art, 1970.

Ryan, Carmelita S. "The Carlisle Indian Industrial School." Ph.D. Dissertation, Georgetown University, 1962.

Sageser, Adelbert Bower. *The First Two Decades of the Pendleton Act: A Study of Civil Service Reform*. Lincoln: University of Nebraska Press, 1935.

Sandoz, Mari. *Cheyenne Autumn*. New York: McGraw-Hill, 1953.

Savage, William W., Jr. *The Cherokee Strip Live Stock Association: Federal Regulation and the Cattleman's Last Frontier*. Columbia: University of Missouri Press, 1973.

Schmeckebier, Laurence F. *The Office of Indian Affairs: Its History, Activities, and Organization*. Baltimore: Johns Hopkins Press, 1927.

Schmitt, Martin F. *General George Crook: His Autobiography*. Norman: University of Oklahoma Press, 1946.

Sell, Henry Blackman, and Victor Weybright. *Buffalo Bill and the Wild West*. New York: Oxford University Press, 1955.

Seymour, Flora Warren. *Indian Agents of the Old Frontier*. New York: D. Appleton-Century Company, 1941.

Sievers, Harry J. "The Catholic Indian School Issue and the Presidential Election of 1892," *Catholic Historical Review*, XXXVIII (July, 1952), 129–55.

Sievers, Michael A. "Sands of Sand Creek Historiography," *Colorado Magazine*, XLIX (Spring, 1972), 116–42.

Sinkler, George. *The Racial Attitudes of American Presidents from Abraham Lincoln to Theodore Roosevelt*. Garden City, New York: Doubleday and Company, 1971.

Slattery, Charles Lewis. *Felix Reville Brunot, 1820–1898*. New York: Longmans, Green and Company, 1901.

Smith, Michael T. "The History of Indian Citizenship," *Great Plains Journal*, X (Fall, 1970), 25–35.

Smylie, John Edwin. "National Ethos and the Church," *Theology Today*, XX (October, 1963), 313–21.

Sprague, Marshall. *Massacre: The Tragedy of White River*. Boston: Little, Brown and Company, 1957.

Sterling, Everett W. "The Indian Reservation System on the North Central Plains," *Montana, the Magazine of Western History*, XIV (April, 1964), 92–100.

Stewart, Edgar I. *Custer's Luck*. Norman: University of Oklahoma Press, 1955.

Straight, Michael. *A Very Small Remnant*. New York: Alfred A. Knopf, 1963.

Talbot, Edith Armstrong. *Samuel Chapman Armstrong: A Biographical Study*. New York: Doubleday, Page and Company, 1904.

Taylor, Samuel. "Origins of the Dawes Act of 1887." Philip Washburn Prize Thesis, Harvard College, 1927.

Thompson, Erwin N. *Modoc War: Its Military History & Topography*. Sacramento: Argus Books, 1971.

Tousey, Thomas G. *Military History of Carlisle and Carlisle Barracks*. Richmond, Virginia: Dietz Press, 1939.

Unrau, William E. "The Civilian as Indian Agent: Villain or Victim?" *Western Historical Quarterly*, III (October, 1972), 405–20.

———. "Indian Agent vs. the Army: Some Background Notes on the Kiowa-Comanche Treaty of 1865," *Kansas Historical Quarterly*, XXX (Summer, 1964), 129–52.

———. "Investigation or Probity? Investigations into the Affairs of the Kiowa-Comanche Indian Agency, 1867," *Chronicles of Oklahoma*, XLII (Autumn, 1964), 300–319.

———. *The Kansa Indians: A History of the Wind People, 1673–1873*. Norman: University of Oklahoma Press, 1971.

———. "A Prelude to War," *Colorado Magazine*, XLI (Fall, 1964), 299–313.

Utley, Robert M. "The Celebrated Peace Policy of General Grant," *North Dakota History*, XX (July, 1953), 131–42.

———. *Custer Battlefield National Monument, Montana*. Washington: National Park Service, 1969.

———. *Frontier Regulars: The United States Army and the Indian, 1866–1891*. New York: Macmillan Publishing Company, 1973.

———. *Frontiersmen in Blue: The United States Army and the Indian, 1848–1865*. New York: Macmillan Company, 1968.

———. *The Last Days of the Sioux Nation*. New Haven: Yale University Press, 1963.

Wallace, Ernest, and E. Adamson Hoebel. *The Comanches: Lords of the South Plains*. Norman: University of Oklahoma Press, 1952.

Waltmann, Henry G. "Circumstantial Reformer: President Grant and the Indian Problem," *Arizona and the West*, XIII (Winter, 1971), 323–42.

———. "The Interior Department, War Department, and Indian Policy, 1865–1887." Ph.D. Dissertation, University of Nebraska, 1962.

Wardell, Morris L. *A Political History of the Cherokee Nation, 1838–1907*. Norman: University of Oklahoma Press, 1938.

Watson, Elmo Scott. "The Last Indian War, 1890–91—A Study of Newspaper Jingoism," *Journalism Quarterly,* XX (September, 1943), 205–19.

White, Lonnie J. "From Bloodless to Bloody: The Third Colorado Cavalry and the Sand Creek Massacre," *Journal of the West,* VI (October, 1967), 535–81.

Whitner, Robert Lee. "Grant's Indian Peace Policy on the Yakima Reservation, 1870–82," *Pacific Northwest Quarterly,* L (October, 1959), 135–42.

———. "The Methodist Episcopal Church and Grant's Peace Policy: A Study of the Methodist Agencies, 1870–1882." Ph.D. Dissertation, University of Minnesota, 1959.

Williams, Robert L. "Tams Bixby," *Chronicles of Oklahoma,* XIX (September, 1941), 205–12.

Wissler, Clark. *Indian Cavalcade: Or Life on the Old-time Indian Reservations.* New York: Sheridan House, 1938. Reprinted as *Red Man Reservations.* New York: Collier Books, 1971.

Woodward, Grace Steele. *The Cherokees.* Norman: University of Oklahoma Press, 1963.

INDEX

449

Rice, Henry M.: 7, 9, 10
Ridge, John: 284
Rochester Theological Seminary: 294
Rogue River War: 5
*Romanism versus the Public School
System*: 307
Rosebud Agency: 173, 274, 362
Ross, John: 284
Ross, Lewis W.: 14n.
Royer, Daniel: 361
"Rules for Indian Schools": 302
Runs, land, in Oklahoma: 385, 390

Sac and Fox Indians: 255
St. Augustine, Florida: 272
Salsbury, Nate: 322, 323, 324
Sanborn, John B.: 19
San Carlos Reservation: 202–203
Sand Creek Massacre: 11–13
Santee Agency: 143, 174
Santee Sioux Indians: 262
Satolli, Francesco: 306
Sayre, Warren G.: 389
Schofield, J. M.: 76
Schools for Indians: 22, 40, 194, 267, 288,
315, 402; *see also* education
Schurz, Carl: 57, 60–61, 97, 98, 102, 119,
128–29, 159–60, 331, 354, 385; and
Ponca affair, 115–17, 134, 162; and Ute
question, 237, 238–39, 240; and sev-
eralty, 242, 243; and Indian education,
271, 273, 279, 284, 289
Seelye, Julius H.: 162
Self-government by Indians: 374, 381
Self-support by Indians: 153–54, 270
Seminole Indians: 373, 400
Seneca Indians: 255
Seventh U.S. Cavalry: 362–63
Severalty, allotment of land in: 40, 90,
153, 154, 159, 166, 178, 179, 186, 191,
194, 221, 227–62, 297, 378, 383, 402;
see also Coke Bill, Dawes Act
Shannon, Peter: 173
Shawnee Indians: 268
Sheridan, Philip: 23, 25, 50, 93, 99
Sherman, William T.: 4, 19, 24, 36, 51–52,
72, 86, 96, 99, 125; and transfer issue,
22, 74–76

Sibley, Henry H.: 8–10
Sioux commissions: *see* Allison Commis-
sion, Crook Commission, Edmunds
Commission, Manypenny Commission,
Pratt Commission
Sioux Indians: 5, 7–8, 19, 110–11, 118,
147, 202, 255, 268, 274; wars with,
7–11, 93–94, 100, 358–64
Sioux Reserve: *see* Great Sioux Reserve
Sitting Bull: 94, 207, 319–20, 361
Slavery: 268, 375, 376
Smiley, Albert K.: 143–44, 174, 180, 191,
224
Smiley, Alfred: 143
Smith, Caleb: 7
Smith, Edward P.: 70–71, 91, 188, 232,
269, 289, 330
Smith, John Q.: 71, 98, 233, 379–80
Social Gospel: 168n.
Society of Friends: *see* Quakers
South Dakota: 184
Southern Utes: *see* Ute Indians
Sovereignty of tribes: 70–71, 329
Spoils system: 355; *see also* Civil Service
reform
Spotted Tail: 274, 333
Springer, William M.: 389
"Squawmen": 213–14
Standing army, danger of: 80
Standing Bear: 114, 162
Standing Bear vs. Crook: 114
Standing Rock Agency: 173, 182, 207, 361
Stebbins, E. N.: 213
Stephan, Joseph A.: 307, 309–12, 316
Stickney, William: 118, 124
Stockbridge Indians: 230
Stuart, George H.: 36n.
Students, leasing of land of: 258
Studies in Pedagogy: 295, 296
Sully, Alfred: 10
Superintendent of Indian education: 305,
357
Superintendent of Indian trade: 266
Superintendents of schools: 366, 368–69
"Supplemental Report on Indian Educa-
tion": 301–302
Surplus lands, sale of: 253
Syphilis: 81